ONE WEEK LOAN

23 FEB 2011

24 OCT 2011

ABCDEFGHIJKLMNOPQRSTUVWXYZ

MICHEL FOUCAULT

In texts such as *Madness and Civilisation* and *The Archaeology of Knowledge*, Michel Foucault established himself as one of the most important figures in the theoretical revolution of the 1960s and 1970s. His influence only grew with later publications and even after his death in 1984, debate continues to rage around his work.

This volume is a refreshingly accessible guide to Foucault's most influential ideas, their contexts and the ways in which they have been put to use by a variety of critics. Examining such key concepts as power, discourse, knowledge, sexuality, subjectivity and madness, Sara Mills guides readers through the theoretical work that underpins so many disciplinary fields today. She also provides a work-by-work guide to Foucault's major texts and an annotated list of further reading, to fully equip those planning to engage with his work at a more advanced level. This volume, crucially, considers how readers new to Foucault's work might integrate some of his approaches to analysis and apply his work to their own studies.

Michel Foucault has been written with students of literature in mind, but its relevance, like that of Foucault's remarkable work, extends far beyond literary studies. For anyone seeking to understand Foucault and the complex debates engendered by his work, this volume is the essential first step.

Sara Mills is Research Professor at Sheffield Hallam University. She has published on feminism, post-colonial theory and linguistics and is the author of *Discourse*, a highly successful volume in Routledge's New Critical Idiom series.

ROUTLEDGE CRITICAL THINKERS

Series Editor: Robert Eaglestone, Royal Holloway, University of London

Routledge Critical Thinkers is a series of accessible introductions to key figures in contemporary critical thought.

With a unique focus on historical and intellectual contexts, each volume examines a key theorist's:

- significance
- motivation
- key ideas and their sources
- impact on other thinkers

Concluding with extensively annotated guides to further reading, *Routledge Critical Thinkers* are the student's passport to today's most exciting critical thought.

Already available:
Roland Barthes by Graham Allen
Jean Baudrillard by Richard J. Lane
Simone de Beauvoir by Ursula Tidd
Maurice Blanchot by Ullrich Haase and William Large
Judith Butler by Sara Salih
Jacques Derrida by Nicholas Royle
Gilles Deleuze by Claire Colebrook
Michel Foucault by Sara Mills
Sigmund Freud by Pamela Thurschwell
Martin Heidegger by Timothy Clark
Fredric Jameson by Adam Roberts
Jean-François Lyotard by Simon Malpas
Julia Kristeva by Noëll McAfee
Paul de Man by Martin McQuillan
Friedrich Nietzsche by Lee Spinks
Paul Ricoeur by Karl Simms
Edward Said by Bill Ashcroft and Pal Ahluwalia
Gayatri Chakravorty Spivak by Stephen Morton
Slavoj Žižek by Tony Myers
Stuart Hall by James Proctor

For further details on this series, see www.literature.routledge.com/rct

MICHEL FOUCAULT

Sara Mills

Routledge
Taylor & Francis Group

LONDON AND NEW YORK

First published 2003
by Routledge
2 Park Square, Milton Park, Abingdon, Oxon OX14 4RN

Simultaneously published in the USA and Canada
by Routledge
270 Madison Avenue, New York, NY 10016

Reprinted 2004 (twice), 2005, 2006, 2007, 2008, 2009 (twice)

Routledge is an imprint of the Taylor & Francis Group,
an informa business

Typeset in Perpetua by
Florence Production Ltd, Stoodleigh, Devon
Printed by the MPG Books Group in the UK

British Library Cataloguing in Publication Data
A catalogue record for this book is available from the British Library

Library of Congress Cataloguing in Publication Data
A catalog record for this book has been requested

ISBN 978–0–415–24568–5 (hbk)
ISBN 978–0–415–24569–2 (pbk)

TO JAN

CONTENTS

SERIES EDITOR'S PREFACE

The books in this series offer introductions to major critical thinkers who have influenced literary studies and the humanities. The *Routledge Critical Thinkers* series provides the books you can turn to first when a new name or concept appears in your studies.

Each book will equip you to approach a key thinker's original texts by explaining her or his key ideas, putting them into context and, perhaps most importantly, showing you why this thinker is considered to be significant. The emphasis is on concise, clearly written guides which do not presuppose a specialist knowledge. Although the focus is on particular figures, the series stresses that no critical thinker ever existed in a vacuum but, instead, emerged from a broader intellectual, cultural and social history. Finally, these books will act as a bridge between you and the thinker's original texts: not replacing them but rather complementing what she or he wrote.

These books are necessary for a number of reasons. In his 1997 autobiography, *Not Entitled*, the literary critic Frank Kermode wrote of a time in the 1960s:

> On beautiful summer lawns, young people lay together all night, recovering from their daytime exertions and listening to a troupe of Balinese musicians. Under their blankets or their sleeping bags, they would chat drowsily about the gurus of the time. . . . What they repeated was largely hearsay; hence my

lunchtime suggestion, quite impromptu, for a series of short, very cheap books
offering authoritative but intelligible introductions to such figures.

There is still a need for 'authoritative and intelligible introductions'.
But this series reflects a different world from the 1960s. New thinkers
have emerged and the reputations of others have risen and fallen, as
new research has developed. New methodologies and challenging
ideas have spread through the arts and humanities. The study of
literature is no longer – if it ever was – simply the study and evaluation of poems, novels and plays. It is also the study of the ideas, issues
and difficulties which arise in any literary text and in its interpretation. Other arts and humanities subjects have changed in analogous
ways.

With these changes, new problems have emerged. The ideas and
issues behind these radical changes in the humanities are often
presented without reference to wider contexts or as theories which
you can simply 'add on' to the texts you read. Certainly, there's
nothing wrong with picking out selected ideas or using what comes to
hand – indeed, some thinkers have argued that this is, in fact, all we
can do. However, it is sometimes forgotten that each new idea comes
from the pattern and development of somebody's thought and it is
important to study the range and context of their ideas. Against theories 'floating in space', the *Routledge Critical Thinkers* series places key
thinkers and their ideas firmly back in their contexts.

More than this, these books reflect the need to go back to the
thinker's own texts and ideas. Every interpretation of an idea, even
the most seemingly innocent one, offers its own 'spin', implicitly or
explicitly. To read only books on a thinker, rather than texts by that
thinker, is to deny yourself a chance of making up your own mind.
Sometimes what makes a significant figure's work hard to approach is
not so much its style or content as the feeling of not knowing where to
start. The purpose of these books is to give you a 'way in' by offering
an accessible overview of these thinkers' ideas and works and by guiding your further reading, starting with each thinker's own texts. To use
a metaphor from the philosopher Ludwig Wittgenstein (1889–1951),
these books are ladders, to be thrown away after you have climbed to
the next level. Not only, then, do they equip you to approach new ideas,
but also they empower you, by leading you back to a theorist's own
texts and encouraging you to develop your own informed opinions.

Finally, these books are necessary because, just as intellectual needs have changed, the education systems around the world – the contexts in which introductory books are usually read – have changed radically, too. What was suitable for the minority higher education system of the 1960s is not suitable for the larger, wider, more diverse, high technology education systems of the twenty-first century. These changes call not just for new, up-to-date, introductions but new methods of presentation. The presentational aspects of *Routledge Critical Thinkers* have been developed with today's students in mind.

Each book in the series has a similar structure. They begin with a section offering an overview of the life and ideas of each thinker and explain why she or he is important. The central section of each book discusses the thinker's key ideas, their context, evolution and reception. Each book concludes with a survey of the thinker's impact, outlining how their ideas have been taken up and developed by others. In addition, there is a detailed final section suggesting and describing books for further reading. This is not a 'tacked-on' section but an integral part of each volume. In the first part of this section you will find brief descriptions of the thinker's key works, then, following this, information on the most useful critical works and, in some cases, on relevant web sites. This section will guide you in your reading, enabling you to follow your interests and develop your own projects. Throughout each book, references are given in what is known as the Harvard system (the author and the date of a work cited are given in the text and you can look up the full details in the bibliography at the back). This offers a lot of information in very little space. The books also explain technical terms and use boxes to describe events or ideas in more detail, away from the main emphasis of the discussion. Boxes are also used at times to highlight definitions of terms frequently used or coined by a thinker. In this way, the boxes serve as a kind of glossary, easily identified when flicking through the book.

The thinkers in the series are 'critical' for three reasons. First, they are examined in the light of subjects which involve criticism: principally literary studies or English and cultural studies, but also other disciplines which rely on the criticism of books, ideas, theories and unquestioned assumptions. Second, studying their work will provide you with a 'tool kit' for informed critical reading and thought, which will heighten your own criticism. Third, these thinkers are critical because they are crucially important: they deal with ideas and questions which can overturn conventional understandings of the world, of texts, of everything we take for granted, leaving us with a deeper understanding of what we already knew and with new ideas.

No introduction can tell you everything. However, by offering a way into critical thinking, this series hopes to begin to engage you in an activity which is productive, constructive and potentially life-changing.

ACKNOWLEDGEMENTS

I would like to thank Tony Brown for discussing Foucault's ideas with me, and remaining sufficiently sceptical about the grandiose claims of critical theory. Thanks are also due to undergraduate and research students at Sheffield Hallam University for approaching Foucault's work with great openness and critical awareness, and drawing attention to what is complex and what is useful in Foucault's work. Robert Eaglestone has been a thoughtful and attentive editor.

> I know, considering how each person hopes and believes he puts something of 'himself' into his own discourse, when he takes it upon himself to speak, how intolerable it is to cut up, analyse, combine, recompose all these texts so that now the transfigured face of their author is never discernible. So many words amassed, so many marks on paper offered to numberless eyes, such zeal to preserve them beyond the gesture which articulates them, such a piety devoted to conserving them in human memory – after all this, must nothing remain of the poor hand which traced them, of that disquiet which sought its calm in them, of that ended life which had nothing but them for its continuation? . . . By speaking I do not exorcise my death, but establish it; or rather . . . I suppress all interiority and yield my utterance to an outside which is so indifferent to my life, so *neutral* that it knows no difference between my life and my death.
>
> (Foucault 1991a/1968: 71)

WHY FOUCAULT?

Michel Foucault (1926–1984) continues to be one of the most important figures in critical theory. His theories have been concerned largely with the concepts of power, knowledge and discourse, and his influence is clear in a great deal of post-structuralist, post-modernist, feminist, post-Marxist and post-colonial theorising. The impact of his work has also been felt across a wide range of disciplinary fields, from sociology and anthropology to English studies and history. However, the iconoclastic and challenging nature of Foucault's theoretical work has meant that his ideas have not simply been accommodated. Instead, they have caused heated – and very productive – debate from the 1960s and 1970s, when he emerged as a key theorist, through to the present.

His work, in books such as *Madness and Civilisation* (1967) and *Discipline and Punish* (1975), can be seen as a historical analysis of social conditions; in the first book, for example, he analyses the development of the distinction between madness and reason, and in the second, he traces the changes that there have been in the way that societies punish those they consider to be criminals. However, his work is not simply concerned to analyse social conditions, but is, at the same time, an analysis of the bases on which we think about analysing social conditions. By that I mean that, because he thinks that the way we approach analysis determines, to a great extent, what we find out and what we can know, in some sense, we must of necessity analyse the perspectives we take on the subject we are analysing, when we undertake an analysis of those social conditions. Thus, his work is not only, for example, an analysis of the difference between madness and reason, but it is also an analysis of the way that we think about insanity and the lengths to which each society goes to regulate the distinction and keep that conceptual distinction in place.

His work has proved disconcerting for many, since he does not offer a simple political analysis. In a way, he seems to be gesturing towards an emancipatory politics, at the same time as undercutting any possibility of such a position. As Charles Taylor puts it:

> certain of Foucault's most interesting historical analyses, while they are highly original, seem to lie along already familiar lines of critical thought. That is, they seem to offer an insight into what has happened, and into what we have become, which at the same time offers a critique, and hence some notion of a good unrealised or repressed in history, which we therefore understand better how to rescue. But Foucault himself repudiates this suggestion. He dashes the hope, if we had one, that there is some good we can *affirm*, as a result of the understanding these analyses give us. And by the same token, he seems to raise the question whether there is such a thing as a way out. This is rather paradoxical, because Foucault's analyses seek to bring *evils* to light; and yet he wants to distance himself from the suggestion which would seem inescapably to follow, that the negation or overcoming of these evils promotes a good.
>
> (Taylor 1986: 69)

Thus, Foucault critically analyses subjects such as: the differences in the way that societies administer punishment (in *Discipline and Punish* (1975)), the categorisation in the nineteenth century of certain women as suffering from hysteria (in *History of Sexuality, Vol. I* (1976)), or the way that homosexuality has been viewed in different societies and at different periods (in *History of Sexuality, Vol. II* (1984)). This critical analysis might lead us to assume that he is approaching analysis with a firm sense of critique, a fully worked out political manifesto, arguing for social change. However, his analysis does not offer us a simple position of critique and those who approach his work in the hope of finding a clear political agenda will be disappointed and will find that Foucault, instead, asks us to question more thoroughly our own sense of the solidity of our political position.

There are many other contradictions in Foucault's work, and it is not the intention of this book to minimise this difficulty in order to represent him as a great critical thinker. It is in the nature of critical thinking that there will be elements which are seen to be contradictions by future thinkers: these contradictions form the basis on which to ground new directions in theoretical work. In fact, Foucault himself was conscious of areas of difficulty in his work and often returned to these questions in order to try to think them through further. In an interview in 1983, he responds to the charge that his refusal to be restricted to one particular type of theoretical position detracts from his work, by saying: 'when people say "Well, you thought this a few years ago and now you say something else", my answer is "Well, do you think I have worked [like a dog] all those years to say the same thing and not be changed?"' (Foucault 1988b: 14). Thus, he sees the changing of a position, the rethinking of past work, as an essential part of the development of his thinking; he certainly does not consider that the progression of one's thought should follow a straightforward trajectory where the author moves from immaturity to maturity and develops and improves on his ideas in a linear fashion. But he does consider it important to be extremely critical of one's own position and not assume that one has ever reached a position where one has discovered the final 'truth' about a subject.

It is, perhaps, the contradictions in his work which have sparked off most debate and most productive critical thinking. For example, his complex and contradictory definitions of the term 'discourse', which will be discussed in Chapter 3, have forced many theorists to define their terms more carefully, and theorists drawing on terms such as 'ideology' have had to make their position clear on the relationship they perceive between discourse and ideology. However, Foucault cannot be reduced to his work on discourse, and it is his wide-ranging lateral thinking on subjects as diverse as the structural features and functions of institutions, the way that our conceptions of knowledge, sanity, madness, discipline and sexuality are maintained and kept in circulation by institutions and by society as a whole, which makes his work of interest to a large number of researchers and students. His iconoclastic approach to disciplinary boundaries and his refusal to be pigeonholed is very appealing to many. In an interview in 1983, he argues 'in France you ha[ve] to be, as a philosopher, a Marxist or a phenomenologist or a structuralist, and I adhere to none of these dogmas' (Foucault 1988b: 8). Characterising these positions as constraining dogmas may be liberating for many who have found that adopting a theoretical position can be a little like joining a religious group or political party, which demands total and unthinking acceptance of a set of ideas or beliefs. We could, however, see this as an overstatement by Foucault, since these political and theoretical positions can be seen rather as simply productive frameworks and tools for creative critical thought. Nevertheless, it is this quality of always surpassing and pushing against the traditional disciplinary boundaries which makes Foucault's work interesting to a wide number of people who feel constrained by the notion of working strictly within the frameworks of their own subject area.

His work has also been drawn on by a wide range of readers because he has managed to attempt to theorise without using the notions of the *subject* and the *economic*: both terms which have been foundational for psychoanalytical theory and Marxist and materialist theory, which together dominated intellectual life at the time that Foucault was writing. The reliance on notions such as the subject or the economic, and also notions such as woman and man, has been seen by many as *essentialism*, an assumption that there are firm foundations for concepts or differences, for example, sexual or racial difference. Foucault has tried to move away from the notion of the subject, that is, he has attempted to think about the forms that human societies take without rooting his analysis in the examination of individuals. He has also tried to move away from the notion of the economic, in that he has analysed social forces without assuming that the ownership of property and the accumulation of capital are the most important elements in any analysis. He does not suggest that the subject and the economy do not play an important role in the way society is organised but, rather, he is interested in not reducing analysis to the importance of one particular feature, which it is assumed is stable. He wants to analyse without drawing on these concepts which have played such an important function in much previous theoretical work. What he is doing is focusing on the way that the subject or the self and the economic are both concepts which are, despite their seeming self-evident nature, in fact, relatively unstable. He argues that these concepts have changed over time, that whatever concepts that we use have a history and motivation for their use and that they must themselves be interrogated.

Perhaps the most interesting part of Foucault's work and one which approximates most closely to a consistent way of approaching analysis is his scepticism. In some senses, Foucault's radical scepticism is part of a more general philosophical and political querying, in the 1960s and 1970s, of those elements which had been taken to be common-sense and which began to be seen as profoundly ideological. While many Marxist critics at the time, such as Louis Althusser (1918–1990), analysed particular concepts and forms of behaviour in everyday life and subjected them to critical analysis, Foucault extended this type of enquiry to the human sciences themselves, the very tools and methods which were generally used in the analysis of everyday life. What appeals to many people in Foucault's work is this almost Zen-like pushing to the limits of what it is possible to say, challenging each element and concept within our theoretical frameworks which we use in order to think.

Together with this scepticism is a concern to think laterally about subjects; this often involves the use of radical reversals and a critique of that knowledge which can be characterised as common-sense. Thus, like many Marxist theorists, such as Louis Althusser, he questions the type of knowledge which we assume that everyone would accept as self-evidently true (Althusser 1984). So, rather than accepting the common-sense view that people who were classified as insane were incarcerated because of a fear that they might harm themselves or others, and in order that they could be treated and cured, in *Madness and Civilisation* (1967), Foucault focuses on the way that the notion of madness performed an essential role in the construction of reason. Rather than accepting that the repression of sexuality during the Victorian period induced a silence around questions of sexual expression, in fact Foucault shows in *The History of Sexuality, Vol. I* (1976) that it brought about a proliferation of discourses about sexuality and brought about the 'transforming [of] sex into discourse' (Foucault 1986b). And finally, instead of considering that language simply reflects an underlying reality, in *The Archaeology of Knowledge* (1972) he asserts that discourse determines the reality that we perceive. While many have seen these aphoristic reversals as a simplification of very complex problems, they have proved instructive to many people in trying to analyse the past without imposing on it our own concerns and stereotypical views. His work involves this, sometimes quite uncomfortable, change of view in relation to familiar notions. However, that is not to say that it is impossible to say anything. Rather, Foucault tries to map out the type of analysis that it is possible to undertake once one has dispensed with all certainties and foundations.

Perhaps one of the more endearing elements in Foucault's work, and one which is singularly lacking in much other theoretical work, is his curiosity. One comes to feel that Foucault was a person driven to question why certain fields of experience are represented in the way that they are. When he tried to formulate what motivated him to write he said:

> it was curiosity – the only kind of curiosity . . . that is worth acting upon with a degree of obstinacy; not the kind of curiosity that seeks to assimilate what it is proper for one to know, but that which enables one to get free of oneself. After all, what would be the value of passion for knowledge if it resulted only in a certain amount of knowledgeableness and not, in one way or another . . . in the knower's straying afield of himself? There are times in one's life when the question of knowing if one can think differently than one thinks, and perceive differently than one sees, is absolutely necessary if one is to go on looking and reflecting at all.
>
> (Foucault 1985: 8)

It is through this almost child-like compulsion to ask difficult questions that Foucault tries to discover more instructive ways of seeing those things which we often consider in our society to be self-evident.

In critical theory, there is often a sense that one has to adopt or align oneself with a particular theorist and, in the process of drawing on their work, one defines oneself as a particular type of person. Thus, using someone's theoretical work is not just a question of being interested in their ideas but also about representing oneself to others. From the 1970s onwards, Foucault has been very much the theorist who was adopted by those on the Left who wished to espouse a radical politics and also by those who wished to represent themselves as iconoclastic. Many theorists and critics have used Foucault's ideas as a way of approaching a subject rather than as a set of principles or rules; as the geographer Daniel Clayton states: 'there are thinkers who you think with to such an extent that they become part of you but are barely mentioned by name. For me that thinker is Foucault' (Clayton 2000: xiv). A further feature of his work which contributes to its popularity is the fact that he does not develop one, fully thought-out theory but, instead, tries to think through ways of thinking without the constraints of a systematised structure. He encourages readers to make what they can of his work rather than feeling that they ought to follow what he has written slavishly; in an interview in *Le Monde* in 1975, he states:

> a book is made to be used in ways not defined by its writer. The more, new, possible or unexpected uses there are, the happier I shall be . . . All my books are little tool-boxes. If people want to open them, to use this sentence or that idea as a screwdriver or spanner to short-circuit, discredit systems of power, including eventually those from which my books have emerged . . . so much the better.

> (Foucault, cited in Patton 1979: 115)

There are obviously serious problems with this approach to theory, attractive though it is to many of us who would simply like an illustrative quotation from Foucault to justify our argument. Not least of these is the fact that, if his books can be used for anything, and if sentences can be taken out of context in order to support whatever argument the reader wishes, there is no sense in which Foucault's theoretical work is any different from any statement which could be made by anyone, without having considered a particular issue at a theoretical level, that is at a level of higher abstraction. Nor is there any reason why Foucault's work could not be used to justify fascism or to deny the existence of the Holocaust.

These remarks about the complexity and contradictory nature of his work should make us cautious about the possibility of 'using' Foucault in any simple way. As I argue more fully in the conclusion to this book, we need also to be careful about the notion of 'applying' Foucault's work. One potential problem is the fact that Foucault is a very androcentric, or male-oriented, thinker. This problem of a sexist focus in his work cannot be solved simply by adding women to his analysis; analysing his androcentrism means that the reader of Foucault's work is forced to fundamentally reconsider the way in which his focus on men alone skews some of the insights which he has to offer. Thus, we should not assume that Foucault has all of the answers to our own theoretical problems; we should draw on his work as a resource for thinking, without slavish adherence, and we should also be very aware of Foucault's weaknesses and theoretical blindspots.

KEY IDEAS

FOUCAULT'S INTELLECTUAL AND POLITICAL DEVELOPMENT

This chapter sets Foucault's intellectual and political development in the context of the wider developments in France during the early part of Foucault's career, since there is an interesting dialectical relationship between his ideas and the political and intellectual climate: the events of 1968 had a crucial defining impact on Foucault's thinking and Foucault played a major role in events and in the focus of theoretical work of the time. However, I imagine that taking the text of Foucault's life or the text of a history of the events of 1968 and bringing them to bear in the task of making sense of his theoretical texts would have seemed to Foucault to be a laughable endeavour. In his essay 'What is an author?', Foucault argues that: 'the task of criticism is not to bring out the work's relationship with the author, but rather to analyse the work through its structure, its architecture, its intrinsic form, and the play of its internal relationships' (Foucault 1986a: 102). However, Foucault himself commented on the way that he focused on particular subjects, not simply because they were theoretically interesting to him, but because these subjects resonated with something from his personal experience: 'Whenever I have tried to carry out a piece of theoretical work, it has been on the basis of my own experience, always in relation to processes I saw taking place around me. It is because I thought I could recognise in the things I saw, in the institutions with which I dealt, in my relations with others, cracks, silent shocks, malfunctioning . . . that I undertook a particular piece of work, a few fragments of autobiography' (Foucault, cited in Eribon 1991: 28–29). Therefore, in drawing on biographical material about Foucault, I do not wish to construct a solid figure of Michel Foucault and attribute to him 'a "deep" motive, a "creative power" or a "design"', almost as if he were a fully rounded character in a novel (Foucault 1986a: 110). I recognise that in focusing on the details of his life as they have been reconstructed by others, 'these aspects of an individual which we designate as making him an author are only a projection, in more or less psychologising terms, of the operations that we force texts to undergo, the connections that we make, the traits that we establish as pertinent, the continuities that we recognise, or the exclusions that we practice' (Foucault 1986a: 110). Nevertheless, there are instances where, for pedagogic and explanatory reasons, using certain biographical details and details of social history can help to make Foucault's work accessible and can help us to understand his work better, without reifying this collection of events which we have labelled 'the life of Michel Foucault'. I, therefore, endeavour in this section to avoid imposing a simple cause-and-effect relationship on events in Foucault's life and the emphases of certain of his texts but, rather, I try to present Foucault's works as emerging from a relationship with, and reaction to, a complex series of tendencies and conflicts in intellectual and political life in France at this period. For those studying Foucault who are not familiar with the events of 1968, there are elements within his work which may seem troubling or difficult to understand, (for example, his relation to Marxism, his own political position and his relation to his own homosexuality). By examining the social context of intellectuals in Paris at this time, it is possible to understand what was 'available' to Foucault as possible forms of behaviour and possible forms of thinking with which he could negotiate and which he could also challenge. But first it is useful to bear in mind a brief outline of Foucault's career from the outset.

He was born in Poitiers, France in 1926. Although most of his academic training was in philosophy, after his first degree he trained for a higher degree in psychology and a diploma in pathological psychology. He was employed as a university lecturer in philosophy and in psychology and also as a teacher of French literature and language when he worked overseas. He worked at universities and cultural centres in Uppsala, Sweden (1954); in Warsaw, Poland (1958) and in Hamburg,

Germany (1959). In the same year he became the head of philosophy at Clermont-Ferrand University, France. He completed his doctorat-d'état (PhD) on madness and reason and published it as *Madness and Civilisation* in 1961. In the following year, he published a book on the work of the poet Raymond Roussel, and in 1963 he published *The Birth of the Clinic*. In 1966, he moved to Tunisia to teach, returning to France to become the head of philosophy at Vincennes University. In 1969 he published *The Archaeology of Knowledge* and in 1970 he became chair of the History of Systems of Thought at the Collège de France. In 1975 he published *Discipline and Punish* and in 1976 be began the publication of the three-volume *History of Sexuality*; he died in 1984. As can be seen from the wide-ranging subjects which Foucault analysed, his work is not easy to pin down. His work reflects the background of intellectual and political activism against which it developed, but it also played a significant part in the process of transformation.

The 1960s and 1970s was a crucial period for Foucault and other radical intellectuals in France and Europe as a whole. It is therefore necessary to describe the events which took place at this time and throughout the 1970s to set Foucault's thought and his political activities in context. It is also important to consider the context of Foucault's ideas in order to see that, in many cases, Foucault acted as a conduit for anti-authoritarian and radical ideas. The Marxist histor-ian, Chris Harman, stresses that 1968 was not, as is often thought, simply the year in which a series of student demonstrations took place in Paris, nor was 1968 simply a year when 'hippie' fashions and ways of living and thinking became especially prominent; instead:

> 1968 was a year in which revolt shook at least three major governments and produced a wave of hope among young people living under many others. It was the year the peasant guerrillas of one of the world's smaller nations stood up to the mightiest power in human history. It was the year the black ghettos of the United States rose in revolt to protest at the murder of the leader of non-violence, Martin Luther King. It was the year the city of Berlin suddenly became the international focus for a student movement that challenged the power blocs which divided it. It was the year teargas and billy clubs were used to make sure the US Democratic Party convention would select a presidential candidate who had been rejected by voters in every primary. It was the year Russian tanks rolled into Prague to displace a 'Communist' government that had made concessions to popular pressure. It was the year that the Mexican

government massacred more than 100 demonstrators in order to ensure that the Olympic Games would take place under 'peaceful' conditions. It was the year that protests against discrimination in Derry and Belfast lit the fuse on the sectarian powder keg of Northern Ireland. It was, above all, the year that the biggest general strike ever paralysed France and caused its government to panic.

(Harman 1998: vii)

In many other countries, Chile, India, Brazil and Palestine, the events which took place in France had a profound effect in political terms in the following years. Although this characterisation of 1968 may be seen by some as overly Marxist and internationalist, it does reflect the real impact of the events on political thinking and activity globally.

During the early 1960s, there was an anti-authoritarian tendency in much political thinking of the time among those who found themselves opposed to the status quo or to the current political regimes, and these ideas gained currency among a wider group of people and began to be drawn on in a general critique of American neo-imperial policy abroad and profound racism in Europe and America. This critique also made its presence felt in terms of the analysis of the more mundane, but perhaps equally important, events of everyday life, such as who lectures to whom in universities and who does the washing up at home, where the personal becomes the political. Foucault sees this shift towards a widening of the definition of politics as significant and he states in 1969 in an interview: 'The boundary of politics has changed, and subjects like psychiatry, confinement and the medicalisation of a population have become political problems' (Foucault, cited in Macey 1994: 217). All of those who protested, even in a minor way, against repression of political activism in the French universities were categorised as being part of this sub-culture or counter-culture which the beatniks and hippies represented with their open rejection of bourgeois values and materialism. There were many anti-war protests, most notably against the American presence in Vietnam. It is against this background of intellectual questioning and political activism that Foucault's work developed, informed by the same radical thinking about common-sense categories, values, policies and forms of behaviour. Foucault's works were bought by large numbers of students and academics, since they seemed to articulate this radical thinking, taking issue with all established ways of thinking and behaving and they provided a framework for thinking about questions of power which were the focus of this larger scale political interrogation.

One of the questions which often dogs critics is about Foucault's political position, partly because Foucault's writings on the subject are so contradictory. Foucault joined the French Communist Party in 1950, like many intellectuals at the time. However, he left the party soon after, along with many others who were disillusioned by the party's doctrinaire stance and also by its support for the Soviet regime after its invasion of Hungary in 1956. The Party also condemned homosexuality as a bourgeois vice. From the moment he left the Party, Foucault became violently anti-Communist.

Foucault's relation to Marxism is complex and should be disentangled from his largely antagonistic and critical relations with the French Communist Party. Indeed, what Foucault argues for is 'an unburdening and liberation of Marx in relation to party dogma which has constrained it' (Foucault 1988c: 45). At many times, Foucault acknowledges his debt to Marxist thought and there are many elements within his work which suggest the profound influence of Marxist analyses of power relations and the role of economic inequality in determining social structures. But equally, just as strong is the sense of Foucault reacting against much Marxist thought. Fundamentally, it is the purely economic and State-centred focus which Foucault distanced himself from, stressing that power needs to be reconceptualised and the role of the State, and the function of the economic, need a radical revisioning. He should, perhaps, best be seen as negotiating with a Marxist framework of analysis which could no longer be applied in any simple way to the more complex social structures of France in the 1960s and 1970s; as he said: 'Marxism exists in nineteenth century thought as a fish exists in water; that is, it ceases to breathe anywhere else' (Foucault 1970: 274).

There has been a great deal of discussion among theorists about the nature and extent of Foucault's political engagement. He himself does not seem to have felt it necessary to have a fully worked-out political position, since in some ways it was precisely this sense of having to hold to a party line which he was reacting against: 'I think I have, in fact, been situated in most of the squares on the political checkerboard, one after another and sometimes simultaneously: as anarchist, leftist, ostentatious or disguised Marxist, explicit or secret

anti-Marxist, technocrat in the service of Gaullism, new liberal, etc.
. . . It's true, I prefer not to identify myself and that I'm amused by
the diversity of the ways I've been judged and classified' (Foucault,
cited in Macey 1994: xix). Such a sceptical apolitical stance is easily
criticised on the grounds that it is simply radicalism pushed to the
extreme of nihilism: Walzer has categorised Foucault's political activity
as that of 'infantile leftism . . . that is less an endorsement than an
outrunning of the most radical argument in any political struggle'
(Walzer 1986: 51). Bartky also criticises Foucault for the essentially
negative critical position which he adopts, which she suggests comes
close to pessimism (Bartky, cited in Sawicki 1998: 97). However, in
a journal article in 1968, Foucault describes his notion of a progressive politics in contradistinction to other forms of politics (such as,
one might assume, Marxism):

> A progressive politics is a politics which recognises the historical and speci-
> fied conditions of a practice, whereas other politics recognise only ideal
> necessities, univocal determinations and the free interplay of individual initia-
> tives. A progressive politics is a politics which defines, within a practice,
> possibilities for transformation and the play of dependencies between those
> transformations, whereas other politics rely upon the uniform abstraction of
> change or the thaumaturgic presence of genius.
>
> (Foucault, cited in Macey 1994: 195)

Thus, rather than seeing a politics as being centred around individual
great leaders who have utopian visions of the future, which entail the
adoption of a set of beliefs by their followers, Foucault is more
concerned to develop and describe a politics which takes account of
the transformative possibilities within the present.

It is clear from this attempt to formulate a progressive politics that
he is not apolitical but simply committed to seeing politics from a
broader perspective than that which sees politics as solely concerned
with party politics. Indeed, the nature of a progressive politics is
something which exercised Foucault greatly; he asks:

> Is progressive politics tied . . . to the themes of meaning, origin, the constituent
> subject, in short to all the themes which guarantee in history the inexhaustible
> presence of a Logos, the sovereignty of a pure subject, the deep teleology of
> a primeval destination? Is progressive politics tied to such a form of analysis

– rather than to one which questions it? And is such politics bound to all the dynamic, biological, evolutionist metaphors that serve to mask the difficult problem of historical change – or on the contrary, to their meticulous destruction? And further: is there some necessary kinship between progressive politics and refusing to recognise discourse as anything more than a shallow transparency which shimmers for a moment at the margins of things and of thoughts, and then vanishes?

(Foucault 1991a: 64–65)

Here, Foucault seems to be trying to establish a basis for productive political activity without necessarily having to agree with a whole range of problematic assumptions about progress and the role of individuals in bringing about political change. It could be argued that a theorist who is interested in the analysis of the anonymous discontinuities in historical and political change is effectively downplaying the role of individuals in transforming society. However, Foucault should not be seen as completely negating the role of the individual in political change; all that he is trying to stress is that humans are not 'the universal operator of all transformations' (Foucault 1991a: 70).

What Foucault is attempting to do in his analysis of the.political is to move away from abstract notions of the political and to ground the political more in local acts and interactions. However, this move does make the analysis of the operation of power relations more complex: 'To say that "everything is political" is to recognise [the] omnipresence of relations of force and their immanence to a political field; but it is to set oneself the barely sketched task of unravelling this indefinite tangled skein' (Foucault 1979c: 72). In a sense, what he is urging us to analyse is what we mean by the political; within his reconceptualisation of what constitutes the political 'one can no longer accept the conquest of power as the aim of political struggle; it is rather a question of the transformation of the economy of power (and truth) itself' (Patton 1979: 143).

While many have criticised Foucault for undermining the possibility of a grounded political position in his theoretical work, they acknowledge that during the 1960s and 1970s he was politically active (although some of them call into question the nature and effectiveness of his political interventions). At the end of 1968 he was appointed head of philosophy at the new experimental University of Vincennes, which became a hotbed of student political activity. Foucault seems to have taken a rather active role in the unrest; his biographer, Didier Eribon, states: 'he had been seen with an iron rod in his hands, ready to do battle with militant Communists; he had been seen throwing rocks at the police' (Eribon 1991: 209). By 1970, the teaching in the philosophy department was criticised by the Minister of Education, since many of the titles of the courses taught contained the words 'Marxist-Leninist'. The Minister decided that the students from Vincennes would not be eligible to become secondary school teachers. The department was then criticised because it did not seem to be holding examinations in the conventional sense. After two years at Vincennes, Foucault left to go to the prestigious Collège de France.

The importance for him of those in dominated positions taking control is particularly evident in Foucault's involvement in setting up the Groupe d'Information sur les Prisons during the 1970s. This group, which consisted of intellectuals, activists and ex-prisoners from a broad political spectrum, tried to draw attention to the inhumane conditions within French prisons. In a classic Foucauldian aphorism, he argues in a press conference: 'They tell us that the prisons are overpopulated. But what if it were the population that were being overimprisoned?' (Foucault, cited in Macey 1994: 258). He wanted to bring about change in the prison structure, not by campaigning on behalf of prisoners as many liberal reformist groups had done before, but by opening up channels of communication for prisoners, so that they could speak for themselves. The group organised demonstrations, discussed conditions with prisoners' families outside prisons and circulated questionnaires to inmates and their families, publishing the results in reports. Foucault was arrested outside La Santé prison when he was distributing leaflets in 1971. The group ceased its activities once it seemed that prisoners' groups were sufficiently well organised. (This concern with punishment and incarceration is further explored in Foucault's book *Discipline and Punish* (1975) and also in his publication of *I, Pierre Rivière* (1973), the 'confession' of a murderer who admitted having killed members of his family.)

In addition to these political activities, he also supported a variety of political campaigns; when he lived and worked in Tunisia he expressed solidarity with the students who were on strike there in 1966 (Macey 1994: 191, 205). Foucault was in Tunisia at the time of the events in Paris in 1968, but he took a keen interest in the events. He returned to France to a teaching post at Vincennes in 1969 and was arrested during one of the student occupations of the university (Macey 1994: 209). During 1971–1973, he took part in a large number of demonstrations against racism and the war in Vietnam and he signed numerous petitions. He also flew to Spain in 1975, as part of a delegation protesting against the execution of two members of the Basque separatist movement by the Spanish government; and he, along with other members of the group, was expelled from Spain. He also took part in campaigns on the treatment of Soviet dissidents and the Solidarity movement in Poland, and wrote about the revolutionary situation in Iran (unfortunately praising, as it turned out, the 'wrong' side) (Foucault 1988f). His acts of political critique did not only extend to those in power or those on the Right as, after his brief membership of the Communist party, he was vehemently anti-Communist.

While Foucault saw sexuality as a profoundly political issue and did write on homosexuality, particularly the sexual practices of males in ancient Greek society, many people have criticised Foucault for not being open about his sexuality and for not taking part in any of the gay rights struggles (Foucault 1978). This reluctance to admit to being homosexual is not surprising given that Foucault was forced to leave Poland because of a homosexual relationship, and was probably not offered a number of high-ranking posts because of his sexuality (Eribon 1991). However, it should be noted that in 1979 Foucault gave a lecture to a gay congress in Paris, and in 1982 he took part in a Gay Pride march in Toronto. There is a sense, however, in which, although engaged in the gay culture of the time, (he had a long-term male partner for the last 25 years of his life), he was also very critical of certain tendencies within gay culture. He wanted gay culture to invent 'ways of relating, types of existence, types of exchanges between individuals which are really new and are neither the same as, nor superimposed on, existing cultural forms. If that's possible then gay culture will be not only a choice of homosexuals for homosexuals. It would create relations that are, at a certain point, transferable to heterosexuals'(Foucault, cited in Macey 1994: 367). He died of an AIDS-related illness in 1984 and has been frequently criticised for not being open about his illness; indeed a number of vicious rumours about Foucault's sexual activities after he discovered he was HIV positive have circulated, notably that he wilfully infected others with HIV. (These stories do seem to be simply part of a fictional backlash response to homosexuality and bear little resemblance to reality.) It is very easy to judge others' actions in the light of a change in the attitudes and actions of those suffering from AIDS-related illnesses, since coming out has become a much more common approach to the disease than it was in the 1980s. And this reluctance may well have had theoretical foundations: when he was criticised by Paul Aron for not 'coming out' about having AIDS, Didier Eribon asks 'was it not precisely the idea of "confession" that Foucault loathed? This loathing left its mark in all the effort expended in his last books to reject, refuse and defuse the order to say, to speak, to make someone speak' (Eribon 1991: 29–30).

It is interesting that, at the same time that Foucault seems to have adopted the classic role of the French intellectual involved in political struggles, he also advised the government on educational policy, sitting on the Fouchet Commission reviewing secondary and higher education in 1965–1966, and he was also invited to serve on a government commission on the reform of the penal code in 1976. At one time, Foucault was considered for appointment as assistant director of higher education in the Ministry of Education, but was turned down because of his homosexuality. It was also suggested that he could be the director of ORTF (Office de Radiodiffusion Télévision Française), the State-run television network. Thus, while he was considered to be a political radical, he was also very much developing his career and being considered for high-ranking administrative positions. He frequently used his position of authority within French society to bring to light political struggles. His engagement seems to be very much that of the 'specific intellectual', a term he developed to describe a new view of political activity whereby, rather than the intellectual assuming that s/he will lead the workers into revolution, the intellectual works within their own field of expertise to undermine oppressive regimes from within (Foucault 1977a). Foucault gives the example of nuclear scientists who criticise government policies in developing nuclear arms. Kritzman describes this form of activism in the following way: 'the analysis of political technologies – in which the intellectual works inside of institutions and attempts to constitute a new political ethic by challenging the institutional regime of the production of truth. Political activism therefore becomes the critical analysis of the conflicts within specific sectors of society without allowing the intellectual to engage with the charade of ideological hermeneutics' (Kritzman 1988: xix). He also drew attention to the intervention made by Dr Edith Rose, a medical psychiatrist, working in the prison at Toul, where there had been revolts in the 1970s. She protested about the conditions in prisons; Foucault comments: 'She was inside a power system and rather than criticise its functioning, she denounced what has just happened, on a particular day, a particular place, under particular circumstances' (Foucault, cited in Eribon 1991: 231). Thus, Foucault exemplified this type of political activity of the 'specific intellectual', using his public position to draw attention to particular political campaigns, while rejecting the utopianism and constraining ideologies of most political parties.

As well as considering the political situation in France in the 1960s and 1970s it is also important to consider the intellectual climate. Macey argues that 'Foucault's life was also the intellectual life of France. There are few changes that are not reflected in his work, and there are few developments that he did not influence' (Macey 1994: 1). One of the things that is striking about French intellectual life of this period, and perhaps even now, is how much more receptive French culture is to philosophy: philosophy is an integral part of the secondary school syllabus and it plays a major role in general intellectual discussions. Philosophy books are published in print runs which can only be dreamed of in Britain. For example, in 1966, when Foucault published *The Order of Things*, the first print run of 3,000 was sold out within a week, the second print run of 5,000 sold out within six weeks, and the book was at the top of a non-fiction best-seller list (Macey 1994: 160). So far, 110,000 copies of this densely argued philosophical work have been sold (Eribon 1991: 156).

At the time that Foucault began to write, the existentialist philosopher Jean-Paul Sartre (1905–1980) still played a major role in French life and culture. Sartre was a politically committed philosopher who was a very active public figure, writing not only philosophical treatises, but also newspaper articles, novels and plays. In many ways, Sartre defined the parameters within which a politically motivated academic could act and influence public opinion. The philosophical position developed by Sartre, existentialism, is concerned with stressing personal experience and responsibility in a seemingly meaningless universe. Foucault was part of the generation who reacted against Sartrean existentialism, and who always, on a personal, political and philosophical level, had great difficulties coming to terms with Sartre. Foucault reacted to what he termed Sartre's 'philosophy of consciousness', since he characterised his own work as concerned to developed a 'philosophy of the concept' (Macey 1994: 33). He also suggested that Sartre was concerned with the analysis of meaning while he was concerned with the analysis of system (Macey 1994: 170).

Hubert Dreyfus and Paul Rabinow see Foucault's philosophical career as taking four stages: a stage where he was exploring the possibilities of Heideggerean thought; an archaeological or structuralist phase; a genealogical stage and, finally, a stage where he was concerned to develop a new model of ethics (Dreyfus and Rabinow 1982). Foucault has been variously categorised as a structuralist, a post-structuralist, a post-modernist, a New Philosopher and also as someone who fits none of these categories easily – being rather a 'non-historical historian, an anti-humanist human scientist, a counter-structuralist structuralist' (Geertz, cited in Dreyfus and Rabinow 1982: iii). He is, thus, not someone who is easily pigeonholed in terms of his academic and theoretical concerns. Furthermore, Foucault's relation to the intellectual conditions of his time are characterised far more by dissent and scepticism than by any passive notions of influence. However, I would like to consider the stages in the development of Foucault's thought as this might help you to have an overall framework for understanding Foucault's ideas, which I deal with in more detail in the individual chapters which follow.

⋅ The idea of discussing the development or progression of his career would have horrified Foucault, since he tried to make clear that these evolutionary concepts are fictional elements which one imposes on events within an author's life after the fact. Human lives are far more random and lacking in cohesion. He argued in his essay 'What is an author?' that 'the author is the principle of a certain unity of writing – all differences having to be resolved, at least in part, by the principles of evolution, maturation or influence. The author serves to neutralise the contradictions that may emerge in a series of texts' (Foucault 1986a: 111). I feel sure that he would have hated the notion that the disparate texts which he published were united under his name, since he argues: 'how can one attribute several discourses to one and the same author?' and he asserts on several occasions, in interviews, that books should be published anonymously (Foucault 1986a: 110). He prefers, instead, to talk about the 'author-function' – that principle which unites the works of an author – rather than talking about the author as a person. Furthermore, in his work on the author he tried to move away from the notion of the oeuvre, seeing the very notion of a completed set of ideas or concerns as fictional and primarily as a concept which is used by critics, commentators and educational institutions to make teaching, examining and critical commentary more manageable and easier to think about.

For these reasons, it is difficult to describe Foucault, perhaps more than any other theorist, within a developmental framework, progressing from a pre-structuralist to a structuralist and then a post-structuralist phase, for example. But we can see a certain focus in Foucault's work which he continually addresses and readdresses, circling back to consider issues which have surfaced in earlier works. From the point of view of readers of his work, this notion of a set of concerns which he circles around is important, not in order to impose on Foucault's work an imaginary cohesion, but to give some sense of larger discursive frameworks within which we can try to understand his work.

As I argued above, we can see that the political and social changes of the 1960s and 1970s had a major impact on Foucault politically and this marked also a major transition in his work. Before the 1960s his work was mainly focused on the analysis of the anonymous production of knowledges and discourse, for example in works such as *The Archaeology of Knowledge*, but after the 1960s, in works such as *The History of Sexuality*, (1976–1984) the internal structures of knowledge and discourse are seen to be produced through inter-relations of power and the effects of those power relations on individuals (see Chapters 2–4). It is at this point in his work that Foucault becomes more profoundly concerned with history. He turns from philosophy and psychology to historical analysis, or perhaps we can see that he tries to combine historical analysis with philosophical/psychological analysis, because, as Donnelly puts it, he sees the focus of history as a way of 'cleansing thought of its transcendental narcissism', and thus as a way of thinking about the present and the past without focusing on the progress of the liberal individual (Donnelly 1986: 16). Foucault's turn to history has not necessarily been applauded by historians, since he makes a very cavalier use of historical records and he is notoriously lax with his documentation and with his references. Furthermore, we might think that conventional history's aim is to offer an explanatory framework for events in the past, an aim which Foucault rejects. He uses historical methods to analyse the development of academic disciplines themselves and to show the triumphalism of their accounts of their own history: 'instead of treating the past as a prologue, as part of an easily comprehensible, continuous series of events unfolding into the present, he tried to establish its radical otherness, its difference' (Donnelly 1986: 17). Thus, for Foucault, the past is not seen as inevitably leading up to the present, a view of history which renders the past banal; it is the very strangeness of the past which makes us able to see clearly the strangeness of the present.

This transition in Foucault's work from the analysis of impersonal, autonomous discourse to one focused on the workings of power is marked by a shift from a type of analysis which he terms 'archaeology' to one characterised as 'genealogy': his earlier works can be seen to be more concerned with archaeology and his later ones with genealogy. These terms, archaeology and genealogy, are the ones most associated with Foucauldian analysis. Archaeology can be regarded as the analysis of the system of unwritten rules which produces, organises and distributes the 'statement' (that, is the authorised utterance) as it occurs in an archive (that is, an organised body of statements). Foucault describes the archive as 'the general system of the formation and transformation of statements' (Foucault 1972: 130). (These terms 'statement' and 'archive' will be discussed in greater detail in Chapter 3, as will the distinctions between archaeology and genealogy.) Kendall and Wickham describe archaeology in the following terms: 'Archaeology helps us to explore the networks of what is said, and what can be seen in a set of social arrangements: in the conduct of an archaeology, one finds out something about the visible in "opening up" statements and something about the statement in "opening up visibilities"' (Kendall and Wickham 1999: 25). In this sense, archaeological analysis can be seen as a historically-based study of what the discourses within the archive allow to be stated authoritatively. This archaeological analysis is a description of regular patterns within a discourse and is concerned to describe the way that statements are transformed into other statements and the way that they are considered to be distinct from others. Thus, this type of analysis is concerned with the relation between different statements, the way that they are grouped together and the conditions under which certain statements can emerge. Archaeological analysis is not interpretative; that is, it does not offer explanations of what happened in the past – it simply describes what happens and the discursive conditions under which it was possible for that to happen. As I show in the final chapter of this book, this lack of interpretation is another element of Foucault's work which many find disconcerting and unsettling, and which many consequently simply ignore.

Genealogy is a development of archaeological analysis which is more concerned with the workings of power and with describing the 'history of the present'. It is a form of historical analysis which describes events in the past but without explicitly making causal connections: as Donnelly states: 'It may not satisfy a certain longing for explanations but that is exactly Foucault's intention, to starve that longing and provide only "documentation"' (Donnelly 1986: 24). Foucault's concern with genealogical analysis is not to focus on an 'analytics of truth' which he argues many philosophers in the past have done, that is, to analyse the conditions under which we might consider certain utterances or propositions to be agreed to be true. Rather, his concern is with an 'ontology of ourselves', that is, to turn that analytic gaze to the condition under which we, as individuals, exist and what causes us to exist in the way that we do (Foucault 1988a: 95). Kendall and Wickham argue that 'taken to its extreme, genealogy targets us, our "selves": it seems we are meant to see beyond the contingencies that have made each of us what we are in order that we might think in ways that we have not thought and be in ways that we have not been; it is a tool we might use on a quest for freedom' (Kendall and Wickham 1999: 30). Smart takes a slightly different slant on the differences between archaeological and genealogical analysis; he argues that: 'the archaeological investigations are directed to an analysis of the unconscious rules of formation which regulate the emergence of discourses in the human sciences. In contrast, the genealogical analyses reveal the emergence of the human sciences, their conditions of existence, to be inextricably associated with particular technologies of power embodied in social practices' (Smart 1985: 48).

There are theorists who argue that genealogy and archaeology are simply two aspects of one type of methodological approach. However, I feel that they can be usefully distinguished as, if not separate methodologies, then distinct perspectives. Kendall and Wickham argue that the distinction between these two approaches can be seen in the following terms: 'where archaeology provides us with a snapshot, a slice through a discursive nexus, genealogy pays attention to the processual aspects of the web of discourse – its ongoing character' (Kendall and Wickham 1999: 31). Foucault argues that: 'if we were to characterise it in two terms, then "archaeology" would be the appropriate methodology of [the] analysis of local discursivities, and "genealogy" would be the tactics whereby, on the basis of the descriptions of these local discursivities, the subjected knowledges which were thus released would be brought into play' (Foucault 1980a: 85).

As well as moving from an archaeological perspective to a genealogical form of analysis, from a focus on the workings of largely impersonal forces to the analysis of the intricate working-out of power relations, Foucault can also be seen to have moved from a structuralist to a poststructuralist phase. In his structuralist phase, Foucault was associated with many members of the Tel Quel (a literary theory journal) group, which included among others Roland Barthes (1915–1980), Julia Kristeva (1941–), and Philippe Sollers (1936–). Macey describes the Tel Quel group as that 'literary Maoist group of thinkers who, perhaps more than any others, radicalised the role of literary and philosophical studies in the academy' (Macey 1994: 151). With Barthes and Kristeva, he became part of that moment of intellectual questioning labelled structuralism, where theorists attempted to move away from concentrating on the genius of the individual creative writer to analyse the underlying structures of literary and non-literary texts. Rather than analysing the intentions of the writer in shaping the text, and assuming an exceptional creative power on the part of the author, structuralist critics turned away from the author, proclaiming that the author was dead. In her/his place, they argued that critics should focus on the text itself and the impersonal forces of discursive structures such as narrative which shaped the text, or critics should turn to the role of the reader in the process of making sense of texts (Barthes 1968; Foucault 1984). Indeed, humanism (that is, the belief that each individual is in essence distinct from others, and that the individual is the key to ways of making sense of phenomena), is one of the main focuses of Foucault's theoretical ire. In an interview, Foucault argues that: 'our task at the moment is to completely free ourselves from humanism and in that sense our work is political work . . . all regimes, East and West, smuggle shoddy goods under the banner of humanism . . . We must denounce these mystifications' (Foucault, cited in Macey 1994: 171).

Thus, Foucault focused not on literary texts and the creativity of their authors, but rather on the anonymous underlying structures and rules of formation of discourse in general. As he says in his introduction to *The Order of Things*, where he analyses the discursive shifts that have occurred through history and which manifest themselves in the regularities in particular types of interpretations across a range of sciences:

> What I would like to do ... is to reveal a positive unconscious of knowledge: a level that eludes the consciousness of the scientists and yet is part of scientific discourse, instead of disputing its validity and seeking to diminish its scientific nature. What was common to the natural history, the economics and the grammar of the Classical period was certainly not present to the consciousness of the scientist; of that part of it that was conscious was superficial, limited and almost fanciful ... but unknown to themselves, the naturalist, economists, and grammarians employed the same rules to define the objects proper to their own study, to form their concepts, and objects of study, that I have tried to reveal, by isolating, as their specific locus, a level that I have called, somewhat arbitrarily perhaps, archaeological.
>
> (Foucault 1970: xi)

Foucault moves away from the individual, towards the discovery of the 'death of Man', towards an analysis of the impersonal determining forces inherent in discourse itself, within what could be labelled his structuralist period. (We must be tentative when suggesting that Foucault was a structuralist, since his relationship with structuralism was always rather tenuous, and theorists such as Louis Althusser, Jacques Lacan (1901–1981), Roland Barthes and Julia Kristeva and Michel Foucault who are generally taken to be structuralist can perhaps be seen as held together only by their negative relationship with liberal humanism rather than being united by a common philosophy.)

The anti-humanist work which Foucault engaged with in this period of structuralism is concerned not to trace the motivations and intentions of individuals but to uncover the workings of discourse over long periods of time. He traces through history the breaks in thinking or 'discontinuities' which occur at particular historical conjunctures; thus, he is not concerned with charting the importance of certain great thinkers, or trends in the history of ideas, but rather the moments when there are radical and shocking changes in direction in the way that phenomena are thought about and the ways that events are interpreted. In order to describe this global way of thinking about events and the general way in which discourse is organised, in *The Archaeology of Knowledge* (1972), he developed the term 'épistèmé', that is, the body of knowledge and ways of knowing which are in circulation at a particular moment. Foucault suggests that there is a significant break at the inauguration of the Classical and the modern periods, where he claims new ways of classifying and ordering information developed. Thus, like many other theorists at this time, Foucault is trying to develop a way of describing events and interpretation without drawing on humanist ideas of the individual. Many other theorists within psychoanalysis focused on the fractured self, rather than the cohesive self of humanism; others influenced by Marxism examined wider social groupings and institutions rather than the individual, since they considered focus on the individual to be a bourgeois concern. Foucault, however, tried to theorise without reference to the individual or subject, focusing at this phase of his thinking on the workings of anonymous discourses which he saw as operating largely under their own momentum and their own system of rules, outside the influence or control of mere humans.

For many theorists who worked within structuralism, the problems inherent in such a position which viewed events and phenomena as autonomous and as governed by internal rules and mechanisms, posed serious theoretical problems. The group of theorists, including Foucault, who found difficulty with structuralist ideas, is generally labelled post-structuralist. Post-structuralism consists of a diverse group of theorists, most notably the deconstructionist, Jacques Derrida (1930–) (who was Foucault's student), Julia Kristeva, Jacques Lacan and Foucault, who reacted against structuralism and the whole notion of inherent structures. Post-structuralism was not united by any particular common theme or beliefs but rather simply by a reaction to the notion of the structure. In fact, Foucault and Derrida engaged in quite violent arguments, which resulted in Foucault dismissing Derrida's work as 'a minor pedagogy' which privileged the authority of the critic (Foucault, cited in Eribon 1991: 121). In some ways, post-structuralism can be seen as the move to theorise without the notion of a centre, core or foundation. In this sense, Foucault's work can be seen to move from a structuralist focus to a more post-structuralist phase, but in many ways, he cannot be seen as wholeheartedly adopting either of these theoretical positions.

IMPACT OF FOUCAULT'S THINKING

Marxist and materialist thinking have changed immeasurably since the 1960s and since the disintegration of the Soviet regime and such events as the fall of the Berlin Wall during the 1980s. Furthermore, the criticism by many post-modernist thinkers of the notion of grand narratives (that is, the notion that it is possible to propose a utopian future which will be achieved by political action) has forced such models as Marxism, which have clear political goals and models of historical progress, to be reconceptualised. However, Foucault's thinking about the theoretical problems of models used by Marxism are of interest in order to be able to reconstruct a model of socialism which can be used to analyse the political problems of the twenty-first century. Foucault's thought 'enlarges the scope of rethinking many of the parameters of socialist struggles and their objectives – the "ends" of socialism – and this in a non-utopian way' (Minson 1986: 107).

Foucault has also been tremendously influential within the fields of post-colonial theory and feminist theory (Mills 1991; 1997). The latter is perhaps rather surprising since Foucault has often been thought of as a misogynist (Morris 1979: 152). However, many feminist theorists have found that Foucault's critical thinking is of use since:

> Both [feminism and Foucault] identify the body as the site of power . . . both point to the local and intimate operations of power rather than focusing exclusively on the supreme power of the state. Both bring to the fore the crucial role of discourse in its capacity to produce and sustain hegemonic power and emphasise the challenges contained within marginalised and/or unrecognised discourses, and both criticise the ways in which Western humanism has privileged the experience of the Western masculine elite as it proclaims universals about truth, freedom and human nature.
>
> (Diamond and Quinby 1988: x)

Thus, both Foucault and feminist thinkers have found it necessary to rethink the conceptual frameworks which underpin much of what is characterised as common-sense within society. The feminist Dorothy Smith, for example, in her work on the discursive construction and negotiation of both femininity and mental illness has used Foucault's thinking about discourse in order to examine the way that individuals negotiate with structures rather than simply submitting to them (Smith 1990).

Post-colonial theory, primarily because Edward Said used Foucault's thought in his extremely influential book *Orientalism*, (1978) has consistently drawn on and reacted to Foucault's work and, in some instances, has tried to make it more profoundly political or materialist and even compatible with psychoanalytical thought (Said 1978; Bhabha 1994; McClintock 1995). The value of his work in this context has been primarily in the reconceptualisation of power relations. As I show in Chapter 2, power is seen by Foucault not as something which is imposed on another but as a network or web of relations which circulates through society (Foucault 1978). Thus, within post-colonial theory, colonialism no longer has to be thought of simply as an imposition of power relations on a passive indigenous population, but can be seen as the enactment through violence and invasion, but also through the production of knowledge and information, of a very fragile hold on another territory, constantly challenged and constantly needing to be asserted and reasserted in the face of opposition (Guha 1994).

Perhaps it is this analysis of power which has most profoundly influenced political thinking, so that rather than simply thinking of power as an imposition of the will of one individual on another, or one group on another, we can see power as a set of relations and strategies dispersed throughout a society and enacted at every moment of interaction.

To summarise then, Foucault should be seen as intervening in political and philosophical debates at a time when there were major shifts and changes taking place both in France and throughout the rest of the world. He was profoundly affected by the events of May 1968 and he made a major impact, both through his writing and through his political actions, on subsequent political changes. He helped to develop theories which could analyse the complexity of the political and philosophical scene after 1968 and, perhaps more importantly, he forced intellectuals to think about the very building blocks of thought that they used to analyse social conditions.

STRUCTURE OF THIS BOOK

Rather than devoting particular chapters to Foucault's major theoretical texts, I have decided to focus chapters of this book to particular concerns of Foucault's which he discusses at different times in his career, in interviews and essays, as well as in books. In Chapter 2, Power and institutions, I examine Foucault's work on power and resistance particularly as it relates to social structures and institutions. His theorising here is important since he takes issue with many of the assumptions that we have about governance and the role of individuals and marginalised groups in resisting oppression by regimes. In Chapter 3, Discourse, I discuss Foucault's work on the autonomous rules and functionings of discourse. In Chapter 4, Power/knowledge, I examine Foucault's work which challenges the common-sense status of knowledge and truth and also his theoretical work which considers the way that these two concepts are held in place by a vast array of mechanisms whose purpose is to exclude other information. In Chapter 5, The body and sexuality, I focus on his theorising of the way that power is enacted and resisted on the site of the body, through an examination of his work on sexuality. His concern with charting the history of sexuality has sparked off a wide range of research primarily within gay, lesbian and feminist theorising. This work has implications for theoretical work on sexuality but also on the nature of the individual and the representation of individual characters in literature. In Chapter 6, Questioning the subject, I analyse Foucault's work on the subject or individual particularly as it relates to notions of madness and sanity. In the concluding chapter, After Foucault, I examine ways of using and reading Foucault's methods and sketch out the ways that Foucault can be used without feeling that one has to adhere strictly to everything he has written. I suggest here that a truly Foucauldian reading or method is one which moves beyond Foucault's writing and thinking.

POWER AND INSTITUTIONS

Foucault's work is largely concerned with the relation between social structures and institutions and the individual. Although, as I mentioned in the previous chapter and will discuss in more detail in Chapter 5, the notion of the individual is problematic for Foucault, nevertheless, it is in the relationship between the individual and the institution that we find power operating most clearly. Throughout his career, in works such as *The History of Sexuality* (1978), *Power/Knowledge* (1980), *The Birth of the Clinic* (1973) and *Discipline and Punish* (1977), he focused on the analysis of the effects of various institutions on groups of people and the role that those people play in affirming or resisting those effects. Central to this concern with institutions is his analysis of power. His work is very critical of the notion that power is something which a group of people or an institution possess and that power is only concerned with oppressing and constraining. What his work tries to do is move thinking about power beyond this view of power as repression of the powerless by the powerful to an examination of the way that power operates within everyday relations between people and institutions. Rather than simply viewing power in a negative way, as constraining and repressing, he argues, particularly in *The History of Sexuality, Vol. 1* (1978), that even at their most constraining, oppressive measures are in fact productive, giving rise to new forms of behaviour rather than simply closing down or censoring certain forms of behaviour.

Foucault, unlike many earlier Marxist theorists, is less concerned with focusing on oppression, but rather in foregrounding resistance to power. Much of this work has provoked a critical debate among critical theorists and political theorists, as the exact mechanics of resistance to power relations is not necessarily clearly mapped out in Foucault's accounts, but his work has, nevertheless, occasioned a very favourable response from a number of feminists and other critical theorists who have found in his work a way of thinking about the forms of power relations between men and women which do not fit neatly into the types of relations conventionally described within theorisations of power which tend to focus on the role of the State, ideology or patriarchy (Thornborrow 2002).

Marxist theory generally uses the term ideology to describe the means whereby oppressed people accept views of the world which are not accurate and which are not in their interests. Ideology, for Marxists, is the imaginary representation of the way things are in a society, and this fictive version of the world serves the interests of those who are dominant in society. Thus, an ideological view of society might be one where the middle classes are portrayed as naturally more intelligent than the working classes, rather than a Marxist economic view which would focus on the fact that schools with a majority of middle class pupils have better facilities.

Marxist theorisations, such as that of Louis Althusser, of the State's role in oppressing people, have been found to be largely unsatisfactory since they focus only on a one-way traffic of power, from the top downwards (Althusser 1984). Althusser is interested in the way that the State oppresses people and the way that ideology constitutes people as individuals. In his model, individuals are simply dupes of ideological pressures. Foucault's bottom-up model of power, that is his focus on the way power relations permeate all relations within a society, enables an account of the mundane and daily ways in which power is enacted and contested, and allows an analysis which focuses on individuals as active subjects, as agents rather than as passive dupes.

POWER RELATIONS

Power is often conceptualised as the capacity of powerful agents to realise their will over the will of powerless people, and the ability to force them to do things which they do not wish to do. Power is also often seen as a possession – something which is held onto by those in power and which those who are powerless try to wrest from their control. Foucault criticises this view, arguing in *The History of Sexuality, Vol. 1* (1978) that power is something which is performed, something more like a strategy than a possession. Power should be seen as a verb rather than a noun, something that does something, rather than something which is or which can be held onto. Foucault puts it in the following way in *Power/Knowledge:* 'Power must be analysed as something which circulates, or as something which only functions in the form of a chain . . . Power is employed and exercised through a net-like organisation . . . Individuals are the vehicles of power, not its points of application' (Foucault 1980: 98). There are several important points to note here: first that power is conceptualised as a chain or as a net, that is a system of relations spread throughout the society, rather than simply as a set of relations between the oppressed and the oppressor. And, second, individuals should not be seen simply as the recipients of power, but as the 'place' where power is enacted and the place where it is resisted. Thus, his theorising of power forces us to reconceptualise not only power itself but also the role that individuals play in power relations – whether they are simply subjected to oppression or whether they actively play a role in the form of their relations with others and with institutions.

As I mentioned earlier, Foucault tends to see power less as something which is possessed but rather as a strategy, something which someone does or performs in a particular context. Power needs to be seen as something which has to be constantly performed rather than being achieved. Indeed, he argues that power is a set of relations which are dispersed throughout society rather than being located within particular institutions such as the State or the government; in an interview entitled 'Critical theory/intellectual theory' he states: 'I am not referring to Power with a capital P, dominating and imposing its rationality upon the totality of the social body. In fact, there are power relations. They are multiple; they have different forms, they can be in play in family relations, or within an institution, or an administration' (Foucault 1988c: 38). Because he is portraying power here as a major force in all relations within society, he seems to have been influenced by the work of Louis Althusser, his teacher at the École Normale, who focuses his analysis of power more on what he terms Ideological State

Apparatuses (that is, the family, the Church, the educational system) rather than the Repressive State Apparatuses, (that is, the legal system, the army and the police) (Althusser 1984). In an interview entitled 'Power and sex', Foucault argues that these multiple power relations are not necessarily easy to observe in play: 'the relations of power are perhaps among the best hidden things in the social body . . . [our task is] to investigate what might be most hidden in the relations of power; to anchor them in the economic infrastructures; to trace them not only in their governmental forms but also in the intra-governmental or para-governmental ones; to discover them in their material play' (Foucault 1988d: 119). Thus, rather than simply locating power in a centralised impersonal institution, such as the army or the police, as earlier Marxist theorists had done, he is interested in local forms of power and the way that they are negotiated with by individuals or other agencies. This concern with the materiality of power relations at a local level can be seen to have influenced many feminist theorists, such as Judith Butler, who have tried to develop models of the relation between gender and power without assuming that power is simply located in institutions and who have tried to see gender identity as something that one performs in particular contexts, not something that one possesses (Butler 1993; Salih 2002).

Foucault's view of power is directly counter to the conventional Marxist or early feminist model of power which sees power simply as a form of oppression or repression, what Foucault terms the 'repressive hypothesis'. Instead, he sees power as also at the same time productive, something which brings about forms of behaviour and events rather than simply curtailing freedom and constraining individuals. He argues in *The History of Sexuality, Vol. I*: 'if power was never anything but repressive, if it never did anything but say no, do you really believe that we should manage to obey it?' (Foucault 1978: 36). Implicit in this quotation is the sense that there must be something else, apart from repression, which leads people to conform. To give an example, he describes in *The History of Sexuality, Vol. I* (1978) the concern that developed in the nineteenth century about male children's masturbation, and the way that this led to the publication of numerous advice manuals on how to prevent or discourage such practices which, in turn, led to a full-scale surveillance of boys. Rather than seeing this as simply the oppression of children and the control of their sexual desires and practices, Foucault argues in *Power/Knowledge*, that this 'was the sexualising of the infantile body, a sexualising of the bodily relationship between parent and child, and a sexualising of the family domain . . . sexuality is far more of a positive product of power than power was ever a repression of sexuality' (Foucault 1980b: 120). Thus, the discussion of the sexuality of children and the watching, advising and punishment of children in relation to sexual practices actually brought into being a set of sexualised relations and the construction of a perverse sexuality – the very sexuality which it was designed to eliminate.

This positive, productive view of power led Foucault to analyse popular uprisings, where individual groups of people take power into their own hands, for example in his interview with a Maoist group where he discusses popular justice in *Power/Knowledge* (1980) and his article on the Iranian revolution entitled 'Iran: the spirit of a world without spirit' (1988f). It is not surprising that Foucault focuses on the analysis of revolution and times of great upheaval, given that the 1960s and 1970s were a time when there were many people who argued that one should try to escape, challenge and overthrow oppressive regimes and cast off all of the rules and trappings of bourgeois capitalist society, as I argued in the previous chapter. In much earlier Marxist thinking the overthrow of the State and the liberation of the working classes through revolution was seen as a fundamental aim of political action. However, in his article 'Truth and Power', Foucault does not argue that revolution is necessarily a simple freedom from oppression, a complete challenge to bourgeois power, and an overturning of power relations, since 'the State consists in the codification of a whole number of power relations which render its functioning possible, and . . . revolution is a different type of codification of the same relations' (Foucault 1980b: 122). Thus, the State should not be seen as possessing power but as constructing a range of relations which tend to position people in ways which make the political system work; as we can see from the example of the French Revolution, a revolution may change certain aspects of the way that society is run, but it will tend to position people in much the same way, imprisoning or executing those who disagree with its policies, taxing people in much the same way as the old regime, and trying, through a range of different methods, to force citizens into conformity with its political programmes. Thus, the notion of liberation from oppression through revolution for Foucault is one which should be treated with extreme caution.

Foucault also analyses, in his essay 'The subject and power', what he terms 'anti-authority struggles' which he sees as something which had developed relatively recently and which he characterises in the following terms: 'opposition of the power of men over women, of parents over children, of psychiatry over the mentally ill, of medicine over the population, of administration over the ways people live' (Foucault 1982: 211). All of these struggles are characterised by him as being 'local' or 'immediate' struggles, since they are instances in which people are criticising the immediate conditions of their lives and the way that certain people, groups or institutions are acting on their lives. He sees these struggles as constituting a refusal of analysis of the wider forces of power: 'the main objective of these struggles is to attack not so much such and such an institution of power, or group, or elite, or class, but rather a technique, a form of power' (Foucault 1982: 212).

Many theorists find extremely problematic Foucault's work on popular justice, for example the interview referred to above (1980). It should be stated that he says on several occasions that we must ask ourselves difficult questions about whether the campaign we are aligning ourselves with is the 'right' one, for example in an interview on 'Power and sex' he states 'to engage in politics – aside from just party politics – is to try to know with the greatest possible honesty, whether the revolution is desirable' (Foucault 1988d: 122). However, this honest approach to the support of political action does not always extend to the analysis of lynch mobs and popular justice: for example, he argues that 'it may be quite possible that the proletariat will exert towards the classes over which it has just triumphed a violent, dictatorial and even bloody power. I can't see what objection one could make to this' (Foucault, cited in Gane 1986: 86). This view of popular justice was fairly common in the 1960s and 1970s and, given his political engagement in various campaigns, can be seen as perfectly consistent. However, when questioned in an interview about the French women who had their heads shaved and who were publicly shamed by mobs, because they had allegedly had relationships with Germans during the Second World War, while the real collaborators escaped public retribution, Foucault suggests that 'it is necessary to find forms through which this need for retribution, which is in fact real among the masses, can be developed, by discussion, by information' (Foucault 1980c: 29). This is a very difficult statement since it seems to suggest that with adequate information people will turn away from lynch mobs and retribution. This certainly is not borne out, for example, in the actions of certain sections of the British population during 2001 who waited outside courts where suspected paedophiles were being tried, in order to attack them, and attacked the houses of those suspected of having been convicted of paedophilia. There were several cases of mistaken identity. For those who were mistakenly accused of paedophilia but still attacked by the mobs, Foucault's blasé attitude to retribution must be rather difficult to take. However, Foucault is at least willing to think seriously about popular acts of retribution without condemning those people as unthinking and brutish, as many commentators in the popular press have done.

Furthermore, Foucault, together with a group of researchers, published *I, Pierre Rivière, Having Killed My Mother, My Sister and My Brother*, which is the confession of a 20-year-old Norman peasant who was convicted in 1836 of murdering three members of his family (Foucault 1978). Foucault organised a seminar to study the 40-page confession detailing Rivière's life, motives, relations with his family, and published the confession along with the reports by contemporary psychiatrists, reporters and reports of the legal proceedings. Even here, in the commentary on the text, Foucault is at pains to be non-judgemental; he describes the confession as 'a strange contest, a confrontation, a power relation, a battle among discourses and through discourses' (Foucault 1978: 12). This dispassionate stance is essential for the type of analysis he does, but it does mean that the systematic nature of male violence towards women is erased. Furthermore, the rights of Rivière's mother, brother and sister, who were brutally murdered, do not seem to figure very large in Foucault's analysis. By the very fact that Foucault has chosen to work on this case, Pierre Rivière is, in a sense, championed. There is a certain risk that one takes in working on problematic topics like this, but for theorists such as Foucault, it seems to add to the daring of his work that he is prepared to work on even those whom society rejects the most. While the analysis of homosexuals, the insane and women seems to be perfectly laudable, since they have not chosen to be socially stigmatised, it seems a very different matter to focus on those who have intentionally acted to disrupt society and deprive others of their rights or their lives. This championing of the power of proletarian groups, lynch mobs and murderers is highly problematic and has been much challenged by other theorists, not only conservatives, but also those on the Left.

POWER AND RESISTANCE

In Volume I of *The History of Sexuality*, Foucault states that 'where there is power there is resistance' (Foucault 1978). This is an important and problematic statement for many reasons. It is productive in that it allows us to consider the relationship between those in struggles over power as not simply reducible to a master–slave relation, or an oppressor–victim relationship. In order for there to be a relation where power is exercised, there has to be someone who resists. Foucault goes so far as to argue that where there is no resistance it is not, in effect, a power relation. Thus, for him, resistance is 'written in' to the exercise of power. However, if we assume that resistance is already 'written in' to power, then this may be seen to diminish the agency of the individuals who do resist oppressive regimes, often at great phys- ical cost to themselves. Given that resistance to oppression is much more difficult than collaborating, (one has only to read the reports contained in Amnesty International briefings or news reports about the Palestinian uprising to realise this), given Foucault's model of power, it is difficult to account for the fact that these individuals have chosen to oppose and challenge oppression, rather than to simply acquiesce. However, perhaps what Foucault is trying to argue in this model of power is that we should not see the way that power relations operate to be simply about the oppression of individuals by an institution or a government. Rather we should see that resistance to oppression is much more frequent than one would imagine; in this way he manages to move away from viewing individuals as only passive recipients.

Certain theorists have worked with Foucault's ideas on power and have tried to capture the complexity of relations of resistance and flesh out Foucault's ideas more. For example, James Scott in *Domination and the Arts of Resistance* has concerned himself with the way that both the powerful and the powerless are constrained in their behaviour within the power relation (Scott 1990). He shows that in their behaviour with each other they may behave as master and slave, maintaining the linguistic rituals for this type of encounter, while when out of each other's presence they behave quite differently. For example, when with his/her peers, the less powerful person will mock the powerful person, invent demeaning nicknames and tell stories of ways in which the powerful person will be humiliated. The powerful person, on the other hand, will tell his or her peers about the difficulties of maintaining control over the powerless and about the strain of maintaini᠁ the steely exterior demanded by his/her role. Scott asks: 'How do we study power relations when the powerless are often obliged to adopt a strategic pose in the presence of the powerful and when the powerful may have an interest in overdramatizing their reputation and mastery? If we take all of this at face value we risk mistaking what may be a tactic for the whole story' (Scott 1990: xii). Thus, Scott suggests that what we need to add to the analysis of the behaviour of the power-less and powerful in each other's presence is an analysis of their behaviour when they are with their equals. There, he suggests, they develop a 'hidden transcript' that is a 'critique of power spoken behind the back of the dominant' (Scott 1990: xii). The powerful also develop a hidden transcript which consists of the claims of their rule which cannot be openly avowed in front of other people. Thus, Scott suggests that at the same time that, for example, Black American slaves might obey their white masters and smile in their presence, among them-selves they would critique that power in folktales, gossip, songs, and in actions such as poaching, petty pilfering, foot-dragging and general non-compliance in their work. Thus, in order to analyse a power rela-tion, we must analyse the total relations of power, the hidden transcripts as well as the public performance.

Theorists have found difficulties in Foucault's method in the analysis of power in that it is, in essence, non-interpretive, and non-evaluative, and yet the situations where Foucault's work is most useful, and where he has done most of his work, are precisely those where there is popular resistance, and where the resistance is one which one feels that Foucault is implicitly supporting. This resistance needs to be charted because of inequalities in access to resources. Take for example, the Subaltern Studies research group in India who have focused on the analysis of the actions of those whom the imperial producers of information and knowledge would largely ignore or cate-gorise only as trouble-makers or rioters (Guha and Spivak 1988; Guha 1994). The sociologists Gavin Kendall and Gary Wickham suggest that 'the task of [a Foucauldian] analysis . . . is to describe the way in which resistance operates as a part of power, not to seek or promote or oppose it' (Kendall and Wickham 1999: 51). However, it might be argued that the very choice of the object of analysis suggests a partic-ular position in relation to which side in a conflict one is supporting. For, as the feminist linguist Deirdre Burton argues, not making one's political position clear and attempting to appear 'objective' in one's analysis often leads one to an analysis which simply supports the status quo (Burton 1982). When the Subaltern Studies group produces information about peasant insurrection, it is not a disinterested account, nor should we necessarily wish it to be so. The production of information for its own sake is a delusion, as Foucault's analyses of the relation between power and knowledge clearly show (see Chapter 4).

DISCIPLINARY REGIMES AND THE DISCIPLINARY SOCIETY

Foucault is also interested in the way that power operates through different forms of regime at particular historical periods. In his work *Discipline and Punish* (1977), he describes the way that power has been exercised in different eras in Europe, moving from the public spectacle of the tortured body of the individual deemed to have committed a crime to the disciplining, incarceration and surveillance of those convicted of crimes in the present day. The book opens with the following description: 'On 2 March 1757 Damiens the regicide was condemned to be . . . "taken and conveyed in a cart, wearing nothing but a shirt, holding a torch of burning wax weighing two pounds" . . . and then "on a scaffold in the Place de Grève the flesh will be torn from his breasts, arms, thighs and calves with red-hot pincers, his right hand holding the knife with which he committed the said parricide, burnt with sulphur and on those places where the flesh will be torn away poured molten lead, boiling oil, burning resin, wax and sulphur melted together and then his body drawn and quartered by four horses and his limbs and body consumed by fire, reduced to ashes and his ashes thrown to the winds"' (Foucault 1991a: 3). After several pages of detailed description of the difficulty of ensuring that the prisoner is in fact executed according to this plan, Foucault juxtaposes a passage from a list of rules for the regulation of the time of criminals in prison written only a century later. By this simple juxtaposition he shows the tremendous change that has taken place – from public execution and public spectacle to confinement and surveillance. However, he argues that this change constitutes a difference in kind rather than a progression or necessary improvement, as in the present day: 'it is the certainty of being punished and not the horrifying spectacle of public punishment that must discourage crime' (Foucault 1991a: 9). The shift in punishment from inflicting intolerable pain to present-day executions in America by lethal injection where no pain is experienced is a shift in the mechanisms of power and punishment and should not be seen to reflect progress or evolution. Nor should the current methods of controlling those considered to be criminals in Britain, such as electronic tagging, be seen as necessarily more humane.

Correlating with this shift in punishment, for Foucault, there is a corresponding shift in forms of power circulating within society, for example, from a system where the king or queen is seen as the embodiment of the nation and power is dispensed from above, to a system where power is exercised within the social body. The meting out of extensive torture and execution in public was a way of publicly displaying the power of the sovereign. Rather than seeing the move away from absolute monarchical power as a result of greater democracy, Foucault argues, in an interview entitled 'Prison talk', that: 'it was the instituting of new, local capillary forms of power which impelled society to eliminate certain elements such as the court and the king' (Foucault 1980d: 39). This is a paradoxical yet challenging view of political change whereby the monarchy becomes redundant because of changes within power relations within the social body as a whole which then make their influence felt from below.

In _Discipline and Punish_ (1977), he also examines the way that discipline as a form of self-regulation encouraged by institutions permeates modern societies. His work on disciplinary regimes is of great interest, since rather than simply seeing regimes as being oppressive, he analyses the way that regimes exercise power within a society through the use of a range of different mechanisms and techniques. He analyses a range of different institutions such as the hospital, the clinic, the prison and the university and sees a number of disciplinary practices which they seem to have in common. Discipline consists of a concern with control which is internalised by each individual: it consists of a concern with time-keeping, self-control over one's posture and bodily functions, concentration, sublimation of immediate desires and emotions – all of these elements are the effects of disciplinary pressure and at the same time they are all actions which produce the individual as subjected to a set of procedures which come from outside of themselves but whose aim is the disciplining of the self by the self. These disciplinary norms within Western cultures are not necessarily experienced as originating from institutions, so thoroughly have they been internalised by individuals. Indeed, so innate and 'natural' do these practices appear that we find it hard to conceptualise what life would be like without this constant checking of appetites and whims, and the constant instilling in children of the need to control their behaviour and their emotional responses, both by the educational system and through parental pressure. Paul Patton suggests that this view of discipline has interesting implications for the analysis of the way that capitalism works: 'It is not perhaps capitalist production which is autocratic and hierarchised, but disciplinary production which is capitalist. We know after all that disciplinary organisation of the workforce persists even when production is no longer strictly speaking capitalist' (Patton 1979: 124). This can clearly be seen to be the case in the forms of disciplinary structures developed within the Soviet system under Communism, where the society as a whole was subject to the most extreme of disciplinary regimes, and while many of these restrictions on personal freedom and self-expression were possibly the result of the practices necessary for intense industrialisation, there is a sense in which it is important to analyse carefully the relation between Communism and extreme forms of restriction of individual liberty.

For Foucault, discipline is a set of strategies, procedures and ways of behaving which are associated with certain institutional contexts and which then permeate ways of thinking and behaving in general. Developed within the setting of the prison, disciplinary regimes now permeate the workplace, the army, the school, the university. Although Foucault suggests that the disciplinary structures of the prison in some ways invade and determine the structures in other institutional settings, he does not describe the process whereby these practices were diffused into other contexts. It is this which is most disturbing in his account and which seems contradictory for some critics. Donnelly comments that: 'Foucault rejects the notion that there is any calculating class of agents behind the scenes pulling the disciplinary strings. But what impersonal force then allows Foucault to talk of discipline univocally, as a strategy by which a whole people are ordered?' (Donnelly 1986: 29). A further problem which can be seen in the description of disciplinary regimes is that the individual subject is seen to be subjected to the point where resistance to these practices and procedures is futile, so ingrained are they in the individual themselves. This seems to conflict with Foucault's ideas developed in *The History of Sexuality* (1978), where he states that where there is power there is resistance.

The feminist critic, Sandra Bartky, argues that 'Foucault seems sometimes on the verge of depriving us of a vocabulary in which to conceptualise the nature and meaning of those periodic refusals of control that, just as much as the imposition of control, mark the course of human history' (Bartky 1988: 79). We need to take Foucault's argument here further than he himself took it, and perhaps see that feminists and other critical theorists have tried to provide us with precisely that vocabulary of resistance.

One of the disciplinary structures which has been most often drawn upon by theorists using Foucault's work is the Panopticon, which he discusses in *Discipline and Punish* (1977) and also in an interview entitled 'The eye of power' (1980f). The Panopticon is an architectural device described by the eighteenth-century philosopher, Jeremy Bentham, as a way of arranging people in such a way that, for example, in a prison, it is possible to see all of the inmates without the observer being seen, and without any of the prisoners having access to one another. Foucault describes it in the following way in 'The eye of power':

> A perimeter building in the form of a ring. At the centre of this a tower, pierced by large windows opening on to the inner face of the ring. The outer building is divided into cells each of which traverses the whole thickness of the building. These cells have two windows, one opening onto the inside, facing the windows of the central tower, the other, outer one allowing daylight to pass through the whole cell. All that is then needed is to put an overseer in the tower and place in each of the cells a lunatic, a patient, a convict, a worker or a schoolboy. The back lighting enables one to pick out from the central tower the little captive silhouettes in the ring of cells. In short the principle of the dungeon is reversed; daylight and the overseer's gaze captures the inmate more effectively than darkness, which afforded after all a sort of protection.
>
> (Foucault 1980f: 147)

From this analysis of a particular way of organising the spatial arrangements of prisons, schools and factories to enable maximum visibility, Foucault argues that a new form of internalised disciplinary practice occurs: one is forced to act as if one is constantly being surveyed even when one is not. Thus, this form of spatial arrangement entails a particular form of power relation and restriction of behaviours.

In the twenty-first century, an example of Panoptical vision might be the use of Closed Circuit televisions in Britain's town centres, where the mere presence of CCTV cameras in the streets, and the knowledge that the videos from these cameras can be viewed by the police, is supposed to be enough to deter petty crime in these areas. The notion of disciplinary structures needing visibility to operate effectively is important. The critic, Barry Smart, argues that 'it is important to remember that the power exercised through hierarchical surveillance is not a possession or a property, rather it has the character of a machine or apparatus through which power is produced and individuals are distributed in a permanent and continuous field' (Smart 1985: 86). The individual within the Panopticon is forced to internalise the disciplinary gaze so that '[s/]he who is subjected to a field of visibility and who knows it, assumes responsibility for the constraints of power; [s/]he makes them play spontaneously upon [her/]himself; [s/]he inscribes in [her/]himself the power relation in which [s/]he simultaneously plays both roles; [s/]he becomes the principle of [her/]his own subjection' (Foucault 1991a: 202–203). Thus, a new form of power relation develops where rather than power being exercised very materially on the body through torture, by someone with authority, someone in power on someone who is powerless, the individual herself now 'plays both roles': the oppressor may well be absent, but the prisoner has internalised the behavioural code of the oppressor, and will behave as though the prison guard were still watching. Using the Panopticon as almost a symbolisation of spatial relations and, at the same time, a new form of power relations has led to productive work within the post-colonial analysis of the description of the colonial landscape since, for example, a particular surveying gaze by the British traveller or colonial official can be seen to be both a place of observation and discipline, as well as the locus for the production of knowledge about future colonial development (Pratt 1992). Thus, the British traveller who produces a description of a colonial landscape, usually from a position of elevation on a hilltop, often in providing an account of an empty landscape stretching off to the horizon may be interpreted as providing an account of a landscape which is ripe for colonial exploitation. Thus s/he can, as in the Panopticon, see all of the people in the landscape below and survey all of the land, and at the same time, she can take up a position of authority over it. However, sometimes the use of this device of the Panopticon can be over-extended, so that the Panopticon can be traced in the design of the shopping mall, the university lecture theatre, the gym and so on (Kendall and

Wickham 1999). However, even if over-enthusiastic Foucauldian analyses have traced the figure of the Panopticon as a disciplinary structure excessively, the notion that architectural arrangements lead to certain configurations of power relations is important.

Foucault is also concerned to describe what he terms governmentality: the analysis of who can govern and who is governed but also the means by which that shaping of someone else's activities is achieved (Foucault 1991c). The critic, Colin Gordon, argues that 'Foucault saw it as a characteristic (and troubling) property of the development of government in Western societies to tend towards a form of political sovereignty which would be a government of all of each and whose concerns would be at once to "totalise" and to "individualise"' (Gordon 1991: 3). Thus, this type of study and focus leads us away from a focus solely upon the State and the government when we analyse governmentality. Perhaps the most productive element in Foucault's analysis of power is the fact that he sees power relations as largely unsuccessful, as not achieving the goal of total domination. If power is relational rather than emanating from a particular site such as the government or the police; if it is diffused throughout all social relations rather than being imposed from above; if it is unstable and in need of constant repetition to maintain; if it is productive as well as being repressive, then it is difficult to see power relations as simply negative and as constraining. At the same time as downplaying human agency in resisting oppressive power relations, through his concentration on the diffusion of power, Foucault also provides the means to formulate resistance. This notion of the diffusion of power and hence the diffusion of resistance has been exploited by resistance groups such as Globalise Resistance, the broad-based alliance of radical anti-capitalist, peace and environmental groups set up around 2000. They have found that diversifying resistance to global organisations such as the World Bank and the International Monetary Fund, and to the globalisation of the economy through the growth of multinational organisations, by bringing together protesters from a wide range of backgrounds and with a wide range of agendas, is most effective. Rather than just demonstrating on single issues or writing petitions to the government, the anti-globalisation movement has used a range of different methods, from the conventional petition to the more innovative mass e-mail networks; they have put on protests ranging from occupying sections of a city outside summit meetings of government leaders from the powerful nations, to boycotting and protesting outside Shell garages and McDonalds' restaurants. Thus, if we assume that the government of the country is not the only source of influence and power, then protest will need to be directed at other targets than the government and will need to find other forms of expression than simply the conventional petition to the Prime Minister. The downside of such a diffuse set of resistance strategies is that with such a broad-based agenda and diversity of aims it is difficult to co-ordinate resistance or even to know, still less agree on, what aims everyone is trying to achieve. But perhaps Foucault would argue that strategies to counter the complex power relations within a globalised economy and society need not be unitary and unidirectional.

INSTITUTIONS AND THE STATE

Foucault attempts to shift the emphasis of analysis away from a simple analysis of institutions as oppressive. The Marxist stress on the centrality of the State in all political analyses is one which Foucault rejects, but perhaps it can be seen as one which had a profound effect on Foucault's thinking, since it seems to be most notable by its absence in Foucault's works. He states that he refrained from producing a theory of the State 'in the sense that one abstains from an indigestible meal' (Foucault, cited in Gordon 1991: 4). What he argues is that theorists often assume a solidity and permanence to the State and institutions which leads them to focus less on the potential for change, the fragility of the maintenance of power: he states in an article on 'Governmentality':

> overvaluing the problem of the state is one which is paradoxical because apparently reductionist: it is a form of analysis that consists in reducing the state to a certain number of functions, such as the development of productive forces of the reproduction of relations of production, and yet this reductionist vision of the relative importance of the state's role nevertheless invariably renders it absolutely essential as a target needing to be attacked and a privileged position needing to be occupied. But the state, no more probably than at any other time in its history, does not have this unity, this individuality, this rigorous functionality, nor to speak frankly, this importance: maybe after all, the state is no more than a composite reality and a mythicised abstraction, whose importance is a lot more limited than many of us think.
>
> (Foucault 1991c: 103)

Thus, he wants to move away from the idea that the State can be discussed as if it were a super-human agent with the same wills and intentions as individuals. To illustrate this we might analyse the complexity of the notion of the State, composed as it is of diverse elected representatives of the people, the MPs, (each with their own personal and political agenda, needs and ambitions, negotiating with the demands of the Party policy as a whole and the Cabinet's discipline) led by the Cabinet and the Prime Minister who are informed and led by the Civil Service which itself is staffed by people and departments each with their own personal agendas. This system is overseen and regulated by the House of Lords which again is staffed by people with their own personal agendas. If we only analyse the government, and obviously the government is only one very small section of the State, since the notion of the State takes in such entities as the police, legal system and all the services provided by the government, then we see clearly quite how difficult it is to see the State as having a single unitary aim. That is not to deny the power that is exercised over individuals by the State, through its various agencies, but rather to suggest that we must recognise the multiple and conflicting agencies involved in the notion of the State.

However, Foucault does not simply want to dispense with the notion of the State in all of his work or to argue that the State is not important; rather, in analysing the relations of power, it is necessary to extend that analysis beyond the limits of the State (Foucault 1979). He argues in an article entitled 'Truth and power' that 'the State, for all the omnipotence of its apparatuses, is far from being able to occupy the whole field of actual power relations' (Foucault 1980b: 122). Thus, relations between parents and children, lovers, employers and employees – in short, all relations between people – are power relations. In each interaction power is negotiated and one's position in a hierarchy is established, however flexible, changing and ill-defined that hierarchy is. The feminist linguist Joanna Thornborrow draws on Foucault's work in order to make a crucial distinction between institutional status, (that is the status one is accorded because of one's position within an institution, for example as a doctor, or police officer) and the status which one manages to negotiate for oneself within particular interactions with others, which she terms local status (Thornborrow 2002). These two statuses interact with, and inform, one another, but they are usefully analysed separately, since while it is often possible to change one's local status, for example by using linguistic strategies more commonly associated with those who have higher institutional status, it is more difficult to change one's institutional status by such means.

Thus, Foucault is keenly aware of the role of institutions in the shaping of individuals, although he does not wish to see the relations between institutions and individuals as being one only of oppression and constraint. Rather, he has led to a focus within much critical theory on the resistance which is possible in power relations.

INTENTIONALITY AND WILL

An important element in Foucault's work on the power of institution is his theorising of the disjunction between intentionality and effect, which he discusses, for example, in his interview 'Power and sex' (1988d). Corporate bodies might present themselves as having a set of intentions, for example in their mission statements, where they claim to have a clear set of aims and guiding principles. However, there is often a crucial disjuncture between those explicit intentions and what actually happens. The notion that complex bodies have intentionality, analogous to individuals, often forces our thinking about the operation of social structures into reductionism. Foucault argues that 'capitalism's *raison d'être* is not to starve the workers but it cannot develop without starving them' (Foucault 1988d: 113). Thus, poverty may be an inevitable effect of capitalism, as Marxist theorists have argued, but Foucault suggests that this cannot be seen as an aim or intention of capitalism. Thus, capitalism cannot be seen to be operating with an overarching plan; capitalism itself as a system, may be made up of a range of conflicting and contradictory forces and institutions each with their own agendas, ways of operating and plans. Thus, in an analysis it is necessary to look at the way in which institutions operate and the way that they are constrained also by the demands and resistance of individuals within the organisation as well as individuals and groups outside it. If we take, as an example of the complexity of organisations and the difficulty of assuming an intentionality, the management of National Health hospitals, we will see that hospitals are constrained in what they can do by government policies and government targets; the amount of money and resources which the government allows the hospitals and their relation to private hospitals. They are also constrained by community groups and health watch-dogs and individuals who have now become influenced by the current notion that it is possible to be compensated financially for medical errors. Although it is clear that hospitals have a management structure and the managers make decisions about their current direction, they can only do so within the constraints imposed by other agencies, and also within the constraints of the previously established procedures for managing hospitals. The managers may intend that the hospital will provide the best service possible to the community, but their policies may have to be modified by forces beyond their control, such as financial constraints; their decisions may have unforeseen consequences, and they may be involved in crises not of their making. Thus, although the manager of a hospital has ultimate responsibility for the way the hospital is run, s/he is not the only person involved in the formulation of management policy. This move away from attributing intentions to institutions in a simplistic way, forces us to reconceptualise the way that we theorise power relations in society.

As I discuss in the final chapter of this book, 'After Foucault', Foucault is interested in a form of analysis which focuses on contingencies rather than simple relations of cause and effect. By this I mean that he argues that when we analyse events in the past, we tend to try to attribute simple, clear causes for those events; for example, it is often argued that the Nazi invaders of the Soviet Union in the Second World War suffered defeat because of the harshness of the Soviet winter for which they were ill-prepared. However, this attributing of cause and effect in this simplistic way masks the fact that there were myriad contingent contributory factors which led to the defeat of the German army: the provision of winter uniforms to the Russians and the lack of such uniforms by the Germans, the use of non-German troops by the Germans in front-line positions, the lack of involvement of German Generals in the planning of the invasion, the overconfidence of Hitler, and so on: no one of these contingent factors being more or less important than the other in bringing about a particular outcome (Beevor 1999). Thus, although finding simple cause-and-effect relations makes thinking and writing about the past much easier, Foucault suggests that we should, rather, try to analyse the complexity and indeed the confusing nature of past events. This notion of analysing contingency instead of a simple cause-and-effect relation is extremely important in the analysis of power relations, since it enables the

Foucauldian analyst to focus more on the way that power is dispersed throughout a society in all kinds of relationship, event and activity; focusing on contingent factors enables us to examine the way that power operates.

CONCLUSIONS

Foucault analyses the relations between the individual and the wider society without assuming that the individual is powerless in relation to institutions or to the State. He does not minimise the restrictions placed on individuals by institutions; in much of his work he is precisely focused on the way institutions act upon individuals. However, by analysing the way that power is dispersed throughout society, Foucault enables one to see power as enacted in every interaction and hence as subject to resistance in each of those interactions. This makes power a much less stable element, since it can be challenged at any moment, and it is necessary to continuously renew and maintain power relations. Thus, his analysis of power has set in motion an entirely new way of examining power relations in society, focusing more on resistance than simple passive oppression.

DISCOURSE

Discourse is one of the most frequently used terms from Foucault's work and, at the same time, it is one of the most contradictory. Foucault himself defines it in a number of different ways throughout his work and, in this chapter, I will explore the way he uses the term in *The Archaeology of Knowledge* (1972) and in 'The order of discourse', (1981). He says in *The Archaeology of Knowledge* that he has used 'discourse' to refer to 'the general domain of all statements, sometimes as an individualizable group of statements, and sometimes as a regulated practice that accounts for a number of statements' (Foucault 1972: 80). By 'the general domain of all statements', he means that 'discourse' can be used to refer to all utterances and statements which have been made which have meaning and which have some effect. Sometimes, in addition, he has used the term to refer to 'individualizable groups of statements', that is utterances which seem to form a grouping, such as the discourse of femininity or the discourse of racism. At other times, he has used the term discourse to refer to 'regulated practices that account for a number of statements', that is the unwritten rules and structures which produce particular utterances and statements. For example, there is no set of rules written down on how to write essays, and yet somehow most students at university manage to learn how to write within the framework of the essay. For Foucault, this set of structures and rules would constitute a discourse, and it is these rules in which Foucault is most interested rather than the utterances and text produced.

A discourse is a regulated set of statements which combine with others in predictable ways. Discourse is regulated by a set of rules which lead to the distribution and circulation of certain utterances and statements. Some statements are circulated widely and others have restricted circulation; thus, within the West, the Bible is a text which is always in print; there are copies of the Bible in many homes. Many political commentators use quotations from the Bible to illustrate points that they have made. There are university theology departments which are devoted to the study of the Bible. Journals are devoted to its analysis, and there are always new interpretations and commentaries on it. In this way, the Bible itself, and statements about it, can be seen to constitute a discourse which is kept in circulation within our society. However, there are other religious texts which are not given such wide circulation and which do not seem to have the type of structural 'supports' that the Bible has. The notion of exclusion is very important in Foucault's thinking about discourse, particularly in 'The order of discourse' (1981). Rather than seeing discourse as simply a set of statements which have some coherence, we should, rather, think of a discourse as existing because of a complex set of practices which try to keep them in circulation and other practices which try to fence them off from others and keep those other statements out of circulation.

The reason that many people find the term discourse to be of use is that Foucault stresses that discourse is associated with relations of power. Many Marxist theorists have used the term ideology to indicate that certain statements and ideas are authorised by institutions and may have some influence in relation to individuals' ideas, but the notion of discourse is more complex than this notion of ideology in that, because of Foucault's ideas on power and resistance which I outlined in the previous chapter, a discourse is not simply the imposition of a set of ideas on individuals. In the *History of Sexuality, Vol. I*, Foucault states that:

> discourses are not once and for all subservient to power or raised up against it, any more than silences are. We must make allowances for the complex and unstable process whereby discourse can be both an instrument and an effect of power, but also a hindrance, a stumbling block, a point of resistance and

> a starting point for an opposing strategy. Discourse transmits and produces
> power; it reinforces it, but also undermines it and exposes it, renders it fragile
> and makes it possible to thwart it.
>
> (Foucault 1978: 100–101)

What I find interesting about this quotation is that, in Marxist theorising, ideology is always assumed to be negative and constraining, a set
of false beliefs about something; whereas here Foucault is arguing that
discourse is both the means of oppressing and the means of resistance.

In considering the term 'discourse' we must remember that it is
not the equivalent of 'language', nor should we assume that there
is a simple relation between discourse and reality. Discourse does
not simply translate reality into language; rather discourse should be
seen as a system which structures the way that we perceive reality.
In his essay 'The order of discourse', Foucault argues that: 'we must
not imagine that the world turns towards us a legible face which we
would only have to decipher; the world is not the accomplice of our
knowledge; there is no prediscursive providence which disposes the
world in our favour' (Foucault 1981: 67). He goes on to argue that
'we must conceive of discourse as a violence which we do to things,
or in any case as a practice which we impose on them; and it is in this
practice that the events of discourse find the principle of their regu-
larity' (Foucault 1981: 67). For example, within Western European
languages, there tends to exist a wide range of terms for colours; yet
not all languages distinguish between colours in the same way and
parcel up the spectrum into blue, red, green and so on as English does.
For example, some languages make no lexical distinction between
green and blue. This does not mean that speakers of that language
cannot tell the difference between blue and green, but that this distinction is not one which is especially significant within that culture. Thus,
the regularities which we perceive in reality should be seen as the
result of the anonymous regularities of discourse which we impose
on reality. Foucault argues that, in fact, discourse should be seen as
something which constrains our perceptions.

Although discourse seems to encompass almost everything, there
does exist a realm of the non-discursive. Foucault has often been interpreted as saying that there is no non-discursive realm, that everything
is constructed and apprehended through discourse. For example, the
body, while it is clearly a material object – our body feels pain, it is

subject to gravity, it can be harmed in accidents – nevertheless, the body can be apprehended only through discursive mediation, that is, our understanding of our body occurs only through discourse – we judge the size of our body through discourses which delineate a perfect form, we interpret feelings of tiredness as indicative of stress because of discourses concerning the relation between mental and physical well-being, and so on. So Foucault is not denying that there are physical objects in the world and he is not suggesting that there is nothing but discourse, but what he is stating is that we can only think about and experience material objects and the world as a whole through discourse and the structures it imposes on our thinking. In the process of thinking about the world, we categorise and interpret experience and events according to the structures available to us and in the process of interpreting, we lend these structures a solidity and a normality which it is often difficult to question. Ernesto Laclau and Chantal Mouffe discuss this question of the non-discursive insightfully in the following quotation:

> The fact that every object is constituted as an object of discourse has nothing to do with whether there is a world external to thought . . . An earthquake or the falling of a brick is an event that certainly exists, in the sense that it occurs here and now, independently of my will. But whether their specificity as objects is constructed in terms of 'natural phenomena' or expressions of 'the wrath of God' depends on the structuring of a discursive field. What is denied is not that such objects exist externally to thought, but the rather different assertion that they could constitute themselves as objects outside any discursive condition of emergence.
>
> (Laclau and Mouffe 1985: 108)

Thus, in Laclau and Mouffe's view, objects exist and events occur in the real world but we apprehend and interpret these events within discursive structures and we are not always aware of the way that discourse structures our understanding. If we return to the example of the body, we can see that we experience our body in what seems like a fairly immediate way – we feel pain, we experience tiredness and hunger – but all of these sensations are filtered through discursive structures which assign particular meanings and effects to them.

When Foucault discusses discourse, he focuses on constraint and restriction; he is aware that we could potentially utter an infinite variety of sentences, but what is surprising is that, in fact, we choose to speak within very narrowly confined limits. He argues that discursive practices are characterised by a 'delimitation of a field of objects, the definition of a legitimate perspective for the agent of knowledge and the fixing of norms for the elaboration of concepts and theories' (Foucault, in Bouchard 1977: 199). Thus, in deciding to say something, we must as speakers focus on a particular subject, we must at the same time make a claim to authority for ourselves in being able to speak about this subject, and we must, in the process, add to and refine ways of thinking about the subject. It is difficult, if not impossible, to think and express oneself outside these discursive constraints because, in doing so, one would be considered to be mad or incomprehensible by others. Foucault alluded to this difficulty of expressing oneself in discourse when he started his inaugural lecture at the Collège de France in 1970: he said: 'I think a good many people have a . . . desire to be freed from the obligation to begin, a . . . desire to be on the other side of discourse from the outset, without having to consider from the outside what might be strange, frightening or perhaps maleficent about it' (Foucault 1981: 51). It is for this reason that Foucault suggests that there are rituals at the beginnings of discourse; to give a banal example, when people begin a conversation in English they will generally begin with 'small talk' that is non-serious talk about the weather or health, before they begin to discuss seriously; on the telephone, there are a series of ritualised openings and closing routines, which help to get conversation going. We do not often think about these ritualised utterances; we only notice them when someone does not use them.

What interests Foucault in his analysis of discourse is the way that it is regulated: 'in every society the production of discourse is at once controlled, selected, organised and redistributed by a certain number of procedures whose role is to ward off its powers and dangers, to gain mastery over its chance events, to evade its ponderous, formidable materiality' (Foucault 1981: 52). It is this sense of the structure of discourse and the control which this exercises on what can be said which interests Foucault. He describes, in his article 'The order of discourse', the procedures which constrain discourse and which lead to discourse being produced: the first set of procedures, he suggests, consists of three external exclusions, and they are taboo; the distinction between the mad and the sane; and the distinction between true and false. Taboo is a form of prohibition since it makes it difficult to speak about certain subjects such as sexuality and death and constrains the way that we talk about these subjects. The second external exclusion is the distinction between the speech of the mad and the sane, as Foucault has shown in his book *Madness and Civilisation* (1967), since the speech of those people who have been considered to be insane is not attended to; it is treated as if it did not exist. To give an example, those people in Britain who have been certified as mentally ill and who have been prescribed certain drugs to help their condition, now, because of changes in the legislation, are not able to state authoritatively that they do not wish to take such medication. They may well state that they do not want to take the drugs but it is now possible that the authorities will ignore their statements and force them to take the medication. In this sense, only the statements of those considered sane are attended to. The division between true and false is the third exclusionary practice described by Foucault; those in positions of authority who are seen to be 'experts' are those who can speak the truth. Those who make statements who are not in positions of power will be considered not to be speaking the truth. The notion of the truth must not be taken as self-evident; he shows in his work how truth is something which is supported materially by a whole range of practices and institutions: universities, government departments, publishing houses, scientific bodies and so on. All of these institutions work to exclude statements which they characterise as false and they keep in circulation those statements which they characterise as true. For Foucault, only those statements which are 'in the true' will be circulated: in *The Archaeology of Knowledge* (1972), he argues that 'it is always possible one could speak the truth in a void; one would only be "in the true" however if one obeyed the rules of some discursive "police" which would have to be reactivated every time one spoke' (Foucault 1972: 224). Thus, even if we are asserting something which as far as we know it is 'the truth', our statements will only be judged to be 'true' if they accord with, and fit in with, all of the other statements which are authorised within our society.

In addition to these external exclusions on the production of discourse, Foucault also asserts that there are four internal procedures of exclusion and these are: commentary; the author; disciplines; and the rarefaction of the speaking subject. These procedures are all concerned with classifying, distributing and ordering discourse, and their function is ultimately to distinguish between those who are authorised to speak and those who are not – those discourses which are authorised and those which are not. The first internal exclusion, commentary, is writing about another's statements. Thus, literary criticism can be considered to be commentary. Foucault suggests that:

> there is in all societies, with great consistency, a kind of gradation among discourses: those which are said in the ordinary course of days and exchanges, and which vanish as soon as they have been pronounced; and those which give rise to a certain number of new speech acts which take them up, transform them or speak of them, in short, those discourses which, over and above their formulation, are said indefinitely, remain said, and are to be said again.
>
> (Foucault 1981: 57)

Most people would consider that a text is commented on and discussed because it is more interesting or of more value than others; for example, Charles Darwin's text *On the Origin of Species* (1859) has been commented on, challenged and interpreted by endless other scientists. But, Foucault, rather than assuming that this is due to a quality within the text, asserts that it is a question of a difference in the way the text is analysed. In the process of commenting on a text, the text itself is given a different and primary status, it is assumed to have a richness, but at the same time the commentary's role is paradoxically to put into words what the text cannot say; as he puts it: 'the commentary must say for the first time what had, nonetheless, already been said, and must tirelessly repeat what had, however, never been said' (Foucault 1981: 58). Thus, commentary on Darwin's work not only keeps Darwin's texts in circulation as ideas which are 'in the true', but also confers status on the author of the commentary, because it demonstrates that they have mastered Darwin's ideas and can even refine those ideas and express them more clearly than Darwin, or relate those ideas more appropriately to the twenty-first century. The second internal exclusionary practice is the author. This may seem quite a paradox, since the author may be seen by many to be simply the person who self-evidently writes a text. However, for Foucault, although he recognises that authors exist, for him the notion of the author is used as an organising principle for texts, and can be considered to be a way of providing a cohesion to diverse texts which have been published by him/her. For example, if we consider the writings of the novelist Kazuo Ishiguro, it is clear that he has produced a wide range of books which vary greatly in terms of their style and subject matter, from *The Unconsoled*, a very stylistically experimental book, to *The Remains of the Day*, a far more conservative book in terms of style and content. It would be difficult to pin him down to a particular way of writing or focus. Yet, because we know that these texts are all published by the same person, we tend to group these very different texts together and we can even begin to assert that there are relations between the books, for example, seeing one book as a reaction to the style or subject matter of another. Yet these books are so different that Foucault would argue, both in 'The order of discourse' and in 'What is an author?' (1986a) that it is we as readers who are using the notion of the author to unite these very diverse texts. Foucault prefers to use the term the 'author-function' rather than focusing on the real author, since it is this organisational aspect of the author-function which interests him. Foucault is very critical of such notions as the progression of an author from immaturity, early works to maturity or later works. If we discuss the 'early' works of Shakespeare, we should interrogate why it is that we are using such a metaphor, implying as it does that these works are less developed than his later texts, and we should simply analyse these texts in their own terms, rather than according to a fictional schema which we have of Shakespeare's life. The third internal exclusion on discourse is the disciplinary boundary, that is, the limits which we place on subject areas. For example, if we work within sociology, we will generally examine a certain range of subjects and we will approach them drawing on a particular range of methodological and theoretical tools. If we approach the same subject from the perspective of another discipline, for example linguistics or psychology, we will approach them and delimit those subjects in different ways and approach them using different tools. Disciplines work as a limit on discourse, because they prescribe what can be counted as possible knowledge within a particular subject area. Because they each have strict methodological rules and a corpus of propositions which are considered to be factual, disciplines allow for the production of new propositions but within extremely tightly defined limits. Thus, academic journals have editorial boards and referees who are responsible for evaluating whether articles which have been sent to them to be published 'fit in' with the disciplinary rules for discussing a particular subject and what it is possible to say within that discipline. They reject those articles which do not. Thus, for Foucault, these practices which are an integral part of disciplines constitute the subject area through rigorously excluding knowledge which might challenge them. The final internal exclusion on discourse discussed by Foucault is what he terms 'the rarefaction of the speaking subject': by 'rarefaction' he means the limitation placed on who can speak authoritatively, that is, some discourses are open to all and some have very limited access. Speaking authoritatively is hedged around by rituals and takes place within particular societies of discourse, where discourses circulate according to prescribed rules. For example, at universities, only certain people can give lectures; these are generally held in specially designed halls where the lecturer is positioned at the front. Only the lecturer speaks for the duration of the lecture. Students do not generally speak to the lecturer or to the rest of the lecture group. Because of the unwritten regulations on who can speak during a lecture, when a student does speak, it is often seen by others as aberrant, or potentially disruptive of the status quo, or if a student is called upon to speak by the lecturer, s/he may well feel nervous or self-conscious and find speaking difficult. Thus, rather than a university simply being an institution in which knowledge is dispassionately circulated, Foucault argues that 'any system of education is a political way of maintaining or modifying the appropriation of discourses, along with the knowledges and powers which they carry' (Foucault 1981: 64). Universities have many unwritten rules about who can speak at certain times (witness the efforts which tutors make to force students to speak in seminars) and whose statements are considered to be authoritative (consider the force of tutors' comments on essays which determine how a particular student is assessed and ultimately the grade that they are given). Indeed, a Foucauldian analysis of the university would focus less on the circulation of knowledge and more on the way certain types of knowledge are excluded, the rigorous process whereby students' ideas are brought into line with the type of knowledge which is considered to be 'academic'. Thus, this whole seemingly self-evident system of silencing and forcing to speak, of commenting on and assessing that work in relation to fixed standards is less about imparting knowledge and is more about the institutionalisation of discourse and the mapping out of power relations between lecturers and students. Thus, this complex system of multiple constraints acts both internally and externally on the production and reception of discourse and it is these constraints which bring discourse into existence.

To sum up, discourse should therefore be seen as both an overall term to refer to all statements, the rules whereby those statements are formed and the processes whereby those statements are circulated and other statements are excluded. Within the theorising of discourse, Foucault also uses some other terms: épistèmé, archive, discursive formation, and statement, which have become important for those drawing on his work and which help us to outline the structure of discourse. I will define these briefly.

Foucault analyses the groupings of discursive formations and the relationships between discourses at any one time. This ensemble of practices he terms an 'épistèmé'. The épistèmé of a period is not 'the sum of its knowledge, nor the general style of its research, but the divergence, the distances, the oppositions, the differences, the relations of its various scientific discourses: the épistèmé is not a sort of *grand underlying theory*, it is a space of *dispersion*, it is an open and doubtless indefinitely describable field of relationships' (Foucault 1991a: 55). Thus, it is not the sum of everything which can be known within a period but it is the complex set of relationships between the knowledges which are produced within a particular period and the rules by which new knowledge is generated. Thus, within a particular period we can see similarities in the way that different sciences operate at a conceptual and theoretical level, despite dealing with different subject matters. For example, Foucault, in *The Order of Things* (1970), analyses the conceptual frameworks, theoretical assumptions, and working methods which certain sciences, natural history, economics and linguistics, have in common; he states:

> what was common to the natural history, the economics and the grammar of the Classical period was certainly not present to the consciousness of the scientist; or that part of it that was conscious was superficial, limited and almost fanciful, but unknown to themselves, the naturalists, economists and grammarians, employed the same rules to define the objects proper to their own study, to form their concept, to build their theories.
>
> (Foucault 1970: xi)

To give an example of the types of 'ways of thinking' that underlie various sciences it is worth considering Foucault's analysis of the épistèmé of the Classical period; he states:

it was resemblance that largely guided exegesis and the interpretation of texts; it was resemblance that organised the play of symbols, made possible knowledge of things visible and invisible and controlled the art of representing them. The universe was folded in upon itself: the earth echoing the sky, faces seeing themselves reflected in the stars and plants holding within their stems secrets that were of use to man. Painting imitated space. And representation ... was positioned as a form of repetition; the theatre of life or the mirror of nature, that was the claim made of all languages, its manner of declaring its existence and of formulating its right of speech.

(Foucault 1970: 17)

He also describes the way that events in the world were interpreted as being signs of the supernatural world: crop-failure, storms, disease and, in fact, any event judged to be exceptional were seen to be indicative of God's anger. Within all natural sciences within the Classical period, diverse scientists shared certain presumptions about the nature of the world and about knowledge which underpinned their scientific work. One of Foucault's biographers, Didier Eribon, describes the épistémé in the following way: 'every period is characterised by an underground configuration that delineates its culture, a grid of knowledge making possible every scientific discourse, every production of statements. . . . Each science develops within the framework of an épistémé, and therefore is linked in part with other sciences contemporary with it' (Eribon 1991: 158). Thus, in his analysis of general grammar, economics and the analysis of wealth and natural history in *The Order of Things*, Foucault aims to analyse the shared presuppositions and theoretical frameworks which organise thought, representation and categorisation.

In analysing an épistémé, Foucault argues: 'I do not seek to detect, starting from diverse signs, the unitary spirit of an epoch . . . a kind of *Weltanshauung* [world-view] . . . [rather] I have studied ensembles of discourse . . . I have defined the play of rules, of transformations, of thresholds, of remanences. I have collated different discourses and described their clusters and relations' (Foucault 1991a: 55). Thus, what Foucault is trying to analyse is not a unified body of ideas or 'spirit of the age' but a set of conflicting discursive frameworks and pressures which operate across a social body and which interact with each other, and these condition how people think, know and write. Rather than there being a smooth transition from one épistémé to another, with scientists building upon the work of others so that there is progress,

Foucault argues that the move from one épistèmé to another creates a discursive break or discontinuity. He suggests that these breaks between épistèmés are sudden, rather than, as they have generally been characterised, an evolution or reaction to previous periods. He asks 'how can it be that there are at certain moments and in certain orders of knowledge these sudden take-offs, these hastenings of evolution, these transformations which do not correspond to the calm and continuist image that is ordinarily accepted?' (Foucault 1979: 31). We can see that Foucault is trying to react against the notion of evolution and progression of traditional historians, whereby it is asserted that knowledge and life in general improve until they reach the highpoint of the present day. Foucault's aim in describing the discursive limits of the épistèmé is to force us to see the strangeness of our current state of knowledge and to question the way that we think, and the conceptual tools which we use to think with.

Foucault's archaeological analysis (discussed in Chapter 1) is focused on the description of the archive, that is 'the set of rules which at a given period and for a given society define . . . the limits and forms of the sayable' (Foucault 1991a: 59). The term 'archive' is used by Foucault to refer to the unwritten rules which lead to the production of certain types of statements and the sum total of the discursive formations circulating at any one time. The term 'discursive formation' is used by Foucault to refer to the regular associations and groupings of particular types of statements; these are groupings of statements which are often associated with particular institutions or sites of power and which have effects on individuals and their thinking. Discursive formations seem to have a solidity about them and yet they are subject to constant change.

Discourses, or discursive formations, are groups of statements which deal with the same topic and which seem to produce a similar effect; for example, they may be groups of statements which are grouped together because of some institutional pressure or association, because of a similarity of origin, or because they have a similar function. They lead to the reproduction of other statements which are compatible with their underlying presuppositions. Discourses should not be seen as wholly cohesive, since they always contain within them conflicting sets of statements; for example, the discourse of masculinity cannot be seen as a simple unitary whole. Within the discourse, or should we say discourses, of masculinity there are sets of statements concerned with the description of machismo (for example, Right-wing statements which extol manly virtues such as strength and confidence), and others which describe the New Man (for example, Left-wing statements which value nurturing and caring). However, these statements, although they have different political intentions and effects, aim to try to characterise men and women as fundamentally different. The effect of these statements is to downplay the similarities between men and women. While the function of asserting these similarities and differences varies, the effect of asserting that men and women are essentially different usually has some advisory function, for example, discourses of masculinity are aimed at describing a situation which an author would like to bring about, (men *should* be tougher as they were in the past, or men *should* be more caring). Thus, discourses should be seen as groups of statements which are associated with institutions, which are authorised in some sense and which have some unity of function at a fundamental level.

The statement can be seen as an authorised proposition or action through speech (Mills 1997). The statement is not simply a sentence because, for example, a map or image could be taken as a statement. The critics, Hubert Dreyfus and Paul Rabinow, argue that 'Maps can be statements, if they are representations of a geographical area, and even a picture of the layout of a typewriter keyboard can be a statement if it appears in a manual or as a representation of the way the letters of a keyboard are standardly arranged' (Dreyfus and Rabinow 1982: 45). Not everyone is able to make statements, or to have statements taken seriously by others. Some statements are more authorised than others, in that they are more associated with those in positions of power or with institutions. What Foucault wants to analyse is 'the law of existence of statements, that which rendered them possible . . . the conditions of their singular emergence' (Foucault 1991a: 59). Thus, rather than assuming that statements simply exist self-evidently, he wants to analyse the process whereby they are brought into being. What makes Foucault's analysis of statements unique is that he tries to analyse statements: 'without referring to the consciousness, obscure or explicit, of speaking subjects; without referring to the facts of discourse to the will – perhaps involuntary – of their authors; without having recourse to that intention of saying what always goes beyond what is actually said; without trying to capture the fugitive unheard subtlety of a word which has no text' (Foucault 1991a: 59). Thus, he is interested in analysing discourse as an impersonal system which exceeds the individual, and he analyses precisely this abstract, anonymous system and structures, and not the individuals who interface with the system. Discourse itself structures what statements it is possible to say, the conditions under which certain statements will be considered true and appropriate. Discourse conditions that certain statements will be more productive of other statements than others.

CONCLUSIONS

Foucault's work on discourse and power is useful in helping theorists to consider the way that we know what we know; where that information comes from; how it is produced and under what circumstances; whose interests it might serve; how it is possible to think differently; in order to be able to trace the way that information that we accept as 'true' is kept in that privileged position. This enables us to look at the past without adopting a position of superiority – of course we know better now – in order to be able to analyse the potential strangeness of the knowledge which we take as 'true' at present.

POWER/KNOWLEDGE

Many of Foucault's writings are concerned with how it is that we know something, and the processes whereby something becomes established as a fact. As we saw in the last chapter on discourse, Foucault is interested in the processes of exclusion which lead to the production of certain discourses rather than others. He is interested in the same processes of exclusion in relation to knowledge and, in the collection of essays entitled *Power/Knowledge* (1980), Foucault explores the way that, in order for something to be established as a fact or as true, other equally valid statements have to be discredited and denied. Thus, rather than focusing on the individual thinkers who developed certain ideas or theories, in works such as *The Order of Things* (1970) and *The Archaeology of Knowledge* (1972), Foucault wants to focus on the more abstract institutional processes at work which establish something as a fact or as knowledge.

The conventional view of knowledge, and particularly scientific knowledge, is that it is created by a series of isolated creative geniuses, for example, Einstein and Pasteur. They are characterised as exceptional people who were able to transcend the conventional ideas of their period and who were able to formulate completely new ideas and theoretical perspectives. In a similar way, the History of Ideas within the philosophical tradition is largely characterised by this concern with individual thinkers, such as Hegel and Wittgenstein, who, it is claimed, changed the course of intellectual endeavour. Foucault would like to produce a much more anonymous, institutionalised and rule-governed model of knowledge-production. As Ian Hunter states:

> Foucault's reformulation of the concept of discourse derives from his attempts to provide histories of knowledge of what men and women have thought. Foucault's histories are not histories of ideas, opinions or influences nor are they histories of the way in which economic, political and social contexts have shaped ideas or opinions. Rather they are reconstructions of the *material conditions* of thought or 'knowledges'. They represent an attempt to produce what Foucault calls an *archaeology* of the material conditions of thought/knowledges, conditions which are not reducible to the idea of 'consciousness' or the idea of 'mind'.
>
> (Hunter, cited in Kendall and Wickham 1999: 35)

Thus, he is not interested so much in what is known at any one period but rather in 'the material conditions of thought' that is the processes which led to certain facts being known rather than others.

Foucault is very aware of how much easier it would be to approach the history of knowledge and ideas by tracing the ideas of 'great thinkers' of Western culture, but instead he has decided to 'determine, in its diverse dimensions, what the mode of existence of discourses (their rules of formation, with their conditions, their dependencies, their transformations) must have been in Europe since the 17th century, in order that the knowledge which is ours today could come to exist, and more particularly, that knowledge which has taken as its domain this curious object which is man' (Foucault 1991a: 70). Thus, he is focusing on the mechanisms by which knowledge comes into being and is produced, and that includes the human sciences in which Foucault, of course, situates his own work. In *The Order of Things* (1970), he is particularly interested in the epistemic shift in the eighteenth and nineteenth centuries in which science turned its attention from the examination of the physical processes within the natural world to the study of 'man'. He argues that:

> Classical thought and all the forms of thought that preceded it, were able to speak of the mind and the body, of the human being, of how restricted a place [s/]he occupies in the universe, of all the limitations by which [her/]his knowledge or [her/]his freedom must be measured, but not one of them was

able to know man as [s/]he is posited in modern knowledge. Renaissance 'humanism and Classical 'rationalism' were indeed able to allot human beings a privileged position in the order of the world, but they were not able to conceive of man.

(Foucault 1970: 318)

So, Foucault wants us to question the self-evident nature of disciplines such as sociology and psychology, consider the way that people thought about humankind before these disciplines developed and analyse the processes whereby it becomes possible to study 'man' as an object.

In *Power/Knowledge*, Foucault describes knowledge as being a conjunction of power relations and information-seeking which he terms 'power/knowledge' (Foucault 1980). He states, in an essay entitled 'Prison talk', that 'it is not possible for power to be exercised without knowledge, it is impossible for knowledge not to engender power' (Foucault 1980d: 52). This is an important theoretical advance in this discussion of knowledge, since it emphasises the way that knowledge is not dispassionate but rather an integral part of struggles over power, but it also draws attention to the way that, in producing knowledge, one is also making a claim for power. For Foucault, it is more accurate to use his newly formed compound 'power/knowledge' to emphasise the way that these two elements depend on one another.

Thus, where there are imbalances of power relations between groups of people or between institutions/states, there will be a production of knowledge. Because of the institutionalised imbalance in power relations between men and women in Western countries, Foucault would argue, information is produced about women; thus we find many books in libraries about women but few about men, and similarly, many about the working classes but few about the middle classes. There are many books about the problems of Black people, but not about Whites. Heterosexuality remains largely unanalysed while homosexuality is the subject of many studies. While this situation is changing radically, where studies of heterosexuality and whiteness have been undertaken, statistically it is still fair to say that academic study within the human sciences has focused on those who are marginalised (see Wilkinson and Kitzinger 1993 on heterosexuality, and Brown *et al.* 1999 on whiteness). Indeed, one could argue that anthropological study has been largely based on the study of those who are politically and economically marginal in relation to a Western metropolis. Thus, although the academic study of a group of people, for example, the analysis of the dialect use of certain groups, often seems self-evident to the researcher, Foucault argues that the object of such research is frequently people who are in less powerful positions. Very few linguists analyse the dialect use of those who speak Received Pronunciation or BBC English; generally, studies are of those with what are seen as regional dialects or accents. In a complex process, this production of knowledge about economically disadvantaged people plays a significant role in maintaining them in this position. But rather than seeing the production of knowledge as wholly oppressive, Foucault is able to see that the production of information by the marginalised themselves can alter the status quo as I discuss later in this chapter.

Foucault characterises power/knowledge as an abstract force which determines what will be known, rather than assuming that individual thinkers develop ideas and knowledge. He asserts that:

> the subject who knows, the objects to be known and the modalities of knowledge must be regarded as so many effects of [the] fundamental implications of power-knowledge and their historical transformations. In short it is not the activity of the subject of knowledge that produces a corpus of knowledge, useful or resistant to power, but power-knowledge, the processes and struggles that traverse it, and of which it is made up, that determines the forms and possible domains of knowledge.
>
> (Foucault 1991a: 27–28)

This is quite a shocking statement in that it dispenses with the myths which in Western society we have formulated for ourselves about the development of knowledge being due to the devotion of innumerable scholars who have worked unceasingly to improve on past knowledge; instead in Foucault's vision, it is power/knowledge which produces facts and the individual scholars are simply the vehicles or the sites where this knowledge is produced. You might think that this is an overstatement, but it is precisely in the most hyperbolic moments of Foucault's writings that his work is most rewarding in theoretical terms. If we allow ourselves to think these 'unthinkable' and seemingly insane ideas about what we know, then we may be able to analyse the extent of the role of individuals and impersonal abstract forces in the production of knowledge.

As I discussed in the previous chapter, Foucault asserts that the set of procedures which produce knowledge and keep knowledge in circulation can be termed an 'épistèmé'. In each historical period this set of rules and conceptual tools for thinking about what counts as factual changes. To give an example of the type of conceptual tool that Foucault has in mind, let us consider what he says about what he terms a 'will to know' which he asserts characterises the épistèmé which developed at the end of the nineteenth century: this will to know is a voracious appetite for information, alongside, or perhaps, prior to which, developed a set of procedures for categorising and measuring objects (Foucault 1981: 55). We should not assume that this will to know or will to truth is universal or unchanging, although it sometimes feels as if it is, in this Information Age where, with the development of the Internet, it seems self-evident that we need more and more space to store information and make it available to as many people as possible. Instead, we should see the will to know reinforced and renewed by whole strata of practices, pedagogies, libraries, institutions, technologies and so on. For example, at the height of the British colonial period in the nineteenth century, there was an outpouring of scholarly, and more popular, knowledge about India and Africa, as the post-colonial theorists Edward Said and Mary Louise Pratt have shown (Said 1978; Pratt 1992). The colonial authorities felt that it was their duty to produce information about the colonised country, by producing detailed maps of the territory, describing architecture in great detail, providing grammars and dictionaries of the indigenous languages, describing the manners and customs of the people. This production of information was also achieved by those who were not employed by the colonial regimes, such as travel writers, novelists, scientists, but who saw in the colonial sphere an opportunity to expand global knowledge. Mary Louise Pratt, in particular, argues that this production of information was not a simple process whereby information about the colonised country was amassed in an objective fashion, as is conventionally assumed; she argues that, in fact, in the process of collecting data, for example about the flora of a country, the Western botanist was setting that information within a Western classificatory system which, in the process, erased the system of classification developed by the indigenous people, which might focus on the use of plants in medicine or in ritual, rather than on the morphological features of the plant, as in the Western model.

Thus, Westerners in the colonial period imposed systems of classification on the colonised countries which they proposed as global objective systems of knowledge, but which were, in fact, formulated from a Western perspective with Western interests at their core (see Foster and Mills 2002, for a fuller discussion). This process of production of knowledge took place through excluding other, equally valid forms of classification and knowledge which were perhaps more relevant to the context. Thus, we must be very suspicious of any information which is produced, since even when it seems most self-evidently to be adding to the sum of human knowledge, it may at the same time play a role in the maintenance of the status quo and the affirming of current power relations.

Foucault argues that rather than knowledge being a pure search after 'truth', in fact, power operates in that processing of information which results in something being labelled as a 'fact'. For something to be considered to be a fact, it must be subjected to a thorough process of ratification by those in positions of authority. As an example of this complex process of exclusion and choice whereby something becomes a 'fact' we might consider the way that, in the West, we tend to assume that the images that we are shown on television news reports must be 'true' and 'factual', but we do not generally consider the complex and lengthy process of editing and exclusion which is enacted on those images before they reach our television screens. To give an example of the way that the information we receive, which we assume to be true, is constrained by governments and other agencies, consider the following comments by the *Washington Post* correspondent, Carol Morello in 2001 on what she was allowed to report from the Anglo-American war in Afghanistan. She describes the way that journalists were only allowed to report if they joined the 'pool' system, whereby the army only gave the journalist accreditation and, therefore, information if they joined the 'pool'; if they joined the pool, they were then allowed very restricted access to certain locations. When Morello was told by the military that some American casualties were arriving she asked the American military forces:

> Could a photographer take photos of the wounded arriving? No. Could print reporters just stand to the side and observe? No. Could reporters talk to the Marine pilots who had airlifted the wounded to the base? No. Could they talk to the doctors after they had finished treating the wounded? No. Could they

talk to the injured Afghan fighters who had also been transported to the base? No. . . . In every war there is an innate tension between the military and the journalists who want to cover the battles up close. With the US troops in southern Afghanistan, however, reporters have operated under limitations more restrictive than those imposed during the Persian Gulf War in 1991.

(Morello, cited in Morgan 2002: 8)

Thus, although, when we watch television we see images which seem to us to be immediate and authentic, these 'true' images of the conflict are the result of a very mediated and stage-managed series of negotiations between journalists and the military and government forces.

In an interview 'Critical theory/intellectual theory', as in his more extended work in the three volumes of *The History of Sexuality*, Foucault suggests that there has developed, within the West since the 1960s, a sense that people should try to find out the 'truth' about themselves. He suggests that it is a common assumption that if one examines one's sexuality, one's past experiences, one could discover the essence of your very being: you could 'find' yourself. However, for Foucault, the moment when you think that you have discovered the 'truth' about yourself is also a moment when power is exercised over you: he puts it in the following way: 'if I tell the truth about myself . . . it is in part that I am constituted as a subject across a number of power relations which are exerted over me and which I exert over others' (Foucault 1988c: 39). In the very process of what seems like constituting oneself as a subject, as an individual, producing knowledge about oneself only makes one an object of discourse, an object of power/knowledge. He takes this thinking about knowledge of oneself a stage further in his essay 'The dangerous individual'; he argues that when those who have been convicted of crimes are being sentenced, it is now deemed essential to know about them in order to judge them. He asks: 'can one condemn to death a person one does not know?' (Foucault 1988e: 127). In the process of convicting someone, a judge needs to be able to assess whether the person's actions were determined by a pathology or whether they were undertaken with full consciousness and intentionality. In each of these cases, the way that the criminal is treated and the type of sentencing is different; for example, in the United States, when a murder is committed, if the cause of the crime is pathological, the murderer will be confined to a mental institution and subjected to treatment, whereas if the murder is considered to be intentional, the murderer is executed or imprisoned.

In an interview entitled 'Truth and power' he examines the way that truth, like knowledge, is not an abstract entity as many within the Western philosophical tradition have assumed. Instead, he asserts that 'truth is of the world; it is produced there by virtue of multiple constraints' (Foucault 1979a: 46). He contrasts the conventional view of truth conceived as a 'richness, a fecundity, a gentle and insidiously universal force' with what he terms 'the will to truth' – that set of exclusionary practices whose function is to establish distinctions between those statements which will be considered to be false and those which will be considered true (Foucault 1981: 56). The true statements will be circulated throughout the society, reproduced in books; they will appear in school curricula and they will be commented on, described and evaluated by others in books and articles. These statements will underpin what is taken to be 'common-sense knowledge' within a society. Those statements which are classified as false will not be reproduced. Each society has its own 'regime of truth', that is, the type of statements which can be made by authorised people and accepted by the society as a whole, and which are then distinguished from false statements by a range of different practices. In an interview, 'Power and sex', he analyses the way that 'truth' or 'facts' are kept in place by a complex web of social relations, mechanisms and prohibitions and argues that 'my aim is not to write the social history of a prohibition but the political history of the production of "truth"' (Foucault 1988d: 112). And furthermore, in 'Questions of method', he adds that 'my problem is to see how [people] govern (themselves and others) by the production of truth . . . (by the production of truth I mean not the production of true utterances, but the establishment of domains in which the practice of true and false can be made at once ordered and pertinent)' (Foucault 1991b: 79). Thus, his analysis of truth and knowledge cannot be seen to be a simple political analysis of the oppressive forces of power/knowledge; he characterises his analysis as one which simply describes rather than criticises.

His analysis of the distinction between fact and falsehood is extended into the literary field by the literary analyst, Lennard Davis, who has shown that before the eighteenth century there was a certain laxity towards the division between fact and fiction (Davis 1983). In the eighteenth century, Davis argues, a number of legal interventions by the government began to make their presence felt on what could be published and this resulted in the division between fact and fiction being clearly established; because the government was trying to restrict criticism in the press, the libel laws defined (and stamp duty taxed) those elements which claimed to be true and factual. Before this, newspapers and chapbooks had contained descriptions of events both natural and supernatural, true and imaginary, which had a moral or religious significance; now, newspapers began to publish reports of events which were recent and which were claimed to be true.

Foucault is not concerned to set up the notion of truth in opposition to a Marxist notion of ideology or false ideas, false consciousness himself, but simply to analyse the procedures which are used to maintain these distinctions. This is one of the difficulties which critics like Edward Said have found in their use of Foucault's work, since for postcolonial theorists it seems indispensable to see the representations by the colonial powers of colonised countries as false (Said 1978). For example, British writers within the colonial period often described the indigenous people of India and Africa as lazy, backward, dirty, inferior, 'primitive', and underdeveloped in comparison to a modern industrialised West. Said struggles in his use of Foucault's work on the question of the truth of these representations, since, at one and the same time, he is forced to see the constructedness of these 'factual' accounts, while wishing to somehow contrast this with a 'true' description of these countries. Such a description of what these countries and their inhabitants were *really* like is, in Foucault's terms, equally fictional and constructed. What Foucault argues is that 'it's not a matter of emancipating truth from every system of power (which is a chimera for truth is already power) but of detaching the power of truth from the forms of hegemony, social economic and cultural, within which it operates at the present time' (Foucault 1980b: 133).

Although hegemony is a term which is much debated within Marxist theory, it can broadly be defined within the following terms: hegemony is a state within society whereby those who are dominated by others take on board the values and ideologies of those in power and accept them as their own; this leads to them accepting their position within the hierarchy as natural or for their own good.

Thus, truth, power and knowledge are intricately connected and what we need to analyse is the workings of power in the production of knowledge. This is especially important for Western feminist theorists who tried initially to document the 'truth' of women's condition or women's experiences to oppose the falsehood of sexist stereotypes of women. However, the 'truth' of these feminist representations was also challenged by other women from marginalised, non-Western groups who did not feel that these images accurately reflected their situations, their concerns and values (Minh-ha 1989). What Western feminists have learned from this debate over who can represent 'women' as a whole, is that the term 'women' is one which it is almost impossible to discuss, since different groups of women will bring different perspectives to what 'women' are. Thus, what Foucault is concerned to assert is that truth is constructed and kept in place through a wide range of strategies which support and affirm it and which exclude and counter alternative versions of events. He is not necessarily concerned to provide alternative versions of events which may be seen by some to be more accurate or which fit in more with his perspective.

However, despite this seeming dispassionate stance on truth and knowledge, Foucault suggests that it is important to counter the types of information which have been disseminated to us by the government and its institutions, and in his own political activism, he considered that the production of knowledge could play an important role. For example, he, along with other campaigners, set up a group in the 1970s which provided information about the conditions in French prisons. This Group d'Information sur Les Prisons, rather than simply critiquing the conditions in prison, provided information about those conditions, written by the prisoners themselves. He stated in a speech setting out the group's manifesto:

> we propose to let people know what prisons are: who goes there, and how and why they go; what happens there; what the existence of prisoners is like, and also the existence of those providing surveillance; what the buildings, food and hygiene are like; how the inside rules, medical supervision and workshops function; how one gets out and what it is like in our society to be someone who does get out.

> (Foucault, cited in Eribon 1991: 225)

This production of unpalatable information, the sort of information that most people would rather not think about, is a form of critique in its own right, forcing to the front of our consciousness the facts about what is entailed when we as a society condemn certain people to confinement.

Yet, it is also important that even this type of seemingly critical knowledge is not seen to be exempt from the workings of power/ knowledge. This is important to bear in mind when we consider the work of white, middle-class, Western sociologists and anthropologists who, perhaps with the best intentions, study working-class communities or communities in other countries: in the process of collecting data and information about those communities they cannot but establish power relations between them and the group. This conjunction of power and knowledge has created great difficulties within sociology, linguistics and anthropology, where studying other communities can be seen to turn them into objects of knowledge. The feminist sociologist, Bev Skeggs (1997), is very aware of this problem in her sociological work about working-class women, as are many of those within the tradition of critical anthropology, who have tried to position themselves alongside the people whom they are studying rather than in a position of superiority. They have had to adopt a range of strategies, for example, giving their research findings to the communities to comment on, including critical comments by members of the study, and writing the research with members of the community, and acknowledging their input. (See, for an example of such a project, Bourdieu *et al.* 1999.) Foucault's decision in relation to the Groupe d'Information sur les Prisons was to attempt to provide the conditions from which the prisoners could speak for themselves; the group talked to prisoners and interviewed their families. He asserts that: 'these investigations are not made from the outside by a group of technicians. Here the investigators and the investigated are the same. It is up to them to speak, to dismantle the compartmentalisation, to formulate what is intolerable and to tolerate it no longer. It is up to them to take charge of the struggle that will prevent the exercise of oppression' (Foucault, cited in Eribon 1991: 228). Here, Foucault seems to be suggesting that in taking the role only of facilitator, he can sidestep the possibility of posing himself as superior to the prisoners; however, he still seems to be determining the form which action on the part of prisoners might take. Serge Livrozet, one of the prisoners who described their experiences in an interview in *Libération* in 1974, clearly felt that Foucault's position was not simply that of a facilitator, when he commented: 'these specialists in analysis are a pain. I don't need anyone to speak for me and proclaim what I am' (Livrozet, cited in Eribon 1991: 234). Thus, every instance of production of knowledge, every instance when someone seems to be speaking on behalf of someone else, no matter how good their intentions are, needs to be interrogated.

Foucault's work on power/knowledge is also, in essence, an analysis of the historical processes at work in the construction of what our society as a whole knows about the past. It is only by critically examining the past that we can defamiliarise what we know about the present. Foucault's notion of history is profoundly antithetical to notions of what is often called Whig history, that is those versions of history which were formulated in the nineteenth century and which assumed that human civilisations (that is for these historians, European civilisations) were inevitably progressing and must necessarily be better than those in the past. Foucault questions this type of triumphalism. In his interview 'Critical theory/intellectual theory', he asserts: 'I think we should have the modesty to say to ourselves that the time that we live in is not *the* unique or fundamental or irruptive point in history where everything is completed and begun again' (Foucault 1988c: 36). Thus, we need to fundamentally question the notion of 'progress'.

Foucault has often been criticised by historians since he is rather cavalier in his generalisations about the past. However, he is using historical material for different purposes than scholarly historians. The sociologists, Gavin Kendall and Gary Wickham, assert that this difference of purpose can be seen in the following terms:

> the Foucaultian method's use of history ... does not involve assumptions of progress (or regress) ... it involves histories that never stop; they cannot be said to stop because they cannot be said to be going anywhere. To use history in the Foucaultian manner is to use it to help us see that the present is just as strange as the past, not to help us see that a sensible or desirable present has emerged ... or might emerge.
>
> (Kendall and Wickham 1999)

The notion that history is not 'going anywhere', that there is no progress, is very disconcerting for many readers. But Kendall and Wickham go on to suggest that within a Foucauldian analysis 'history should not be used to make ourselves comfortable, but rather to disturb the taken-for-granted' (Kendall and Wickham 1999: 4). Rather than characterising the present as an inevitable outcome of events in the past we must see the present as one possible outcome of those events: to analyse the present then, 'does not consist in a simple character-isation of what we are but instead – by following lines of fragility in the present – in managing to grasp why and how that-which-is might no longer be that-which-is' (Foucault 1988c: 36). In a sense, what we have to bear in mind is that the present is both 'a time like any other' as well as 'a time which is never quite like any other' (Foucault 1988c: 37). Perhaps, what Foucault's form of analysis teaches us is that in some senses the present is unanalysable since it seems as if it is too complex to see clearly what is happening, and because it is too familiar. However, if we are to analyse it at all, and this does seem to be Foucault's aim, to analyse the present by discussing the past, then we must begin by treating it as if it were more like the past, in all its strangeness.

CONCLUSIONS

Foucault in a number of his writings is concerned to establish the interconnectedness of power and knowledge and power and truth. He describes the ways in which knowledge does not simply emerge from scholarly study but is produced and maintained in circulation in societies through the work of a number of different institutions and practices. Thus, he moves us away from seeing knowledge as objec-tive and dispassionate towards a view which sees knowledge always working in the interests of particular groups.

THE BODY AND SEXUALITY

Foucault wrote on the impact of institutional and discursive forces on the body, particularly in books such as *The History of Sexuality* (1978–1986). He suggests that the body should be seen as the focus of a number of discursive pressures: the body is the site on which discourses are enacted and where they are contested. He also analysed, in *The Order of Things* (1970) and in *Discipline and Punish* (1977), the changes consequent on the academic and governmental analysis of the population as a whole, what he terms 'bio-power', that is, the 'increasing organisation of population and welfare for the sake of increased force and productivity' (Dreyfus and Rabinow 1986: 8).

His analysis of the interaction between the body and institutions has been very influential among feminists and Queer theorists from the 1980s onwards. Jana Sawicki suggests a reason:

> among the many influential French critical theorists Foucault was distinct in so far as his aim was to intervene in specific struggles of disenfranchised and socially suspect groups such as prisoners, mental patients and homosexuals. In so far as Foucault's discourse appeared to be more activist and less narrowly academic than those of his post-structuralist counterparts, it compelled activist feminist theorists to take a serious look at his work.
>
> (Sawicki 1998: 93)

Thus, theorists of marginalised groups have found his work useful because it lends itself to being put to use in a political cause.

THE BODY, DISCOURSE AND SEXUALITY

Many analyses of power have focused on the role of institutions, but Foucault analyses the operation of power largely outside the realm of institutions; for this reason, the body is one of the sites of struggle and discursive conflict upon which he focuses. Rather than a top-down model of power relations which examines the way the State or institutions oppress people, he is concerned to develop a bottom-up model, where the body is one of the sites where power is enacted and resisted. Smart argues that:

> An analysis of the techniques and procedures of power at the most basic level of the social order which then proceeds to a documentation of changes and developments in their forms and their annexation by more global forms of domination is radically different from an analysis which conceptualises power as located within a centralised institutional nexus and then seeks to trace its diffusion and effect in and through the social order.
>
> (Smart 1985: 79)

This first type of analysis is a Foucauldian one, focusing on the way that mundane power relations at a local level feed into the constitution of institutional power relations. Maybe it would be more accurate to say that Foucault is attempting to privilege neither side of the power relation, but is concerned to describe the interaction of institutions and the individual without assuming that one of them is primary in the relation.

The focus in Foucault's work on the body rather than the individual is important. The individual in Foucault's framework is considered to be an effect rather than an essence, as Gary Wickham puts it: 'the notion of bodies as the target of power is part of Foucault's attempt to avoid the liberal conception of individuals as unconstrained creative essences' (Wickham 1986: 155). Foucault argues that 'the individual is not to be conceived of as a sort of elementary nucleus . . . on which power comes to fasten . . . In fact, it is already one of the prime effects of power that certain bodies, certain gestures, certain discourses, certain desires, come to be identified and constituted as individuals'

(Foucault 1980a: 98). Thus, rather than seeing individuals as stable entities, he analyses the discursive processes through which bodies are constituted. This is a particularly useful notion for feminists and Queer theorists who wish to theorise the forms of oppression of women, gays and lesbians without falling into false assumptions about essentialism (the notion that sexual or other difference is due to biological difference). Foucault suggests, in an essay entitled 'Nietzsche, genealogy and power' that the body should be seen as 'the inscribed surface of events', that is, political events and decisions have material effects upon the body which can be analysed. He also described the body as 'the illusion of a substantial unity' and 'a volume in perpetual disintegration', thus emphasising that what seems most solid is, in fact, constructed through discursive mediation; for him the task of genealogical analysis 'is to expose a body totally imprinted by history and the processes of history's destruction of the body' (Foucault 1986b: 83). As well as questioning the seeming solidity of the body, Foucault also draws attention to the body as 'an historically and culturally specific entity', that is, one which is viewed, treated and indeed experienced differently depending on the social context and the historical period. In this sense, bodies are always subject to change and can never be regarded as natural, but rather are always experienced as mediated through different social constructions of the body.

In his work on 'bio-power', Foucault argues that it is at the level of the body that much regulation by the authorities from the nineteenth century onwards is enacted: knowledge is accumulated, populations are observed and surveyed, procedures for investigation and research about the population as a whole and of the body in particular are refined. Here, he argues, the aims of government in their attempts to control populations and the social sciences in their investigations of population growth and large-scale trends across societies seemed to coalesce. The view of the population as a whole as a resource was a new one; as the critics Hubert Dreyfus and Paul Rabinow put it: 'The individual was of interest exactly insofar as [s/he] could contribute to the strength of the state. The lives, deaths, activities, work and joys of individuals were important to the extent that these everyday concerns became politically useful' (Dreyfus and Rabinow 1986: 139). Thus, while ostensibly surveys of the population were undertaken by the government to improve the welfare of the population as a whole – for example, eradicating venereal disease and incest among the working classes, they in fact had the effect of tightening the disciplinary regime, so that the population was more strictly controlled.

Bio-power is not simply concerned with analysis of populations as a whole but also with the analysis of sexuality. Foucault's focus on the analysis of sexuality has played an important role in challenging preconceived notions of sexual identity. In a statement which exemplifies the Foucauldian approach to analysis, he argues that his study *The History of Sexuality* (1978–1986):

> was intended to be neither a history of sexual behaviours nor a history of representations, but a history of 'sexuality' – the quotation marks have a certain importance. My aim was not to write a history of sexual behaviours and practices, tracing their successive forms, their evolution, and their dissemination; nor was it to analyse the scientific, religious or philosophical ideas through which these behaviours have been represented. I wanted first to dwell on that quite recent and banal notion of 'sexuality': to stand detached from it, bracketing its familiarity, in order to analyse the theoretical and practical context with which it has been associated.
>
> (Foucault 1985: 3)

In the three-volume *History of Sexuality*, he focuses on views of sexuality and the consequent conceptualisation of the self since the Greeks. In the first volume, he analyses in particular the views of sexuality which developed within the nineteenth century which he argues still have an influence on contemporary notions on sexuality. He contrasts the 'frankness' and 'publicness' of people in the seventeenth century around sexual matters to the prudery and attempts to confine discussions of sexuality behind closed bedroom doors in the Victorian era. What makes his analysis of sexuality important is that he argues that while, within the nineteenth century, there was an attempt to silence discussion of sexuality and restrict sexual practices, we should not assume that this repression was effective, or effective in the ways in which it was envisaged it would be. The seeming repression of sexual discussion and sexuality itself had an unintended effect, that is to increase the desire to speak about sexuality and increase the pleasure gained from violating these taboos:

> if sex is repressed, that is condemned to prohibition, non-existence and silence, then the mere fact that one is speaking about it has the appearance of a

deliberate transgression. A person who holds forth in such language places himself [/herself] to a certain extent outside the reach of power; he [/she] upsets established law; he [/she] somehow anticipates the coming freedom.

(Foucault 1986c: 295)

This is a paradoxical analysis of the repression of sexuality and indeed of the liberalisation of views on sexuality, since it has led to people in the twenty-first century imagining that freedom lies in unfettered sexual expression.

He argues, in an essay entitled 'We other Victorians', that:

since the end of the sixteenth century, the 'putting into discourse of sex', far from undergoing a process of restriction, on the contrary has been subjected to a mechanism of increasing incitement . . . the techniques of power exercised over sex have not obeyed a principle of rigorous selection, but rather one of dissemination and implantation of polymorphous sexualities . . . the will to knowledge has not come to a halt in the face of a taboo that must not be lifted, but has persisted in constituting – despite many mistakes of course – a science of sexuality.

(Foucault 1986c: 300)

Thus, rather than closing down the possible forms of sexuality, the repressive discourses which circulated around sexual behaviour in the eighteenth and nineteenth centuries actually had the effect of constituting seemingly perverse forms of sexuality as *possible* and, perhaps more importantly, as *desirable* (since forbidden) forms of behaviour. Thus, homosexual activity, which before the nineteenth century had been seen as a series of stigmatised acts engaged in by males, began to be seen to constitute a particular sort of individual who would engage in those acts and no other. Thus, for the first time homosexuals and heterosexuals were constructed as distinct categories. Homosexuals began to be seen as particular types of people who were born as 'inverts', that is, pathologically perverse. Thus, homosexuality as a categorisation of individuals was invented. Because of this seeming solidity of the construction of this categorisation of sexual preference, sex and sexuality became the legitimate object of scientific study.

In *History of Sexuality, Vol. I* (1978), Foucault analyses the changes in the focus of the analysis of sexuality and the way that perversity became of great importance in the eighteenth and nineteenth centuries.

In the seventeenth century, Foucault argues, the focus of concern was on the matrimonial couple: 'the sex of the husband and wife was beset by rules and recommendations': when it was possible and not possible to have sex (Foucault 1986d: 317). However, other forms of sexual practice 'remained a good deal more confused: one has only to think of the uncertain status of "sodomy", or the indifference regarding the sexuality of children' (Foucault 1986d: 317). In the eighteenth and nineteenth centuries, the sexuality of the couple came under less overt scrutiny: instead, the focus was on:

> the sexuality of children, mad men and women and criminals: the sensuality of those who did not like the opposite sex; reveries, obsessions, petty manias, or great transports of rage. It was the time for all these figures, scarcely noticed in the past, to step forward and speak, to make the difficult confession of what they were.
>
> (Foucault 1986d: 318)

Foucault analyses the process of confession, whereby in order for past actions to be atoned for, they must be spoken about to an author- ised person. This practice developed within the Christian Church but can be seen in a wide range of practices today, ranging from thera- peutic counselling, testimonia/autobiographical writing and reality-TV and in gay and lesbian 'coming out'. He argues that 'the Christian West invented this astonishing constraint, which it imposed on everyone, to say everything in order to efface everything, to formulate even the least faults in an uninterrupted, desperate, exhaustive murmuring, from which nothing must escape' (Foucault 1979d: 84). Foucault's tracing of the history of the confessional to the religious ritual of atonement and forgiveness suggests that 'coming out' is constrained by similar views of homosexuality as sin. However, perhaps gay and lesbian theorists have managed to recontextualise coming out as a liberatory movement where a gay or lesbian becomes openly a member of a different sort of community and becomes a different sort of person, rather than being someone who is publicly admitting their sins.

Foucault describes, in Volume II of the *History of Sexuality* (1985), the ways in which, for ancient Greek society, homosexual acts were seen in very different ways, not as defining oneself as a particular type of individual, but as indicating one's control of one's appetites. He analyses the sexual codes of the Greeks in order to show that our notion of sexuality 'applies to a reality of another type', rather than sexuality being seen as a constant (Foucault 1985: 35). For the Greeks, 'what differentiates men from one another . . . is not so much the type of objects toward which they are oriented, nor the mode of sexual practice they prefer; above all, it is the intensity of that practice' (Foucault 1985: 44). Thus, moderation of sexual practice and control of lust were seen as more important and more defining of a moral self than whether men chose to have sexual relations with women, men or with boys. Thus, Foucault is not simply interested in the way subjects come to recognise themselves as sexed individuals, but also in the way that this analysis of one's sexual behaviour leads one to judge oneself morally. Rather than assuming that there is some necessary link between sexual behaviour and moral standards, Foucault asks 'why is sexual conduct, why are the activities and pleasures that attach to it, an object of moral solicitude?' (Foucault 1985: 10). Foucault describes the way in which, for the Greeks, through mastery of one's sexual behaviour and sexual appetite one formed oneself as a moral or ethical subject: 'a process in which the individual delimits that part of himself that will form the object of his moral practice, defines his position relative to the precept he will follow, and decides on a certain mode of being that will serve as a moral goal' (Foucault 1985: 28).

Foucault argues that not only was homosexuality invented in the nineteenth century but so was sexuality itself. Until the eighteenth century, there was a concern with the regulation of the 'flesh', that is the control of desire and demand; in the nineteenth century this develops into a concern with sexuality. Since the nineteenth century, this has had the effect of determining that in a sense one *is* one's sexual preference; the sex of the person that one sleeps with determines the identity category that you inhabit. Foucault saw the construction of sexuality being constituted along three axes: 1) knowledges about sexual behaviour; 2) systems of power which regulate the practice of sexual acts; 3) 'the forms within which individuals are able, are obliged, to recognise themselves as subjects of this sexuality' (Foucault 1985: 4).

In *The History of Sexuality, Vol. I* (1978), and in an essay 'The repressive hypothesis' (1986d), Foucault discusses the way that children's sexuality was discussed in the eighteenth and nineteenth centuries; he shows that in the seventeenth century there had been a certain 'freedom' between adults and children to talk about sexual matters which was lost in the repressive moves to prevent male children masturbating; however, 'this was not a plain and simple imposition of silence. Rather it was a new regime of discourses. Not any less was said about it; on the contrary. But things were said in a different way and in order to obtain different results' (Foucault 1986d: 309). He suggests that one has only to look at the architecture of schools built during this period to see:

> that the question of sex was a constant preoccupation. The builders consid-
> ered it explicitly. The organisers took it permanently into account. All who held
> a measure of authority were placed in a state of perpetual alert . . . The space
> for classes, the shape of the tables, the planning of the recreation lessons, the
> distribution of the dormitories (with or without partitions, with or without
> curtains) the rules for monitoring bedtime and sleep periods – all this referred,
> in the most prolix manner, to the sexuality of children.
>
> (Foucault 1986d: 310)

Not only did the sexuality of (male) children become an issue which had to be confronted and managed in schools, but it became a general and public problem which required parents, doctors and schoolteachers to be advised:

> doctors counselled the directors and professors of educational establishments,
> but they also gave their opinions to families; educators designed projects
> which they submitted to the authorities; schoolmasters turned to students,
> made recommendations to them, and drafted for their benefit books of exhor-
> tation, full of moral and medical examples. Around the schoolboy and his sex
> there proliferated a whole literature of precepts, opinions, observations, med-
> ical advice, clinical cases, outlines for reform and plans for ideal institutions.
>
> (Foucault 1986d: 310)

In this sense, rather than repressing and silencing male children's sexuality, those very children were drawn into a 'web of discourses which sometimes address them, sometimes speak about them' and which shaped their sexual responses (Foucault 1986d: 311).

This treatment of boys' masturbation as an epidemic which needed to be eradicated entailed:

> using these tenuous pleasures as a prop, constituting them as a secret (forcing
> them into hiding so as to make possible their discovery), tracing them back to

their source, tracking them from their origins to their effects, searching out everything that might cause them or simply enable them to exist. Wherever there was a chance they might appear, devices of surveillance were installed; traps were laid for compelling admissions; inexhaustible and corrective discourses were imposed; parents and teachers were alerted, and left with the suspicion that all children were guilty, and with the fear of being themselves at fault if their suspicions were not sufficiently strong ... an entire medico-sexual regime took hold of the family milieu

(Foucault 1986d: 322)

What is interesting about this analysis of children's sexuality is precisely the reversal which Foucault's analysis makes: what seems to be repressed and silenced is, in fact, brought to light and discussed endlessly; and further, what the authorities seem to wish to repress, they in fact depend on for their functioning. This is quite different from the conventional notion of repression or prohibition, as he puts it:

the child's 'vice' was not so much an enemy as a support; it may have been designated as the evil to be eliminated, but the extraordinary effort that went into the task that was bound to fail leads one to suspect that what was demanded of it was to persevere, to proliferate to the limits of the visible and the invisible, rather than to disappear for good. Always relying on this support, power advanced, multiplied its relays and its effects, while its target expanded, subdivided, and branched out, penetrating further into reality at the same pace.

(Foucault 1986d: 322)

Thus, this analysis of sexuality can be seen to be, at one and the same time, an analysis of the workings of power and the way that, despite the intentions of those acting to control children's sexuality, certain other effects ensued.

As part of his analysis of sexuality, he analyses what we would now term 'child abuse' but which he labelled 'inconsequential bucolic pleasures' (Foucault 1986d: 312). He describes the case of a French male farmhand in 1869 who was indicted for indecent assault (in Foucault's words: 'he had obtained a few caresses from a little girl'); he was arrested and his case was reported by gendarmes, a doctor and two experts. Foucault suggests that the only significance of this case is the pettiness of it all, that 'this everyday occurrence in the life of village sexuality . . . could become from a certain time, the object not only of a collective intolerance but of a judicial action, a medical intervention, a careful clinical examination, and an entire theoretical elaboration' (Foucault 1986d: 313). The authorities acquitted the farmhand of any crime but locked him away in a hospital where he remained until his death. It is clear with whom Foucault's sympathies lie: he refers to 'these barely furtive pleasures between simple-minded adults and alert children', and 'this village half-wit who would give a few pennies to little girls for favours the older ones refused him', but particularly in the current concern about paedophilia, these 'furtive pleasures' do not seem so inconsequential. Foucault asks us to analyse the way we categorise these sexual acts and those who engage in them without resorting to categorisations such as paedophiles.

Some feminist theorists have found this type of analysis of sexuality productive, forcing us to reconsider the seemingly self-evident nature of our responses to sexual acts. For example, Nicola Gavey surveyed a wide range of heterosexual women and asked them whether they had ever had unwanted sex with their partners (Gavey 1993). While most of them admitted that they had had sex with their partners when they had not wanted to, they did not classify this as rape because of their views about the difference of male and female sexual needs and drives. Because of the way relations between men and women are still often structured around notions of unequal power, Gavey argues that some women find it difficult to refuse to have sex with their partners. This is because many heterosexual women view sexual relations in terms of contradictory notions of consent and availability: 'when dominant discourses on women's sexuality are structured around consent, and they neglect more active notions such as desire, it is little wonder that women often don't really understand the concept of consent in a way that is meaningful to us' (Gavey 1993: 105).

In another feminist study, Linda Grant questions that date rape should always be presumed to have the devastating effects which media-reports and therapists assume it does. She analyses the construction of the concept of date-rape in the last fifteen years, and contrasts the way that date-rape is considered now and the way that she herself experienced a sexual encounter she had in the 1970s, where she felt forced into having sex against her will. Although she categorised this sexual experience as unpleasant and it made her angry, she was surprised, when telling another person, to be informed that she had been raped. She says, describing herself in the third person – perhaps a telling strategy:

> By the end of the afternoon she'd pretty well forgotten about the night before. She did not feel defiled. She did not shower a dozen times, scrubbing at her skin. She did not feel her identity evaporate. She did not call the police. She did not inform the university authorities. She did not confront the man. What she did do was to tell a number of people what had happened and it was agreed that it was typical of him – he was an arrogant, egocentric bastard . . . no one suggested that the woman should go for counselling. No one held her. She didn't develop an eating disorder and she was never afterwards able to feel that the event had been a trauma. She just had it down as a bad night.
>
> (Grant 1994: 79)

While this type of analysis does not aim to question the traumatic effect of violent rape on women, as it is clear that such rape and sexual abuse is a brutal violation of women and does have serious psychological consequences, what Grant is drawing attention to is the way that date-rape has been constructed as a form of sexual behaviour which entails a number of different types of behaviour in response to it. She is questioning whether this set of behaviours need necessarily be consequent to this type of sexual experience. Thus feminists working with Foucault's ideas have tried to question the self-evident nature of our thinking about sexual assault and our responses to it.

This focus on the body as a place where discourses are acted out and acted upon is one of the ways that Foucault manages to consider the way that identities are constructed without falling prey to a simple liberal humanism (that is, an assumption that there is a stability to the individual and that each individual is unique). He is interested in examining the way that power relations produce particular types of identities. However, rather than seeing power as simply a site of oppression, or as simply determining certain identities, Foucault sees that it is in negotiation and play that identities are formed. Foucault suggests that it is possible to construct what he calls counter-discourses and counter-identification, that is, individuals can take on board the stigmatised individualities that they have been assigned, such as that of 'perverse sexuality' and revel in them rather than seeing them in negative terms. Thus, some lesbians can use terms such as 'dyke' to refer to themselves, and some gay men can use the word 'queen' or 'poof' in a positive way. Indeed, the very use of the word 'Queer' to describe anti-essentialist lesbian and gay theorising is an instance of counter-identification, of celebrating the terms which have been used to condemn us. Foucault analyses the stereotypical image of the homo-sexual: 'in nineteenth century texts there is a stereotypical portrait of the homosexual or invert: not only his mannerisms, his bearing, the way he gets dolled up, his coquetry, but also his facial expressions, his anatomy, the feminine morphology of his whole body are regularly included in this disparaging description' (Foucault 1985: 18). Foucault focuses on the way that this image of homosexuality comes to stand for homosexuality as a whole and argues that it has a complex relation with the behaviour and self-representation of homosexuals since 'actual behaviours may have corresponded [to this image] through a complex play of inductions and attitudes of defiance' (Foucault 1985: 18). This notion that individuals can take this negative stereotype and use it productively to form elements of their own individuality has been drawn on by lesbian theorists in particular. For example, Robyn Queen has analysed the way that lesbians represent themselves in an often complex mixture of parodies of stereotypical heterosexual behaviour together with ironised stereotypes of lesbian and gay, butch and femme behav-iours (Queen 1997). William Leap describes an incident where, when confronted with the phrase 'Death to Faggots' written on a lavatory wall, a gay male had written in response, 'That's Mr. Faggot to you, punk'. As Leap puts it: 'Using an appeal to appropriate verbal etiquette to a death threat is an especially delicious moment of queer phrase-making' (Leap 1997). Thus, rather than assuming that the identities that we seem to have at the present moment are stable and only to be seen from one perspective, Foucault suggests that there are ways of subversively using these positions which have been mapped out for us by others. For many Queer theorists, identity is best seen as performa-tive, something which we do and act out, something which we assem-ble from existing discursive practices, rather than as something which we possess (Butler 1990).

One of the issues which Foucault consistently draws attention to is the way that, since the 1960s, people have sought the truth about themselves in their sexuality. If one is sexually liberated and freed from all prudish constraints, it was argued, one will in a sense be more truly oneself. In the nineteenth century, through the force of knowledges about sexuality, individuals 'were led to focus their attention on them-selves, to decipher, recognise and acknowledge themselves as subjects of desire, bringing into play between themselves and themselves a certain relationship that allows them to discover, in desire, the truth of their being, be it natural or fallen' (Foucault 1985: 5). However, in *The History of Sexuality, Vol. I*, Foucault shows that this notion of liberation through sexuality is an illusion as 'where there is desire, the power relation is already present: an illusion, then to denounce this relation for a repression exerted after the event; but vanity as well to go questing after a desire that is beyond the reach of power' (Foucault 1978: 151).

As well as analysing the way that homosexuality and children's sexuality has been constructed, Foucault also considers the way that women's bodies and sexualities are shaped by social pressures. Women's bodies, particularly middle-class women's bodies have been the subject of a vast array of different practices and discursive regimes. Feminist theorists have taken the notion of disciplinary regime, discussed in Chapter 1, and used it to analyse the workings of femininity on the female body. A disciplinary regime is one where one's comportment is overseen and subjected to a series of rules and regulations relating to control of appetite, movement and emotion. Foucault, in *Discipline and Punish*, describes the disciplinary structures which were put in place in prisons and armies in the nineteenth century in order to ensure the smooth running of these institutions; people within the institutions were forced to obey commands and perform even mundane actions according to a rigid set of rules which were internalised to such an extent that they began to seem part of the individual's personality. Capitalist production has colonised a great number of techniques from such institutions, and others, in its construction of the work ethic, ensuring that notions such as punctuality, self-discipline and precision are internalised by workers as desirable qualities. In a similar way, some feminists have argued that femininity can be viewed as a disciplinary regime. Femininity is achieved (if it is ever achieved) through a long process of labour to force the body into compliance with a feminine ideal, through depilation, cosmetics, exercise, dieting and attention to dress. It is this working on the body which is of interest to feminist theorists.

However, some feminist theorists have also remarked upon the fact that the notion of the disciplinary regime is perhaps unhelpful in this context since it appears to operate outside of an institutional context. And, as Sandra Bartky argues, 'no one is marched off for electrolysis at gunpoint' (Bartky 1988: 75). While noting that there are a number of experts who are consulted for advice on how best to manage one's femininity, we still need to ask who 'is the top sergeant in the disciplinary regime of femininity? . . . The disciplinary power that inscribes femininity in the female body is everywhere and is nowhere; the disciplinarian is everyone and yet no one in particular' (Bartky 1988: 70). Thus, although there are elements of disciplinary regime in femininity, it is the fact that no one particular agency can be held responsible which differentiates it from other disciplinary regimes. This lack of institutional agency behind the regulation of femininity is also what makes it difficult to critique and change – hence when the British Labour government made a commitment to try to change young women's views on body size recently, they turned to trying to influence the images represented in women's magazines.

One of the ways in which the bodies of women within particular contexts seem to be subjected to particular discursive frameworks is in relation to eating disorders as Sandra Bartky and Susan Bordo describe in their essays on anorexia nervosa (Bartky 1988; Bordo 1989). Here we see in action what Foucault terms a 'microphysics of power' that is the very minute operations of power, in this case upon the body. Disciplinary practices of, for example, exacting routines of body and object co-ordination train the body in certain ways to 'become docile' (Bartky 1988: 61). Bordo describes the way that, drawing on Foucault's work, we can trace a number of themes which have been seen to operate as ways of seeing the body and for her these are particularly important in the analysis of anorexia nervosa (Bordo 1989). The body is experienced as alien to the true self of the soul or the thinking self; it is experienced as confinement and limitation; and the body is the enemy and as something which eludes our control. These ways of thinking about the body have all been used at different periods of history, sometimes in conjunction or opposition. Anorexics aim to reverse these oppositions in order to put themselves (that part of them which is not their bodies) in control.

Bartky argues that feminist campaigns against certain disabling forms of femininity are not likely to be successful since many women have invested in these procedures:

> Women . . . like other skilled individuals have a stake in the perpetuation of
> their skills, whatever it may cost to acquire them and quite apart from the
> question of whether as a gender they would have been better off had they
> never had to acquire them in the first place. Hence, feminism . . . threatens

women with a certain de-skilling, something people normally resist; beyond this, it calls into question that aspect of personal identity that is tied to the development of one's sense of competence.

(Bartky 1988: 77)

CONCLUSIONS

Thus, a Foucauldian analysis of the body and sexuality is concerned to defamiliarise those elements which are taken for granted and challenge any statement which argues for the unchanging nature of the body. Foucault's ideas about sexuality have led to a radical questioning of the relation between sexual choice and sexual preference and identity. His work has also been influential in rethinking identity itself and has led to a concern with performative rather than essentialist views of identity. He analyses the relation between institutions and the body and the way that power relations are played out on the body, but he does not see the body as passive in this process and is as much concerned with charting the possible forms of resistance to control as with describing disciplinary control itself.

QUESTIONING THE SUBJECT: MADNESS AND SANITY

Foucault wrote many books and articles which challenged the stability of the individual subject. For example, as I discussed in the previous chapter, his work in *The History of Sexuality* aimed to question whether one's preference for certain types of sexual acts with certain types of people marked one out as a particular type of individual, thus destabilising the very notion of gendered and sexual identity. In *The Archaeology of Knowledge* (1972) and *The Order of Things* (1973), he tried to develop a form of analysis which focused on the impersonal and abstract forces of discourse in structuring the individual, thus calling into question the notion of the individual as any more than a site where discourses are played out, as I discussed in Chapter 2. In addition, Foucault also analysed a subject which is perhaps at the heart of the notion of the individual: the construction of the notion of mental illness. Although most of Foucault's academic training was in philosophy, after his first degree he trained for a higher degree in psychology and a diploma in pathological psychology, and he worked for a short period in a mental hospital and psychologically assessed prisoners; this interest in psychology persisted in many of his works, most notably in *Madness and Civilisation* (1967). He himself suffered persistently from depression and attempted suicide on several occasions. This may have been partly due to the great difficulty at this time about being openly homosexual, but it does suggest that 'his pronounced interest in psychology stemmed from elements in his own life' (Eribon 1991: 27). These concerns with challenging our conventional views on mental illness and sexuality have led him to emphasise the importance of trying to analyse without employing the notion of the individual subject and to see the subject as an effect of discourses and power relations.

Foucault's work in *Madness and Civilisation* (1967), on the way that madness is constructed by society and its institutions has been profoundly influential, his work appearing at a time when the alternative psychiatric movement in Britain and America, which tried to challenge the medicalisation of mental illness, was beginning to develop. He aimed to try to demonstrate that rather than madness being a stable condition, mental illness should rather be seen as 'the result of social contradictions in which [humans are] historically alienated' (Foucault, cited in Eribon 1991: 70). These social contradictions change from era to era. He saw madness as being constructed at a particular point in history; madness is constituted to ring-fence reason or sanity and to create clear distinctions between madness and sanity. Madness is also constructed as part of a wider process of the development of modernity, and hence as a part of a process whereby the épistémé moves from explanations based on religion, to those based on medical analysis: the feminist geographers, Liz Bondi and Erica Burman, argue, drawing on Foucault's work: 'The move from a moral-religious to a secular and medical approach to the production and evaluation of individual experience is what – according to Foucauldian analyses – makes the shift to modernity, along with all those other practices of production and consumption that mark the birth of the rational bourgeois – and we might add culturally masculine – individual subject' (Bondi and Burman 2001: 7). Donnelly even argues that 'early psychiatry helped to constitute the object "madness" which it then developed to treat' (Donnelly 1986: 18). This seems to be a little too intentionalist an account of the development of psychiatry, but there is a certain truth in the statement. Foucault's method in analysing the history of madness is 'rather than asking *what* in a given period, is regarded as sanity or insanity, as mental illness or normal behaviour, [instead] . . . to ask *how* these divisions are operated' (Foucault 1991b: 74). Thus, just as in the case of his analysis of the constitution of truth and knowledge, (discussed in Chapter 3) he is interested in how madness is kept in place, what tools are used to keep madness in circulation as a category, and what processes are used to distinguish between the mad and the sane.

Rather than reifying madness, Foucault traces the way that madness has been constructed in different forms and judged in different ways throughout history. Thus, rather than seeing madness in the negative way that we do in the West at present, David Cooper suggests that in reading Foucault's *Madness and Civilisation*, 'one is awakened to a tragic sense of the loss involved in the relegation of the wildly charismatic or inspirational area of our experience to the desperate region of pseudo-medical categorisation from which clinical psychiatry has sprung' (Cooper, introduction to Foucault 1999: viii). Behaviour such as hearing imaginary voices, hallucinating, hysteria, speaking in tongues, which would, in other periods of history, have been seen as possessions by spirits or God, or visions inspired by angels, instead of being valued and sanctified by the Church, became something which needed to be treated by confinement and the administering of drugs. Foucault identifies a shift in the way that madness is conceptualised:

> in the Renaissance, madness was present everywhere and mingled with every experience by its images or its dangers. During the classical period, madness was shown, but on the other side of the bars; if present, it was at a distance, under the eyes of a reason that no longer felt any relation to it and would not compromise itself by too close a resemblance.
>
> (Foucault 1999: 70)

Foucault also shows that during the Classical period, rather than madness being considered as an illness as it now is, it was seen as a manifestation of animality; in *Madness and Civilisation*, he comments that: 'the animality that rages in madness dispossesses man of what is specifically human in him; not in order to deliver him over to other powers, but simply to establish him at the zero degree of his own nature' (Foucault 1999: 74). This is important to bear in mind when analysing the way that madness is treated and interpreted in the twenty-first century as the medicalisation and confinement of those considered to be mentally ill, and even the care of those people within the community, presupposes a very different model of madness and cure. If madness is considered to be the epitome of animality then the only cure is discipline and brutality to curb these passions; if madness is considered to be the result of chemical imbalance in the brain, or of repression of trauma during childhood, then the only cure is the use of drugs to restore the chemical balance, and/or therapy. Foucault confronts us with the strange treatments of madness which developed in the eighteenth century, when madness was seen as due to imbalance within the system of humours. Patients were given blood transfusions, were shocked by sudden immersion in cold water, were forced to ingest bitters. This focus on the strangeness of the way that madness was treated in the past forces us to consider the strangeness of the way that we treat mental illness, with madness now functioning as a pathology, treated by confinement, drugs or the use of electric shock therapy.

Rather than assuming that the distinction between madness and sanity self-evidently exists, Foucault examines, in *Madness and Civilisation* (1974), the way that institutional changes, such as the availability of houses of confinement, contributed to the development of such a distinction. Foucault describes the way that the institutionalisation of those considered to be insane developed from the practice in the twelfth century of confining those who were suffering from the highly infectious disease leprosy. Leper houses were built in Europe from the twelfth century onwards to prevent leprosy from spreading to the rest of the population. In England and Scotland alone, 220 leper houses were built during the twelfth century. Because of this segregation and because, with the cessation of the Crusades the contagion from sources in the East was largely eliminated, by the sixteenth century leprosy was less widespread in Europe. In the seventeenth century, hospitals which had been built to house lepers were taken over to be used as asylums for those who were categorised as 'socially useless'; this included the idle, the poor, those who had scandalised their families, together with those whose behaviour was considered to be in any way abnormal. All those who could not, or would not, work, were placed in this category and confined. Foucault sees the confinement of those who did not work as partly determined by economic conditions of the time, but he does not reduce this measure simply to economic forces, since he shows that even when the economy improved, the poor were still confined and forced to labour. What strikes Foucault about this process of confinement, which he terms 'the great confinement', is just how many people were confined: he claims that 'more than one out of every hundred inhabitants of the city of Paris found themselves confined [in one of the houses of confinement]' (Foucault 1999: 38). The Hôpital Général in Paris alone contained 6,000 people. The confinement of this very diverse group of people was not enacted on grounds of medical incapacity or with the aim of curing the confined. This draws attention to the relative recentness of the medicalisation of madness – the categorising of madness as a mental *illness*.

In the nineteenth century, these houses of confinement began to be used solely for the confining of those who were considered insane: in *Madness and Civilisation*, Foucault argues that:

> the asylum was substituted for the [leper] house, in the geography of haunted places as in the landscape of the moral universe. The old rites of excommunication were revived, but in the world of production and commerce. It was in these places of doomed and despised idleness, in this space invented by a society which had derived an ethical transcendence from the law of work, that madness would appear and soon expand until it had annexed them. . . . The nineteenth century would consent, would even insist that to the mad and to them alone be transferred these lands on which a hundred and fifty years before, men had sought to pen the poor, the vagabond, the unemployed.
>
> (Foucault 1999: 57)

While most critics would see the reform of the asylums in the nineteenth century, and the move away from the harsh treatment of patients, where inmates were chained up, to one where patients were treated more compassionately, where their complaints were listened to, and they were no longer viewed as a 'freakshow' for the middle classes, as a period of liberalisation and as a time when those who were judged to be mentally ill were treated with more care, Foucault argues that this should not be seen as a simple improvement of conditions: 'the asylum no longer punished the madman's guilt . . . but it did more, it organised that guilt. It organised it for the madman as a consciousness of himself' (Foucault 1999: 252). Thus, unlike with any other illness, the diagnosis of mental illness seems also to imply a failing on the part of the individual for which they can be blamed: Foucault claims that:

> the asylum . . . is not a free realm of observation, diagnosis and therapeutics; it is a juridical space from where one is accused, judged and condemned, and from which one is never released except by the version of this trial in psychological depth, that is by remorse. Madness will be punished in the asylum, even if it is innocent outside of it. For a long time to come, and until our own day at least, it is imprisoned in a moral world.
>
> (Foucault, cited in Eribon 1991: 97)

This has led to the stigmatisation of mental illness, so that even when it is clear that psychological damage is the result of social conditions, sexual abuse or poverty, the individual is held to be at fault or to blame. As some feminist theorists have argued, the 'mental health services . . . have helped to maintain the social status quo by naming and managing as "madness" the psychological damage and distress caused by social inequalities' (Williams *et al.* 2001: 98). In a similar way, we need to question critically whether the releasing of people into 'care in the community' from the 1980s onwards in Britain is necessarily better for those people. The closing of the asylums seems for many a radical improvement, but the conditions of those in the community, living in hostels or on the street, without sufficient support or funding, with the possibility of enforced medication, means that we cannot necessarily see this supposed liberalisation as making these people more free. Furthermore, while many consider that those people undergoing mental crises are now treated with more respect and dignity than in previous periods, Foucault asks us to question our assumptions yet again. The medicalisation of madness has resulted in the alleviation of suffering for many, but this has also resulted in a greater stigmatisation of mental illness, and has placed the 'cure' of madness in the hands of professional psychiatrists and therapists.

As I have shown above, Foucault charts the way that certain types of behaviour have thus begun to be characterised as aberrant and indicative of mental illness. Feminist theorists such as Dorothy Smith (1990), in her article on mental illness entitled 'K is mentally ill', have drawn on Foucault's work to describe the complex process of distinguishing what behaviour we are prepared to tolerate and what behaviour we feel needs to be categorised as indicative of mental illness. She analyses the way that a group of friends gradually begin to notice certain forms of withdrawn behaviour on the part of an individual she calls K. Through discussion with one another, they come to the decision that she is suffering from a mental illness and must therefore be referred to a doctor, and in the end confined to an asylum. Smith should not be seen as suggesting that K is not suffering distress, but what she is focusing on is the process whereby it is decided that she is mentally ill. This process is a discursive one where reference is made to the norms of society, and how we expect people to behave. This change in the view of aberrant behaviour has consequences as Foucault has shown; in previous periods, if people displayed aberrant behaviour, they were largely left alone or stigmatised as being non-productive, but the medicalisation of mental illness results in sometimes enforced confinement and treatment and what, in the special issue of *Feminist Review* on mental illness, was termed 'an individualising, apolitical, biologistic understanding of [distress]' (Alldred *et al.* 2000: 1). Thus, what may in fact be seen to be primarily emotional problems are now categorised as problems of mental illness requiring medical intervention. Many feminists, such as Elaine Showalter, have analysed the way that those women who have rebelled against the social conventions and restrictions on women's behaviour have sometimes been labelled as mentally ill (Showalter 1987). Thus, the fact that the distinction between madness and sanity has been confused with the socially constructed distinction between the normal and the abnormal means that any instances of seemingly aberrant behaviour can be labelled as an instance of mental illness.

Feminist theorists drawing on Foucault's work have challenged the way that drugs are administered to those suffering from mental distress to 'cure' them, and indeed some feminists have tried to celebrate, or at least view in different ways, the behaviours which have been considered by others to be aberrant. In a clear case of counter-identification which I discussed in the previous chapter, feminist theorist and activist Sasha Claire McInnes states:

> Today, as I recover my Self, I am elated (Manic), shy introverted and reflective (Social Phobia) irritable and frustrated (PMS) whelmed and stressed (Post Traumatic Stress Disorder) sad and melancholic (depression) passionate, joyful, extroverted in utter abandon (Mania) wanting and expecting respect (Borderline Personality Disorder) and fearful (anxiety disorder). All of these feelings and others are now precious to me. I want these feelings. I want them all. It's the 'messiness' of my humanity and of being alive that I choose and cherish over the half-life offered by brain, mind and heart-numbing legal drugs.

> (McInnes 2001: 164)

In this quotation from McInnes we can see someone who is keenly aware of the way that their behaviour has been described by those within the medical establishment and by psychiatrists, who would see these 'symptoms' as in need of treatment and cure. McInnes' alternative vision of these behaviours, classified as physical and social disorders by others, stresses the positive elements, even when they seem to bring her some distress.

Foucault's work on the distinction between madness and sanity and the constructed nature of mental illness has been enormously influential for both those such as feminist theorists who are concerned to analyse the way that women are judged to be mentally ill, as well as those people who have suffered mental distress and have found themselves treated in particular ways by the medical establishment. This challenging work by Foucault is in essence, a fundamental analysis of the nature of the human individual and a call to destabilise the subject.

THEORISING WITHOUT THE SUBJECT

Thus, as both of these discussions of Foucault's work on sexuality and on madness have shown, Foucault is concerned with the radical questioning of the stability of the individual subject or self in *The Archaeology of Knowledge* (1972) and *The Order of Things* (1973). This move away from the analysis of the individual subject to an analysis of the constitution of the subject, led him also to be interested in what led academics to turn to the analysis of 'Man' when the human sciences developed in the nineteenth century and, indeed, he suggests that this focus was not coincidental but that it was a necessary relation. He states, in an interview entitled 'Critical theory/intellectual theory', 'while historians of science in France were interested essentially in the problem of how a scientific object is constituted, the question I asked myself was this: how is it that the human subject took itself as the object of possible knowledge? Through what forms of rationality and historical conditions? And finally at what price?' (Foucault 1988c: 29/30). Rather than the focus on the self appearing to be a natural progress in the development of knowledge, he suggests that the analysis of the self needs to be scrutinised, and perhaps that this analysis of the subject need not necessarily be seen in positive terms.

Foucault sees the emergence of 'Man' as an object of knowledge as an epistemic shift, a dramatic change in the way that societies conceptualise. This emergence of 'Man' has profound consequences for representation, as the critics Hubert Dreyfus and Paul Rabinow put it:

Representation suddenly became opaque. As long as discourse provided a transparent medium of representation whose linguistic elements corresponded to primitive elements in the world, representation was not problematic. God had arranged a chain of being and arranged language in pre-established correspondence with it. Human beings happened to have a capacity to use linguistic signs, but human beings as rational speaking animals were simply one more kind of creature whose nature could be read off from its proper definition so that it could be arranged in its proper place on the table of beings. There is no need for any finite being to make representation possible: no place in the picture for a being who posits it.

(Dreyfus and Rabinow 1986: 27)

Foucault argues, in *The Order of Things*, that from this Classical épistèmé where 'Man' is not represented, there is a shift to a focus on representing and analysing 'Man': 'In the general arrangement of the Classical épistèmé, nature, human nature and their relations are definite and predictable functional moments. And man as a primary reality with his own density, as the difficult object and sovereign subject of all possible knowledge, has no place in it' (Foucault, cited in Dreyfus and Rabinow 1986: 27).

For me, the most forceful element of his thinking about the focus on 'Man' in the analysis of the development of medical science is one of his more successful reversals of conventional wisdom: he shows the way in which the dissection and examination of the corpse led to the beginning of medical knowledge about the processes within the living body. To be able to decipher symptoms which were only displayed on the outside of the living body, the doctor had to examine the inside of the dead body. Once the discovery of the use of dissection is made, he comments in *The Birth of the Clinic* (1973), 'life, disease and death now form a technical and conceptual trinity'. And he goes on to say:

it will no doubt remain a decisive fact about our culture that its first scientific discourse concerning the individual had to pass through this stage of death. Western man could constitute himself in his own eyes as an object of science, he grasped himself within his language and gave himself in himself and by himself, a discursive existence only in the opening created by his own elimination: from the experience of Unreason was born psychology, the very possibility of psychology; from the integration of death into medical thought is born a medicine that is given as a science of the individual.

(Foucault, cited in Eribon 1991: 154)

In an extension of his analysis of the emergence of 'Man' as the object of the human sciences, he also argues that 'one has to dispense with the constituent subject . . . to attain an analysis which can account for the constitution of the subject within the historical texture' (Foucault 1978: 35). Thus, in examining the development of the human sciences, his aim is to develop a form of analysis which does not focus on the subject at all, but which focuses on the discursive processes which brought it into being. In *The Birth of the Clinic* (1975), Foucault begins the process of tracking down the concern with the analysis of human nature; he argues that 'it is within medical discourse that the individual first became an object of positive knowledge'(Foucault 1975: 27). In one of Foucault's challenging aphorisms, he then goes on to propose the death of Man, by analogy with Nietzsche's death of God:

> one thing in any case is certain; man is neither the oldest nor the most constant problem that has been posed for human knowledge. Taking a relatively short chronological sample within a restricted geographical area – European culture since the sixteenth century – one can be certain that man is a recent invention within it. It is not around him and his secrets that knowledge prowled for so long in the darkness . . . As the archaeology of our thought easily shows, man is an invention of recent date. And one perhaps nearing its end.
>
> (Foucault, cited in Eribon 1991: 159)

Thus, not content with theorising without the subject, he suggests that our current obsession with analysing human nature in human sciences such as sociology and psychology will soon end. In an interview in 1966, when asked what or who he considered to be behind the system which structuralists describe, he replied:

> What is this anonymous system without a subject, what thinks? The 'I' has exploded . . . this is the discovery of the 'there is'. There is a *one*. In some ways one comes back to the seventeenth century point of view, with this difference: not setting man but anonymous thought, knowledge without a subject, theory with no identity, in God's place.
>
> (Foucault, cited in Eribon 1991: 161)

Thus, Foucault is concerned with what enables certain things to be thought and said rather than the individuals who articulate those thoughts. He is concerned more with analysing the impersonal discursive processes at work rather than the way that individuals carve out for themselves a place within these abstract discourses.

This intriguing analysis which aims to dispense with the subject is at odds with much critical thinking and, indeed, with much common-sense thinking, which seems 'naturally' to be focused on the individual and identity. However, Foucault forces us to consider the specificity of this focus on the individual within the West, determined as it is by the particular set of discursive structures which make the individual seem self-evident.

CONCLUSIONS

Foucault's focus on the changing way in which the distinction between madness and sanity is made, and the invention of mental illness, rather than on the individual subject makes us analyse the process of subjection and resistance at work in the relation between institutions, the government, the family and individual subjects. His anti-psychoanalytic stance is productive at a theoretical level, making us see the subject as an effect of power relations rather than as something which precedes those relations and which is constrained by them. Foucault is the only theorist who analyses mental illness without being concerned with the development of an alternative system for analysing the psyche and emotional distress; in some senses, for him, the self and the individual are not of interest and, in fact, constrain our thinking on the subject.

AFTER FOUCAULT

Is much better than his grades – will have to free himself of a tendency to be obscure.

(Foucault's secondary school report, 1945, cited in Eribon 1991: 22)

In any book of this type which aims to introduce readers to the work of a particular theorist, it is only possible to give a general overview of Foucault's work and suggest ways in which Foucault might be approached and put to use. The aim of this chapter is to try to bring together the suggestions which have been made over the course of the various chapters on Foucault's work, to suggest ways in which his theoretical positions might be brought to bear in the analysis of texts and more general analysis. However, it should be borne in mind that Foucault does not have one theoretical position. Indeed, Foucault suggests that the reason that he irritates a wide group of people is precisely because he does not have a unitary position (Foucault 1991b). Others may argue that that is, in fact, the basis of his appeal.

READING FOUCAULT

Foucault, like many other French theorists of this era, has been found by many to be quite difficult to read for a variety of reasons, some of them stylistic and some of them to do with content. In terms of content, he assumes a familiarity on the part of the reader, in much of his work, with a very wide range of philosophical ideas and theorists, such as Nietzsche, Heidegger, Hegel and Marx, which for many readers within the English speaking world, is not always shared. He also assumes an ability on the part of his readers to engage in interdisciplinary thinking (that is, for example thinking about issues pertaining to psychology from a historical and philosophical perspective) which for many people, accustomed to disciplinary-bound work, may prove difficult. Furthermore, he approaches subjects which are not theoretically 'mapped out' in the way that other theoretical work is, and as such he may be seen as establishing ways of approaching a subject which are radically new.

In terms of stylistic difficulties, the very complex grammatical structures of his sentences can be off-putting, but are characteristic of a certain French discursive tradition in philosophical work and particularly in French post-structuralist theory. He himself remarks in response to criticism of one of his books on the grounds of the opacity of his argument and style that 'I willingly concede that the style is unbearable; one of my flaws is not being naturally clear' (Foucault, cited in Eribon 1991: 84). For these and many other reasons, Foucault's writing style and the form of his argumentation sometimes does deter all but the most intrepid reader.

USING FOUCAULT'S METHODS

Some theoretical work is not easy to 'apply'. Indeed, there are problems in thinking that theory should always, and only, be applied. Foucault himself tried to question the distinction between theory and analysis when he said 'theory does not express, translate or serve to apply practice: it is practice' (Foucault, cited in Kritzman 1988: xix). However, generally when we read theoretical work in an academic context, there is sometimes a disjunction between the theory that we are reading and the uses which we are able to make of it. Foucault's work is often insightful, but it is sometimes difficult to know how best to use it. Sometimes, the reader is led to use certain decontextualised elements from Foucault's work: this is the 'application' of Foucault at its worst, where the Panopticon is examined as a structuring principle in the layout of libraries, railway stations, supermarkets and so on, and the distinction between madness and sanity is investigated in a particular genre of books (women's writing, post-colonial writing and so on) as if Foucault's work were simply descriptive. For example, some critics have described Foucault's analysis of the constructed nature of mental illness and the way the parameters and constituents of insanity vary over time and then have traced in an analogical way the literary texts of writers such as Charlotte Perkins Gilman (1973/1899) in *The Yellow Wallpaper*, or Ken Kesey's (1973) *One Flew Over the Cuckoo's Nest*. In this type of analysis, Foucault's work is used at a thematic level, where his findings are seen to be analogous to the sort of explorations which literary writers have been engaged in. Foucault's work here is used as a sort of catalyst for literary exploration. This thematic approach to Foucault simply repeats Foucault's ideas rather than making use of him. Since Foucault was very concerned to question ways of thinking rather than simply locating themes to apply, it seems best to concentrate on the critique of thinking and concepts.

There are certain elements of Foucault's thought which are particularly productive to draw on when analysing texts or events. There are also particular methodological stances which Foucault takes which it is worth focusing on, although it is important to bear in mind that Foucault did not develop a fully worked out methodological position, and criticised the very notion of formulating one type of position. These stances and approaches include the following elements:

1 DRAW ON ARCHIVES

In all of Foucault's theoretical work, use of an archive figures very large. He worked in a wide range of libraries, for example the Bibliothèque Nationale in Paris but also more obscure university libraries in Uppsala, Sweden and Hamburg, Germany, drawing on their archives and finding most insight in the most obscure texts. In his work on the confession of the murderer Pierre Rivière, he commented that he had used such an obscure text for the following reasons:

> documents like those in the Rivière case should provide material for a thorough examination of the way in which a particular kind of knowledge (e.g. medicine, psychiatry, psychology) is formed and acts in relation to institutions and the roles prescribed for them (e.g. the law with respect to the expert, the accused, the criminally insane and so on). They give us a key to the relations of power, domination and conflict, within which discourses emerge

and function, and hence provide material for a potential analysis of discourse (even of scientific discourses) which may be both tactical and political, and therefore, strategic. Lastly, they furnish a means for grasping the power of derangement peculiar to a discourse such as Rivière's and the whole range of tactics by which we can try to reconstitute it, situate it and give it its status as the discourse of either a madman or a criminal.

(Foucault, cited in Eribon 1991: 235)

Throughout his career, Foucault chooses to work on non-canonical, obscure texts precisely because they offer such rich possibilities for analysis.

Foucault tends to examine those subject areas which others did not consider worthy of attention, for example, the confessions of murderers, the case notes on child molesters, the documentation around children's masturbation, and so on. In current theoretical work in a wide range of subject areas this sense of examining the more banal, mundane and perhaps more ephemeral texts has become a major shift in attention, undoubtedly partly due to Foucault's work. Foucault does not analyse these diverse resources in order to be able to capture trends or themes in a particular period, but rather to examine the possible forms of expression which circulate within a given period.

2   BE SCEPTICAL

Foucault advocates a profound and radical scepticism; he describes his project as aiming:

to give some assistance in wearing away certain self-evidences and common-places about madness, normality, illness, crime and punishment; to bring it about, together with many others, that certain phrases can no longer be spoken so lightly, certain acts no longer, or at least no longer so unhesitat-ingly performed; to contribute to changing certain things in people's ways of perceiving and doing things; to participate in this difficult displacement of forms of sensibility and thresholds of tolerance.

(Foucault 1991b: 83)

This radical scepticism towards one's material has always caused the most difficulties for theorists drawing on Foucault's work, since it can be confused with cynicism. However, what Foucault's work does is to suspend judgement; rather than assuming that a particular analysis of events is 'true' and therefore marshalling a series of 'facts' to back up an argument, Foucault suggests that we should be critical of our own position.

Judgement is one of the hidden elements which are present in a great number of critical positions within the humanities and social sciences, even those which pride themselves on their supposed objectivity. Foucault argues that:

> it's amazing how people like judging. Judgement is being passed everywhere all the time. Perhaps it is one of the simplest things mankind has ever been given to do. And you know very well that the last [person], when radiation has finally reduced [their] last enemy to ashes, will sit down behind some rickety table and begin the trial of the individual responsible . . . I can't help but dream, about a kind of criticism that would try not to judge.

> (Foucault 1988: 326)

Thus, assuming that the past is inferior to the present and that we have made great progress is a value judgement, and within a Foucauldian framework needs to be avoided. This assumption may be made explicitly or it may be located at the level of presupposition, for example, in assertions about the 'primitive' or 'simple' nature of life in countries outside Europe which are described as 'developing countries' or 'pre-industrialised'; here we are implicitly assuming a linear trajectory for the development of all countries' economies along the lines of Western capitalist countries; implicit in this assessment of 'developing' countries is an assertion that being 'developed' and 'industrialised' is necessarily better than other forms of economic development. Thus, Foucault calls on us to suspend our judgement when we analyse.

3 DON'T MAKE SECOND ORDER JUDGEMENTS

Gavin Kendall and Gary Wickham argue that 'the suspension of judgement involved in good Foucaultian use of history is largely about suspending judgements other than those you happen to recognise as your own': these judgements which you have not made yourself are what are termed second order judgements (Kendall and Wickham 1999: 13). They argue that this type of judgement may creep into our analysis 'when any aspect of any object being investigated is granted a status (perhaps this status is labelled a "cause", perhaps something else, which draws its authority from another investigation'(Kendall and Wickham 1999: 13). This form of analysis is at the meta-theoretical level, one which analyses the value judgements which have infiltrated our arguments because we have unwittingly adopted someone else's theoretical perspective. This rejection of second order judgements can lead to a type of analysis which does not make political claims. However, while this is a Foucauldian strategy par excellence, you might ask in your own analysis whether this is adequate as a form of analysis – simply to provide a description of techniques without interpretation or claiming some status for the material that you have amassed.

4   LOOK FOR CONTINGENCIES RATHER THAN CAUSES

One of the most significant elements of Foucault's thought is that he did not seek to explain why something happened in any simple way, but rather saw that events were overdetermined, that is, that they had a multiplicity of possible causes, the conjunction of which brought the event to occur. What Foucault's thought makes us realise is that the event that we are analysing need not necessarily have happened, or may have happened in a different way, if conditions had been slightly different. Major political changes have been triggered by the conjuncture of a range of different political and non-political events. For example, when Neil Kinnock was leader of the Labour Party in the 1980s, various explanations were given for the fact that the party was not elected. Journalists and political analysts tend to focus on one of these as the main factor, for example, that his rhetorical style seemed anachronistic; that his economic policies were not in tune with the needs of the middle classes; that the trade unions seemed to form too close an alliance with the Labour party; and so on. None of these causes can be seen within a Foucauldian analysis as the sole cause of electoral defeat. All of these elements played a role in the defeat and, thus, it only takes one insignificant non-political element, for example, the style of Kinnock's rabble-rousing speech to the Labour Party rally in Sheffield before the election, which for some inexplicable reason is always given as the reason why the Labour Party did not win, to mobilise those other elements into a particular type of result. What Foucault is interested in is what he calls 'eventalisation', that is:

> making visible a *singularity* at places where there is a temptation to invoke a
> historical constant ... to show that 'things weren't as necessary as all that'
> ... eventalisation means discovering the connections, encounters, supports,
> blockages, plays of forces, strategies and so on which at a given moment estab-
> lish what counts as being self-evident, universal and necessary. In this sense,
> one is indeed effecting a sort of multiplication or pluralisation of causes.
>
> (Foucault 1991b: 76)

We are accustomed in our research to look for clear causes and effects, but Foucault argues that we should simply trace the way that certain events happened and examine the contingent events which may, or may not, have played a role in their development. Thus, rather than seeing capitalism as a determining force in the way that events take place, we should see capitalism as one force among many others which lead to certain types of event occurring. Similarly in some research into gender, there is an assumption that gender causes difference in behaviour – the fact that certain people are male causes them to behave in certain ways. A Foucauldian analysis of gender would see sexual identity as being only one of the many factors which plays a role in particular types of behaviour and, indeed, would see that gendering process as shaped by the activity itself (Mills, forthcoming). In his genealogical analyses, Foucault suggests that we need to analyse contin- gencies so that we may move beyond the ways in which we currently limit ourselves.

5 INVESTIGATE PROBLEMS RATHER THAN A SUBJECT

When trying to use Foucault's work, if we begin with the notion of investigating a historical period or a subject, we may discover that we do not find Foucault of much use. If however, we focus on problems, such as the relation between ethnic minorities and institutions, or the social stigmatisation of those with disabilities, Foucault's way of thinking is more likely to be of use. That is not to suggest that Foucault necessarily offers solutions to the problems that he focuses on, since his method is non-interpretive. Nevertheless, while Foucault aims not to produce general solutions to the problems he isolates, we may still find that the choice of examples that he makes does have implicitly within it an argument and an interpretation. His choice of the study of the way the sexuality of women, homosexuals and children is discussed is not unmotivated, and may be considered to have already built into it a judgement or political position.

6   DON'T OVERGENERALISE FROM YOUR FINDINGS

Foucault is very aware of the problem of generalising from analysis of specific texts, and he says: 'I don't try to universalise what I say: conversely, what I don't say isn't meant to be thereby disqualified as being of no importance' (Foucault 1991b: 73). Despite the difficulty of the multiple negatives in this statement, what Foucault is arguing here is that although generalisations are difficult to make, given the complexity and overdetermined nature of events, that does not mean that it is impossible to say anything at all, except the most specific statement about the particularities of one event. Yet, although generalisations are possible, great care must be taken in making grand statements about culture at a particular time. Nevertheless, Foucault himself is prone to generalise about the status quo at particular times, but perhaps his analyses are supposed to be taken as indicative of certain trends rather than as truly representative of a whole culture.

These six pointers should not be taken to be a definitive guide to Foucault's methods, but should help you to work out a form of Foucauldian analysis which is not simply a repetition of Foucault's themes but rather a way of working with his ideas and modifying them in line with your own concerns.

IMPLICATIONS OF FOUCAULT'S WORK FOR LITERARY ANALYSIS

Many students of literature, having read this book, will be left thinking 'What has all this to do with the analysis of literature?' for in no sense could Foucault be considered a *literary* theorist. Indeed, many students of a Critical Theory course which I lecture on have stated – 'Foucault is fascinating at a philosophical and abstract level, but how can I make this work for the analysis of literature, and how can I integrate this sort of theoretical work into an essay?' As I have stressed throughout this book, the answer comes through the use of a form of lateral thinking. Rather than trying to shoehorn Foucault's work into an analysis of literary texts, we should rather turn our attention to the way that Foucault makes possible an analysis of the grounds on which we analyse literature. Foucault's work is useful in analysing literature at a meta-theoretical level (that is, enabling us to describe how it comes about that literature is produced in the way that it is – taught in universities, written about by critics, discussed reverentially by the middle classes, made to appear to be distinct from popular culture and so on) rather than at an analytical level (that is, enabling us to comment or explain what is going on in literary texts). There are those who consider that it is possible to use Foucault in literary textual analysis but I hope that in this section I will be able to demonstrate that this type of analysis generally uses Foucault's theoretical work in an analogical way, rather than an analytical way; that is, their aim seems to be to show that these ideas are played out in literature at a thematic level, in ways which show similarities to Foucault's ideas.

1   LITERATURE AS DISCOURSE

Foucault's tastes in literature tended, like his tastes in music, to be rather towards the avant-garde end of the spectrum, and his commentaries on this type of literature tend to be rather surprisingly descriptive. His theories have been used by critics such as the post-colonial critic, Edward Said, to argue that we should analyse literary texts as part of a larger discursive formation rather than assuming that literature has a separate and privileged status in relation to other texts (Said 1978; 1993). Said, in particular was instrumental, along with New Historicist critics such as Stephen Greenblatt (see below) in suggesting that literature was best studied alongside other texts, such as travel writing, scientific writing, essays, in order to relate the literary text to its discursive context. Historians, such as Hayden White, have argued that historical texts have to be seen to share linguistic codes with literary texts; thus, both make use of narrative, focalisation and point of view and both literary and historical texts draw on similar discursive resources within a particular context (White 1987).

Critics drawing on Foucault's work have tried to map out the way that literature was constituted as a subject worthy of study in the nineteenth century (Eagleton 1983). When literature was first introduced for study at university level, it was necessary to authorise it by aligning it with religious study (making parallels between biblical criticism and literary criticism) and trying to make the study of literature appear more scientific. In this way, literature could be seen to be a serious subject of study. This analysis of the constitution of literature as a proper university subject forces us to analyse particularly carefully the efflorescence of 'scientific' trends in literary theory, from New Criticism through structuralism and post-structuralism. A Foucauldian analysis of literary criticism would analyse the authorising moves which are made by literary critics and theorists to carve out powerful positions for themselves.

A Foucauldian analysis might question the stability and inevitability of the literary text. For example, McGann analyses the complex publishing history of Byron's *Don Juan* in 1818, where because of the fear of accusation of libel and blasphemy the text was published first in a very expensive edition without the author's name, only then to be published in pirated cheap versions by the radical press, which had very different impacts on their different audiences. For McGann, this example of publishing history:

> illustrates how different texts, in the bibliographical sense, embody different poems (in the aesthetic sense) despite the fact that both are linguistically identical. In the second place, the example also suggests that the method of printing or publishing a literary work carries with it enormous cultural and aesthetic significance for the work itself. Finally, we can begin to see, through this example, that the essential character of a work of art is not determined *sui generis* but is, rather, the result of a process involving the actions of a specific and socially integrated group of people.
>
> (McGann 2001: 293)

Thus, a Foucauldian analysis might focus on the way that the interpretation of a text depends in part upon the form in which it is published.

2   THE AUTHOR

As I have mentioned several times during this book, Foucault questioned the status of the author, particularly when the figure of the author is drawn upon to make coherent a body of diverse work, and to impose simplistic ideas of progression on them. Conventional literary analysis often tries to find out about the author and their concerns in order to enrich our understanding of the texts. But for Foucault, this information is, in essence, irrelevant. He would argue that biographies of authors are constructed very selectively; biographers impose a narrative cohesiveness on events and describe only those events which are of interest to their particular perspective on the person's life. Particularly in the case of literary biographies, the information we know about an author may, in fact, be selected by biographers very much with the explication of literary texts in mind, and may draw on the literary texts themselves. A Foucauldian analysis would focus on the way in which we put that biographical and contextual information to work in interpretation. Foucault would suggest that the study of literature be undertaken without reference to the text of the author's life, but that what might be of interest is the author-function, that is the role the figure of the author is made to play in the analysis of literary texts.

3 CREATIVITY AND ORIGINALITY

Within traditional literary criticism, it is assumed that literature is a supremely creative sphere of writing. Post-structuralist theorists, and particularly Foucault, have forced us to see that literature, like any other discourse, has regularities of expression, genre and form at any particular moment. For him, it is not the notion of creativity which is of interest but those elements of a literary text which are repetitive, those which seem to be produced in relation to other texts, which seem to appear in many other texts. He is not arguing that it is not possible to be creative, but that given the creative possibilities – the fact that writers could say *anything* they liked – they, in fact, tend to say so little, and within such constricted limits. A Foucauldian analysis would be interested in the structural features of the discourses of literature which tend to produce similar features in texts at the level of narrative voice, style, genre and so on.

4 INTERPRETATION AND COMMENTARY

In a preface to a revised edition of *Madness and Civilisation*, Foucault stated that when a book is published:

from that moment on it is caught up in an endless play of repetitions; its doubles begin to swarm. Around it and far from it; each reading gives it an impalpable and unique body for an instant; fragments of itself are circulating

> and are made to stand in for it, are taken to almost entirely contain it, and
> sometimes serve as a refuge for it; it is doubled with commentaries, those
> other discourses in which it should finally appear as it is, confessing what it
> had refused to say, freeing itself from what it had so loudly pretended to be.
>
> (Foucault, cited in Eribon 1991: 124)

He included this preface, because his work on madness had had such a surprising response from the reading public; he had not intended the book to be adopted as a rallying call to the anti-psychiatry movement, nor to be read widely outside academic circles, but this statement seems to sum up the notion that interpretations of texts cannot be constrained by the intentions of the author. Once completed, the book is no longer within the author's control and the reader can make of it what they will. Thus, Foucault's work can be seen as a critique of those types of analysis which are concerned with reconstructing the author's intentions from the text itself.

Another Foucauldian concern, which I discussed in Chapter 2, which can be brought to bear on literary texts, is his concern with the role of commentary, that is critical evaluations or explications of texts. Foucault shows that there are certain texts, such as Shakespeare's, which are persistently commented on by critics, and these commentaries ensure that Shakespeare is kept in circulation and, in the process, give status to the commentary itself. Such texts are kept in print by publishing houses and therefore are readily available for further commentary. In recent years, publishers have made available texts by Black British authors and women writers because of the wealth of critical writing that there now is on these writers. Canonical literature is that which has the greatest number of commentaries and, as a literary scholar, one is always encouraged to research those texts which are canonical as one gains prestige for oneself in the process of analysing them. Thus, a Foucauldian analysis of literature might well focus on the role that literary criticism plays in the process of publishers maintaining books in print and in the process of canon-formation, rather than analysing literary texts themselves.

5 HISTORICAL ANALYSIS

New Historicism, which developed in the 1980s, was influenced directly by, among others, Foucault's thought and can be seen as an attempt to put Foucault's ideas to work on literature. His integration of historical method and analysis into philosophical work was important in enabling literary scholars to attempt such historical work in their own field. Literary work has traditionally always included a great deal of straightforwardly historical information – setting a text in its historical context – but this work has generally been rather descriptive and historical information has been used only to provide explanations for certain thematic concerns in literary texts. Foucault's work showed the way that historical analysis could be exciting and focus on thematic concerns such as power relations and sexuality rather than simply contextual information for the understanding of the literary work. It is Foucault's work on power, in particular, which has played a major role in New Historicist accounts, as critics Philip Rice and Patricia Waugh comment:

> his writings have consistently shown how so-called objective historical accounts are always products of a will to power enacted through formations of knowledge within specific institutions. His 'histories' resist the allure of 'total theories' which offer overarching narratives and instead focus attention on the 'other' excluded by and constructed by such accounts.
>
> (Rice and Waugh 2001: 253–254)

New Historicists, such as Stephen Greenblatt, felt that it was possible for them in their historical work to do as Foucault had done in his philosophical analyses – to juxtapose texts from different genres and provenances and make them illuminate literary texts and to examine 'the embeddedness of cultural objects in the contingencies of history' (Greenblatt 2001: 308). The collection of essays edited by Nancy Armstrong and Lawrence Tennenhouse (1987) on conduct literature was motivated by the realisation that 'the literature of conduct and the conduct of writing known as literature share the same history. Both literature and conduct books, especially those written for women, are integral and instrumental to the history of desire' (Armstrong and Tennenhouse 1987: 1). For them, analysing texts in their discursive context, relating them to other texts, provides a more fully historicised account. Where their work differs from Foucault's is perhaps in their stress on agency and the self, for example Greenblatt argues that New Historicism is interested not in abstract universals but 'in particular contingent cases, the selves fashioned and acting according to the generative rules and conflicts of a given culture' (Greenblatt 2001: 308). Nevertheless, this focus on agency is tempered by a very Foucauldian concern with the limits on agency: Greenblatt states that: 'actions that appear to be single are disclosed as multiple; the apparently isolated power of the individual genius turns out to be bound up with the collective, social energy; a feature of dissent may be bound up in a larger legitimation process, while an attempt to stabilise order on things may turn out to subvert it' (Greenblatt 2001: 308). New Historicist critics, thus, analyse the literary texts as the manifestation of certain discursive processes at work within the cultural context as a whole.

PROBLEMS WITH FOUCAULT'S WORK

Throughout this book, rather than assuming that Foucault has the status of a guru whose teachings need to be followed unthinkingly, I have tried to draw attention to the problems which many theorists have found with Foucault's work. In some ways, Foucault is very seductive as a theorist because he seems to ambush and forestall every problem that you pose for him. However, I have already drawn attention in earlier chapters to the problems which are inherent in the notion of not developing a fully worked out methodology. If Foucault's theories are simply sets of ideas which can be drawn on if they prove to be useful, rather than fully cohesive analytical frameworks, how are they to be preferred to any set of uninformed, bigoted ideas which might prove useful? The fashionable nature of his work has meant that some people have used Foucault's work in a rather uncritical way, and the style of sweeping generalisation that Foucault often makes and which his followers have copied has irritated many people. Jean-Luc Godard, the French film director, said that he wanted to make films to contest the views of people like 'the Reverend Father Foucault' who asserts that ' "At such and such a period, they thought . . ." That's fine with me, but how can we be so sure? That is exactly why we try to make films; to prevent future Foucaults presumptuously saying things like that' (Godard, cited in Eribon 1991: 156).

I have also drawn attention to the problems which historians have found in Foucault's work because of his rather unscholarly use of historical material. Many historians find it difficult to accept the disinterested stance that Foucault takes towards his material. Those who are politically committed find his work deeply flawed. For example, Jean-Paul Sartre, the French philosopher with whom Foucault clashed on several occasions, commented on his archaeological analysis:

> An archaeologist is someone who studies the traces of a vanished civilisation ... What Foucault presents us with is ... a geology, the series of successive layers that make up our 'ground'. Each of these layers defines the conditions of possibility of a certain type of thought prevailing throughout a certain period. But Foucault does not tell us the thing that would be most interesting, that is, how each thought is constructed on the basis of these conditions, or how mankind passes from one thought to another. To do so he would have to bring in praxes, and therefore history, which is precisely what he refuses to do.
>
> (Sartre, cited in Eribon 1991: 163)

This criticism of Foucault's seeming ahistoricism and lack of political analysis is typical of many on the Left.

His androcentrism, that is the centring of his analysis on male experience alone, has posed problems for feminist theorists, yet many of them have tried to modify his work to make it work for them, since many feminists have found his analysis of power relations productive. As I mentioned earlier in this book, it is not sufficient simply to add women in to a Foucauldian analysis; in some sense this androcentrism needs to be analysed and a modified framework needs to be developed which does not focus on the analysis of men or Man in isolation from the analysis of women, and which does not assume that by analysing the behaviour and concerns of men one is analysing human culture as a whole. It may be possible to see Foucault's sexism as determined by the cultural milieu in which he worked, but using Foucault's work in the twenty-first century means that we must address the gender-specific nature of his work.

Foucault's conception of power also poses difficulties for some critics. While it is important that he has focused on the possibility of resistance rather than only describing oppression, he has located resistance within power itself, thus denying the agency of those who oppose oppressive regimes. For some, the focus on power leads to repetition as if all cultural phenomena are reduced to power relations. One such critic, Robert Castel, criticised *Madness and Civilisation*, because he argued: 'the breadth of theoretical detours and the subtlety of analyses of situations close up around several simplified formulas, and the argument in the hands of epigones becomes repetitive: every-where and always there is nothing but repression, violence, the arbi-trary, confinement, police control, segregation and exclusion' (Castel, cited in Eribon 1991: 126). Thus, for some critics, despite Foucault's stated aim to move away from the repressive hypothesis, in fact his work seems to chart only repression and does not focus very much on the productive mechanisms of power.

He has also been criticised by those working within the psychiatric profession for his work deconstructing the notion of madness. His work has proved immensely useful to the anti-psychiatry movement, since it has had the effect of suggesting that madness is constructed by society. However, for those suffering from mental illness, while it may be useful to know that the medicalisation of madness has a history, this knowledge does not offer them alternative remedies, since Foucault was equally sceptical of psychotherapy, seeing it as simply another form of confessional. Thus, his critique of madness has been productive, but erasing the materiality of mental illness may pose significant problems.

A further problem with Foucault's work can be seen in his analysis of discourse, for he seems to be ambivalent in his discussion of the non-discursive, at one and the same time asserting that everything is discursively constructed and yet also wanting to maintain that there are certain elements which are non-discursive. There are other funda-mental problems which someone using Foucault's thought must address, for example as Barry Smart asks: 'Can the archaeologist in practice avoid questions of truth and meaning? Is it not necessary to differentiate between accurate (i.e. "true") and distorted descrip-tions or interpretations?' (Smart 1985: 54). Furthermore, Foucault's supposed disinterested stance belies the fact that, while he argues against relying on cause and effect to describe events, he somehow manages to smuggle these notions into his argument implicitly. This notion of simply describing is difficult to accept; the very fact that elements from the past have been assembled together implicitly consti-tutes an argument or narrative which stands as an explanation, however provisional, for some phenomenon in the present. For example, in *Madness and Civilisation*, Foucault seems to suggest that economic condi-tions were the driving force behind the confinement of the poor and the insane in the eighteenth century (Foucault 1991a). At other points in his analyses the reader is left at a loss as to how to explain the phenomena described without resorting to notions of causality. Donnelly suggests that 'he comes ironically close to the perils of arguing from origins – as if to understand an object one need discover its pristine origins and hence the key to or germ of its subsequent development – which is precisely the fallacy genealogy is contrived to correct' (Donnelly 1986: 25).

However, rather than seeing these problems as flaws in Foucault's argument, many theorists see contradictions as theoretical stepping stones, ways of moving Foucault's work onwards, so that it may more adequately describe a world which has changed since Foucault wrote. We should not imagine that Foucault can offer us simple solutions to the problems which face us now, but we may be able to draw on his approach and methods in order to construct our own solutions.

In summary, then, there are a number of theoretical stances which can be taken when using a Foucauldian analysis of an event or a text. Not all of these particular positions will prove useful, but it is hoped that by isolating them in this way it will be possible to make Foucault's ideas work on the analysis of events and texts. One problem which is often faced in using Foucault's work is that one is led to draw on the images, themes or symbolisations that he uses, or quote from him at length only to be faced with the impossibility of saying anything further. What is essential is to use Foucault's methods in your reading of Foucault: be sceptical about the value of Foucault; do not accept any of his sometimes bold but often unjustified generalisations, and do not assume that he is telling you the 'truth' of the situation.

FURTHER READING

WORKS BY MICHEL FOUCAULT

In this section, Foucault's works are ordered by their original publication date, to give an idea of his publishing history. All of Foucault's works first appeared in French, but the publication details here indicate the English-language translations you are more likely to consult. For this reason, two dates will appear: the first, in square brackets, is the original publication date, while the second date and all other details refer to the translation. (Where translations are not available, only a date in square brackets will appear, and all details refer to the French text.)

It is advisable to read one or two short commentaries on a theorist's work before reading their work: Dreyfus and Rabinow's book on Foucault devotes a chapter to each of his major works and gives the reader a sense of a framework within which to approach Foucault's work as a whole (Dreyfus and Rabinow 1982). Foucault's interviews are significantly easier to digest than his more considered theoretical work. Therefore, it is advisable to read these before going on to the major works (see collections of essays and interviews below such as Bouchard 1977; Morris and Patton 1979; Kritzman 1988). It is also advisable to try to tackle the more readable books by Foucault before going on to the more difficult ones: *The History of Sexuality, Volume 1* (1978/1976), is a particularly easy text to try first. The collections of essays by Foucault, such as that by Paul Rabinow, *The Foucault Reader*, and *Power/Knowledge* edited by Colin Gordon (1980) are also useful, as you can choose which elements of Foucault's work appeal to you most before deciding which books you will go on to read. However, at some stage you will need to read the major texts such as *Archaeology of Knowledge* (1994/1972), *The Order of Things* (1970/1966), *Madness and Civilisation* (1999/1967) and *Discipline and Punish* (1991/1975).

BOOKS

Foucault, M. [1961] (1967) *Madness and Civilisation: A History of Insanity in the Age of Reason*, (trans. R. Howard), New York: Pantheon.

This is a fairly accessible book on the way that Western societies have divided sanity from insanity. It is a very clear analysis of the changes that there have been in what counts as madness in different historical periods. The most accessible parts of the book are the first chapter on the way that houses of confinement developed from hospitals set up to house lepers and the second chapter on the Great Confinement in the seventeenth century when large numbers of French people were confined because of poverty or insanity. The fifth chapter, Aspects of Madness, is an interesting analysis of the way that madness manifests itself differently in different contexts.

—— [1962] (1986) *Raymond Roussel*, Paris: Gallimard.

An analysis of the writings of the surrealist French poet, Raymond Roussel; translated into English by Charles Ruas as *Death and the Labyrinth*, Garden City, NY: Doubleday. For Roussel specialists only.

—— [1963] (1973) *The Birth of the Clinic: An Archaeology of Medical Perception*, (trans. A.M. Sheridan Smith), New York: Pantheon.

Although this book is essential for those interested in the development of Foucault's ideas, it is perhaps a little specialised for many readers. It does however contain within the introductory chapter a marvellous description of the 'cure' for hysterics in the eighteenth century which involved being immersed in baths for 10 hours a day for 10 months. Unlike *Madness and Civilisation* which analyses the way that madness and sanity are conceptualised over a vast time-scale, *The Birth of the Clinic* focuses only on the late eighteenth century and analyses in rather technical language the relations between medical discourse and institutions.

—— [1966] (1973) *The Order of Things: An Archaeology of the Human Sciences*, (trans. A. Sheridan), London: Tavistock.

As always with Foucault, this book opens with a tremendous vignette: a description by the novelist Jose-Luis Borges of a Chinese encyclopedia which classifies animals into a) those belonging to the Emperor; b) embalmed; c) tame; d) suckling pigs; e) sirens; f) fabulous and finally n) that from a great distance look like flies. This outlandish categorisation scheme underlies the driving principle of the book, which aims to force the reader to critically analyse the way that knowledge is organised within different historical periods. Although a complex book, in that Foucault is dealing with analogies between different sciences in the way that they organise ways of knowing, it is, nevertheless, a book which contains many illustrative examples.

—— [1969] (1972) *The Archaeology of Knowledge*, (trans. A.M. Sheridan Smith), New York: Pantheon.

This is one of Foucault's more difficult texts. Here he is grappling with the theoretical problems brought about through the use of the notion of discontinuity, that is the sense that there are sudden breaks in history, where regimes, ideas and ways of organising knowledge change. It is here that Foucault maps out the notion of a discursive formation, and describes the way that discourses emerge and are regulated. He describes the constitution of the archive and the statement here, and he describes the archaeological method.

—— [1973] (1978) *I, Pierre Rivière, Having Killed My Mother, My Sister and My Brother*, Paris: Gallimard.

This book consists of the memoir by Pierre Rivière, a nineteenth-century French peasant, who was convicted of killing three members of his family, together with one short essay by Foucault, six essays by members of the study group which he set up to examine this confession and contemporary material by doctors, psychiatrists, newspaper reports, letters and court proceedings. This book is a good introduction to the way a Foucauldian analysis can be made to work on a text.

—— [1975] (1977) *Discipline and Punish: The Birth of the Prison*, New York: Pantheon.

Foucault analyses here the changes there have been in the way that people considered to have committed crimes have been punished, from public torture and ritual disembowelling and branding to the current disciplinary regime where those considered to be criminals are locked away in prisons or mental hospitals. Rather than assuming that there has been progress in the way that criminals are treated, Foucault suggests throughout this book that we need to critically analyse the confinement of criminals. The first two chapters on torture in the eighteenth century make for grim reading, but they usefully force us to reflect on current disciplinary regimes. The third section on discipline is very readable and the section on the examination is particularly insightful.

—— [1976] (1978) *The History of Sexuality, Vol. I An Introduction*, (trans. Robert Hurley), New York: Pantheon.

This is by far the most accessible book by Foucault. He writes in a fairly informal way here and discusses sexuality and the way that we think about sexuality and repression giving a range of different examples, such as children's masturbation, homosexuality and women's hysteria. In this book, more than any other, he lays out his ideas on power relations and the way power functions in society. Because it is a fairly slim volume, and relatively easy to read, this is the book with which to start your study of Foucault.

—— [1984] (1985) *The History of Sexuality, Vol. II: The Use of Pleasure*, (trans. Robert Hurley), New York: Pantheon.

Both in this volume of the *History of Sexuality* and Vol. III, Foucault seems to be trying to formulate a new ethical framework. In this volume, rather than writing a history of sexual desire, Foucault focuses on what he calls 'a hermeneutics of the self', that is, an analysis of the relation between pleasure and the moral concerns that sexual pleasures lead to, in this case, in ancient Greek culture. This concern with Greek and Greco-Roman sexual practices and moral codes may seem fairly alien to some readers, but Foucault's general concerns with an 'aesthetics of existence' are very pertinent to contemporary cultural analysis.

—— [1984] (1986) *The History of Sexuality, Vol. III: The Care of the Self*, New York: Pantheon.

Although this volume is entitled 'The care of the self' it is very much concerned with the interaction between the self and others. In fact it could be seen more as an analysis of the concern with the care that others should take of themselves. This later work is less drawn on than others by critics, although there are several critical works devoted to both of the last volumes of *History of Sexuality*, for example, Moss (1998).

ESSAYS AND INTERVIEWS

Essays by, and interviews with, Michel Foucault are so numerous that it is impossible to list and annotate them all here. A full bibliography may be consulted at www.theory.org.uk which also contains some useful commentaries and links to sites. The Foucauldian web site also contains an extensive bibliography: www.thefoucauldian.co.uk. Possibly the best bibliography can be found at www.nakayama.org/polylogos/philosophers/foucault/index-e.html.

Certain essays and interviews make essential reading, and these have been collected into several key collections in English. You may like to consult the following:

Foucault, M. (1977) *Michel Foucault: Language, Counter-memory, Practice: Selected Essays and Interviews*, (ed. D. Bouchard, trans. D. Bouchard and S. Smith), Oxford: Blackwell.

—— (1980) *Power/Knowledge: Selected Interviews and Other Writings 1972–1977*, (ed. C. Gordon), Brighton: Harvester.

Contains essays, lectures and interviews given by Foucault between 1972–1977; perhaps the most interesting of these is his interview 'On popular justice' where he maps out his ideas on power, and the interview on 'The eye of power' where he describes the Panopticon in some detail. This is a good introduction to Foucault since many of the ideas contained in these essays and interviews are treated in more detail and in more technical, dense language in his major works.

—— (1984) *The Foucault Reader*, (ed. P. Rabinow), Harmondsworth: Penguin.

This is a collection of some of the more important essays by Foucault, including 'What is an author?'; 'Nietzsche, genealogy, history'; and selections from texts such as *The Order of Things* and *Power/Knowledge*.

All essays and interviews cited in this study are listed in the Works Cited section.

WORKS ON MICHEL FOUCAULT

Couzens Hoy, D. (ed.) (1986) *Foucault: A Critical Reader*, Oxford: Blackwell.

This collection of essays considers a wide range of difficult issues in Foucault's work, for example his problematic use of historical material, his political position, his relationship to the philosophical tradition and so on. Although the essays themselves are fairly demanding intellectually, they all take a critical position in relation to Foucault's work, which is productive.

Diamond, I. and Quinby, L. (eds) (1988) *Feminism and Foucault: Reflections on Resistance*, Boston: North Eastern University Press.

An excellent collection of essays, all of which engage in analysing the productiveness of Foucault's thinking about power and the body, particularly for feminist theory. The essays are, on the whole, very readable and very easily applied to other contexts. There are useful essays on anorexia.

Dreyfus, H. and Rabinow, P. (1982) *Michel Foucault: Beyond Structuralism and Hermeneutics*, Brighton: Harvester.

A very thorough yet readable introduction to Foucault's ideas. It is worth reading this book before you read any of Foucault's works because it provides you with a framework within which to approach the 'development' of his ideas. It traces the stages of Foucault's intellectual career in a productive way without oversimplifying Foucault's work.

Kendall, G. and Wickham, G. (1999) *Using Foucault's Methods*, London: Sage.

Despite an extremely irritating series of interspersed comments supposedly by their students, this is a very useful (but very prescriptive) book about how to use Foucault's ideas. There are a series of exercises, some of which are useful and enable you to think through how Foucault's ideas might be applied, and others which are not.

Kritzman, L. (ed.) (1988) *Michel Foucault: Politics, Philosophy, Culture: Interviews and Other Writings, 1977–1984*, London: Routledge.

Contains a number of interviews with Foucault, most notably 'The minimalist self', and 'Critical theory/intellectual theory', 'Power and sex', 'Iran: the spirit of the world without', together with a useful introduction by Lawrence Kritzman. There is also an essay by Foucault 'The dangerous individual' in which he examines the role of the confession and knowledge of the criminal in trials, and the pathologisation of criminals. Because this book collects together a number of interviews by Foucault which are not easily available, and because the interviews are generally more accessible than his major works, and comment usefully on the ideas he has developed in those works, this book is a very good introduction to Foucault's ideas.

Macdonnell, D. (1986) *Theories of Discourse*, Blackwell: Oxford.

Sets Foucault's ideas about discourse against other theorists such as Pecheux, Volosinov/Bakhtin, Althusser, and Hindess and Hirst. A very clear explication of some of Foucault's ideas and useful in that it gives details of other theorists against whom Foucault defined himself and/or who have defined themselves in relation to Foucault.

Macey, D. (1994) *The Lives of Michel Foucault*, London: Verso.

This is a very thorough, beautifully written and extremely well researched book on Foucault and his ideas. It is a very readable book and acts as an introduction to his biography and his ideas in the context of the different personae that Foucault adopted.

Mills, S. (1997) *Discourse*, Routledge: London.

A survey of Foucault's definitions of the term discourse in relation to other discourse theorists' work.

Morris, M. and Patton, P. (1979) *Michel Foucault: Power/Truth/Strategy*, Sydney: Feral Publications.

A collection of interviews with Foucault and critical essays on him by Morris and Patton and others. Despite being a fairly early collection of theoretical essays the standard of critical analysis here is very high and the essays by Patton and by Morris are excellent.

Smart, B. (1985) *Michel Foucault*, London: Tavistock.

A readable introductory text which discusses the major texts and which contains sizable extracts from Foucault's works with commentaries.

INTERNET RESOURCES

There are many internet sites on the works of Michel Foucault and these can be accessed by typing Michel Foucault into any search engine such as 'google'; many of the sites only consist of rehashing of Foucault's basic ideas; the following consist of resources on Foucault and bibliographical material:

www.theory.org.uk/foucault

This contains a good introduction to Foucault's ideas, a bibliography and a fair selection of links to other sites devoted to Foucault. Possibly the best internet site on Foucault.

www.thefoucauldian.co.uk

A good up-to-date bibliography of books by, and on, Foucault together with a Frequently Asked Questions page for those new to Foucault's work.

www.nakayama.org/polylogos/philosophers/foucault/index-e.html

Contains a full bibliography of Foucault's works and interviews compiled by Michael Karskens, together with a number of on-line papers on Foucault by a variety of scholars.

www.excite.co.uk/directory/society/philosophers/foucault-info

Contains a well organised site on Foucault's works and life; with links to other sites of interest; there are quite a few down-loadable extracts from texts by Foucault.

WORKS CITED

Note: details for works by Michel Foucault refer to the editions cited. More information on these works, including original publication dates, appears in the Further Reading section.

Alldred, A., Crowley, H. and Rupal, R. (2000) 'Introduction', *Feminist Review* 68 pp. 1–5.

Althusser, L. (1984) *Essays on Ideology*, London: Verso.

Armstrong, N. and Tennenhouse, L. (eds) (1987) *The Ideology of Conduct: Essays in Literature and the History of Sexuality*, London: Methuen.

Barrett, R. (1997) 'The homo-genius speech community', in A. Livia and K. Hall (eds), *Queerly Phrased: Language Gender and Sexuality*, Oxford and New York: Oxford University Press, pp. 181–201.

Barthes, R. (f. pub.1968, 1991) 'The death of the author', in P. Rice and P. Waugh (eds), *Modern Literary Theory: A Reader*, London: Edward Arnold, pp. 109–122.

Bartky, S. (1988) 'Foucault, femininity and the modernisation of patriarchal power', in I. Diamond and L. Quinby (eds), *Feminism and Foucault: Reflections of Resistance*, Boston: North Eastern University Press, pp. 60–85.

Beevor, A. (1999) *Stalingrad*, Harmondsworth: Penguin.

Bell, D., Binnie, J., Cream, J. and Valentine, G. (1994) 'All hyped up and no place to go', *Gender, Place and Culture* 1/1 pp. 31–47.

Bhabha, H. (ed.) (1994) *The Location of Culture*, London: Routledge.

Bondi, L. and Burman, E. (2001) 'Women and mental health', *Feminist Review* 68 pp. 6–33.

Bordo, S. (1989) 'Anorexia nervosa: psychopathology as the crystallisation of culture', in I. Diamond and L. Quinby (eds), *Feminism and Foucault: Reflections of Resistance*, Boston, North Eastern University Press, pp. 98–114.

Bouchard, D. (ed.) (1977) *Michel Foucault: Language, Counter-memory, Practice: Selected Essays and Interviews*, (trans. D. Bouchard and S. Smith), Oxford: Blackwell.

Bourdieu, P., Johnson, J., Ferguson, P.P. (trans.), Emanuel, S. (trans.) and Accardo, S. (eds) (1999) *The Weight of the World: Social Suffering in Contemporary Society*, London: Polity.

Brown, H., Gilkes, M. and Kaloski-Naylor, A. (eds) (1999) *White? Women: Critical Perspectives on Race and Gender*, York: Raw Nerve Books.

Burchell, G., Gordon, C. and Miller, P. (eds) (1991) *The Foucault Effect: Studies in Governmentality*, Chicago: University of Chicago Press.

Burton, D. (1982) 'Through glass darkly, through dark glasses', in R. Carter (ed.), *Language and Literature*, London: Allen and Unwin, pp. 195–214.

Butler, J. (1990) *Gender Trouble: Feminism and the Subversion of Identity*, London: Routledge.

—— (1993) *Bodies that Matter: On the Discursive Limits of Sex*, London: Routledge.

Clayton, D. (2000) *Islands of Truth: The Imperial Fashioning of Vancouver Island*, Vancouver: UBC Press.

Crawford, M. (1995) *Talking Difference: On Gender and Language*, London: Sage.

Culler, J. (1975) *Structuralist Poetics: Structuralism, Linguistics and the Study of Literature*, London: Routledge and Kegan Paul.

Darwin, C. (1859/1968) *On the Origin of Species*, ed. J.W. Burrow, Harmondsworth: Penguin.

Davis, L. (1983) *Factual Fictions: The Origins of the English Novel*, New York: Columbia University Press.

Donnelly, M. (1986) 'Foucault's genealogy of the human sciences', in M. Gane (ed.), *Towards a Critique of Foucault*, London: Routledge Kegan and Paul, pp. 15–32.

Dreyfus, H. and Rabinow, P. (eds) (1986) *Michel Foucault: Beyond Structuralism and Hermeneutics*, Hemel Hempstead: Harvester Wheatsheaf.

Dumm, T. (1996) *Michel Foucault and the Politics of Freedom*, London: Sage.

Eagleton, T. (1983) *Literary Theory: An Introduction*, Oxford: Blackwell.

Eribon, D. (1991) *Michel Foucault*, (trans. Betsy Wing), Cambridge, MA: Harvard University Press.

Foster, S. and Mills, S. (2002) *Women's Travel Writing: An Anthology*, Manchester, Manchester University Press

Foucault, M. (1962) *Raymond Roussel*, Paris: Gallimard.

—— (1970) *The Order of Things: An Archaeology of the Human Sciences*, London: Tavistock.

—— (1972) *The Archaeology of Knowledge*, (trans. A. M. Sheridan Smith), London: Routledge.

—— (1973) *Moi, Pierre Rivière, ayant égorgé ma mére, ma soeur et mon frère*, Paris: Gallimard.

—— (1975) *The Birth of the Clinic*, New York: Vintage.

—— (1977a) 'The political function of the intellectual', *Radical Philosophy* 17 pp. 12–14.

—— (1978) *The History of Sexuality, Vol. I: An Introduction*, (trans. Robert Hurley), Harmondsworth: Penguin.

—— (1979a) 'Truth and power', interview with Fontano and Pasquino, in M. Morris and P. Patton (eds), *Michel Foucault: Power/Truth/Strategy*, Sydney: Feral Publications, pp. 29–48.

—— (1979b) 'Powers and strategies', interview with Revoltes Logiques collective, in M. Morris and P. Patton (eds), *Michel Foucault: Power/Truth/Strategy*, Sydney: Feral Publications, pp. 48–58.

—— (1979c) 'Interview with Lucette Finas', in M. Morris and P. Patton (eds), *Michel Foucault: Power/Truth/Strategy*, Sydney: Feral Publications, pp. 67–75.

—— (1979d) 'The Life of infamous men', in M. Morris and P. Patton (eds), *Michel Foucault: Power/Truth/Strategy*, Sydney: Feral Publications, pp. 76–91.

—— (1980a) 'Two lectures', in C. Gordon (ed.), *Power/Knowledge*, Brighton: Harvester, pp. 80–105.

—— (1980b) 'Truth and power', in C. Gordon (ed.), *Power/Knowledge*, Brighton: Harvester, pp. 107–133.

—— (1980c) 'On popular justice', interview with Pierre Victor, in C. Gordon (ed.), *Power/Knowledge*, Brighton: Harvester, pp. 1–36.

—— (1980d) 'Prison talk', in C. Gordon (ed.), *Power/Knowledge*, Brighton: Harvester, pp. 37–52.

—— (1980e) 'The history of sexuality', in C. Gordon (ed.), *Power/Knowledge*, Brighton: Harvester, pp. 184–191.

—— (1980f) 'The eye of power', in C. Gordon (ed.), *Power/Knowledge*, Brighton: Harvester, pp. 147–165.

—— (1981) 'The order of discourse', in R. Young (ed.), *Untying the Text: A Post-structuralist Reader*, London: Routledge, Kegan and Paul, pp. 48–79.

—— (1982) 'The subject and power', in H. Dreyfus and P. Rabinow (eds), *Michel Foucault: Beyond Structuralism and Hermeneutics*, Brighton: Harvester, pp. 208–226.

—— (1985) *The History of Sexuality, Vol. II: The Use of Pleasure*, (trans. Robert Hurley), Harmondsworth: Penguin.

—— (1986) *The History of Sexuality, Vol III: The Care of the Self*, London: Allen Lane/Penguin.

—— (1986a) 'What is an author', in P. Rabinow (ed.), *The Foucault Reader*, Harmondsworth: Peregrine, pp. 101–123.

—— (1986b) 'Nietzsche, genealogy, history', in P. Rabinow (ed.), *The Foucault Reader*, Harmondsworth: Peregrine, pp. 76–100.

—— (1986c) 'We "other Victorians"', in P. Rabinow (ed.), *The Foucault Reader*, Harmondsworth: Peregrine, pp. 292–300.

—— (1986d) 'The repressive hypothesis', in P. Rabinow (ed.), *The Foucault Reader*, Harmondsworth: Peregrine, pp. 301–329.

—— (1988a) 'The Masked Philosopher', in L. Kritzman (ed.), *Michel Foucault: Politics, Philosophy, Culture: Interviews and Other Writings, 1977–1984*, London: Routledge, pp. 323–330.

—— (1988b) 'The minimalist self', interview with Stephen Riggins, in L. Kritzman (ed.), *Michel Foucault: Politics, Philosophy, Culture: Interviews and Other Writings, 1977–1984*, London: Routledge, pp. 1–19.

—— (1988c) 'Critical theory/intellectual theory', interview with Gerard Raulet, in L. Kritzman (ed.), *Michel Foucault: Politics, Philosophy, Culture: Interviews and Other Writings, 1977–1984*, London: Routledge, pp. 20–47.

—— (1988d) 'Power and sex: discussion with Bernard-Henri Levy', in L. Kritzman (ed.), *Michel Foucault: Politics, Philosophy, Culture: Interviews and Other Writings, 1977–1984*, London: Routledge, pp. 110–124.

—— (1988e) 'The dangerous individual', in L. Kritzman (ed.), *Michel Foucault: Politics, Philosophy, Culture: Interviews and Other Writings, 1977–1984*, London: Routledge, pp. 125–151.

—— (1988f) 'Iran: the spirit of a world without spirit', in L. Kritzman (ed.), *Michel Foucault: Politics, Philosophy, Culture: Interviews and Other Writings, 1977–1984*, London: Routledge, pp. 211–224.

—— (1991a) *Discipline and Punish: The Birth of the Prison*, Harmondsworth: Penguin.

—— (1991b) 'Questions of method', in Burchell, G., Gordon, C. and Miller, P. (eds), *The Foucault Effect: Studies in Governmentality*, Chicago: University of Chicago Press.

—— (1991c) 'Governmentality', in Burchell, G., Gordon, C. and Miller, P. (eds), *The Foucault Effect: Studies in Governmentality*, Chicago: University of Chicago Press, pp. 85–103.

—— (1999) *Madness and Civilisation: A History of Insanity in the Age of Reason*, London: Routledge.

Gane, M. (1986) 'Introduction', in M. Gane (ed.), *Towards a Critique of Foucault*, London: Routledge, Kegan and Paul, pp. 1–15.

Gavey, N. (1993) 'Technologies and effects of heterosexual coercion', in S. Wilkinson and C. Kitzinger (eds), *Heterosexuality: A Feminism and Psychology Reader*, London: Sage, pp. 93–119.

Gilman, C. (1899/1973) *The Yellow Wallpaper*, London: Virago.

Gordon, C. (1991) 'Governmental rationality: an introduction', in G. Burchell, C. Gordon and P. Miller (eds), *The Foucault Effect: Studies in Governmentality*, Chicago: Chicago University Press, pp. 1–51.

Grant, L. (1994) 'Sex and the single student: the story of date rape', in S. Dunant (ed.), *The War of the Words: The Political Correctness Debate*, London: Virago, pp. 76–96.

Greenblatt, S. (2001/1990) 'Resonance and wonder', in P. Rice and P. Waugh (eds), *Modern Literary Theory*, 4th edn, London: Arnold, pp. 305–324.

Guha, R. (1994) *Elementary Aspects of Peasant Insurgency in Colonial India*, Oxford: Oxford University Press.

Guha, R. and Spivak, G. (1988) *Selected Subaltern Studies*, Oxford and New York: Oxford University Press.

Harman, C. (1998) *The Fire Last Time: 1968 and After*, London: Bookmarks.

Jefferson, A. (1991) 'Structuralism and post-structuralism', in A. Jefferson and D. Robey (eds), *Modern Literary Theory: A Comparative Introduction*, London: Batsford, pp. 92–122.

Kendall, G. and Wickham, G. (1999) *Using Foucault's Methods*, London: Sage.

Kesey, K. (1973) *One Flew Over the Cuckoo's Nest*, London: Pan.

Laclau, E. and Mouffe, C. (1985) *Hegemony and Socialist Strategy*, London: Verso.

Leap, W. (1997) 'Performative affect in three Gay English texts', in A. Livia and K. Hall (eds), *Queerly Phrased: Language, Gender and Sexuality*, Oxford and New York: Oxford University Press, pp. 310–325.

Macey, D. (1994) *The Lives of Michel Foucault*, London: Vintage.

McClintock, A. (1995) *Imperial Leather: Race, Gender and Sexuality in the Imperial Contest*, London: Routledge.

McGann, J. (2001/1985) 'The text, the poem and the problem of historical method', in P. Rice and P. Waugh (eds), *Modern Literary Theory: A Reader*, 4th edn, London: Arnold, pp. 289–305.

McInnes, S. (2001) 'The political is personal: or why have a revolution (from within or without) when you can have soma?', in *Feminist Review*, 68 pp. 160–180.

McNay, L. (1992) *Foucault and Feminism*, London: Polity, pp. 160–180.

Mills, S. (1991) *Discourses of Difference: An Analysis of Women's Travel Writing and Colonialism*, London: Routledge.

—— (1997) *Discourse*, London, Routledge.

—— (forthcoming) *Rethinking Gender and Politeness*, Cambridge: Cambridge University Press.

Minh-ha, T. (1989) *Woman, Native, Other: Writing Postcoloniality and Feminism*, Bloomington: Indiana University Press.

Minson, J. (1986) 'Strategies for socialists? Foucault's conception of power', in M. Gane (ed.), *Towards a Critique of Foucault*, London: Routledge, Kegan and Paul, pp. 106–148.

Morgan, P. (2002) 'Tales from the tabloids', *Socialist Review*, January, pp. 8–10.

Morris, M. (1979) 'The pirate's fiancée', in M. Morris and P. Patton (eds), *Michel Foucault: Power/Truth/Strategy*, Sydney: Feral Publications, pp. 148–168.

Morris, M. and Patton, P. (eds) *Michel Foucault: Power/Truth/Strategy*, Sydney: Feral Publications.

Moss, J. (ed.) (1998) *The Later Foucault*, London: Sage.

Murphy, L. (1997) 'The elusive bisexual: social categorisation and lexico-semantic change', in A. Livia and K. Hall (eds), *Queerly Phrased: Language Gender and Sexuality*, Oxford and New York: Oxford University Press, pp. 35–57.

Patton, P. (1979) 'Of power and prisons', in M. Morris and P. Patton (eds), *Michel Foucault: Power/Truth/Strategy*, Sydney: Feral Publications, pp. 109–146.

Poster, M. (1984) *Foucault, Marxism and History*, London: Polity.

Pratt, M. (1992) *Imperial Eyes: Travel Writing and Transculturation*, London: Routledge.

Queen R. (1997) 'I don't speak Spritch: locating lesbian language', in A. Livia and K. Hall (eds), *Queerly Phrased: Language, Gender and Sexuality*, London: Routledge, pp. 233–242.

Rabinow, P. (ed.) (1986) *The Foucault Reader*, Harmondsworth: Peregrine.

Rice, P. and Waugh, P. (eds) (2001) *Modern Literary Theory*, 4th edn, London: Arnold.

Rivkin, J. and Ryan, M. (eds) (1999) *Literary Theory: An Anthology*, Oxford: Blackwell.

Said, E. (1978) *Orientalism*, London: Routledge and Kegan Paul.

—— (1993) *Culture and Imperialism*, London: Chatto and Windus.

Salih, S. (2002) *Judith Butler*, London: Routledge.

Sawicki, J. (1998) 'Feminism, Foucault, and "subjects" of power and freedom', in J. Moss (ed.), *The Later Foucault*, London: Sage, pp. 92–107.

Scott, J. (1990) *Domination and the Arts of Resistance: Hidden Transcripts*, New Haven and London: Yale University Press.

Sheridan, A. (1980) *Michel Foucault: The Will to Truth*, London: Tavistock.

Showalter, E. (1987) *The Female Malady: Women Madness and English Culture*, London: Virago.

Skeggs, B. (1997) *Formations of Class and Gender: Becoming Respectable*, London: Sage.

Smart, B. (1985) *Michel Foucault*, London: Tavistock.

Smith, D. (1990) 'K is mentally ill', in *Texts, Facts and Femininity: Exploring the Relations of Ruling*, London: Routledge.

Taylor, C. (1986) 'Foucault on freedom and truth', in D. Couzens Hoy (ed.), *Foucault: A Critical Reader*, Oxford: Blackwell, pp. 69–103.

Thornborrow, J. (2002) *Power Talk: Language and Interaction in Institutional Discourse*, Harlow: Pearson.

Walzer, M. (1986) 'The politics of Michel Foucault', in D. Couzens Hoy (ed.), *Foucault: A Critical Reader*, Oxford: Blackwell, pp. 51–69.

Wex, M. (1979) *Let's Take Back Our Space: Female and Male Body Language as a Result of Patriarchal Structures*, Berlin: Frauenliteraturverlag Hermine Fees.

White, H. (1987) 'The value of narrativity in the representation of reality', in P. Rice and P. Waugh (eds), *Modern Literary Theory: A Reader*, 4th edn, London: Arnold, pp. 265–272.

Wickham, G. (1986) 'Power and power analysis: beyond Foucault?', in M. Gane (ed.) *Towards a Critique of Foucault*, London: Routledge, Kegan and Paul, pp. 149–179.

Wilkinson, S. and Kitzinger, C. (eds) (1993) *Heterosexuality: A Feminism and Psychology Reader*, London: Sage.

Williams, J., Scott, S., and Waterhouse, S. (2001) 'Mental health services for "difficult" women', *Feminist Review* 68 pp. 89–104.

Young, I. (1989) 'Throwing like a girl: a phenomenology of feminine bodily comportment, motility and spatiality,' in J. Allen and I. Young (eds), *The Thinking Muse: Feminism and Modern French Philosophy*, Bloomington: Indiana University Press, pp. 51–70.

Young, R. (ed.) (1981) *Untying the Text: A Post-structuralist Reader*, London: Routledge, Kegan and Paul.

INDEX

Contents

ACKNOWLEDGEMENTS

For this book I interviewed a number of individuals who had fascinating civilian and military roles in World War Two: amongst them, a teenage Bevin Boy, a very young secretary in the Cabinet War Rooms, and an underage Home Guard recruit who later went on to become a navigator in a Wellington bomber. Given the passage of time, it was always improbable that I would get to meet a significant, living, former member of Churchill's war ministry – politician or civil servant. But I did interview many people in the course of my research who knew a good deal about the book's main characters, either through family connection or other association. In particular I wish to thank Lord Woolton, Charles Sandemann-Allen, Earl Attlee, Lady Attlee, Lord Beaverbrook, Baroness Linklater, John Thurso MP, John Julius Norwich and Mrs Jane Kerr for their time and their various vital insights into their famous ancestors, and for giving me access to important documentary material. Lord Carrington served in Churchill's 1951–5 administration, and he gave me splendid character sketches of some of the wartime ministers he personally knew who had survived to serve WSC again.

Caroline Balcon and her staff made me very welcome in the Prime Minister's Room in the House of Commons, where one particular crucial, memorable scene takes place – although a number of other War Cabinet meetings were also held there between 1940 and 1945. Equally, I must thank Jane Ford and Nicky Luscombe for allowing me to spend a fascinating few hours looking round Cherkley Court, Lord Beaverbrook's dramatically situated old 'pile' in Surrey.

I am also indebted to a good many others who provided stories, guidance and help of one kind or another – Lord (Michael) Dobbs, Dr Paul Addison, Prof. Stuart Bell, Dr Anthony Seldon, Prof. Robert Self, Kenneth Baxter, Liz Todd, Eric Johnson, Joy Hunter, Derrick Clewley, Peter Fleming, Clive Robey, Nick Kerr, Diana Mackenzie, Martin Kinna, Ashley Cooper and Ben Perkins. Edmund Bradbury was an excellent, assiduous researcher on the subject of the 'Bevin Boys'.

First and foremost, though, this was a book that relies heavily on written memories and government documents of the time. A good deal of the very best archival material of British political life resides in the Churchill Archives at Churchill College, Cambridge, where I spent very many happy and fruitful hours. I owe a special debt to Allen Packwood and his superb staff who handled all my enquiries with expert efficiency and great good humour. Over at the Bodleian Library in Oxford, Colin Harris and his colleagues were equally welcoming and knowledgeable, and I thank them hugely for all their help. I also received great help and advice at the Imperial War Museum, Warwick University, Cambridge University Library, Trinity Library, Cambridge, and the BBC Archives at Caversham.

My excellent agent Andrew Gordon has, as ever, offered wise counsel throughout this project. I must also thank everyone at Aurum for their continuing backing and encouragement – Richard Green, Melissa Smith, Jessica Axe, Jennifer Barr and Katherine Josselyn. My copy editor, Steve Gove, did splendid work in the closing weeks. But most of all I would like to thank my brilliant editor Sam Harrison; I could not have wished for a more incisive mind at work on this book, nor anyone so supportive.

PROLOGUE

Friday, 10 May 1940

'Where is Hitler going for Whitsun?' the leader writer of the *Daily Mirror* had asked in half-jocular, half-serious vein that morning when writing about Britain's lack of preparation for war. 'To Holland, Belgium, Sweden, Switzerland? Or on a round trip through the Balkans – with Musso, perhaps, in attendance, personally conducting his Fuehrer? What would happen thereupon?'

His answer had arrived all too quickly, even as his newspaper was landing on the doormats of millions of British homes. At first light Hitler launched his long-awaited invasion of western Europe, choosing the Low Countries as his entry point. In Operation *Fall Gelb*, the Luftwaffe carried out sustained attacks on airfields across Belgium and the Netherlands, while daring raids by German airborne troops, dropped by gliders behind enemy lines, captured vital strategic and defence installations in the two countries. Meanwhile the Panzer and infantry divisions of General Fedor von Bock's Army Group B began to advance, meeting little resistance, certainly not from hapless little Luxembourg, protected by just four hundred infantry and twelve cavalrymen.

At this most perilous moment in Europe's history, Britain's political class appeared dangerously divided. The nation was facing its greatest

3

external threat since Napoleon one hundred and thirty-five years before and it was unclear who could lead it to safety. After a tumultuous week in Westminster, the Prime Minister, Neville Chamberlain, had been left clinging onto power by his fingertips, with most expecting him to fall by the end of the coming day. 'CHAMBERLAIN TO RESIGN' was the morning headline in the *Daily Express*. 'PM'S LAST BID FAILS' was the *Daily Mirror*'s take on matters. Only the *Daily Worker* offered him a glimmer of hope, with 'PREMIER HOPES TO SURVIVE "RE-ORGANISATION"'

This tall, lean seventy-one-year-old, with greying moustache, curved nose and penetrating dark eyes, had never relished the responsibility of being Prime Minister during wartime. He was naturally shy, and his meticulous mind and social conscience were better suited to the field of domestic reform: improving factory conditions, clearing Britain's slums, empowering local government. His domain was the committee room rather than the grand stage. Exhorting a nation, sending young men to the battlefield and shaping military strategy were uncomfortable duties.

Thus, since the start of his premiership, on 28 May 1937, much of Chamberlain's time had been spent trying to avoid an armed conflict – and not without popular support. His quest for a diplomatic agreement with Hitler had reflected a general yearning for peace; just twenty years on from the end of the last war, and with Britain barely recovered from a worldwide economic depression, few had any real desire to take up arms again. The strategy of so-called 'appeasement' reached its apogee at the Munich conference of September 1938, when Hitler – seemingly satisfied with Germany's annexation of the 'Sudetenland' region of Czechoslovakia – promised to make no further territorial demands in Europe. Upon his return, Chamberlain triumphantly waved a piece of paper, proclaiming he had won 'peace for our time'. But as that conceit unravelled over the course of the next eighteen months, in the face of the Nazis' undisguised aggression, the criticism of his leadership in Parliament – and certain sections of the press – built with increasing vehemence. By the time of Germany's invasion of Poland, on 1 September 1939, his government's failure to put the

ountry on a proper war footing had been exposed as imprudent at
est, negligent at worst.

Matters had come to a head on 7–8 May 1940 in an extraordinary
wo-day debate in the House of Commons. What had been billed as an
ccasion to analyse Britain's disastrous military campaign in Norway,
rom where troops had been forced into a desperate evacuation while
nder heavy attack from the Luftwaffe on 2 and 3 May, had become an
nquiry into the entire military record of Chamberlain's Conservative-
ed national government since the declaration of war on Germany
he previous September. Members of Parliament crowded excitedly
nto the green benches, the galleries were packed to overflowing, and
he atmosphere – in turn tense, raucous and emotional – was unlike
nything seen or heard in the chamber before.

From the moment he stood up to present the government's case
n Wednesday everything had gone wrong for Chamberlain. His own
peech was a poor effort, balancing advantage and disadvantage in
he Norway campaign, admitting errors but denying complacency.
There was no emotion, no flight of fancy, no glimmer of light atop the
mountain. 'He seemed tired and embarrassed,' observed government
parliamentary private secretary Henry 'Chips' Channon.

Speaking for His Majesty's Most Loyal Opposition had been the
Labour Party leader, Clement Attlee. Small, trim and bald, with a
izeable toothbrush moustache and round, steel-rimmed spectacles,
he was by nature undemonstrative, and even now, after five years in
charge, he still struggled to impose his authority on his colleagues.
But that day he had begun the attack on the government with a calm,
ncisive speech all the more damaging for being unadorned.

Attlee's impressive army record – he had fought bravely in the ill-
fated Gallipoli campaign in the First World War – lent him moral
gravity. Referring to that experience in his criticism of the calibre of
troops – a good proportion of them 'territorials' – who had been sent
to fight in Norway, he had observed, 'We had an experience in the
Dardanelles of having young men sent out. They did not last long. It
was seasoned men, capable of responsibility and enterprise, who were

wanted for this Norwegian affair'. He bemoaned the lack of suppor
from fighter aircraft – 'surely a sine qua non of the whole adventure' –
and concluded that the people of Britain 'want different people at the
helm' from those who had led them into the conflict.

The leader of the Liberal Party, Sir Archibald Sinclair, focused
his criticisms on reports he had received from serving soldiers about
a desperate lack of equipment. 'The minister of supply appeared in a
press picture in a becoming white fur coat – but the troops at Namsos
had no white coats at all. Apparently he had the only one. They had
no snow shoes . . . and in the fighting which occurred at Namsos I
understand that men were caught up to their waists in snow.' Turning
to the shortfalls in the production of guns and planes, he asserted that
'the government is giving us a one-shift war while the Germans are
working a three-shift war. Foreigners are shocked by our complacency
and by our failure to rouse ourselves out of our peacetime routine.'

In the course of the two days Chamberlain had been assailed by
MPs on all sides of the house. Herbert Morrison, the unsuccessful
candidate when Attlee became leader of the Labour Party in 1935,
and Albert Victor Alexander (usually known as 'A.V.' or 'Bert'), First
Lord of the Admiralty in the 1929–31 Labour administration, kept up
the pressure from the Labour ranks, while Alfred Duff Cooper made
an eloquent adversary among the rebel Tories. The feeble defence
mounted by Chamberlain's close confidants in the War Cabinet, Sir
Samuel Hoare, air secretary, and Sir John Simon, Chancellor of the
Exchequer, merely imperilled his government further.

It was left, however, to two veterans of the First World War to fatally
wound Chamberlain. His old colleague Leo Amery, now the leader of
a group of backbench Tory rebels, concluded his speech by quoting
Oliver Cromwell's denunciation of the Rump Parliament in April
1653: 'You have sat too long here for any good you have been doing.
Depart, I say, and let us have done with you. In the name of God, go.'
David Lloyd George, the man who had steered the nation to safety
over twenty years before, and bore only loathing towards Chamberlain,
struck the final, debilitating blow. 'This was a half-prepared, half-baked

xpeditionary force, without any combination between the army
nd the navy,' he told members. 'Here we are in the worst strategic
osition in which this country has ever been placed.' Echoing Amery
ne day before, he concluded, 'I say solemnly that the prime minister
nould give an example of sacrifice, because there is nothing which
an contribute more to victory in this war than he should sacrifice the
eals of office.'

Only Winston Churchill, First Lord of the Admiralty and chairman
f the new military co-ordinating committee, made the best of a bad
tuation, rallying some doubters with his defence of the naval strategy.
fter much agonised debate, the Labour Party decided to press a
vision on the motion for the adjournment, effectively provoking
vote of censure on the government's conduct of the war. If they
ad misjudged the mood, and Chamberlain had won a comfortable
ajority, his authority might have been enhanced and the chance to
ust him would have been squandered. But when the result came, the
overnment's majority of 250 was whittled down to just eighty-one (281
 200), with a fifth of its backbenchers (around ninety) either voting
gainst the administration or abstaining. Technically, the government
ad won; morally, it had been an abject defeat, and Chamberlain left
ne chamber to cries of 'Resign, resign', a few excitable Tory rebels
reaking into a chorus of 'Rule Britannia'.

The mood in Downing Street the day after was gloomy and recrim-
atory. 'Jackals' was Samuel Hoare's contemptuous description of the
bellious backbenchers. Chamberlain himself made efforts to concil-
te the dissenters, including an unsuccessful offer of a senior cabinet
le to Amery. Sir Herbert Williams, a senior Tory backbencher who
d a delegation of supporters to Number 10 after lunch, found the
rime Minister in a demoralised state. 'It was a pathetic interview. He
ad been terribly shaken both by the debate and the voting. It was
 if he had been struck a severe blow, because as we walked into the
om he seemed unable to get out of his chair. We stated our case and
e listened with great care, and by the time we had finished he was in
uch better form'.

Later in the afternoon the Prime Minister hosted two crucia[
meetings in the Cabinet Room. In the first, joined by foreign secretar
Lord Halifax, Winston Churchill, and Conservative chief whip Davi
Margesson, he had considered the drastic changes needed to restor
confidence.

If there had to be a new leader, Chamberlain's loyal lieutenar
Halifax looked to be first in line. The tall, quietly spoken, easy
mannered aristocrat, known as the 'Holy Fox' for his twin passions o
religion and fox hunting, was held in high esteem throughout the Tor
party. There had been evidence too, in recent days, that senior Labou
figures preferred him to the other candidates, principally Churchil
Hugh Dalton, Labour's foreign policy spokesman, had noted in h
diary on 8 May, 'I thought, and a number of others shared the view
that there was much to be said for Halifax.' Judging from a letter in *Th*
Times that morning from A.L. Rowse, historian and prospective Labou
candidate for Penryn and Falmouth, many in the wider party agreed
'I believe the Labour Movement would serve under Lord Halifax a
Prime Minister, who has defined the moral issues of the war as no on
else has done and gives the nation the right moral leadership.'

Chamberlain had at last been convinced that Labour – the secon
largest party in Parliament, commanding 154 MPs out of 615 – neede
to be brought into a coalition government. At that moment, too, h
had finally appeared ready to relinquish the premiership. 'The P]
recapitulated the position, and said he had made up his mind to g
and that it must be Winston or me,' recorded Halifax. 'He would serv
under either.' But by the end of the meeting the foreign secretar
had effectively talked himself out of the job. He had argued that h
position in the House of Lords would prove isolating during wartim
with Churchill running defence matters in the Commons, he woul
be too far from the 'centre of gravity'. More likely is that, at the ver
moment of opportunity, Halifax had feared the burden of responsibili
would prove too great for him to bear.

Whatever the real reason, his colleagues supported his act of sel
denial. 'Winston, with suitable expressions of regard and humility, sai

e could not but feel the force of what I said, and the PM reluctantly, and Winston evidently with much less reluctance, finished by accepting my view.' And so the question of the future leadership of the country was left to rest. Halifax and Churchill retired to the garden of Number 0 for a cup of tea while Chamberlain kept other appointments. Then at 6.15 p.m. Clement Attlee and his deputy, Arthur Greenwood, arrived, and the three Conservative and two Labour leaders sat facing each other across the Cabinet table.

Chamberlain, revealing nothing of his earlier discussions, told Attlee and Greenwood that a new national government was now a necessity; although he had begun by asking directly if they would join it, and serve under *him*. According to Halifax, the Labour leaders were a 'bit evasive' when faced with this request. Attlee had told Chamberlain, 'Mr Prime Minister, the fact is our party won't come in under you. Our party won't have you and I think I am right in saying that the country won't have you either.'

Pressed by Chamberlain, the Labour leader expressed the opinion that his party would likely serve under another Conservative, but he would need to consult it first. Thus it was agreed that Attlee would convene a meeting of Labour's National Executive Committee the following day, when delegates would be gathering for their delayed party conference in Bournemouth, and put two questions to them. First, would they be prepared to serve in a national government under Neville Chamberlain? Second, would they be prepared to serve under someone else?

On Friday, as the news of the German invasions came in, Whitehall lurched into a flurry of meetings. By seven o'clock Halifax had received the Dutch minister and Belgian ambassador, with their formal requests for help, at the Foreign Office. Over at the Admiralty, the three services ministers – Churchill for the navy, Oliver Stanley for war (the army) and Sir Samuel Hoare for the air force – gathered for an early breakfast together. During the Military Co-ordination Committee meeting that followed, they and the chiefs of staff authorised the dispatch of two additional fighter squadrons to France. They also ordered the execution of Royal Marine, a long-planned operation to mine the

River Rhine. Then, at the emergency War Cabinet meeting at 8 a.m.
ministers were told that the British Expeditionary Force, 'although no
at the highest state of readiness', would soon be on the move toward
the Belgian front.

Now, paradoxically, with his government's military and politica
strategy in ruins, Chamberlain viewed the catastrophe as an
opportunity to prolong his premiership. He had retired to bed the
previous night in the firm belief that his tenure at Number 10 had
just hours to run. But at this time of grave national crisis, he began
to reason, a radical and distracting reconstruction of his government
would not be in the best interests of the country. 'I propose to remain,
he wrote to one of his senior ministers that morning. 'The next three
or four days' battle will determine the fate of civilisation for the nex
one hundred years.'

This was not vanity on Chamberlain's part, but he had failed to
grasp that power had already slipped away from him; that his momen
had come and gone. He had a strong sense of patriotic duty, and h
genuinely believed that he should continue to lead the country through
the next, difficult hours. And he was by no means alone in this: ove
at the Foreign Office 'Chips' Channon sensed a turn in fortunes fo
the Prime Minister. 'It was the popular view [here] this morning tha
Neville was saved, for after all his policy had been vindicated swiftl
and surely within twenty-four hours. Had he sent an army to Finland
where should we be now?'

Newly energised, Chamberlain sought to bolster his position
First he turned to Sir Archibald Sinclair – a tricky task as ther
had been much bad blood between them in the past. When calle
to Downing Street at ten o'clock that morning, however, Sinclai
gave Chamberlain's argument that the political status quo should b
maintained a fair hearing. Emerging half an hour later, watched by
crowd of several hundred, he promptly issued a statement to the medi
which began, 'Recent events have proved the necessity of prompt an
radical reconstruction of the British Government, but the opening o
the first critical battle in the West is not the moment.' The Libera

ader then walked straight over to the Commons to explain his about-
urn to Attlee and Greenwood.

Heartened by his old foe's support, Chamberlain was now telling
nyone and everyone that he would carry on – at least for now.
'Neville is inclined to hold up his resignation until the battle is over,'
oted Hoare. However, his change of heart was inciting anger in the
anks of the disaffected. Sir Kingsley Wood, Lord Privy Seal in the
War Cabinet, and a recent, unexpected recruit to the rebels – having
reviously been a staunch Chamberlain supporter – had observed the
rime Minister's new mood and relayed his fears to the plotters in
heir familiar haunts around the clubs and restaurants of Westminster.
rendan Bracken, Churchill's parliamentary private secretary, fumed
nd told friends, 'It's as hard getting rid of him as getting rid of a corpse.'

Yet there was still the Labour Party for Chamberlain to consider. In
is round of calls that morning he had phoned Clement Attlee at the
House of Commons, explaining his view that he should continue in
ffice for the time being because of the German attack. 'Not at all,'
Attlee had replied; Chamberlain should make way as soon as possible.
The Labour leader, Dalton and Greenwood had then addressed
he issue of a statement of support Chamberlain had requested the
revious evening. The announcement they drafted fell far short of
what the struggling Prime Minister needed: 'The Labour Party, in view
f the latest series of abominable aggressions by Hitler, while firmly
onvinced that a drastic reconstruction of the Government is vital
nd urgent in order to win the war, reaffirms its determination to do its
tmost to achieve victory. It calls on all its members to devote all their
nergies to this end.'

Dalton and Attlee then shared a taxi to Waterloo station, where they
ere set to join other party delegates on the 11.34 train to Bournemouth.
There on the platform to see them off was Herbert Morrison, MP for
outh Hackney and the powerful leader of London County Council.
Morrison planned to delay leaving the capital until as late as possible:
t would look bad if he . . . was down at Bournemouth when the first
ombs fell here'. Such was the level of panic and uncertainty that day.

In Downing Street, the import of the statement Labour had just pu
out – the withholding of the party's support for the government despit
the crisis – had not been lost on those gathering for the day's secon
meeting of the War Cabinet. Horace Wilson, head of the civil servic
and Chamberlain's *eminence grise*, was particularly irate at the wordin;
Outside the Cabinet Room, Anthony Eden, the Dominions secretar
discussed the political state of play with Chamberlain loyalists Olive
Stanley, war secretary, and Lord Hankey, minister without portfolic
Stanley was 'indignant', having learned that Churchill was pressin;
for early changes to government, but Hankey's response was mor
surprising: 'Personally, I think that if there are to be changes, th
sooner they are made the better.'

The War Cabinet's discussion centred once again on whether t
commence bombing raids on Germany. Chief of the Air Staff Sir Cyr
Newall informed those present that while early reports suggested th
Luftwaffe had confined their operations to strictly military target;
evidence was now starting to emerge that French towns had bee;
bombed. It was agreed, in principle, that it would be justified for th
RAF to start attacking the Ruhr, but a final decision was delaye
until 5 p.m. while further information was gathered. Zero hour for th
advance of British land forces into Belgium was set for one o'clock
The home secretary, Sir John Anderson, warned his colleagues t
expect the arrival in boats of around 300,000 refugees from Belgiu
and Holland. It was decided to cancel the Whitsun holiday and as
people to return to work, and information minister Sir John Reith wa
instructed to put out an official announcement later that day.

At 1.40 Chamberlain and his wife Annie headed off to th
Dorchester Hotel for luncheon with Lord and Lady Halifax, who wer
temporary residents there; the party was made up by Sir John Dil
vice chief of the Imperial General Staff, and Princess Olga of Greec.
Beforehand, a number of Conservative MPs had visited the Prim
Minister to apologise for voting against the government on Wednesda
At lunch, Chamberlain seemed outwardly relaxed. Princess Olga foun
him 'calm and charming', showing 'little effects of the battle that ha

een waging about him'. He did, however, remain bitter about Lloyd George's personal attack on him in the debate, which had 'surpassed nything he had ever seen in Parliament'.

Chamberlain and his government were still holding on to power. Their fate would be decided in just over an hour's time, a hundred miles away in a basement room in a south coast hotel.

The English weather appeared blissfully unconcerned by the political nd military storms that were raging across Europe in spring 1940. 10 May had brought yet another glorious day, bathing Bournemouth in arm and golden sunlight, and many of the Labour Party delegates athering in the fashionable art deco Highcliff Hotel for their annual onference elected to take afternoon tea in deckchairs beneath olourful awnings on the garden terrace. Inside the hotel, their epresentatives on the party's National Executive Committee had o time for pleasantries. They had assembled in a large conference oom in the basement to consider the future of Chamberlain and his overnment. For an opposition party that commanded just a quarter of ne MPs in Parliament, this was a startling responsibility.

At 3.30 p.m. the chairman, Barbara Ayrton Gould, called the eeting to order. A former suffragette, who had once been arrested nd incarcerated in Holloway Prison for her part in a window-reaking campaign in Whitehall, Gould was one of five women in ne thirty-strong gathering. The atmosphere in the smoke-filled oom was lively, with even normally silent members contributing agerly to a lengthy debate. The sense that they were about to make istory was palpable. That the group would reject any collaboration ith a government led by Chamberlain, however reformed, was rtually assured. The Prime Minister was a bogey figure to many in ne Labour movement, reviled for helping to defeat the general strike ' 1926, resented for his key role in the hated national government ' 1931, and condemned for aiding and abetting the introduction of ne means test, the intrusive inquiry into the finances of unemployed eople who sought benefits.

Chamberlain had formally proposed a coalition with Labour whe
war broke out, on 1 September 1939, but the offer had been made wit
little enthusiasm, as he had scant regard for the qualities of the oppositio
leaders. The feeling was mutual, and the idea had been dismissed wit
equal contempt by a unanimous vote of the Parliamentary Labou
Party. Later, at the end of March 1940 – even before the Norway cris
– Chamberlain had told the King, George VI, of his plan to build a ne
War Cabinet whose members would be 'concerned with co-ordinatio
rather than departmental duties', and that it was his intention to fin
places for opposition parties. It was widely rumoured he had offere
Labour three seats in that Cabinet, but Attlee had dismissed th
proposal and nothing had come of the initiative.

If Labour loathed Chamberlain, there was no deep enthusiasm fo
either of the alternatives, Churchill or Halifax. But the pendulu
now appeared to be swinging in the direction of the former. Aft
the debacle of the Norway debate, Halifax had been tarnished b
association with Chamberlain, and the worrying developmen
across the Channel were convincing Labour's leaders that, i
Dalton's words, 'the strongest and most vigorous man' must now lea
the country. Attlee put to the executive the two questions agreed a
Number 10. The answers to both were unanimous: no to the first, bu
yes to the second.

It was a momentous moment, this effective toppling of a prim
minister. But just as the committee were absorbing the ramifications,
messenger entered the room with equally dramatic news: the Germar
were bombing Canterbury.

The information would later turn out to be false. Although this wa
indeed the very first attack on the English mainland in the war,
was no full-scale blitz. The Kent city had not been hit; a lone plar
had dropped five incendiary bombs that had landed harmlessly enoug
in a farm and a wood near the villages of Chilham and Petham a fe
miles away. But at that moment the men and women around the tab
were unaware of this. As far as they were concerned, Hitler ha
launched his long-feared bombing campaign against the people o

Britain. 'It helped some of us to insist that this was a day, not for words, but for action,' reflected Dalton.

A statement was quickly drafted – and agreed unanimously – that read, 'The National Executive Committee of the Labour Party is prepared to take its share of responsibility as a full partner in a new government under a new prime minister which could command the confidence of the nation.' Dalton claimed credit for inserting the words 'under a new prime minister'. He told his colleagues, 'If you don't make it absolutely plain, the Old Man will still hang on.' Crucially, they also made clear among themselves that this was a *decision*, not a *recommendation*; albeit with the proviso that to be binding, it would need the approval of the whole conference on Monday morning. Attlee told the executive he would ring Chamberlain immediately to inform him of the vote, and that he and Arthur Greenwood – not in the room – would thereafter return to London and begin negotiations about a future government.

The Labour leader had just returned to the lobby of the Highcliff at 4.45 p.m. when a phone rang. Chamberlain's private secretary in Downing Street was on the line: did the Labour leadership have answers to the Prime Minister's two questions? By way of response, Attlee read out the resolution. With a taxi waiting, he then asked Dalton if he would remain in Bournemouth and act as a liaison between him and the executive. He arrived at the station just in time to catch the 5.15. His party had made its decision; events had been set in train.

While the private secretary was taking down Attlee's statement in one corner of Downing Street, in the nearby Cabinet Room ministers were half an hour into their third meeting of the day. They had already been told about the Kent bombs, and now they were being updated on how German paratroopers had seized Rotterdam airport, paving the way for the landing of troop-carrying aircraft. General Sir Edmund Ironside, chief of the Imperial General Staff, struck an optimistic note. Although parachutists had clearly been dropped widely in Belgium, there had been no rush of armoured divisions across that country's border and he was doubtful whether a full-scale invasion was actually taking place.

As progress reports on the action along the Western Front were being completed, the private secretary came into the Cabinet Room and handed Chamberlain the dictated note from Bournemouth. The Prime Minister glanced at it, his expression unchanging, then put it to one side while he continued with the meeting.

Then, at around 5.30, with the main business on the agenda over, the Prime Minister brought up the 'additional' item. He revealed the contents of the piece of paper he had just been handed, reading out the Labour Party's statement that they would serve under an alternative Conservative leader. With some emotion in his voice, he told his ministers he now proposed to go to the Palace and offer his resignation to the King.

That evening, after the main BBC bulletin of the day at 9 p.m., Chamberlain made his final broadcast to the nation as Prime Minister. Eight months earlier, his speech announcing war with Germany had been a flat, uninspiring affair. Now he found the right words, showing magnanimity in his hour of defeat and displaying surprising emotion and resolution in the face of a formidable foe. Mindful of the public's unease over the recent discord in Westminster, he began with a pledge of unity. 'He [Hitler] has chosen a moment when, perhaps, it seemed to him that this country was entangled in the throes of a political crisis and he might find it divided against itself. If he has counted upon our internal division to help him, he has miscalculated the mind of this people.' Chamberlain acknowledged that 'some new and drastic action must be taken if confidence was to be restored to the House of Commons and the war carried on with the energy and vigour essential to victory'. The action needed, he made clear, was the formation of a national, coalition government with Labour and Liberal Party members joining the Conservatives. Then, for the first time, the country learned who was to be their new war leader. 'His Majesty has now entrusted to my friend and colleague, Mr Winston Churchill, the task of forming a new administration on a national basis, and in this task I have no doubt he will be successful.'

Churchill's accession, after what had been, to all intents and purposes, a parliamentary coup, undoubtedly gladdened the hearts of
many beyond Westminster. And within its walls, too, there was much
excitement – although some contemplated the prospect of his premiership, and the government he was to lead, with trepidation. Rab Butler,
Lord Halifax's ministerial colleague at the Foreign Office, declared that
'The good clean tradition of English politics, that of Pitt as opposed to
Fox, had been sold off to the greatest adventurer of modern political
history.' But within the ranks of Churchill's long-standing supporters
there was a mood of elation. 'What a moment to take on! He will
indeed have to ride the whirlwind and direct the storm,' recorded his
friend Violet Bonham Carter.

A few minutes before Chamberlain began his address to the nation,
Attlee and Greenwood had stepped off the train at Waterloo, to be
met by the *Daily Herald* journalist Maurice Webb and a naval officer
from the Admiralty. The Labour leaders now learned, for the first time,
the effect of their vote four hours earlier. Chamberlain had resigned,
and the new Prime Minister wished to see them immediately. Thus
they set off to the Admiralty, to play their part in forming the coalition
government that would win the war.

Chapter One
'A Ministry of all the Talents'
10 to 15 May 1940

In May 1936 Winston Churchill, then a backbencher, had pressed the Conservative-led national government of Stanley Baldwin to sharpen its defence policy in the face of the aggressive intent of Japan, Italy and, above all, Germany. The MP for Epping, in the latest of a series of speeches on rearmament, told the House of Commons that a new ministry of supply was needed to co-ordinate the work of the three service ministries – army, navy and air force – and put them on a stronger footing. To accusations that he was warmongering, he responded, 'Is there a man in the House who would not sacrifice his right hand here and now for the assurance that there would be no war in Europe for twenty years?'

Baldwin and Churchill had been close allies in government in the 1920s, as Prime Minister and Chancellor of the Exchequer respectively, before drifting apart over the issues of dominion status for India and rearmament. In the face of this latest attack, Baldwin, who regarded Churchill as an exasperated uncle might view an unruly nephew, confided to the deputy Cabinet secretary, Thomas Jones, a pointed insight into the character of his old ally: 'When Winston was born lots of fairies swooped down on his cradle gifts – imagination, eloquence, industry, ability, and then came a fairy who said "No one person has a right to

many gifts", picked him up and gave him such a shake and a twist
that he was denied judgement and wisdom. And that is why while we
delight to listen to him in this House we do not take his advice.'

Four years on, even as Churchill finally reached the 'top of the
greasy pole' – as Benjamin Disraeli had once put it – those doubts still
persisted among many at Westminster. While his courage, drive and
charisma were undeniable, and it could be hoped that age – he was now
sixty-five – had brought him the wisdom Baldwin had felt was lacking,
politicians of all parties still viewed Churchill as troublesome, and
worried about his impetuosity and egotism. 'Winston the adventurer'
had an innate relish for warfare, born of the feats of his famous ancestor
John, Duke of Marlborough, and his own military exploits in Cuba,
India and Sudan. On the eve of the First World War he had written
to his wife Clementine, 'I am interested, geared up and happy. Is it
not horrible to be built like that? The preparations have a horrible
fascination to me. I pray to God to forgive me for such fearful moods of
levity.' On 10 May 1940 this was a great strength, but also a potential
danger. He had been proved right about the threat posed by the Nazis,
so it was grudgingly accepted that he at least ought to be given the
chance to lead his country against it. He was not trusted, however, and
he began his premiership very much on trial.

In forming a coalition government it certainly helped that Churchill's
own career had never been circumscribed by party affiliation. He had
entered Parliament in 1900, as the Conservative MP for Oldham;
a predictable choice, given the Tory circles he had moved in, and
the example provided by his father, Randolph, who had served as
Chancellor of the Exchequer in Lord Salisbury's administration in the
1880s. But Winston had become disaffected with the Tories, vigor-
ously denouncing their association with wealth and property. He had
left the party in 1904, after which had followed twenty years with
the Liberals under the premierships of Henry Campbell-Bannerman,
Herbert Henry Asquith and David Lloyd George. In 1924, however,
increasingly alarmed by the spread of socialism and the rise of the

Labour Party, he had 're-ratted' to the Conservative fold; his retur
had been greeted reluctantly, although he had remained there eve
since.

Lord Beaverbrook, the newspaper magnate who was a close frien
and kindred spirit, once put Churchill's shifting loyalties in th
characteristically blunt, if inflated fashion. 'He has been everythin
in every party. He has held every view on every question. He has bee
apparently quite sincere in all his views. Perhaps he has convince
himself. But he is utterly unreliable in his mental attitude.' If Churchi
had a consistent political vision, it was wrapped up in a sense of Britain
historical continuity stretching back way beyond the Victorian er
into which he was born. For him, the history of England was that c
the onward march of individual liberty; fought for at home, but als
spread throughout the world with the British Empire. As a domesti
politician, he adhered to Edmund Burke's view that 'a state withou
the means of some change is without the means of its conservation
Hand in hand with that awareness of the necessity for occasiona
reform went his upholding of the ideal of 'noblesse oblige', by whic
enlightened men of his (aristocratic) class had a clear public duty t
govern justly, and address the sufferings of the poor and disadvantaged

Whatever political label might be bestowed on him – libera
reactionary, eighteenth-century Whig, Victorian Tory paternalist
Churchill's experience in government was unmatched. Having gaine
his first post as under-secretary of state for the colonies in 1905, he ha
thereafter, in both Liberal and Conservative administrations, serve
in almost every important Cabinet and government position, bar tha
of foreign secretary. After a reforming stint as President of the Board c
Trade, during which he introduced unemployment insurance and labou
exchanges (1908), Churchill had gone on to become home secretar
(1910), First Lord of the Admiralty (1911), Chancellor of the Duch
of Lancaster (1915), Minister of Munitions (1917), Secretary of Stat
for War and Air (1919), Secretary of State for the Colonies (1921
and Chancellor of the Exchequer (1924), before finally returning t
the Admiralty in 1939 in Chamberlain's War Cabinet.

Discussions about his 'judgement' often harked back to his first spell
at the Admiralty, to the Gallipoli campaign in early 1915. As First
Lord he had conceived a bold plan to forge an indirect route to victory
from the east, while the two sides were bogged down in interminable
trench warfare on the Western Front. The Royal Navy was to force its
way through the Dardanelles Straits and take Constantinople, thus
knocking Turkey out of the war, securing a supply route for Britain's
hard-pressed ally Russia, and inspiring the Balkan states to join the
Allied war effort against Austro-Hungary, thereby pressuring Germany.

When the naval assault foundered and the subsequent land attacks
disintegrated into a bloody mess on the Gallipoli peninsula in early
1916, with up to a quarter of a million Allied casualties, the generals
and politicians ran for cover, leaving the architect of the campaign
to shoulder nearly all the responsibility for its failure. Among those
who led the retreat from the battlefront in December 1915 had been
Major Clement Attlee of the 6th South Lancashire Regiment. The
last-but-one man to be evacuated from Suvla Bay, he refused to pin the
blame on Churchill. Many years later he would say of Gallipoli that
'he strategic conception was sound – the trouble was that it was never
adequately supported'.

So when the Labour leader arrived at the Admiralty late on Friday,
10 May 1940, to start negotiations over the new coalition, he bore no
resentment over the new Prime Minister's past military 'adventures'.
And since Labour had jettisoned its pacifist foreign policy, he and
his deputy Arthur Greenwood had stood shoulder to shoulder with
Churchill in opposition to appeasement.

For his part, Churchill recognised the debt he owed Labour for
administering the final, knockout blow against Chamberlain. He knew
he needed all the friends and allies he could find, as many in his own
party were furious at Chamberlain's departure and willing him to fail.
On a deeper level, at this moment of national crisis, he understood
that his administration had to command the broadest possible support.
As the talks commenced, therefore, Attlee and Greenwood would find
him in receptive mood.

Few rooms in Whitehall resonated with such history as the magnificen[t] Admiralty Board Room. It was here on the night of 6 November 180[5] that an exhausted, sweat-stained officer had arrived to tell Willia[m] Marsden, first secretary to the Admiralty, 'Sir, we have gained a grea[t] victory, but we have lost Lord Nelson.' A huge portrait of the admira[l] painted in 1799 by Leonardo Guzzardi after the Battle of the Nil[e] occupied a large portion of one wall.

The three men who sat down to business, overlooked by Nelson, o[n] that Friday evening in May 1940 hailed from a wide spectrum of Britis[h] life. Churchill was blessed with the accident of privilege. After hi[s] upbringing in the monumental surroundings of Blenheim Palace, cossete[d] by servants, he had been naturally drawn into high society through hi[s] vivacious mother, Jennie, while his father Randolph's dealings at th[e] very top of government had given him some early awareness of politic[s.] For a man with Churchill's talents and pedigree, entry into the inne[r] sanctums of British life had been virtually guaranteed.

Labour's leaders came from humbler backgrounds, although Attlee'[s] in particular, had not been disadvantaged. The son of a respected Londo[n] solicitor, he had at first followed the natural course of a comfortabl[e] conventional middle-class life: attending Haileybury College, a publi[c] school; reading history at Oxford; and being called to the bar by th[e] Inner Temple. His 'conversion' to socialism had come only after his firs[t] exposure to the raw poverty in London's East End while helping out a[t] a boys' club in Stepney. Greenwood, by contrast, had received a mor[e] obvious Labour upbringing. The son of a painter and decorator fro[m] Hunslet, Leeds, he had been educated at the local board school befor[e] winning a scholarship to Yorkshire College (later Leeds University[)] where he had studied history and economics. While Attlee, the socia[l] worker, had helped to improve basic living conditions among the poo[r] of London, Greenwood, the teacher, had sought to raise aspiration[s] when lecturing for the Workers' Educational Association in Leeds.

Both men had cut their teeth in government as members of Ramsa[y] MacDonald's ill-fated 1929–31 administration. As Minister of Healt[h] Greenwood had been one of its more successful members, improvin[g] idows' pensions and introducing the Housing Act (1930), which ermitted slum clearance and rebuilding. Attlee had served in the less gnificant roles of Chancellor of the Duchy of Lancaster and Postmaster eneral. Yet when Labour eventually called time on the leadership of ne pacifist George Lansbury in 1935, it was the diffident Attlee who pped the ballot, with the gregarious Greenwood third (after Herbert Iorrison). Even so, the tall, thin Greenwood, with his ready smile nd hearty laugh, was undoubtedly one of the country's best-liked oliticians; his weakness, which was by now well established, was drink. ttlee, sober, seemingly shy, with a laconic manner of speaking, was less fable and harder to read. His critics had repeatedly underestimated im, however; his quiet leadership had been efficient and effective, not ast during the dying days of the Chamberlain administration.

Attlee and Greenwood had arrived for their negotiations ith Churchill determined to claim Labour's reward for toppling 'hamberlain, but not to be obstructive. 'I was very conscious that in ne First World War there had been a lot of haggling over places,' Attlee :called. 'It seemed to me that this was the reason for some of the fail-:es of the military show then, and I was determined we would not aggle this time.' In the event there was no need for him to worry. Both e and Greenwood were offered places in a War Cabinet of five, and 'hurchill reassured them that Labour would be allocated more than a ird of the positions in the government. For a party with just a quarter ' the seats in Parliament, these were rich spoils.

The sticking point was the future of Neville Chamberlain. Churchill ad originally wanted to offer his predecessor – who remained leader ' the Conservative Party – the post of Chancellor of the Exchequer, a :ospect that horrified not just Labour, but the various groups of Tory bels. Instead he now proposed to make him Leader of the House of ommons. But again, Attlee 'was absolutely opposed to that. I didn't iink the House would stand it and certainly our people wouldn't.' hurchill quickly dropped the idea, although it was eventually agreed hamberlain would stay in the War Cabinet in the still important role ' Lord President of the Council.

There was swift agreement about the 'service' ministers: S
Archibald Sinclair (air), Labour's A.V. Alexander (navy) an
Anthony Eden (War Office). Then the discussion moved on to th
home and economic portfolios, with Churchill indicating he was kee
to have Herbert Morrison, Hugh Dalton and particularly Ernest Bevi
on board. Mobilising the country's workforce for the war effort woul
be crucial, and popular consent could not be gained by appointin
Tory ministers tainted by the hardship and unemployment of th
1930s. Churchill saw Bevin, general secretary of the Transport an
General Workers' Union, and a giant in the Labour movement, as th
man best placed to command the respect of the working class. Attle
agreed to sound out 'Ernie' in the morning. Bevin was not an MP, s
if he were willing to join the government he would quickly need to b
found a constituency.

'It is probably easier to form a Cabinet, especially a Coalitio
Cabinet, in the heat of battle than in quiet times,' Churchill woul
observe later. 'The sense of duty dominates all else, and person:
claims recede.' The process was further oiled by Attlee's pragmatisn
He did not press Churchill to include colleagues he believed fe
short of the mark. So there was no position for Frederick Pethwic
Lawrence, former Financial Secretary to the Treasury: 'too old', w:
Attlee's judgement (at sixty-eight he was just three years older tha
the Prime Minister). Nor did he recommend a place for so senic
a figure as Hastings Lee-Smith, former President of the Board (
Education: 'too slow'. These were 'bourgeois' MPs – like himself
and Attlee was keen to ensure a strong working-class representatio
in the new government.

Amicable and productive, this first session of coalition-building wer
on until the early hours. Attlee and Greenwood then left to report th
results, by telephone, to their colleagues at the Labour conference i
Bournemouth; Churchill, with no similar party obligations, conferre
with his inner circle before retiring to bed at 3 a.m. It had been
'pleasant talk', he reflected later; there would be much more of it i
the days to come.

he new Prime Minister received a sympathetic press on Saturday orning. 'OUR WAR PREMIER CHURCHILL' was the front-page headline the *Daily Mirror*, whose leader writer asserted that 'He is one of ose who have never been deceived by the character and purpose of ir treacherous enemies.' In similar vein, the *Daily Express* opined, lo man is better fitted to form a wartime Cabinet. He understands e mind of Hitler. He is capable of developing the powers of ingenuity d resource that this war demands. He will answer daring with ring.' The most glowing praise of all came, perhaps unexpectedly, om the *Manchester Guardian*, which asserted that Churchill 'has the onfidence of the nation even more than had Mr Lloyd George when became prime minister [in 1916]'.

Around Westminster, in offices emptied of civil servants for the hitsun bank holiday, anxious ministers spent a lonely day waiting r a telephone call or, even better, a summons from the Admiralty. eanwhile, the clubs and restaurants in St James's were unusually sy. Groups of MPs sat around disseminating the latest rumour and ssip – as well as the occasional hard fact – about the composition of e new government.

At 11 a.m., following fresh discussions with Churchill at Admiralty ouse, Attlee returned to the Commons and phoned Ernest Bevin at ansport House (the TGWU's headquarters on Smith Square), where e union boss had arrived to collect his papers before his journey wn to Bournemouth. Bevin told Attlee he approved of Labour's cision to join the Tories in coalition. 'You helped to bring the her fellow down; if the party did not take its share of responsibility, ey would say we were not great citizens but cowards.' But on the ea that he should join the government, as Minister of Labour, he avered: 'You have sprung it on me.' When they met face-to-face a w hours later, in Attlee's office, Bevin confided his fears that the inistry of Labour would remain 'a glorified conciliation board'. The bour leader assured him that it would be central to the war effort th added, substantial powers, so Bevin agreed to talk it through with e Trades Union Congress that weekend.

Over at the Liberal Party's headquarters in London's Gayfere Stree[t] Sir Archibald Sinclair was delighted to receive an offer to becom[e] Secretary of State for Air, although he was perturbed that such a seni[or] role did not merit a place for himself – and thus his party – in the W[ar] Cabinet. He wrote to Churchill, 'this is a formidable difficulty, an[d] unfortunately it is emphasised by the fact that I gave this as my reaso[n] for refusing the invitation of your predecessor at the beginning of th[e] war'. Sinclair would be assuaged, however, by assurances that he wou[ld] be invited to War Cabinet when there were 'major questions of polic[y] to discuss, and that this would be made clear when the announcemen[t] of his position appeared in the newspapers.

At 5.30 p.m. Attlee phoned Dalton and his colleagues [in] Bournemouth to keep them abreast of developments, and to seek th[e] approval of the National Executive Committee for the governmen[t] posts he had been offered. Herbert Morrison was unimpressed, sayin[g] 'it didn't sound like a Government which would stand up any bett[er] than the last one, and that it would not impress the public'. Others o[f] the NEC wanted assurances that MPs with backgrounds and experti[se] in industry would find places in the new government. On this, Attle[e] after consultation with Churchill, was able to satisfy them, and [at] 6 p.m., by a vote of 17 to 1, the committee finally agreed that Labo[ur] should join the coalition under the terms offered.

So at 9 p.m. on Saturday night, the first appointments to the ne[w] government were released to the press. The five-man War Cabin[et] was to comprise Churchill (Prime Minister and Minister of Defence[)], Chamberlain (Lord President), Attlee (Lord Privy Seal), Lord Halif[ax] (Secretary of State for Foreign Affairs) and Greenwood (Minist[er] without Portfolio). The others were Sinclair (Secretary of State f[or] Air), A.V. Alexander (First Lord of the Admiralty) and Anthon[y] Eden (Secretary of State for War). From these appointments season[ed] political onlookers deduced that Churchill had learned two key lesso[ns] from his experience in government in the previous war. First, th[e] smaller a War Cabinet the more quickly and efficiently decisions cou[ld] be made. Second, having witnessed the then Prime Minister Herbe[rt]

quith's failure to control his generals on the Western Front, he was
termined that military policy should stay in the hands of politicians,
t soldiers or sailors. To the latter end, appointing himself Minister
Defence as well as Prime Minister made him the permanent chair
the Defence Committee of the Cabinet, which included the service
nisters (war, air and the Admiralty) and their chiefs of staff. In
dition, it would emerge that Churchill was also to lead the Chiefs
Staff Committee, where he could deal with the heads of the armed
vices directly, in the absence of their political masters.

At noon on Sunday, Churchill's first appointees were summoned
Buckingham Palace to be formally sworn in to their new offices.
these, Eden was the one with reason not to be entirely satisfied
h his position. At the outbreak of war, he was disappointed not
be given a service ministry; now he had one, but without a place
the War Cabinet where many felt he belonged. The charming,
alistic yet hard working forty-three-year-old already had significant
vernment experience, as Lord Privy Seal with a special brief for the
ague of Nations (1933–5), and then as foreign secretary (1935–8).
hile Churchill had his own group of loyal followers in the House
Commons dubbed 'The Old Guard', Eden had his devotees too –
isively named 'The Glamour Boys' by the irritated Tory whips.

Eden had resigned as foreign secretary in protest over Chamberlain's
gotiations with Mussolini, and then established his place firmly in
e anti-appeasement camp by opposing the Munich agreement. Now,
h the army in what he described as an 'inglorious state', he was
prehensive about his new role and anticipated his relationship with
urchill would be 'choppy'. But for the moment he was content to
uckle down to the job and wait patiently for preferment.

Due to some novel convention, Eden – together with Sinclair
d Alexander – found themselves taking the oath of office before
ville Chamberlain, instead of the King. The war secretary found
former leader in a depressed state. 'He looked ill and was clearly
ting it all. He said that he was staying in the new Government
h a heavy heart.'

One of the most crucial appointments still to be made was the Minis
of Supply. Britain's armed services needed equipping comprehensiv
and urgently, and early on in their discussions Churchill and Attlee h
identified Herbert Morrison as by far the most suitable candidate
the job. In his interview with 'Mr London' that afternoon, the Pri
Minister left the Labour man under no illusion about the burden ab
to be placed on his shoulders. 'He said, I don't offer you cheerfulne
I don't offer you good fortune: I don't offer you quick successes,' v
Morrison's memory of the conversation. Churchill added, 'I offer y
nothing but tears and blood and sweat and toil,' a sentiment tl
would become familiar to a number of Cabinet ministers over the n
twenty-four hours. 'Nevertheless, he did it in such a way,' Morris
remembered, 'that, although it was a most cheerless invitation to a l
of anxiety and stress and trouble, you just felt you would have beer
worm if you had said "No" – and that's how he meant it to be.'

Over at the Ministry of Information, Sir John Reith learned tl
he was to be moved on from his job – and out of the Cabinet – bef
he actually received the official call from the Admiralty. 'How filt
this treatment – and what a *rotten* government,' was the reacti
of this fiercest of Churchill's critics, on hearing of his departure
BBC radio's evening news. His replacement, Alfred Duff Cooper, v
a popular choice, however, widely admired as a principled politici
(he had resigned as First Lord of the Admiralty over the Muni
agreement) and a gifted writer and journalist.

Just three other appointments were released to the press tl
evening: Morrison's, together with those of Sir Kingsley Wood
Chancellor of the Exchequer, and Lord George Lloyd, a dieh;
imperialist, as Secretary of State for the Colonies. But one other v
as good as signed and sealed: Churchill had devoted a good part
the weekend to wooing Lord Beaverbrook for the post of Minister
Aircraft Production, and the peer had left Admiralty House havi
given his word that he would accept the job.

Their deliberations with Churchill complete, Attlee and Greenwc
travelled back to Bournemouth so that Attlee could prepare his spee

Labour's conference, the party's ultimate authority, the following
y. His one remaining task was to inspire Labour's rank and file to
ly behind the new coalition.

onday's newspapers by and large approved of the emerging team.
averbrook's *Daily Express* described Sir Archibald Sinclair as not
erely an affable aristocrat with a gift for oratory' but a man 'of force and
e who sticks to his principles'. Anthony Eden's 'liking for innovations'
ould be a virtue at the War Office, while Herbert Morrison's was 'a
ost admirable appointment' for a man who had 'managed the London
ounty Council with great skill'. Elsewhere, the response bordered on
e eulogistic. For the *Yorkshire Post* the new government was 'in itself a
vid symbol of national solidarity. Every type of home in the land from
e country mansion to the meaner back-to-back home in Leeds or
anchester may feel itself represented in it . . . this is something much
ore than a Ministry of All The Talents; it is a ministry embracing all
at is sturdy and true in British democracy.'

That morning Attlee addressed Labour's annual conference. His
reements with Churchill had already been endorsed by every other
y body in Labour's complex bureaucracy – including the general
ouncil of the Trades Union Congress and the executive of the
rliamentary party – and few doubted that he would get the backing
the delegates assembled in Bournemouth. But there remained scope
r embarrassment from Labour's hard left and pacifist wings. As it was,
ttlee made short work of them, declaring that he had 'little patience
ith those who today, in face of these tremendous events, talk clap-
ap about imperialist wars and so on'. He assured his audience Labour
as joining the government 'as partners and not as hostages', although
e warned bluntly, 'We shall none of us get all that you want.'

Attlee was not a gifted orator, but he spoke with a quiet resolve and
oquence that befitted the occasion. The final flourish was that of the
rincipled internationalist. 'Friends, we are standing here today to take
decision not only on behalf of our own movement, but on behalf of
abour all over the world. We have to stand today for the souls in prison

in Czechoslovakia, in Poland, yes, and in Germany . . . life witho
liberty is not worth living. Let us go forward and win that liberty a
establish that liberty forever on the sure foundation of social justic
He left the stage to resounding applause and a standing ovation, a
the vote on the NEC's recommendation – taken in his absence, af
he had hurried from the hall to hear the Prime Minister's speech in t
Commons that afternoon – was won overwhelmingly, by 2,413,0
votes to 170,000.

While Attlee was speaking in Bournemouth, Churchill, st
ensconced at the Admiralty, had been interviewing prospecti
members of the new Government. Around mid-morning three can
dates took their seats in the dining room adjacent to his study to aw
their call. The trio were markedly different from each other in ch
acter and background, the embodiment of the *Yorkshire Post*'s talk c
'symbol of national solidarity'.

The most experienced was Leo Amery, aged sixty-six, an c
friend of the Prime Minister's from as far back as their schooldays
Harrow. In their first meeting, Churchill, the bumptious new boy, h
inexplicably pushed Amery, head of the house, into the swimmi
pool, although no grudges had arisen from this unpromising encount
young Winston would write Leo's English essays for him, while L
had reciprocated by helping Winston with his Latin prose. A few ye
later they had both been journalists during the Second Boer Wa
Amery for *The Times*, Churchill for the *Morning Post* – and at o
point had narrowly escaped capture together.

Elected to Parliament as Conservative MP for Birmingham Sou
in 1911, Amery had held Cabinet posts as First Lord of the Admira
and colonial secretary under Andrew Bonar Law and Stanley Baldw
respectively. During the 1930s he had joined Churchill in advocati
significant rearmament. But the two old friends, despite mutual Tc
instincts, disagreed about much else – free trade, the gold standard a
especially the best future for the dominions and colonies of the Briti
Empire. On the latter subject, Amery favoured self-government
India, an idea anathema to Churchill.

Second in line outside the Prime Minister's study that morning was lcolm John MacDonald, aged thirty-nine, MP for Bassetlaw, and of Labour and then national government Prime Minister Ramsay cDonald. Like Churchill, he was used to being reviled by large tions of his former party, having deserted it to follow his father o the National Labour ranks in 1931. MacDonald and Churchill fered on nearly every political issue, but Churchill appreciated the inger man's personality – bright, entertaining with a marvellous se of humour and an explosive laugh. MacDonald played as rd as he worked, and had many friends in London's theatreland, :luding Laurence Olivier, Ivor Novello and actress and singer rothy Dickson.

The third interviewee was Ellen Cicely Wilkinson, aged forty-nine. our MP for Jarrow and a writer of polemical novels, she was known Red Ellen' – a moniker that owed as much to the flaming colour of hair as to her commitment to socialism. The daughter of a cotton rker from Manchester, Wilkinson's fiery soapbox oratory had won urchill's admiration; during his discussions with Attlee two days lier, he told the Labour leader he was 'very keen' to have her in his vernment. Like the Prime Minister, she had spotted the dangers of zism very early on. In 1933, she had written a pamphlet entitled *The* *ror in Germany*, outlining Nazi outrages against ordinary people, and had served on a legal enquiry into the faked Reichstag fire. (The zis duly took note and denounced her as 'a red-haired agitator'.)

Wilkinson emerged from her audience with Churchill as parliamen- y secretary at the Ministry of Pensions. Amery was disappointed, wever. Because of his seniority and his influence, he had been ping for a post central to the war effort. It had been intimated to n the day before that he would be made Secretary of State for the minions, with added responsibilities as the Prime Minister's deputy the military chiefs of staff. Instead he was offered Secretary of State India; an important job, but ultimately bound to bring him into iflict with Churchill, and not a post that would take him into the r Cabinet.

When MacDonald followed Amery into the office, he was surpris
to see Churchill striding up and down, head bowed in deep thoug
hands clutching the lapels of his jacket, as if in the throes of a speech
the House of Commons. The Prime Minister looked up quizzically, th
resumed pacing, before turning to face MacDonald. 'My dear Malcolr
he declared, 'I'm glad to see you. I've nothing to offer you except .
and then, after a brief hesitation, 'blood and toil, tears and sweat.'

After a moment or two the Prime Minister emerged from I
declamatory diversion and snapped back into friendly informali
'I want you to be Minister of Health in my government,' he tc
MacDonald, explaining it would be a crucial role once Hitler launch
an all-out attack on Britain and the casualties swelled. As MacDona
left the room and passed through the private secretary's office,
stopped to chat to Amery, who had lingered on. 'Did he also offer y
blood and sweat and toil and tears?' the new India secretary asked.
MacDonald's affirmative, Amery observed, 'He must be rehearsing I
speech for Parliament this afternoon.'

When Churchill stood up to address the Commons for the fi
time as Prime Minister, a few hours later, the words were not lc
in coming. Those with an appreciation of oratory past detect
resonances of Garibaldi's speech to his 4,000 legionaries as the Fren
were poised to enter Rome in 1849. 'Let him who wishes to contin
the fight against the foreigner follow me,' the Italian freedom figh
had urged his troops. 'I cannot offer him either money or food. I of
him hunger, thirst, forced marches, battles and death.'

Of his new government, Churchill said it had been necessary
appoint the War Cabinet and the service ministers in just a single c
'on account of the extreme urgency and rigour of events'. Moreov
it was 'the evident wish and will of Parliament and the nation that
should be conceived on the broadest possible basis and that it shou
include all parties'. After the speeches had finished, and the vote h
been taken, the result was 381 to 0.

The House gave a welcoming cheer as Churchill led his new te;
of ministers into the chamber from behind the Speaker's chair. Attl

lexander and Sinclair sat to his left, while Kingsley Wood and
orrison flanked him on the right, leaving room for one more body
1 that side. A few moments later Neville Chamberlain entered the
ouse and filled the space, his ecstatic reception easily overshadowing
at given to his successor. Later, when one of the Chamberlain
yalists, Patrick Spens, MP for Ashford, referred in his speech to 'Our
ader, the lord president of the council', there was a further outburst
f applause for the deposed Prime Minister – with which Churchill,
emonstrably and loudly, joined in. This vehement demonstration of
yalty was proof, if any was needed, of the long road Churchill still
ad to travel to win the trust of his party.

The new Prime Minister's handling of the appointment process was
ot without setbacks. Oliver Stanley, dismissed as war secretary, had
een offered the alternative, if lesser, post of Dominions secretary by
ay of consolation, but had also been reminded of his shortcomings.
'ou may be right when you say I lack drive and initiative,' Stanley
esponded hotly, 'but if I do, I ought not to be a Minister, and if you
nink I do, then you ought not to ask me to be one.' Nor was the former
ar leader, Lloyd George, in a mood to succumb to blandishments.
Despite the seventy-seven-year-old's irritation at Churchill's decision
ot to offer him a place in the War Cabinet (because he refused to work
rith Chamberlain), he had made it known that he would be willing
o take on the Ministry of Food. But Lord Woolton, a Chamberlain
ppointment, was already in place, and on advice from others Churchill
ras not minded to move him. When Lloyd George was offered a
ifferent role, as Minister of Agriculture, he turned it down.

Churchill received better news from another, more vital quarter.
After much discussion with union colleagues in Bournemouth, and
eassurances from Attlee and Greenwood, Ernest Bevin decided to
vrite to the Prime Minister and accept the post of Minister of Labour
nd National Service. Here, arguably, was the most telling proof that
he new government would indeed be as broadly based as possible; no
ruly national coalition would have been complete without a leading
rade unionist.

All his life Churchill had been a ferocious critic of socialism: 'monstrous and imbecile conception which can find no real footho in the brains and hearts of a sensible people'. And yet the pragmatist him recognised that in wartime a planned sharing of resources acro society would be essential. During the First World War, in a speech his Dundee constituents, he had dared to use the 's' word in favourab terms. For the purpose of destroying the German military system, l had told his audience, 'Our whole nation must be organised – must l *socialised*, if you like the word.' He knew that he needed someone in h cabinet to do that 'socialising' for him in the fight against Hitler, ar the choice of Bevin was little short of inspired.

What was more remarkable was that these two men were o adversaries, and had never been more so than during the general stril of 1926, when workers across industry downed tools in protest again the worsening lot of Britain's coal miners. Bevin blamed Churchi then at the Treasury as chancellor, for having destroyed the chances a peace settlement between trade union leaders and the pit owners. I concluded from that bitter experience, making reference once more Churchill's ill-fated Dardanelles campaign, 'It is not that Mr Church is not a brilliant man, but it is not safe to leave the destinies of millio of people in the hands of a man with an unstable mind, a man wl can fly off at a tangent as he did in the war, with such terrible resul for millions of men.'

By May 1940, however, Churchill and Bevin had put their differenc aside and were working well together, driven by the common aim defeating Germany and bound by the necessities of wartime. Church had recently sought Bevin's assistance in mobilising part of the trawl fleet for war service as minesweepers and auxiliary minelayers, and had been willingly given. Bevin had also recruited a 'flying column' dockers who could be moved from one port to another to ensure th swift delivery of food, munitions or raw materials for the war industrie

Bevin accepted in a letter to Churchill on 13 May, on conditic that the post should have the widest possible brief. 'It is imperativ that its position and place should be strengthened in order to de

ith the problem of labour organisation and supply, and the Ministry
ust therefore be in a position to make its contribution to the actual
ganisation of production so as to secure the right utilisation of labour,
d not merely be regarded as an institution to supply the personnel.'

he first full meeting of the new War Cabinet, scheduled for 6.30
e same evening, was held in its traditional gathering place in the
abinet Room at 10 Downing Street, the heart of British government
cision-making ever since Sir Robert Walpole, the original First
ord of the Treasury (Prime Minister was a derogatory term in those
ays) had taken up residency in the 1740s. Just inside the entrance
this 'cramped, close space', as Lord Salisbury, Prime Minister in
e 1880s, described it, stood two Corinthian columns, supporting a
oulded entablature which wended its way around the entire room.
ominating the rest of the space was a 25ft table around which stood
venty or so curved, leather-upholstered mahogany chairs, dating back
William Gladstone's time. Only the Prime Minister's seat, with its
ack to the mottled grey marble fireplace, had arms. Cabinet ministers
ere allotted a chair according to rank, and black blotters inscribed
ith their titles marked their places.

On two of the walls were large bookcases that housed the Prime
Minister's library. On the wall at the far end of the room a huge map
isplayed the state of the war. Above the fireplace, on the adjacent
all, a portrait by the French artist Jean-Baptiste van Loo captured
e physical likeness, and much of the character, of Number 10's
rst occupant; from here Sir Robert, the coarse, convivial political
anipulator, with his thick, arched eyebrows, brown eyes, protruding
wer lip, double chin and ruddy complexion, dressed in the black and
hite robes of the chancellor, kept proud watch over his successors.

Nineteen gathered around the Cabinet table that evening. On
Churchill's left sat Chamberlain, and next to him Attlee and then
Duff Cooper. To the Prime Minister's right were the Cabinet secretary
ir Edward Bridges, General Hastings 'Pug' Ismay (Churchill's military
ecretary) and Air Chief Marshal Sir Cyril Newall. Directly facing

Churchill, across the table, was Lord Halifax, the foreign secretar
On his right was Sir Alexander Cadogan, permanent under-secretar
of state at the Foreign Office, with A.V. Alexander, First Lord of th
Admiralty, and Sir Dudley Pound, First Sea Lord, further along. Le
of Halifax were Arthur Greenwood, Anthony Eden and General S
Edmund Ironside. At the head of one end of the table sat Sir Archiba
Sinclair and Lieutenant-Colonel Ian Jacob, assistant military secretar
to the War Cabinet: at the other end were home secretary Sir Joh
Anderson (a Chamberlain appointment whom Churchill had bee
content to retain), Minister of Shipping Robert Hudson, and Captai
Angus Nicholl of the Royal Navy (the fourth member of the Cabine
secretariat present).

The meeting began with much uncertainty about Germany's nex
move. Ironside was in no doubt that 'the battle that could decid
the Empire was beginning'; it was clear the enemy's heavy armou
continued to advance at various points across the Western Front. B
as yet there were no signs of infantry columns mobilising in support.
was impossible to determine whether the main German effort woul
be directed 'through Luxembourg against the left of the Maginot Lin
or through Maastricht'.

Thereafter the discussion moved on to the unresolved questic
of whether this was the right time to bomb Germany. Churchi
led a lengthy debate, putting the pros and cons. There was mor
justification: 'the enemy by the many atrocities he had alread
committed, had given ample justification in the eyes of the wor
for an attack on the Ruhr'. Then there was the military rational
an attack now would force the Germans to retaliate when they wer
unprepared to do so, and before Britain's fighter and bomber strengt
had been worn down by prolonged operations. Sir Cyril Newall, th
prime advocate of bombing the enemy's industrial heartland, believe
the military initiative needed to be wrested away from German
in this he won support from Arthur Greenwood, who thought 'th
arguments in favour of making the attack were very strong'. But range
against them were Chamberlain, Sinclair and Halifax. The ex-Prim

inister led the way, saying all the RAF's fighters and bombers should
concentrated on supporting the army in Belgium and France. He
orried that if and when the Germans retaliated, they would find the
fences of Britain's aerodromes and aircraft factories in too weak a
ate to resist.

Sinclair too was concerned about Britain's weakness in the air. The
r staff had calculated that sixty fighter squadrons were needed for
'adequate' defence of the country, and at present there were just
irty-nine. Halifax felt that 'it was in the interest of the nation in the
eaker position, especially if it had great potential development, to
frain from exposing that potential to damage'. He would be 'gravely
neasy' if the decision were made to bomb Germany at this time. The
ime Minister summed up by saying that in view of the 'balanced
guments' for and against an attack, it would be best to postpone a
cision for a further three or four days. By that time it would be clear
hether the great battle had started or not'.

After two hours, and a final word from Churchill that he planned
write to the American president, Franklin Roosevelt, to ask for
ar material, in particular fighter planes, the meeting closed. First
pressions of the new personnel were mixed. 'Do Greenwood,
ttlee, Sinclair and Alexander strengthen the party so?' wrote the
eptical Cadogan. According to Halifax, 'there is no comparison
tween Winston and Neville as a chairman'. But Ironside, for one,
d been impressed by the contributions of the new recruits. 'Attlee,
reenwood and Alexander are definitely better than the men we
d before.'

15 May the greater part of Churchill's government was in place,
th just a handful of positions – mainly of His Majesty's Household
to be filled. There would eventually be eighty-four members of the
tional coalition: forty-eight Conservatives, eighteen from Labour,
e Liberals, six Liberal Nationals, two from the National Labour
rganisation, three Nationals and two Independents. Appropriately,
e pair who had drawn up the suggestions for much of this great

coalition were to all intents and purposes sworn foes: Churchil‍
parliamentary private secretary Brendan Bracken, a slick, energet‍
and amusing operator, had been the new premier's loyal politic‍
supporter and close friend for the greater part of twenty years, whi‍
Captain David Margesson had been an urbane, charming, prefectori‍
chief whip to four successive prime ministers.

Behind Margesson's back, Bracken would disparagingly refer to hi‍
as 'The Parachutist', in reference to how this arch Chamberlaini‍
had now landed in the enemy camp, but together they collaborat‍
effectively. Harold Nicolson, who was one of the final appointment‍
as junior minister to Duff Cooper at the Ministry of Information, w‍
given an entertaining account of the Cabinet-making process.

> [Bracken] sat up until three in the morning with David Margesson
> going through lists. Winston was not in the least interested once
> the major posts had been filled, and kept on trying to interrupt
> them by discussing the nature of war and the changing rules
> of strategy. Meanwhile they would come back to their list, and
> Brendan would say, 'Well what about So-and-So?' Margesson
> would reply, 'Strike him out. He's no good at all.' 'Why then,'
> Brendan would ask, 'did you appoint him?' 'Oh well,' Margesson
> said, 'he was useful at the time.'

It was Bracken, though, who was the more proactive during t‍
selection process, often slipping scribbled submissions on to Churchil‍
desk at the Admiralty. 'Humble Suggestions', read one, proposi‍
Chamberlain for a job of 'Co-ordinating Economics', Conservati‍
Captain Euan Wallace as a peer and Secretary of State for Scotlan‍
and Labour's Hugh Dalton as Minister for Shipping. These were amo‍
the ideas that never came to pass, but many others did.

With the Labour members on board, Churchill's ministry was a f‍
more diverse group than the previous administration, with mark‍
contrasts of generation, class, education, occupation and region. T‍
classic public schools still had plenty of representatives – a third of t‍

oalition government (twenty-eight) had been educated at Eton and
Iarrow – but there were also alumni from the likes of Stockwell Road
oard School (Herbert Morrison), Barton Hill Elementary School
A.V. Alexander), Penyrheol Board Elementary School (David
Grenfell, Labour's secretary for mines), Ardwick Higher Elementary
Grade School (Ellen Wilkinson) and Leeds Grammar School
Conservative Patrick Munro, Lord of the Treasury).

An aristocrat may have led the government, and there were still
iumerous descendants of politicians, diplomats, administrators and
oldiers in its ranks, but working-class MPs – urban and rural – had
lso found places. Six of the latter had been miners – two of them,
George Hall (Labour's Under-secretary of State for the Colonies)
nd David Grenfell, had gone down the pit at the age of twelve –
vhile Sir Walter Womersley, Conservative MP for Grimsby, had been
mployed to drive a horse and cart at a Bradford mill when only ten.
The coalition included the son of a blacksmith (A.V. Alexander),
he son of a grocer (Labour education minister James Chuter Ede), a
isherman's boy (Ernest Brown, Liberal National Secretary of State for
icotland), a draper's apprentice (Labour's Joseph Westwood, Brown's
unior minister), a police constable's son (Herbert Morrison) and, most
notably, the son of an agricultural labourer and a domestic servant
Ernest Bevin).

Parliament in 1940 was largely composed of the generation of MPs
who had fought in the First World War. They had all lost family and
riends in the conflict, and their views had been profoundly shaped by
heir gruelling experiences on the Western Front and in other theatres
of war. Thus Churchill's government contained several men who
nad performed with great courage on the battlefield. Seven had won
he coveted Military Cross: Anthony Eden, Herwald Ramsbotham
President of the Board of Education), William Morrison (Postmaster
General), Sir Edward Grigg (Under-secretary of State for War), John
estyn Llewellin (Minister of Aircraft Production), Ernest Brown and
Harold Balfour (air minister), who had flown Sopwith Camels for the
Royal Flying Corps.

Hugh Dalton, Labour's Minister of Economic Warfare, had won th
Italian government's Medaglia al Valore Militaire when serving wit
the Royal Artillery, in recognition of his 'contempt for danger' durir
the retreat that followed the Battle of Caporetto. The Liberal Nation
Geoffrey Shakespeare (junior minister in the Dominions ministr
had like Clement Attlee fought with great distinction at Gallipo
while Harold Macmillan and Alfred Duff Cooper had displayed simil
bravery under fire in the trenches in Flanders. Herbert Morrison ha
shown courage of a rather different kind. Blind in one eye from birth
his disability would have granted him exemption from service in th
First World War, but instead he had chosen to register as a conscientio
objector on socialist grounds, applying to do civilian work for th
national benefit, as a gardener at Letchworth Garden City.

What Churchill's ministry lacked, in any numbers, were wome
They were still uncommon in frontline British politics, the breakthroug
having come only as recently as 1929, a year after universal suffrag
when Margaret Bondfield was made the first ever female Cabin
member, as Minister of Labour, by Ramsay MacDonald. Church
chose just two women for his administration: Ellen Wilkinson ar
Florence Horsbrugh, MP for Dundee, who was appointed parliamenta
secretary at the Ministry of Health. A third, Janet 'Jennie' Adamso
MP for Dartford, was made a parliamentary private secretary – a nor
governmental role – at the Ministry of Pensions. But there were son
outstanding candidates among the other twelve who sat among th
615 MPs in the House of Commons. The talents of the redoubtab
social reformer Eleanor Rathbone (Independent), who had also bee
an early critic of Nazism, could have been harnessed to the governmer
cause. And although there was already one Lloyd George – Gwilyr
the second son of the former Prime Minister – in the government,
place might equally have been found for his sister Megan, Liberal M
for Anglesey.

Churchill had historically been uncomfortable with the presenc
of women in the Commons, though. The only female politician in h
social circle, indeed, was Violet Bonham Carter, Asquith's daughte

hom he had given a key role in his anti-fascist group 'The Focus' in
ie 1930s. Bonham Carter, one of the most effective parliamentary
>eakers of her day, had been introduced to Churchill at a dinner party
1 1906 and they had remained close friends ever since.

There was one other key recruit to the administration: Churchill's
mg-standing scientific adviser, the eccentric Sir Frederick Lindemann,
rofessor of Experimental Philosophy at Oxford. To his close-knit
ircle of friends, which included the Churchill family, 'the Prof' was
>yal, affectionate and generous. But to others – especially scientific
vals – he could be chilly, arrogant and boastful. He had a deep dislike
>r the country of his birth, Germany, and his political views were
om the far right, with a firm belief in inherited wealth, inequality
nd white supremacy. Teetotal, vegetarian and non-smoking, he was
n outstanding sportsman, a tennis player who had won tournaments
ll over Europe and even competed at Wimbledon in both the singles
nd doubles tournaments in 1920.

The Prof's scientific method was both practical and imaginative.
During the First World War he had worked out how a pilot might
xtract himself from a spin by personally testing his theory, learning to
y and risking his own life in the process. His great value to Churchill
- other than feeding Winston's curiosity about science – was his ability
o translate long, complex tracts and papers into short, succinct notes,
>erfectly tailored to Churchill's preferred tool of written communi-
:ation, the brief minute. For this reason, at the beginning of the war,
Churchill had asked the Prof to form a small statistical branch at the
\dmiralty to analyse and interpret data bearing on naval matters.
There Lindemann had gathered around him a group of young, brilliant
nen from the universities (mainly economists and a scientist or two).
When Churchill moved to Downing Street, so Lindemann and his
boys' went with him, though here the scope of their work was greatly
:nlarged. They were now to evaluate all the key trends in the war
:conomy: manpower requirements, armaments output, ship produc-
:ion, the losses inflicted on shipping in the Atlantic, food production
nd rationing.

The Prof was by no means the only outside expert Churchill drafte
in to the heart of government. Indeed, one of its key features would b
the crucial (yet often unnoticed) roles that 'technocrats' played on th
Home Front – men such as shipping specialist Lord Leathers, industri:
administrator Andrew Rae Duncan and banknote manufacturer Lor
Wyndham Portal. Like Lloyd George in the previous war, Churchi
valued the fresh invention and imagination these men brought to th
dusty corridors and the often closed minds of Whitehall, and if h
could place them in ministerial positions, he would.

As the Prime Minister surveyed his government, he proclaimed
to be the most broadly based in British political history. 'From Lor
Lloyd of Dolobran on the right to Miss Ellen Wilkinson on the left
he would proudly tell anyone who asked.

On Tuesday, 14 May, the day after his 'blood, toil, tears and swea
speech in the House of Commons, the *Evening Standard* published th
latest cartoon by David Low, the left-leaning New Zealander whos
relationship with Churchill had been a chequered one until the tw
men were united by their opposition to appeasement in the 1930s. B
now, Low believed Churchill was the only man with the energy an
appetite to sustain Britain through the battle ahead. To that end, an
with the purpose of helping to bolster public morale, he drew a cartoo
entitled 'All Behind You, Winston'. It depicted the Prime Ministe
rolling his sleeves up and marching determinedly forward, followed b
Attlee, Bevin, Morrison, Chamberlain, Halifax, Greenwood, Sinclai
Eden, Amery, Duff Cooper and Alexander – the Cabinet appointe
to that date. Behind them loomed endless ranks of men and wome
the people of Britain, marching in their wake, seemingly willing the
political leaders on to meet the danger.

It was an inspiring image, although its optimism was at odds wit
the reality of events on the continent. France and Belgium were no
under the most severe strain from the advancing German army, and
they were to fall, the invasion of Britain would surely follow. Churchi
and his ranks of ministers had a herculean task on their hands.

Chapter Two

'No longer two nations but one'

14 May to 5 July 1940

The defence of western Europe was unravelling at terrifying speed. By nightfall on day one of Operation *Fall Gelb*, almost all of the Grand Duchy of Luxembourg was under German occupation. Four days later, the Luftwaffe's relentless bombing of unprotected Rotterdam persuaded the Dutch to surrender. In Belgium, after the early capture of the Liège forts – including the massive Eben-Emael, reputedly the strongest in the world – the Allied armies were in retreat; Brussels could hold out no longer than 17 May.

Meanwhile, in France, the Maginot Line, eighty-seven miles long and the most extensive, elaborate system of defensive fortifications ever constructed, had been exposed as a folly. The German high command had merely ignored it, instead sending its finest Panzer divisions crashing through the supposedly impenetrable Ardennes, with its thick woods and narrow winding roads. There the ten weakest, least-trained, worst-equipped divisions of the French army proved incapable of holding the line, and the RAF's efforts to destroy the vital bridges over the River Meuse failed. By 15 May, the way was clear for the Wehrmacht to push on deep into France, and cut off and surround the Allies' withdrawal from Belgium.

Day after day, Churchill and his ministers faced desperate demands from the French government to send more fighter planes across the

Channel to aid the beleaguered Allied troops. On 15 May Air Chief Marshal Sir Hugh Dowding was invited to the War Cabinet to make his case for resisting those entreaties. It was a compelling performance; he dramatically pulled from his pocket a graph illustrating the scale of losses of the Hawker Hurricane, Britain's prime fighter plane. Pointing to a red line on the diagram that clearly plummeted downward, he told ministers, 'This red line shows the wastage of Hurricanes in the last few days. If the line goes on at the same rate for the next ten days, there won't be a single Hurricane left in France or England!'

The War Cabinet's thoughts had already begun to turn from the defence of western Europe to the protection of Britain. A growing fear of the arrival of German paratroopers – fed by lurid newspaper reports – had spurred the war secretary, Anthony Eden, to propose a volunteer force to defend the country's small towns and villages. In a BBC broadcast on 14 May he asked for men aged between seventeen and sixty-five to call at their local police station and offer their services. 'I expected the response . . . to be prompt. In fact it was overwhelming, the first recruit arriving within four minutes of the end of the broadcast,' he recalled. Within twenty-four hours, no fewer than 250,000 had registered to join his Local Defence Volunteers (later renamed the Home Guard).

Earlier, the home secretary, Sir John Anderson, had been forced to respond to the public's growing fears about spies and collaborators. On 11 May he had agreed to detain all male Germans and Austrians – numbering around 2,000 – who lived in coastal areas between Scotland and Hampshire. On 17 May, he reluctantly extended detention to encompass a further 7,000 borderline cases and recent arrivals.

At a salutary meeting on Saturday, 18 May the War Cabinet acknowledged that in order to fight a dictatorship, a democracy like Britain had to be prepared, in some respects, to act like its enemy. Neville Chamberlain, in charge of strategy on the Home Front, had drawn up plans for a scenario in which Britain had to hold out against the Nazis alone, without any prospect of help from America. He conceded it would be 'impossible and undesirable immediately to effect complete and revolutionary change in the whole structure and social system of this country'. But it was imperative, he told ministers, 'that we should abandon our present rather easy-going methods and resort to a form of government which would approach the totalitarian'.

Chamberlain worried that the 'drastic' legislation his Lord President's Committee envisaged would come as a shock to British people unless they had been prepared for it. He recommended that Churchill broadcast to the nation the following day to 'indicate we were in a tight fix and that no personal considerations must be allowed to stand in the way of measures necessary for victory'. And this the Prime Minister duly did, telling his listeners, 'After this Battle of France abates its force there will come a battle for our island, for all that Britain is and all that Britain means. In that supreme emergency, we shall not hesitate to take every step, even the most drastic, to call forth from our people the last ounce and the last inch of effort of which they are capable.'

Chamberlain and his officials had liaised closely with Ernest Bevin over the 'totalitarian' measures required, as their implementation would fall to his ministry. The details were revealed to the House of Commons, on 22 May, in the revised Emergency Powers (Defence) Bill, which was presented by Clement Attlee as Bevin was not yet an MP. The new Minister of Labour was to be given, by rule of law, powers that a dictator would have envied. Specifically, the bill required 'persons to place themselves, their services, and their property at the disposal of His Majesty, as appear to him to be necessary or expedient for securing the public safety, the defence of the Realm, the maintenance of public order, or the efficient prosecution of any war in which His Majesty may be engaged, or for maintaining supplies or services essential to the life of the community'.

As Attlee put it, 'The Minister of Labour will be given power to direct any person to perform any services required of him.' *Time* magazine observed, with some levity, 'Horny-handed Ernest Bevin could – if he chose – walk into London's stuffy Athenaeum Club, tap the Archbishop of Canterbury on his bald pate and order him to Sussex to dig trenches.' *The Times* reflected, more gravely, that the measures 'came near to suspending the very essence of the Constitution as it ha[s] been built up in 1,000 years. Our ancient liberties are placed in pawn for victory: nothing less than the destruction of Hitlerism will redeem them.' Yet the bill passed through the Commons and the Lords with only the merest murmurs of opposition. Indeed, it took just two hour[s] and thirty-four minutes to gain Royal Assent.

Bevin could now say with some legitimacy that he had absolute authority over the lives of every civilian between the ages of fourteen and sixty-four. He was confident, however, that coercion would not be needed and that 'voluntaryism' alone would mobilise Britain's worker[s] to deliver that victory.

By 22 May German forces had reached the Channel ports of Boulogne and Calais. The Wehrmacht's Panzer divisions had scythed their way across northern France, splitting the Allied armies and trapping the best French units and most of the British Expeditionary Force in a small coastal pocket. Despite help from the Royal Navy and the RAF, Boulogne surrendered on 25 May. The following afternoon, after five days of heroic defence by troops led by Britain's Brigadier Claude Nicholson – who had been ordered not to evacuate, but to fight on to the end – Calais fell too. That left Dunkirk as the only available exit port, and here the retreating 400,000 strong British Expeditionary Force now headed.

The War Cabinet had to face the consequences of the impending fall of France. General Lord Gort, commander of the BEF, had warned that his army would almost certainly lose all of its equipment and doubted whether more than a small proportion of men could be evacuated. Already the chiefs of staff had been asked to draw up a paper envisaging a French surrender and considering how Britain could fight on without most of her army. Euphemistically titled 'British Strategy in a Certain Eventuality', the report deemed Britain's remaining force[s] and civil defence utterly inadequate to the challenge of repelling the Wehrmacht should it ever come ashore.

The chiefs' central conclusion was that 'the crux of the whole problem is the air defence of this country'. They calculated th[e]

Luftwaffe's numerical superiority over the RAF at something like four to one. It was vital that the war effort concentrate 'primarily on the production of fighter aircraft and crews, and the defence of those factories essential to fighter production should have priority'. Ultimate survival depended on America, however. One of the report's key assumptions was that 'The United States of America is willing to give us full economic and financial assistance, *without which we do not think we could continue the war with any chance of success*' (emphasis original).

With the military situation so dire, the War Cabinet began a critical discussion of whether to fight on alone, or consider the circumstances in which the country might sue for peace. A battle of wills developed between Churchill, the advocate of the former path, and Lord Halifax, who coolly, logically and persistently presented the case for the latter. Neville Chamberlain positioned himself somewhere in between, while Clement Attlee and Arthur Greenwood – to begin with – listened rather more than they spoke. The issue dominated most of five War Cabinet meetings held over Sunday, 26 and Monday, 27 May, with debate centred on whether to accept Italy – hostile, but still neutral – as a mediator in negotiations. 'We had to face the fact that it was not so much now a question of imposing a complete defeat upon Germany out of safeguarding the independence of our own Empire and, if possible, that of France,' the foreign secretary asserted.

Mindful of Chamberlain and Halifax's continuing political sway, Churchill was careful, at least initially, to appear not to reject the idea of talks. He 'doubted whether anything would come of an approach to Italy, but the matter was one which the war cabinet would have to consider'. And at the end of a lengthy, four-hour meeting on Sunday afternoon – held following discussions with the French premier, Paul Reynaud, who had flown over from Paris – he still seemed to equivocate: 'Herr Hitler thought that he had the whip hand. The only thing to do was to show him that he could not conquer this country. If, on Monsieur Reynaud's showing, France could not continue, we must part company. At the same time, he [Churchill] did not raise objection to some approach being made to Signor Mussolini.'

In truth, he was entirely hostile to the idea. At the second of three War Cabinets that day, he first allowed Sinclair, Attlee and Greenwood to make the case against negotiations. Sinclair told Halifax bluntly that it would be a 'futile' exercise. 'Being in a tight corner, any weakness on our part would encourage the Germans and the Italians, and would tend to undermine morale both in this country and in the Dominions.' Attlee weighed in with the view that 'the suggested approach would be of no practical effect and would be very damaging to us'. Greenwood's language was even stronger: 'If it got out that we had sued for terms at the cost of ceding British territory, the consequences would be terrible . . . it would be heading for disaster to go any further with those approaches.' Churchill then stepped in to make his position abundantly clear. He said he was 'increasingly oppressed with the futility of the suggested approach to Mussolini, which the latter would certainly regard with contempt . . . at the moment our prestige in Europe was very low. The only way we could get it back was by showing the world that Germany had not beaten us.' Chamberlain remained undecided, cautioning that Halifax's strategy should not be abandoned just yet.

The foreign secretary was furious at the meeting's events and the ambush he had walked into. 'I thought Winston talked the most frightful rot, also Greenwood, and after hearing it for some time I said exactly what I thought of them, adding if that was really their view and if it came to the point, our ways would separate.' Halifax told Sir Alexander Cadogan, also present at the meeting, that 'I can't work with Winston'. Cadogan sympathised, but attempted to steer him away from thoughts of resignation: 'Nonsense; his rhodomontades probably bore you as much as they do me, but don't do anything silly under the stress of that.' When Churchill and Halifax talked further, in the garden at 10 Downing Street, the Prime Minister was 'full of apologies and affection', attempting to smooth things over. But nothing had been resolved, and the two men merely regrouped to continue their political struggle the next day.

* * *

A partial news blackout on the progress of the battle across the Channel had led the British public to believe that the German advance was still being strongly resisted. So when the announcement came on BBC radio, on the morning of Tuesday, 28 May, that King Leopold III of Belgium had ordered his troops to surrender, the Ministry of Information's Home Intelligence officers reported that people were 'stunned, bewildered, anxious and recriminatory'.

At the morning's War Cabinet, information minister Duff Cooper urged his colleagues to be more 'frank' about the desperate plight of the British Expeditionary Force. Unless the grim reality was spelt out, 'public confidence would be badly shaken and the civil population would not be ready to accept the assurances of the Government of the chances of our ultimate victory'. In his latest update on the evacuation from Dunkirk, the First Sea Lord Sir Dudley Pound told ministers 11,400 men had so far made it back to Britain, and a further 2,500 were on their way. But the prospects of getting a significant number of the remaining 400,000 British soldiers to safety were not great. Churchill took Duff Cooper's advice and went to the House of Commons early in the afternoon to make a brief but sombre speech. He told MPs that the situation of the British and French armies, attacked on three sides and from the air, was 'extremely grave' and that the surrender of the Belgians 'adds appreciably to their grievous peril'. He concluded with the ominous words, 'The House should prepare itself for hard and heavy tidings.'

Two hours later the ongoing debate about whether Britain should go it alone shifted from Number 10 to the Prime Minister's room behind the Speaker's chair in the Commons. At 6.15 p.m. twenty-five anxious ministers crammed into the small, archetypal Westminster Palace chamber, with its dark wooden panels and flocked wallpaper. One of those present, Malcolm MacDonald, later painted a vivid picture of the scene. 'The sky out of doors was a mixture of blue heaven and grey clouds, which caused sunbeams to keep alternately slanting brightly and dissolving gloomily through tall windows into the room – a display of Nature's indecisive mood of mixed optimism and pessimism which seemed appropriate to the occasion.'

Churchill urgently required this 'outer' Cabinet to come to his aid. The War Cabinet had just vacated the room, after another hour and a half of intense debate over Halifax's peace initiative. The arguments had again swung back and forth between Churchill and the foreign secretary, with Attlee, Sinclair and Greenwood once more backing the former's clear rejection of negotiation, while Chamberlain continued to hover in the middle, unconvinced any approach should be made immediately, but prepared to accept that 'it might be that we should take a different view in a short time, possibly even a week hence'.

The meeting had ended in some testy exchanges. Greenwood brusquely concluded that he 'did not feel that this was a time for ultimate capitulation'. An irked Halifax responded that there was 'nothing in his suggestion [that] could even remotely be described as ultimate capitulation'. Churchill's last comment had been that 'the chances of decent terms being offered to us at the present time were a thousand to one against'. By now, with Chamberlain inching towards his side, he was determined to bring the argument to a swift end. If the wider Cabinet could be persuaded to give him a unanimous endorsement, it would provide him with the ammunition he needed to finally overcome Halifax and dispel all notion of a negotiated peace.

Addressing that group of twenty-five, he summoned a commanding performance. He first laid bare in some detail the history of the disastrous military campaign, before, with his journalist's eye, vividly capturing the current scene on the beaches at Dunkirk as the evacuation took place under a great pall of black smoke, deliberately augmented by a cloud of artificial cover from the British ships in order to conceal from the German planes the scale of the withdrawal. The RAF, he assured them, was holding off the German fighters and making great inroads into the enemy's bombing strength, but he was being as realistic as he could bear. He was hopeful of evacuating 50,000; if 100,000 could be saved, it would be a 'magnificent performance'.

Outlining the case for negotiation, he admitted that Hitler might well be ready to offer peace, as he had gained all he wanted in Europe – for the moment – and had no particular ambition to conquer Britain.

On the face of it, this could appear an honourable settlement for a beleaguered nation. But it would be idle to expect the German dictator to stop at that; sooner or later, once Britain had been disabled and disarmed, Hitler would request her fleet, her naval bases, and much more. Ultimately she would become a slave state, with a Nazi puppet – 'Mosley or some such person' – in charge.

Churchill then reviewed Britain's prospects if she continued to fight. An early invasion could not be ruled out, but the Royal Navy was in good shape, and could inflict considerable reverses on the Germans once they attempted the crossing. Massive bombing assaults from the Luftwaffe should be expected, and people must expect to live and work for days on end in air raid shelters underground; but the RAF, so capable until now, would surely respond effectively. In the last resort, if there was to be a long, drawn-out siege, vast sections of the population might be evacuated across the Atlantic Ocean. Britain should never surrender, and in the blackest possible scenario her remaining forces would continue the war relentlessly from Canada and other friendly countries, with 'confident certainty' of ultimate victory, even if such an eventuality was still years away.

As he reached the climax of his half-hour speech, the Prime Minister put his position to the room in language that evoked Cicero's Third Philippic to the Senate in 44 BC. Two thousand years earlier the great Roman orator had sought to stiffen sinews against another dictator, Mark Antony: 'If the final episode in the history of the Republic has arrived, let us behave like champion gladiators: they met death honourably: let us . . . see to it that we fall with dignity rather than ignominy.' Now, Churchill declared, 'We shall go on and we shall fight it out, here or elsewhere, and if this long island story of ours is to end at last, let it end only when each of us lies choking in his own blood upon the ground.'

After this peroration, there were loud murmurs of approval. Churchill told his ministers that they were free to resign, with every mark of friendship from him, if they disagreed with his decision. None came forward. 'We had a little question and answering after that and

then left, all of us tremendously heartened by Winston's resolutio
and grip of things,' Leo Amery reflected that night. 'He is a rea
war leader and one whom it is worthwhile serving under.' Malcoln
MacDonald felt it was 'the most unforgettable hour', describin
how, with 'a gleam in his eyes during his passages about fighting o
the beaches and in the streets, he spoke of himself carrying a gu
and shooting at the enemy – almost as if this would be the mos
enjoyable moment in his whole life'. For Hugh Dalton Churchill wa
'the only man we have, for this hour'. Patting him on the should
in appreciation, Dalton suggested that the Low cartoon of 14 Ma
should be placed on the wall of the Prime Minister's room. 'Ye
that was a good one, wasn't it,' a smiling Churchill acknowledge
There was just one (silent) dissenter. Churchill's old foe John Reith
the new Minister of Transport, felt the speech had been 'dramatic
unreal, insincere', and that his fellow ministers had been guilty o
'some rather humbugging and sycophantic remarks'. But his was
lone, jaundiced voice that day.

Immediately after the twenty-five left the room, the other fou
members of the War Cabinet, again joined by Sinclair and S
Alexander Cadogan, returned. Churchill wasted no time in drivin
home his advantage. He revealed that the rest of the Cabinet ha
expressed no alarm at the reversals in France, and instead had show
'great satisfaction' at the prospect of Britain fighting on. Pointedl
he told them he did not recall ever having heard such a gathering o
politicians express themselves 'so emphatically'.

His plan worked: Halifax's resistance was overcome. It was agree
that the French government should be told the idea of peace talk
had been rejected, and that 'in reaching this decision we were lookin
at the matter from the point of view of France as well as ourselves
Sir Edward Spears, Churchill's personal representative to the Frenc
Prime Minister, was at Monsieur Reynaud's side when the communiqu
arrived in Paris, and saw the 'magical' effect it had on him. Reynau
had been under pressure from his own war cabinet to pursue the Italia
option, but the news from London 'evidently reinforced his own inne

onviction that this was the right course to pursue, and he straightaway
etoed any further communication being sent to Rome'.

ineteen-year-old RAF auxiliary pilot Hugh Spencer Lisle Dundas,
f 616 (South Yorkshire) Squadron, was having breakfast at RAF
econfield on Wednesday, 29 May when he received orders to leave
mmediately and make the 220-mile trip to RAF Rochford, near
outhend. Upon arrival at the fighter base that afternoon, he and his
olleagues were instructed to relieve a hard-pressed regular squadron
nd soon found themselves plunged into the Battle of Dunkirk. As his
pitfire circled the beaches, Dundas was totally unprepared for what
e saw.

'I had perhaps an unreal view, at that age, of what war was about,
nd it wasn't until I saw the mess at Dunkirk that I began to get a
limpse of reality.

'It was a terrifically confused and murky scene. There was this enor-
nous pillar of smoke rising from some oil tanks that had been set on
re and, although levelling off, went down the Channel for a distance
f 75 to 100 miles, and underneath that there was a lot of haze and
eneral mayhem. Clouds, smoke – I think that was one of the reasons
vhy the army didn't think the air force was there half the time.'

Down in the harbour, Ron Tomlinson and his brother Alan arrived
n a 40ft motor yacht named *Tom Tit* that they had stolen for the task
n Ramsgate harbour. It was their second day of relief work at Dunkirk
fter a stint in the trawler *Tankerton Towers*. Altogether they made
ixteen trips, all on one engine, taking on fifty soldiers each time and
offloading them onto bigger cargo, passenger and paddle boats for the
rip back to England. Ron's perspective of the conditions was markedly
lifferent from that of Hugh Dundas: 'You couldn't have had a better
lay for it, the sea was dead calm, just as if it had to happen for this
pecial occasion.

'The soldiers were all whacked out, we could see they had had a
very tough time. It was a bloodbath on the beaches – I've seen it once
nd I never want to see the like again.'

When the evacuation concluded on Tuesday, 4 June, a total
338,226 British and French troops had been rescued, 240,000 from th
harbour and 98,000 from the beaches. At 3.40 p.m., Churchill stoc
up in the House of Commons to relay the unexpectedly good news. A
he often did, he had rehearsed his speech in the garden at Number 1
that morning, striding up and down with Lord Halifax and his junic
minister Rab Butler in tow, uttering, 'We shall fight them on th
beaches.' But before he reached that stirring line, he warned MPs tha
'our thankfulness at the escape of the army and so many men . . . mu
not blind us to the fact that what has happened in France and Belgiu
is a colossal military disaster'.

Nor was it over. When the German tanks reached the French coas
at Abbeville on 20 May, they had split the British Expeditionary Forc
in two. The troops escaping through Dunkirk were those who had bee
trapped north of the German armies, but a significant number remaine
stuck south of the River Somme, including the 51st Highland and 1
Armoured Divisions. These were pressed into action alongside the
French counterparts when the Wehrmacht launched phase two of th
Battle for France, codenamed Operation *Fall Rot*, on Wednesday,
June, attacking along the line of both the Somme and Aisne.

The Allied soldiers fought tenaciously, despite the Germans' fa
greater numbers and firepower. Soon enough, however, the thin, 16(
mile 'Weygand Line' had broken and there was nothing to stop th
inevitable German assault on Paris. The British troops, along with pa
of the French army, began to pull back to the coast, and Operatio
Cycle was mounted to evacuate them from the ports of Le Havre an
Saint Valery.

On Monday, 10 June, Mussolini declared war on Britain and Franc
committing 1.5 million men, 1,700 aircraft and six capital ships to th
Axis cause. Italy was relatively weak in terms of men and materie
but the Italian dictator was determined to take a share of the spoil
On the same day, General Weygand told the war cabinet he intende
to declare Paris an open, undefended city, supposedly free fro
enemy attack under international law. When the proclamation wa

ade three days later, three-fifths of the French capital's five million
sidents simply fled.

Thursday, 13 June was also the date of Churchill's fifth – and final
trip across the Channel to Tours, where the retreating French gov-
nment had based itself. The occasion was a meeting of the Supreme
'ar Council, and accompanying the Prime Minister were Halifax,
:averbrook, Cadogan, General Ismay and the interpreter Captain
:rkeley. They arrived in the middle of a thunderstorm, and to a
:lcome that seemed symbolic of both the state of the war and Anglo-
ench relations. 'Tours airfield had been heavily bombed the night
fore; but we landed safely and taxied around the craters in search
someone to help us. There was no sign of life, except for groups of
ench airmen lounging about the hangars,' Ismay recalled.

Churchill rebuffed requests from the French to be released from their
ligations not to make a separate peace with Germany, and he pledged
lobby President Roosevelt to make a crucial last-minute interven-
on. The meeting ended on an emotional note, with Churchill saying
is was almost certainly the 'darkest hour' for the Allies. 'Whether or
ot this be so,' he went on, 'my conviction that Hitler and all that he
ands for will be smashed, and that Nazism will not reign over Europe,
mains entire.' Reynaud responded that his confidence remained
ually firm, 'else he could not endure to go on living'.

Yet events were swiftly outstripping the actions, let alone the wishes,
the politicians. Operation Cycle had been completed at dawn that
y, with around 15,000 British and Allied troops evacuated, although
: thousand men from the Highland Division had been forced to
rrender. The following morning Parisians awoke to the sound of a
erman-accented voice announcing that a curfew was being imposed
r 8 p.m. that evening. German tanks had rolled into the city and a
ant swastika now flew beneath the Arc de Triomphe.

At 8.20 p.m. General Alan Brooke, commander of the remaining
itish Expeditionary Force of around 150,000, managed to get through
the telephone to Downing Street to challenge Churchill over the
ea of any new initiatives or reinforcements. Brooke had been back in

France for just twenty-four hours, and yet he already knew his task w
hopeless. Churchill reminded him that he had been sent to France '
make the French feel that we were supporting them'. 'I replied that
was impossible to make a corpse feel, and that the French Army wa
to all intents and purposes dead, and certainly incapable of registeri
what was being done for it,' Brooke recalled some years later. Th
argument continued back and forth down the line for half an hour. 'F
gave me the impression that I was suffering from "cold feet" because
did not want to comply with his wishes,' wrote Brooke. 'At last, whe
I was in an exhausted condition, he said "All right, I agree with you"

Now orders would begin to go out for the final withdrawal
troops. Codenamed Operation *Aerial*, it was a task comparable in sca
to Dunkirk and in many ways more complicated, spanning as it d
ten days and eight different ports. British military operations on th
continent had effectively been brought to an end.

Around the same time as Churchill had been trying to stiffen th
resolve of the French cabinet in Tours, three men had sat down
lunch in an elegant flat in Mayfair, London, to discuss a plan to achiev
the same objective by very different means.

Leo Amery and Arthur Salter, Independent MP for Oxfo
University and a junior minister in the Ministry of Shipping, were th
guests of Jean Monnet, the French diplomat who headed the Angl
French Co-ordination Committee – a body charged with furtheri
the two countries' economic needs in the war against German
Monnet and Salter were old friends, having worked together at th
League of Nations during the 1920s, and both were ardent believe
in European political union. Encouraged by Amery, the two men no
seized the moment of crisis to put their beliefs into practice. It cou
be argued that Britain and France had not been bound together in ar
real constitutional, economic, linguistic or geographical sense sin
July 1453, when the Battle of Castillon effectively ended the Hundr
Years' War and sent the two countries firmly on their separate path
what was needed now was a 'dramatic gesture emphasizing our unit

o Monnet and Salter set to work on a memorandum that would plot truly revolutionary course for the future.

On Friday, 14 June, Amery began lobbying in support of their plan. 'ollowing a ministers' meeting chaired by Churchill, he thrust a copy f Salter's paper into the Prime Minister's hand, highlighting one f its less controversial ideas – a joint British/French War Cabinet. Amery followed this up in a talk with Attlee, and later that evening lispatched further copies to Neville Chamberlain and Lloyd George.

By the 15 June meeting of the War Cabinet, the first full draft of the vhat was titled the 'Franco-British Union' was ready for consideration. Chamberlain read some extracts aloud; he agreed, with much of the hinking, although it took 'too gloomy a view' in certain passages, and le remarked that the idea of joint parliaments and a joint cabinet 'did lot seem to be very fully thought out'. Of the others present, Churchill nd Sinclair remarked only that the Supreme War Council already provided a forum for the two cabinets to meet. With the complete collapse of France looming, their major preoccupations were whether o release her government from its agreement not to make a separate peace with Germany, and the possibility, even at this eleventh hour, of persuading America to intervene in some shape or form. Nevertheless, ime was granted for further modifications.

When Monnet and Salter submitted their final draft to Amery, ate that evening, the India secretary was startled by their ambition. I thought it a little fantastic, with its references to the absolute unification of the two nations including such things as customs and currency.' Among those who cast their eyes over the document at Downing Street the following morning were Churchill's special adviser Sir Desmond Morton and the visiting French government representative Brigadier General Charles de Gaulle. Conversation about the proposal continued over lunch at the Carlton Club. 'It is an enormous thing,' Churchill told de Gaulle of the proposed union. 'Yes,' the general replied. 'But the declaration can be made immediately. With things at the point they are, you should neglect nothing which can sustain France and maintain our alliance.'

At that, Churchill returned to Downing Street and summoned a special meeting of the War Cabinet for 3 p.m., where the document was unveiled. Its contents were quite breathtaking. Paragraph two stated baldly, 'The two Governments declare that France and Great Britain shall no longer be two nations but one. There will thus be created a Franco-British Union. Every citizen of France will enjoy immediately citizenship of Great Britain; every British subject will become a citizen of France.'

All customs were to be abolished, and there was to be a single currency. There would be one single war cabinet, one parliament, and a constitution would be drawn up 'providing for joint organs of defence and economic policy'. The armies of Britain and France would be placed under a single, supreme command.

It finished with a flourish. 'This unity, this union, will concentrate the whole of its strength against the concentrated strength of the enemy, no matter where the battle may be. And thus we will conquer.'

The eight politicians round the table, faced with this proposal for a political revolution – the establishment, in effect, of a new country – responded with remarkable equanimity. Sir Archibald Sinclair expressed his 'warm support', and said he was in favour of anything that would tighten the alliance between the two countries. Lord Halifax said risks had to be taken, and the only phrase with which he would take issue was 'France and Great Britain shall no longer be two nations but one'. Only Viscount Caldecote, Secretary of State for Dominion Affairs, seemed to worry unduly. If the document was intended to cover the peace after the war, then it raised issues which were 'too stupendous' to consider at such short notice.

Churchill told his colleagues his first instinct had been against the idea, but that in such a serious crisis the War Cabinet must show imagination; a spectacular initiative was needed to shore up the French. After some discussion, the plans for the abolition of customs and the establishment of a single currency were dropped, as was the idea of a single parliament, although joint sessions of the two might take place

om time to time. It was agreed, however, that a written constitution
ould be drafted, provided it was kept to 'very broad lines'.

After further minor amendments, Salter and Monnet's plan was
pproved. The resulting document, 'The Declaration of Union', was
stounding, in some ways inspiring. When De Gaulle – who had
mbraced it 'with an air of unwonted enthusiasm' – read its contents
ver the telephone to Reynaud in Bordeaux, the French premier was
) astonished that he asked, 'Does he agree to this? Did Churchill give
ju this personally?' De Gaulle then handed the receiver to the British
rime Minister, who assured Reynaud the document was the decision
f the whole Cabinet. 'He was transfigured with joy,' recalled General
dward Spears, who was standing next to the French leader. 'The sense
f the generosity of the offer was overwhelming, the sincerity of the
esture completely convincing.'

The atmosphere in the private secretary's office at Number 10
as also one of elation. John 'Jock' Colville was Churchill's assistant
rivate secretary at the time, having performed the same role for
Ieville Chamberlain, and would be a vivid chronicler at the heart of
overnment over the ensuing years. With barely disguised excitement,
e pondered mischievously, 'Who knows, we may yet see the "Fleurs
e Lys" restored to the Royal Standard!'

That night Churchill, Attlee, Sinclair and the chiefs of staff
ere to be transported by the cruiser Galatea to Concarneau, off the
>ast of Brittany, to discuss with Reynaud and his colleagues the
rolonging of the battle – and the future of this new nation. They got
; far as Waterloo, where a special train had been primed to depart for
outhampton at 9.30 p.m. Not long after they had taken their seats,
hurchill received a hand-delivered note from a private secretary
iforming him that the trip was off because of a 'ministerial crisis' in
ordeaux. What he discovered, on returning to Downing Street, was
iat Reynaud had been ousted from power. Despite the support of
'resident Albert Lebrun, he had run into a wall of criticism over the
eclaration, led by eighty-four-year-old Marshal Philippe Pétain from
ie pro-armistice grouping.

The French Prime Minister had read the document to his cabinet twice, to be greeted on each occasion by silence. As he recounted 'Some were astonished, others taken aback, more were hostile.' Pétain described the proposal as 'fusion with a dead corpse'. In the end, a motion from deputy premier Camille Chautemps that 'The Declaration of Union' should be rejected won the day, by thirteen votes to eleven. Reynaud resigned. Pétain, his successor, immediately announced his intention to seek a separate peace.

The resulting armistice was signed on Saturday, 22 June. Hitler carefully choreographed the moment to humiliate France, deliberately setting it at Compiègne, in the very same railway carriage – brought out of its museum for the occasion – in which German representatives had surrendered to their French conquerors in 1918. The Führer even sat in the same chair from which Marshal Ferdinand Foch, commander-in-chief of the Allied armies, had dictated terms to Matthias Erzberger, secretary of state and head of the German delegation.

When he received the details of the armistice at Chequers that day, Churchill hurried back to London for an emergency Cabinet meeting at 9.30 p.m. There he condemned Hitler's 'murderous' terms, which included the takeover of Paris, the complete disarming and demobilising of the French army, and the payment of compensation by France to Germany for the full cost of the occupation. But what interested the War Cabinet most, as it contemplated the battle ahead, was Article 8, on the subject of the French fleet. Hitler had demanded that all French warships be 'collected' in specific ports, demobilised and kept under German or Italian control. The article continued, 'The German Government solemnly declares to the French Government that it does not intend to use the French war fleet, which is in harbours under German control, for its purposes in war, with the exception of units necessary for the purposes of guarding the coast and sweeping mines.'

No one around the Cabinet table that night placed any faith in this assurance. The prospects for the battle at sea now looked bleak. The Italian ships in the Mediterranean could cut across Britain's lines

f communication to the Middle East and India; while the Japanese
ight see this as the right moment to attack the British Empire in the
ar East. For the French fleet now to join Hitler would mean the Royal
Navy was stretched and threatened across all the world's oceans, and
ess able to defend Britain against invasion.

Churchill's mind was already racing ahead to the practicalities of
ealing with the problem. He voiced particular worry about two new
attleships, *Richelieu* – the most powerful afloat in the world – and
an Bart. The former was en route for Dakar in French West Africa,
ne latter to the Moroccan port of Casablanca. The Prime Minister
ggested the Royal Navy could track them on the high seas and pull
longside to 'parley' with their captains. If they refused to negotiate,
ney should be treated as traitors to the Allied cause. 'The ships
ight have to be bombed by aircraft from the *Ark Royal* or they must
e mined into their harbours . . . in no circumstances must they be
llowed to escape.'

The key to the affair was presumed to be Admiral François Darlan,
ne commander of the French navy. But Darlan was now minister of
narine in Pétain's government; the final decision was ultimately out
f his control. 'We could not afford to rely on his word,' Churchill told
ne War Cabinet on 22 June. 'However good his intentions, he might
e forced to resign and his place taken by another Minister who would
ot shrink from betraying us.'

All the while, the War Cabinet remained mindful of attitudes
cross the Atlantic. On 15 May, in his first significant communication
vith President Roosevelt as Prime Minister, Churchill had asked for
he loan of forty or fifty destroyers. The request had been turned down,
nd not simply because the Neutrality Act limited America's ability to
rovide aid for Britain and France: the White House had to consider
he risk that these ships would end up in German hands. Roosevelt
vas watching and waiting to see how the war progressed. By 29 June,
Washington was urging the British government to take decisive action
o prove it had the resolve to continue the fight against Germany. As
Lord Halifax reported, 'any action which we might take in respect of

the French Fleet might be applauded in the United States.' So wa
launched Operation *Catapult*, designed to secure the 'neutralisatior
of the French fleet either by taking the ships under British control, (
by destroying them.

Happily, the new battleships, *Richelieu* and *Jean Bart*, proved to be n
immediate threat. The former, shadowed by a British naval squadror
was by now stationed at Dakar, and *Jean Bart*, still to start her engine
was safely tucked away in Casablanca. And at Alexandria, where th
battleship *Lorraine*, four cruisers, three destroyers and a submarin
were berthed, the French commanding officer, Admiral René-Émil
Godfrey, would eventually accede to a diplomatic solution. But ther
would be no such amity at the port of Mers-el-Kébir in French Algeri;
Here, under the command of Admiral Marcel-Bruno Gensoul, wer
the First World War-era battleships *Provence* and *Bretagne*, the moi
modern *Force de Raid* battleships *Dunkerque* and *Strasbourg*, th
seaplane tender *Commandant Teste* and six destroyers.

On Tuesday, 2 July, Admiral Sir James Somerville, in comman
of 'Force H', the task force sent to 'neutralise' the French flee
received the final text of the ultimatum he was to deliver t
Gensoul. It stated that the French admiral could either join wit
the British; be escorted to internment at a British port; sail und(
escort for demilitarisation in the Caribbean; or scuttle his ships. I
difficult negotiations the following day Gensoul rejected all of thes
options outright, despite numerous visits from the French-speakin
captain Cedric Holland, Somerville's representative.

At 4.46 p.m. on 3 July, Somerville received a communiqué from th
Admiralty instructing him 'to settle matters quickly'; French reinforc(
ments were on their way. He wasted no time. At 5.15 p.m. Somervil
signalled that if his proposals were not met within fifteen minutes h
would have to destroy the French ships. Again Gensoul rejected th
ultimatum, saying 'the first shot fired would alienate our two navie
and do untold harm to us, and that he would reply to force by force
Holland left the battleship at 5.25, and half an hour later the Roya
Navy began its bombardment.

The first salvo smashed into the side of the *Bretagne*, inflicting tal damage that consigned the battleship to the depths, along with 77 of its crew. The *Dunkerque* was crippled, with two hundred dead nd many injured. The destroyer *Provence* ran aground, and *Mogador* as also badly mauled. The battleship *Strasbourg* was a rare survivor, aking it back to Toulon and into French hands. The final death toll f French sailors was 1,297, with around 350 wounded.

When Churchill stood up in the House of Commons at 3.54 p.m. n 4 July to explain the action, he expressed his 'sincere sorrow' over e decision he and the War Cabinet had taken. He concluded, 'I leave e judgment of our action, with confidence, to Parliament. I leave it the nation, and I leave it to the United States. I leave it to the world nd to history.' Finally, he affirmed that 'The action we have already ken should be, in itself, sufficient to dispose once and for all the es and rumours which have been so industriously spread by German ropaganda and Fifth Column activities that we have the slightest ntention of entering into negotiations in any form and through any annels with the German and Italian governments. We shall, on the ontrary, prosecute the war with the utmost vigour by all the means at are open to us until the righteous purposes for which we entered pon it have been fulfilled.'

With that call to arms, he sat down. The whole House rose to their et and cheered loudly, waving their order papers and handkerchiefs appreciation.

The ovation lasted for two minutes, and at the end of it Churchill as visibly moved, tears rolling down his cheeks. 'This is heartbreaking r me,' he told former war minister Leslie Hore-Belisha as he left the amber. Reflecting on the significance of Mers-el-Kébir, Leo Amery oncluded, 'It will wake the world up to a realization that we are now ghting for our lives and have taken our gloves off.'

Britain had lost an ally, but had gained the respect of America. The attle of France – the battle with France – was over. Now the Battle f Britain would begin.

Chapter Three

The Beaverbrook Effect

10 July to 7 September 1940

At 1.50 p.m. on Wednesday, 10 July 1940, Flying Officer Thomas Peter Kingsland Higgs received the order to 'scramble' and climbed into his Hurricane at the Croydon satellite airfield. He and his eight fellow pilots from 111 Squadron had been instructed to join the battle against the largest number of German bombers yet observed over the Channel; the Luftwaffe was clearly bent on destroying a merchant convoy bringing vital supplies of food and raw materials to Britain.

Peter, aged twenty-three, had been in service with 111 Squadron for little more than six weeks. He had learned to fly while reading for a degree in modern history at Merton College, Oxford, before joining the Royal Air Force as a direct entry commission in October 1938. Peter's squadron leader John Thompson was a strong advocate of the relatively new, terrifying and highly risky 'head-on' tactic for confronting a bomber formation. This required the pilot to fly through the pack of enemy planes at a speed of 500 miles per hour, leaving time for no more than a three-second burst of gunfire. The aim was to provoke an instinctive reaction to break ranks in the bombers' pilots, and thus cause them to collide with their compatriots. Even if the Germans swerved safely, the formation would be broken up, and the British fighter planes could then pick them off one by one.

Peter was about to join a massive dogfight involving more than
hundred aircraft. The sky between Dover and Dungeness quickly
ecame a twisting, turning melee of fighters, vapour trails snaking in
l directions, but with neither side gaining the upper hand.

Then Peter and the other eight Hurricane pilots rolled into the
tack with the head-on manoeuvre, their seventy-two .303 calibre
achine guns spewing tracer bullets. As anticipated, the German
anes dodged the incoming fire and their orderly 'V' formations
sintegrated. The scattering bombers rained their payloads all over the
hames Estuary, but of 150 bombs dropped, only one hit the convoy;
1 Squadron's daring tactic had saved the lives of scores of sailors.

As the Hurricanes tore through the German formation once more,
eter 'rammed into' a plane piloted by the Luftwaffe's *Staffelkapitän*,
auptmann Walter Krieger. The collision sheared off the wing of the
urricane and Peter was sent spinning out of control into the Channel.
/hen a rescue launch arrived on the scene not long afterwards it was
le to pick up Krieger and one of his colleagues, but there was no sign of
eter. Reports suggested his parachute had failed. The Air Ministry stated
mply that 'Two British machines were lost, but the pilot of one was safe.'

The next day's newspapers were jubilant. 'RAF'S BATTLE SCORE – 37,'
outed the front-page headline in the *Daily Mirror*. 'THREE SPITFIRES
TACK FIFTY – AND WIN,' proclaimed the *Daily Express*. The ministry
aimed the RAF had shot down fourteen German machines and so
riously damaged twenty-three others that they were unlikely to
ach home. Although the real statistics may have been a little less
mforting, the propaganda value of the air force's success over the
hannel was immense, both militarily and psychologically. It also
nt out a reminder to the Americans, a week after Mers-el-Kébir, that
ritain was up for the fight.

A month later, Peter Kingsland Higgs' body was found washed
hore on the Dutch coast at Noordwijk. He was the first British
lot to die during the first heavy engagement between the RAF and
e Luftwaffe over English soil – effectively, the beginning of the
attle of Britain.

* * *

On the same day Peter died for his country, Lord Beaverbrook wa
seeking to engage the people of Britain more closely with the pilot
struggle. With his fertile mind and flair for publicity, the Minister c
Aircraft Production would, in the coming months, come up with sever.
schemes to promote the idea of a 'People's War'. On this occasion, h
issued an appeal to the nation's housewives to scour their homes fc
every piece of aluminium they could find – from pots, pans and kettl.
to vacuum cleaners, bathroom fittings and cigarette boxes – and han
it over to the local headquarters of the Women's Voluntary Servic.
from where the donations would be dispatched to smelting facilitie
and turned into material for Spitfires and Hurricanes, Blenheims an
Wellingtons. 'Very few of us can be heroines on the battlefront,' Lad
Reading, head of the WVS, said in a BBC broadcast that evening, 'bu
we can still have the tiny thrill of thinking as we hear the news of a
epic battle in the air, "Perhaps it was my saucepan that made part c
that Hurricane."'

If the dominant Luftwaffe was to be defeated, 'The Beaver', as h
was known to all and sundry, had to ensure Britain produced plane
at a rate significantly quicker than ever before in the history of th
aviation industry. Working closely alongside him, to deliver the pilots
ground staff, weapons and supplies to keep the machines flying, wa
Sir Archibald Sinclair, Secretary of State for Air. Both had a long
standing interest in aviation. Sinclair had been an accomplished pilo
in the pioneering days of aviation, and at one point during the Firs
World War he had come close to enlisting in the Royal Flying Corps
Beaverbrook too had tried his hand in the cockpit, before settling fo
the safer option of merely owning aircraft. Unfortunately, despite a
mutual fascination with their subject, and beneath a surface cordiality
the two were at odds and Sinclair had already incurred Beaverbrook'.
wrath. The first major clash within the Cabinet was under way.

There could scarcely have been two characters more dissimilar ir
background, appearance, moral outlook, political views or method
Here was the old order versus the new: an inheritor of wealth anc

ivilege in contrast to a self-made millionaire; an establishment
sider pitted against a buccaneering outsider; an idealist alongside a
ustler.

Archibald Henry Macdonald Sinclair was high-minded and patriotic.
e had the courteous, if slightly aloof, manners of the aristocratic
ighland gentleman, and he liked to retain Edwardian standards of
ess, notably with his trademark wing collar. Endowed with striking
ood looks, he might have been 'the complete tragic actor . . . with
ng black hair, deep-set greenish-brown eyes and a pale face'. His
ssured manner and natural charm had won him the respect of men
nd the admiring looks of women. But his life had not always been
asy: orphaned at an early age, the young Sinclair had led a wandering
xistence, without a regular guardian or a settled home. Fortune had
rived in 1912, however, when – on the death of his grandfather, a
iberal Party politician – he had acquired, at the age of just twenty-
vo, a baronetcy, and with it the ownership of 120,000 acres at the
orthernmost tip of Scotland. Not that he had previously been a
ranger to high society: his aunt, Mrs Owen Williams, knew Edward
'II and Sinclair himself mixed in influential political circles under the
ing of Liberal leader Herbert Asquith and his daughter, Violet.

It had been around this time that Sinclair first encountered
Churchill, at the Maidenhead home of Maxine Elliott, an American
ctress and theatre owner. Despite a sixteen-year age difference –
Churchill was then thirty-nine – the two men had discovered much
ommon ground. Sinclair's mother, like Jennie Churchill, had been
n East Coast American, and he too had lost his father to venereal
isease. As boys, both had been nurtured by nannies, and as young men
hey had pursued similar careers, enrolling at Sandhurst and training
s cavalry officers. Each had also struggled with a speech impediment
 Churchill with a lisp, unable to pronounce his 's's, Sinclair with a
light stammer.

They had formed a natural, instinctive bond, never quite one of
quals because of the differences in age and experience, but deep-seated
onetheless. 'They delighted in one another's society even when both

poured out a Niagara of words, as often happened, simultaneousl
observed their mutual friend Violet Bonham Carter. Indeed, in lat
years, Sinclair's oratorical skill would be compared favourably wit
Churchill's. 'He [Churchill] is like a great liner ploughing throug
the storm,' wrote the correspondent for the *Manchester Evening Neu*
'while Sinclair is like a sailing vessel which rides the waves. He is mo
graceful in his lines and more buoyant.' Churchill, quick to recogni
this talent, had become Sinclair's political godfather, encouraging hi
to stand for Parliament.

In November 1915, following the disastrous Gallipoli campaig
Churchill had found himself out of the War Cabinet. Rather tha
languish in the outer ranks of government, he had chosen to head f
Flanders, and upon being appointed lieutenant colonel in the 6th Roy
Scots Fusiliers, stationed close to the front line near Ploegsteert Woc
(referred to as 'Plugstreet'), he had demanded – and got – 'Archie' as h
second in command. Unlike Ypres to the north, or Loos to the soutl
there were no major set-piece battles at Ploegsteert. It was attrition
work, neither safe nor easy, but it didn't involve 'going over the top
the Royal Scots Fusiliers were holding the line. Nonetheless, fiftee
men were killed and 123 injured in the trenches under Churchil
hundred-day command, while he and Archie narrowly escaped tw
shelling attacks on their HQ at Laurence Farm.

After the war, their friendship had evolved into a politic
relationship. From 1919 to 1921, Sinclair served as personal milita
secretary to Churchill at the War Office and then, in 1921–2, as h
private secretary at the Colonial Office. Thereafter their paths bega
to diverge. The 1922 general election saw Sinclair elected as Liber
MP for Caithness and Sutherland, whereas Churchill lost his Dund
seat and started his journey back to the Conservative Party.

Sinclair's first cabinet post, in 1931–2, had been that of Scottis
secretary in Ramsay MacDonald's 'national government'. Three yea
later, while his erstwhile mentor was brooding through his 'wilderne
years', he had claimed the greater prize of leadership of the Liberal Part
However, his long allegiance to Churchill was far from over. Despi

heir political differences, Sinclair shared his friend's fears about the
hreat posed by Nazi Germany, and as the subject of rearmament began
o trouble the Commons the two men maintained a united front, often
peaking in close proximity during debates.

At the outbreak of war, in September 1939, Neville Chamberlain
nvited Sinclair – despite their mutual distrust – to join his government
nd thus enter into a wartime coalition. Sinclair refused because the
ffer did not include a seat in the War Cabinet. But when Churchill
ame calling eight months later with a similar proposal – the Air
Ministry, but again, no place in the inner circle – Sinclair did not
esitate to accept.

Beaverbrook was as different to Sinclair in appearance as he was in
haracter. Sometimes crudely described as 'gnome-like', he had a large
ead, with a short neck, atop a small, slight body. He also had a boyish
ace, full cheeks and a wide forehead, and his characteristic expression
vas an impish grin, spread across a wide mouth. He had no apparent
artorial ambitions; his usual daily garb was provided by a wardrobe of
ndistinguished dark blue suits. And rarely was he described as affable.
His best side was energetic, innovative and motivational, especially in
ublic, but behind closed doors his Cabinet colleagues had to contend
with an individual who was deeply competitive and manipulative, used
o having his way, and prone to nursing resentment when thwarted.

William Maxwell Aitken – as he was then – had first met Churchill
round the same time as Sinclair, in 1911, at the dining table of the
brilliant barrister and Conservative MP F.E. Smith. But Churchill's
riendship with Aitken developed more slowly, and without the
naster–pupil dynamic; there were just five years between them,
besides which, at this stage Aitken, the recently elected Unionist MP
or Ashton-under-Lyne, was hitching his political wagon to Andrew
Bonar Law, leader of the Conservatives and a fellow Canadian. There
vas, moreover, little in Aitken's background that would naturally draw
nim and Churchill together. The latter's upbringing in Blenheim Palace
nad been a world away from Aitken's childhood in the small town of

Newcastle, New Brunswick, where his father, a Presbyterian ministe
and his mother, the daughter of a farmer, had raised their ten childrer
And while Churchill, upon becoming a man, had sought action an
adventure in the army, Aitken's battles had been fought around th
boardroom table, first in the booming town of Halifax, Nova Scotia
and then in Montreal, where he had put his growing wealth to worl
buying and selling companies, investing in the newspaper and magazin
trade, and becoming involved in ventures in Cuba and Puerto Rico.

What they shared – beyond a similar restless drive to live life a
principal actors on the world stage – was an aversion to official educa
tion. Both had been unruly, mischievous boys, with a mutual dislik
of traditional subjects such as mathematics and the classics; at sixteer
Aitken failed an examination for Dalhousie University because h
declined to sit the Latin and Greek papers. Like Churchill, though
his self-education, through voracious reading, was extensive, with th
Bible – especially the Old Testament – providing his moral instruc
tion, Edmund Burke his political lodestar, and the likes of Rudyar
Kipling, Arnold Bennett, H.G. Wells and Somerset Maugham source
of light relief.

When Aitken moved to Britain in 1910, the options for 'colonial
in London were either to be meek or polite, in which case the
were likely to be ignored, or aggressive and eccentric, thus makin
themselves rare and admirable freaks. Aitken was quickly perceive
as the latter, 'dislocating the pattern of British society, rupturing th
continuity, pushing traditions and institutions around'. By 1940, a
Lord Beaverbrook (he had been ennobled in 1917), his meteori
progress into the heart of British life had included a spell in th
Cabinet during the First World War (he was the original Minister o
Information) and a role as kingmaker to the highest office in the lan
(he claimed credit for helping to propel his hero Bonar Law to th
premiership in 1922). But his greatest achievement – and the source o
much of his political power – had been his transformation of the *Dail*
Express group, a previously dull set of newspapers, into well-writter
opinionated, mass-circulation daily journals.

When Churchill became Prime Minister, he had been intimate
friends with both Sinclair and Beaverbrook for a quarter of a century, but
while his affection for 'Archie' knew no bounds, 'Max' had taken root
– like a little devil, some said – in his soul. In the tightest of moments,
when high policy had to be decided, Churchill trusted Beaverbrook's
instincts more than those of any other man. So, in preparation for the
battle of Britain it was Beaverbrook he chose to empower and, as a
direct consequence, Sinclair whom he emasculated. For the former,
he plucked a rib off the Air Ministry and created a whole new body,
assuring him of a free hand and full support; with Sinclair, he not only
ripped away the productive element of his department, but by himself
taking on the role of Minister of Defence as well as Prime Minister,
he effectively denied Sinclair any real strategic influence on the war.
Churchill never doubted that his preference for Max over Archie was
the right one, but in the months to come it would test his government
and his friendships with both men to the limit.

When William Crozier, the editor of the *Manchester Guardian*, went to
interview Sinclair at his second-floor office in King Charles Street, just
off Whitehall, at 2.45 p.m. on Friday, 26 July 1940, he was alarmed by
the secretary of state's appearance. The air war over Britain was in its
early stages. 'I asked him if he was keeping well in spite of his strenuous
job, and he said very well,' Crozier recorded. 'In point of fact he looked
ill, his face was white and I thought fallen as compared with the time
I saw him last, and his clothes hung loosely on him.'

The hours Sinclair worked contributed to his strain. A normal
working day would stretch from 10 a.m. to 3 a.m., the latter end of
his schedule largely designed to accommodate the Prime Minister's
nocturnal habits; it was not unusual for the air minister to be summoned to see Churchill at Downing Street in the early hours. After
dinner each night Sinclair would return to his office at 9 p.m. and stay
there until his paperwork was complete. He made life more difficult for
himself by not delegating authority, and by writing overlong memos
and letters. Neither could he relax on weekends; he would spend

Sunday going through a mass of statistics he had ordered from his civil
servants. He was careful, however, not to transmit his anxieties to his
colleagues, or to apply to his department the pressure he inflicted upon
himself. 'Archie was a grand fellow,' recalled Harold Balfour, his junior
minister. 'He was the soul of honour, brave, kind and considerate. In
foul weather or fine he would give me his support.'

At Stornoway House, an elegant six-storey townhouse overlooking
Green Park, Lord Beaverbrook spared neither himself nor his staff
for the cause. The house was his own private residence, which he
temporarily converted into the offices of his government department
for the first month in the job. A former Prime Minister, Lord Grenville
had been a previous occupant, and Beaverbrook would later joke
'Grenville lived in Stornoway House and in 1807 abolished the slave
trade. I lived in Stornoway House in 1940 and re-established the slave
trade at the Ministry of Aircraft Production.' Beaverbrook did not
run his department like a trained administrator or politician; he ran
it as he ran his business interests, off the cuff and with as much direct
personal involvement as possible. Over his desk hung three slogans
'Committees Take The Punch Out Of War', 'Organisation Is The
Enemy Of Improvisation' and 'All Things In War Are Simple, But
The Simple Is Always Difficult'.

Evidence of his unconventional style could be seen throughout the
building. Upstairs, secretaries and typists were forced to commandeer
beds for desks, set up typewriters in the bathrooms, and answer a
multitude of telephones that seldom stopped ringing. Downstairs, air
marshals and representatives of every branch of the aircraft industry
regularly filed in for interviews in the big bow-windowed library, where
they would usually find the minister carrying on three conversations at
once and, in spare moments, talking into his Dictaphone. Beaverbrook's
world was a 'diverting comedy of bell-pushing, a loud harsh voice, and
abrupt orders for men and papers'.

He had one overriding objective – to get as many planes as
possible built and in the air in the shortest possible time. The RAF
had started the war with two excellent fighters, the Hurricane and

e Spitfire. The question was whether the factories would be able
 turn out sufficient of these aircraft to fill the gaps in the squadrons
at would soon result from the German onslaught. So Beaverbrook
viftly abandoned medium-term objectives, statistical planning and
ly rational allocation of resources. Success hinged on informality,
ontaneity and inventiveness.

To that end, senior, conventional figures like Sir Wilfrid Freeman and
ir Vice-Marshal Arthur Tedder were pushed into the background, and a
oup of industrialists were brought in to replace them, men Beaverbrook
usted to apply the necessary drive, ruthlessness and know-how. The
ost important of these brash newcomers – many of them his past, or
esent, associates – were Patrick Hennessy and Trevor Westbrook.
ennessy, an exuberant forty-two-year-old Irishman, had helped
versee a surge in sales as general manager at Ford Motors. Westbrook,
notoriously volatile character, had been dismissed in March as general
anager of the Vickers-Armstrong aircraft works at Weybridge, Surrey,
ter a quarrel with his director. Such was his standing among the 7,000
nployees that there was a brief strike in sympathy over his departure.

The old production wing of the Air Ministry, based in Harrogate,
orth Yorkshire, had by no means been neglectful of the RAF's needs.
ut Beaverbrook's new administration identified a number of ongoing
oblems. There was a shortage of materials and components on
e production line; both a repair organisation for damaged aircraft
id an adequate system for the repair of engines were lacking; and,
eanwhile, numerous aircraft stood idle for lack of vital instruments.
ennessy and Westbrook began quickly to address these failings, with
eir master at their shoulder, day and night.

'It was the most exciting time of my life,' Hennessy recalled. 'We
oke all the rules.' Beaverbrook formed action squads to enter likely
ores of spare parts and remove them, despite furious protests. He
ommandeered aircraft to fly to France to pick up damaged engines
id components for use in repairs. He even commissioned the
tandard Motor Company to manufacture a light armoured vehicle –
cknamed the 'Beaverette' – to defend his factories.

Beaverbrook imposed his will at every level of the ministry. Manager and foremen in aircraft plants were liable to be roused in the dead of night and told, 'If we're up, there's no reason why you shouldn't be Other departments – notably Ernest Bevin's Ministry of Labour an Herbert Morrison's Ministry of Supply – were often circumvented i the rush for men, materials and constant production. Beaverbrook aggression and cunning were perfectly illustrated in early July, whe he instructed Hennessy to order two shiploads of special steel allo from Edgar Lewis, a contact of his in Pittsburgh, in the United States All orders of this kind were supposed to go via the British Purchasin Commission in Washington, and from there to be handled by th Ministry of Supply, but Lewis was told simply to stamp this deliver for the Ministry of Aircraft Production and to send it to Liverpoo When the shipment reached the now bombed-out north-west port, i could not be taken ashore. Hennessy recalled Beaverbrook saying h would get John Reith to arrange it.

'The Beaver then put on one of his great persuasive acts. "You ar the man who can do something vital and important for the country · nobody else. These ships and their contents can save us. Help me.' This appeal to Reith's vanity worked a treat, and he promptly gave th necessary orders through his transport ministry to have the materia moved out and delivered to the aircraft factories.

A few weeks later Hennessy received a call from Beaverbrook, who told him to report at once to his country house, Cherkley Court. Ther he found his boss with an irate Herbert Morrison, who was on the poin of resigning. 'What have you landed me in? Why have you bypassed m department? Explain,' demanded Morrison. Hennessy, after a knowing glance from Beaverbrook, shouldered the blame and told Morrison he had ordered the steel alloy himself, and was unrepentant because the aircraft industry could not afford to wait. Morrison soon withdrew his threat to quit.

Beaverbrook's focus on the aircraft production figures was unwa vering. Every Saturday afternoon he would have the weekly chart brought to his room at Stornoway House. After reading them, he uld send them by dispatch rider to the Prime Minister, who would ually be at Chequers. If they were good, Beaverbrook would get a ply by letter; if they were outstanding, he would receive a telegram. 27 May 1940 he submitted the latest tally to Churchill with an blogy for sending such a depressing account, but pointing out that ch 325 fighters built, as opposed to the 261 originally estimated, it s at least an improvement. Acknowledging the progress in a letter wrote to Sinclair on 3 June, Churchill also rebuked the air minister er his disclosure to the War Cabinet that day of a shortage of pilots: ord Beaverbrook has made a surprising improvement in the supply d repair of aeroplanes, and in clearing up the muddle and scandal of e aircraft production branch. I greatly hope that you will be able to as much on the Personnel side, for it will indeed be lamentable if we ve machines standing idle for want of pilots to fly them.'

It would be a recurring theme of the next few months: praise, on the hole, for Beaverbrook; admonition, from time to time, for Sinclair. th, in reality, were making massive contributions to the battle raging the skies.

ck in early January, with Chamberlain still ensconced at Number , Beaverbrook had invited Sinclair to dinner. 'I would like to have u alone as I want to tell you of my grievances against the present nduct of the war,' he explained. 'By all means, let us compare griev- ces!' Sinclair replied. This initial rapport had continued, reaching zenith on the first weekend of Churchill's premiership, when they ld amicable discussions about how their departments would work gether. Within weeks, however, all that early goodwill had evapo- ted. Beaverbrook was putting it about to Churchill's aides that 'the ir Ministry was a rotten ministry' and that Sinclair was 'a thoroughly d minister, who was hoodwinked by his subordinates'.

Sinclair faced two disadvantages when vying with Beaverbrook for e Prime Minister's favour. The first was Churchill's historic enmity wards the Air Ministry, which he felt was bureaucratic, slow to nbrace innovation, and top-heavy at senior level. He distrusted the

air marshals, and would bypass ministers by asking Professor Lindema.
and his Statistical Office to provide him with information on which
judge the progress on pilots and planes.

The second problem was the difference in Churchill's bonds w
the two men. Sir Ronald Melville, the air minister's private secreta
suggested that 'Churchill treated Sinclair like a son and Beaverbro
like a father – relationships which were never likely to produce
effective partnership'. Perhaps familiarity led Winston to treat t
younger man, his former adjutant, too casually, with a 'half-serio
levity'. Herbert Morrison, observing the dynamic in Cabinet, saw it
merely affectionate: 'Churchill had his favourites among his minist
for gentle leg pulling. One was Archibald Sinclair, who always to
it very well.' Others viewed the Prime Minister's behaviour rath
differently. John Moore-Brabazon, Minister of Transport and la
Beaverbrook's successor as Minister of Aircraft Production, thoug
'the abuse and insults Winston heaped upon him [Sinclair] w
unbelievable, which was strange, for he was devoted to Archie, a
had a very real affection for him. But never in the smallest way c
Sinclair show his resentment to these outrageous assaults; they seem
to pour off him like water off a duck's back.'

The patient, long-suffering Sinclair respected and admir
Churchill and was willing to absorb any manner of punishment fro
him. '[H]e receives at least three violent prods from the PM every d
demanding immediate explanations of this and that and a variety
immediate actions,' wrote Hugh Dalton. 'This, he says, is the PM's w
and it has much to be said for it, from the point of stimulation.'

Inside Cabinet, Sinclair found himself short of real allies. I
persistent, if well founded, criticism of appeasement had made h
enemies in Halifax and Chamberlain. 'Archie Sinclair at the A
Ministry seems to be a major disaster,' Halifax opined on 12 May, ev
before Sinclair had had time to show his worth. In a letter to his sis
Hilda on 15 June, Chamberlain wrote: 'Max makes the most bit
complaints of Sinclair who he is, he says, nothing but "blah". He
blocked by him at every turn and can't say anything bad enough

n. I told him that I had always had a very poor opinion of Sinclair
d had told Winston so . . .'

Churchill liked to play Beaverbrook and Sinclair off against one
other, believing that the creative tension this generated spurred
e two men on. 'There is one thing about the warfare between AM
e Air Ministry] and MAP [the Ministry of Aircraft Production]
ich is helping the public interest, namely that I get a fine view of
at is going on and hear both sides of the case argued with spirit,'
told Sinclair. He said much the same thing to Beaverbrook on
December. 'I am definitely of the opinion that it is more in the
blic interest that there should be sharp criticism and counter-
ticism between the two departments than that they should be
nding out ceremonious bouquets.'

In this developing battle Beaverbrook invariably had the upper
nd. He could decide what types of aircraft were produced and in what
mbers; the Air Ministry had no say until the Beaver's department
d delivered the planes to the squadrons. But even this was not
ough for Beaverbrook. The Air Ministry had developed a carefully
anned programme for its reserve aircraft, and another for those
anes allocated for training; it also exercised strict control over the
ocks of engines stored for future use and the quantities of spare parts
quired at each operational airfield. Beaverbrook demanded influence
if not the final say – in all of these areas. On the latter he affirmed:
etter a stringency in spares and a bountiful supply of aircraft than a
rplus of spares and a shortage of aircraft.' When Sinclair attempted
retain control of the stock of spare parts, Churchill rebuked him.
earnestly trust you will see Lord Beaverbrook's wishes are met fully
d immediately in the matter of these spares. I really could not endure
other bickering over this, considering the gravity of the situation.'

Early on in the feud, Beaverbrook resorted to a tactic that would
come common during his time in Churchill's war ministry, that of
signation. He tried it first on 30 June, saying, 'I am not suited to
orking with the Air Ministry or Air Marshals.' Churchill would have
one of it, replying, 'I require you therefore to dismiss this matter from

your mind, and to continue the magnificent work you are doing
which to a large extent our safety depends.'

Some of the Beaver's complaints against Sinclair and the A
Ministry were valid, but others were synthetic. This was a man w
liked to be in control at all times, to impose his will on others;
relished conflict, he needed an opponent, and if there wasn't a dispu
available, he would create one. When the good-natured, imperturba
Sinclair declined to step into the ring, it merely infuriated Beaverbroo
He was punching thin air. He had one of his assistant secretari
E.G. Compton, keep a list of 'Noes' from the air minister. By ea
September 1940 there were eleven, which he attached to a letter
proposed to send to Lord Halifax. 'I am distressed by the situation
which I find myself at the Cabinet. My colleagues and I are not worki
well together,' the letter started. 'It seems to me that when you ha
a good Minister of Aircraft Production, you should treat him as su
trusting his judgment in matters which concern his own Ministry.
fact, it is my view that I should have complete authority over aircr
and that I should not be obstructed in my business, either by deba
in the Cabinet or by difficulties from the Air ministry.' It ended w
the now familiar threat: 'I have reached the conclusion that the Pri
Minister should find a Minister who will get on more agreeably w
his colleagues.' In the end, Beaverbrook thought twice about it a
never sent the letter.

Whatever the merits of these political tussles, it gradually becam
apparent that Beaverbrook's ruthless methods were paying off, wi
a dramatic increase in the numbers of fighters produced: 446 in Ju
496 in July and 476 in August. It came just in time, for on 1 Augu
in Führer Directive No. 17, Hitler told his military commanders th
the first phase of probing and reconnoitring the British defenc
was over. Now the plan was to 'intensify air and sea warfare agair
the English homeland'. This time, the directive stated, the attac
would be aimed at RAF squadrons, their airfields and their suppli
and also against the aircraft factories, particularly those maki
anti-aircraft equipment.

This new assault was codenamed *Adlerangriff* ('Eagle Attack'). different weather persuaded Göring to delay *Adlertag* until esday, 13 August, but when 'Eagle Day' finally came 1,485 sorties re launched against a multitude of targets on the south coast and ther inland. The Luftwaffe's aim was to deal Fighter Command a ppling blow, so the raiders paid particular attention to Eastchurch nistakenly believing it to be a key Fighter Command base, when it s actually a station of Coastal Command, the RAF's maritime arm – Royal Aircraft Establishment at Farnborough, and airfields in the a of Middle Wallop (Sector HQ for Wales and the West Country) :h as Boscombe Down, Worthy Down and Andover.

The biggest single disaster occurred at RAF Detling in Kent, where ere was no air raid warning and no alarm. The Stuka bombers caught men queuing for their evening meals. Sixty-seven base personnel re killed, the hangers set ablaze, and twenty-two bombers destroyed some of them ready for a mission. By the end of the day Fighter mmand had lost forty-seven aircraft of various kinds on the ground out its losses in combat numbered only thirteen, and ten of those ots had survived. Though damaging, Göring's blow had missed.

At 10 Downing Street the mood was one of elation: 'I heard the onishing result of today's air battle: seventy-eight German planes stroyed for certain and we only lost three pilots,' recorded Jock lville. 'This is indeed a victory and will do much for the public rale.' That was true, but *Adlertag* was just the first of many strikes at : RAF over the critical month that followed, and by now Churchill s preoccupied not just with the need for more planes, but also with ack of pilots. 'W[inston] is convinced that the shortage is partly due the Air Ministry's policy of keeping too many pilots for training and und jobs,' Colville wrote that same day. 'Beaverbrook and Archie clair are, as ever, at it hammer and tongs.'

r those watching the life and death struggle between the fighter planes m the ground, the distant battle had, at times, an ethereal, dreamlike ality. It was a peerless summer; the skies were consistently clear and

flawlessly blue. 'You lay in the tall grass with the wind blowing gen
across you and watched the hundreds of silver planes swarming throu
the heavens like clouds of gnats,' recorded the American journa
Virginia Cowles on a visit to Dover. 'You could see the flash of wir
and the long white plumes from exhausts; you could hear the whine
engines and the rattle of machine-gun bullets. You knew the fate of civi
sation was being decided fifteen thousand feet above your head in a wo
of sun, wind and sky. You knew it, but even so it was hard to take in.'

At the War Cabinet meeting on 14 August there was considerable
excitement when Sinclair relayed a dramatic police report detail
how the first contingent of German parachutists, forty-five in a
had landed in different parts of the country – Scotland, Derbyshi
Staffordshire and Yorkshire. In one case, a box containing maps an
instructions had been found. Churchill suggested a reward shou
be offered for the invaders' capture, a proposition rejected by l
colleagues in favour of a more general publicity campaign. The ne
day, however, the home secretary, Sir John Anderson, discovered th
all was not as it appeared. The landing had been a hoax; there were i
German infiltrators, but up to eighty parachutes had been dropped
part of an enemy plan to sow confusion and undermine morale. It a
added to the jittery mood pervasive in Whitehall.

Thursday, 15 August also marked the Luftwaffe's most determine
effort yet to saturate the British defences. With 1,000 fighter plan
and 800 bombers at their disposal, the Germans unleashed a concerte
onslaught against major towns and cities on the north-east coast
England. The theory was that eight hundred German aircraft wou
pin down the RAF in the south, leaving the unguarded airfield
aircraft factories, radar stations, ports and shipping in the north wid
open to attack. But what German intelligence had failed to anticipa
was the strategic foresight of Air Chief Marshal Sir Hugh Dowdin
who had earlier moved seven Hurricane and Spitfire squadrons nort
to counter this very eventuality.

The less experienced radar operators in the north initially put th
number of enemy planes on approach at thirty, which was quick

vised to over fifty. In fact there were sixty-five Heinkel He III ombers and thirty-four Messerschmitt Bf 110s on their way from bases Norway, and fifty Junkers Ju 88s from Denmark. Fighter Command's Group scrambled the Spitfires of 72 Squadron Acklington to meet e enemy and once the full scale of the onslaught was known, 605 quadron Drem's Hurricanes and 41 Squadron Catterick's Spitfires nt to join them. Marshalled with skill and flair by the officer mmanding 13 Group, Air Vice-Marshal Richard Ernest Saul, the tack was turned back. In all, twenty-three German aircraft were shot wn that afternoon, while just two RAF pilots were injured. RAF riffield was destroyed, however, with seventeen deaths and the loss twelve Whitley bombers, and in the worst of the civilian casualties even were killed and forty injured by Heinkel bombs in Dawdon, ounty Durham. Even so, this 'Battle of Tyneside' represented a severe tback for Göring; never again was a daylight raid attempted on the orth English coast.

Further south, the battles raged on into early evening, with fierce ogfights over Swanage, Portland and the Straits of Dover, and onstant attempts by the Junkers and their escorts to hit the airfields ound Middle Wallop. This was also the day when London received its st foretaste of the Blitz. As the Messerschmitt fighter bombers tried escape pursuing Hurricanes, two German planes crashed into the eavily populated suburbs around Croydon and Purley. The Bourjois erfume factory was hit and sixty people were killed, 180 injured.

When word of the day's dramatic events was transmitted to Downing reet, Churchill, 'consumed with excitement', together with General may and Lord Beaverbrook, decided to head out to Fighter Command Q at Bentley Priory, near Stanmore, to watch developments from e RAF's nerve centre, the central operations room. At one moment, ith the lights that denoted planes in action flashing continuously, it came clear to the trio that every single available RAF squadron was agaged, with nothing in reserve. 'I felt sick with fear,' recalled Ismay. Once the Prime Minister was satisfied the battle had turned in ritain's favour, he returned to Number 10 and reported to his staff that

there had been well over a hundred German losses – in fact, the fin
revised figure would be seventy-six – with just thirty-four machine
and eighteen pilots lost on the British side. He asked Colville to rela
the good news to Neville Chamberlain, who was recuperating afte
illness at his country home. 'The Lord President was very grateful t
you,' Colville said to the Prime Minister. 'So he ought to be,' replie
Churchill. 'This is one of the greatest days in history.' The followin
afternoon he was back at Stanmore. The effects of two days sper
watching Britain's defences on the brink, protected by this small grou
of skilled airmen, left him drained. 'Don't speak to me: I have neve
been so moved,' he told Ismay. A few minutes later he leaned forwar
and said, 'Never in the field of human conflict has so much been owe
by so many to so few.'

He carried that vivid phrase with him into the House of Common
on 20 August, making his tribute to the RAF the rousing centrepiec
of a masterly summary of twelve months of war. Just as emboldenin
as the powerful rhetoric, though, was Churchill's news of increase
co-operation with America, first through negotiations over th
use of British defence bases in Newfoundland and the West Indie
and second in the form of the delivery by the US of vital guns an
ammunition to replenish Britain's stocks after the Dunkirk disaste
'Like the Mississippi, it just keeps rolling along,' the Prime Ministe
reassured MPs on the growing transatlantic alliance.

The task of winding up the debate, five long hours later, fell t
Sinclair. The support act ensured the mood of optimism did not wane
First, he saluted the performance of each branch of the armed service
– the 'power' of the navy, the 'dogged fighting spirit' of the army, an
the 'superb prowess and audacity' of the pilots and crews of his ow
Royal Air Force. Next, he paid tribute to the fighter and bomber pilot
who had rallied to the cause from all parts of the Empire, and from th
conquered nations in Europe. Then, Sinclair mocked Goebbels ove
his 'hard lying' about British casualties: 'If the German claims had been
true, the British navy would now have consisted of four submarine
and sixty-three destroyers, minus three aircraft carriers, twenty-one

uisers and seventeen battleships. This ghost navy certainly puts up a
onderful defence of our coasts and trade!'

Sinclair concluded with a vow that would prove a hostage to fortune
later years. 'We shall never use our powers in the air as an instrument
mass terrorism. Our blows are, and will continue to be, directed
ainst the enemy's aerodromes, aircraft factories, aero-engine factories
d other centres of his military industry and supply. Wherever the
struments of cruelty and oppression are forged . . . there the strong
m of the RAF will reach out.'

that Commons speech of 20 August, Sinclair had responded to
iticism by one MP, John Moore-Brabazon, of Churchill's recent
omotion of Lord Beaverbrook. Noting the acclaim expressed by most
her MPs for his adversary's 'energy, devotion and drive', Sinclair had
oncluded that 'The House would scarcely [have been] surprised' at
eaverbrook's elevation to the War Cabinet.

Whatever his characteristically loyal public utterances, privately
inclair was fighting his bitterest battle yet with Beaverbrook, this time
ver the issue of the training of pilots. Sinclair believed that a steady
pply of qualified pilots could only be guaranteed if they could train
ee from the limitations imposed in Britain by lack of space and the
reat of enemy attack; far better to send them abroad, to the open
ies of the prairie and the veldt in Canada, South Africa, Australia
d New Zealand, as part of the new Empire Air Training Scheme.
here they could train safely in Anson and Battle aircraft no longer
onsidered worthy of the front line. But with Britain anticipating
vasion, Beaverbrook bitterly opposed the movement of even one
ilot, one aircraft, out of the country. The idea that inexperienced
rmen tended to crash more often was not one he ever countenanced.
\s far as he was concerned, even one man throwing a bomb out of a
aining aircraft was better than nothing,' reflected Sir Ronald Melville.

This row over the training of pilots abroad dominated many a
/ar Cabinet meeting in July and August. On the day Sinclair spoke
the Commons, Beaverbrook had composed his strongest critique

yet of the proposal. 'The Air Ministry anticipates a transfer overse:
of 2,500 aircraft in the last half of the year. This cannot be done.
would congest the ports and overburden terminal facilities. And th
packing required would be a wilful squandering of valuable materia
As for the airmen themselves: 'The departure of good pilots, no
flying instructors here, is a serious consideration. At present, we ca
call upon these men in emergency to serve the country as operation:
pilots. They are a valuable reserve.

'Similarly, training machines represent a last reserve of aircra
If we send them abroad, we dissipate this reserve.' Halifax note
'Max . . . always paints a gloomy picture in Cabinet in order to restra
the Air Ministry from sending aircraft out of the country.' But no
Beaverbrook added a psychological objection to his case, playing o
Churchill's role as the defiant leader of a besieged homeland. 'The
have been many rumours concerning evacuation of Canada in th
past, and also about Government and other intentions in futur
There have been suggestions about the Fleet. The departure of a larg
Air Force, partly to the American continent, would cause a renewal
false rumours in many directions.'

Matters came to a head in the War Cabinet meeting on Friday, 3
August. 'We must take a long view and consider our preparations fc
the air battles of 1941,' Sinclair argued. 'Navigation and night flyir
were arts in which our pilots had an undisputed technical superiori:
over the Germans, but the latter were making a big bid to catch us u
Our advantage might disappear if we confined our training of pilots t
this country, under the hampering conditions of German air attack ar
an English winter.' Once again, Beaverbrook made it plain that he wa
opposed to any pilots or machines being sent out of the country. He d
not accept that Ansons and Battles were obsolescent machines: 'Ou
reserves of these aircraft might yet save us in the event of invasion.'

The minutes of the discussion show that Clement Attlee an
Arthur Greenwood lent some support to Sinclair, saying that the Wa
Cabinet should not concentrate on the 1940 campaign so exclusive
as to 'find ourselves unable to wage the campaign of 1941'. Churchill

ompromise – favouring Beaverbrook – was that the position would be
viewed in a month's time, but that the scheme should be postponed
ntil December. His concession to Sinclair was that one navigational
aining school could go to South Africa, but the air minister was
early frustrated. 'We had no time to waste if we intended to gain the
upremacy of the air in 1941. The decision of the War Cabinet might
ell make it impossible to recover lost ground.' He insisted he had a
sponsibility to Parliament for the training of the RAF.

Churchill's curt response was that, first and foremost, Sinclair's
sponsibility was to him and the War Cabinet. At that, Sinclair
alked out, asking Churchill, as he left, if he could see him privately
ter in the day. 'Archie came back much, much earlier to the office
an anybody expected that day,' recalled Melville. 'He was absolutely
hite and quivering with anger. The reception that Beaverbrook had
ot at the Cabinet was so favourable that he had no alternative but to
y that if this happens, I shall leave my position as Secretary of State
r Air.' Resignation was usually Beaverbrook's tactic; for the placid
inclair to be stirred to such anger was rare indeed.

Churchill brought both men together at the weekend and managed
o broker a settlement. Sinclair's paper for the War Cabinet of Monday,
September showed he had won agreement to send just nineteen
lots and thirty-eight planes (Ansons) abroad that month, but the
gures increased in October (38 pilots, 102 planes), November (85,
24), December (95, 181) and January 1941 (86, 124). The uneasy
ompromise agreed by Churchill by and large stuck. While the Battle of
ritain raged, some airmen with relatively few hours of flying experience
ad to be pushed into action earlier than the air marshals and Sinclair
anted. In the longer term – particularly during Britain's bombing war
n Germany – the Empire Training Scheme would pay major dividends.

n Tuesday, 3 September, the Combined Intelligence Committee
ported 'sudden and startling' increases in the concentration of barges
coastal ports and waterways on the other side of the Channel. British
notographic intelligence had spotted fifty vessels at Ostend, a hundred

and forty at Terneuzen and ninety at the south end of the Bevelan
Canal. On that same day General Wilhelm Keitel, commander-in
chief of the German armed forces, issued a directive setting out th
revised timetable for Operation *Sealion*, Hitler's master plan for th
invasion of the United Kingdom. The earliest date for the departure c
the transport fleet was to be 20 September, with 'S-Day' on the 21st.

Meanwhile, the Luftwaffe had begun to prowl by night. Assaul
were made on Bristol, Cardiff, Swansea, Liverpool and Newcastle, an
they were starting to test the spirit and resilience of the populatior
Twenty-three-year-old Liverpudlian Doris Melling, shorthand typis
and hospital library assistant, recorded in her diary, 'Everyone gettin
very mad about these raids. Apparently we are just here to be hit a
It said in one of the papers that it was a fine sight to see the Spitfire
taking off after the Germans. I dare say it is. I would like to see
around here.' Yet the damage had scarcely begun. That the lives c
Doris and the other inhabitants of Britain's towns and cities wer
about to become far more dangerous was signalled by Hitler himsel
on Wednesday, 4 September in a surprise speech in Berlin's *Sportpalas*
where an adoring audience of thousands, largely made up of femal
workers, had come to hear the Führer open his second wartime winte
relief campaign.

Hitler was clearly incensed by the RAF's pinprick raids, which had
culminated in an attack on Berlin on 25 August. As the Americar
correspondent William L. Shirer observed, 'The Berliners are stunned
They did not think it could happen. Göring assured them it couldn't.

The Führer told his crowd that for three months he had held back
from ordering any retaliatory action, 'thinking that they would stop thi
nonsensical behaviour. Mr Churchill has taken this to be a sign of ou
weakness. You will understand that we shall now give a reply, night fo
night, and with increasing force.' In mocking fashion, Hitler continued
'The English are wondering when the attack is going to begin. The
English ask: "Why doesn't he come?"' Hitler then stepped back, raised
his arms and said: 'Be calm. Be calm. He's coming. He's coming.'

On Friday, 6 September, at Chequers, Churchill played war game

ith his guests Generals Ismay, Alan Brooke and Sir John Dill. 'First
° all he placed himself in the position of Hitler and attacked these
hores while I defended them,' Brooke recorded. 'He then revised the
hole of the air-raid warning and gave us his proposals to criticise.
inally, at 1.45 we got off to bed.' The following evening, Hitler
imself made good what he had promised three days earlier. Air
id warnings would be irrelevant: the Führer had sent an armada of
ombers to lay London waste.

Chapter Four

'A troglodyte existence'

7 September to 31 December 1940

On Saturday, 7 September, the peace of a late summer's evenin
in the ancient village of Horsell, Surrey, was shattered by th
unaccustomed sound of the bells ringing out at the twelfth-centur
church of St Mary the Virgin. Traditionally one of the most evocative
comforting rituals of country life, the bells had not been heard in th
parish – or anywhere else in Britain – since 13 June, when a governmen
ban had been imposed. Now it was a sound to strike fear into loca
inhabitants, as it had been designated as the first official warning tha
an invasion by the Germans was under way.

Sixteen-year-old Derrick Clewley and his father William mad
their way to the old oak tree on the corner of Brewery Road an
Arthur's Bridge Road, with no idea if they were about to encounte
enemy parachutists – or even, perhaps, German Panzer tanks. Youn
Derrick was a member (although technically a year under age) o
the local branch of the Home Guard, Britain's one-million-stron
volunteer army, formed as a second line of defence, principally i
coastal areas and in towns and villages in the south and east, wher
it was expected that the Wehrmacht would begin its attack. O
their way out, Derrick and his father had grabbed from behind th
garage some pea sticks, designed only to prop up plants. Armed wit

ese inadequate weapons, they headed off to join twelve others in onfronting the enemy.

In a state of apprehension and some confusion, the men of the Iorsell Home Guard waited at the oak tree for a couple of hours before became clear that there were no German tanks or paratroopers dvancing on the village after all. Eventually they drifted off back to heir homes and turned on the wireless, hoping for more information n the invasion – if, indeed, there really was one.

That evening the codeword 'Cromwell', ordering 'action stations' or the coastal divisions, had been issued by General Headquarters Iome Forces to the Eastern and Southern Commands. Having also een sent to all formations in the London area and to the 4th and th Corps in General Headquarters Reserve, instructing a state of eadiness at short notice, it had been repeated, for information, to all ther commands in the United Kingdom.

The message was to prepare for an invasion, *not* that it was under ay. But in Horsell – and some other parts of the Home Counties – Iome Guard commanders, acting on their own initiative, had decided) ring the church bells regardless. Unsurprisingly, rumours began preading: not only were parachutists landing, but German E-boats vere approaching the south coast.

Sadly, the rumours were correct: the Germans were coming – but ot by sea.

During a meeting at 5.30 that afternoon in Downing Street, the chiefs of taff had decided to activate Operation *Cromwell* after being presented vith compelling evidence that the invasion could happen at any time n the next three days. Admiral of the Fleet Sir Dudley Pound was in the hair, joined by Air Chief Marshal Sir Cyril Newall, General Sir John Dill (the new Chief of the Imperial General Staff – CIGS), General Sir Alan Brooke (commander in chief, Home Forces) and Major-General Frederick Beaumont-Nesbitt (director of military intelligence).

It was Beaumont-Nesbitt who outlined the reasons to expect an ttack on Britain. A large number of barges and small ships had been

moved to ports all along the Belgian and French coasts, from Osten
to Le Havre; the Luftwaffe, based between Amsterdam and Brest, ha
been substantially augmented by the transfer of 160 long-range bombe
from Norway, while short-range dive bombers had been redeployed t
forward airfields in the Pas de Calais region; a few days earlier fo
Dutch spies, captured on landing in a rowing boat on the south-ea
coast, had confessed to having been sent to report on the movemer
of British reserve formations in the areas of Oxford, Ipswich, Londo
and Reading; and finally, the moon and tide conditions would be mo
favourable for a seaborne invasion between 8 and 10 September.

All this intelligence, yet none of it led them to suspect what wa
happening right then, just four miles east of where they sat. As the mi
itary chiefs discussed whether they should deploy a massive fog scree
in the English Channel to help repel invaders, the Luftwaffe's bombe
and fighters were causing devastation in the East End of London.

Nearly 500 bombers – Heinkels, Dorniers and Junkers – escorted b
600 Messerschmitt fighters, had flown to the capital over the Channe
in an astonishing block 20 miles wide, filling 800 square miles c
sky. Although Fighter Command eventually committed twenty-on
squadrons to the air, the element of surprise allowed the Luftwaffe t
strike with relative impunity, ultimately raining down more than thre
hundred tons of high explosives and many thousands of incendiaries i
the first hour and a half of the raid.

First the sky was filled with huge clouds of smoke that billowed int
the air from burning oil storage tanks, then it turned an iridescen
orange from the light of the blazing fires which raged uncontrollabl
among the goods yards and warehouses along the banks of the Thames
Tugs and barges were set alight and sank in the river, while the stron;
wind whipped up by the heat caused small flaming planks of woo
to be tossed around like matchsticks. The fires raged as far upriver a
Tower Bridge where St Katherine's Dock, which lay almost opposite
was engulfed in flames.

This was indiscriminate terror bombing: although London's dock
land infrastructure was the main target, the Nazi hierarchy scruple

ot at all over the fate of the thousands who lived in the area. The orking-class residents of Southwark, Bermondsey, East and West Ham, oplar, Plaistow, Barking, Hackney, Rotherhithe and Stepney were ummelled, and the area around Limehouse was particularly badly hit.

The lucky ones headed for their basements. Some sought protection eneath the table in the front room or under the stairs, while others und communal safety in the brick-built street shelters. Not many ouses had gardens, so there were few domestic shelters in which take cover. Large numbers of shocked and frightened East Enders ecided to trek away from the danger. Some went eastwards to Epping rest and the open country of Essex, where thousands camped out in akeshift tents. Others headed west, towards the centre of London, here it was believed the shelters were deep and safe and the bombing ss severe.

When the day raiders had finished their work, the night assault egan. At 8.20 p.m. the second wave of 250 bombers – this time ithout a fighter escort – crossed the Sussex coast at Beachy Head. ith their target lit by the vivid glare of a hundred dockside fires, their sk was, if anything, even easier.

Barrage shooting by the anti-aircraft batteries being forbidden, and any of the guns having been moved to protect the aircraft factories, ondoners heard only a few brief and pitiful bursts of shellfire to relieve e drone of the planes and the steady crash of the bombs. In all they dured eight hours of bombing, and when the all clear sounded at 40 a.m. on Sunday, the toll was 436 killed and over 1,600 injured. ghter Command had managed to bring down forty-one German anes, but had lost twenty-three of its own fighters, with six pilots lled and seven injured.

Early the next morning, Soviet ambassador Ivan Maisky and his wife ok their car and drove from Kensington to the East End to survey the amage at first hand. They encountered 'crowds of frightened people, ying to salvage something from their broken property . . . terrible ies coming from somewhere below, from the foundations of houses ollapsed into heaps of stones and earth . . . mothers sobbing over the

mutilated bodies of their children . . . men cursing with furious glance
at the sky'.

As he peered into the ruins of a three-storey house, Maisky spotte
a child's cot in an alcove, miraculously hanging in the air, suspende
by its corner from the wall. 'On the cot lay a large doll with a re
ribbon in its hair . . . one's heart momentarily froze with the though
"Where is the mistress of that doll?" I could not forget this scene, s
simple and so pathetic.'

Government ministers spent Sunday surveying the wreckage of th
East End, taking soundings on the work required to clear the debri
the urgent need to house the homeless, and how to prepare for futur
attacks. Malcolm MacDonald, Minister of Health, visited West Har
where a shaken group of five councillors demanded a general evacuatio
of the area – a demand with which MacDonald, not wishing to appea
to panic, was unwilling to comply.

The Prime Minister headed for the docks, where he found fires sti
raging and scores of houses reduced to rubble. He stopped at an a
raid shelter in which forty people had been killed, and a large crow
mobbed him. General Ismay, accompanying Churchill, feared th
residents might harbour resentment over a lack of protection. Instea
they appreciated his visit in their hour of distress. 'Good old Winnie
they cried. 'We thought you'd come and see us. We can take it. Giv
it 'em back.' Churchill, as so often in these situations, was moved t
tears. Londoners would indeed have to take it, though: the Luftwaf
returned that evening, killing a further 412 and severely injuring 74
and would continue to come for a further fifty-six consecutive night

Such a prolonged offensive came as a surprise to most in Whitehal
The bombing war had been anticipated, but it had always been suppose
that it would consist of lightning raids, carried out in the daytime
much like the First World War. It was for this reason among others tha
deep shelters had been ruled out: they would be too far apart to provid
quick access, and there would be an increased risk of a major accident a
hundreds of people attempted to use the stairs down to them at the sam

ime. Now, the sustained bombardment began to reignite the arguments or using – or building – underground shelters; although those arguments were heard neither in Parliament, where London MPs seemed eluctant to criticise the government except in secret session, nor in the mostly compliant national press. Instead the case for deep shelters found ts champion in the communist-backed *Daily Worker*, where Professor B.S. ('Jack') Haldane wrote a series of campaigning articles.

Haldane was a flamboyant geneticist and physiologist, one of the rst effective popularisers of science. As befitted a communist, he ook a collectivist approach to the bombing threat and insisted that unkers built deep underground were the answer. Not only would they rovide protection from high explosive bombs, but they would meet he psychological need of humans under attack to go below ground nd support each other in times of stress. Haldane had been a witness o the aerial warfare of the Spanish Civil War and the success – as e saw it – of the Republican defenders of Madrid and Barcelona in stablishing a network of over 1,400 deep, 'bombproof' shelters.

The government's case continued to be made by Sir John Anderson. he home secretary's coldly analytical approach was concerned with ne straightforward technical problem above all else: how best to rotect the citizen from splinter, blast and falling debris. He felt that uestions of psychological comfort were beside the main point.

The philosophy behind the government's shelter strategy was ne of individualism, as opposed to Haldane's collectivism, and the Anderson shelter' epitomised that approach perfectly. 'The hard core f the problem is to provide protection for the citizen in, or close to his wn house,' insisted the man who gave it its name. Here, within the orrugated steel panelled walls of this vaulted structure, 6ft high, 4ft in wide and 6ft 6in long, the 'common man' and his family – maybe queezing in a friend or two – could shelter from the bombs, at home or n his own garden. The shelters had been made free to all householders ho earned less than £5 a week, while those with a higher income ad to pay £7. By the outbreak of war one and a half million had been rected, and during it a further 2.1 million were put up.

Anderson had made clear his views on Haldane's alternative when he spoke in a Commons debate on air raid shelters on 21 December 1938. In the blunt, unconsciously patronising tone that could lead him into trouble on parliamentary occasions – sounding more like the instructing senior civil servant he had once been than the engaging politician he was now supposed to be – he declared 'Apart from the difficulties and delays involved in any extensive scheme for deep bombproof shelters, I do not think we are prepared to adapt our whole civilisation so as to compel a large proportion of our people to live, and maintain their productive capacity, in a troglodyte existence deep underground.' Thus the government was committed to a policy of 'dispersal'. Individuals and their communities were to take refuge at home in the shelters that bore Anderson's name, in brick-built communal street shelters with reinforced concrete roofs that might house twenty to fifty people in trench shelters in public parks, or in other medium-sized refuges based around the workplace.

The *Daily Worker* had consistently harried the home secretary over this thinking. In April 1939, after Anderson rejected Haldane's 'Finsbury Plan' for deep shelters in that district, the newspaper informed its readers, 'you have received your death sentence'. And on 7 September the following year, the morning before that first London attack, the paper had returned to the fray with a front-page article on safety in Birmingham, headlined 'SHELTER SCANDAL IN MUCH RAIDED CITY'. Now, as the Blitz wore on, it was able to resume its campaign as the evidence began to accumulate in its favour.

Just hours after the King had visited Bethnal Green on Monday, 9 September, in a successful morale-boosting tour of the East End, the public mood took a less deferential turn. Around 5,000 local residents attempted to storm the entrance of the unfinished Bethnal Green tube station, and were only beaten back by the combined effort of the police and the Home Guard. By now the idea of using the London Underground for dormitories had taken hold and it would never be relinquished.

Churchill was no natural advocate of deep shelters, but on 12 September, just five days into the attack on London, he began to give the idea serious consideration. As Captain Euan Wallace, Conservative MP for Hornsey and the new senior commissioner for London's civil defence, wrote in his diary that night, however, 'This proposal was very carefully discussed when I was Minister of Transport and turned down for a variety of reasons. Reith [the current transport minister] has been asked to recapitulate them for the benefit of the Prime Minister.' Reith discussed the tube dilemma on the telephone with Churchill at 11 p.m.; he, like Wallace, was not keen to open up any part of London's transport system to those he described as 'refugees'.

The next morning, after a breakfast meeting at the Home Office with Sir John Anderson, Reith walked back to his office at the Ministry of Transport only to discover that the building was on fire, smoke billowing from the roof, after a bomb strike.

The German bombers hit an even more prestigious target just a few hours later. The War Cabinet meeting, which was being held underground in the recently reinforced Central War Room on King Charles Street, beneath the Treasury, was halfway through proceedings when a message was delivered to Churchill to say that Buckingham Palace had been dive bombed. The King and Queen were safe, but it had been the closest of escapes for the royal couple. 'There was . . . a tremendous explosion, and we and our two pages who were outside the door, remained for a moment or two in the corridor away from the staircase, in case of flying glass,' was the Queen's description. 'Then came a cry for bandages, and the first aid party rose magnificently to the occasion, and treated the three casualties calmly and correctly.' One of those badly hurt, Alfred Davies, who had been working below the chapel, later died of his injuries.

Just before this dramatic interruption, the War Cabinet had been discussing the question of opening up the tube during air raids. Malcolm MacDonald warned his colleagues that people in certain parts of London were 'showing reluctance' to use Anderson and street shelters. They preferred underground shelters, such as the basements of churches, schools and public buildings. But these were becoming overcrowded, and outbreaks of infectious disease were feared.

Sir John Anderson was having none of it. He told his colleagues firmly that the public had been 'educated' to use the various shelters available, and that there was enough accommodation for the majority of the population. His meeting earlier that morning with Reith had won him a valuable ally, as the transport minister added that he had examined the arguments, but he too remained convinced the tube must be kept free for transport services. So the Anderson strategy continued. The authorities actively discouraged shelter in the Underground, and some station gates were even locked and guarded, while soldiers evicted 'trespassers' at others. But morale in the blitzed areas was in serious danger of cracking.

In Berlin that same day, Hitler had met with Field Marshal Erhard Milch and Grand Admiral Erich Raeder to plot the way ahead. He was determined that the air attacks should continue without interruption, at the expense of Operation *Sealion*, the long-planned land invasion of the United Kingdom. 'Even though victory in the air should not be achieved before another ten or twelve days, Britain might yet be seized by mass hysteria,' he suggested. 'If, within the coming ten or twelve days we achieve mastery of the air over a certain area, we could, by a landing operation, compel the enemy to come out with his destroyers against our landing fleet.'

The stage was set for what would prove to be the deciding hour in the Battle of Britain. On Sunday, 15 September the Luftwaffe launched its biggest attack yet against London, hoping along the way to draw out the RAF and deal it a fatal blow. But its huge force of 1,100 planes faced an aggressive, defensive line of fighters under the expert command of Air Vice-Marshal Keith Park at 11 Group Headquarters in Uxbridge. All the RAF planes were up in the air quickly thanks to the radar system, which the Germans consistently underestimated.

The raids continued throughout the day, the Luftwaffe flying a staggering thousand sorties against the capital. 11 Group put up ts entire force of twenty squadrons, and called for assistance from 2 Group (covering the Midlands) and 10 Group (the south-west). n all nearly forty RAF fighter squadrons – 480 aircraft – were engaged n fierce combat at any one time.

Churchill had been at RAF Uxbridge most of the day and watched nervously – but mightily impressed – as Park and his colleagues plotted their moves. Having returned to nearby Chequers for his customary fternoon nap, he was awoken at 8 p.m. to be given the astonishing news that 187 German planes had been brought down, for the loss of no more than twenty-five RAF fighters and twelve pilots. Lord Beaverbrook, on hearing of the day's events, telephoned Peter Howard, one of his investigative journalists on the *Daily Express*, and exclaimed triumphantly, 'This day our country has won a victory that will be recorded in the annals of history in the same terms as Trafalgar or Waterloo are recorded.' In fact the figures were inflated, as they often were in that period. The real German combat losses were eventually calculated as fifty-six planes – as opposed to twenty-eight on the British side – with eighty-one aircrew killed, thirty-one wounded and sixty-three taken prisoner. Fighter Command's dead numbered twelve, with fourteen injured and just one taken prisoner.

Nonetheless, it had been a well-planned, well-executed defence from the RAF. Yet despite this success, most of Churchill's ministers believed an invasion was still probable. The following day, 16 September, General Raymond E. Lee, military attaché at the American embassy, gauged opinion from Sinclair, Eden and Beaverbrook. Sinclair felt Hitler will invade because of prestige reasons, and because he must do it now or never.' Eden thought 'it will be in the next fortnight', while Beaverbrook said simply: 'Hitler will attack.'

They were all wrong, although they would not know it for some weeks. On Tuesday, 17 September, Hitler held a meeting in the Chancellery in Berlin with Göring and Field Marshal Gerd von Rundstedt, at which he reluctantly decided to postpone Operation *Sealion*. He ordered the dispersal of the invasion fleet, which included some two thousand barges held in Belgian, French and German harbours. The Führer did, however, dictate that the bombing of London should continue, and over wider areas than ever before.

The skill and resilience of the RAF, combined with the inclement weather, had put a stop to Germany's invasion plans. But rumours and misleading intelligence would continue to keep politicians on both sides of the Atlantic on edge for several more weeks. Indeed, on the morning of Sunday, 22 September, President Roosevelt sent a message to Churchill reporting that 3 p.m. that very day was zero hour for the attack.

Churchill telephoned Eden, who was quietly going through some papers in the study of his rented house in Dover. The war secretary told the Prime Minister it was wet and windy, hardly good conditions for a crossing, and that he felt safe enough. But even so, he decided to step outside and take a closer look. 'I went to the top of the hill which overlooked the Channel and afterwards sent a further message reporting it was so rough that any German who attempted to cross would be very seasick.' Such sangfroid would be required in large doses over the next few weeks.

Meanwhile resentment towards the government's shelter policy continued to build. A dramatic expression of it came on the evening of Saturday, 14 September, when a crowd of fifty East Enders – men, women and two children – marched into the Savoy Hotel after an air raid alert and occupied the basement shelter.

'If it's good enough for the rich it's good enough for the Stepney workers and their families,' declared their leader Phil Piratin, the tenacious Jewish communist who had brought 100,000 Londoners on to the streets in the Battle of Cable Street in 1936. The police were called, but a tense confrontation was eased when the hotel manager was content for the invaders to stay.

The group settled themselves into armchairs and deck chairs, and on the unoccupied floor space of the shelter, while the bewildered waiters brought them pots of tea, bread and butter. Piratin announced that he and his colleagues would pay only 2d a head – the same price s that displayed at a Lyons Corner House – rather than the Savoy's sual minimum charge of 2s 6d.

The demonstrators left peaceably enough when the all clear sounded ss than half an hour later. But the incident received more publicity an the government would have liked; the London correspondent f the American broadcaster CBS described the events vividly to his illions of listeners the next day. Meanwhile, the Nazi paper *Völkischer eobachter* relished Churchill's discomfort: 'Londoners have become ve dwellers. Life has stopped. The working population is fleeing from e east and south of the city to the West End. Desperate men and omen have stormed the luxurious Savoy hotel.'

At Monday's War Cabinet an aggrieved Churchill brought up the avoy incident, saying that 'episodes of this kind could easily lead to rious trouble'. Sir John Anderson acknowledged that there were gns of organised demonstrations from East Enders in the West End. ogether, he and Churchill convinced the Cabinet that 'strong action' ould, if necessary, be taken to prevent further demonstrations.

Yet thousands of Londoners were ignoring Anderson's strictures to ay close to home. Many began queuing up at the various deep tube ations at midday to buy a 1½d ticket to gain access to a platform to eep on for the night. The high point of the flight to these stations me on Friday, 20 September, when an estimated 117,000 headed derground.

On Tuesday, 17 September Professor Haldane had led a deputation the National ARP Co-ordinating Committee to the Home Office, eading for the government to step up deep shelter protection. he following day the *Daily Mirror* joined the *Daily Herald* and the *aily Worker* in fierce attack on the current policy, this time targeting s fire on the Ministry of Health. 'There is still time – but not too uch – to get on with further evacuation schemes and with provision deep shelters hitherto rejected, with unparalleled obstinacy, by Sir hn Anderson,' its editorial boomed.

That same day Anderson defended his shelter strategy effectively a secret session of the Commons. But with Churchill becoming

increasingly concerned and preoccupied by the issue – his wii
Clementine was receiving many letters on the subject, and had starte
to visit shelters unannounced – the home secretary was comir
under severe pressure to change course. A conference he held t
try to convince newspaper editors of his position was a disaster. I
uncompromising fashion, he told them he would not embrace a polic
of deep shelters and advised them to halt their campaign against hin
'Is that the policy of the Government?' asked one of those present. 'D
you think I should have said what I have said were that not so?' wi
Anderson's angry response.

His generally aloof attitude would cost him dear. The workings (
the popular press were alien to Anderson, and he was unwilling t
woo reporters and editors to win their support. He should not hav
been surprised when the *Daily Worker* published a cartoon of hin
showing him running for a deep shelter pursued by members of th
public demanding their own entry. Over his shoulder was a shotgu
and a brace of game birds – a reference to an earlier report by the pape
that in the first week of the Blitz he had gone on a shooting holida
in Scotland.

Lord Horder, doctor to Kings George V and VI and chairman of th
British Medical Association, had been asked by Anderson to quickl
draw up a report on the state of London's shelters. In just four days h
and his committee had travelled the length and breadth of the city t
visit every kind of refuge. Despite pockets of good practice, his finding
gave cause for grave concern.

He was disturbed by conditions in many of the public shelter
both purpose-built and improvised. The crypt shelter below St John
Church in Bethnal Green was 'dusty, dirty and gloomy . . . there wi
an unpleasant smell and the ventilation of the whole shelter was nc
good'. In Charrington's Brewery in Stepney where 1,800 men, wome
and children gathered, 'the atmosphere at 8.50pm was like the tropi
and extremely close . . . the noise of people talking was tremendoɪ
and the children were quite unable to sleep. They showed signs o
tiredness and being on edge and many of them were crying bitterly.'

Like Anderson, Horder believed that scurrying to shelters every night
as bad for people – and for morale. Yet when he submitted his early
ndings, having witnessed the growing discontent at first hand, he con-
·ded that 'we must take into account the herd instinct of the masses
nd their desire in the face of danger for human companionship'. To
at end, he grudgingly conceded among his recommendations that 'the
ssibility of using the Tube system for shelters during the night should
· considered, provided that this does not interfere with the traffic'.

The problem, though, was now as much about perception as it was
out policy. The impression was of an unbending government unable
unwilling to address people's fears. Anderson may have commissioned
e Horder Report and begun to put its recommendations in place, but
e public's confidence in him – driven by the relentless press criticism
was at a low ebb. If the still new government's reputation was to be
eserved, it would have to sacrifice him.

Not that the home secretary was totally without supporters. The
pular humorist, novelist and playwright A.P. Herbert composed this
tle poem in his honour, and it appeared in the *Sunday Graphic* in
ctober.

> You will not mind as many do,
> The foolish things the clever say.
> You saw the grim decisions through,
> The sticky jobs all came your way.
>
> But millions, from your armoured nest,
> Emerging safe, defiant, free.
> Will say 'John Anderson knew best,
> 'And we can be as tough as he.'

t the Prime Minister no longer needed a tough guy. What he
nted was a charismatic leader who was close to Londoners
d would invigorate them through these grim times; a capable
rliamentarian who could defend the government's evolving strategy;
d a minister who could win over the disgruntled press.

The failing health of Neville Chamberlain – stricken with cancer presented Churchill with an opportunity to reshape his government a just the right moment. And so he made the obvious choice. He aske Herbert Morrison to move from the Ministry of Supply to becom home secretary and Minister of Home Security.

Having gone into hospital in late July for what he believed was routine colostomy operation, Chamberlain discovered he was actual suffering from terminal cancer of the bowel.

After convalescing throughout August, he returned to work in ear September, warning Churchill that he would 'not attain full efficienc all at once'. In the event, he chaired one War Cabinet on 12 Septembe and attended his final Cabinet meeting in the Prime Minister's roo at the House of Commons on Wednesday, 18 September, bowing ou after over seventeen years of virtually continuous service. Churchi paid him generous tribute in their exchange of letters, applaudir his 'unshaken nerve and persevering will', and acknowledging tha 'the help you have given me since you ceased to be my chief tided u through what may well prove to be the turning point of the war'.

In the reshuffle of 3 October Anderson took Chamberlain's plac in the War Cabinet as Lord President of the Council; his remova from the Home Office had hardly been a demotion. Joining him the top table were Ernest Bevin (a universally popular appointmen and Kingsley Wood, Chancellor of the Exchequer (an underwhelmin choice in the eyes of many). Thus – with Beaverbrook's elevation i early August – the War Cabinet now comprised eight, compared to th original five back in May.

Bevin's upward move may have stolen many of the headline the following day, but it was Herbert Morrison's that captured th imagination. 'No one should be better able to deal with London's a raid problems than Mr Herbert Morrison,' reflected the *Yorkshire Post*. '. municipal leader and administrator of proved quality . . . Londoners i particular may feel that they have a man whom they know and trust i charge of their "front line",' *The Times*' editorial declared. 'When I hear u had been appointed Home Secretary I went home and slept soundly,' oclaimed Ritchie Calder, campaigning journalist on the *Daily Herald*.

Though their son was born in Brixton, Morrison's father (a police nstable) and mother (a maid servant) had been pure East End ckneys, and he had inherited all the best characteristics of that eed of Londoner – a quick mind, a clever tongue, wit and joviality. is childhood had been difficult; having lost his right eye when just ree days old, he had left elementary school at fourteen, taking jobs an errand boy, 'live-in' shop assistant and telephone switchboard erator. But his ferocious self-education included Marx, Engels, erbert Spencer, Darwin and – his favourite – *Riches and Poverty* Sir Leo Chiozza Money, a compelling assessment of the unequal stribution of wealth in Britain. Morrison discovered a gift for public eaking through a chance soapbox appearance in Brockwell Park, uth London, and a career in politics first began to develop in 1906 en he joined the Independent Labour Party.

A founder member of the London Labour Party, Morrison became ayor of Hackney in 1920, and three years later entered Parliament MP for South Hackney. He was an effective Minister of Transport Ramsey MacDonald's 1929–31 administration, and in the 1930s – en out of Parliament – he cemented his reputation and his political wer base while leader of London County Council, overseeing the velopment of the capital's housing, health, education and transport rvices. Highly ambitious, he was hugely disappointed to be beaten r the leadership of the Labour Party by Clement Attlee in 1935.

Now in his early fifties, Morrison was one of the better recognised liticians – short in stature, he had a deeply lined face, with a wave unruly hair parted to the left, and an earnest expression that would eak out into a pleasing, if slightly self-satisfied, smile. He wore rtoiseshell glasses, and would tilt his head on one side so as to focus etter with his single eye.

At the Ministry of Supply Morrison had found himself being pulled st one way and then another by competing claims for raw materials d labour from his senior colleagues – and fierce rivals – Bevin

and Beaverbrook. But his ebullient self-confidence and energy h
impressed many, and was coupled with a happy knack of inventir
snappy phrases with which to stimulate production in the factorie
'Go To It', with its later variant 'Stick To It', was a sub-editor's deligh
He was a naturally gifted communicator, by voice or by word, and
constant presence on newsreels and in newspapers – way ahead of th
majority of his colleagues in understanding the vital importance
public relations.

But on pure policy, the new home secretary knew that at best l
could only tweak the government's approach. So in his first maj
broadcast on Sunday, 3 November – ironically the first night sin
the start of the Blitz when the air raid sirens did not sound – he ma
it clear that 'anything like a universal policy of deep shelter, for th
whole population or the greater part of it, is beyond the bounds
practical possibility'. The 'offensive' war effort had to come first. Ste
cement and bricks, not to mention labour, were needed for munitio
and aircraft factories and aerodromes.

Morrison paid tribute to the 85 per cent of Londoners, the 'quie
determined people' who did not crowd into big shelters, who sle
in their own homes, in Anderson shelters or in communal domest
shelters. But he knew he had to assuage the critics, so he promise
to use a good deal of whatever resources remained to carve out ne
tunnels linked to the tube system for more deep shelter places (100,0C
in six months was his estimate in a Cabinet paper), as well as buildir
more communal brick surface shelters, strengthening the Anderso
shelters, and adapting a large number of 'strong modern buildings'
London for shelter both above ground and at basement level.

In the meantime, he began to further implement Lord Horde
recommendations, which included a ticketing system and th
allocation of bunks (over 1.7 million had been ordered) for the regul
occupants of the larger shelters, plus chemical lavatories, bett
ventilation, lighting and running water. Permanent canteens were
be introduced in the big shelters, while regular entertainment in th
form of night classes, film shows and music was being organised.

Predictably, the *Daily Worker* excoriated Morrison, saying his broadcast 'promised his listeners more bunks and ladled out more bunkum'. Most of the other papers tended to agree with the *Yorkshire Post*, however, that the new home secretary was tackling the whole shelter problem with 'realistic energy'.

Morrison was not alone in his task. Supporting him were two of the most able and empathetic members of the coalition. That they were also both women – the only members of their sex in Churchill's ministry – made their accomplishments even more admirable.

'I do so like that little spitfire,' Harold Nicolson observed of Ellen Wilkinson on 20 November. 'She and Florence Horsbrugh are really the only two first-class women in the House. I should like to see both of them made Cabinet ministers.'

With Churchill at the helm, that prospect was unlikely. Yet, despite their political differences, he was shrewd enough to see the value of having Labour's Ellen Wilkinson at the Home Office at such a sensitive time. This ex-communist who had led the Jarrow March, the 'Fiery Particle' admired for her energy, dynamism and passionate oratory, was just the person he needed on board to restore public confidence in his administration's shelter policy. And the appreciation was mutual. 'After I had been interviewed by Mr Churchill I felt I had been in the presence of a very great man and a very great leader,' Wilkinson said following her appointment to the government in May. She was moved from the Ministry of Pensions to become one of Morrison's three parliamentary secretaries and given specific responsibility for shelters.

Florence Horsbrugh had successfully made the transition from the Chamberlain to the Churchill government, retaining her post as junior minister at the health ministry. This daughter of an Edinburgh chartered accountant first came to public attention in the First World War, when her pioneering work in developing a network of kitchens and canteens won the approval, among others, of Queen Mary, and gained her an MBE.

Elected MP for Dundee in 1931, she had consistently impressed

her colleagues with confident speeches in Parliament, delivered in
fine, contralto voice. In 1936, dressed in an evening gown of brow
velvet, she became the first woman to move the address in reply t
the King's Speech – the new monarch Edward VIII's first opening o
Parliament. 'WOMAN TRIUMPHS IN THE COMMONS, SETS BARE ARM
FASHION' was the faintly condescending headline in the *Daily Expres*.
A woman who preferred low tones to highlights, understatemen
to exaggeration, Horsbrugh had brought to her tasks in the healt
ministry an 'impressive mixture of ministerial authority, politica
sagacity, feminine gentleness and maternal fussiness'.

She had already played a crucial role in civil defence, helping t
arrange the successful evacuation in September 1939 of one and a ha
million women and children from the major cities – one of the bigge
social experiments in British history. Now, with mass evacuatio
over – although much smaller numbers were leaving London again
Horsbrugh turned her attention to the victims of the Blitz. Specificall
she had to organise the casualty clearing services in London, set u
hostels for those rendered homeless and ensure the smooth runnin
of rest centres, while – liaising closely with Wilkinson – she wa
responsible for health and sanitation in the shelters. She would als
completely restructure the British Civil Nursing reserve.

On her first evening in office Ellen Wilkinson headed for the notor
ous Tilbury shelter in the underground goods yard beneath the railwa
arches in Stepney. Originally established by the local authority as a sa
haven for 3,000 people, on some nights it was occupied by as many a
16,000. At first there was no sanitation and poorer families were force
to occupy floors covered with excrement and discarded margarine.

'This has been tidied up a bit, hasn't it,' Wilkinson remarked t
the warden upon arrival. 'It's a palace to what it was,' he replied
As she made her way round the shelter, she stressed to the reporte
accompanying her the three 'S's: 'safety, sanitation and sleep'.

'My job is to put to bed each night, outside their own homes, on
million people,' was Wilkinson's typically vivid description of her tas
The new minister's first foray into the East End certainly impresse

ilde Marchant, journalist and East End commissioner: 'No distasteful
orner, no story of misery was overlooked . . . I liked her energy and
er natural touch with these people.'

Up to then, Wilkinson's war had been dogged by illness and injury.
t the end of July she had undergone an appendix operation at
Mary's Hospital, London. Barely was she up and about again before
e suffered a minor fracture of the skull when a lorry hit her car in
e blackout on 5 August. Wilkinson had an especially keen sympathy
r the plight of those forced to use the shelters, because, just a few
ays after that first round of visits, a bomb destroyed her own flat in
uildford Street, Bloomsbury. She was eventually rehoused at Hood
ouse in Dolphin Square, but continued to spend many nights in
bed in her office as she refused to enter the deep shelters used by
embers of Parliament.

Wilkinson and Horsbrugh now saw a lot of each other, both when
t and about inspecting civil defences in London and across the table
Whitehall in various Cabinet committees. They frequently clashed,
though not always because of their ideological differences (which
ere largely subdued at this stage of the war); more because of their
ry contrasting personalities.

Wilkinson had inherited her father Richard's quick temper as well
his keen sense of justice. Although generous and warm-hearted to
fault, a lack of inches and a certain awkwardness of manner were
erhaps responsible for her occasionally pugnacious and aggressive
anner. Horsbrugh, by the same familial token, exhibited the qualities
precision and love of facts shown by her accountant father Henry.
all, smiling and unflustered, it was only when irritated that she
lopted what the more cruel commentators described as her 'maiden
nt' demeanour.

Their first clash, just two days after Wilkinson's appointment to
e Home Office, came over the subject of the possible compulsory
acuation of London's children. Wilkinson felt parents would be
ntent for their offspring to leave the city if the government simply
ade it clear that it was their duty; Horsbrugh pointed out that a

quarter had indicated they would refuse to send their children away, s
a stricter policy of compulsion was required.

'There seems to be the making of some pretty passages at arn
between these two ladies,' observed Captain Euan Wallace, 'and it
interesting to contrast Miss H's solid sympathetic commonsense wit
the rather theatrical statements of the new Under Secretary.'

As Göring's Heinkels, Dorniers and Junkers pounded oth
industrial centres, the two women's work took them further outsic
London. The shipbuilding centres of Barrow, Hull, Clydebank an
Belfast were heavily bombarded, as were the ports and manufacturir
cities of Liverpool, Manchester, Birmingham, Bristol, Plymoutl
Sheffield, Cardiff, Nottingham, Portsmouth and Southampton. Ar
then there was the smaller town of Coventry, with its population
just under a quarter of a million.

The Luftwaffe had already targeted many of the metalworking indu
tries of the West Midlands, and had visited Coventry sixteen tim
between 1 October and 8 November. Ernest Bevin had personally con
plained to Churchill about the 'undefended state of the town', while th
chiefs of staff had recognised that 'the morale of the workers in Covent
has unquestionably deteriorated as a result of enemy air attacks'.

On the evening of 14 November 1940 Hitler launched Operatic
Mondscheinsonate (Moonlight Sonata) – quite probably in retaliatic
for a recent RAF attack on Munich – with the intention of destroyir
the cathedral city's factories and industrial infrastructure with delibera
disregard for the damage inflicted on residential and cultural areas.

Around five hundred German planes rained down torrents of bomb
500 tonnes of high explosive and 36,000 incendiaries, turning tl
centre of the city into a firestorm. Around two-thirds of its buildin
were destroyed – including the iconic fourteenth-century St Michae
cathedral – and 4,300 families were made homeless. The tram syste
was destroyed. Almost every factory, if not actually hit, was put out
action by the complete obliteration of water, gas and electricity supplie

Amid such destruction, a precise accounting of the death toll prove
exceedingly difficult. Much later, it was estimated that 568 were kille

the raid with another 863 badly injured; thousands had managed to escape, either by trekking out of the city to nearby towns and villages, or remaining safe in the seventy-nine public air raid shelters. Florence Horsbrugh took her car and drove into Coventry on Friday, before the flames had died down. There she joined Herbert Morrison and his wife Margaret, who had by coincidence been staying at nearby Himley Hall with the regional commissioner Lord Dudley when the bombs started to fall. Lord Beaverbrook also paid a visit to the blitzed city that afternoon, worried about the effect of the attack on its vital aircraft production factories.

The following day the King arrived to lend his psychological support to the shocked population. In his field marshal's uniform, he spent five hours picking his way through the smoking mountains of rubble and talking to survivors, who reported that he was moved to tears by what he witnessed. 'I was horrified at the sight of the centre of the town,' George VI recorded in his diary that night, 'the cathedral, hotels, shops, everything was flat and had been gutted by fire. The people in the streets wondered where they were, nothing could be recognized.'

After he departed, Morrison, Horsbrugh and Lord Dudley met to plot the way ahead for the stricken city. Morrison ordered up the Pioneer Corps to clear the damage, mobile canteens were brought in, and a house-to-house distribution of bread and milk started. Royal Engineers began work to restore the electricity supply, which they achieved within three days. Horsbrugh's main challenge was to find beds for the thousands who were now homeless. Some were billeted with obliging families in unscathed houses, while others stayed outside the city with relatives, or strangers who let out rooms for very low rents.

Morrison told the War Cabinet on Monday, 18 November that local people had been shaken by their experiences, and had been bitter at what they regarded as the lack of active defences. Nevertheless, they had kept their heads.' He reported that, on the whole, damage to munitions production was less extensive than at first feared.

While the home secretary was the visible face of the government during the Coventry crisis, Horsbrugh, largely unheralded, went about

her business, quietly dealing with the housing and health issues an
enabling the distraught residents to put together their lives agai
The *Daily Mirror* described her role as 'mothering the city', and a fe
years later her boss Malcolm MacDonald acclaimed her as 'one of th
heroines of the Battle of Coventry'.

Morrison and Horsbrugh – and Wilkinson too, although n
directly involved in the reconstruction efforts in Coventry – learne
valuable lessons from that terrible experience. An army of firewatche
was swiftly instituted; the major administrative reform of establishin
the first National Fire Service would soon follow.

Churchill and his ministers were themselves increasingly driven unde
ground as the German bombers kept on coming. Of the seventy-tw
War Cabinet meetings held between September and December, thirty
four took place in the Cabinet War Room, seventeen in the House (
Commons, and just twenty at 10 Downing Street. One of them – o
3 October – was at 'Paddock', codename for the government's reserv
meeting place in west London should it be forced to leave the princip:
emergency Cabinet War Rooms beneath the Treasury in Whitehall.

'Paddock' was a vast subterranean complex built directly beneat
the Post Office Research and Development Station in Dollis Hil
Willesden. It was a two-storey building, forty feet underground, wit'
a five-foot layer of concrete forming a protective roof and making
near impossible to destroy. Its warren of thirty-seven rooms included
mix of offices, kitchens and living quarters, together with a long ma
room, teleprinter room and cabinet room (with BBC studio adjoinin
it), and one room which had pinned to its door the words 'Captai
David Niven'. No one was ever sure, but it was thought that the acto
a friend of Churchill's, would be called upon to impersonate the Prim
Minister in radio broadcasts, to maintain the pretence he was sti
running the country in London – even if by then he had been force
to flee to Canada or America.

But Churchill disliked what he felt was the damp, oppressiv
atmosphere of 'Paddock', and was reluctant to contemplate the life (

'troglodyte'. After October's meeting, it was used by the War Cabinet who gathered there in March 1941 – just once more in the war.

The Prime Minister, his wife and staff had by now abandoned Number 10 as living quarters, and moved instead into a set of rooms known as the 'Number 10 Annexe', over the Cabinet War Rooms in the Board of Trade building. These were above ground, overlooking St James's Park, but protected inside with steel girders and outside with steel shutters.

Beleaguered as he was, nevertheless Churchill's political pre-eminence was reinforced on 9 October when, at a party meeting at Westminster's Caxton Hall, he was elected unanimously as leader of the Conservative (and Unionist) Party in succession to Chamberlain. Lord Halifax, presiding, suggested that the outgoing leader might have failed to preserve peace but the 'historian will, perhaps, record . . . a more informed and balanced judgement than is always attainable today'.

On 9 November Neville Chamberlain died at his home at Highfield Park in Hampshire. At the service at his local church of St Michael's in Heckfield the next day, the village vicar took as the text of his sermon 'Blessed are the peacemakers, for they shall be called the children of God'. Four days later Chamberlain's ashes were interred alongside those of fellow Conservative Prime Minister Andrew Bonar Law in the nave at Westminster Abbey; among the pallbearers at his funeral service were Cabinet colleagues Churchill, Lord Halifax, Sir Kingsley Wood, Sir Archibald Sinclair and Clement Attlee.

As the year drew to a close, the Prime Minister was asked to consider the merits of fresh proposals from the Ministry of Home Security for a new shelter to protect the public in their own homes. At 6 p.m. on Tuesday, 31 December, he strode into a room in 10 Downing Street where he was greeted by Herbert Morrison and his scientific adviser, thirty-nine-year-old Professor John Fleetwood Baker, already carving out a reputation as an innovative structural engineer.

Churchill was asked to cast his eye over two competing prototypes for a household shelter. One was a steel construct with a cross-section in the shape of a gothic arch, covered all over with steel plate and with flaps closing the ends. In the opinion of Professor Baker it was a 'death trap'. Its design, however, was based on a sketch Churchill himself had drawn for Morrison a few weeks earlier.

The other one, Professor Baker's invention, was a flat-topped, cage-like 'table shelter', with a steel roof, welded wire-mesh sides, and metal lath 'mattress' type floor. This, Baker demonstrated to Churchill, would absorb energy far better than the arch design, and escape from it – via the sides – would be much easier. It was 6ft 6in long, 4ft wide and 2ft 6in high, and could accommodate two or three people. It would also be very economical to manufacture in bulk, and could be put together with just a spanner and a hammer.

Morrison and his keen young designer put the case for the flat-topped shelter persuasively and at some length, and eventually won over their listener. Churchill – always receptive to scientific expertise and himself a skilled bricklayer – was fascinated by the structural theory behind the construction.

Any allegiance to his own back-of-the-envelope proposal now disappeared. He eventually thumped the top of the table shelter. 'That's the one, make 500,000 in the next three months and give them to the people. Show them that it is safe, blow a house up on one, put a pig in it, put the inventor in it,' he said, digging Baker in the ribs.

Thus was born the 'Morrison shelter', as it came to be known. Introduced within three months, it would prove an invaluable extra means of protection against the German bombs, and would also play its part when new weapons were targeted on London homes later in the war. By the end of the year Morrison could justifiably claim that 'the worst of the overcrowding in the big shelters is now a thing of the past'. Two hundred thousand new bunks had been installed, and Lord Horder's new standards of cleanliness had been fully rolled out. The big programme of tunnel construction to shelter thousands more Londoners was well under way.

Morrison never overturned the original shelter strategy – he merely modified it. But the perception was that he and his industrious group of ministers had rolled back the tide of government indifference and stubbornness. And that, to the public, made all the difference.

Chapter Five

'A New Magna Carta'

1 January to 11 March 1941

On four days in late January 1941 the War Office carried out one of those 'paper' exercises, so beloved of military planners, designed to envisage as authentically as possible a real-life scenario. Codenamed Operation *Victor*, it imagined nothing less than a full-scale German invasion of Britain, with the enemy first carrying out a diversionary landing in Ireland before launching assaults on the south and east coast by sea, land and air.

Ingeniously put together by Brigadier Sir Ronald Weeks, it even featured an imaginary speech by the Prime Minister to be delivered on the eve of invasion, presumably from an underground bunker outside London. 'The crazy villain who has brought so much suffering upon the world has now set foot upon our outposts and, very shortly now, will break himself and end his own wicked tyranny in a disastrous attack upon this island,' the premier would say in an attempt to rouse the nation.

Jock Colville read out the doomsday broadcast after dinner at Chequers to an amused Churchill and his guests. 'The PM promised he would produce a far better one in the event,' recorded Colville. 'If he did have to make such a speech he would end it, "The hour has come; kill the Hun".'

The threat of invasion had in fact receded markedly since lat
October, when a Bletchley Park decrypt of a Luftwaffe transmissio
disclosed that Hitler had ordered the dismantling of crucial air loadin
bays in Holland. As a result Churchill and his chiefs of staff were pe
suaded that an assault on the British Isles had become highly unlikel
the War Office summary at the end of that month concluding that 'th
invasion of UK has been either abandoned or postponed until 1941'.

With that fear cast aside for the moment, the question of how t
persuade the United States to more actively back the war effort, and, i
doing so, prevent Britain from sliding inexorably towards bankruptc
became the British government's paramount concern. Fortunatel
President Roosevelt's special envoy, Harry Hopkins, had seen enoug
in the first two weeks of a visit to Britain to report back favourabl
to the President. He planned to inform Roosevelt that Britain wa
prosecuting the war with great resolve, and to advise him that th
financial means to enable her to continue so doing should be mad
available as quickly as possible.

Despite their long careers close to the apex of power in thei
respective countries, Churchill and Roosevelt had met just once
in July 1918, at a dinner hosted by Churchill's friend F.E. Smith, a
Gray's Inn, London, for Allied ministers prosecuting the First Worl
War. Roosevelt, very much the honoured guest, had been assistan
secretary in the US Navy Department, while Churchill was the
Minister of Munitions, rebuilding his reputation after the Dardanelle
fiasco. It had not been an auspicious meeting. In later years Churchi
could remember nothing of the encounter, but the reverse wa
certainly not the case. 'I always disliked him since the time I went t
England,' Roosevelt told Joe Kennedy, the American ambassador t
London, in conversation in 1939. 'At a dinner I attended he acte
like a stinker.' His opinion would hardly have been improved by a
article Churchill wrote in the *Evening Standard* in December 1937
in which he characterised Roosevelt's New Deal as a 'ruthless wa
against private enterprise, destined to lead America back into th
'trough of depression'.

Since the end of the First World War, Anglo-American relations
in general had been marked by a large degree of unease and mistrust.
Britain had hoped that the United States – now the world's leading
creditor nation – might agree to a general cancellation of war debts,
but President Woodrow Wilson and the American banks had made it
clear they expected to be repaid in full. The chill between the former
allies had only worsened as each adopted what the other perceived as
protectionism.

But on security and foreign policy, Churchill's consistent opposition
to appeasement and his stand against the Munich agreement
struck a chord with Roosevelt, a commander-in-chief who grasped
that America could not hide from the rest of the world's troubles.
'Passionately though we may desire detachment, we are forced to
realize that every word that comes through the air, every ship that sails
the sea, every battle that is fought, does affect the American future,' he
told his people in a speech from the White House on the day Britain
declared war on Germany. Indeed, it was Roosevelt who had initiated
the relationship between the two men, with a letter on 11 September
1939: 'How glad I am you are back again in the Admiralty . . . I shall
at all times welcome it if you will keep me in touch personally with
anything you want me to know about.' Thereafter a regular trickle of
correspondence passed between them, and this grew – when Churchill
became Prime Minister in May 1940 – into a veritable torrent; one
that would flow through the next five years of the war.

On 15 May, as the German army swept through the Low Countries
and advanced on France and Belgium, Churchill warned Roosevelt:
'I trust you realise, Mr President, that the voice and force of the
United States may count for nothing if they are withheld too long.
You may have a completely subjugated Nazified Europe established
with astonishing swiftness, and the weight may be more than we
can bear.'

With the powerful rhetoric came specific requests. Churchill asked
for the 'loan of 40 or 50 of your older destroyers', 'several hundred of
the latest types of aircraft', anti-aircraft equipment and ammunition, a

substantial quantity of steel, a visit from a United States squadron
police the Irish ports, and finally a request to 'keep that Japanese d
quiet in the Pacific, using Singapore in any way convenient'. Even
this stage, however, Churchill knew what a struggle it would be to p
America for such huge quantities of materiel, and in a phrase towar
the end of the telegram he presaged events many months down t
road. 'We shall go on paying dollars for as long as we can, but I shou
like to feel reasonably sure that when we can pay no more, you wi
give us the stuff all the same.'

Back in November 1939, the President had won a significant victo
over America's isolationists with the passage of a fourth Neutrali
Act. This had been presented as a peace measure, but in fact it ha
allowed the American government to sell war materials to 'belligeren
nations, provided they paid cash and carried the goods away in the
own ships. The intent had been to aid Britain and France, countri
with substantial foreign exchange reserves and large merchan
fleets, but even then Roosevelt had been unable – and unwilling
to hand over 'the stuff' unless payment had already been made, an
often punitive conditions were attached. By May 1940, wary of th
significant isolationist opposition in Congress and reluctant to try
sway public opinion until he calculated the time was right, there wa
no likelihood of him soon declaring America a non-belligerent. In a
opinion poll published on 29 May, only 7.7 per cent of responden
favoured entering the war there and then.

Thus Churchill's request for fifty destroyers of First World Wa
vintage, wanted as escorts for merchant convoys, was initially turne
down. Roosevelt cautioned, 'A step of that kind could not be take
except with the specific authorisation of Congress, and I am n
certain that it would be wise for that suggestion to be made . . .
this moment.' But as the summer wore on, as the RAF resisted th
Luftwaffe so impressively, and the Royal Navy further demonstrate
Britain's intent to fight on at all costs with the sinking of the Frenc
fleet at Mers-el-Kébir, Roosevelt and his advisers increasingly came
the conclusion that Britain was no lost cause.

By this point Churchill and the War Cabinet had become anxious about the rate of attrition in merchant shipping in the Atlantic from dive-bomber and submarine attacks. A large building programme of destroyers and anti U-boat craft was under way, but no ships were due to come off the production line until well into 1941. In a plaintive telegram to Roosevelt on 30 July, Churchill listed the ships hit over the previous ten days: *Brazen, Codrington, Delight, Wren* all sunk, and *Beagle, Boreas, Brilliant, Griffin, Montrose* and *Walpole* damaged. 'I cannot understand why, with the position as it is, you do not send me at least 50 or 60 of your oldest destroyers.'

Fortunately, Roosevelt was slowly coming round to a plan to give Churchill what he wanted. For some time certain non-interventionists had been promoting the idea – first proposed by the *Chicago Tribune* – that Britain should hand over some of her colonies in the western hemisphere in return for the cancellation of her First World War debts. Now an organisation called the Century Group, linked to the interventionist Committee to Defend America and with strong connections to the White House, took up that idea but turned it into something much more palatable to Britain in her hour of need. The destroyers should be offered in exchange for naval and air concessions in British possessions. When the initial framework for a deal was eventually worked out, it proposed the transfer of fifty destroyers plus a number of motor torpedo-boats and planes, in return for leases on British naval and air bases in Newfoundland, Bermuda, the Bahamas, Jamaica, Trinidad, St Lucia and British Guiana.

Spurred on by Sir Philip Lothian, Britain's ambassador to Washington, foreign secretary Lord Halifax urged his fellow ministers not to haggle over the conditions of the deal. 'We are already heavily in debt to America as a result of the last war, and . . . we shall shortly be still further in her debt as a condition of winning the present war. We have no hope of ever repaying the enormous sums which will be involved, nor do well-informed Americans ever expect this of us . . .'

But there was considerable disquiet among several members of the War Cabinet about this sacrifice of British interests. Lord Lloyd,

the colonial secretary, and Lord Caldecote, the Dominions secretar
fretted about the considerable loss of sovereignty; the former sai
caustically of Britain's ambassador to the US, 'All this is the doing o
Philip Lothian. He's always wanted to give away the Empire and now h
has the perfect opportunity to do so.' A.V. Alexander at the Admiralt
argued that any concessions to the Americans would encourag
them to concentrate on the defence of their own hemisphere an
neglect help to Britain. All three put together a draft Cabinet pape
demanding a more substantial quid pro quo, including an even greate
number of destroyers, the abolition of the 'cash and carry' clauses o
the Neutrality Act, and the promise of landing rights on Hawaii for a
eventual British trans-Pacific air service.

Churchill himself was particularly perturbed by a telegram fron
Roosevelt asking for a public guarantee that if Britain were overrur
the Royal Navy would neither be surrendered nor sunk; he was equall
annoyed by an American suggestion that Britain transfer her ships t
Canada in the event of defeat. The Prime Minister believed that suc
assurances were quite out of the question, partly because they concede
too much to the United States, but primarily because he feared tha
further public mention of the matter would unsettle domestic moral
at a perilous time. 'Only a war alliance,' he wrote, could justify 'an
stipulations about the disposition of the fleet.'

As he studied the final drafts of the agreement over the followin
days, Churchill reluctantly and at times grudgingly acquiesced to th
bulk of America's demands. 'Those bloody destroyers,' he frequentl
muttered to advisers, and recalled the story of the girl who remarked t
the magistrate, 'And all that for twopence and an orange!' Eventuall
after a fraught few days' negotiations, agreement was reached that th
British territories would be made available on ninety-nine-year lease
with no rent to be paid.

The 'Destroyer-Bases Deal', as it became known, was sealed o
2 September by an exchange of notes between US Secretary of Stat
Cordell Hull and British ambassador Lord Lothian. Its practical valu
was limited; only nine of the mothballed ships were actually put int

rvice by the Royal Navy before the end of the year, and these were
r less seaworthy than anticipated. The symbolic value was crucial,
hough. In Rome Italian foreign minister Galeazzo Ciano thought the
ay of direct American involvement in the war was close at hand,
hile in Berlin the provision of the destroyers was seen as 'an openly
ostile act against Germany'.

In London, however, despite the comfort given by the deal,
oncern persisted about the broader financial situation. On Thursday,
2 August, the Chancellor, Kingsley Wood, had presented a deeply
epressing paper to the War Cabinet entitled 'The Exchange
osition', which made no attempt to disguise the country's plight. He
old colleagues he was seriously perturbed by the rate at which gold
nd exchange resources were disappearing, and that they should be
ully aware of the dangerous financial possibilities of the near future'.
ritain's total reserves amounted to just £490 million, compared to
775 million at the beginning of January. At the current rate of losses
ritain would run out of gold by the end of December, and, in addition
o that, holdings of United States securities totalled just £200 million
although these were 'almost unsaleable' at present.

The Chancellor held out little hope that America would loosen the
urse strings. 'It appears prima facie unlikely that American financial
id, when forthcoming, will be given without conditions and without
mit.' Measures were already being taken to press the governments of
elgium, Holland and Norway for some of their gold, spirited away to
afety after the Nazi invasions. Even more drastically and humiliatingly,
he Chancellor suggested he might order the requisitioning, up and
own the country, of wedding rings and other gold ornaments; but he
alculated that would not produce any more than £20 million.

Herbert Morrison, Minister of Supply, warned that it would be a
ery serious matter if his department had to slacken the rate of orders
o America. It would be better to take a gamble on the financial side,
ather than risk losing the war. Beaverbrook backed him, saying 'we
ught to do everything in our power to fill American factories with
3ritish orders. No American Government would dare to tell those

factories to cease production, with all the consequences in the shap
of unemployment and industrial derangement.'

'American sympathy is an amazing thing,' an exasperated Lor
Woolton recorded in his diary. 'Newspapers, broadcasts, America
conversations are all full of it, but still they won't allow their ships t
come into England carrying either food or munitions, and they sti
don't give us one dollar's worth of goods unless we pay cash for them

For all their private resentments, the War Cabinet knew the
had few – if any – cards to play in financial negotiations with th
Americans. By December Sir Kingsley Wood was telling Sir Frederic
Phillips, the senior Treasury official based in Washington, 'We ar
deeply concerned at the possibility of finding ourselves at the end o
February with all reserves exhausted after having drawn upon Frenc
and allied gold . . .'

'Well, boys, Britain's broke: it's your money we want.' A frank admis
sion, and especially startling when uttered by Philip Henry Kerr, 11t
Marquess of Lothian, the supposedly discreet representative of He
Majesty's government in Washington. When he touched down a
LaGuardia Airport in New York City on Saturday, 23 November, th
Ambassador was met by a phalanx of reporters, eager for the Britis
government's current assessment of the war, especially now that rela
tions with America had been put back on an even keel following th
re-election a few weeks earlier of President Roosevelt.

The press pack who followed him out of the airport picked u
further comments, in particular that 'available gold and securities ha
been virtually used up and that this factor figured in the calculatio
for 1941'. Whether he used the actual words 'Britain's broke', howeve
is uncertain. The phrase the British newspapers reported consistentl
over the next few days was 'Britain is beginning to come to the en
of her financial resources.' The semantics mattered less than th
message, of course, and Lothian had put that across with all the nou
of a former journalist with the *Daily Chronicle* and *Christian Scienc
Monitor*. He never intended to make a direct appeal for immediat

edit, merely to intensify the public debate. His remarks generated front-page headlines in newspapers all over the US, and the American public were genuinely shocked to learn that Britain's economic circumstances were so dire.

Back home, his remarks irritated some in the War Cabinet, prompting Churchill to send an admonitory telegram: 'I do not think it wise to touch on very serious matters in newspaper interviews to reporters at the landing stage. The Chancellor of the Exchequer complains that he was not consulted about your financial statements, and Treasury does not like their form.' But despite the mild reproof, Churchill knew the value of his ambassador. Lothian had played a major part in the negotiations over the destroyers, encouraging his reluctant Prime Minister to cede British sovereignty over the bases for the greater prize of closer American involvement in the war.

Lothian had been Chamberlain's appointment (on the strong recommendation of Lord Halifax) in August 1939, and, despite their shared belief in the primacy of the British Empire, he and Churchill had had their differences. Lothian, in 1919, had incurred Churchill's wrath when, as Lloyd George's private secretary, he had persuaded his master to reject the then war secretary's scheme for larger-scale intervention in the Russian Civil War. He had also been on the opposing side in the appeasement debate. In 1935 he had returned from meeting Hitler and Göring to declare that 'Germany does not want war and is prepared to renounce it absolutely . . . provided she is given real equality.' A subsequent reading of Mein Kampf, with the Munich Crisis providing a further dose of reality, persuaded him to completely re-evaluate Hitler and his motives.

Fortunately, Churchill recognised that here was a man who loved America and Americans; who knew the country as well as any other British politician or diplomat. As a young man Lothian had travelled extensively throughout the United States just before the First World War and had promoted from early on the idea of an Anglo-American alliance. He had established valuable contacts with politicians, judges and journalists, and had even met President Theodore Roosevelt,

Franklin's distant cousin.

Previous occupants of the British embassy had given it a reputatic for unmerited swagger and fusty aloofness, the old colonial masters sti frowning on their upstart conquerors. Lothian blew away all the cobwel with his aristocratic charm and self-confidence, and by commo consent was the most popular ambassador since the charismatic Lor Bryce in 1913. 'He was not so deeply troubled, or rather confine by their [English] public school and caste system,' observed Gener Raymond E. Lee, America's military attaché to London.

Tall, fair-haired, with a broad forehead and high-arched Roma nose, Lothian was invariably rumpled but never dishevelled. Thoug born into a devout Roman Catholic family – he had once considere the priesthood – he was now a committed Christian Scienti: (inspired by Lady Astor) and allocated an hour or two every day t religious reading.

While in England earlier in November, Lothian had spent time wit the Prime Minister, drafting a long letter to Roosevelt that he hope would correct powerful American misconceptions about Britain position and strength, and stir the President and his advisers – wh had been distracted over the past month or so – into examining the conscience over Britain's plight. The principal areas of need Lothia and Churchill identified were support from the US in acquiring Iris' naval bases, help in guarding Singapore, more ships, and the loan, gi or, at worst, sale at a reduced charge of weapons and aircraft.

By 2 December, after many consultations and revisions, a draft wa ready for the War Cabinet. On the same day, President Roosevelt le Washington bound for a post-election Caribbean cruise on the US *Tuscaloosa*, taking with him only his immediate staff and his specia adviser, Harry Hopkins. Churchill informed his ministers of Lothian advice that the letter should be held back a week and only delivere to the President when he was fully settled and relaxed on his cruise.

War secretary Anthony Eden thought the section on Britain munitions production painted too optimistic a picture. Churchi retorted that if it were painted too darkly, isolationist elements i

merica would say it was 'useless to help us, for such help would be
sted and thrown away'. Lord Halifax wondered if now was the time
ask for more than fifty destroyers – but A.V. Alexander advised
inst it, saying it would be unwise in view of America's own limited
stroyer strength.

When the letter was finally sent on 8 December it was 4,000 words
g, covering in great detail the whole of the war situation from
North Sea to Gibraltar to Suez and Singapore. Most of it – on
urchill's insistence, and against Lothian's advice – was concerned
h shipping and the dangers to Britain's merchant fleet from
sistent attacks by bombers and U-boats.

Only in the final three paragraphs was the broad financial crisis
lained. But this was also the most blunt and dramatic section of
document. 'The moment approaches when we shall no longer be
e to pay cash for shipping and other supplies . . . I believe you will
ee it would be wrong in principle and mutually disadvantageous in
ect if, at the height of the struggle, Great Britain were to be divested
all saleable assets, so that after the victory was won with our blood,
ilization saved, and the time gained for the United States to be
ned against all eventualities, we should stand stripped to the bone.'

The style was Churchillian, but the logic was Lothian's. The
nbassador seemed to be at the height of his powers. Then a few
ys later Alistair Cooke, special correspondent for *The Times*, arrived
the embassy in Washington to interview Lothian. The door was
ened by the butler, who responded to Cooke's request gravely: 'I'm
ribly sorry, Sir, that will be quite impossible. The Ambassador died
ly this morning.'

It was known Lothian had been taken ill because the night before
colleague at the embassy, first secretary Nevile Butler, had been
ced to step in and deliver an important set-piece speech before the
nerican Farm Bureau in Baltimore. The shocking manner of his
ath, however, only emerged days later.

Lothian had clearly been fatigued over recent months, sometimes
ling asleep in important meetings, but this had been put down to

overwork. Then, on Sunday, 8 December, he had fainted, and ov
the next few days had remained in very poor condition with intern
pains. He had made it clear, however, that because of his religic
beliefs he did not want a conventional doctor to tend to him, b
would rely instead on treatment from a Boston 'healer' whom he h
known for many years. Three of his personal staff were also Christi
Scientists, only reinforcing his determination not to turn to medici
for an illness that, to his faith, was real to the material world, yet unr
to the world of the spirit.

Lothian had grown steadily weaker and badly short of breath, a
had died at 2 a.m. on Thursday, 11 December, the cause eventually giv
as uremic poisoning. Back in London the government was stunned:
is a blow over the heart,' wrote Harold Nicolson. In public, in t
House of Lords, Lord Halifax applauded Lothian's 'instinctive ser
and sureness of touch on all questions that arose . . . no-one, I thin
has ever served this country at Washington more wisely'. Private
Halifax was bitter at the manner of his colleague's death, observi
that he was 'another victim for Christian Science'; while Churchill,
similar vein a couple of days later, said it was a 'monstrous thing' th
Lothian had not allowed a doctor to be called. 'I had at last come
like Philip, after years of prejudice.'

The Prime Minister's first choice replacement for this critical job w
Lloyd George, whom he had tried to persuade to join his governme
back in May. His 'knowledge of munitions and his fiery personali
marked him out, Churchill observed to Jock Colville, adding that
would find him a place in the War Cabinet so he would have equ
status with Halifax. But Lloyd George declined the offer, ostensibly
the advice of his doctor, Lord Horder, who believed the strain wou
be too great for the seventy-seven-year-old.

Lord Cranborne and Sir Archibald Sinclair briefly enter
Churchill's thoughts, but eventually he alighted on Halifax. Thou
the Foreign Secretary had no appetite for the post, Churchill thoug
the appointment of such a senior figure in Washington, at a criti
period for Anglo-American relations, would impress the Wh

ouse. Moreover, it would finally rid him of a powerful rival who still even with the passing of Chamberlain – enjoyed enough support in e Conservative Party to cause trouble for Churchill if the war started go badly. The resulting vacancy would also enable him to bring his n man, Anthony Eden, into the Foreign Office, where he could ep a close eye on him.

Halifax initially resisted Churchill's entreaties. On Thursday, December he recorded, 'It is an odious thought if he decides for me.' is was a man who was English to his marrow, an upper-class Tory mfortable in his accustomed surroundings of high office, church and untry retreat. America, its history, its culture and its people were en to him; it had to be explained to him at one luncheon why the hite House, the most famous building in the United States, had quired its name. 'I got the distinct idea that he did not know the war 1812 had ever happened,' General Raymond E. Lee observed.

Desperately, Halifax pushed other candidates: 'The US would like iberal! This supports perhaps your possibility of A.S [Sinclair]'; and en 'Another suggested to me last night was Woolton, who is said to ve many of the more important qualities.' But it was all to no avail. a conversation with the Prime Minister after Lothian's funeral, lifax was persuaded, indeed instructed, to take the job. It was 'an portunity . . . to do a piece of work that would reflect great credit on personally', Churchill told him, while also suggesting that there re 'certain currents of opposition against my being at the Foreign fice and that, from my own point of view, I should gain by taking e other work'.

In Washington, enthusiasm for the appointment was in short pply. Henry Morgenthau Jr, Treasury secretary, brought Roosevelt's ention to an article in the New Republic entitled 'The Halifax nder'. The editorial commented, 'We still hold that America serves to be something more than a pocket in which to store old peasers; many Americans will want to know what sort of war this is he answer now given them is a poor one.'

For Clement Attlee, it was a clear advantage to see the back of the last

of the appeasers. But Hugh Dalton regretted his departure: 'I have work
very hard at my personal relations with the Viscount and now all the
hours of studied suavity will have been thrown away. I have now got
make a new start, on somewhat different lines, with Master Anthony.'

On 17 December President Roosevelt, tanned and relaxed after I
Caribbean cruise, and having absorbed all the arguments put
Churchill and Lothian, decided to host a press conference at t
White House. He proceeded, in the folksy language that the pub
found so reassuring, to propose a radical change to America's financ
relationship with Britain.

The President told his audience that his desire now was to 'get r
of the silly, foolish old dollar sign' and substitute for it 'a gentlema
agreement to repay in kind'. After all, he repeated, the arms a
munitions that America lent would not only be for Britain's defen
but would also be the best, immediate defence of the United States

Roosevelt invoked an inspired homily to help the public understa
the new arrangement he had in mind, and the moral force behind
It is as if you have a neighbour whose house is on fire, he explaine
The neighbour comes running to you and shouts over the gard
fence, 'Neighbour, neighbour, my house is on fire, help me out, le
me your garden hose.' Well of course, being a good neighbour, you le
the garden hose to your neighbour and he puts out the fire – and th
he gives you the hose back.

If that analogy was unpicked, it made little sense. The 'hose' re
resented tanks that in all likelihood would be blown up, planes th
would be shot down and ships that would be sunk, so how could it
handed back in any shape at all? But in these early moments of 'Len
Lease' – as it would swiftly become known – the disarming nature
Roosevelt's metaphor obscured any ambiguities it contained. Brita
would be doing America's work while enabling her to stay out of t
war, and that was what mattered; handing back the 'hose' – or payme
– could wait until later.

This piece of homespun invention showed early signs of goi

wn well with the public. The President sought to build on the
omentum in one of his 'fireside chats' on 29 December. Emphasising
at American security – and her chances of staying out of the war
were dependent upon British survival, he warned that current
dustrial efforts were insufficient. In a telling phrase, he described
e role America should now play: 'We must be the great arsenal of
mocracy,' he told listeners.

This apparent commitment to full, unequivocal aid was music to
e ears of the British government, facing at that moment a bill for
ns purchases to the value of $1,000 million, with combined gold
d dollar reserves of only $574 million with which to pay. But the
rds were still yet to be matched by deeds, as far as Churchill and his
lleagues were concerned. Two days after Roosevelt's fireside chat,
e heavy cruiser USS *Louisville* was en route to the naval base of
mon's Town, near Cape Town in South Africa, to take on board the
0 million of Britain's gold reserves held for safe keeping there since
ly in the war.

The Prime Minister was affronted by this latest heavy call on Britain's
indling liquid assets. 'I am much puzzled and even perturbed by the
oposal . . . to collect whatever gold there may be in Cape Town,'
d the initial draft of a telegram he planned to send to Roosevelt.
his would inevitably become known to the world, and it would wear
e aspect of a sheriff collecting the last assets of a helpless debtor.'

It was the frustration of a man still desperately anxious about
itain's financial predicament, not the usual familiar and deferential
nguage he employed to the President. And in the end, Churchill
ought better of it, erasing the grumbling passage. He wanted to get
e pitch and tone of his first message of the New Year just right, so he
ked Kingsley Wood, Chancellor of the Exchequer, Anthony Eden,
e new foreign secretary, and Lord Beaverbrook to join him on New
ar's Eve at the Number 10 Annexe and help compose the telegram.
The quartet began their message with a straightforward thank you.
'e are deeply grateful for all you said yesterday. We welcome especially
e outline of your plans for giving us the aid, without which Hitlerism

cannot be extirpated from Europe and Asia.' But worries remaine
'What would be the effect upon the world situation if we had to defau
in payments to your contractors, who have their workmen to pa
Would this not be exploited by the enemy as a complete breakdov
in Anglo-American co-operation?' But, they added reassuringly, 'V
shall be entirely ready, for our part, to lay bare to you all our resourc
and our liabilities around the world, and we shall seek no more he
than the common cause demands.'

Their work done and the telegram dispatched, Kingsley Wood a
Beaverbrook headed off into the night. Churchill took Eden on
the roof and together they looked at the stars and the new moon, a
kept an eye on the enemy air activity. 'It was raining and the firi
that evening was slight,' Eden noted. 'I could not help wonderi
what fate would have in store for us before the next New Year's D
came around.'

Churchill and his ministers need not have worried. Just twenty-fo
hours after he had delivered his 'arsenal of democracy' fireside cha
Roosevelt sat down in the White House to get things moving wi
two men who were already integral to Anglo-American financi
diplomacy.

One was Henry Morgenthau Jr, US Secretary of the Treasu
since 1934, who had played a crucial role in framing the New De
legislation. The only Jew in the Cabinet, he was also one of Roosevel
closest friends. The other, representing Churchill's interests, was or
of the unsung allies of his administration: Arthur Blaikie Purvis,
London-born industrialist who had been given leave of absence fro
his position as president of Canadian Industries Limited to take t
work as Britain's key buyer of war supplies.

A sharp-faced man with an eager air, fair hair and big, black, bus
eyebrows, Purvis had come a long way from his humble beginnings
Tottenham. Having won a scholarship to the local grammar school, l
had been forced to leave at the age of thirteen on the death of his fath
William, whereupon he had started as a five-shillings-a-week office b

the City. At nineteen he had moved to Glasgow, to join the Nobel Explosives Company (later ICI), and by the age of twenty-four was in charge of the company's New York office. During the First World War he had been responsible for buying explosives for the company throughout America, and had made one of the largest war purchases, 25 million of acetone, which at the time was in acute shortage in the United Kingdom.

From mid-1940 Purvis, 'a man of the highest integrity with no enemies and, indeed, no critics', had been given a free hand in his role as director-general of the British Purchasing Commission to secure whatever contracts he could from US firms for his country's war effort. In two dramatic days, 16–17 June, in New York, he had pulled off one of the greatest deals of the war. At the time American factories had been choked with orders for arms for France, but it had become clear that within a few hours Marshal Pétain would sign an armistice and that those contracts would be frozen and lost to Britain – a nation whose army had discarded all its munitions on the beaches of Dunkirk. This really was the proverbial race against time. So Purvis had scoured the city to round up the three French officials who dealt with the purchases, and by late evening had managed to gather them all in his apartment. There he got to work drafting and redrafting the contracts, until by 3 a.m. they were ready for signature.

The War Cabinet's instructions had been that Purvis should buy only the limited number of armaments the country needed – and could afford – but the French insisted Britain should take on all of the contracts, or nothing. With no time to consult London, Purvis hesitated momentarily, and then signed away $612 million, at a stroke of the pen doubling Britain's dollar liabilities. Lord Woolton admitted to the House of Lords a few weeks later, 'Never have wider powers to commit this country been delegated to any Mission, and indeed it is true also to say that no Mission has ever carried so grave a responsibility.' Purvis's decisive, unilateral action had ensured his country acquired the tanks, guns and planes necessary to continue to wage war.

Now, in the Oval Office with Roosevelt and Morgenthau,

Purvis prepared carefully for the start of the Lend-Lease negotiation
Nominally he reported to a small inner War Cabinet grouping
three: Beaverbrook, A.V. Alexander and Sir Andrew Duncan, the ne
Minister of Supply. He had guessed the President would want to kno
the precise value of the goods Britain needed, but Duncan's departmen
the co-ordinating ministry in Whitehall for munitions, had so far faile
to give him an accurate estimate. So Purvis and his staff had done th
arithmetic and come up with their own figure – a staggering fiftee
billion dollars. When he nervously handed a balance sheet containir
the sum to Roosevelt, he was relieved at the President's calm reactio
Roosevelt told Morgenthau to ready himself to draw up the necessa
legislation for when he gave it the 'green light'.

The isolationists on Capitol Hill and their supporters in the pre
had by no means given up the fight. On 1 February the *Chicago Dai
Tribune*, which had dubbed Lend-Lease the 'Dictator Bill', pounce
upon a meeting held between Lord Halifax and Senator Walter
George, chairman of the Senate committee on foreign relations and
key player in steering the bill through Congress.

The *Tribune* claimed the new British ambassador had 'urged quic
action on the measure' and its massive front-page headline screame
'HALIFAX STEERS F.D.R. BILL'. In fact Halifax had merely enquire
about the bill's timetable, in what was more of a social encount
than one involving serious diplomacy. The embarrassment to th
Lend-Lease cause was momentary, but Halifax learned his lesson. 'It
an example of how boggy the ground may easily become,' he ruefull
reflected that night.

Back in England, Roosevelt's personal envoy Harry Hopkins w
about to arrive on a fact-finding mission. The former social worke
one of the principal architects of Roosevelt's 'New Deal' legislatio
had been tasked with taking a long, hard look at Churchill's govern
ment to assess whether the President would get value for money fro
the largesse he was about to put Britain's way via Lend-Lease. As we
as assessing the state of Britain, Hopkins was there to establish a rel
tionship between Churchill and Roosevelt. As he told Ed Murrow, th

olumbia Broadcasting System's London correspondent, he wanted to
ry to get an understanding of Churchill, and the men he sees after
idnight'. On his first weekend Hopkins was invited to stay at Ditchley
ark, the home of Conservative MP Ronald Tree and now Churchill's
ternative weekend retreat 'when the moon was high' – i.e., when
hequers was too conspicuous to night bombers. There he met the
ey figures in the Prime Minister's entourage – including Bracken and
indemann – and he felt for the first time the full force of Churchill's
rsonality.

After dinner on the Saturday night, the party made their way into
e beautiful library, with its marble fireplaces, bookshelves right up to
e cornices, six Georgian armchairs, immense sofa, and two Alfred
unnings paintings hung over the mantelpiece.

Churchill launched into a lecture of exceptional virtuosity, even
his standards. Oliver Lyttelton, President of the Board of Trade and
e of his rapt audience, judged it to be one of his very best: 'His
norous eloquence, his sense of history, of man's destiny and Great
ritain's part in it were enthralling.' The monologue ended with just
e sort of folksy image Roosevelt would have admired, of a humble
bourer returning home at night, 'smoke curling upwards from his
ottage home in the serene evening sky', content in the knowledge
at there was no secret police to knock upon his door and disturb
is leisure. 'A government with the consent of the people, and man's
eedom to say what he will – war aims other than these we have none,'
e Prime Minister concluded.

Asked how the President would respond to all this, Hopkins replied
an exaggerated drawl, 'Well Prime Minister, I don't think the
resident will give a damn for all that.' Lyttelton recoiled: 'Heavens
live, it's gone wrong, thought I. There was another pause, and then
arry said, You see, we're only interested in seeing that Goddam
onofabitch, Hitler, get licked.' The gathering dissolved into laughter,
nd driven by Churchill's loquaciousness and Hopkins' dry humour,
e Anglo-American alliance made great strides. That same weekend
Churchill read the preliminary text of the Lend-Lease Bill, and told

Hopkins it 'had made him feel that a new world had come into being

When Hopkins picked up his pen in his suite at Claridge's three da
later, he had already made up his mind. 'The people here are amazir
from Churchill down, and if courage alone can win – the result wi
be inevitable,' he wrote to Roosevelt. His view of where the power la
was unequivocal. '*Churchill* is the government in every sense of th
word . . . I cannot emphasize too strongly that he is the one and on
person over here with whom you need to have full meeting of minds

Hopkins stayed in England for six weeks. In his final thirty-pa;
cabled report to the President, he concluded, 'The most importa
single observation I have to make is that most of the Cabinet and a
of the military leaders here believe invasion is imminent. They a
straining every effort night and day to meet this. They believe that
may come at any moment, but not later than May 1.'

Back in Washington, the congressional hearings on the Lend-Lea;
Bill saw the Republicans attack the President for assuming quas
totalitarian powers. Equally there were many who feared Britain w.
about to take America for a free ride, just as she had done after the Fir
World War when she had failed to meet all her debts. But Rooseve
prevailed. On 8 February the House of Representatives passed the bi
by a vote of 260 to 165. By the time it reached the floor of the Sena
it was clear that the sound and fury from the isolationists was fadin
away. But the White House wanted further commitments from th
British government to ensure its final passage. If Britain was to quali
for unlimited, open-ended aid, she had to be seen to be hurting, ar
'stripping' herself of her remaining financial resources.

Morgenthau had asked Purvis and Sir Frederick Phillips, he;
of the Treasury mission in Washington, to examine direct Britis
investments in America, such as Shell Oil, American Viscose, Lev
Brothers, Dunlop Tire and Brown & Williamson Tobacco, and advise
that some should be sold off to convince American politicians – ar
the American public – of Britain's good faith. The War Cabinet we
reluctant to commence the sale, but Lord Halifax, the recipient
much of the pressure in Washington, began to see that it was vital. H

nt a startlingly frank telegram to Churchill, stating that 'we should, ithout delay, hand over to America our remaining financial resources that country'. All that could be hoped for were half-decent prices, id not a knockdown sale.

Roosevelt followed this up by sending a message to Churchill 4 March, requesting a spectacular sale that would demonstrate Congress that Britain was doing all she could. Six days later 1orgenthau was running short of patience. He paid an unsolicited ill on the British ambassador, dragging him out to dinner at asey's and demanding swift action. 'A financial problem – not too isy to solve,' noted Lord Halifax in his diary that night. But after late-night call to one adviser, Robert Brand of Lazard Brothers, id conversations the next day with another, Sir Edward Peacock om the Bank of England, it was decided to 'offer up' the Viscose orporation of America, a firm that was 97 per cent owned by the ritish company Courtaulds.

Viscose, Britain's largest and most profitable holding, would ventually be sold for $54 million, only about half of its market value. his satisfied Morgenthau, but the humiliating sale angered the British overnment, in particular its key economic adviser, John Maynard eynes. He accused Morgenthau of 'stripping us of our liquid assets the greatest extent possible *before* the Lend-Lease Bill comes into peration, so as to leave us with the minimum in hand to meet during ie rest of the war the numerous obligations which will not be covered y the Lend-Lease Bill'.

Keynes was right. Morgenthau was a good friend to the 'English' is he always referred to Britain), but not without reservations, and e was always first and foremost a staunch defender of American iterests. He had an eye on the future and the battle for world iarkets after the war, so he had little desire to leave Britain with ountiful caches of gold and dollars. In fact by 11 March she was olding just $12 million in unscheduled reserves. But this was the ay the financial lifeline finally arrived, as President Roosevelt signed ie Lend-Lease Bill into law, having achieved a comfortable margin of success, 60 to 31, in the Senate a couple of days earlier, followed by an equally decisive 317 to 71 victory in the House of Representatives to which the bill had been sent back for a final time to consider some Senate amendments.

Churchill had history in mind when he addressed the House of Commons the following day: 'The Government and people of the United States have in fact written a new Magna Carta, which not only has regard to the rights and laws upon which a healthy and advancing civilisation can alone be erected, but also proclaims by precept and example the duty of free men and free nations, wherever they may be to share the responsibility and burden of enforcing them.'

Lend-Lease as Magna Carta was not Churchill's idea. That part of his speech had been written by an enterprising official at the Foreign Office, Professor Thomas North Whitehead, an economics graduate from Trinity College, Cambridge, who, two days later, wrote a paper for his minister, Rab Butler, that took the notion one step further. The Lincoln copy of Magna Carta had been in America for the past two years, on display in the British Pavilion of the New York World Fair before moving to the Library of Congress.

'Many thousands of Americans have waited daily in long queues to view it with a reverence and pride scarcely believable,' wrote Whitehead. So why not offer it as a gift to the American nation? 'It would represent the only really adequate gesture which it is in our power to make in return for the means to preserve our country.' But more than that, it might have significant political advantage: 'The immediate effect of such an action would be greatly to increase the emotional interest of Americans in this country, which would thereby assist the President in his task of carrying public opinion with him in giving us increasingly greater assistance.'

Whitehead suggested that the dean and chapter of Lincoln be offered one of the 'less perfect' British Museum copies of the great charter, together with war bonds of £100,000 towards the upkeep of the cathedral, or, alternatively, just paid a straight £250,000 in bonds

he gift could be announced by the Prime Minister in the House
Commons, or alternatively by the King in a special broadcast.
n appropriate handover ceremony would follow in Washington.

Roosevelt had been delighted when Magna Carta had arrived at
ongress in late 1939, joking that there might have been criticism if it
ad been 'turned over to the executive branch of the government, i.e.,
e King John of modern days'. In the Library of Congress, however,
he precious document has been retained in the safe hands of the
arons and the commoners'.

Ministers were now enthused by Whitehead's idea. 'I have always
anted to do this,' noted Anthony Eden. His suggested overture was,
ill you accept it as a symbol and a seal of our compact to fight to
e last against the forces of evil?' Rab Butler, his bright young junior
inister, agreed, noting that the handover would require an Act of
arliament that 'would give an opportunity for airing democratic
inciples here'. This was 'as good a psychological moment as any' to
ake the gift.

Churchill asked Butler to bring the matter before the War Cabinet
n Monday, 17 March. But at that meeting opinion was divided. Some
lt if it was to be done, it should be done quickly; others doubted
hether it would make much impact on public opinion in the United
ates, but worried that it might attract unfavourable reaction in the
ominions.

Butler was told to go away and make discreet inquiries of the dean
nd chapter of Lincoln. Meanwhile Leo Amery, who had not attended
e War Cabinet but had quickly learned of the proposal, wrote to
hurchill informing him that two years earlier *he* had put a very similar
ea to Neville Chamberlain, who had doubted if the dean could be
ersuaded to give up the charter. Nonetheless, Amery pointed out that
ncoln Cathedral needed a lot of money for restoration and believed
ought not to be impossible to overcome their resistance'.

The India secretary suggested nothing should be done at that
oment and instead offered up 15 June, Magna Carta Day, as a much
ore auspicious occasion for the gesture. The Prime Minister, in his

view, should announce the gift in a special broadcast to America an the Empire, extolling Magna Carta 'as the foundation of our commo liberties'. 'I prefer this,' Churchill noted to Butler. 'Will you get i touch with Mr Amery to discuss the gift with him?'

So discreet were the enquiries, however, that history does not recor the views of the Dean of Lincoln, R.A. Mitchell. The copy of Magr Carta sent to America remained in the Library of Congress until it wa returned to its home in early 1946. Whitehead's imaginative idea ha come to nothing.

Chapter Six
'Uncle Fred's Recipe for Survival'
11 March to 21 June 1941

A week after the signing of the Lend-Lease Act, Churchill paid court to the latest important American to arrive in London, the ew United States ambassador, Republican New Yorker John Winant. he venue was the Savoy Hotel, although in keeping with the sober mes the occasion was a luncheon rather than a lavish dinner.

The hotel's maître chef de cuisine for the past twenty-two years, rançois Latry, was renowned for the extravagance of his dishes; he ad once filled crayfish with foie gras and braised turbot in vintage urgundy for the table of writers Arthur Conan Doyle and Hilaire elloc. Now, however, he had to adapt his talents to the strictures f the times, and the Ministry of Food was using his expertise and nagination to create a series of new recipes.

That afternoon one of those dishes was placed in front of the Prime Minister and his fellow guests, who included most of the Cabinet, arious press proprietors and other high-ranking men in British public fe (the Pilgrims Society, which was hosting the luncheon, was a aale-only body). It was an early outing for a very different kind of ie, consisting of boiled diced vegetables – potato, parsnip, cauliflower, wede and carrot – in a gravy flavoured with spring onions and thick-ned with oatmeal, under a wheatmeal crust.

Monsieur Latry had christened this stodgy if nutritious offerin
'Woolton Pie', in honour of Lord Woolton, the Minister of Food; *Tl*
Times published the recipe a few weeks later, and it would become
symbol of austerity in the kitchen. 'Steak and kidney pie without th
steak and kidney,' joked the man who inspired the dish. Churchill
palate was attuned to richer fare, however. '[I thought] it was extreme
good,' Woolton noted. '[But] when it was offered to the Prime Ministe
he sent it away, and asked for some cold beef. I told him afterwar
that I thought he treated my pie with less than respect, and he replie
"Yes, I thought it was one of your synthetic productions".'

Fortified by the meat, Churchill went on to make 'an absolute
first-class speech, full of vigour and imaginative phrasing', helping t
bind the new ambassador to the British war effort. Of equal importanc
with the Prime Minister's dazzling oratory, though, was the fact tha
the two most instantly recognisable – indeed, the two most popula
– members of the government had shared a joke, an indication of
developing relationship. Britain needed them both working in uniso
in the ongoing struggle for control of the Atlantic seaways; Churchill, a
Minister of Defence, to deploy the right resources to fight it, Wooltor
as the guardian of the nation's larder, to ensure that the essentia
supplies that got through would prevent the country from starving.

Things had not always been so relaxed between the two mer
Woolton had been Chamberlain's appointment, in April 1940, an
after his first meeting with the new Prime Minister six weeks later h
had been left with the distinct impression that Churchill doubted hi
ability to do the job: 'It was clear that he had very little confidence i
me and I heard some time afterwards that he had said to some of hi
friends, "We shall have to be ready with a rescue squad for Woolton"
Churchill seemed unconvinced that his food minister could handle th
administrative burden of controlling a staff of over 13,000 and, mor
crucially, did not think this businessman would operate effectively i
Parliament and in the full glare of the public spotlight.

For the next six months Churchill and Woolton met occasionall
in Cabinet, but mostly communicated by note and letter. It was nc

auspicious start. The Prime Minister, whose instincts were against
tioning and only accepted it grudgingly as a necessary evil, fired off a
umber of stinging missives to his food minister whenever he thought
ew restrictions were excessive. On 12 July, Churchill objected to
Woolton's instructions to hotels and restaurants to shorten their menus
nd to serve either a fish or a meat course, but not both: 'Is it worse
r the country for a man to eat a little of three or four courses of food,
aintily cooked out of scraps, or a good solid plate of roast beef? Is it
ore patriotic to avoid luxury by having the food, whatever it is, badly
ooked? Is it wrong to eat up the luxury foods which are already in the
ountry, or ought they to be wasted? This is just the sort of criticism
at will be raised in Parliament.'

Woolton stood firm, writing in reply the next day: 'My mail, which I
ad every morning, shows that the working class is concerned that the
ch and poor should be treated alike, and the reason why I introduced
e phrase about luxury feeding into my broadcast was in order to
alance the rationing of tea and margarine, which understandably
fects the poorer classes the most.' Churchill had the last word, of
ourse, retorting sardonically, 'Almost all the food faddists I have
er known, nut eaters and the like, have died young after a period
senile decay. The British soldier is far more likely to be right than
e scientists. All he cares about is beef . . . the way to lose the war is
try to force the British public into a diet of milk, oatmeal, potatoes
c, washed down on all gala occasions by a little lime juice.' Having
ade his point, the Prime Minister pressed his case no further. Indeed,
Woolton's exhortation on 'luxury' eating – 'I am asking you for a hard
e', he told his radio audience – would eventually be extended in May
42, with an order restricting the price of a meal in a restaurant to a
aximum of 5s, and limiting it to three courses.

Woolton held his ground on numerous other issues. But he was,
an extent, intimidated by Churchill. 'I always felt like a small
y when he used to reprove me for having taken action without
nsulting either him or the Cabinet.' His business career had been
void of the dead hand of government bureaucracy, and he was apt

to make swift decisions on the spot without going through the variou
committees.

'Lunched with Woolton. He isn't very happy in government an
doesn't propose to stay after the war,' observed Sir John Reith in lat
July. Beaverbrook sought to reassure the Food Minister that he wa
'one of the PM's favourites', while the Chief Whip, David Margessor
soothed his worries by telling him, 'Churchill is not really intereste
in spite of his long experience, in any of the civil or social problem
His whole interest is in war organisation – hence his lack of intere
in the Ministry of Food.' But by late November 1940 Woolton wa
fretting that he had been given only one proper tête-à-tête with th
Prime Minister, and – perhaps because of this distance – in privat
he was entertaining serious, and extremely gloomy, reservations abou
Churchill's government.

Woolton had asked if he could make a speech warning tha
shipping space for non-essential foods might have to be given up fo
military purposes that winter. 'The Prime Minister wrote back the so
of letter a headmaster might send to a 5th form boy, telling me tha
I had all the powers and to ration – showing that he had completel
failed to understand anything about the food situation . . . There is n
centralised government in the country, and no control . . . Chamberlai
succeeded in getting a personal allegiance from the members of h
Government, because although he was not strong he was absolutel
reliable and trustworthy. There's no allegiance to Churchill; there
nobody in the Government whom the public would trust.'

Just before Christmas 1940, Woolton decided to take the initiativ
and wrote to Churchill requesting an interview, saying the time ha
come for the Prime Minister to learn more about the food situatior
Invited to lunch at Chequers on Boxing Day, Woolton 'saw a nev
Winston, in the midst of his family, where the relationship was obvious
that of the father and not of the Prime Minister'. More significant wa
the lengthy discussion afterwards, when Woolton's complaints abou
the shortcomings of the Economic Policy and Food Committees wer
listened to carefully, and the Prime Minister – who had laid out o

he table a host of documents and diagrams illustrating the threat to
Britain's merchant convoys – was 'receptive and helpful'. One of the
outcomes of their talk was the setting up of an import executive, a
group of ministers headed by Sir Andrew Duncan (Minister of Supply),
whose remit was to improve shipping, the repair and the control of
ships, and the unloading of food at the country's docks.

That Boxing Day meeting was a turning point for Woolton. Rather
than being assured of it by others, he could now see for himself that
he had the essential confidence of the Prime Minister. Disputes would
continue – Churchill's attitude to the rationing of food was very
different, and he would often bring in his scientific adviser Professor
Lindemann as a counterweight to Woolton – but though he was
unlikely to invite his food minister to Number 10 for a late-night
brandy and cigar, the Prime Minister recognised his huge value to the
government. In fact, he might even have felt a tinge of jealousy at
the attention that Woolton had attracted, and the plaudits he was
increasingly receiving. Churchill was undeniably the leader of the
nation, the great orator loftily inspiring the people and maintaining
their spirit, but Woolton was the consummate communicator,
dispensing advice and encouragement on the radio on a daily basis as
the country tried to make ends meet.

He seemed a natural performer, as if born to the role. But in truth,
he had been equipped for his task by a lifetime of experience in the
real world, far removed from Westminster.

Frederick James Marquis was born on 23 August 1883 in a terraced
house in Salford, near Manchester, the only surviving child of Thomas
Robert, a wandering saddler, and his ambitious wife Margaret. He
attended Ardwick Higher Grade School, where his government
colleague Ellen Wilkinson was later educated – he would lecture her
when he returned for a brief spell as a pupil-teacher. After winning
a county council exhibition to Manchester Grammar School, he
initially developed a keen interest in the arts, studying Greek in order
to qualify for a Cambridge scholarship. The story told was that the day

eighteen-year-old Frederick was informed he had won the place, hi
father confided in him that the doctor had given him just six month
to live. The son tore up the letter and stayed at home to look afte
his fading parent; as it turned out, the invalid was to survive anothe
forty-four years.

Instead of journeying to the gleaming spires, young Marquis went t
the University of Manchester, graduating in 1906 with a combinatio
degree (mathematics, chemistry and science), and returning in 191
to take up a research fellowship in economics; he was awarded his M
two years later. The formative moment of his life arrived a couple o
years after that when he was living in digs in the slums of Liverpool, a
a member of the city's university 'settlement' – a reformist movemen
aimed at bringing together the volunteer middle class and the poverty
stricken working class. His next-door neighbour in grim Park Street
a 'woman of some refinement both of speech and appearance', wa
found dead, her body having lain undiscovered for several days
The coroner's shocking verdict was that she had died of starvation
Woolton would recall many years later, 'Few things affected my lif
more surely . . . here was a problem of poverty on our very doorstep
We were young men . . . expounding economic history and theory
yet here we were, living in this sordid street, the surrounding house
of which were insanitary and verminous, where the sickening smell o
overcrowded humanity was such that, as I write now, it still seems t
nauseate me.

'Was the problem that confronted and disturbed us economic o
moral or endemic to human nature? Here was a challenge to a youthfu
mind.'

Marquis was determined to play his part in confronting tha
poverty. He was soon made warden of the university settlement
where he showed his reforming zeal by establishing a free dental car
unit and maternity and prenatal clinics. Around the same time h
also assumed management responsibility for the David Lewis Hote
and Club Association in Liverpool, where local retail firm Lewis'
provided cheap beds for the homeless, recreation in a 'people's palace

- comprising a club, library, billiard room and temperance bar – and a
large theatre.

Through the work during the First World War of his new wife,
Maud, and women doctors in the university settlement's innovative
maternity clinic, Frederick witnessed at first hand the remarkable
results social action could bring. Infant mortality per thousand families
was reduced to a third of the previous local average, through a careful
scientific approach to child welfare, diet in particular. These were
lessons Marquis would apply in his work in the next war.

The young Clement Attlee was also deeply involved in social
work at that time, at the Toynbee Hall 'settlement' in London's East
End. The two, who would sit round the Cabinet table three decades
later, met briefly in 1909, when Attlee listened to Woolton deliver a
paper on his work in Liverpool. Both would publish books on their
experiences: Woolton's *Recreation for the Poorest* in 1913, Attlee's *The
Social Worker* in 1920.

Attlee sought political solutions to the poverty he encountered
through the Independent Labour Party (ILP). Marquis, too, leaned
leftwards for a period and was especially impressed by the work of
Beatrice Webb of the Fabian Society on reform of the Poor Law. But
an encounter with the founder of the ILP, the legendary Keir Hardie,
helped push Marquis in the opposite direction to his future coalition
colleague.

Hardie came to speak at a meeting hosted by the Liverpool University
settlement, and afterwards was invited to dine at the home of one of its
wealthy supporters. After a lavish supper, Hardie approached Marquis
and told him this was a 'very dangerous house for a young man to be
in'. When the young social worker asked him why, Hardie replied, 'I
am a vegetarian, a teetotaller, a non-smoker, and I always sleep on
a hard bed. I have reduced my wants to a minimum and no one can
buy me.' Those words left a big impression on Marquis: 'Here was an
ardent reformer and a Puritan, but not a deep thinker.' He realised
that, unlike Hardie, he had no difficulty reconciling socialist principles
with the possession of wealth, or indeed the pursuit of it. 'The other

thing that Mr Keir Hardie did not notice was that the love of powe
was probably at least as great a temptation as the love of luxury.'

By the end of the First World War – during which he was a civi
servant in the War Office, turning out boots for the Allied armies -
Marquis's engagement with democratic socialism had cooled. He
resigned his membership of the Fabian Society, now believing that
the abolition of poverty could only be achieved through business
efficiency. Social problems would be solved by reducing the cost o
living and by increasing employment; better labour conditions should
be pursued, not only out of human decency, but because they would
bring in more profit.

This philosophy he preached, and practised, during a long and
highly successful career at Lewis's department store, which he joined in
1920 and where he swiftly rose through the ranks, becoming a director
in 1928 and chairman in 1936. Marquis forsook a political career
but increasingly established himself as one of the 'great and good'; a
respected voice at the interface between business and government
He was appointed to committees studying the future of the General
Post Office, civil aviation, overseas development, industry and air raid
shelters. On the latter, a controversial subject before the war as wel
as during the Blitz, he backed Sir John Anderson in pointing out the
dangers of 'psychological dependence' on deep shelters.

Knighted in 1935, Marquis was awarded a peerage in 1939 for his
services to industry, taking the title Baron Woolton after the leafy
Liverpool suburb in which he lived. His connections to government
had grown strong but that did not stop him, in the spring of 1938, from
announcing that Lewis's – a largely Jewish-run firm – would boycot
German goods in protest over the annexation of Austria. Woolton wa
summoned by Chamberlain to Downing Street, where he received a
'high-powered rocket . . . I was told that the Prime Minister strongly
disapproved of my action and that I had no right to interfere in the
foreign policy of the Government.'

With war looming, however, no sensible government was going to
ignore the skills of one of the most highly regarded businessmen of his

ay. Woolton was first given the post of honorary technical adviser on extiles to the Secretary of State for War, Leslie Hore-Belisha. Simply ut, he was the 'Army's wardrobe master', charged with clothing the ation's soldiers for battle. 'It was the most difficult job I have ever one in my life, and the one that caused me the greatest anxiety,' he ould later claim. But by drawing on experience from his previous artime role, and utilising all his contacts in industry, the task was ompleted within four months: over a million khaki suits, overcoats nd pairs of boots, delivered and ready for action.

A natural progression followed, with Woolton's appointment as irector-general at the Ministry of Supply, overseeing the provision f equipment and stores for the war machine. Then, in April 1940, he topped being one of the government's 'back room' boys, as he described , and was handed the key Home Front appointment of Minister of ood. On just his second day in the job, in a speech at the Queen's Hall central London, Woolton launched the National Food Campaign nd delivered the first of many memorable sound bites. He appealed to is audience of mainly women to mobilise themselves on the 'Kitchen ront', to eschew the comfortable habits of peacetime and to avoid aste. Sixty shiploads of tea a year could be saved if the maxim 'one poonful for each person . . . and none for the pot' were adopted.

'I made it clear that "food" was going to be a difficulty which overnment and people alike would share.' The philosophy of the ettlement' would now be translated into executive action. Woolton ould be a constant visitor to the nation's kitchens.

eldom have I seen a face with so much benevolence,' remarked the ortrait photographer Yousuf Karsh after his first session with Lord Voolton. His camera captured a tall, grey-haired, affable-looking an with a commanding presence, who carried an exaggerated air of rbanity and polish' with him while in the company of his cabinet olleagues, but resembled a kindly if occasionally stern uncle in his ealings with the general public. Indeed, as his many millions of radio steners got to know him, 'Uncle Fred' became his sobriquet.

Some of those who sat round the table at his Cabinet committee – like Herbert Morrison – found his manner on occasions 'somewha portentous' and 'rather exasperating'. But his junior ministers thrive on the responsibility – and freedom to make decisions – that he gav them. 'Lord Woolton was not only a great administrator, but he kne how to treat his Under-Secretary as few ministers ever do,' remarke Robert Boothby. Most government colleagues agreed with the genera verdict of Oliver Lyttelton, Minister of Production, who describe him as 'A man of transparent honesty. I can recall no instance of hin saying an unkind word about anyone. It was because of these grea qualities that his associates worked happily under him.'

By the time Woolton moved into the Ministry of Food's headquar ters in April 1940, rationing was already well under way. First to be hi – on 8 January – had been bacon and ham (which were limited to 4o a week), butter (4oz) and sugar (12oz). Then on 11 March meat wa rationed too – in shillings and pence rather than pounds and ounces beginning at 1s 10d. An opinion poll carried out by the British Institut of Public Opinion in November 1939, after Woolton's predecesso William 'Shakes' Morrison had announced the introduction of ration ing, showed that 60 per cent thought it was necessary, as against 2(per cent who were opposed and 12 per cent of 'don't knows'. Wooltor could draw on this bedrock of support when further austerity measure had to be introduced. The public appreciated that there would be n queues for essential foods and that they would get the ration withou fail, while the system seemed fair enough as it was the same for every one, rich or poor.

Woolton was also fortunate to inherit a fairly well-run ministr under the experienced permanent secretary Sir Henry French. It main failings were a poor public image and low staff morale. Wooltor strategy for dealing with the latter was to set off round the offices in Portman Square, meeting each and every employee and hearing a first hand their concerns. 'I made the staff feel that we were engage on a task that was essentially a personal one for the people of thi country; that our high organisational efficiency had to prove itself b

emonstration on the breakfast table in millions of homes.' After that,
is door was always open to those with either suggestions or complaints.

Soon after taking over Woolton persuaded King George VI to tour
he ministry, where the monarch met civil servants and inspected the
Chart Room, the hub of the whole organisation. 'That short morning
isit did more good for the internal morale . . . than anybody could
ave done in a year,' Woolton reflected. Another early move was to
ut up a sign over the staff entrance that read, 'We not merely cope,
e care'.

He set out to rectify the ministry's indifferent public image with
he help of Howard Marshall, its first ever director of public relations.
Marshall shared Woolton's interest in improving conditions for the
isadvantaged, and was concerned in particular for the lot of poor
enants. In the 1930s he had joined a national campaign against slum
ousing, even co-writing a book on the subject. But it was the sound of
is deep, warm, unhurried voice commentating on Test Match cricket
n BBC Radio for which he was best known. His insight into the game
vas sharp, yet just as important was the air of expectation and drama he
rought to a great sporting occasion. On 23 August 1938 millions had
rowded around their radios, riveted by his thirteen-hour description
f Len Hutton's world record score of 364 at The Oval. Marshall's
onversational, lyrical style drew audiences in, making listeners feel as
hough they were sitting across the table from a friend.

Woolton's growing prowess on the radio drew heavily on Marshall's
echnique. 'I always kept a picture in front of my mind of the man in
cottage house, sitting without a collar, with slippers on, at the end of
he day's work, with children playing on the rug, with his wife washing
p in an adjoining room with the door open; that was my audience –
nd it was interrupted by a ring on the front door bell, and a visitor
rriving in the middle of my broadcast. If I was fortunate, and success-
ıl, the man said, "Sit down and shut up; we are listening to Woolton".'

Listen to him they certainly did. From July 1940, as rationing
ightened even further, his avuncular presence was hardly ever absent
rom the airwaves. Woolton was no stranger to the routine and practice

of public relations from his time at Lewis's department store, of course
but his experiences as a social worker and a teacher gave him a kee
understanding of the 'ordinary folk' huddled round the wireless, wh
in turn felt he recognised their concerns.

The BBC established a short programme called *The Kitchen Fron*
over which the Ministry of Food retained substantial control. It wa
broadcast six mornings a week, at 8.15 after the morning news, to
listening public of 5.5 million. Hosted by familiar cookery experts sucl
as Marguerite Patten, it gave housewives ideas on how to stretch ver
little a long way, explaining how to make cakes without flour, suga
or lard, rissoles without beef, and tea without tea leaves. Wasting an
kind of food was subliminally portrayed as unpatriotic. Not only thar
on 12 August 1940 a Waste of Food Order was introduced, with
maximum penalty of two years' imprisonment or a fine of £500, fo
squandering precious rations. Later the ministry introduced *Food Flas*
information films in cinemas. These lasted just fifteen seconds an
relayed simple, unambiguous messages designed to encourage thrift.

Woolton and Marshall assailed the public with adverts in news
papers, bright posters, catchy phrases and rhymes. 'The only way t
influence the public mind through leaflets and posters is by direc
simple statement,' Woolton asserted, so the likes of 'Grow Your Own
(onions), 'Waste Not, Want Not', 'Eat Up Your Greens' and 'Kee
a Pig' were born. Cartoon characters such as 'Potato Pete' and 'D
Carrot' appeared in the pages of every woman's magazine, encourag
ing children to eat their vegetables, and there was even a popular ditt
that featured Uncle Fred himself:

> Those who have the will to win,
> Cook potatoes in their skin,
> Knowing that the sight of peelings,
> Deeply hurts Lord Woolton's feelings

It was sung by Betty Driver, whose Lancashire hotpot would later fin
a place in most housewives' recipe books. Well-known music hal

tistes like 'Gert and Daisy' – Elsie and Doris Waters – and Tommy
rinder were also recruited to the cause, appearing with Woolton on
ublic platforms.

The Ministry of Food occasionally veered from information and
xhortation to sheer propaganda, as in the case of the carrots and the
AF ace. Woolton responded to an oversupply of carrots – 100,000 of
hem – by suggesting that the RAF's exceptional night-flying was due
o its pilots consuming, via the vegetable, large amounts of carotene,
hich improved their night vision. He impressed on the public that
hey would see much better in the blackout if they followed their heroes'
ad and took in extra quantities of vitamin A by doing the same.

The vehicle for this benign deception – in truth the introduction
f airborne radar was the main reason for the pilots' success – was
venty-three-year-old Flight Lieutenant John Cunningham, who
as quickly dubbed 'Cat's Eyes' as the number of enemy aircraft he
owned steadily mounted. It was a nickname Cunningham privately
oathed, especially because he gave substantial credit for his twenty-
lus kills to his brilliant onboard radar operator 'Jimmy' Rawnsley.
Nevertheless, he went along for the ministry's ride. 'CARROTS DFC
NIGHT BLITZ HERO' was the headline in the Daily Express when
Cunningham received his first medal. Herbert Morrison – himself
ell versed in the tricks of public relations – thought the episode a
nasterstroke' on the Food Minister's part.

Effective publicity was one thing, but if Woolton was to save Britain
om malnutrition he also needed the very best scientific advice.
he nation's diet was now likely to be hugely dependent on home
griculture. With such limited resources, how could he supply all the
alories and vitamins needed to sustain not only the country's fighting
ervices but also its heavy manual workers, its housewives, babies,
hildren and pregnant and nursing mothers? The Food Minister was
scinated by the rapid advance of science in the area of nutrition, and
ought to recruit the best and the brightest. Among others, he brought
a to advise him Sir Henry Dale, Nobel Prize winner in physiology in
936, and Lord Horder, the King's physician.

Already in place as the ministry's chief scientific adviser was th
noted biochemist Jack Drummond, and it was he who drew up the soun
nutritional principles that guided Woolton's wartime decision-makin
In pioneering work in the early 1930s, Drummond had succeede
in isolating pure vitamin A. His involvement with the new scienc
of nutrition, combined with his interest in gastronomy, led him
undertake a comprehensive study of the English diet stretching bac
over five hundred years. In 1939, on the eve of war, he published th
results of his work in a book – co-authored with Anne Wilbrahan
later his second wife – called *The Englishman's Food: A History of Fi*
Centuries of English Diet. This eminently readable mix of social histor
and biochemistry demonstrated that malnutrition was not just a soci
issue, but would be a pressing wartime concern, too. It was vital
particular to identify the correct food that would fortify soldiers on th
battlefield and workers in the munitions factories.

Prior to his appointment, Drummond had sent a memorandum to th
Ministry of Food outlining what would turn out to be his and Wooltor
basic strategy. In it, he recognised that any wholesale experiment
creative nutrition had to work hand in hand with national habit ar
tradition. With that in mind, he advocated the provision of bread
high nutritive value (the National Wholemeal Loaf, disliked by th
public), an increase in the consumption of potatoes, oatmeal, chees
and green vegetables, the supply of not less than a pint of milk a da
to expectant and nursing mothers (and to all children up to the age
fifteen) and the fortification of margarine by adding vitamins A ar
D. He also ensured that pregnant women and the youngest childre
– in the almost complete absence of citrus fruits – received rations
blackcurrant and rosehip syrup as an alternative source of vitamin C

Valuable as Drummond's advice proved, however, hard politic
choices had to be faced. The advantage in the Atlantic lay firmly wi
the U-boats and the Luftwaffe, which by spring 1941 were inflictir
huge losses on Britain's merchant convoys. Woolton's larder w
shrinking dramatically.

* * *

n Wednesday, 26 February, Convoy OB 290, sailing off the west
ast of Ireland, was attacked by four Focke-Wulf Condor bombers.
even merchant ships with a total capacity of 35,107 tons were sent
the bottom of the Atlantic Ocean. The following day, the U-47,
ommanded by the legendary Günther Prien, took advantage of the
sulting chaos to penetrate the remaining escorts in the convoy and
nk three more. It was Germany's greatest single triumph of the main
tlantic campaign.

The success of the Condors so far out to sea, the havoc caused
the concentration of U-boats between Britain and Iceland, and
e impunity with which two battle cruisers from the German navy,
harnhorst and *Gneisenau*, were operating along the convoy routes,
ere all preying on Churchill's mind. On the night of the OB 290
saster, Brendan Bracken suggested to Jock Colville that the Prime
inister should not be told, as it would prevent him from sleeping.
it at 3 a.m. Churchill asked Colville what the latest information was
om the Admiralty. When Colville relayed the news, commenting
at it was 'distressing', Churchill replied: 'Distressing! It is terrifying.
it goes on it will be the end of us.'

With setbacks in North Africa and the Balkans, there was much to
ncern the Prime Minister at this point in the war. But it was the
ipreme menace' of the U-boats that now dominated most of his
aking hours. Woolton was no less concerned: Britain was hugely
liant on imports of food. Two-thirds of it was brought in from over-
as, requiring twenty million tons of shipping a year. Fifty per cent of
eat was imported, 70 per cent of cheese, sugar, cereals and fats, 80 per
nt of fruits and 91 per cent of butter. Of this, one-sixth of meat
ports, one-quarter of butter imports and half of all imported cheese
me from New Zealand alone. A giant map of the world on the wall
Woolton's office showed the great distances food had to travel to
ach the shores of Britain: meat, butter and cheese, for example, jour-
eyed up to 13,500 miles, sugar 4,000 to 11,200 miles, milk products
700 to 13,500, jam 6,000 to 12,000, tea 11,500, rice 11,200, wheat
700 to 11,000, palm oil 9,000 and oranges and lemons 1,500 to 6,000.

Before the war Britain's total imports of food and raw materia[l] excluding oil, had amounted to 60 million tons. Professor Lindeman[n] Statistical Branch calculated that by the end of 1940 this had falle[n] to 45.4 million tons, and in 1941 the country was on course to lo[se] another 15 million tons. Woolton's monthly report on the 'Foo[d] Situation' to the War Cabinet in January 1941 made for grim readin[g] Part one was headlined, with some understatement, 'Arrivals Muc[h] Below Programme'. At 914,000 tons the amount imported was 29 p[er] cent lower than the revised 1940/41 schedule, and there was a ple[a] from the Food Minister for more tankers to be allocated to carry whe[at] and oilseeds. There were plenty of potatoes – a 'substantial surplu[s] from the 1940 crop – but the outlook for animal protein foods w[as] 'poor'. The weekly meat ration had been reduced from 1s 2d to 1s, a[nd] consumers 'did not accept corned beef willingly'. Home production [of] bacon was calculated to plummet from the February rate of 4,000 to[ns] a week to half that by August. Fresh and frozen fish was in short supp[ly] because of the suspension of sailings from Iceland.

Even if the convoys survived the German attacks, unloadin[g] their cargo was becoming ever more difficult. The Luftwaffe's late[st] onslaught was aimed at the docks, leaving the Port of London (whic[h] handled a quarter of Britain's imports) closed for a time, whi[le] Glasgow and Liverpool were particularly badly hit. By May, all b[ut] twelve of the latter's deep-sea berths were damaged. At the beginnin[g] of March, more than 1.7 million tons of shipping was out of action an[d] awaiting repair, while a further 930,000 tons was undergoing repa[ir] while loading. The convoys that made it into port encountered th[e] problem of congestion. Too many were arriving at the same time, an[d] in late January Churchill received a minute from Lindemann pointin[g] out that these delays were making 'the average round voyage la[st] about one and a half times as long as formerly'. The Statistical Branc[h] estimated that a saving of fifteen days in the turnaround of ships cou[ld] deliver the country an extra five million tons of imports.

In his speech welcoming the new US ambassador on 18 March – [at] the lunch where he first tasted 'Woolton Pie' – Churchill had done h[is]

evel best to draw America further into what he was starting to refer to
s the Battle of the Atlantic. He revealed to his audience that German
ubmarines and cruisers were raiding as far west as the forty-second
egree of longitude, two-thirds of the way across the ocean. Lord
Halifax, in Washington, then tipped off the US State Department
hat one of these cruisers was already well inside America's 600-mile
eutrality belt. 'The fire will catch,' Churchill assured William Crozier,
vhen the editor of the *Manchester Guardian* visited him in the Annexe
wo days later for an off-the-record interview. But whether it would be
s straightforward as a declaration of war by the United States after
ne of her ships was sunk, he could not say.

In the meantime Britain had to survive on her own. Churchill had
lready, on 6 March, drafted a Battle of the Atlantic directive, setting
ut what could be done over the next four months 'to enable us to
efeat the attempt to strangle our food supplies and our connection
vith the United States'. He ordered that the fight should be taken
o the U-boat and the Focke-Wulf 'wherever we can and whenever
ve can'. 'Extreme priority' should be given to providing ships with
Hurricane fighters – launched by catapults – to combat the German
ombers. He suggested that faster boats capable of speeds between
welve and thirteen knots might be 'liberated' from convoys for a
while, as an experiment. He wanted the 'maximum' defence to be
rovided for the ports under attack – Mersey, Clyde and Bristol – and
vished to hear back about the details within a week. And – responding
o Lindemann's minute – he required 'every form of simplification and
cceleration of repairs and degaussing, even at some risk' to be applied
n order to reduce the 'terrible slowness of the turnaround of ships in
British ports'.

Such was his concern for the convoys that the Prime Minister decided
o set up another ad hoc committee – one of his favourite responses to
n ongoing weakness in the war effort. The Battle of the Atlantic
Committee held its first meeting at 5 p.m. on Wednesday, 19 March
vith Churchill in the chair; the ministers attending were Beaverbrook,
Bevin, A.V. Alexander, Sinclair, Moore-Brabazon (transport minister),

Margesson, Sir Andrew Duncan and Lord Woolton. All the measure
ordered in the directive of thirteen days ago were discussed, with
emphasis on the need to quicken the turnaround of ships in port. 'Ever
effort must be directed to this end,' Churchill demanded.

Over the coming weeks, this committee would see the Prime
Minister's mood become darker, more demanding, more bullying than
in virtually any other setting of the war. For the long-suffering General
Ismay, who attended many of these tense encounters, Churchill wa
'perhaps too impatient and self-willed to be an ideal chairman', but a
least he compensated with 'enthusiasm, drive and imagination'. Other
thought very differently. According to Moore-Brabazon, these were the
most unpleasant meetings he ever attended. 'The issue was grave, bu
the way Churchill treated everyone was almost unbearable. He usually
appeared after his early afternoon sleep in the vilest of tempers, and
having such a problem to face did not improve it. He behaved as if he
were a bullying schoolmaster. Everyone, in his opinion, was a halfwit
and if anyone said anything he was jumped upon and snubbed.'

The Prime Minister's black moods were an understandable response
to a grim outlook. The attacks on the convoys, setbacks in Libya
Crete and Greece, and now the systematic assault by the Luftwaffe or
Britain's cities, exposed the country's continuing isolation. On Good
Friday, 11 April, having decided to get out of London to see the damage
for himself he visited Swansea, inspecting detachments of civil defence
workers in a city whose centre 'had not a house standing'. The following
day he arrived in Bristol, where many homes were still smoking from
a severe raid the night before. Colville observed that they 'walked and
motored through devastation such as I had never thought possible'.

Back in Westminster, the odd murmur of discontent about the
direction of the war was now being heard. Lord Hankey, a powerful
Whitehall figure for many years, but now banished by Churchill to
relative obscurity as Chancellor of the Duchy of Lancaster, was often
the recipient of these complaints. He collected two of them on 1 May
First, General Sir John Kennedy, director of military operations
approached him on Horse Guards Parade. 'He at once tackled me

bout the Supreme Control of the War; said he was very anxious about
; believed we should lose the war if it was not put right.' Then a few
ours later, on Park Lane, he encountered Sir Robert Menzies, the
rime Minister of Australia. 'He burst out at once about Churchill and
is dictatorship and his cabinet of "Yes-men".'

Minor sniping in the House of Commons – mainly from old
upporters of Chamberlain – irked Churchill sufficiently that he
ecided to call a vote of confidence. The debate effectively turned
ito a dramatic rhetorical battle between the leader of the current
ar and the winner of the last. In an hour-long speech, Lloyd George
ocused his criticism on Churchill's management of his cabinet: 'The
rime Minister must have a real War Council . . . he is a man with
very brilliant mind, one of the most remarkable who have graced
iis House with their presence. There is no doubt about his brilliant
ualities, but for that very reason . . . he wants a few more ordinary
ersons, against whom he can check his ideas, who are independent,
ho will stand up to him and tell him exactly what they think.'

In response, Churchill was contemptuous: 'It was not the sort of
eech which one would have expected from the great war leader
f former days, who was accustomed to brush aside despondency and
larm . . . it was the sort of speech with which, I imagine, the illustrious
nd venerable Marshal Pétain might well have enlivened the closing
ays of Monsieur Reynaud's Cabinet.'

'Never have I heard him in such brilliant form,' observed 'Chips'
hannon. Others admired the performance, but were not totally
onvinced by the content. 'Winston . . . made an effective speech
om a debating point of view, but said little to convince me that he
new much more about how to win the war than myself,' reflected
Conservative backbencher Sir Cuthbert Headlam.

Nevertheless, the government motion was carried by a resounding
47 votes to 3 (with Lloyd George himself abstaining). It was exactly
year since the debate that brought about Chamberlain's downfall and
iis time his successor comfortably vanquished his critics. 'He went to
ed early, elated by his forensic success,' noted Colville.

Three days later that euphoria turned to despair. On the nigh of 10 May the chamber of the House of Commons, the epicentre of British democracy and Churchill's spiritual home for forty years, wa destroyed by German bombs. When the Prime Minister visited th scene with Beaverbrook the next day he was overcome with emotio at the destruction wrought to the chamber, Pugin's great gothi masterpiece. The spot where he and Lloyd George had jousted ove the future conduct of the war had been obliterated; the Speaker's Cha lay hidden among twisted girders and huge chunks of fallen masonr the green-padded benches were charred and drenched, and there wa no sign of the famous dispatch box from where he habitually displaye his mastery.

For five minutes he stood silently among the smouldering ruins an gazed around, all the while grinding his walking stick into the cinder 'At last he moved, and in the dim light I could see that tears wer running unchecked down his cheeks,' observed Guy Eden, politica correspondent of the *Daily Express*. 'Turning abruptly to an official, h controlled his voice with an effort and said quietly; "This Chambe must be rebuilt – just as it was. Meanwhile, we shall not miss a singl day's debate through this".'

The barrage of Luftwaffe bombs that fell on the Palace of Westminst was replicated all over the capital, and the damage to historic propert was as nothing compared to the fate of ordinary Londoners. This wa the deadliest attack in the whole of the Blitz, lasting over seven hou and killing 1,500 people, destroying 11,000 homes and setting off ove 2,000 fires. The next day one-third of London's streets were impassabl all but one railway station line was blocked, and only two bridges ove the Thames were usable.

The sheer randomness of life and death during wartime was neve more evident. In Clapham, fifteen-year-old Maggie Meggs got out o bed to tell her parents they had to leave the house. 'Something bad going to happen,' she insisted. Muttering at the whims of teenagers, M and Mrs Meggs escorted their daughter to their Anderson shelter. O their return they found a two-foot spear of glass embedded in Maggie

llow. In Walworth, nineteen-year-old Hereward Barling was guiding
doctor to an incident in Rodney Road when a bomb dropped. The
octor survived; Barling was killed instantly.

lthough in public he scorned his critics, Churchill had been
ontemplating making changes to his government for some time. On
nd, the main concern of the War Cabinet was the Western Desert in
ibya and Egypt and the need to provide General Archibald Wavell,
ommander-in-chief Middle East, with both the political backup and
nproved military resources to withstand the fierce counter-attack from
eneral Erwin Rommel's Afrika Korps. Randolph Churchill, recently
ected MP for Preston, had suggested to his father that a minister of
ate in the Middle East should be appointed to lighten Wavell's load.
he Prime Minister turned to his old friend Oliver Lyttelton, whom
e had first met in the trenches during the previous war.

Lyttelton was first and foremost a successful businessman, notably
managing director of the British Metal Corporation. But Churchill
anted this witty, urbane holder of the Military Cross by his side in
artime, so he found him a safe seat as MP for Aldershot – he was
turned unopposed – and then a post in government as President of
e Board of Trade. Over a champagne lunch in the Annexe, Churchill
kingly encouraged Lyttelton with the prospect that he would
ecome the 'Satrap of the Middle East' and 'hold the gorgeous East in
e'. A place in the War Cabinet was also dangled before him, and –
aving been assured that its other members backed the appointment
Lyttelton accepted.

Another old friend Churchill wanted nearer the heart of government
as Beaverbrook. The Beaver had left the Ministry of Aircraft
oduction, exhausted, in April, and since then had been kicking his
eels as a minister of state with loosely defined powers of supervision
ver war production. Too much of his time was spent gossiping about
olleagues. Urgency was a prerequisite of good wartime government
d this one was singularly lacking in it, Beaverbrook told William
rozier in an off-the-record interview in late May. He praised John

Anderson as 'bold and bloody', but criticised Ernest Bevin, saying h
took ten days to make decisions on important schemes, while Sinclai
although a 'nice man', was merely a defender of the air marshal
'No-one has a true sense of urgency except Churchill himself,' h
concluded.

Unfortunately the post Churchill offered to Beaverbrook wa
Woolton's, at the Ministry of Food. Sacrificing his most effective mini
ter made little sense, regardless of his desire to have his closest politica
ally back in a role with 'direct executive authority'. Beaverbrook imme
diately turned him down. 'I do not know anything about food, an
cannot grasp the problem in a short time,' he wrote to the PM on 2 Jun
'Experience is needed. I have none. It is not even a production job.'

Three days later Churchill was still toying with the idea, wonderin
if Beaverbrook might be persuaded to reconsider if Food was combine
with Agriculture. He summoned Woolton, his ploy being to sugge
that Woolton seemed tired of being Minister of Food, and then to hol
out the prospect of a fresh brief.

'Truth to tell, I'm a little tired of it . . . but I don't think it's a goo
thing to take another job because you're tired of the one you've go
unless the new one is one for which you've a special qualification o
desire,' Woolton recorded. 'I had neither for the one that was offere
to me, and I told the PM that I thought it was a good thing to hav
continuity of control in food supplies during a war.'

Churchill acknowledged defeat in a letter to Beaverbrook late
the same day. He was not in a position to offer him stewardship o
a Ministry of Agriculture and Food, 'as it does not appear that Lor
Woolton has any desire to relinquish his work at Food – a difficu
task which he does very well'. The hunt for a worthwhile role fo
Beaverbrook went on.

In late March 1941, George Orwell thought, the crisis now coming '
going to be a crisis of hunger, which the English people have no rea
experience of . . . it will be devilish difficult to get the people to fac
hunger when, so far as they can see, there is no purpose in the wa

hatever, and when the rich are carrying on just as before'. By the
ummer jam and sweet spreads, cheese and eggs had all been put on
ne ration. Churchill had strongly objected to the former, in another
vely War Cabinet meeting, but had been forced, in the end, to give
ay when Woolton's proposal met with otherwise unanimous support
round the table.

Fortunately, Orwell's prediction proved unduly pessimistic. The
nnovations devised by Woolton and his team were going from
rength to strength, keeping the spectre of starvation well away from
ne door. In the towns, the 'British Restaurant' (originally the drab-
ounding 'Community Feeding Centre', until renamed by Churchill),
 basic cafeteria run by local government or voluntary agencies to
rovide cheap, filling meals, was expanding month by month. In the
ountryside, the 'Pie Scheme', run by the Women's Voluntary Service,
upplied meat pies to agricultural workers.

In the Battle of the Atlantic, moreover, the Royal Navy had pulled
ff a remarkable series of coups that began to make life much easier for
ne merchant ships bringing in Britain's food supplies. In early March,
)peration *Claymore* saw the capture of the German trawler *Krebs*,
ielding two Enigma machines and the settings for the naval codes
or the previous month. This allowed the cryptographers at Bletchley
ark to read German naval communiqués by April. Then on 7 May,
ne destroyer HMS *Somali* captured the German weather ship *München*
ff the coast of Ireland, along with another Enigma machine and more
odebooks. This time the British had won a still greater prize, as the
odes were for the following month of June.

Two days later, on 9 May, Operation *Primrose* gathered in yet more
ntelligence booty. The German submarine U-110 was attacked by
n Allied convoy that included the British HMS *Bulldog*. Damaged
y depth charges, U-110 surfaced and was boarded by the *Bulldog*'s
rew, who collected all the papers and charts they could find, and a
hird Enigma machine. More crucial codes were acquired, together
vith grid charts that provided vital information on the position of
J-boats throughout the Atlantic, and of all German minefields and

swept channels. 'Hearty congratulations,' the First Sea Lord, Admir
Sir Dudley Pound, signalled to Captain Joe Baker-Cresswell of HM
Bulldog. 'The petals of your flower are of rare beauty.'

In April 1941 British shipping losses were 688,000 tons. In Jun
with the German naval codes broken, that figure was down to 432,00
and by July it had plummeted to 121,000 tons. On 31 May, togeth
with the US secretary of commerce Robert Hinkley and special env
Averell Harriman, Woolton watched the first consignment of food t
arrive under Lend-Lease being unloaded at a British port: four millio
eggs, 120,000 pounds of cheese and 1,000 tons of flour. The minist
had his picture taken with the dockers unloading the ship. 'To celebra
I broke my own regulation – and handed over, for division amongst th
unloading staff of two hundred and forty, a twenty-pound cheese.'

American largesse in food and munitions was one thing, but the Wa
Cabinet's ultimate goal of bringing the US into the war still prove
elusive. On 21 May SS *Robin Moor* was sunk by German submarin
U-69 in the tropical Atlantic as she made her way to Mozambiqu
without a protective convoy. But though President Roosevelt tol
Congress that the Germans had 'flagrantly violated the right of Unite
States vessels freely to navigate the seas', and despite his view tha
Germany was 'responsible for the outrageous and indefensible sinking
he would not be drawn into retaliation.

Three weeks later, in his first broadcast for five months, Lor
Woolton assured his audience that despite the Battle of the Atlanti
the nation's health was as good as ever and the food situation wa
'sound'. Stocks of essential ingredients were as replete after twent
months of war as they had been after nine. Even so, he announced tha
the butter ration was to be reduced from four to two ounces, a cut h
was able to sweeten by putting extra jam (one pound) and cheese (tw
ounces) on the table. 'There wasn't much to tell them, but they like t
be reassured occasionally,' he admitted in his diary that night.

The following weekend, on Midsummer's Day, Saturday, 21 Jun
Woolton joined a crowd of 18,000 at Lord's cricket ground to watch
splendid day's play in a charity match between the Army and the Roya

ir Force. Some of England's finest players were on show, including
yril Washbrook, Charlie Barnett and Denis Compton. 'Cricket gives
e a greater sense of relaxation than anything else I can do in London,'
/oolton reflected.

Within hours this feeling of respite from the grind of government
ould be replaced by sudden relief and optimism, as news came through
events that were to change the entire dynamic of the war.

Chapter Seven

'Riding the dung cart'

22 June to 7 December 1941

At 7.30 on the morning of Sunday, 22 June 1941, there was
knock on the door of foreign secretary Anthony Eden's room
Chequers. Churchill's valet Frank Sawyers entered and, presentin
Eden with a large cigar on a silver salver, announced: 'The Prim
Minister's compliments and the German armies have invaded Russia
Putting on his dressing gown, Eden walked along the corridor t
Churchill's bedroom. 'We savoured the relief – but not for me at tha
hour the cigar – and discussed what was immediately to do.' Afte
almost exactly a year of isolation, Britain – and the British Empire
was no longer alone in facing the might of Hitler's forces.

The invasion came as no surprise to the two men. Indeed, just
week earlier Churchill had warned President Roosevelt, 'from ever
source at my disposal, including some most trustworthy, it looks as if
vast German onslaught on Russia was imminent'. It should not hav
come as a shock either to Russia's leader, Joseph Stalin. Persister
intelligence from, among others, his diplomats in Berlin, his be
agent, Richard Sorge, in Tokyo, and from decrypts at Bletchle
Park (although he was told only that the information came from
'trusted agent') had alerted Stalin to the near certainty of an invasio
sometime in mid to late June. Yet so reluctant had he been to fac

cts, so willing was he to believe it was disinformation from Western
opagandists, that when the moment actually arrived he was too
nned to respond.

He left it to his people's commissar for foreign affairs, Vyacheslav
olotov, to rally the nation. In his fifteen-minute broadcast the old
lshevik, the man whose name was on the non-aggression pact signed
th Germany two years previously, told his audience that history was
their side. The Germans would be expelled just as the French were in
12: 'our cause is just. The enemy will be defeated. Victory will be ours.'

Anticipating the moment – although not certain it would happen
at very weekend – Churchill had included among his party at
hequers not just Eden, but the United States ambassador John Winant,
d his good friend and Secretary of State for Dominion Affairs Lord
3obbety') Cranborne. The American's initial smile of satisfaction at
e dramatic news gave way to some doubts. 'Winant . . . suspects it
ay all be a put-up job between Hitler and Stalin,' observed house
est Jock Colville.

Fifty miles south at Lord Beaverbrook's home, Cherkley Court,
ere were no such reservations. On hearing the news bulletin, twenty-
ven-year-old Michael Foot, one of his lordship's journalist protégés
d co-author of the recent, hugely successful *Guilty Men* (a polemic
ainst the appeasers), ran downstairs and rummaged through the
amophone cupboard. The household was then roused by the sound,
top volume, of 'The Internationale' ('No more deluded by reaction,
tyrants only we'll make war'). 'I was happy to inform the bleary-
ed household, guests and butlers alike, that they were now allies of
e Soviet Union,' Foot recalled.

Eden left for London to confer with Ivan Maisky, the Soviet
nbassador, while Beaverbrook hurried over to Chequers to join his
'ar Cabinet colleagues. Churchill also invited Sir Stafford Cripps,
s ambassador to Moscow, who had been recalled for consultations
few weeks earlier. At the previous Monday's meeting, Cripps had
formed his colleagues that the prevailing view in diplomatic circles
Moscow was that Russia could not hold out against Germany for

more than three or four weeks. At dinner on Saturday night Churchi[ll]
had agreed, saying 'Russia will assuredly be defeated.'

Nonetheless, elated by finding an ally, and despite having be[en]
a foe of the communist regime from the moment of its inceptio[n]
Churchill set out to draft a speech for broadcast that night that wou[ld]
offer unequivocal support to the Soviets. This message would be [a]
the more powerful coming from a fierce ideological adversary, someo[ne]
who had tried to strangle communism at birth, but it needed to be se[nt]
quickly. To that end Churchill chose not to convene a full War Cabin[et]
meeting to confer with the likes of Attlee, Bevin and Greenwood, b[ut]
instead remained at Chequers to work on the address with Cripp[s,]
Beaverbrook and the returning Eden.

Such was the care and attention given to the drafting that it w[as]
finished only twenty minutes before Churchill was due to go on a[ir.]
When it was delivered, he made it clear he would 'unsay no word' [of]
criticism he had levelled against the Soviet regime over the past quart[er]
of a century. But he then went on to lend his support with some of t[he]
most vivid, folksy imagery he had used in any of his wartime speeche[s.]

'I see Russian soldiers standing on the threshold of their nati[ve]
land, guarding the fields which their fathers have tilled from tim[e]
immemorial. I see them guarding their homes where mothers and wiv[es]
pray – ah yes, for there are times when all pray – for the safety of the[ir]
loved ones, the return of the breadwinner, of their champion, or the[ir]
protector. I see the ten thousand villages of Russia, where the means [of]
existence was wrung so hardly from the soil, but where there are st[ill]
primordial human joys, where maidens laugh and children play.'

Advancing upon this bucolic bliss was the 'Nazi war machine, wit[h]
its clanking, heel-clicking, dandified Prussian officers, its crafty expe[rt]
agents fresh from the cowing and tying down of a dozen countrie[s.]'
Churchill's conclusion was that 'Any man or state who fights [on]
against Nazidom will have our aid . . . it follows, therefore, that w[e]
shall give whatever help we can to Russia and the Russian people.'

The language was a little too melodramatic for some. Twenty-yea[r-]
old garage assistant Muriel Green, listening in Snettisham, Norfol[k,]

bserved, 'It seems grand they [the Russians] will fight with us. We
stened to Churchill's speech. The Gs say they get sick of his rambling
escriptions.' But for Maggie Joy Blunt, a thirty-one-year-old
rchitectural writer from Slough, it was one of the 'cleverest speeches'
f Churchill's career. 'I smoke my last cigarette to him; think this is the
ost important day of the century.'

At the Soviet embassy in west London ambassador Maisky listened
ith special care to the Prime Minister's words. 'After hearing
hurchill I thought: "For today I may be content; my wishes have
een fulfilled . . . but what help [will Britain give]? In what forms? To
hat extent?"'

For one man at the table at Chequers that weekend the help had
o be wholehearted, and volunteered free of conditions. The following
orning Lord Beaverbrook's *Daily Express* urged the country to offer
hatever aid was necessary. 'We are the next on the list, and next
utumn is to be the time,' the opinion column suggested. 'Every shot
e Russians fire, every bomb they drop helps us; and every shot we
re, every bomb we drop, helps Stalin.'

Beaverbrook, the arch-capitalist, would soon prove to be the com-
unist country's most vocal ally. But for Churchill and the rest of the
Var Cabinet an enduring aversion to the Soviet Union was hard to
row off, and there was uncertainty over the correct approach towards
is new 'ally' – not that that was a word the government used in those
rly days. It could hardly be forgotten that Britain had gone to war
defence of Poland – one of whose attackers was the Soviet Union.
ories in the Cabinet like Eden and Cranborne felt words of support
ould be phrased purely in the military context; 'politically Russia
as as bad as Germany and half the country would object to being
ssociated with her too closely'.

Churchill was anxious about the stance of his Labour colleagues, and
War Cabinet the day after his broadcast he urged that any speeches
ey made 'should continue to draw a line of demarcation between
e tenets of the Labour Party and those of Communism'. Attlee told
im not to worry – he was proposing to emphasise exactly that in

a BBC broadcast the following evening. Further reassurance came i
the attitude of Herbert Morrison, who said that despite the change
circumstances, he saw no reason to lift the ban on the communis
backed *Daily Worker*. But the image of Russia would gradually b
transformed from one of grimly quiescent masses toiling for a harsl
industrialised socialist order, to one of resolute, independent peasan
bravely resisting Germany's might.

While the government attempted to get to grips with this chang
it stumbled occasionally. The playing of 'The Internationale' was
case in point.

Every Sunday evening before the nine o'clock news the BB
broadcast a popular programme called *National Anthems of the Allie*
now the song of a new ally had to be added to the list. But the worker
anthem, this rallying call of communists, socialists and anarchists, wa
hardly music to Churchill's ears. So on Thursday, 10 July the son
forced its way on to the War Cabinet's agenda. Eden and Minister c
Information Duff Cooper were instructed to talk to the BBC abou
playing Tchaikovsky's 1812 Overture (dedicated to Field Marsha
Kutuzov, who had resisted Napoleon's Grande Armée) instead of th
revolution-stirring 'Internationale'. The BBC duly obliged, and thre
days later the Soviet national anthem vanished from the airwaves.

The press was scornful. The *Daily Express* noted that the recordin
of the Tchaikovsky overture was 'poor, overlain with the surging an
fading normal to short-wave broadcasts'. Cassandra in the *Daily Mirro*
under the heading 'Age of Cant', said the Foreign Office's skirmishe
over playing 'The Internationale' were 'one of the most amusing an
ludicrous farces we have had for some time'. As the British public
solidarity with the Russian people deepened during the life-and-deat
struggle that unfolded over the following months, so did the clamou
for 'The Internationale' to return, which it did, six months later.

On the day the War Cabinet discussed its new approach to th
Soviet Union, there was one other pressing item on the agenda
the future of the Ministry of Information itself. Alfred Duff Coope
the minister in charge, had come to Cabinet that day with a plea – an

ear proposals – for more powers to put an end to the erosion of
onfidence, credibility and influence that had beset his department
ver the previous twelve months.

he Ministry of Information was based at Senate House, in Malet
treet, Bloomsbury, at arm's length from Whitehall. It had enjoyed a
rief but colourful existence in the First World War under the stew-
dship of Lord Beaverbrook, who had strong characters like novelist
ohn Buchan and Liberal MP Charles Masterman to help him raise
orale at home and influence opinion abroad.

It was brought back into the fold on 4 September 1939, the day
ter Britain's declaration of war on Germany. Now, for sheer grandeur,
beit in a modernistic style, its headquarters – normally the admin-
trative centre of the University of London – could rival anything
 Whitehall. Senate House was a seemingly indestructible building
at reeked of boundless authority and ambition. While the Luftwaffe
ombs left many homes in adjoining streets in ruins, this pyramidal art
eco structure of white Portland stone, standing 209ft tall, remained
scathed and continued to dominate – or 'insult', as one of its occa-
onal employees, Evelyn Waugh, described it – the London skyline.
Another writer was just starting to visualise it as a forbidding 'Ministry
 Truth' in a frightening, totalitarian world.)

During the first two years of the war its new inhabitants,
oliticians and civil servants, had laboured in an anxious, fractious
nvironment. Fairly or unfairly, the Ministry of Information had too
ften become a byword for confusion, incompetence and impotence
nong parliamentarians, the press and the public alike. 'Hush, hush,
uckle who dares, another new Minister's fallen downstairs' was
 popular little refrain among the 2,500 Senate House employees.
ince the start of the war they had witnessed the downfall of
oth the dull, unimaginative Lord Macmillan and the inflexible,
ntankerous Sir John Reith, and now Duff Cooper, comfortably the
ost suited of the three for the job, was becoming disenchanted at
is lack of influence.

A man with a distinguished war record, a politician of princip
(witness his resignation over Munich) and an administrator
great experience (at the Foreign Office, War Office, Treasury ar
Admiralty), the urbane, sophisticated Duff Cooper seemingly had a
the requisite qualities for office. He was also a master of fluent, excitir
English prose, exemplified in his original and insightful biography
the French diplomat Talleyrand. Indeed, his felicitous broadcasts
the desperate days of May 1940 had been second only to Churchill'
Like his great friend, his romantic, Macaulayesque view of Britis
history permeated every defiant sentence. Perhaps his style was tc
literary at times for a mass audience, but he was capable too of a mo
robust, populist touch.

One broadcast – on the evening of 28 May, as the Britis
Expeditionary Force began its evacuation of Dunkirk – had bee
singled out for praise. The Home Intelligence Report the following da
bore testimony to the confidence listeners now placed in the ministe
'His best yet . . . reports indicate that people were impressed by h
confident manner and that his speech had a steadying effect . . . th
increasing prestige of the Minister and his abilities as a broadcaster ar
becoming obvious . . . the people are beginning to rely on him to te
them how the situation should be looked at.'

Unfortunately, those days of May and June 1940 were the high
water mark of Duff Cooper's tenure at the MoI. Initially 'delighted'
his appointment – he had just returned from a successful lecture tou
of America where he had skilfully promoted the British cause – Du
Cooper found his enthusiasm beginning to drain away in the face
constant wrangling with other government departments, attacks k
the press, arguments with the BBC, and, crucially, weak support fro
Churchill. His natural inclination to provide as much uncensore
news as possible was frequently thwarted by the service departments
War, Army, and especially Navy – with the obstructive presence of th
Prime Minister looming in the background.

It all started badly for Duff Cooper when an early attempt to gathe
information on the state of public morale – through the newly create

artime Social Survey – turned into accusations, fuelled by the *Daily* *erald*, that he 'had instituted a system of espionage which gave certain ·ople the right to pry into the affairs of the neighbours'. The popular ess had made much of 'Cooper's Snoopers', as did the odd Member Parliament. In a lively debate on 1 August, Sir Archibald Southby, onservative MP for Epsom, likened the canvassing to Gestapo ethods in Germany at the start of the Hitler regime.

Invasion had always been on the government's mind in those xious days of summer and autumn 1940, and exhortation of the blic in the face of this impending threat was essential. But the inistry of Information found itself in trouble for a series of ill-judged, ten patronising campaigns. 'Careless Talk Costs Lives' had been the ception, an early, successful anti-gossip exercise at the height of mours of spies and fifth columnists. It had a lightness of touch to ide it and a brilliant collection of cartoons by the editor of *Punch*, yril Bird ('Fougasse'), to back it up. But then came the disastrous ilent Column', the name given to a propaganda exercise urging crecy in all military matters.

There was nothing new in this, and it appeared eminently sensible wartime. But the public's tolerance diminished rapidly in the face a deluge of short cinema films, coloured posters, and quarter-page verts in 108 newspapers and 72 magazines. These featured a cast unlikely characters, all portrayed as letting down the country: 'Mr crecy Hush Hush', 'Miss Leaky Mouth', 'Mr Pride in Prophecy', 1r Know All', 'Miss Teacup Whisper' and 'Mr Glumpot'.

The notion that a loose word here and there should be considered patriotic or dangerous rankled with many people. But what really itated Britons was the enforcement. In one week in July 1940, venteen people were sentenced and fined a total of 123 weeks and 62 for defeatist chatter. A young engineer, Henry Blessingdon, as jailed for three months and fined £60 for telling a vicar about an port he had helped to build. A Leicester schoolteacher, Kathleen ary Bursnall, received a two-month sentence and a fine of £20 for ying to soldiers, 'You are bloody fools to wear that uniform.'

'This is spreading suspicion and unhappiness,' Home Intelligen[ce]
recorded. People asked, 'If we can't talk, what can we do?' Eventual[ly]
even Churchill realised these arbitrary arrests were counter-productiv[e.]
The 'silent column' campaign has 'passed into innocuous desuetud[e,']
he told a relieved House of Commons on 23 July.

Then there was the structure and make-up of the ministry itse[lf.]
'A monster had been created, so large, so voluminous, so amorphou[s]
that no single man could cope with it,' Duff Cooper later reflected.
handful of civil servants tried in vain to marshal an army compose[d]
of some of the brightest minds in the country, including professor[s,]
writers, artists, journalists, retired ambassadors, retired admirals, fil[m]
producers, barristers, anthropologists and theologians. Unfortunate[ly]
there were just too many brilliant amateurs at Senate House, and t[oo]
few ordinary professionals.

The Prime Minister's belligerent attitude towards the med[ia]
presented Duff Cooper with many restless moments during his ste[w]
ardship of the MoI. Churchill was an avid consumer of newspape[rs]
(the first editions would be sent to him every night), but quick to ta[ke]
offence at any personal slight, or criticism of his government. His ow[n]
experience as a war reporter, which included brushes with the cens[or]
and attacks on those in power, had not left him with a relaxed pe[r]
spective. The *Daily Mirror* and the *Sunday Pictorial* were particul[ar]
targets of his ire, and Duff Cooper often had to play the role of peac[e]
maker and talk the Prime Minister out of intemperate plans for pre[ss]
censorship.

Churchill regularly fulminated against the BBC, too. At a W[ar]
Cabinet meeting on 6 November 1940 he had described the Corporatio[n]
as 'the enemy within the gate; continually causing trouble; more har[m]
than good'. John Reith, sitting across the table, had watched a plia[nt]
Duff Cooper agree with the Prime Minister that 'more control' w[as]
needed and that 'BBC employees ought to be civil servants'.

Then there was the Prime Minister's particular bête noire, J.[B.]
Priestley. When the writer resumed his popular *Postscript* broadcas[ts]
on Sunday, 26 January 1941, he called for a radical declaration of w[ar]

ns. The population was being asked to 'take it'; 'tell them exactly
at they are taking it for', demanded Priestley. 'Do something now.
ve us a sign that a new democratic order is on the way.'

Churchill was irritated and three days later wrote to Duff Cooper:
m very sorry that you have got Mr J.B. Priestley back, and that his
t broadcast should have been an argument utterly contrary to my
own views. How many more has he got to do? Have you any control
er what he says? He is far from friendly to the Government, and I
all not be too sure about him on larger issues.'

The bizarre flight of Rudolf Hess, Hitler's deputy, to Scotland
10 May 1941 ought to have provided the MoI with a golden
portunity. 'I feel that we should make it quite clear that whatever
lue Hess may be as a prisoner of war, he is fifty times more valuable
a propaganda carrier. He ought to be our bird before he is anyone
e's bird,' wrote an anxious Harold Nicolson.

But the MoI was largely excluded in the Hess affair. Duff Cooper
s not even informed of Hess's arrival until two days afterwards. By
en, Munich Radio had been the first to broadcast the news and
y propaganda value had been severely dented. The War Cabinet –
l by Churchill and Beaverbrook – was never persuaded to put out
statement about the deputy Führer. The public were never given
e reasons for his arrival, so confusion, ignorance and rumour were
owed to rule.

The ministry's long-running struggle to avoid being sidelined by
e service departments came to a head at that War Cabinet meeting
23 June 1941. Duff Cooper was frustrated that his ministry had
come a 'Post Office', merely distributing the news as supplied to it.
e war, air and navy ministries had kept a tight grip on the release of
ws from within their own spheres; the MoI felt useless and powerless
a result.

In cabinet, Duff Cooper discovered to his surprise that he could
unt on the wholehearted support of Beaverbrook, who perhaps
called his own struggles in 1918. The new Minister of Supply sub-
tted a memorandum whose central point was a call for all contact

between newspapers and government departments to be conduct
through the MoI. 'In future, the Ministry of Information becomes t
propaganda battle-front, and the Service Ministries are to be regard
as the supply . . . the Ministry of Information [is] to root hog or die.

Duff Cooper's paper to the same meeting put the matter plain
'The Cabinet has to decide whether the head of the Ministry
Information is to be a very important minister . . . or whether he is
be a high official with the duty of carrying out the direction of otl
departments.' He pleaded in his concluding paragraph, 'Unless it
given the authority which it demands there is danger of [the minist
ceasing to be an object of ridicule in order to become one only of pit

But in his own memorandum Churchill showed no intention
bowing to the central demand. 'The publication of war news fro
the fighting departments . . . must be subject in the event of dispt
to the veto of the departmental minister concerned.' He also insist
that the MoI should not be able to change the form of communiqu
from the Admiralty or War and Air Ministries unless those departmer
were consulted first, and declared that their press officers shou
continue to have separate dealings with the newspapers.

Beaverbrook was unimpressed by the Prime Minister's views. 'T
Ministry of Information comes to the Cabinet for improvement, and
gets a plan that makes things worse . . . I advise enlarging the powe
of the Ministry of Information, or abolishing it. The ministry cann
go on in its present form.' But Beaverbrook's protests were to no ava
At the 23 June and 30 June War Cabinet meetings only Lo
Cranborne, the Dominions secretary, rallied to his and Duff Coope
side, the rest supporting the Prime Minister. A despondent D
Cooper told Churchill afterwards that had it not been wartime
would have resigned.

The end was not far away, however. Duff Cooper left office in mi
July with a final, uncharacteristic act. During a long, boozy lunch wi
journalists, he was fiercely criticised by William Connor, author
the Daily Mirror's 'Cassandra' column, for failing to act over a coup
of broadcasts made by P.G. Wodehouse, then in France in effecti

:rman captivity. The comments appeared to be no more than mild :monstrations of the old writer's remoteness from the real life and ood of the British people; but to the columnist, they were akin to achery. Greatly riled by Cassandra's taunts, Duff Cooper invited him respond by way of a broadcast. When the BBC governors saw the ipt they were horrified, deeming it vulgar, extravagant and almost tainly libellous; they refused to put it on air. Duff Cooper, conscious his brandy-fuelled lunchtime pledge, felt duty-bound to overrule em by way of a written order, the only one issued to the Corporation wartime.

'I have come to tell you tonight of the story of a rich man trying to ke his last and greatest sale – that of his country,' Cassandra's riposte gan. 'It is a sombre story of honour pawned to the Nazis for the price a soft bed in a luxury hotel.' In a letter to *The Times* on 22 July Duff oper acknowledged the 'distress' caused to many by the broadcast, d admitted that it had been his sole responsibility. 'The Governors leed shared unanimously the view expressed in your columns that : broadcast was in execrable taste. *De gustibus non est disputandum.* casions, however, may arise in time of war when plain speaking is re desirable than good taste.'

As for Cassandra, he told *Times* readers the following day that over per cent of his readership at the *Daily Mirror* – 'fighting men, factory rkers, miners and ordinary people' – 'completely approved' of what had said. 'When Dr Goebbels announces an apparently new and ling propaganda recruit to further this slaughter, I still retain the ht to denounce this treachery in terms compatible with my own nscience – and nothing else.'

It was a sour end to Duff Cooper's term at Senate House. In July 41 he was replaced, the Prime Minister offering him a new challenge the War Cabinet's representative in the Far East. 'He was a curiously red political figure and had by now become also rather an idle one. : preferred talking over lunch to doing anything,' was the judgement Francis Williams, former editor of the *Daily Herald* and Duff Cooper's :ss relations officer. Churchill was less damning but more colourful:

'Here is a man with a fine war record, with experience of politics a
government, and a fine reputation as a writer. He is just the man for
And what happened? He failed completely. It just shows that it does
do to harness a thoroughbred to a dung cart.'

The cart would now be ridden by an out-and-out newspaperma
Brendan Bracken, Churchill's parliamentary private secretary, wa
press proprietor with interests in such quality titles as *The Econom*
The Banker, *Investors Chronicle* and the *Practitioner*. Printing t
Stock Exchange List (as chairman of *Financial News*) and the Bi
(as director of publishers Eyre and Spottiswoode) meant he was 't
provider of Mammon and Manna'.

Equally important for any prospect of success was his relationsł
with the man in Number 10; no one had fought harder to get Church
into power, and few had such a close and influential political a
personal relationship with the Prime Minister. 'They quarrelled li
husband and wife,' recalled Harold Macmillan, 'but WSC expect
that – and it never lasted or affected their true harmony. Few oth
had the entrée or privilege to do it with impunity.'

Bracken was one of the more extraordinary individuals to penetra
the inner sanctum of power in British politics. The son of an Iri
builder and Republican activist, as an unruly teenager he w
despatched to Australia, where he spent a precarious, nomadic thr
years, working on a sheep farm, travelling widely, reading avidly a
visiting religious establishments.

After he returned, aged 18, a career as a teacher was briefly pursu
before he beat a path to London, where he began to carve out his care
in the newspaper world. Soon, through his native wit and rough char
he had inveigled himself into the upper echelons of British socie
and by 1929 had won a parliamentary seat for the Conservatives
North Paddington.

Bracken's unconventional background was matched by an arresti
appearance. He was an imposing, unusual looking man – tall, bur
bespectacled , with a big, pale face, brown eyes and a shock of wiry r

ir that stretched over his forehead like a wig. There was a simian-
e quality about him that both attracted and repelled. Always there
s an air of mystery about 'Dear Brendan', as Churchill affectionately
lled him: Bracken did not discourage the persistent – if utterly
proven – rumour that he was the Prime Minister's illegitimate son.

Despite the logic of his appointment, Bracken was very reluctant
accept the position. Perhaps he feared losing such privileged access
his master, with the byzantine workings of a troubled department
w set to occupy his time. But Churchill persuaded him, cracking a
ke to try and make light of the challenge. 'He had the hardihood to
y that it was worse than manning a bomb disposal unit,' Bracken
orted to his friend Lord Wolmer. He would, however, continue to
e at 10 Downing Street and thus remain in close contact with the
me Minister.

Bracken had set out his views on the future role of a Ministry of
ormation in a Commons debate on 28 July 1939. 'I hope that the
ntrollers of this Ministry will realise that the world is dazed and bored
propaganda . . . the only effective work the Ministry of Information
n do is to establish good relations between the Government and the
itish and Foreign Press.'

Two days after taking office he held his first briefing with home and
erseas media and spelt out his credo even more succinctly. 'I am a
essman. I am interested in news: and if I cannot get news into the
pers, the sooner I depart from these premises the better for you,
e country and all of us.' The era of inspirational propaganda would
on be over.

The cultivated Edwardian charm of the aloof Duff Cooper gave way
the wisecracking, talkative, plain-speaking Bracken. Churchill's
ela' might be a rogue, but he was a clever rogue, and he was never
ll. A conversation with the new minister would leave the listener
ounded by his near total recall of figures and his encyclopedic
owledge of diverse subjects – especially the large houses and
urches of Britain. Bracken spoke in public in the same informal
nner and conversational tones that made him such an engaging

talker in private, which quickly helped him to win the trust and resp
of MPs. Although when taking questions in the Commons, he co
dismiss them in much the same manner as a 'drill sergeant rebuking
awkward squad'.

On his first day at Senate House Bracken walked into every ro
and met every occupant, using his retentive memory to store deta
about them all. On a return visit a few days later, he was able to addr
everyone correctly by name and position – and tell them whether th
still had a future in the department.

The new minister's first impressions of 'Bloomersbury', as he quic
dubbed his new domain, were not favourable. A week later, follo
ing a conversation with Bracken, Nicolson recorded that 'he see
to be sacking everybody'. But he was also making some shrewd n
appointments, including the promotion of Francis Williams to be
new controller of press and censorship.

As a young reporter Williams, with a colleague, had once boug
a horse and caravan and set off on a journey to chronicle the sta
of England for the editor of the Daily Herald, George Lansbury, w
subsequently became leader of the Labour Party. Later Willia
worked for Beaverbrook's Daily Express as a financial reporter. H
was a resourceful and experienced newspaperman, one of whose jo
was – when Bracken was unavailable – to argue Churchill out of
worst obsessions about the press.

Another inspired appointment by Bracken was Cyril Radcliffe
the ministry's director-general. Radcliffe, a gifted lawyer, may ha
been distant in manner but was lucid, tough and eager to engage
intellectual or administrative battle. Bracken's energy and dash co
bined with Radcliffe's calmness and judgement made them a formida
team. 'The result was that the Ministry of Information assumed a n
status,' observed Ronald Tree. 'Instead of being a whipping boy an
butt for the cartoonist, it began for the first time to feel a sense of pr
in its achievements, and a force to be reckoned with.'

The vast majority of the press rallied to Bracken's side. Th
recognised that here at last was a minister who genuinely believed

ess freedom, and who would fight robustly for the release of more ews from the Foreign Office and the service departments. Bracken ersuaded Sinclair's Air Ministry to release details of the numbers of rcraft involved in raids, and he won round the War Office, which lowed journalists to accompany the troops in North Africa for the 'st time.

As for relations with the BBC, there had been pressure from many uarters early in the war for the Board of Governors to be abolished its charter scrapped. Churchill had written to Duff Cooper on 7 May 1940, 'I should be glad to receive some proposals from you for tablishing a more effective control over the BBC. Now that we have Government representing the Opposition as well as the Majority, we ould have a much freer hand in this respect.'

Bracken had no desire to muzzle the Corporation. He put it on cord in the House of Commons on 23 October 1941 that 'in wartime is necessary and right that the Government should control the olicy of the BBC in matters affecting the war effort, the publication of ews, and the conduct of propaganda'. But, recognising the popularity d growing strength of the BBC's news coverage, and the vital ntribution it was making to fostering national unity and morale, e wanted it to retain a large measure of independence, at least for omestic programming.

For overseas broadcasting he insisted on closer scrutiny. In this e relied greatly upon the skilled diplomat and spymaster Ivone irkpatrick, whom he moved from the post of director of the foreign vision of the MoI to that of controller of the European Service of e BBC. Kirkpatrick had witnessed the rise and rise of the Nazis as st secretary at Britain's Berlin embassy in the 1930s, and it was he ho first interviewed Rudolf Hess soon after Hitler's deputy landed May 1941. The European Service, which was by now broadcasting over twenty languages for around thirty hours a day, was essentially news, not a propaganda, operation. But the boundaries between this d a new body, proposed by Bracken, called the Political Warfare xecutive, would become very porous.

The birth of the PWE was announced by Churchill in the Hous of Commons on 11 September, in suitably clandestine fashion. Litt information was given as to the make-up and remit of the organisatio and answers to questions were refused on the grounds of nation security. Finally Tory MP Rupert De la Bère asked the Prime Ministe 'What is the difference between a secret question and an awkwa question?' Back came the reply, 'One is a danger to the country, an the other is a nuisance to the Government.' He might have said tha the PWE was the body tasked with waging psychological warfare the Germans, through the use of both 'white' (overt) and 'blac (covert) propaganda. The former included leaflets dropped by th RAF over occupied territory and messages broadcast by the Europea services of the BBC. The latter would come in the form of secret radi stations – eventually around forty – that gave the impression transmitting from occupied Europe, whereas in fact they were a based on British soil. The PWE would also publish 'black' printe material (leaflets, newspapers, fake astrological magazines and forge ration books), spread rumours, and, later in the war, drop sma incendiary devices into Germany with appeals to ordinary German to use them against the authorities. At this stage of the conflic psychological warfare was one of the few weapons Britain could us against her enemy.

Later on, Bracken decided to introduce to the War Cabinet regular summary of morale and public opinion. In his first report F restated his beliefs about information and propaganda. 'There must h more explanation; not only about the Armed Forces and the war si uation, but also about production, labour, wartime restrictions an the big problems that affect the life of everyone today. When th public is bewildered by something new a failure to explain mear the risk of driving a wedge between Government and public. We mu stop appealing to the public or lecturing at it.'

Bracken brought stability and authority to the MoI. Above all els it was his relationship with Churchill that was the key to his succes Now the Prime Minister was more willing to try and understand th

oblems of a department he had once scorned. When Churchill set
o a cabinet subcommittee on censorship without consulting Bracken,
he minister protested angrily. 'You know perfectly well how glad I shall
e to hand over this task to a more competent person. Why could you
ot have asked for my resignation instead of appointing a committee
inspection?'

The Prime Minister immediately abandoned his plan, replying
eekly: 'Now please leave off scolding me on paper, and if you have
ny griefs come and beat me up personally.'

t the start of November 1941, there was a lull in offensives on the
ar's principal battlefronts. Hitler's troops had penetrated deep inside
e Soviet Union, reaching Leningrad and Kiev, but the German
igh Command had ordered a halt to Operation *Typhoon* (the
dvance on Moscow) as the weather worsened and the roads to the
ty turned to mud. This gave Stalin's generals the chance to reinforce
s defending army with tanks and aircraft from the Soviet Far East
nd Siberia. Meanwhile, in the North African desert, the summer had
en something of a phoney war, with only the odd skirmish along the
byan frontier.

There had also been significant progress towards the War Cabinet's
ime objective of drawing America into the war. In August in
acentia Bay, Newfoundland, the American heavy cruiser *Augusta*
nd Britain's newest battleship *Prince of Wales* had moored side by side,
nd Churchill and Roosevelt had held their first face-to-face meeting
nce that brief, unpromising encounter in London in 1918. For four
ays they talked about help for Russia, the conduct of the desert war
North Africa, the danger of Spain joining the Axis, the threat from
pan in the Pacific and much else besides.

Concrete commitments were made, including American pledges
supply bombers and provide convoy escorts west of Iceland, and a
int agreement on a massive aid package to sustain Russia's war effort.
grand-sounding accord was also signed; the Atlantic Charter was
statement of joint principles and values for the post-war world that

included national self-determination, free trade, the disarmament
aggressor nations and an end to territorial aggrandisement. It was a
important, symbolic document. Yet the Americans were still out of th
fight. While the two leaders were talking in Newfoundland, the Hou
of Representatives had passed the Selective Service Bill – inauguratir
the very first peacetime draft – by just one vote.

Then in late September, in his guise as Minister of Supply, but al:
as an increasingly vociferous champion of Russia, Beaverbrook set c
across the Norwegian Sea on the cruiser *London* for Archangel, fro
where he flew to Moscow to confer with Stalin, along with Americ;
envoy Averell Harriman and General Ismay. 'Make sure you are n
bled white,' Churchill warned him. Stalin's more extravagant reques
– like asking Britain to send troops to fight in the Ukraine – we
rejected. His demand that Britain should recognise Russia's frontie
as they existed in 1941 – incorporating the Baltic States and Poland
was politely listened to. All Beaverbrook was able to offer was materi
– a wealth of it: 500 tanks a month, and 200 fighters and 500 anti-tar
guns within nine months.

'Beaverbrook has been a great salesman. His personal sinceri
was convincing. His genius has never worked more effectively,' w
Harriman's assessment. Sir Archibald Rowlands, another member of th
party, observed that Beaverbrook got on 'amazingly well' with Stal;
because they were 'both racketeers' and thus understood each other.

Beaverbrook noted that Stalin drew pictures of wolves while talkir
and filled in the background with a coloured pencil. After eight hou
in continuous conversation, 'We had got to like him – a kindly m;
with a habit when agitated of walking about the floor with his han
behind his back.'

In a triumphant BBC broadcast soon after he returned, the Beav
fired the first shots in his 'second front' appeal. 'Stalin must be sustaine
The Soviet Union must be enabled to enter the spring campaign wi
adequate supplies of all munitions of war . . . these are the promises v
made to Stalin in Moscow in your name. These are the pledges th
we shall carry out.'

His diplomatic triumph complete, Beaverbrook returned to the hard
grind at the Ministry of Supply. As Minister of Aircraft Production, he
had been obliged to work closely with both his predecessor in his new
role, Herbert Morrison, and the Minister of Labour, Ernest Bevin. By
and large his relationship with the former was amicable and mutually
beneficial; with the latter, cordiality and effective partnership were
sadly lacking. Bevin jealously guarded his position as controller of the
nation's manpower; demands for greater productivity and flexibility
from 'his' workers were met with great suspicion, especially when they
came from the cunning Beaverbrook. Bevin liked to play everything
by the trade union rulebook, and had an ingrained suspicion of all
capitalists. By contrast Beaverbrook was the improvising individualist,
always seeking to cut corners and evade convention, believing
extraordinary times required exceptional working hours and practices.
Such was Bevin's fury over Beaverbrook's 'meddling' in his domain
that at one point he even threatened to launch a prosecution of his
War Cabinet colleague, accusing him of breaking the Factory Acts.

This developing battle was unlike the one Beaverbrook had fought
with Archibald Sinclair, which had been, at root, a conflict of strategy
and policy. The clash with Bevin was one of personality and power,
pitting against each other two remarkable self-made men – both vain,
egotistical and ruthless – who were unaccustomed to playing second
fiddle to anyone. What they were fighting over was control of vast
areas of the country's war production.

Harold Macmillan, Beaverbrook's junior minister, likened his master's teasing of his solid Labour opponent to a scene from the bullring:
'Bevin was the bull with many taurine qualities: Beaverbrook was the
Matador.' For his part, the Minister of Labour made little secret of
his dislike for Beaverbrook and his methods. 'Bevin said the PM had
called him [Beaverbrook] a magician, so he had replied that the magician's stock-in-trade was illusion,' Sir John Reith recorded.

In August 1940 Bevin and Beaverbrook had spent a weekend
together with Churchill (and others) at Chequers, where, after an
initial stiffness, they talked civilly enough, despite their obvious

differences in outlook. Yet since then the antipathy had grown, suc
that friends of the two men had become anxious about its effect on th
national cause. Efforts were made to bring them together in congeni
surroundings away from Whitehall to cultivate a better workir
relationship. Early in July 1941 Beaverbrook agreed, reluctantly, ·
invite Bevin and his wife Florence to dinner at Cherkley Court.

The mediator was Trevor Evans, industrial correspondent f·
Beaverbrook's *Daily Express*, who was present when the Bevins arrive
at 6 p.m., to be greeted formally by Beaverbrook's valet, Albert Nockel
As they passed by Beaverbrook's office to enter the lounge, they wou
have gazed at an imposing portrait of his lordship, painted in heav
impasto by Harry Jonas in 1919, which depicted the sitter in an arm
chair, correcting proofs of a copy of the *Daily Express* with a red pen.

After only four or five minutes, Evans, who was in the office makir
some calls on Beaverbrook's behalf, was astonished to see Bev·
walking ponderously yet purposefully to the front entrance, followe
rather meekly by Mrs Bevin. He heard Beaverbrook call Nockels ·
help the couple on with their coats, and then bid them farewell. Evar
later spoke to both men and discovered what had gone wrong.

Bevin had taken a few moments to admire one of the most breathtal
ing views in all England, out across the resplendent yew woods of th
950-acre parkland to the Mole Valley beyond, with a glimpse of th
150ft spire ('Cubitt's Finger') of St Barnabas' Church along the wa
Turning to Beaverbrook, he had remarked, 'What a wonderful scene yo
have displayed in front of your window.' Beaverbrook, busy prodding th
fire into life, had responded with a joke: 'Yes, and when your party ge
into power, all you'll do is take it away from me one day!' Whereupo
the prickly Bevin had suddenly jumped up and snapped, 'Come on, Fl·
let's go. I won't stay here and have the Labour cause insulted.'

In the autumn of 1940, with invasion looking more and more likel·
Churchill had suggested to his inner circle that if the governmer
were forced to take to the hills, his favoured triumvirate to lead th
resistance would be Beaverbrook, Bevin and himself. A year later th·
proposition looked fantastical. Such a committee would be destined ·

the way of Caesar, Pompey and Crassus; it would be 'very *unsafe* for inston', one wag remarked.

Despite Bevin's quick temper, however, Beaverbrook was the eater source of complaint, even threatening to stay away from abinet meetings when Bevin was present. He felt powerless with vin as chairman of the Production Executive – a clearing-house for erlapping interests in the supply departments – and meetings of this dy were frequently stormy. 'Lord Beaverbrook does not attend the oduction Executive because he says at two meetings you shouted him wn,' Harold Macmillan wrote to Bevin on 10 November. 'He suffers m asthma and, in a shouting contest, he is bound to come off worse,' averbrook pointed out to Churchill that if any disputes between e Ministry of Labour and the supply ministries were referred to the oduction Executive – as Bevin wanted – then that would mean 'any pute with Mr Bevin is to be referred to Mr Bevin'. But a few days er, he had seemingly undergone a complete volte-face, suggesting it a new Production Ministry should be created (as Parliament had ggested) with Bevin at its head. 'I would serve under him for the sent and as a means of enabling him to establish his authority,' he d the Prime Minister.

By now Churchill was tiring of the feud, and of Beaverbrook's nstant manoeuvring. 'I do not understand why in one breath u object to the Production Executive under Mr Bevin, who you urself proposed for the Chair . . . and at the same time advocate as 'roduction Minister the same Mr Bevin of whom you would be a ect subordinate,' he wrote testily on 13 November. 'The Production ecutive has no power to overrule you against your will, because you 1 at once carry the matter to Cabinet or me. On the other hand, the sake of a quiet life, one would hope that a good many matters uld be discussed and cleared up there.' Beaverbrook responded on November, 'I have done everything possible to persuade you that conduct in relation to Mr Bevin is entirely correct. His complaints ainst me are founded on pressure for labour which I have directed ainst him.'

Getting nowhere, the Beaver eventually resorted to an extraordina
personal plea to his foe. In a hastily written letter on 22 Novemb
starting with the unusually familiar 'Dear Ernie', he asked, 'Can
make a platform for you where I can stand at your side? I am sure y
can do so if you determine to build it. With your leadership of men a
women in the industrial centres, supported by the principal Supp
minister, the war effort can be increased.'

It appeared Beaverbrook was suggesting that the two of them shou
exhort the workers together at factory meetings. Bevin, bemused
his rival's olive branch, was nonetheless having nothing to do wi
it. 'Dear Max' was the courteous opening, before the somewhat st
evasive reply. 'I welcome what you say . . . [but] your reference
making a platform for me puzzles me a little and I am not sure I foll
what is in your mind. I have no policy or platform except that of t
Government as a whole, arrived at through the War Cabinet, a
came into the Government not for any personal position but solely
contribute what I could to our common effort under the leadership
the Prime Minister.'

Beaverbrook tried again, writing that he was 'sorry that I failed
make my meaning clear'. He tried to spell out his offer, but it remain
ambiguous: 'It is my hope to persuade you to lead all the people
hard work. It is my belief that you can do more in that direction th
anyone else. And there is a desire on my part to serve you in such
movement in any capacity you wish. It is my resolve to support a
sustain you to the full in that leadership.' There was no reply fr
Bevin. But a truce, of sorts, was to hold until the final act was play
out early in 1942.

There was a more pressing matter for Bevin to address as 1941 drew
a close – Britain's crippling lack of manpower. 'Voluntaryism' had be
the foundation of his policy since the start of the war: the British peop
were to do the jobs they wanted to do, or were called on to perfor
without compulsion. This strategy had already been compromised, b
thanks to a manpower survey made available to the War Cabinet
the autumn it was cast aside irrevocably. Britain now needed a massi

njection of labour: two million additional men and women by June 1942, in all areas of the armed forces and the war industries.

The War Cabinet argued long and hard about the level of conscription required. Eventually, on 28 November, a comprehensive package of measures was thrashed out. The call-up age for men would be raised from forty-one to fifty, and lowered from nineteen to eighteen and a half. Most strikingly, single women aged between twenty and thirty would be conscripted for non-combatant duties in the armed services, civil defence or industry.

There were dissenters against the plan, for a variety of reasons. A.V. Alexander opposed the principle of compulsion; Archibald Sinclair thought men in the forces would disapprove of women joining them; Beaverbrook felt it was a mistake to recruit so many women into the army when they were desperately needed in the factories. All agreed, however, that one particular proposal should be left on the table: the conscription of married women for the services and civil defence. In the three-day Commons debate on the new National Service Bill, there was surprisingly little opposition. The questions were not about why conscription had to be introduced, but why it had not been introduced earlier.

There was some criticism from the women who spoke in the debate. Mavis Tate, Conservative MP for Frome, objected to talk of absenteeism on the part of women in the factories, complaining it was because of a 'disgraceful' lack of nursery schools and day nurseries, as well as a shortage of transport to and from work. Eleanor Rathbone, Independent for the Combined Universities, felt the twenty-to-thirty age limit was mistaken, as it was 'working on the analogy of men . . . That is the very age when a woman is likely to have a baby in the cradle and a husband in the forces.'

It fell to Bevin to wind up the debate. When the pacifist MP John McGovern mocked one of the other measures introduced, the registering of all sixteen- to eighteen-year-olds for community work, as the 'Churchill Youth Movement', Bevin replied, 'I would rather have a Churchill youth movement than leave the children in slums unattended.'

Pressed, mainly by Labour MPs, to consider nationalisation as

a quid pro quo for this extension of compulsion, he responded, 'M
entry into this Government and that of everyone else concerned
had as its supreme object the winning of the war . . . it is a cardina
point of policy for the Government as a whole that neither interes
property, persons, nor prejudice will be allowed to stand in the way o
our achieving that great objective.'

'The best speech I have heard him make,' was the verdict of Tor
MP Sir Cuthbert Headlam. The National Service Bill was passed b
326 votes to 10. Brendan Bracken's MoI had worked hand in han
with Bevin to ensure that the measures – which were presented und
the banner 'Maximum National Effort' – had a favourable receptior
'A stirring call to war', wrote the *Daily Mirror*. 'After twenty-seve
months we are ready for this great move forward', was the *Yorkshir
Post*'s view. It was a significant moment, but two days later it wa
eclipsed by an event that was to change entirely the course of the wa

At 7.48 a.m., Hawaiian time, on 7 December 353 Japanese fighte
planes and bombers launched a surprise attack on the US Pacific Flee
anchored in Pearl Harbor. Within ninety minutes, eighteen ships
including five battleships – were sunk or run aground, and 188 aircra
were destroyed. In total, 2,403 Americans – sailors, soldiers an
civilians – died; 1,178 were wounded.

The following day the United States and Great Britain declare
war on Japan. Two days after that, Germany and Italy declared war o
America, an act that was swiftly reciprocated. 'Today all of us are i
the same boat with you and the people of the Empire and it is a sh
which will not and cannot be sunk,' Roosevelt assured Churchill. Th
Prime Minister told the Commons, 'In the past we have had a ligh
which flickered, in the present we have a light which flames, and i
the future there will be a light which shines all over the land and sea

Leo Amery was apprehensive. 'The next few months will be ve
anxious for us . . . the whole world is now practically at war.' B
Anthony Eden shared Churchill's optimism. 'I could not conceal n
relief . . . before, we had believed in the end but never seen the mean
Now both were clear.'

Chapter Eight

'The Ascendancy of Stafford Cripps'

8 February to 15 June 1942

he magnificent, baroque-style Bristol Hippodrome was packed to overflowing on the afternoon of Sunday, 8 February 1942. Fortunate have escaped the bombing that had wrecked so much of the south-est port city, the theatre's stalls and boxes hummed with anticipation over 2,500 men and women, with another 2,000 outside clamouring get in, greeted the arrival of the latest star turn. The audience sang or He's a Jolly Good Fellow', Alderman William Hennessy called for ree cheers, and the subsequent applause echoed around the ornate uilding for many minutes.

The tall, slim, bespectacled man who was the focus of their acclaim as not one of the famous actors who regularly graced the theatre, like oël Coward, Robertson Hare or John Gielgud; nor was he one of the opular entertainers of the time, such as Hughie Green, Jimmy James or e promising young Ernie Wise. He was instead a politician, with no arty, no government position, and he had barely been seen on British il for eighteen long months. And yet Sir Richard Stafford Cripps, MP r Bristol East, was able to stride out on to that 80ft stage and receive e crowd's tumultuous acclaim as if he were an all-conquering hero.

It was easy to see why his constituents – and many beyond th
boundaries of Bristol – viewed him in this light. Just two weeks earli
Cripps had returned from the war's fiercest battlefront, Russia, whe
he had acted as Churchill's ambassador through the most difficult
times. As Britain's fortunes continued to plummet, with Malaya c
the verge of being completely overrun by the Japanese, and Bengha
having fallen to Rommel's troops in the latest calamity in the Weste
Desert, the contrast with the Red Army's recent valiant defence
Moscow could not have been greater.

Many in the country gave Cripps huge credit for his foresight
fighting Russia's corner long before anyone else had been prepared t
Britain's new alliance with the Soviet Union was ascribed by son
almost entirely to his efforts. The fact that he had been a 'fellow travelle
before the war, supporting the idea of a broad left-wing front, includir
the communists, was now quickly forgotten. Even his air of asceticis
seemed to symbolise the spirit and self-sacrifice of Soviet resistance.

While Churchill's own popularity remained largely undiminishe
by the continual setbacks on the military front, there was a feelir
abroad that the government, its style and its personalities, needed
shake-up. It was the moment for the quintessential outsider to mak
his case.

'God Save The King' and 'The Internationale' were sung lusti
by the Hippodrome crowd, and then, with the Union flag and th
hammer-and-sickle banner as his backdrop, Cripps lobbed some politic
hand grenades into 10 Downing Street. Since his return to Britain c
23 January, he told his audience, he had noticed a 'lack of urgency'
the country. 'It is almost as if we were spectators rather than participant
I might compare it to the difference between a keen and enthusiast
supporter of a football game and one of the team. We do not seem
realise how total the effort is that is required if we are to win this war, ar
we have not yet put aside our partial interests in order to concentrate c
that total war.'

He thanked Lord Beaverbrook for his support for Russia, and salute
the workers who were making munitions for the Soviet war machin

Hitler's armies could be defeated, perhaps in a year's time, but only 'if we work with a 100 per cent effort, sacrificing our personal interests'.

He then cast an eye to the future, choosing words that were likely to infuriate Churchill. 'Our war aims are negative – to defeat Hitler and destroy the Nazification of Europe. But what are we to put in its place? Are we bent on returning to the old system of organisation which brought us into the last two wars, or are we really determined to build something new and better for the world?'

At 9 p.m. that night Cripps repeated his Bristol speech almost word for word on the BBC's *Postscript*. If anything, his lecture – for that is what it sounded like – was now even harsher. 'Your individual effort is your personal responsibility and you cannot get out of it by criticism of others . . . we are out to win the war and to win it as quickly as may be. In that determination there must be no reservations arising out of personal interests or comforts.'

It was calculated that half the adult population of Britain heard Cripps' radio broadcast, with over 90 per cent of listeners approving of it. His local paper, the *Gloucester Citizen*, applauded his sentiments: 'Last night he brought home to millions in this country the blunt truth, which for so long politicians have shirked. In praiseworthy contrast to the blah-blahs and mollycoddling of some of our Cabinet ministers, he declared in effect that we were not pulling our weight. And who can deny it?'

Churchill might grumble about Cripps mapping out the future before the present had been secured, but he knew he had to find some way of accommodating this independent-minded politician who had turned up on his doorstep. Cripps was not 'shop-soiled' by participation in a failing government, and he had a moral authority that probably only the Prime Minister otherwise possessed at this moment.

There was some history between the two. During Churchill's time as Minister of Munitions in the First World War, Cripps, a research chemist by training, had expanded output when put in charge of one of the country's biggest munitions factories in 1916, although he stepped down only months later because of ill-health. His father, like

Churchill's, had sat in the Cabinet: Charles Cripps (Lord Parmoor) had been Lord President of the Council in Ramsay MacDonald's 192 and 1929 Labour governments, and when, in 1930, Stafford, age forty-one, was appointed Solicitor General they had become the firs father and son to serve together in government since Joe and Auste Chamberlain in 1903.

Stafford Cripps had been a forceful opponent of appeasemen contributing powerfully to the debate on 8 May 1940 which began th process of toppling Chamberlain. But the reality was, in Eden's vivi phrase, that Churchill and Cripps 'had always been as disparate as lion and an okapi'. Their lifestyles were poles apart: Churchill, th hearty eater, prolific drinker and cigar smoker, Cripps the vegetarian teetotaller, and now – after doctor's orders – non-smoker.

Cripps' 'exploratory' mission to the Soviet Union in May 1940 ha not been Churchill's idea, but that of foreign secretary Lord Halifax Cripps and Halifax – despite their obvious political differences – knew each other well through their association with the World Alliance fo Promoting International Friendship through the Churches; Halifa was a staunch High Anglican, while Cripps practised a very indivic ual, evangelical form of Christianity. The mission, with Cripps initiall a 'hybrid politician-ambassador', had turned into a full-time role tha continued throughout 1940 and the whole of 1941. 'A lunatic i a country of lunatics – it would be a pity to move him,' had bee Churchill's dismissive response, in December 1940, to a suggestio that Cripps might return to play a part in the coalition government.

Cripps himself, largely denied access to Stalin and his inner circle his advice often set aside by the War Cabinet, had endured a difficu year and a half and had been desperate to come home. But sinc December 1941 he had been fortified by a good working relationshi with Eden, who gave him a significant part to play in his summit wit Stalin in Moscow.

When he arrived back in England in the New Year, Cripps foun himself hailed by the public, lauded by the press, and reluctantl wooed by the Prime Minister. The political landscape had change ver the past few months, and he was – at least for the moment – he principal beneficiary of this new environment. To a good number n Westminster Cripps was remote, self-righteous, pompous and even ranky, earning the sobriquet 'Christ and Carrots'. A gag circulating he tearooms mocked his supposed sense of humour: 'Stafford saw a ke last week – by appointment'.

But the public merely observed an austere, principled man with esh ideas about how to manage the war. Cripps was a clear threat to Churchill, because his proposed changes – especially on the military ont – would require the Prime Minister to devolve a fair amount of is power. The whisper in Westminster was that it might soon be the Winston and Sir Stafford' show – and that was something Churchill as not prepared to tolerate.

he sense of euphoria that had followed America's entry into the war n 7 December evaporated swiftly as the Allies faced the new enemy's assive, co-ordinated assaults on their possessions right across the Far ast. The following day Japanese forces attacked the British colonies f Hong Kong and Malaya, as well as Siam (Thailand), while simulta- eously striking against US defences in the Philippines and Guam.

At 10 p.m. on Tuesday, 9 December, the Prime Minister called n emergency meeting of his chiefs of staff in the Cabinet Room at Downing Street to consider the crisis in the Far East, in particular he plight of the two capital ships *Prince of Wales* and *Repulse*, on their ay to provide protection for Singapore, but without air cover and angerously exposed to attack from the rampant Japanese planes. Churchill's proposals had been that either 'they should vanish into he ocean waves and exercise a vague menace like rogue elephants', or at they should head south and join what was left of the US fleet. The guments had raged back and forth until midnight, but nothing was ecided and it was agreed to address the problem again the next day.

By then it was too late. As the ships and their escort of three estroyers approached Kuantan on the east coast of Malaya, shortly efore midday on 10 December, they were attacked by waves of torpedo bombers from the Japanese Genzan Air Group. At the end of the ninety-minute onslaught, the *Prince of Wales* and *Repulse* had both been sunk with the loss of 840 sailors.

Churchill was badly shaken by this setback. He felt a close affinity for the *Prince of Wales* as the battleship had transported him to Placentia Bay for his historic first meeting with President Roosevelt. He had special affection too for its drowned commander, Admiral Tom 'Thumb' Phillips, whom he had promoted when First Lord. The decision to deploy the two ships without air cover had been taken by the Defence Committee, but driven by Churchill, against Admiralty advice.

The Prime Minister had made the decision some time ago that the 'impregnable fortress' of Singapore – a £60 million naval base protected by 15in guns and 60,000 troops – would have to hold its own. Britain's tanks and fighter planes would be better concentrated on the North African theatre, and on helping the beleaguered Russians. Now, however, the east coast of the Malayan peninsula was exposed and the Japanese could launch their amphibious landings against the Allies' soft underbelly.

Militarily unprepared for the Japanese advance, senior British officials in Singapore also appeared to be in the grip of political paralysis. After his unfortunate spell at the Ministry of Information, Alfred Duff Cooper found his new job as Churchill's Cabinet envoy to the Far East scarcely less taxing. He filed his first full dispatch on 18 December, while the Prime Minister was sailing to America on board the *Duke of York*. It was a typically lucid and colourful report but highly damning of most of the men entrusted with the safety of the Singaporeans.

Sir Robert Brooke-Popham (commander-in-chief Far East Command) was a 'very much older man than his years warrant and sometimes seems on the verge of nervous collapse'. Sir Shenton Thomas (governor) was 'one of those people who find it quite impossible to adjust their minds to war conditions. He is also the mouthpiece of the last person he speaks to.' Stanley Jones (colonial secretary) was a 'sinister figure .

universally detested in the Colony, where he is accused of having been defeatist since the beginning of the war.'

Perhaps most worrying was Duff Cooper's portrait of the general officer commanding Malaya, Lieutenant-General Sir Arthur Percival, a man who had served brilliantly and courageously in the previous war, with the Military Cross and Croix de Guerre to his credit, but who was now apparently struggling to assert his authority. 'A nice, good man who began life as a schoolmaster. I am sometimes tempted to wish he had remained one,' Duff Cooper told Churchill.

In secret session in the Commons the following day, 19 December, MPs were scathing about the lack of preparation that had led to the loss of the two ships and the RAF aerodromes at Kota Bharu and Alor Star in northern Malaya. George Harvie-Watt, Churchill's new parliamentary private secretary and his eyes and ears around Westminster, recorded in his latest report for the Prime Minister that both Mr Attlee and A.V. Alexander were batting on sticky wickets and the speeches did not please the House at all'.

Disconcerted as he surely was by these reports, Churchill's chief desire on his latest US trip was to keep Roosevelt to his commitment that the Atlantic and European theatres of war should be the principal focus of the Allies' efforts. Once Germany was defeated, it was anticipated that the collapse of Italy and the defeat of Japan would follow. In this respect, Churchill was successful, despite opposition from elements of Roosevelt's military circle who wanted to concentrate efforts in the Pacific.

On Boxing Day Churchill became the first British Prime Minister to address a joint session of Congress. He read the mood almost perfectly, his peroration bringing the Congressmen to their feet, cheering and waving their papers. But the strain of the war had taken its toll and that night, while attempting to open the window of his bedroom in the White House, he became short of breath and felt a 'dull pain' over his heart that travelled down his left arm.

Churchill's doctor, Sir Charles Wilson (who would be ennobled in March 1943 as Lord Moran), examined him and interpreted his

symptoms as those of 'coronary insufficiency' (more commonly angina)
although he told his patient only that he had been overdoing thing
and that his circulation was 'a bit sluggish'. Wilson resolved that no one
should know about the attack – not even Churchill's wife Clementine
or the President. 'The textbook treatment for this is at least six week
in bed. This would mean publishing to the world . . . that the PM wa
an invalid with a crippled heart and a doubtful future,' Wilson recorded
in his diary later. 'The effect . . . could only be disastrous.'

The prime ministerial party returned to England on Saturday, 1'
January. Beaverbrook's *Sunday Express* reported large cheering crowd
at Plymouth, where Churchill's entourage landed in a flying-boat from
Bermuda. 'CHURCHILL WILL ANSWER CRITICISM OF FAR EAST WAR' wa
the paper's defiant headline. The next day the *Daily Mirror*'s politica
correspondent Bill Greig put it more soberly and realistically: 'Event
have brought him back to a reckoning rather than a festival.'

Sir Stafford Cripps had not been the first politician to discern a growing
national lethargy in the bleak days of January 1942. Lord Woolton
while noting that freedom from air raids had seen life in Englanc
'almost back to normal', with restaurants and theatres crowded anc
West End hotels full, worried that nobody seemed to care very mucl
about 'getting the war moving'. 'We hear of labour troubles, strikes
absenteeism in factories engaged on vital war work, because the
workers won't continue to work after they have earned up to the wage
that will attract income tax. And on the continent people are literally
dying in thousands from starvation.'

In Parliament the grumbling continued unabated. Sir Cuthbert
Headlam, following a conversation with the chairman of the 1922
Committee of Tory backbenchers, reflected, 'There is no doubt today a
feeling of great unrest in the Party, and in the House generally, agains
the Government.'

Prime ministers returning home with a foreign policy triumpl
habitually fail to read the mood back home. Churchill, flushed witl
success at the Washington conference, initially indicated to Harvie-Wat

at he wished to confront his doubters head on. 'He said there would be
o Government changes and strongly objected to any criticisms. He said
e country and America were behind him'. Egged on by the ever-
heming Beaverbrook, Churchill even flirted with the idea of calling a
eneral election. 'This sounded ridiculous. I didn't see what good it could
o,' Harvie-Watt recalled. 'It would finish up as a "coupon election" and
ould savour too much of the Nazi pre-war elections to the Reichstag.'
lmost certainly never a serious proposal, it nonetheless revealed
hurchill's unsteady grasp of the political mood.

Aircraft losses were rising, plane production was falling, and the
apanese were closing in on Singapore. So Churchill resorted to
e tactic he had employed the previous spring following the fall of
reece and setbacks in the Middle East: he called for a vote
f confidence to clear the air. At the end of the three-day debate, from
7 to 29 January, the government had a majority of 464 to 1, but the
gures obscured the full story.

Churchill had given ground, indicating to MPs that he would
ollow the American lead and appoint a new Minister of Production.
e had also admitted that 'wrapped up in the bad news will be many
les of blunders and shortcomings, both in foresight and action',
lthough he had insisted that the decision to send the *Prince of Wales*
nd *Repulse* into dangerous waters had been the 'policy of the War
abinet and the Defence Committee, initiated by the Naval Staff'.
dmiral Phillips' decision to press on, without fighter protection, had
een 'audacious and daring' and the prize might have been 20,000 of
e enemy drowned in the sea. On the central criticism of his military
rategy, he had responded that 'to aid Russia, to deliver an offensive
Libya and to accept a consequential state of weakness in the then
eaceful theatre of the Far East was sound and will be found to have
layed a useful part in the general course of the war'.

Some critics had directed their fire at Churchill's advisers and
e structure of government. 'It is not that his judgment is bad, but
at his information is often bad . . . is the present system of the War
abinet the right one?' asked Sir Herbert Williams, Conservative MP

for Croydon. Sir John Wardlaw-Milne, an old foe and the influenti[
chairman of the Select Committee on National Expenditure, had mac
his attack more personal. 'I say that any criticism of any member of th
Government, as the Government is at present constituted, become
unfortunately, a criticism of the Prime Minister. If you live under
dictatorship, that must happen.'

Churchill had hoped to appease his detractors by reshaping h
government, but his efforts stalled when Stafford Cripps turne
down an invitation to become Minister of Supply. Churchi[
started to work on Cripps over the course of a convivial weeken
at Chequers on 25 and 26 January, but the returning ambassad[
refused to commit himself to joining the government because th
offer lacked a place in the War Cabinet. Cripps realised he woul
be subordinate to the new Minister of Production, Beaverbrook,
man he could not trust, and who had treated him with disdain th
previous autumn in Moscow.

When the minor reshuffle was announced on 4 February, and
became clear that it revolved around Beaverbrook's new role, th
response was underwhelming, inside and outside Westminster alik
The *Yorkshire Post*, rarely critical of the government, drily observe[
'We have passed the time for relying on theatrical efforts an
spectacular spurts to whip up production of particular weapons,' whi[
the *Spectator* opined that, 'For an imaginative man, Mr Churchi[
shows himself surprisingly unimaginative in the periodical reshufflin[
of his administration.'

On 15 February, the 'impregnable' fortress of Singapore surrender[
Churchill had given General Wavell in Java the brutal instructio[
five days before: 'There must at this stage be no thought of saving th
troops or sparing the population. The battle must be fought to th
bitter end at all costs . . . commanders and senior officers should d[
with their troops.' Right up to the final hours, with Japanese forc[
on the outskirts of the town, Wavell continued to obey these order
exhorting his commander on the ground, 'so long as you are in positio[

to inflict losses and damage to the enemy and your troops are physically capable of doing so you must fight on.'

But in this telegram, sent to Percival on 15 February, Wavell had added, 'when you are fully satisfied that this is no longer possible I give you the discretion to cease resistance.' Percival and his officers had received the message while in conference at 9.30 a.m. It was what they needed to seek surrender terms. 'Owing to losses from enemy action, water, petrol, food and ammunition practically finished,' he wrote in a final telegram to Wavell. 'Unable therefore to continue the fight any longer.'

The 85,000 troops taken prisoner – British, Australian, Indian and Malayan – represented the largest surrender in British history. Churchill announced Singapore's fall in a 9 p.m. broadcast on the BBC. While acknowledging a 'heavy and far-reaching military defeat', he sought to accentuate the positive. 'We must remember that we are no longer alone. We are in the midst of a great company. Three-quarters of the human race are now moving with us.'

But many thought it an unpersuasive performance. 'It was a foolish and unpleasant speech . . . the use of words won't win the war, and I'm afraid that the feet of clay are beginning to be discerned,' Lord Woolton reflected. 'Unfortunately he appeals for national unity and not criticism, in a manner which recalls Neville Chamberlain,' wrote Harold Nicolson. 'I do not think his speech will have done good, and I feel deeply depressed and anxious.'

Within the government individual grumbles and more serious discontents began to undermine confidence in Churchill's leadership. Brendan Bracken, the most steadfast of allies, wrote to the Prime Minister requesting to resign from the Ministry of Information 'because he didn't feel he was properly treated'. The atmosphere in Whitehall was thick with gossip and intrigue. Oliver Harvey, Eden's private secretary, wrote that 'Bracken now knows [about the] state of [Churchill's] health and doctor's report, so it will soon be known all over Fleet Street. A.E [Eden] and I both very worried at turn of events . . . A.E feels he [Churchill] is more and more obstinate and at the same time losing grip.' Beaverbrook, writing to Sir Samuel Hoare in Madrid, gave his perspective: 'We are in the midst of a political crisis in Britain. The newspapers made it. But the Prime Minister keeps it alive.'

Woolton, under pressure as the sinking of merchant convoys reached a new height, was in the blackest of moods. 'If I were clear that we had personnel to replace the present Cabinet I would myself resign in order to break the present one,' he confided to his diary. 'There's little talent: the Cabinet was formed solely on political issues and without regard to ability . . . Beaverbrook is always at the Prime Minister's elbow instead of being on his own job, and one wonders how much his judgement affects Winston's.'

Beaverbrook was the problem, not only for Woolton, but also for Bevin and Attlee, who had looked on his appointment as production minister with dismay. Bevin, determined to maintain his control over manpower and labour, set out right from the start to enfeeble Beaverbrook in his new role. By the time Churchill spelled out the details of the post to the House in a White Paper, on 10 February, it was clear who had won most of the arguments. 'Mr Bevin has evidently got himself completely detached. He proudly survives the imperious and impetuous, but possibly powerless, control of Lord Beaverbrook,' wrote the *Daily Mirror*.

Churchill's wife was urging him to go further, and wrote to her husband two days later, saying, 'leave Lord B entirely out of your Reconstruction'. She acknowledged he might then work against the government. 'But is not hostility without, better than intrigue and treachery and rattledom within? Exorcise this bottle imp and see if the air is not clearer and purer.'

Despite his deep loyalty to friends, Churchill was wearying of this particular political struggle. He told Beaverbrook on the day he promoted the White Paper, 'I have reached the end of my patience. I have lavished my time and strength during the last week to make arrangements which are satisfactory to you and to the public interest, and to allay the anxieties of the departments with whom you will be brought in contact. I can do no more.'

The Cabinet in the garden of 10 Downing Street on 24 October 1941, together with military chiefs and other officials.

Front Row (from left): Ernest Bevin, Lord Beaverbrook, Anthony Eden, Clement Attlee, Winston Churchill, Sir John Anderson, Arthur Greenwood and Sir Kingsley Wood.

Back Row (from left): Sir Edward Bridges (secretary to the War Cabinet), Sir Charles Portal (Chief of Air Staff), Sir Archibald Sinclair, Sir Dudley Pound (Admiral of the Fleet), A.V. Alexander, Lord Cranborne, Herbert Morrison, Lord Moyne, David Margesson, Brendan Bracken, General Sir John Dill (Chief of the Imperial General Staff), General Sir Hastings Ismay (Military Secretary) and Sir Alexander Cadogan (Permanent Under-Secretary of State for Foreign Affairs).

ALL BEHIND YOU, WINSTON

ft: Churchill's long and varied political
e made him uniquely qualified to lead
wartime coalition. His air of defiance
d optimism rallied the nation in a
y no other could.

Above: The famous Low cartoon in the
Evening Standard on 14 May 1940,
portraying national unity in the war
effort. Striding out with Churchill are
his Labour colleagues Attlee, Bevin
and Morrison. Close behind (from
left) are Chamberlain, Greenwood,
Halifax, Sinclair, Duff-Cooper,
Alexander and little Leo Amery.

Churchill visits a bomb-damaged home at the height of the Blitz in late 1940.
He could provide stirring words on these occasions, but was also easily moved
to tears by what he witnessed.

Sir Archibald Sinclair, Liberal leader and Secretary of State for Air. He had fierce tussles in cabinet with Lord Beaverbrook during the Battle of Britain.
© PICTORIAL PRESS LTD/ALAMY STOCK PHOTO

The irrepressible and unconventional Brendan Bracken, Churchill's close confidant and a successful Minister of Information.
© MARIE HANSEN/THE LIFE PICTURE COLLECTION/GETTY IMAGES

"The need is great,
the time is short,

URGENCY

must be the watchword."

LORD BEAVERBROOK

IT'S A FULL TIME JOB TO WIN

Lord Beaverbrook was at the forefront of propaganda to mobilise the Home Front in the dark days of 1940. This was one of hundreds of posters produced by the Ministry of Information.

Churchill leaves Downing Street with Sir John Anderson after a War Cabinet meeting in May 1940. Anderson was an indispensable figure: towards the end of the war Churchill advised the King that if he and Eden were killed, Anderson (then Chancellor) should become Prime Minister.

The redoubtable Ernest Bevin at his office in the Ministry of Labour. Emergency legislation gave him absolute control over the working lives of every Briton.

Above: Lord Halifax, then Foreign Secretary, and Anthony Eden, War Secretary, leave Downing Street after a tumultuous War Cabinet meeting on 28 May 1940. Halifax had just presented the case for suing for peace with Germany.

© Fox Photos/Getty Images

Right: Herbert Morrison, master of the photo opportunity and the pithy phrase, ferrying a sack of coal outside the Ministry of Supply headquarters in July 1940.

© Popperfoto/Getty Images

The only two women in Churchill's war ministry. Florence Horsbrugh (seated) and Ellen Wilkinson confer in April 1945 during the conference in San Francisco that established the United Nations.

Above: Sir Stafford Cripps. In early 1942 he was the most popular politician (bar Churchill) in the country, and even briefly viewed as his possible successor.

Right: Lord Woolton, Minister of Food (1940-43) and then Minister of Reconstruction (1943-45). 'Uncle Fred', here taking charge of a soup kitchen during the Blitz, was one of Churchill's best-recognised and most admired ministers.

Left: As the war developed, Clement Attlee and Anthony Eden formed a powerful axis in the area of foreign affairs - where they saw it as their task to resist some of Churchill's wilder impulses.

© David E. Scherman/The LIFE Picture Collection/Getty Images

Above: A preoccupied Lord Beaverbrook prepares to address a conference on the conscription of labour in January 1941: his great rival, Ernest Bevin, in more jocular mood, stands behind him. Other Government ministers present are Oliver Lyttelton (left) and Sir Andrew Duncan, with Bevin's junior minister Ralph Assheton alongside him.

© Keystone/Getty Images

Consulting amicably enough early in 1945, but Bevin and Morrison nursed a deep-seated mutual dislike. However, their personal differences did not prevent them joining forces to harry Churchill over reconstruction.

REMEMBER, GENTLEMEN, NO QUESTIONS ASKED ABOUT OUR PRIVATE LIVES OUTSIDE ..... BUT ALL IS PEACE AND LOYALTY WITHIN

JUST A BIG HAPPY FAMILY

Top left: A night off at the Opera House on 1 May 1945 for four of Britain's delegation to the United Nations meeting in San Francisco – Clement Attlee, George Tomlinson (junior minister in Labour department), Ellen Wilkinson and Florence Horsbrugh.

Bottom left: Clement Attlee takes tea with his constituents in Limehouse. He grew in stature as the war progressed, valued especially for his efficient committee work and expert chairing of War Cabinets when Churchill was absent.

Above: David Low's cartoon in the *Evening Standard* on 12 April 1945 captured the open conflicts that had started to beset the coalition. Bevin and Bracken are pictured, arms in slings after their public (verbal) . jousting, while a gnomic Beaverbrook hides under the table.

Victory at last. The War Cabinet takes the applause on the balcony of the Ministry of Health in Whitehall on the afternoon of 8 May 1945. From the left, Oliver Lyttelton, Ernest Bevin, Churchill, Sir John Anderson, Lord Woolton and Herbert Morrison. © CENTRAL PRESS/HULTON ARCHIVE/GETTY IMAGES

Beaverbrook's irresistible force had met Bevin's immoveable object. The main changes in the most extensive reshuffle of the government so far, on 19 February, showed the results of Bevin and Attlee's stubborn resistance. Having lasted just two weeks in his new job, Beaverbrook was out of government entirely. The more emollient but very capable Oliver Lyttelton was recalled from Cairo to replace him as Minister of Production, while Attlee was promoted to Deputy Prime Minister and given the post of Dominions secretary. Moreover, Churchill finally bowed to the popular pressure to bring Cripps into the government, giving him a place in the War Cabinet as Leader of the House of Commons (hitherto one of Churchill's own responsibilities) and the nominal title of Lord Privy Seal. Bevin, Eden and Sir John Anderson all stayed in their old positions, but Arthur Greenwood, whose drinking had become an inconquerable problem, left the War Cabinet. There was also an unexpected change at the War Office where Captain David Margesson, one of the old Chamberlainites whom Churchill had tolerated, was replaced by Sir James Grigg, previously the chief civil servant in the same department.

Beaverbrook's exit was explained away partly because he had now been assigned special duties in America, and partly because his health – asthma being a particular problem – had been suffering. But the day after the reshuffle Churchill made it clear to William Crozier of the *Manchester Guardian* that Beaverbrook's departure was not what he had wanted. 'He could have had any one of three or four offices if he had liked to stop. I didn't want him to go. He was good for me! Any number of times, if things were going badly, he would encourage me, saying, "Look at all the things on your side. Look at what you have accomplished."'

He may have misjudged the Westminster mood, there were grumbles behind his back from colleagues, the state of his health was troubling, and he had to confront continuing military setbacks. But there was no serious threat to Churchill's pre-eminence. However, as *Time* magazine suggested, 'for the first time millions of Britons began to doubt his abilities', while in the War Cabinet the balance of power had tilted, just slightly, away from him. Markers had been laid for the future, and there were signs it would now no longer be the largely quiescent body it had been since the coalition's inception two years before.

'Hide them in caves and cellars, but not one picture shall leave this island,' Churchill had exhorted Kenneth Clark, director of the National Gallery, when it was suggested in June 1940 that the nation's masterpieces should be shipped abroad to Canada. The Prime Minister's words were heeded and the artworks were stored safely underground at the disused slate mine of Manod, near Blaenau Ffestiniog in Wales. Now, in safer times, they were being brought back home one by one to take their place in the new 'Picture of the Month' display at the gallery.

'Because London's face is scarred and bruised these days we need more than ever to see beautiful things,' sculptor Charles Wheeler told *The Times*. The first work to be shown, from early March, was Titian's *Noli me Tangere*, a profoundly moving representation of Mary Magdalene reaching out towards the recently resurrected Christ, set against a background of tumbling hills and a rich, melancholy Venetian sunset. One interpretation viewed Christ's self-sacrifice for humanity as a metaphoric depiction of the nation's sacrifices, and of the people's faith in ultimate victory over totalitarianism.

Meanwhile the totalitarian regime currently sweeping all before it in the Pacific had reached Burma. On 7 March, the Japanese took the capital Rangoon. They now had the jewel in the crown of the British Empire – India – in their sights.

The War Cabinet was desperate to secure India's full support in repulsing the advance. Tens of thousands of Indian volunteer servicemen were already fighting alongside British troops in Africa and Asia, but there was concern over the anti-colonial sentiment among the population as a whole; in the event of an invasion, it was not impossible that the Japanese would be welcomed as liberators. Churchill's government would surely have to make significant concessions on the principle of self-government. The Indian case had been strengthened by the Atlantic Charter and its 'right of all peoples to choose the form of government under which they will live', and was also of keen interest to the instinctively anti-colonial Americans.

Relations with India had been poor from the moment war on Germany was declared in September 1939. On that same day the Viceroy, Lord Linlithgow, without consulting political leaders, had simply declared India a belligerent state alongside its colonial master. In particular this dismayed the pacifist-inclined Congress Party, which withdrew from all the provincial legislatures set up in 1935.

Churchill's jaundiced view of Congress's spiritual leader – he once referred to him as a 'seditious Middle Temple lawyer now posing as a fakir' – had scarcely been improved when Mahatma Gandhi published an open letter to the British people in July 1940, suggesting they lay down their arms to the Germans and Italians. 'Invite Herr Hitler and Signor Mussolini to take what they want of the countries you call your possessions. Let them take possession of your beautiful island with your many beautiful buildings. You will give all these but not your souls or your minds.' Nonetheless, Churchill had sanctioned a government White Paper, in August 1940, promising an independent Indian Constituent Assembly with completely indigenous representation and some power to frame the future constitution of the country; safeguards for minorities, especially Muslims, would also be put in place. Since these changes were only to be instituted *after* the war, however, the proposals had been promptly rejected by all sides.

Eighteen months later it was Attlee, in a paper to the War Cabinet on 2 February, who suggested it was time 'for an act of statesmanship', time for 'some person of high standing' to be sent out with wide powers to negotiate a settlement for India. Surprisingly perhaps, having had his feet under the Cabinet table for just two weeks, the man chosen to make that journey was Cripps. Finding accord in the fractious relationship between Congress and the Muslim League, appeasing the fiercely imperialist Lord Linlithgow, and satisfying the conflicting demands of Churchill, Dominions secretary Attlee and Amery (India secretary) back home would be the trickiest of tasks. Yet Cripps had already built up valuable contacts and a sound understanding of Indian affairs. Crucially, he had established a close personal and political relationship with Jawaharlal Nehru: the leader of Congress had stayed, along with his daughter Indira, at Cripps' country home, Goodfellows, in 1938, and Nehru had been Cripps' host for a good part of a private visit to India in 1939. On that same trip Cripps had also met Muhammad Ali Jinnah, leader of the Muslim League.

Cynics wondered if Churchill saw the mission as an opportunity to hand a dangerous rival an impossible task. Perhaps more important, though, was that Roosevelt was pressing for progress in the matter, equating India's position with that of his own country between 1783 and 1789, when, post-revolution, the welding of the original thirteen states into a federal union had proven far from easy or harmonious. In a letter to Churchill, on the eve of Cripps' departure, the President wondered if a 'temporary dominion government', covering different castes, occupations, religions and geographies, might be immediately established which could then plan for a longer-term federal future. But he cautioned, 'For the love of Heaven don't bring me into this, though I do want to be of help. It is strictly speaking, none of my business, except insofar as it is a part and parcel of the successful fight you and I are making.'

Cripps' mission lasted less than a month, from 22 March to 10 April, and ended in failure. Working to the brief settled by the War Cabinet, he proposed a post-war Indian Union with full dominion status. Thereafter, India would be free to leave the Commonwealth and pursue complete independence. A constituent assembly would frame a constitution, and any province not willing to join the Union could establish a separate constitution and form a separate Union. But Congress wanted immediate self-government. Gandhi described dominion status after the war as a 'post-dated cheque and drawn on a crashing bank', and his party feared India's disintegration if provinces were allowed to opt out. There was also disagreement about the powers of a future Indian minister of war.

It was thought in some quarters that Cripps had strayed from his instructions and had offered Gandhi and Nehru self-government earlier than the end of hostilities. But few in Whitehall really blamed him for the collapse of the talks. 'The truth is we have wet-nursed India so long in our grandmotherly way that Indians perforce have lost all sense of political realism,' wrote Oliver Harvey.

'We have done our best under the circumstances here,' Cripps wrote to Churchill on 11 April; 'we are not depressed though [we are] sad at the result. Now we must get on with the job of defending India.' The reply was sympathetic: 'You have done everything in human power and your tenacity, perseverance and resourcefulness have proved how great was the British desire to reach a settlement.' Churchill added that 'The effect throughout Britain and in the United States has been wholly beneficial.'

Time would only tell whether Cripps' failure had dented his political progress. For the moment, he was still riding high. In April a Gallup survey asked, 'If anything should happen to Mr Churchill, whom would you like to succeed him as Prime Minister?' It showed Cripps, with 34 per cent, behind only Eden on 37 per cent. The organisation revealed in a separate poll that for the first time since the beginning of the conflict, more people were dissatisfied (50 per cent) than satisfied (38 per cent) with the government's conduct of the war. The 'Picture of the Month' in April was El Greco's *Christ Driving the Traders from the Temple*; something similar was needed on the battlefields of North Africa and the Far East.

At 7.22 a.m. on Thursday, 21 May, a high-speed London and North Eastern Railway locomotive, the *Golden Fleece*, pulled up at the quiet country station of Brookmans Park, just eighteen miles outside London. From the door of the sleeping compartment stepped a stocky man in a smart brown suit with a distinctive black moustache and round spectacles. He wore a frosty smile and looked every inch the suburban bank manager. Accompanying him, umbrella in hand, was a tall, elegant-looking individual, sporting a lighter moustache and slicked-back hair, who would not have been out of place on a Hollywood movie set.

Vyacheslav Molotov, people's commissar for foreign affairs, and Anthony Eden, British foreign secretary, were meeting on this unremarkable branch line in conditions of great secrecy; not a word of the Soviet politician's trip had been made known to the wider world. This 'mystery man thriller', as the *Daily Express* would later dub it, was partly a product of the natural paranoia of an aide to Stalin, but due also to Molotov's unwillingness to publicise a set of negotiations that might well fail and reflect badly on him.

After extracting a guarantee of confidentiality from a resourceful *Daily Mirror* photographer who had turned up on a tip-off, Eden led his guest to a waiting car and they drove out of the village, heading for Chequers, where Churchill was waiting to meet them. There the Soviet contingent would remain for the whole of their week in England.

The Wehrmacht advance towards Moscow had been halted for now, but the Soviet counter-offensive at Kharkov was going very badly wrong. From the outset, Molotov pressed strongly his two main demands: for the Allies to open up a 'second front' in Europe, landing sufficient combat troops to draw off forty German divisions from the Soviet front; and for recognition of the Soviet Union's June 1941 borders, which incorporated the Baltic states and east Poland. The talks appeared to stall, but then, on Sunday, 24 May, Stalin unexpectedly sent a telegram instructing Molotov to accept the uncontroversial British draft proposals and not press for the 1941 frontiers. 'I don't know what obliged Stalin so sharply to change his attitude,' reflected Soviet ambassador Ivan Maisky. Perhaps the Russian leader had concluded that half a treaty was better than none. With the Germans attacking hard again, adequate supplies of aeroplanes and tanks were more important than hypothetical borders, and discussion of a second front could continue when Molotov went on to Washington for talks with Roosevelt.

Even so, the Anglo-Soviet Treaty of Mutual Assistance, signed in secrecy on 26 May, locked in – in general terms – a military and political alliance between the USSR and the British Empire for the remainder of the war, and for twenty years thereafter. When Molotov and Eden put pen to paper that day, in the latter's office in Whitehall, they did so before the full glare of the cameras, although the pictures were only to be made public two weeks later once Molotov had returned to London from the US. Churchill was delighted with Eden, congratulating him at War Cabinet for his 'skilful handling of the negotiations', and the following day he thanked Stalin for 'meeting our difficulties in the Treaty as you have done'. But the elephant in the room had not gone away: 'A SECOND FRONT IN 1942', the *Daily Mirror* proclaimed on 12 June when the embargo was lifted; 'BRITAIN, USA AND RUSSIA AGREE SECOND FRONT THIS YEAR,' read a *Daily Express* front-page headline.

This was no newspaper hype. Eden had been forced to read out to the Commons a communiqué Molotov had brought back with him from Washington, stating that 'full understanding was reached between the two parties with regard to the urgent task of creating a second front in Europe in 1942'. Roosevelt had told Molotov that the Allies were already consulting on landing craft, food for troops and other issues. The President had agreed that the date of 1942 be included in the joint statement, so Eden had no alternative but to swallow it. The War Cabinet lacked both the appetite and the means to conduct a cross-Channel operation that year, but – intent both on ensuring Hitler retained his troops in France and on bolstering Russian morale – it acceded to the unattainable pledge nonetheless.

Ministers had already been doing their best to dampen down expectations about the likelihood of a second front before the year was out. Sir Stafford Cripps told his Bristol constituents that the government was 'as keen and anxious for this to materialise as you are'. But he stressed that, first, it had to be organised 'at the proper time and place', and, second, the War Cabinet had to make sure 'not to give the enemy any information about our intention'.

On his return from his failed mission to India Cripps had cut an increasingly forlorn figure. He was largely ignored by Churchill outside War Cabinet meetings, and was frustrated by his minimal influence on day-to-day decision-making. 'Cripps was annoyed about the lack of work involved in his office of lord privy seal and made needless toil out of his leadership of the House of Commons,' Herbert Morrison later reflected.

That 'toil' included having to defend the absent Prime Minister in a stormy two-day debate on the war situation in May. This proved doubly difficult for Cripps as he shared many of the MPs' criticisms – chief of which was that Churchill was struggling to combine the roles of Prime Minister and Minister of Defence, and ought to be replaced in the latter by a new and independent chairman of the Chiefs of Staff Committee.

But Cripps, brushing off some heckling about the Prime Minister's absence, stuck loyally to his brief. No 'superman' existed, he said, who could control the military chiefs, Prime Minister and War Cabinet. Rallying to Churchill's side, he added that 'the War Cabinet desires to have the advice of a first-class defence minister, and there is no-one in the country with wider and larger experience of defence problems than the Prime Minister'. He assured the House that 'the Prime Minister as minister of defence submits to the Cabinet just as other ministers do in their sphere of activity'.

But his restlessness drew Cripps into composing another speech about his vision of post-war Britain that undoubtedly irked Churchill. In the BBC Sunday night *Postscript* slot that had served him so well in the past, he staked out partisan territory. 'There must be, after this war, none of the gross inequalities that there were in the aftermath of the last one, none of that disgraceful contrast of great poverty and great wealth . . . the waste of humanity which our education and social system has permitted in the past will no longer be tolerated.' Harold Nicolson thought that the broadcast was 'uncompromisingly and radically socialist . . . that will much annoy the Conservatives, and [which] was not wholly in keeping with the party truce'.

But such was Cripps' enigmatic nature and quixotic behaviour that others formed a different impression of his mood and views in this period. George Orwell, who with a group of other writers spent a long evening with the Lord Privy Seal – 'about two and a half hours of it, with no drink' – was not convinced, for all his bold rhetoric, that the Labour maverick would stay true to his beliefs. 'I cannot help feeling a strong impression that Cripps has already been got at. Not with money or anything of that kind, of course, nor even by flattery and the sense of power . . . but simply by responsibility, which automatically makes a man timid.'

For the time being, with any second front some way off, and the immediate search for military success on land proving elusive, attention focused more and more on the need for progress in the air. A report by David Bensusan-Butt in August 1941 – commissioned by Professor Lindemann – had first cast great doubt on the efficiency of the RAF's bombing campaign. An examination of 633 photographs in June and July that year showed that only one in four planes got within five miles of their targets in Germany, and over the industrialised Ruhr it was just one in ten.

Nor, in May 1942, despite an improvement in navigation aids, was a report by High Court judge Mr Justice Singleton able to reassure the War Cabinet either that the bombers were destroying targets effectively, or that the morale of the German people was likely to crack. He recorded that 'a very large proportion [of bombs] have fallen on open ground', and did not think that great results could be hoped for within six months from 'air attacks on Germany at the greatest possible strength'.

Nonetheless Bomber Command, now with Sir Arthur Harris as commander-in-chief, stepped up its campaign, launching heavy raids on the north German port of Lübeck in late March, and hitting nearby Rostock a month later. Strategic bombing had given way to area bombardment, threatening the civilian populations of the towns attacked as much as the specific military targets. Goebbels noted in his diary, 'The British are publicising their last raid on Rostock in the grand manner. It has been, it must be admitted, pretty disastrous.'

Then on the night of Saturday, 30 May the first 'thousand bomber raid' took place when the RAF attacked Cologne, dropping 1,455 tons of bombs and losing just forty-one aircraft in the process. When the War Cabinet met on Monday morning to review the success of the operation, Air Chief Marshal Sir Charles Portal said simply that 'there was little to add to the statements in the press'. Indeed, he and the Air Minister, Archibald Sinclair, had enjoyed a huge propaganda coup. The newspapers had seized on the 'good' news with enthusiasm. '1,500 PLANES IN BIGGEST RAID YET' was the headline in the *Daily Mirror*. 'THE VENGEANCE BEGINS! ONE BOMBER EVERY SIX SECONDS, 3,000 TONS IN 90 MINUTES', screamed the *Daily Express*.

A fortnight later the War Cabinet ruled out a very different sort of bombing raid. In response to the Lidice massacre in Czechoslovakia – where the Germans had massacred 173 men, and transported women and children to concentration camps, in retaliation for the assassination of Reinhard Heydrich, Reich Protector of Bohemia and Moravia – Churchill suggested wiping out three German villages in revenge. The justification for this drastic action would be announced afterwards.

Ernest Bevin, Anthony Eden and Leo Amery volunteered differing levels of support. '[The] German responds to brute force and nothing else,' said the Minister of Labour. Eden felt 'there might be a deterrent element in this'. Amery inquired, 'Why a village? Why not a quiet residential town?' But everyone else around the table was against the idea. Archibald Sinclair felt it was a 'diversion of effort from military objectives'. Clement Attlee, drily, doubted 'if it is useful to enter into competition in frightfulness with Germans'.

Churchill withdrew the suggestion. 'I submit – unwillingly – to the view of Cabinet against,' he concluded. The meeting then moved on to other points, including a discussion of public morale. The Prime Minister forecast that the 'likely news for the next few months will cure undue optimism' in the country. This War Cabinet meeting had been the gloomiest for many months, with reports of severe losses to Coastal Command as the Battle of the Atlantic continued, and crippling blows to the Malta convoys. Nor were there any developments in the land war to give cause for optimism. 'The news from Africa has become ominous, and it looks like another defeat for us there,' Lord Woolton recorded in his diary that night. Britain was no longer short of allies, but what was desperately needed was a victory – any kind of victory – that would signal the turning of the tide.

Chapter Nine

'Ringing the bells of victory'

21 June to 1 December 1942

On the afternoon of Sunday, 21 June, four days into another visit to America, Churchill was talking with Roosevelt, General Sir Alan Brooke and General Ismay in the President's study at the White House, when General George C. Marshall walked in with a pink slip of paper and handed it to Roosevelt. The President absorbed it quickly and then, without a word, passed it to Churchill. It read, 'Tobruk has surrendered, with twenty-five thousand men taken prisoners'.

Churchill visibly winced. The news was then confirmed by a second telegram from Admiral Harwood, commander-in-chief of the British naval forces in the Mediterranean. For a few moments no one spoke, then the silence was broken by Roosevelt, who simply asked, 'What can we do to help?'

Churchill's response was instinctive. 'Give us as many Sherman tanks as you can spare, and ship them to the Middle East as quickly as possible.' Although the new battle tank was only just coming into production, and America's own armoured divisions had barely got their hands on it, Roosevelt promised three hundred plus a consignment of one hundred 105mm self-propelled guns.

The Prime Minister then phoned Attlee and asked him to convene a meeting of the War Cabinet that evening – it was Sunday, so not all members were close by – to consider some practical solutions to the crisis. At the 10.30 p.m. gathering in Downing Street, Ernest Bevin led the recriminations. He bemoaned the 'defeatist attitude' of the telegrams received that day from General Claude Auchinleck – Commander-in-Chief Middle East Command – and others, adding that 'we should not tolerate the suggestion that Rommel and his troops were superior to our own'. The time had come, he suggested, to consider changes in the high command. But Oliver Lyttelton, Minister of Production and not long back from his role in the Middle East, rejected Bevin's demand for sackings. 'When General Auchinleck had been urged two months ago to stage an offensive . . . he had constantly affirmed that he was too weak in armour to do so with any prospect of success,' he told his colleagues. 'Recent events might well confirm the correctness of this view.'

By midnight, the War Cabinet had agreed on one immediate measure. One hundred and twenty tanks and twenty-four Hurricane fighters intended for India were now to be diverted to Suez. Together with the Shermans, it was at least a start. The broader issues of military leadership, strategy, and the efficiency of the equipment would have to wait for another day. For now, Rommel's progress had to be halted by whatever means were available.

The New York newspapers scented blood – 'ANGER IN ENGLAND', 'TOBRUK FALL MAY BRING CHANGE OF GOVERNMENT', 'CHURCHILL TO BE CENSURED', were among their headlines – although Eden reassured the Prime Minister that the mood back home suggested nothing of the kind. 'Of course there was much grief. No doubt there would be blame for the government,' he conceded. But much had been happening in London while Churchill was away. Four days later, a motion was put down in the House of Commons by Churchill's old opponent, Sir John Wardlaw-Milne. Reading 'This house, while paying tribute to the heroism and endurance of the Armed Forces of the Crown in circumstances of exceptional difficulty, has no confidence in the central direction of the war,' it was eventually signed by twenty-one other MPs: seven Conservatives, seven from Labour, six Independents and one Liberal.

On the same day the government suffered yet another by-election defeat, its fourth, and heaviest, since March. At Maldon in Essex, the Independent candidate Tom Driberg (gossip columnist 'William Hickey' of the *Daily Express*) overturned an 8,000 Conservative majority from 1935 to register his own 6,000 majority over the Coalition candidate, agricultural engineer Reuben Hunt; the turnout of 45 per cent was the highest in the whole of the war.

Driberg was a member of the left-leaning 1941 Committee, a grouping of progressive intellectuals – such as J.B. Priestley, Edward G. Hulton (the owner of *Picture Post*), H.G. Wells, Richard Acland, Michael Foot and Julian Huxley – which urged that the government should seek to 'win the peace' as well as the war. They wanted Britain's social system rebuilt, advocating – among other reforms – works councils, public control of the railways, mines and docks, and a national wages policy.

There were persistent rumours around Westminster that Beaverbrook was taking soundings about Churchill's position. 'Undoubtedly the opposition to Winstonian control is gathering force,' wrote Sir Cuthbert Headlam. 'Beaverbrook is said to be behind a lot of this – influencing, so they say, Winston's critics who sit on both sides of the house.' In fact Beaverbrook had approached his bête noire Bevin to canvass his views on the formation of an alternative government, should Churchill be forced out. An angry Bevin had interrupted Beaverbrook before this flight of fancy developed too far, warning him he would go at once to Churchill to tell him about the approach. Whether he carried through with his threat is unclear, but what is known is that on Sunday, 28 June, at a mass meeting in Liverpool's Philharmonic Hall, an impassioned Bevin sought to rally support for the Prime Minister and his government on the eve of the vote of confidence. In an apparent reference to Beaverbrook, he told his audience, 'This wicked, filthy business of trying to break our national unity by playing off Winston Churchill against his colleagues on the part of newspaper millionaires is a most diabolical thing.'

The Prime Minister retained the support of the public – opinion polls (still in their infancy) put his approval rating at just below 80 per cent – but his backing in Westminster remained shallow. Harvie-Watt spelt out the mood of the House to him thus: 'It is being said that every time the Government has asked for anything the demands have been met; the House agreed to the conscription of men and women, high taxation, full supplies of supply and production, and yet the results as proved in Libya have been not only disappointing but disastrous.'

Meanwhile the Tory party was divided over the proposed vote. The 1922 Committee was adamantly opposed to any censure debate, and Wardlaw-Milne himself began to have second thoughts. Realising he had stirred up a crisis, he suggested to government whips that it should be deferred while a major battle – the first El Alamein – was going on. But Attlee, sensing the government would get the approval it needed, ensured it went ahead.

Nevertheless the 'Great Debate' or 'Great Inquest' was a testing moment, and would prove to be a gripping piece of parliamentary theatre, lasting two long days with simultaneous debates in the House of Commons and House of Lords. In the Commons on the first day, Wednesday, 1 July, the benches and galleries were more crowded than on any day since the Norway debate that had brought down Neville Chamberlain. Dozens of MPs stood up to speak, and consequently broke the record for the longest sitting of the war: over fifteen hours, until the House broke up at 2.45 a.m. the following morning.

In the Lords, Beaverbrook startled his fellow peers by admitting that the British Army in the Western Desert had more tanks than the Germans and Italians put together. He also informed them that the coalition had made no provision for the dive-bomber – seen by many as a critical piece of equipment in this theatre of war – when it had taken over in May 1940.

Yet this was Beaverbrook at his most effective and most loyal. He suggested that recent setbacks could be attributed to 'too many committees in Cairo . . . committees are always a cause of delay [cheers and laughter]. And organisation is the enemy of improvisation.'

Confronting the criticism that Churchill had taken on too much by combining the roles of Prime Minister and Minister of Defence, he responded, 'If you create a separate Ministry of Defence you will either duplicate the functions of the Prime Minister or you will create a dual Premiership. The first would be useless, and the second would be intolerable and fatal.'

The debate in the Lords was considered and good-humoured. In the Commons, where the votes mattered, there was acute tension, high farce, an ineffective display from the government's lead speaker Oliver Lyttelton, and scintillating contributions from critics as otherwise far apart as Leslie Hore-Belisha and Aneurin Bevan.

Sir John Wardlaw-Milne, opening the case for the prosecution, was a tall, dignified man, who delivered his speech at a measured pace in a gentle west-of-Scotland accent. His detractors considered this former Indian civil servant and financier to be a pompous bore, but on this day he spoke authoritatively and held the House's attention, at least to start with. Claiming his motion had 'one object, and one object only, of assisting us to win the war in the shortest possible time', he went on to present the nub of his argument: that Churchill should give way to a new minister of defence, who would be an independent leader of the armed forces, not beholden to the War Cabinet, and 'strong enough to see that his generals and admirals are allowed to do their work in their own way'.

Then, in an instant, he lost the respect of the House. 'I do not know whether Members have thought of it,' he said, 'but it would be a very desirable move, if His Majesty the King and the Royal Highness would agree, if His Royal Highness the Duke of Gloucester were to be appointed Commander-in-Chief of the British Army.'

If Wardlaw-Milne had been allowed to finish his sentence with the words 'without, of course, administrative duties', and then gone on to explain that the King's younger brother would be a figurehead only, all might have been well. As it was, the thought of the Duke of Gloucester – an amiable country gentleman type – assuming a position of power caused his fellow MPs to dissolve into gales of laughter.

The seconder of the motion, Sir Roger Keyes, only made matters worse. Whereas Wardlaw-Milne had argued Churchill had too much power and must be stripped of some of it, Keyes' argument was the opposite. He said the problem with the central direction of the war was that the Prime Minister was surrounded by ministers who lacked courage or ability, specifically naming Morrison, Bevin and Alexander. In Keyes' view, Churchill needed to assume *greater* responsibility.

With the vote's Conservative sponsors confused over strategy, it was left to Aneurin Bevan, the firebrand Labour MP for Ebbw Vale, to make the most coruscating speech. Britain's military setbacks were due to three things, he said: the main strategy of the war was flawed; the wrong weapons had been produced; and those weapons were being commanded by men who had not studied their use. In a memorable phrase, he accused Churchill of winning debate after debate yet losing battle after battle. 'The country is beginning to say that he fights debates like a war and the war like a debate.'

When Churchill stood up to make his closing statement – watched in the gallery by his wife Clementine and daughters Diana and Mary – he exploited the House's residual loyalty as expertly as ever. First, he dealt with his critics, in particular the 'bitter animosity' of Bevan's 'diatribe'. Next he continued quietly, without emotion, in a half-conversational manner, to respond in detail to the criticisms of equipment failures and oversights. Thereafter, he pointed to the advantages the Allies possessed, even at this dire moment: airpower was developing rapidly; British tanks were bolstering Russia's defensive shield; convoys to the east had grown; India had been reinforced; the US Navy had won victories in the Coral Sea and at Midway Island.

'We have no right to assume that victory is certain,' he concluded. 'It will be certain only if we do not fail in our duty. Sober and constructive criticism, or criticism in Secret Session, has its high virtue; but the duty of the House of Commons is to sustain the Government – or to change the Government. If it cannot change it, it should sustain it.'

His government was sustained, by 475 votes to 25, with 35 abstentions. Churchill left the chamber to a loud ovation, brandishing his

V for victory sign. Eden was relieved: 'Winston wound up with one of his most effective speeches, beautifully adjusted to the temper of the House.' Others were not so sure the boil had been lanced: 'the House was quite won over in spite of itself,' noted Lord Woolton. 'Their cheers indicated that they had quite lost sight of the gravity of the position of the country . . .'

The following day Churchill received a first-hand account of the army's difficulties in the Middle East from a young captain based at Britain's headquarters in Cairo. Twenty-three-year-old Julian Amery, son of Leo, had been sent back to London to brief senior War Office officials on the plans being drawn up in the event of Egypt being overrun. Granted this unexpected opportunity to brief the Prime Minister through his father, Amery did not hold back. Painting a picture of poor morale, both at HQ and in the field, he urged the Prime Minister to go out to Egypt and see the situation for himself. 'Your presence among the troops in the battle area would be enough. It would have an electric effect.' Churchill – who never needed a second invitation to head for the scene of the battle – had already been contemplating such a move, and would act on it very shortly.

In a letter to his old friend Samuel Hoare in May 1941, Beaverbrook, observing Clement Attlee and Arthur Greenwood as they sat alongside Churchill during a parliamentary debate, had described the two Labour men as 'a sparrow and a jackdaw, perched on either side of the glittering bird of paradise'. It was a typically colourful, disparaging description from a man who might himself have been likened to a black crow: cunning, mischievous and destructive. But while the jackdaw – and indeed the crow, albeit only temporarily – had now left the garden, the unobtrusive sparrow had settled down well among the bigger birds.

Attlee's profile with the public was still not high in the summer of 1942. On the newsreels they saw an unassuming man, pipe in hand and flat cap on his head, following in the wake of the flamboyant Prime Minister, while on the BBC his unremarkable voice offered only dry, cautious tones where Churchill served up bold rhetoric. In April, when Eden and Cripps were riding high in the public's estimation as potential replacements for Churchill in the event of his death, only 2 per cent thought the designated Deputy Prime Minister should be the successor. In fact, before setting off for Washington in June, Churchill had written to the King to nominate Eden for the task. 'He is the outstanding candidate in the largest political party in the House of Commons . . . with the resolution, experience and capacity which these grievous times require.'

Attlee was aware of his limitations, in Parliament and on the radio. In August 1941 he had found himself in charge of the War Cabinet for a lengthy period while Churchill was away meeting Roosevelt in Placentia Bay. 'I had to take the place of the PM . . . as the reviewer of the war situation, no easy thing to follow such an artist,' he had written to his brother Tom. 'I eschewed embroidery and stuck to a plain statement. It is no use trying to stretch the bow of Ulysses.' On announcing the Atlantic Charter six days later, he had confessed, 'I felt that I was taking the place of Bruce Belfrage [a BBC news presenter] rather than making any original contribution.'

In the early stages of the war Attlee's strength had been in making the machinery of Whitehall work more efficiently. He had culled the number of ministerial and official committees, and transformed the Lord President's Committee into the governmental hub of the Home Front, in the process taking a lot of weight off the War Cabinet. Eden, for one, had watched his early reticence in the War Cabinet and Defence Committee and wished he would contribute more, as his succinct interventions were always full of sound common sense. But now, with the Prime Minister out of the country increasingly often, Attlee's skill as a committee chairman came to the fore. He had looked on as Churchill became prone to treating the War Cabinet simply as a debating society, testing out new ideas and developing arguments for speeches; when he was in charge, he would make sure it stuck to its core role as an instrument of decision.

The chiefs of staff were especially grateful for the Deputy Prime

Minister's brisk methods. General Alan Brooke, often driven to distraction by Churchill's rambling if entertaining discourses, recorded, 'PM now away and meeting run by Attlee very efficiently and quickly.' Others outside the Cabinet Room appreciated his collegiate approach. 'Attlee . . . does what I wish Winston would do, see other Ministers and talk things over with them,' noted Leo Amery.

As the government suffered that summer in the wake of the constant stream of military defeats, so Attlee came under pressure from elements in his own party, disgruntled at what they perceived as his uncritical loyalty to the Tory leadership. Chief among these was Professor Harold Laski, the intellectually brilliant political science lecturer at the London School of Economics, and a key member of Labour's National Executive. In a series of articles in *Reynolds News*, Laski upbraided the Labour members of the coalition for failing to implement socialist reforms. 'No one . . . can point to any serious effort by Mr Attlee to make the idea of a partnership with the people a conscious part of the Prime Minister's policy,' he wrote.

Inside Westminster, such frustrations were usually voiced by the formidable duo of Aneurin Bevan and Emmanuel 'Manny' Shinwell, the feisty left-wing MP for Seaham, and it was the latter who led the way in an acrimonious debate on 29 July over increases in old-age pensions. The government had proposed an increase of 2s 6d a week, but Attlee and Bevin assured Labour MPs that this was just an interim proposal pending the recommendations of the eagerly awaited Beveridge Report later that year.

This promise of 'jam tomorrow' failed to assuage Shinwell. He indulged in a particularly acrimonious exchange with his old sparring partner Ernest Bevin, suggesting at one point the minister 'would prefer the friendship of members of the Tory party' to himself, before he joined another sixty-two Labour members in voting against the government. This was the largest opposing vote since the coalition had come into being in May 1940. Yet despite such party irritations, and the rise of a potentially dangerous rival, the popular Stafford Cripps, Attlee's calm and self-confidence appeared unperturbed. 'He gives me an impression of greater strength and on-the-spotness,' noted Hugh Dalton after a lunch at the Lansdowne Club.

Attlee had not hitherto ventured far into the field of military strategy, however. As a member of the Defence Committee and the War Cabinet, he had long held nominal responsibility in this area, but he had been largely excluded from the major decisions by Churchill's tight ownership of the military campaign. Moreover, Attlee appreciated and deferred to the Prime Minister's imaginative understanding of the battlefield, even if he and Eden had to dissuade Churchill from some of his wilder schemes. Having never thought Churchill's most ambitious project of all, the Dardanelles campaign in the First World War, the disaster conventional history painted it to be, he had no objection in principle to Churchill's dual role as premier and Minister of Defence in the current struggle. What was wrong now, to Attlee's mind, was not the speed of decision-making but the fact that too many of the decisions taken were based on outdated strategical thinking.

So he put together his thoughts in a wide-ranging four-page paper, which he sent on 6 July initially to Eden, by this time a key ally in the Cabinet. 'I am a good deal disturbed at our failures in the field,' he told the foreign secretary. 'We are still very largely bound by conceptions of fighting before the present war which express themselves in the establishment and equipment we maintain.' Static warfare, with the division (40,000 men) as the 'cumbrous' unit, supported by an 'immense litter of ancillary services', was outdated. Military chiefs were still thinking 'in terms of lines, although linear warfare has been largely stultified by the air and to a lesser degree by the tank'.

Attlee observed the mobility of the Japanese forces – 'highly trained guerrillas' – and noted the success of both the Germans and the Russians in using planes to supply troops and maintain advanced air forces. The Air Ministry, he wrote, still regarded such use of aircraft as 'an illegitimate filching away of resources. Their attitude continues to be dominated by the conception that the war can be won by big bombers.' As for generals, Rommel 'like Cromwell and Marlborough is with the forward troops . . . this is the right place. The general far in the rear is applicable to the days when wars were fought with masses of infantry.'

After receiving Eden's comments, Attlee made revisions and then, on 10 July, sent his paper to the Prime Minister. A considered reply of all the points came back on 29 July, with Churchill conceding the need for a more significant commando force, for a brigade group rather than a division where operations were on a small scale, and for a reduction in the 'excessive standards of transport'. But given the lack of progress on land, he would not be moved from the tactic he currently favoured: 'to withdraw our Bomber force from the cities, factories and seaports of Germany to be a mere handmaid of the Army, bombing airfields and railway junctions behind the hostile front, would be a great relief to the enemy.'

The Attlee–Eden axis on foreign policy and strategy would continue to gain strength. But the Deputy Prime Minister's criticisms about the bombing campaign made no headway in War Cabinet. Indeed, the night before Churchill gave his response to Attlee's memorandum, Air Marshal Sir Arthur Harris, chief of Bomber Command, had broadcast on the BBC, in a forbidding message to the German people, that he intended to 'scourge the Third Reich from end to end . . . We are bombing Germany, city by city in order to make it impossible for you to go on with the war. That is our object. We shall pursue it remorselessly.'

At 1 a.m. on Thursday, 30 July, following a Cabinet dinner with the King at Number 10, Churchill broke the news to his ministers that he intended to visit Cairo to see the problems of the Eighth Army at first hand. At the same time the Foreign Office had received a telegram from the British ambassador in Moscow, Sir Archibald Clark Kerr, suggesting there would be 'immense advantages' in the Prime Minister visiting the Soviet Union to meet Stalin and discuss the second front.

Churchill jumped at the idea of a double mission, and it was put to the War Cabinet the same day. Remembering the incident in Washington eight months before, however, Eden privately worried about the risks posed to the Prime Minister's health by the journey, and persuaded Churchill to consult his doctor, Sir Charles Wilson, before any final decision was taken. Churchill passed the doctor's test, and a little after midnight, on Sunday, 2 August, he set off from Lyneham airfield in an unheated, four-engined US Liberator bomber named *Commando*. He went with two objectives at the forefront of his mind: in Cairo, to make sweeping changes to the high command; in Moscow, to convince Stalin that Operation *Torch*, the intended North African landings, would be a more than adequate substitute for a second front on the European mainland.

No member of the War Cabinet accompanied the Prime Minister. Churchill was content to take Sir Alexander Cadogan and General Alan Brooke as his principal advisers, with his old friend South African president Field Marshal Smuts joining them for the Cairo leg. The friendship between Smuts and Churchill had been forged in unlikely circumstances in the Second Boer War, when the former, a key commando leader, interrogated the latter, a captured journalist, and a mutual respect developed. Churchill had little time for the leaders of other Dominion countries, but he greatly admired Smuts and his wise counsel, encouraging his attendance at War Cabinet.

The Prime Minister's delight at escaping the shackles of Whitehall and heading for the thick of the action was self-evident. 'Winston was bubbling with enthusiasm,' observed one of the first men to brief him, Air Marshal Sir Arthur Tedder, head of RAF Middle East Command. 'He was like a schoolboy just out of school and off for a really wonderful holiday.'

A few days later, after a full round of conferences and a visit to inspect the Eighth Army at El Alamein, Churchill's mind was made up. General Auchinleck had to go, to be replaced by Lieutenant General William Gott, whose aggressive personality appealed to the Prime Minister, and who came with a recommendation from Eden, the pair having served together in the First World War. Back in London, on Friday, 7 August, Attlee convened the War Cabinet three times; at 9.30 a.m., 5 p.m. and 11.15 p.m. – only in the desperate days of May 1940 had ministers met so often in a twenty-four-hour period. There was unrest in India and the fate of the Atlantic convoys to consider, but Churchill's proposed changes in the military hierarchy in the Middle East were the main focus of their attention.

Around midnight Attlee, Cripps, Eden, Anderson, Lyttelton and Bevin were among those critically examining the plan when an ashen-faced secretary entered and handed a piece of paper to Attlee with the comment, 'I fear this is bad news.' It was a message from Churchill that Gott's plane had been shot down and the general killed. Eden in particular was badly shaken by the loss of his old regimental colleague. The war had been going badly for us and it seemed we could never get the right commanders in the right places. Now that we thought all was set fair, this unexpected blow had fallen.'

The Prime Minister's determination to remove Auchinleck was unaltered by the tragedy. The Eighth Army command would instead go to Lieutenant General Bernard Montgomery, commander of the South-Eastern Army in Britain, who had already been earmarked to take control of British forces in Operation *Torch*. General Sir Harold Alexander, mentioned in dispatches earlier in the year during the desperate retreat in Burma, was to become commander-in-chief Middle East Command. Auchinleck was offered the newly created Persia and Iraq Command but, deeply hurt by his dismissal, refused it and retired to India to lick his wounds.

Montgomery assumed command of the Eighth Army at 2 p.m. on 13 August – an act of 'disobedience', as he took charge two days before he was officially due to do so. Right from the start he sought to instil a new resolve. 'I issued orders that in the event of enemy attack there would be *no* withdrawal; we would fight on the ground we now held, and if we couldn't stay there alive we would stay there dead,' he recalled. This was music to the ears of Churchill, who by then had reached Moscow – via Teheran – to begin the delicate task of informing Stalin there would be no second front. The Soviet Union was facing a grave crisis, with Hitler's summer offensive in full flow and the German Sixth Army rapidly approaching the outskirts of Stalingrad.

The War Cabinet was apprised daily – sometimes hourly – as to each twist and turn of Churchill's first ever face-to-face meeting with Stalin. The Soviet leader's mood was dark to begin with, after the Prime Minister frankly informed him that the 'great offensive' in Europe could not be launched until 1943. He was only partly assuaged when Churchill pledged to intensify the bombing campaign instead, putting twenty more German cities in the firing line.

Churchill won a more favourable response when he outlined the strategy behind Operation *Torch* by taking up his pen and drawing a picture of a crocodile – one of his favourite metaphors – on a piece of paper. Once North Africa was in the possession of the Allies, it was 'our intention to attack the soft belly of the crocodile as we attacked its hard snout'; the clear implication being that Sicily and Italy was the belly, while northern France and western Europe remained the snout. Now Stalin's mood changed. 'May God help this enterprise to succeed,' he remarked enthusiastically.

But apparent harmony at the end of that first meeting quickly evaporated, to be replaced by a provocative, accusatory approach from the Russians the following night. Stalin called for 'higher sacrifices' from the western Allies. Operation *Torch* was all well and good, but it demonstrated that Britain and America thought the Russian front was of 'secondary importance'. On the recent sinking of two-thirds of Convoy PQ 17, which had been bringing vital supplies to the Soviet Union, he bluntly told Churchill, 'This is the first time in history the British Navy has ever turned tail and fled from the battle. You British are afraid of fighting. You should not think the Germans are supermen. You will have to fight sooner or later.'

The Prime Minister kept calm in the face of this provocation. He then launched into an oratorical tour de force lasting five minutes, in which he complained that he had travelled all across Europe to 'meet the hand of comradeship' and that it grieved him to think the Russians did not believe the Allies were doing their utmost for the cause. 'If, by the loss of 150,000 British and American soldiers on the shore of France, real help could be given to Russia and something useful chieved, the Americans and the British would not hesitate to give he order.' Transfixed by Churchill's 'magnificent performance', the nterpreters failed to translate it properly. Stalin, however, had no need to grasp the speech fully to appreciate the passion with which it was delivered. 'I do not understand the words,' he said, smiling broadly or the first time that evening, 'but by God I like your spirit.'

Churchill deduced that Stalin, for all his bluster, would accept the postponement of the second front. 'It is my considered opinion that in his heart – so far as he has one – Stalin knows we are right . . . moreover I am certain that his sure-footed and quick military judgement will make him a strong supporter of "Torch".' He was correct. By the time Churchill left on Sunday, 16 August, after two further meetings, he was able to tell the War Cabinet that 'the greatest goodwill prevailed, and for the first time we got on easy and friendly terms'. Stalin had swallowed the bitter pill; now everything turned on the Allies defeating Rommel and launching the *Torch* invasion as soon as practicable.

Churchill had hinted to Stalin at their first of their meetings in the Kremlin that in the absence of a fully fledged second front, 'something could be done in September . . . on the stretch between Dunkirk and Dieppe.' In fact this attack, Operation *Jubilee*, took place sooner, on Wednesday, 19 August. The following day its principal author, Acting Vice Admiral Lord Louis Mountbatten, chief of Combined Operations the body that oversaw amphibious offensives carried out jointly by army and naval personnel), great-grandson of Queen Victoria and a favourite of Churchill, was invited to Downing Street to give the War Cabinet an account of the operation. Its target had been the French port of Dieppe, and it involved the landing of 5,000 Canadian infantry, ,000 British commandos and fifty US rangers, supported at sea by the Royal Navy, in the air by seventy-four RAF squadrons – mainly Spitfires – and on land by fifty-eight of the new Churchill tanks.

The Chief of Staffs Committee had approved the plan, when it was Operation *Rutter*, back in May. Since then, Mountbatten had run the operation – significantly modified in the meantime – with great secrecy; the Prime Minister and a majority of his military chiefs had been aware (to varying degrees) of its progress, but there is no evidence that the ministers around the table that evening – Attlee (in the chair) Cripps, Eden, Anderson and Amery – had been brought into the loop Even Sir Archibald Sinclair, air minister, who had signed off the RAF squadrons for the mission, was thought to have been briefed only at the last minute. It was a typical example of Churchill's preference for secrecy where unconventional, risky operations were concerned.

Mountbatten presented the ministers with a positive story. He said two-thirds of the 6,000-plus force had been accounted for and returned to Britain. Planning, organisation and co-operation between the services had been excellent; the air support had been 'faultless' The personnel of one enemy coastal battery had been wiped out, while another was neutralised. All in all, despite very heavy air fighting, the 'lessons learned in this large-scale raid would be invaluable in planning for Operation *Round-Up*' – a reference to the major cross-Channel invasion planned for the spring of 1943.

Attlee praised Mountbatten for the planning and execution which 'reflected the greatest credit on all concerned'. Lord Halifax noted later, 'I don't think it sounds at all bad – one or two things went wrong . . . but the troops [are] in good heart, and the Air Force having had a real good fight at everything the Germans had to put up.'

In fact, the assault was a disaster. Of the Canadian contingent, 3,367 were killed, wounded or taken prisoner; of the British commandos 247. The Royal Navy lost the destroyer HMS *Berkeley* and thirty three landing craft, suffering 550 dead and wounded. The RAF which flew 2,617 sorties in the largest single-day battle of the war lost 106 aircraft, over double the number it took from the Luftwaffe The German army suffered 591 casualties. Perhaps the only accurate part of Mountbatten's presentation was the capture of the Hess coastal battery on 'Orange Beach', six miles west of Dieppe.

Mountbatten nevertheless remained bullish. 'The air support was faultless . . . morale of returning troops reported to be excellent; all have seen are in great form,' he telegraphed Churchill on the day of is appearance before the War Cabinet. For the moment, Churchill greed with Mountbatten on the value of the operation. 'My general mpression of Jubilee is that the results fully justified the heavy cost,' e telegraphed the War Cabinet on 21 August while still in Cairo. The large scale air battle alone justified the raid.'

The British press dutifully painted a glowing picture of the failed ttack. 'LORD LOUIS: OUR TANKS PENETRATED THE TOWN', was the front-age headline in the *Daily Express* two days after the operation, which laimed 273 German planes had been destroyed. A reporter for the German paper *Deutsche Allgemeine Zeitung*, who was visiting a nearby Luftwaffe airbase, unsurprisingly viewed things in a very different light - but arguably with more accuracy. 'As executed, the venture mocked ll rules of military logic and strategy.' And as more information about he raid seeped out, the gloss on the events of 19 August wore off. our days after *Jubilee* Hugh Dalton was offered a worrying second pinion when dining with his friend, the military intelligence officer Christopher Mayhew. 'He takes rather a gloomy view of the operation. n the centre, he says, it was just a massacre, and there was a muddle t one of the other landing places . . . our tanks got stuck against a sea vall.' A week on and General Alan Brooke admitted, 'The casualties vere undoubtedly far too many – to lose 2,700 men out of 5,000 on uch an enterprise is too heavy a cost.'

Later, as he read detailed reports of the day's events, Churchill's atisfaction over Dieppe would diminish too. He even considered onstituting a full-scale inquiry. But the raid's failure – or benefit, if iewed from the perspective of tying down the Germans and learning essons for D-Day – faded from the memory as the more momentous nilitary events of autumn 1942 began to unfold.

On Sunday, 23 August Vasily Grossman, special correspondent for he *Red Star* newspaper, reached Stalingrad just as General Friedrich Paulus's Sixth Army prepared to launch the Germans' major offensive n the city. Months of bombing from the Luftwaffe had already taken ts toll. 'Stalingrad is in ashes. It is dead,' Grossman wrote. 'People are in basements. Everything is burned out. The hot walls of the building are like the bodies of people who have died in the terrible heat and haven't gone cold yet . . . there are children wandering about, there are many laughing faces. Many people are half insane.'

A week later in the Western Desert, Field Marshal Erwin Rommel prepared to launch his offensive against the Allied Eighth Army at Alam el Halfa, calculating that Montgomery's troops, yet to receive reinforcements or to settle down under their new command, would be at their most vulnerable. The residents of Stalingrad, protected by the depleted Soviet 62nd and 64th Armies, would face months of siege and starvation. But by 2 September the Eighth Army, aided by vital Ultra intelligence – which enabled the sinking of German fuel cargoes – and supported superbly by the Desert Air Force, had finally halted Rommel. If not a victory, the British government at last had a successful defence to boast of.

The situation further east remained ominous, however. In August and September the government had to confront Gandhi's 'Quit India' campaign, whose renewed call for immediate independence had sparked rioting across the country. Even with Churchill absent, the War Cabinet – save for some half-hearted opposition from Cripps – was unanimous in adopting a tough line. With Japan still threatening India, it fell to Attlee, Secretary of State for the Dominions, and one of the more liberal-minded ministers in this area, to approve the imprisonment of Gandhi, Nehru and other Congress leaders.

The question of what to do about Gandhi's latest hunger strike did, however, provoke dissent. On 10 August Sir James Grigg, war secretary, led the hardliners: 'I would leave him to die where he is – at Poona where he is in a palace not a prison.' Others disagreed. 'Whatever the disadvantages of letting him out, his death in detention would be worse,' Lord Halifax averred. Later, the government offered to release Gandhi while he fasted. Gandhi replied that if he were released, he would have no need to fast. In the event, his fast lasted twenty-one days; by the end of the year, 60,000 people had been arrested in the crackdown.

The man who had grappled with the seemingly intractable Indian problem in the spring was now a frustrated and isolated power in the War Cabinet. 'Stafford Cripps' shares have gone down rather with his colleagues,' his friend Violet Bonham Carter had observed in early July. Cripps told aides he had been permitted only one face-to-face meeting with Churchill since his return from India. Slowly but surely he was being frozen out. Worse, his heavy, at times hectoring, tone in the Commons won him scant affection from MPs, one particular incident, on 8 September, underlining his status as an irritant to both his peers and his master.

Churchill's speech on the war that morning had so disarmed his critics that there were few volunteers for the debate that followed. But later Cripps, as Leader of the House, took it on himself to give MPs a sharp dressing down for this pliancy, accusing them of preferring their luncheon to their duty of scrutinising the government. 'This has enraged everybody, and will, I fear, do the House much damage in the country,' noted Harold Nicolson. In War Cabinet the following day Churchill displayed his annoyance.

'Why encourage criticism?' he asked Cripps.

'I didn't. I regretted the lost opportunity [for MPs] to express support,' replied the Leader of the House.

'Silent support is perhaps best. The House of Commons is in a very good mood – better to have left them alone,' retorted the PM.

'The general effect was bad,' came back Cripps.

'I disagree,' replied Churchill.

Two weeks later an unhappy Cripps forced the issue. 'I do not now feel you place reliance on my help,' he wrote to Churchill. 'I feel increasingly out of touch with your mind on a wide range of subjects of which, as Leader of the Commons, I should have an intimate knowledge.' Cripps attached a memorandum containing familiar criticisms of the machinery of Churchill's ministry.

Churchill replied that he was 'surprised and somewhat pained' to receive the letter. 'I thought we were on the most cordial terms when I set out on my journey at the beginning of August. . . I have always found our conversations agreeable and stimulating.'

A solution to Cripps' discontent had to be found. At 11 p.m. or Wednesday, 30 September, he was summoned to Downing Street where he and Churchill had a 'lively' discussion until 2.30 a.m Eden was given a first-hand account later that day. 'The first hour W attacked him, so SC says, told him he had raked up criticism from al quarters, that if he went out he would have no future, neither Tories nor Socialists supporting him. SC retorted; then matters were calmer but without agreement.'

Churchill told Eden he was convinced Cripps had devised some 'Machiavellian political plot'. The foreign secretary and Attlee then stepped in to act as peacemakers, urging Cripps not to resign at such a critical moment for the government, with Operation *Torch* about to be launched. They also floated the idea – without consulting Churchill – of Cripps taking a new job outside the War Cabinet, as Minister of Aircraft Production, a prospect that had evidently excited his interest

The matter was resolved the next day. Churchill liked the sug-gestion that Cripps might move to aircraft production, while the unhappy minister acknowledged the need not to rock the boat at a crucial juncture. 'If "Torch" failed, we were all sunk, if it succeeded, he was free to act as he wished. If it were fifty-fifty, we could think again, had been Eden's advice to his colleague. On 3 October Cripps wrote to the Prime Minister, telling him, 'You have not convinced me that the changes which I have suggested in the central direction of the war are unnecessary.' He was, however, withholding his resignation because of the 'special circumstances to which you and my other colleagues have drawn my attention'.

'If "Torch" fails, then I'm done for and must go and hand over to you,' Churchill confided in Eden. But salvation was not far away Twelve days after Montgomery launched Operation *Lightfoot* in Egypt Rommel's Afrika Korps was routed on the battlefield at El Alamein Hitler refused his general's request to retreat, but the 'Desert Fox' disobeyed orders and by 8 November had fallen back to the port of Sidi Barrani, close to the Libyan border. On that same day, further west along the African coast, some 63,500 US and 10,000 British troops had made dawn landings at Algiers and Oran in Algeria and Casablanca in Morocco.

At the War Cabinet meeting at 6 p.m. the following day, Churchill's excitement at Montgomery's success and his relief that *Torch* was finally under way were palpable. As General Alan Brooke reported the capture of 40,000 German prisoners and the destruction or seizure of nine-tenths of the enemy's tanks and three-quarters of their guns, the Prime Minister proclaimed El Alamein to be 'one of the greatest victories ever won by the British Empire in the field'. He proposed that church bells – silenced since 1940 – should ring out in celebration of the first British military success of the war. As for *Torch*, he was equally upbeat. 'It is the biggest combined effort since the attack on the Low Countries – and the largest amphibian operation ever undertaken . . . I beg my colleagues and the military authorities to look on this as a springboard . . . this is the moment for the offensive.'

In the House of Commons on 11 November, after he had given a dramatic, detailed description of Montgomery's triumph, Churchill informed MPs of the fall of Casablanca, the last of the vital North African ports to be taken by the Allies. He brought news, too, of Hitler's decision to march into Vichy France, 'thus breaking the Armistice which the Vichy Government had kept with such pitiful and perverted fidelity'.

After all the misery of the previous ten months, Churchill was now able to reassert himself, and on 22 November he carried out a Cabinet reshuffle on his own terms. Cripps was sent to the Ministry of Aircraft Production as promised, and Herbert Morrison was promoted to the War Cabinet in his place. Eden succeeded Cripps as Leader of the House, while Lord Cranborne took his role as Lord Privy Seal.

Morrison learned of his promotion in unusual circumstances. Invited to Chequers for the weekend, he was surprised when he sat down for dinner to see a small radio on the table by Churchill's side. 'He switched on the BBC news bulletin and the announcement of Cripps' resignation came through – the first inkling I had of it. There was a twinkle in the Prime Minister's eyes when he switched off the set and without any comment about the Cripps affair, invited me to join the Cabinet.'

Hugh Dalton, certainly no friend of Cripps, thought the departing minister had been 'very skilfully played by the PM . . . Seldom has anyone's political stock, having been so outrageously and unjustifiably overvalued, fallen so fast and so far.' In press coverage on Monday, 23 November, the Labour-supporting *Daily Herald* asserted that the War Cabinet had been clearly strengthened. But *The Times* worried that the reconstruction of Britain might be now set back by the 'withdrawal from the War Cabinet of a minister peculiarly identified in the public mind' with the necessary 'freshness' in policy outlook that was now needed.

The sudden optimism inspired by the African victories had set many ministers' thoughts turning towards post-war policy. For some in the War Cabinet, there was apprehension at the impending publication of Sir William Beveridge's long-awaited report *Social Insurance and Allied Services*. Sir William had been reported in the *Daily Telegraph* on 13 November suggesting that his welfare proposals would take Britain 'half-way to Moscow'. The quote was, in fact, erroneous, but it voiced precisely the fear of many Conservative members of the government.

Brendan Bracken had told colleagues in the War Cabinet meeting of 16 November that Beveridge was 'working up a political campaign'. The author wished to brief lobby correspondents two weeks before publication, and to follow this with a full press briefing on the day. Churchill appeared relatively emollient at first, merely responding, 'It was a pity if such a comprehensive scheme failed to get a fair chance because of the propaganda of its author.' Later in the meeting, though, he emphasised more severely, 'The report is Government property. Beveridge must be told he is not to expound it – threaten him with [parliamentary] privilege.'

Ten days later the battle lines were more sharply drawn. The chancellor, Kingsley Wood, estimated the cost of implementing the Beveridge Report to be as much as £100 million. For Labour, an enthusiastic Attlee suggested, 'US reaction may be good – they may be impressed by our boldness.' Stafford Cripps warned, 'When opinion crystallizes, it would be a pity to let it appear the Government is being dragged reluctantly to support it,' adding, 'Could we not welcome it in principle?' Churchill and Kingsley Wood firmly disagreed with that approach.

The struggle for national survival had been the glue holding the coalition together. Huge differences in political philosophy had been put to one side in the common interest. Now that it seemed the fight might not be lost, the old fissures were opening up again, as thoughts turned to what sort of peace could be constructed from the ruins of war.

Chapter Ten

'Slaying the five giants'

1 December 1942 to 18 May 1943

Late on the evening of Monday, 30 November 1942, long queues began to form outside the London headquarters of His Majesty's Stationery Office at York House, Holborn. Government publications are rarely bestsellers, and *Social Insurance and Allied Services* was a particularly unpromising title. The main text was 150,000 words long, and it was followed by pages and pages of appendices containing surveys, statistical tables and various memoranda.

But those who braved that cold winter's night were not doing so out of a desire to immerse themselves in technical details about provisional rates of benefit, compulsory insurance contributions or comprehensive health and rehabilitation services. They had joined the mile-long line because they wanted to buy a vision of the future – of a Britain far removed from the rationed, cramped, controlled country of 1942; of a new order where, in the heroic language of sections of the report, the 'five giants' of Disease, Ignorance, Squalor, Idleness and Want had been slain.

Freedom from want cannot be forced on a democracy or given to a democracy. It must be won by them. Winning it needs courage and faith and a sense of national unity: courage to face facts and difficulties and overcome them; faith in our future and in the ideals of fair play and freedom for which century after century our forefathers were prepared to die; a sense of national unity overriding the interests of any class or section.

The author of those stirring words was sixty-three-year-old Sir William Beveridge, a renowned economist and social reformer all the more respected by the British public because they viewed him as an idealist untainted and unconstrained by party affiliation. With his exuberant white hair, avian profile, rubicund complexion and gently smiling face, Beveridge looked more like an amiable farmer or reassuring family doctor than some wild-eyed revolutionary. Yet his supremely lucid and logical report, written out in neat longhand at the disciplined rate of 1,000 words a day, spelt potential trouble – as well as opportunity – for the coalition government. This was a Magna Carta for the working classes.

From early on in the war, even as all efforts were concentrated on Britain's survival, ideas of what sort of country should emerge in the aftermath of the conflict had flourished in people's minds. 'The European House cannot be put in order unless we put our own house in order first,' wrote *The Times* in July 1940. 'The new order cannot be based on the preservation of privilege whether the privilege be that of a country, of a class or of an individual.'

The miseries of the 1930s, of unemployment and the hated household means test, had to be left behind. Long waiting lists at hospitals needed to be reduced, and the cursory examinations and hasty diagnoses given by many panel doctors dispensed with. Above all, there was a growing chorus of disapproval over the social welfare system; a seminal report by Seebohm Rowntree, based in York, had found that whereas in 1901 poverty had been principally caused by low earnings, now it was in large part due to unemployment and inadequate provision for childhood and old age.

Back in June 1941, when Arthur Greenwood, Minister without Portfolio, asked Beveridge to chair an obscure interdepartmental inquiry into social insurance, the expectation had been that this would be just another 'patching up' exercise. There were issues of compensation for industrial injury and sickness to consider, as well as the long overdue rationalisation of the chaotic and inconsistent mix of social security that had accumulated over the previous half-century. No less than seven government departments were directly or indirectly concerned with administering cash benefits for different kinds of need.

But beyond that, the inquiry had been an excuse for Ernest Bevin and other ministers, tired of the restless ambition of this undoubtedly brilliant but somewhat vain and overbearing civil servant, to cast Beveridge into a backwater where he would be unable to disturb their work on the war effort. He had not been expected to report back until the return of peacetime.

That plan had now backfired. Beveridge was at first deeply disappointed with his new brief, believing he had been 'kicked upstairs' for the remainder of the war. But with time he came to see how his inquiry could be transformed into a major work of social reconstruction, enabling him to become the pioneering architect of a more enlightened age. He could not, he told ministers as he prepared his report a year later, confine himself to the narrow issue of social insurance. There were three principles without which his plan for social security would not work. All were politically controversial, especially to a Conservative-led government.

First, there had to be a National Health Service, free at the point of use to prevent medical bills causing poverty. Second, there had to be family allowances paid at the same rate in and out of work, because purely means-tested help would leave those with large families better off unemployed. And third, there had to be full employment – or at worst, a jobless rate of no more than 10 per cent – to ensure wages were high enough to pay the contributions needed to fund the scheme.

The mixture of private cover and means-tested dole that had existed before the war would be replaced by a comprehensive scheme of social insurance, administered by a new Ministry of Social Security. All working people would pay a single weekly contribution to the state, and in return flat-rate benefits would be paid out to support the unemployed, the sick, the retired and the widowed.

Yet in some ways this central pillar of Beveridge's report was not as radical as his supporters claimed, or as his critics feared. This was the proposal of a liberal collectivist, not an out-and-out socialist. He did not establish a principle that people were entitled to free allowances simply because they were members of a community. The contributory principle still reigned: people were only entitled to 'what they paid for'. 'The state in organizing security should not stifle incentive, opportunity, responsibility,' Beveridge emphasised. 'In establishing a national minimum, it should leave room and encouragement for voluntary action by each individual to provide more than that minimum for himself and his family.'

It was not the level of benefits per se that attracted such popular support, but the democratic intent behind them. 'All social insurance . . . for all citizens without income limit – from duke to dustman,' proclaimed the *Daily Mirror*. 'Cradle to grave benefits for all, including free medical, dental, eyesight and hospital treatment.' *The Times* recorded that an incredible 70,000 copies of Beveridge's report were sold in its first three days (the final tally would be 635,000). Details were broadcast by the BBC from dawn on 1 December in twenty-two languages. Gallup noted that after two weeks, 95 per cent of the population knew about the proposals, and the vast majority supported them. Members of the public questioned for the Ministry of Information's 'Home Intelligence Weekly Report' were insistent that Sir William's core ideas must be acted upon. 'If not, things will be damned unpleasant for whatever government is in power; if it's mucked up, there will be hell to pay.'

Some, of course, had reservations. 'People in all walks of life fear that the high rate of benefits may prove an incentive to laziness and thriftlessness,' the Ministry of Information reported. Oswald Falk, nephew of social reformer Arnold Toynbee and a former colleague of John Maynard Keynes, wrote a hostile letter to *The Times* on 2 December. 'The Beveridge Report is the road to the moral ruin of the nation . . . it is the way of sleep, not a symptom of the vitality of our civilization, but of its approaching end.' But these were minority views. Even a large number of backbench Tory MPs were won over. After Beveridge delivered a 'concise and brilliant speech' to the 1922 Committee, Harvie-Watt reported to Churchill, 'The younger members are prepared to go a long way with the suggestions contained in the report . . .'

Nevertheless, Beveridge would have to manoeuvre adroitly if he was to persuade the coalition government to implement any part of his scheme. The estimated cost – £700 million by 1945, and up to £850 million twenty years thereafter – was seen as prohibitive by many, especially the Chancellor, Sir Kingsley Wood, whose lot it was to contemplate the colossal scale of Britain's post-war debt. Meanwhile, for some on the right of British politics, the principle of an enlarged social role for the state was simply anathema. What the man who 'fathered' the first scheme of unemployment insurance in Britain would make of it, no one was quite sure.

Beveridge and Churchill had first met at the political salon of Fabian Society founders Sidney and Beatrice Webb at 41 Grosvenor Road, on 11 March 1908. Like Clement Attlee a few years later, Beveridge, a leader writer on the *Morning Post*, had spent time at the pioneering Toynbee Hall settlement – where university dons and students lived alongside the poor of the East End of London – and was interested in long-term solutions for unemployment; Churchill, about to become President of the Board of Trade, was working to usher in rapid social change as a member of Herbert Asquith's reforming Liberal government.

Their introduction had gone well. They talked about decasualisation and other ways of helping the jobless, and Beveridge was impressed by Churchill's 'brilliance and restlessness'. A few days later Beatrice Webb urged the new minister, 'If you are going to deal with unemployment, you must have the boy Beveridge.' Soon Churchill invited 'the boy' to a departmental seminar on labour exchanges, and not long afterwards he drafted him into the Board of Trade. Working alongside the masterful permanent secretary Sir Hubert Llewellyn Smith, Beveridge had shaped two groundbreaking pieces of legislation for Churchill: the Labour Exchanges Act (1909), which set up offices to inform employers of available labour and workers of available jobs, and the National Insurance Act (1911), which brought in the first system to protect the British working class against sickness and unemployment, and applied to two and a quarter million employees in heavy industries.

This was the zenith of Churchill's radicalism: a period of mighty legislative accomplishment (although the latter act was actually ushered in by Lloyd George) that also included his 1909 Trade Boards Act, establishing for the first time the concept of a 'minimum wage'. The Beveridge Report could be viewed as a logical extension of those earlier measures, but by the 1940s Churchill's reforming instincts had long since dimmed. Increasingly irritated by those who planned for peace before first winning the war, he now viewed his erstwhile colleague as 'an awful windbag and a dreamer'.

On 15 December Beveridge married Juliet ('Jessie') Mair, mother of four children and widow of David Mair, his first cousin. Churchill did not attend the ceremony, but sent as a wedding present a four-volume edition, in green and gold, of his panegyric on his great ancestor Marlborough, *His Life and Times*. Though it was in fact a well-worn piece of Churchillese, used on numerous occasions when talking or writing about social security, the inscription must have encouraged Beveridge that his ideas might yet get a fair wind: 'May he bring the magic of averages to the rescue of millions'.

On the eve of a trip to Casablanca in January, to plan the next stage of the Allied European strategy with President Roosevelt, the Prime Minister circulated a memorandum to the War Cabinet that sounded a more cautious note. Headlined 'Promises About Post-War Conditions', it attempted to dampen down the euphoria created by the Beveridge Report.

'A dangerous optimism is growing up about the conditions it will be possible to establish here after the war,' the document began. The

Prime Minister went on to list all the potential benefits outlined in the Beveridge Report – the abolition of unemployment and low wages, better and prolonged education, great developments in housing and health, the abolition of 'want' – but observed sceptically that all this was to be achieved without raising the cost of living, or reducing the value of sterling. 'It is because I do not wish to deceive the people by false hopes and airy visions of Utopia and Eldorado that I have refrained so far from making promises about the future,' he wrote.

Beveridge wrote to Churchill on 30 January. 'Can you spare me a few minutes of your time at any time in the future? I would like the chance of a word with you about the "magic of averages" in relation to social security.' His entreaty fell on deaf ears.

For Attlee, Morrison and Bevin, who for two and a half years had laboured under a self-denying ordinance in the interest of national unity, it was no doubt galling to see their radical thunder stolen by Beveridge; an arrogant academic – as they perceived him – who was a Liberal to boot. Even so, they remained publicly loyal to the Churchill line of caution over his proposals. For Bevin, at least, this was not purely out of adherence to collective Cabinet responsibility. He had his own issues with the report, regretting that there was no mention of a guaranteed weekly wage, disliking the notion of job training (which sounded to him too reminiscent of the old workhouse test) and believing family allowances would undermine wages. 'Man cannot live by Beveridge alone' would be his watchword. Attlee and Morrison found such self-restraint in discussing and promoting social change more difficult, however, especially with the Labour Party so enthusiastic about the contents of the report. In private, the gloves could come off.

With a date set for a full-scale Commons debate on Beveridge, on Monday, 16 February, Churchill issued another warning note in a second memorandum to his colleagues. Using the same phrase written on Beveridge's wedding present – 'bringing the magic of averages nearer to the rescue of millions' – he acknowledged that the report constituted 'an essential part of any post-war scheme of national betterment'. But he also made it quite clear that a general election was required – 'a House of Commons refreshed by the people' – before any major changes could be implemented.

Attlee fired back immediately, writing that he was 'disturbed' at the claim that it would be 'unconstitutional or at least improper' for the government to legislate for social change. In a rebuke to the Prime Minister for his detachment from Home Front matters, he wrote, 'I doubt whether in your inevitable and proper preoccupation with military problems you are fully cognizant of the extent to which decisions must be taken and implemented in the field of post-war reconstruction before the end of the war.' Refusing to accept that further change would be catastrophic, he warned, 'I am certain that unless the Government is prepared to be as courageous in planning for the peace as it has been in carrying on the war, there is extreme danger of disaster when the war ends.'

On the eve of the Commons debate, the War Cabinet assembled at Downing Street with the Prime Minister's fresh memorandum in front of them, and Attlee was ready to lock horns with him in response. The exchanges were robust.

Sir John Anderson told colleagues his interpretation of Churchill's memorandum was that there would be no reconstruction legislation at all – or reform of the social security system would be given a lower priority than other projects. To this Attlee said bluntly, 'If the PM's line is taken, it will provoke demand for a General Election.' He again disputed the argument that it was not the job of a wartime coalition to introduce social legislation, pointing out, 'In the last war an education bill [The Fisher Act] was passed by an even older Parliament.'

But Churchill asserted, 'Our first promise should be to ensure that the demobilized will get back to their old jobs – ie, under the old regime . . . no promises, no commitments, [yet] every conceivable preparation.'

'Preparations all involve decisions of policy,' retorted Attlee.

'I would agree to legislation by this Parliament to prepare for post-war; but not to legislation taking decisions binding the future,' Churchill went on.

Now Morrison contested him: 'If we accept the view that we can have no enabling legislation dealing with post-war problems – then we shall be in an indefensible position.'

By the end of the meeting Churchill had reluctantly been forced to concede that the government's speaker the next day, Sir John Anderson, should not have his hands tied by a blanket refusal to legislate during the current parliament.

As it turned out, what Anderson said mattered less than the manner in which he said it. He addressed MPs as if in his natural role of civil servant reporting to the government, rather than as a minister engaging a political assembly. His words by themselves suggested real enthusiasm: this 'is indeed a bold and imaginative conception . . . any Minister who . . . could come and accept it in its entirety might justifiably feel both proud and happy . . . I have made it clear that the Government adopts the scheme and principle.' Anderson was in fact committing the government to universal healthcare and an employment policy. But this was an object lesson in how to alienate the House of Commons. Reading entirely from a script, the Lord President was stiff in manner, humourless, pompous in response to interruptions, and gave the impression that the report was a heavy load to bear, not a gift to be welcomed.

The mood of the Labour Party hardened as a result of this inept display. When its administrative committee met that night, a critical amendment was drawn up to challenge the government's motion, demanding 'early implementation' of the Beveridge Report. Attlee and Morrison struggled to defend their position at a fractious party meeting early the following morning. By the time they went on to attend a session of the War Cabinet at Downing Street, at 12.30, all the evidence suggests they were prepared for a fight. It would be one of the more acrimonious meetings of the war.

Around the table were all the members of the War Cabinet: the Prime Minister, Attlee, Eden, Anderson, Bevin, Morrison and Lyttelton – together with Kingsley Wood, Archibald Sinclair, and James Stuart and William Whiteley, the joint Tory and Labour parliamentary secretaries to the Treasury. This would be Churchill's last major engagement for over a week. He was visibly sick. A heavy cold and sore throat had dogged him for several days, and the night before his temperature had risen sharply. His doctor, Sir Charles Wilson, had diagnosed inflammation on the base of a lung, which a specialist would confirm the following day as pneumonia.

The meeting began with Whiteley's assessment of the mood at Westminster and in the country. '[The] general public is expecting more from the Government than has been offered. The temper of the [Labour Party] meeting this morning was very unsatisfactory.' The chancellor then pitched in, outlining how the various government departments would draw up plans for implementing Beveridge's proposals. With those complete, the government would review them, together with other claims on the Treasury's purse, in the light of the prevailing financial situation. 'That is what every Government does before introducing a bill. What's wrong with that?' Kingsley Wood asked.

Then, as Whiteley later put it to colleagues, Attlee 'fought like a tiger'. '[I] didn't come into this Government on the basis only of dealing with the war,' the Deputy Prime Minister asserted. '[I] always understood that we would concern ourselves with preparations for post-war problems. Moreover, the public are very much interested in their post-war conditions.' Most cuttingly, he continued: 'The mandate of this government is not limited to "blood, tears and sweat". This government must either govern or get through a general election a government that will.'

Churchill hit back, saying that any commitments to Beveridge's report would be 'irresponsible' and a 'peril to financial security . . . We must get our soldiers home and into employment.' Attlee retorted, 'The Labour Party are not irresponsible about this.' To which Churchill responded, 'Everyone wants it; but can you pay for it?'

At this point, Herbert Morrison weighed in. 'If we said "no legislation until after the war" the House of Commons wouldn't have it. [This is] a political crisis; [there is a] solid Labour vote in favour of the motion tabled.' He added, 'If this Government leaves its successor with no legislative preparations for the post-war period we shall be treacherous to the country.'

Later Churchill seemed keen to take the heat out of the meeting. 'My plan was to win the war and keep the government united for the purpose of putting through [afterwards] a programme of four or five projects of social importance. However, if an Appointed Day can be left blank, I wouldn't oppose the introduction of a bill. Though I think it would be unwise – occupying much Parliamentary time and provoking much controversy. So long as we reserve the right to decide at the end of the war when to bring it into operation.'

While this uneasy compromise hung in the air, it fell to Herbert Morrison, on day three, to demonstrate that the coalition had been inspired by Beveridge's plan and intended to respond positively to the public mood. In an accomplished, energetic speech, he told MPs that the Beveridge Report should be 'classed as a great state document that will live long in our social and economic history . . . a landmark, not only in Britain but in the world'. But despite this generous praise, there was still the government line to be maintained: 'We cannot give a date when the Bill will be produced. We are not going to do it.'

When the House divided, Labour's amendment expressing dissatisfaction with the government's approach was defeated by 335 votes to 119. But it had been the biggest total of votes yet cast against the coalition; the protests were led by ninety-seven Labour MPs, including former War Cabinet member Arthur Greenwood, who had commissioned Beveridge's report. David Lloyd George, now eighty years old – and, along with Churchill, the 'father' of the welfare state – came up from his country home, Churt, specifically to vote against this 'watering down' of social reform; he marched into the 'No' lobby with his daughter Megan on his arm.

The vote opened up a serious rift between Labour ministers and the party's backbenchers. Jim Griffiths, MP for Llanelli, who had moved the critical amendment, summed up the views of the party's rank and file. 'The Beveridge Plan has become in the minds of the nation both a symbol and a test . . . a symbol of the kind of Britain we are determined to build when the victory is won . . . Frankly, I am terribly disappointed at the fact that the Government has not risen to the opportunity offered to them this week of giving a real message to the people of this country.'

Regardless of Labour's enthusiasm for Beveridge – some of which he shared, quite a lot of which he did not – Ernest Bevin was furious with the party for what he believed was its disloyalty. He viewed Griffiths' amendment as a vote of censure on him and his fellow Labour ministers, toiling away in government under the necessary strictures of collective responsibility. He even briefly threatened to resign from the War Cabinet, but in the end reserved his sanction for his supposed comrades; for the next year he stopped attending party meetings, viewing his place in the government as the representative of the trade unions alone.

Home Intelligence reports suggested that most people now feared Beveridge's proposals had been put on the back burner. In a series of by-elections in February, Conservative candidates fared badly, with the party's vote down on average 8 per cent in four of the six seats contested. While recovering at Chequers from his bout of pneumonia, Churchill thought more and decided to wrest back the initiative. He began to consider making a speech about the Home Front – his first significant foray into this territory since the start of the war – with the possible title 'A Four-Year Plan for England'. He took soundings from a number of ministers, with 'Prof' Lindemann – ennobled in June 1941 as Lord Cherwell – constantly at his side to evaluate the statistical information. Robert Hudson, Minister of Agriculture, was the first to be summoned to Chequers, followed by Rab Butler, President of the Board of Education.

At a specially convened War Cabinet meeting on Friday, 19 March, the discussion was entirely devoted to the Prime Minister's speech, now to come live from Chequers on the BBC on Sunday evening. Attlee, Bevin, Anderson, Lyttelton and Bracken all helped to add finishing touches. The familiar warnings about the need to win the war first remained, with a pledge 'not to make all kinds of promises and tell all kinds of fairy tales' about social reform in the future. But now Churchill said that he was 'very much attracted' to the idea of a four-year plan, once Germany and Italy had been defeated, which would be the 'right length for the period of transition and reconstruction'. There was also, for the first time, an acknowledgement of 'my friend Sir William Beveridge'. He gave an endorsement of his protégé's new system, which 'should have a leading place in our four-year plan'.

Churchill appeared ready to don once more the mantle of Liberal reformer he had cast off several decades earlier. In the speech's most resounding section, after a reprisal of that familiar phrase 'bringing the magic of averages to the rescue of millions', he proclaimed that 'the time is ripe for another great advance . . . you must rank me and my colleagues as strong partisans of national compulsory insurance for all classes, for all purposes, from the cradle to the grave'. Once again, however, came the warning. 'For the present during the war our rule should be no promises but every preparation . . . all our improvements and expansion must be related to a sound and modernized finance.'

Not everyone listening was swayed by the stirring rhetoric. 'It was a foolish broadcast,' recorded Lord Woolton. 'He said nothing specific . . . he has effectually damped down any public effort at planning for the post-war period.' *The Times* thought very differently. It was a 'proclamation of much vigour and sincerity . . . that may well mark an epoch in the social policy of this country'.

Churchill's intervention had not, however, drawn a line under the matter. Attlee, Morrison and Bevin continued to be frustrated by the lack of legislative initiative, invariably defended by Kingsley Wood and the Prime Minister on the grounds of prudence while uncertainty remained about the post-war financial burdens on the exchequer. In June the three wrote a critical joint memorandum for the War Cabinet entitled 'The Need For Decisions'. They argued that detailed policies should be pursued *now* to find homes and employment for 'all those who had served the country'.

'We refused to make definite decisions on the Beveridge Report without having considered other demands. The principle of refusing to make piecemeal decisions is sound, but the moral cannot possibly be to make no decisions at all . . . we shall be hopelessly impeded if no decisions have been reached on the use of land, development rights, compensation, water supply, the financing of the building programme, reorganization of transport, heat and power.'

The political momentum was now with the party straining for change. A Gallup poll in June showed a twelve-point Labour lead over the Conservatives on voting intentions at the next general election. At the same time, 76 per cent were satisfied with the government's conduct of the war, and a remarkable 93 per cent approved of the performance of the Prime Minister. Those figures demonstrated Churchill's continuing popular appeal, but they also reflected a series of crucial successes on the battlefield in the first half of 1943; at long last, the public had been given a tantalising glimpse – albeit still far on the horizon – of the end of hostilities.

Of all these victories, the monumental triumph of General Georgy Zhukov's Soviet forces over General Friedrich Paulus's Sixth Army at Stalingrad was by far the most significant. This pitiless battle had endured for nearly six months while Hitler pursued the strategic prize of southern Russia and the Caucasian oilfields, as well as the symbolic triumph of crushing the industrial city – a maker of armaments and tractors – that bore the name of the Soviet leader.

Over two million men, 2,300 planes, 24,000 artillery guns and 1,500 tanks had been hurled by the two armies into one of the most brutal battles in history. 'Not a step backwards,' Stalin had ordered, and the final months had seen hand-to-hand combat for the control of individual streets. General Paulus and his staff were captured on Sunday, 31 January; two days later, the remainder of the Sixth Army – 90,000 men – capitulated.

The surrender of German troops at Stalingrad had raised the stakes for Hitler in North Africa. Rommel, after repelling the Allied drive into southern Tunisia at Faid Pass in early February, launched a last, desperate counter-attack at Medenine on 6 March. Montgomery, who had been forewarned by Ultra intercepts, scornfully told Sir Alan

Brooke, 'He is trying to attack me in daylight with tanks, followed by lorried infantry . . . I have 400 tanks . . . good infantry . . . and a great weight of artillery. It is an absolute gift, and the man must be mad.'

The Desert Fox, suffering from jaundice and exhaustion, returned to Germany three days later. His efforts to persuade Hitler to abandon North Africa and instead concentrate on reinforcing Italy had failed: the Führer kept on pouring men into the region. But throughout April the better organised American and British forces pushed back the Axis troops – more than half of them Italian – to a small pocket on the northern tip of Tunisia. At the same time, the RAF and American fighters began to break the back of the Luftwaffe, while the Royal Navy strangled the enemy supply line across the Mediterranean, depriving General von Arnim of armour, fuel and food. The end came on 7 May, when tanks of the British 7th Armoured Division rolled into Tunis, while further North American and Free French troops captured the city of Bizerta. Within a week, the German and Italian forces in Tunisia – nearly 250,000 men – had surrendered. Finally thoughts could turn to Operation *Husky*, the invasion of Sicily, the 'soft belly of the crocodile'.

For millions, however, these checks on the fascists' advance came far too late. By now all the evidence indicated that the Nazis had embarked upon a policy to systematically exterminate Europe's Jews.

William Sampson Cluse was one of the least noticeable MPs in Westminster. The Labour member for South Islington had as colourful a background as anyone in the Commons – orphaned at the age of five, he had taken up part-time work by eleven and been apprenticed to the printing trade at fifteen – but the retired compositor, now sixty-seven years old, made only fleeting contributions to debates, usually restricting himself to questions about the value for money of matters such as cinema ticket prices, the Home Guard's travel expenses, or the productivity of Italian prisoners of war. Cluse was, in the eyes of the *Daily Express*, 'Strube's Little Man', after the character created by the paper's cartoonist, Sydney Strube. With his umbrella, bow tie and bowler hat, the 'Little Man' was a national symbol of the long-suffering 'man in the street', struggling with everyday grumbles and problems, yet always trying to keep his chin up. But on Thursday, 17 December 1942, the unassuming Cluse was to provoke an extraordinary moment, the like of which Lloyd George later told Anthony Eden he 'could not recall in all my years in Parliament'.

Cluse had listened to speeches by Eden and the Liberal MP Jimmy de Rothschild, and had been profoundly moved by them. First the foreign secretary, in tones of deep solemnity, had read out the text of a declaration by a group of twenty-six 'United Nations' – including the 'Big Four' of the USA, Great Britain, the USSR and China – established at the Washington conference of 1942, citing 'reliable reports' of the barbarous and inhuman treatment of the Jews in occupied Europe, where the able-bodied were being worked to death in labour camps, and the infirm 'left to die of exposure and starvation or deliberately massacred in mass executions'. De Rothschild, the MP for Ely, had applauded Eden's 'eloquent and just denunciation' – his voice quivering with emotion and his eyes filled with tears – before moving on to say that His Majesty's Jewish subjects 'will feel that, but for the grace of God, they themselves might be among the victims . . . they might be in those ghettos, in those concentration camps, in those slaughter houses'.

Five other MPs made brief contributions, and then Cluse stood up. In a calm, measured voice, he said simply, 'Is it possible, in your judgment, Mr Speaker, for Members of the House to rise in their places and stand in silence in support of this protest against disgusting barbarism?'

There was no precedent for such a gesture, but the Speaker, Edward Fitzroy, suggested it could be allowed if it was a spontaneous act by the House as a whole. On his word, over two hundred members rose as one and bowed their heads. 'We stood for a few frozen seconds. It was a fine moment, and my back tingled,' wrote Henry 'Chips' Channon.

Evidence that the Germans were committing widespread atrocities in eastern Europe had been reaching the British government, albeit in piecemeal fashion, since mid-1941, when code breakers at Bletchley Park had intercepted reports from the German *Ordnungspolizei* (regular uniformed police) documenting large-scale killings of Jews by *Einsatzgruppen* (SS execution squads) in the newly occupied Soviet territories. Whether prompted by the details contained in those decrypts or by reports from various other sources, Churchill had referred to the growing horror in his broadcast to the world on 24 August, days after he signed the Atlantic Charter with President Roosevelt. Speaking of 'whole districts being exterminated' and 'methodical, merciless butchery', he had concluded that 'We are in the presence of a crime without a name.'

Fragments of information about German atrocities had continued to reach the British government in the closing months of 1941. On 19 November it received a disturbing report from David Kelly, head of the British legation in Switzerland. Relaying news from two valued sources back to the Foreign Office in London, he stated, 'The Pole . . . says that about one and a half million Jews who were living in Eastern [recently Russian] Poland have simply disappeared altogether; nobody knows how or where. The Dutch Minister tells me that fifty per cent of the Dutch Jews sent to camps are now dead.'

The Nazi leadership's intentions had been well enough known, even if never expressed with complete candour. Yet on the day before Kelly filed his report, Alfred Rosenberg, newly appointed Reich Minister for the Occupied Eastern Territories, had held an off-the-record press conference in Berlin. The East, he said, had been 'called to solve a question that has been put to the peoples of Europe; that is, the Jewish Question. About six million Jews live in the East and this question can only be solved by a biological eradication of the whole of Jewry in Europe.'

Two months later, on 20 January 1942, the Wannsee Conference of senior Nazi officials had met in secret and agreed on the implementation of the 'final solution' to this 'Jewish Question': the industrial slaughter of Jews in German-occupied Europe. The first trainloads of Jews had arrived at the biggest of the death camps, Auschwitz in

German-occupied Poland, in late March, and the gas chambers there had claimed their first victims six weeks later. Although the detail and scale of the murders at Auschwitz would not be known for another two years, by the spring of 1942 evidence of the killing programme at the specially designated death camps had already started to emerge. One of the more detailed early reports came in May from Leon Feiner, an underground activist for the Polish Jewish socialist party Bund. Feiner described the extent of the murders, town by town and district by district, and he was among the first to report the use of gas – in mobile vans – as one of the Germans' means of killing large numbers of Jewish prisoners.

General Wladyslaw Sikorski, head of the Polish government-in-exile, broadcast the contents of Feiner's report on the BBC on 24 June. The following day the *Daily Telegraph* carried the story on its principal inside news page, under the bold headline 'GERMANS MURDER 700,000 JEWS IN POLAND,' with an accompanying subtitle 'TRAVELLING GAS CHAMBERS.' Combined with pressure from Jewish groups, the widespread newspaper coverage soon forced the War Cabinet to act. On Thursday, 9 July Brendan Bracken called a press conference at the Ministry of Information, appearing with Stanislaw Mikolajczyk, deputy prime minister of the Polish government-in-exile, and two members of the Polish national council.

'I can assure our Polish friends that those responsible will be tried as murderers, which they are, and these gangsters will be punished with the utmost rigidity of the law,' Bracken told reporters. But his comments received very little attention in the next day's press. Instead the main stories concerned a massive tank battle as the Wehrmacht launched a new offensive against the Red Army on the Kharkov front, and a lull in Rommel's quest to push British forces back to the Egyptian border. With Allied forces struggling on all fronts, it appeared that the plight of the Jews in occupied Europe took second place in the minds of both the government and general public.

Prior to Eden's declaration on 17 December, Bracken's statement had been a rare public acknowledgement by the government of its growing knowledge of the mass round-ups and killings – although even on that occasion he had not specifically referred to the Jews. Churchill remarked on the deportation of Jews from Vichy France in his war report on 8 September, calling it the 'most bestial, the most squalid and the most senseless of all their [German] offences'. Then on 7 October the Lord Chancellor, Lord Simon, made a fleeting reference to the 'ferocity . . . with which the aged, the Jews, the women, the children have been treated', when announcing the establishment of a 'United Nations' Commission for the Investigation of War Crimes.

Although news of atrocities committed against the Jews had steadily accumulated from midsummer onwards, the government was initially reluctant to go public with a wholesale condemnation. The memory of the First World War, when propaganda about German atrocities in Belgium had proved entirely false, had not yet faded from the memory. Civil servants in the Foreign Office were particularly sceptical of the reports, and ministers were guided by their advice.

'At first it was very difficult to assess their accuracy – indeed, so horrible were they that it was hard to believe they could be true,' Anthony Eden remarked later. But by the autumn any doubts in the minds of the War Cabinet were being erased. It was one thing, however, to condemn the slaughter of the Jews – even to promise retribution for the perpetrators at a later date – it was quite another to seek to prevent it. Even before Eden's speech, the War Cabinet had been compelled to consider whether anything at all could be done to stop the killings; more realistic, at this stage, would be the granting of refuge to those Jews who might be able to escape the horrors.

Responsibility for the latter lay primarily in the hands of the home secretary, Herbert Morrison. On 28 October he received a major deputation of church leaders – including the Archbishop of Canterbury, William Temple, and Cardinal Arthur Hinsley, Roman Catholic Archbishop of Westminster – as well as MPs, peers and representatives from the major refugee and relief organisations. They had come to the Home Office specifically to plead the case of 2,000 Jewish children in Vichy France threatened with deportation to Poland, but they had also hoped to gain a more general insight into government policy on refugee immigration.

They left not merely disappointed, but incensed. After listening to an impassioned appeal by Eleanor Rathbone, MP for the Combined English Universities, Morrison reassured her that the government 'did not underestimate the magnitude of the horrors which Vichy were committing or the difficulties of the unfortunate refugees'. But he went on to remind his guests that Britain and the Empire had already made what he regarded as a generous contribution to solving the refugee problem: taking in 50,000 Jews between 1933 and 1939.

He then made his position clear: wartime Britain could offer very little to those seeking sanctuary. She was a small country whose towns and cities had been massively damaged by German bombers. The government had enough problems finding places for the indigenous population to live, with a large influx of American soldiers starting to put an additional strain on what accommodation remained. He also dwelt at some length on a theme he would return to time and time again in the coming months, warning that 'anti-Semitism was just under the pavement and that if we let in large numbers of Jews this would cause an anti-Semitic outburst that we would be incapable of controlling'.

The home secretary had already set out his position to the War Cabinet that autumn: 'There are many foreign persons, both Jews and others, who are anxious to come to this country, and the general policy has been not to admit during war additional refugees to the United Kingdom unless in some quite rare and exceptional cases it can be shown that the admission of the refugee will be directly advantageous to the war effort.' His refusal to budge from the policy might appear uncharitable, but it ought not to be seen specifically as a lack of sympathy for the Jews, or as evidence of anti-Semitism. Morrison's record in this regard suggests otherwise.

In 1935 he had returned from a visit to Palestine convinced by the Zionist cause. In the House of Commons the following year he waxed lyrical about the spirit of the Jewish people, and in particular about the kibbutzim. 'I have seen these Jewish agricultural settlements . . . they are one of the most wonderful demonstrations of the moral capacity of the human race in the whole of the civilized world . . . I have seen these fine young people, coming from various countries where they have been persecuted . . . I have eaten their humble food with them and have witnessed their fine morale.' Three years later, these sentiments led him to oppose a White Paper which contained a limit on Jewish immigration to Palestine of 75,000 over five years, in effect suspending the 1917 Balfour Declaration's commitment to foster an independent Jewish state. 'I ask honourable members to remember the sufferings of these Jewish people all over the world,' he implored. 'I ask them to remember that Palestine, of all places in the world, was certainly the place where they had some right to expect not to suffer or to have restrictions imposed upon them.'

Morrison was also sensitive to the needs of the large Jewish population in his constituency of South Hackney. But memories of how Oswald Mosley, his former colleague in the Labour government of 1929–31, and more recently leader of the British Union of Fascists, had stirred racist tensions in the East End of London remained fresh. Rightly or wrongly, Morrison feared that an influx of Jewish refugees could threaten national cohesion at a time when anti-Semitism still festered just below the surface.

Britain had taken in a sizeable number of Jewish refugees on the eve of war – most notably through the *Kindertransport* programe, which started in December 1938 and gave homes to nearly 10,000 mainly Jewish children from Germany, Austria, Czechoslovakia and Poland. Then there were outstanding acts from individuals like Nicholas Winton, a twenty-nine-year-old stockbroker of German-Jewish origin, who had helped bring out 669 Jewish children from Czechoslovakia by the start of the war.

Within the government's own ranks there were examples of charity towards refugees. In October 1938 Harold Macmillan had provided homes on his Birch Grove estate for forty Czechs, a number of them Jews, who had fled the Nazi occupation of the Sudetenland. In early

1940 Clement Attlee and his wife Violet had invited a twelve-year-old German Jewish boy, Hans-Paul, who had arrived on the *Kindertransport*, to live with them and their four children at their home in Stanmore, Middlesex. Hans-Paul had stayed with the Attlees for six months until the Blitz, when he had been evacuated to the countryside. But worthy gestures from these and many other British families could only make a tiny dent in the massive overall threat to the Jews.

As the calls for action grew louder following Eden's declaration, it fell to Attlee to shore up the government line in the Commons. On 19 January 1943, he explained that although consultations with other governments on how to tackle the growing refugee problem were under way, the fact remained that 'the only real remedy for the consistent Nazi policy of racial and religious persecution lies in an Allied victory; every resource of all the Allied nations must be bent towards this supreme object'. By this point the War Cabinet had set up a new 'committee on the representation and accommodation of Jewish refugees', and the Political Warfare Executive was seeking to make the slaughter of the Jews the central theme of British propaganda in Europe, but the perception beyond Whitehall remained that of inaction.

Meanwhile the group that had come away so dismayed from that 28 October meeting with Herbert Morrison had formed the National Committee for Rescue from Nazi Terror, and was stepping up its lobbying and campaigning. In January 1943 the vice-chairman of the new body, the radical publisher Victor Gollancz, wrote and published a 16,000-word polemical pamphlet which almost rivalled Beveridge in terms of public interest, selling 250,000 copies in three months. Titled *Let My People Go: Some Practical Proposals for Dealing with Hitler's Massacre of the Jews*, it grabbed the attention right from the start:

Of the six million Jews or so who were living in what is at present Nazi-occupied Europe, a high proportion – say between one and two million – have been deliberately murdered by the Nazis and their satellites . . . all this is part, not of war, but of a quite deliberate policy, openly proclaimed, of exterminating the Jewish population of Europe.

This policy . . . is now reaching its climax. *Unless something effective is done*, within a very few months these six million Jews will be dead.

Gollancz acknowledged the 'genuineness and warmth' of Eden's statement in the Commons, but argued that the government's 'policy' of vengeance at a later date 'will not save a single Jewish life'. Instead he urged the 'United Nations' to negotiate with Germany to allow the Jews to emigrate. Jews could be exchanged for similar categories of enemy nationals; the 'doors of Palestine must be opened . . . and the policy of treating Jewish refugees to Palestine as illegal immigrants immediately reversed'; temporary camps should be immediately established in North Africa, Cyprus and Kenya; and an approach should be made to the South American states to see how many refugees they might be willing to receive.

The Church also kept up the pressure for a more 'energetic' policy. Archbishop Temple wrote to Churchill, asking him to pronounce publicly on the right of asylum, while the Archbishop of York, Cyril Garbett, spoke angrily and passionately to a public meeting in Leeds, referring to Nazism as the 'Fourth Horseman of the Apocalypse'. Elsewhere, more secular luminaries spoke up, including Beveridge, who wrote in the *Observer* on 7 February that 'the United Nations . . . should ask Germany, in place of exterminating the Jews, to set them free to leave Germany and lands under German control . . . Hitler might think he saw an advantage in throwing a large mass of people upon the resources of the Allies to use their food and transport, instead of sending the inhabitants of the ghettoes to slaughter houses in Poland and Germany.' At the same time, he urged Britain and all other signatories of the United Nations declaration on 17 December to revise their regulations for the entry of refugees – to 'open the door to safety'.

In fact, there were already signs that the government had been persuaded to soften its position. On 3 February, Oliver Stanley had announced plans for Palestine to take 4,500 refugees from Bulgaria and five hundred children from Rumania and Hungary. Richard Law told his counterpart at the US State Department that 'public opinion in Great Britain has been rising to such a degree that the British Government can no longer remain dead to it . . . [there must be] some reply to the persistent demands to know what it is doing to help the Jews'.

At the War Cabinet meeting at Number 10 on Monday, 22 February, Eden was still searching for an acceptable international strategy. 'There has been no progress with the United States, and no immediate chance of direct conversations . . . We here can do so little that it is difficult to take it up internationally unless the US cooperates.' Morrison replied, 'I could take 1,000 or so as part of a United Nations move – but only to bring the others on [board] . . . My feeling is we've done too much already without guarantees that other nations will help.' The home secretary finished with his familiar mantra, warning of the 'danger of anti-Semitic troubles here'.

At the White House in March the likely extermination of around 70,000 Jews in Bulgaria came up during talks between Eden and Roosevelt. On the idea of an offer of evacuation, the foreign secretary urged caution: 'If we do that, then the Jews of the world will be wanting us to make similar offers in Poland and Germany. Hitler might well take us up on any such proposal and there are simply not enough ships and means of transportation in the world to handle them.' But later the same month, the Joint Emergency Committee on European Jewish Affairs and the Committee for a Jewish Army sponsored major demonstrations in New York's Madison Square Garden, which helped to persuade Roosevelt that something more had to be done. A joint conference with the British on the refugee problem was finally arranged in Bermuda for 19 April.

It commenced just hours after the start of the Warsaw ghetto uprising, a desperate bid by that city's surviving Jews to resist their imminent transportation to the Treblinka death camp. The contrast could not have been starker. 'You go to heaven if you want – I'd rather stay here in Bermuda,' wrote Mark Twain in the nineteenth century. To choose this island paradise as the venue for discussing the starving, tortured and murdered victims of Nazism seemed singularly inappropriate, but Bermuda had been selected as much for its isolation as for its climate. It was a place from where the world's press could be kept away and low expectations maintained.

Leading the British delegation was Richard Law, Eden's junior minister, who was instructed not to discuss increasing the numbers of Jewish refugees allowed into Palestine. When the conference wound up after twelve days it was clear very little had been achieved, even though the final report was kept secret until December. All that was left on the table by 30 April were suggestions for helping escaped Jews to leave Spain – the fortunate few who had already saved themselves – and a vague declaration on the post-war repatriation of refugees. While the delegates sat round tables in the cool of the Mid Ocean Club and Manor Hotel, in Warsaw the Nazis were razing buildings and burning the inhabitants alive. On 21 April a secret transmitter in the ghetto flashed a final four-sentence message to the West; it ended with the words 'save us'.

Despite the secrecy, enough news from the conference filtered out to fill Jewish and humanitarian organisations with despair. One of them took out an advertisement in the *New York Times* under the headline 'TO 5,000,000 JEWS IN THE NAZI DEATH-TRAP BERMUDA WAS A "CRUEL MOCKERY".' On 10 May the War Cabinet discussed Bermuda, and considered tactics for a forthcoming parliamentary debate on refugees planned in the wake of the conference. Eden told his colleagues that agreement had been reached on three main points: neutral countries would take more Jewish refugees, a camp would be set up in North Africa to relieve the pressure on Spain, and the inter-governmental conference on refugees would be revived. The foreign secretary seemed satisfied. '[It was] encouraging that we and the US delegates – which is not easy – got on very well together.'

Morrison – after once more cautioning 'that when you get more than a certain number you begin to generate anti-Semitism' – clearly realised the Home Office could expect a rough ride in the impending debate. What was needed was some manipulation of the speakers. 'Could the Whips get some balanced speeches on the other side – so long as they aren't too extreme? Supporting the middle line?'

The Chief Whip, James Stuart, was able to oblige, and a number of pliant, mainly Conservative, backbenchers lined up to support the government spokesmen, Home Office Minister Osbert Peake and Eden. But they nonetheless took a ferocious battering. Peake unnecessarily infuriated the government's critics by declaring that the 'rate of extermination' was such that 'no measures of rescue or relief, on however large a scale, could be commensurate with the problem'. He also scorned Victor Gollancz's suggestion of a direct offer to the German government, saying, 'There is no indication whatever that any such offer, if made, would meet with anything but a negative response.' ('Make it!' shouted a voice from the opposition benches.)

Eleanor Rathbone countered by telling the House that the 'dreadful' opening speeches of the Bermuda conference had 'breathed the very spirit of defeatism and despair'. She proposed approaching neutral countries like Argentina, and establishing a new Ministry for Refugees, before launching a personal attack on Herbert Morrison. 'Why does he always make us feel in his Parliamentary answers, and even more in our approaches to him privately, as if the whole question of refugees was becoming a bore and an irritation to him and that he was transferring to refugees the dislike which he quite openly feels for ourselves?'

But it was left to Victor Cazalet, Conservative MP for Chippenham, liaison officer between the Polish government-in-exile and the British Cabinet, to produce the most impassioned speech of the day. Although not Jewish himself, Cazalet was of Huguenot descent and a wholehearted advocate of the refugee cause; in particular, he was a vehement champion of a Jewish national home in Palestine. He warned fellow MPs, 'All I can say is that the threat of Goebbels is no idle boast. The Jews are being exterminated today in tens of thousands. The stories of the horrors of the massacres at a camp called Treblinka would put to shame the massacres of Genghis Khan or the suffering of the Albigenses in the past.'

Concluding the debate, Eden attempted to strike a conciliatory note. 'I know some honourable members think that the Government are perhaps insensitive in this matter. I can assure them that we are not . . . I do not know whether ministers can contribute to the problem if they wear their hearts on their sleeves for the jackdaws to peck at, but I believe they will do all that is humanely in their power to help the matter forward, short of any major interference with our war effort.'

The Times, the *Manchester Guardian* and the *Daily Express* all covered the debate at some length the next day – but on pages two, three and four, as all the front pages were taken up by Churchill's speech to Congress. None chose to cover the matter as purely – or even mainly – a Jewish tragedy; it was about 'the refugees' – Jews, Poles, Czechs and other races. *The Times*' leader writer said the 'painful and heartbreaking fact is that the saving hand cannot reach the majority of the refugees, and it is neither a shelving of responsibility nor a salving of conscience to say that the only certain hope for them is allied victory at the earliest moment'. The *Manchester Guardian* thought differently: 'We have had 200,000 prisoners suddenly thrown on us in Tunisia and no one talks of there being no ships and food available. But there is no sign that we are bringing that sort of spirit to the question of the refugees.'

That same month, a young SS doctor named Josef Mengele had arrived at Auschwitz and begun to conduct medical experiments on the inmates, injecting them with phenol, petrol, chloroform and air. And on 25 June the newly built gas chamber opened, bringing the daily capacity at the four new crematoria to 4,756 bodies. The mass slaughter would continue, much of it still unknown to the outside world.

Chapter Eleven

'A grand job to be done for the nation'

19 May to 17 December 1943

On the morning of 19 May 1943 a German submarine from the *Donau 2* 'wolf pack' attacked a large Allied convoy, SC 130, in the north Atlantic Ocean off Cape Farewell, Greenland. The convoy comprised thirty-eight merchant ships and was bound for Liverpool with a cargo of vital supplies for the war effort – wheat, flour, fuel oil, steel, sugar, ammunition and explosives.

U-954 fired off two torpedoes towards the rear of the convoy, narrowly missing their mark. A few weeks earlier such an attack might have left SC 130 feeling isolated and vulnerable. But now its escort ships, equipped with cutting-edge sonar, radar and high-frequency direction finders – and backed in the sea by aircraft carriers and in the sky by long-range B-24 Liberator bombers – had been quick to turn defence into attack. U-954 was forced on the run for several hours.

When the leading pursuers, the frigates HMS *Jed* and HMS *Sennen*, eventually located their quarry, they continuously fired their new 'Hedgehog' mortars into her. These small forward-throwing bombs created a dense explosive field more accurate than the usual depth charges. Some while later a large pool of oil rose to the surface of the water, together with splintered white-painted wood and pieces of blue paper and cloth, evidence that U-954 had been sunk with all hands.

One of the U-boat's crew was its twenty-one-year-old watch officer Lieutenant Peter Donitz, the youngest son of Grand Admiral Karl Donitz, commander-in-chief of the German navy and the man ultimately responsible for the direction and welfare of all his country's submariners. The failure of his son's boat and the rest of the packs that day to make any sort of dent in the Allied convoy – not one ship was lost – persuaded Admiral Donitz that the game was finally up. Five days later, Donitz ordered his submarines to pull out of mid-ocean operations against the convoys and to retreat to waters south-west of the Azores.

Donitz would send the 'wolf packs' back into action in September, better equipped and protected; but they would never pose the same threat again. A crucial moment had passed – far more significant than any individual land battle like El Alamein. No church bells would ring out for this victory, but the British people would not starve, British industry would receive the vital raw materials it needed, and Bomber Command could bank on the fuel to keep up its offensive on Germany. Moreover, Operation *Bolero*, the build-up of American troops and materiel for the planned cross-Channel invasion, would continue unimpeded.

Nine days later the First Lord of the Admiralty stepped up to the dispatch box in the House of Commons and signalled the War Cabinet's belief that this was the beginning of the end of the Battle of the Atlantic. A.V. Alexander did not couch his statement on the U-boat war in such climactic terms, but the evidence he presented and his barely disguised sense of relief spoke volumes.

May was the best month of 'kills' so far in the war, he told MPs (the actual figure, which he could not publicly disclose, was forty-six), and he attributed the improved situation to the 'growing size of our escort forces – both ships and aircraft – and the growing deadliness of our weapons and devices'. He reported that Allied bombing of the U-boat construction yards in Germany and of their operational bases in the Bay of Biscay was now reaping rewards. He denounced Hitler's propagandists as 'quite wrong' in ascribing the low rate of Allied losses in April to the small number of ships at sea; instead, Alexander insisted, imports of food and munitions in that month had been the highest since the beginning of 1942.

What Alexander could not say was that while better technology, more accurate bombs, continuous long-range air cover, and enhanced convoy escorts had all been vital in turning the tide, intelligence had been perhaps the crucial factor. After ten barren months, a raid on U-559 by the British destroyer HMS *Petard* in October 1942 had recovered valuable documents, enabling Bletchley Park to break Enigma's latest and more complicated 'Triton' system (dubbed 'Shark' by the British).

This moment of triumph for Alexander and the Admiralty had been a long and difficult time in coming. For months they had been outvoted on one of the central arguments of the war: whether to use bomber aircraft in offensive mode against Germany, or in a defensive role to protect shipping in the Atlantic. It had always been an unequal contest, with Churchill, 'Prof' Lindemann, Sir Archibald Sinclair and Air Chief Marshals Sir Charles Portal and Sir Arthur Harris (commander-in-chief Bomber Command) on one side, and on the other Alexander, First Sea Lord Admiral Sir Dudley Pound and Air Chief Marshal Sir Phillip Joubert de la Ferte, commander-in-chief of Coastal Command. Churchill's dictum had always been, 'The Navy can lose us the war, but only the Air Force can win it.' Only after the Casablanca conference, at which the combined chiefs of staff had asserted that 'the defeat of the U-boat must remain a first charge on the resources of the United Nations', had the defence of trade taken priority.

With the war at sea now being demonstrably won, the military focus could shift in earnest to the land, and to Operation *Husky*, the invasion of Sicily. At dawn on 10 July, some 2,700 ships and landing craft disgorged 180,000 men along with hundreds of vehicles along the 105-mile stretch of coastline between the Gulf of Gela and the Gulf of Noto. In a robust counter-attack, German armoured forces almost drove the Americans back into the sea at Gela. Nevertheless, within forty-eight hours, all the beachheads had been secured. By 17 August enemy resistance in Sicily had been totally crushed; though not before 100,000 German and Italian troops, and a great deal of military equipment, had been successfully transferred to the mainland. The fight up the Italian peninsula would be considerably more difficult.

With supplies of food and raw materials across the Atlantic now uninterrupted, the principal preoccupation on the Home Front became the coal crisis. On 20 July Ernest Bevin had to convince a silent, suspicious gathering of miners in a conference hall in Blackpool that their already beleaguered industry was in need of immediate and drastic change.

Much of the labour minister's speech dealt with the general progress of the war and the reforms planned for social services after the cessation of hostilities. Eventually Bevin turned to the mining industry, and, mopping his forehead with a handkerchief – whether because of the heat of the summer's day, or the anxiety of the moment – sought to explain that every piece of territory the Army took in Italy resulted in fresh calls on the scanty reserves of the coal industry, and that if the continent was invaded successfully, the demand would go up by millions of tons. He drew much laughter when he quipped about the land campaign, 'I cannot mention the other places to which we shall have to go, because the tourist programme is not yet out.'

He then came to the crux of the matter. 'At the end of this coal year there won't be enough men and boys in the industry to carry it on. It is a serious problem. It is the one great difficulty in our war effort. I am up against it . . . I shall have to resort to some desperate remedies during the coming year.' The drastic solution he proposed was to compulsorily recruit between 30,000 and 60,000 youths aged sixteen to eighteen into the mines.

Miners' leaders were stunned by Bevin's proposal; some wondered whether he had Cabinet approval or if he was acting on his own initiative. Ebenezer Edwards, general secretary of the Miners' Federation, felt the plan would fail in its main objective of boosting productivity in the short term. He was against forcing youngsters into the pits unless they were well guarded against accidents and given 'a fair, honest and just deal'. Joe Hall, president of the Yorkshire mineworkers' association, was similarly disparaging: 'My boy did not go down the mines because my experience in the mines tells me conditions have not improved. They are getting worse.'

At the start of the war, coal had been the one raw material which everyone in Britain had assumed would always be abundant. The first inkling that something was amiss came on 28 May 1941 when David Grenfell, secretary of mines and himself a former south Wales pitman, told an astonished House of Commons that the country was facing a severe shortage – just at the time when the power stations, shipyards and steel mills were crying out for more coal. Grenfell revealed to MPs that in the winter just gone he had been 'very worried for weeks' about the coal supply to the population of London: 'I was afraid that we had come to the end, and would find that disaster had overtaken us in this large centre of population here.'

The crisis had begun after the German advances of May and June 1940 closed off important export markets. Nearly a hundred pits shut overnight and 34,000 miners were made idle, mainly in south Wales and the north-east. In order to find them work, Bevin was persuaded in the autumn of 1940 – contrary to Grenfell's advice – to allow men to leave the pits, either to join the forces or to seek alternative employment in the growing munitions and construction factories. Most, if not all, of the coal shortage of 1943 could be traced back to this particular decision. In the year to April 1941 the work force had dropped from 764,000 to 690,000. Bevin had tried all manner of means to halt the exodus, including, in spring 1941, using the Essential Work Order, under which – in return for a guaranteed week and an extra shilling per shift – miners had been prevented from leaving the industry and their employers from dismissing them.

In June 1941 Bevin broadcast an appeal for 50,000 ex-miners to return to the pits. He couched his plea in strong language: 'This

Government has played straight with the miners and the mining industry, and the nation is entitled to a square deal from you in return. If any man stays away from his job other than for genuine and unavoidable cause, he is acting criminally against his fellow men, the nation and the forces. He is helping Hitler, and we cannot allow it to continue.'

Despite this stern exhortation only a trickle returned, yet still the government refused to recall miners, even temporarily, from the services. To many in the major mining areas this appeared short-sighted: 'Those responsible for the direction of our war effort must ask themselves continually whether a proportion of the millions of men now being trained in the use of arms would not be better employed in making arms for their comrades,' the Yorkshire Post argued on 24 June.

Then in July 1941 Bevin ordered the registration of all men with mining experience (since 1935) who had taken up other employment. This added 30,000 more to the workforce, but by April 1942, when Sir John Anderson, Lord President of the Council, submitted a paper on coal production to the War Cabinet, the labour force was still fifteen thousand short of the figure needed to raise the weekly production of coal to 4.35 million tons for the coming year.

A Cabinet committee, once more chaired by Anderson, was then set up to consider the essential question of how to increase coal output. What emerged eventually from its deliberations, in June 1942, was a White Paper proposing a number of changes to the management of the pits that it was hoped would spur greater production. Most significant was the institution of a new system of 'dual control': the government would exercise a greater say through powerful regional controllers, while the colliery owners were still responsible for the finances of the mines.

At work at the same time as Anderson's committee had been the Board of Investigation into Wages and Machinery of the Coalmining Industry, which had taken just two weeks to bring forward its proposals: a flat-rate increase in pay of 2s 6d a shift; an output bonus; and a national minimum wage of 83s a week for underground workers and 78s for those above ground. The board was chaired by Lord Wilfred Greene, Master of the Rolls, but its report's principal architect was a bright, twenty-six-year-old statistician, J.H. (Harold) Wilson, who had previously worked with Beveridge but was now a temporary civil servant in the mines department. His recommendations were adopted immediately and in full.

The final administrative change in the government's attempt to revive the industry had come on 12 June with the creation of a new Ministry of Fuel, Light and Power, under the control of Gwilym Lloyd George. But the Greene/Wilson plan produced the more immediate results. At a stroke it raised the miners from fifty-fourth to twenty-third in the league table of industrial earners, and thus did more than anything else to stem the increasing number of strikes in the coalfields. With Bevin's ongoing efforts to transfer men back to the pits, it also helped to raise the labour force to 711,000 by the end of 1942.

Unfortunately, the revival was short-lived. Plans to concentrate manpower in the most productive mines and seams largely failed; men were reluctant to move even relatively short distances from their villages to work in different pits. And absenteeism among miners was rife, due to a combination of factors, including pay differentials, continuing resentment of the mine owners, and a general weariness at the increasing demands placed upon them after four years of war.

In the folklore of the British working class, the miners had always commanded a special place. For writers like George Orwell, the powerful imagery of their dark, hot underground existence was irresistible. Modern civilisation had been founded on coal and the miner was 'a sort of caryatid upon whose shoulders nearly everything that is not grimy is supported . . . all of us *really* owe the comparative decency of our lives to the poor drudges underground, blackened to the eyes, with their throats full of coal dust, driving their shovels forward with arms and belly muscles of steel'. But for the Minister of Labour, struggling to deal with the miners' increasing propensity to strike, there was precious little romance.

In January 1942 Bevin decided to prosecute over a thousand pitmen at Betteshanger Colliery in Kent under Order 1305 (which banned strikes and lockouts in wartime) after they had struck for nineteen days over the level of allowances for working difficult seams. Three local union officials were jailed and the rest of the workforce hit with fines of £1 or £3, most of which were never paid. Now, in the late summer and early autumn of 1943, further trouble was brewing in the coalfields of Scotland, Wales and the Midlands.

In the biggest industrial action in the coalfields, 15,000 miners in Nottinghamshire stopped work after an eighteen-year-old surface worker, Sidney Page, was jailed for refusing to work underground. At the Penrhiwceiber colliery, Mountain Ash, in Glamorgan, 4,600 men walked out after the alleged non-payment of the minimum wage to three miners.

But it was not just the pits – strike action dogged all quarters of industry in August and September. Liverpool dockers walked out after refusing to work overtime, Clydeside shipwrights struck over wages, and electricians and engineers from the Vickers-Armstrong shipyard in Barrow-in-Furness were also in dispute over a long-deferred pay increase. Bevin, the self-styled representative of the trade unions, spoke darkly of 'anti-war people' in the labour movement 'kicking over the traces in wartime, when people are fighting for their lives'.

Workers' strikes were almost always over the bread and butter issues of pay and conditions – but the elephant in the room in the coal industry was nationalisation. Miners' leaders expected Labour ministers to deliver it sooner rather than later, and the radical feeling stirred by Beveridge encouraged them to revive their interest.

At the War Cabinet meeting on 8 October, the new minister Gwilym Lloyd George pinned his colours firmly to the mast of nationalisation. His memorandum stated that 'dual control' between the government and colliery owners had not improved the efficiency of the nation's mines. 'I am convinced that more coal can be got with the present manpower, provided that the limitations of the present organization and in the practical use of my powers are removed.' But the issue was too politically explosive, and the assembled ministers swiftly sidestepped it. Indeed, if nationalisation was ever considered a viable solution to the crisis, it was killed stone dead five days later when the Prime Minister rounded off a special two-day debate on mining in the Commons.

'The principle that we work on is "Everything for the war, whether controversial or not, and nothing controversial that is not bona fide needed for the war",' Churchill declared. 'It would raise a lot of argument, [a] lot of difference of opinion, and it would be a tremendous business to nationalize the coal mines . . .'

In the same debate Gwilym Lloyd George admitted that a change of policy was now urgently needed: 'It is clear that voluntary recruitment will not of itself produce the numbers required, and it will now be necessary to call up men for the coalmines in the same way as they are called up for the Armed Forces.'

Conscription to the pits had finally, inevitably, come to pass. But before it was enforced, Bevin made a final plea, this time specifically to the nation's schoolboys. In a radio broadcast to schools on 12 November he urged sixth-formers to volunteer for the mines. 'There's a grand job to be done for the nation . . . none of you would funk a fight with the enemy, and I do not believe it will be said of any of you boys that you failed to respond to the call for coal upon which victory so much depends.'

'We were deeply impressed by Bevin's earnest, if unpolished manner, but none of us responded,' recalled Norman Longmate, then aged seventeen and a pupil at Christ's Hospital, an independent boarding school in West Sussex. And it appears the appeal met with a similarly unenthusiastic response in other schools. Bevin had, however, finished with pleading. Compulsion was the only course left to him, and he would shortly impose one of the more remarkable recruiting schemes in British labour history.

The Chancellor of the Exchequer, Sir Kingsley Wood, had died suddenly, aged sixty-two, in the early hours of Tuesday, 21 September.

His fatal heart attack had denied him the opportunity to introduce the most innovative and important proposal drawn up during his time at the Treasury. Later that day, he had been due to tell MPs about his new PAYE (Pay As You Earn) scheme, a compulsory deduction of income tax from current pay packets – rather than retrospectively – that would cover all the nation's employees and guarantee more money for the exchequer. It would prove to be his enduring legacy.

The bespectacled Wood had been short – just five feet tall – plump, cherubic and curly-haired, with a thin, high speaking voice. His appearance, together with a certain geniality and conviviality, had inevitably resulted in him being described as 'Pickwickian'. But despite his high position in the government, he had made little impact on the public, and his sudden death barely made it to the front pages of most newspapers, which were more concerned with Churchill's war update in the Commons, the sacking of Naples and the Red Army's successful summer offensive.

Wood had built a reputation in Whitehall in the 1930s as a highly capable administrator, reviving the Post Office and expanding the telephone service, as well as introducing an effective slum clearance programme when Minister of Health and Housing. While at the Air Ministry, from 1938 to 1940, he had also launched the valuable Empire Training Scheme, although dispute remained over whether he had satisfactorily quickened the pace of aircraft production in time for war.

In peacetime the Treasury would have been the dominant department in Whitehall. But since the onset of hostilities the influence of the chancellor had been diminished. Even in economic policy Wood had been far from supreme, as this was now co-ordinated by the Lord President's Committee, currently chaired by Sir John Anderson. And though Wood had become a member of the War Cabinet in October 1940, he had been removed from it in February 1942.

Yet within the more limited confines of his role, Wood's impact had been impressive. Not only had he kept the economy stable, he had successfully generated the finance needed for the war effort, aided by an outstanding group of advisers including John Maynard Keynes and Lord Catto, a future governor of the Bank of England. He had also been Churchill's ideological bedfellow in the Cabinet, and an important barometer of feeling within the Conservative Party.

Now that 'Little Joe' – as Bracken and Beaverbrook had conde-
cendingly called him – was gone, a limited but important reshuffle
was necessary. Some, like Leo Amery, wondered whether 'the Labour
wing of the coalition may possibly wish to press their claims to the
vacancy'; one or two newspapers tipped Herbert Morrison for the
post. But in the end, Churchill went for the logical, safe option of Sir
John Anderson, with Attlee replacing him as Lord President, Lord
Cranborne assuming Attlee's role as Dominions secretary, and Richard
Law, Britain's representative at the Bermuda conference, receiving a
promotion to minister of state at the Foreign Office.

The controversial appointment was not the new chancellor, but
the return of Lord Beaverbrook, back in the Cabinet – although not
the War Cabinet – in the free role of Lord Privy Seal. Churchill had
been petitioning him to rejoin the government for many months, but
Beaverbrook had repeatedly turned the Prime Minister down: he was
determined to preserve his independence and continue pressing for an
immediate second front.

Three days after Wood's death, the Beaver had been preparing to
table a hostile motion on this very subject in the House of Lords; his
fear was that preparations for the cross-Channel invasion had stalled
during Churchill's recent meeting with Roosevelt in Quebec. Upon
receiving word of his old friend's move, the Prime Minister summoned
him to Downing Street the evening before the debate. Beaverbrook,
having received a clear assurance that the operation would go ahead
the following spring, agreed to withdraw the motion. Churchill then
persuaded him, finally, to rejoin the government; as ever he valued his
companionship, as well as his intuitive advice.

The Prime Minister was just beginning to plan for a big summit
meeting towards the end of the year at which he, Roosevelt and Stalin
would co-ordinate military strategy against Germany and Japan, and
start to make decisions about the post-war order in Europe. But the
Labour ministers in the coalition were determined to drag his focus
back to Britain's future, and the task of realising the spirit – and some
of the letter – of the Beveridge Report. One piece of draft legislation

was already making particularly good progress through the Cabine
committees: an Education Bill, designed by Rab Butler with the aid o
his energetic and highly capable junior Labour minister James Chute
Ede, a former school teacher.

Forty-year-old Richard Austen Butler (known to all as 'Rab') ha
travelled a long distance since May 1940. Then, as Halifax's under
secretary at the Foreign Office and closely associated with Chamberlain
policy of appeasement, he was viewed with suspicion by Churchill
supporters. But Churchill himself had come to recognise the youn
minister's administrative and political flair, while Butler's disdain o
the man he had called the 'greatest adventurer' turned to admiratio
on viewing his direction of the war. On appointing him President o
the Board of Education in July 1941, Churchill told Butler, 'I thin
you can leave your mark there.'

Butler's visit to Chequers in March had paved the way for th
Education Bill, and Churchill had included some lyrical passage
on schooling in his 'Four-Year Plan' speech a week later, asserting, '
hope our education will become broader and more liberal.' Butler an
Chuter Ede's draft bill would certainly achieve that: it advocated fre
secondary education for all, raising the school leaving age to fifteen
the creation of three different types of secondary school, and bringin
church schools into the national sector. Its promise was greater socia
mobility, and although Churchill grumbled that the measures wer
'leftish', he also viewed them as a great success.

Attlee, Bevin and Morrison wholeheartedly backed Butler's bil
Bevin had been especially engaged, offering suggestions on furthe
education to Chuter Ede, and proving a powerful supporter of th
bill in Cabinet. But the lack of progress in the contentious areas o
health, social insurance and planning was threatening to destabilis
the coalition.

On the evening of 14 October, Attlee arrived at the War Cabine
ready for battle. His resolute approach, aided by Bevin and Morrisor
led to a 'frightful row, and loud explosions from the prime minister
Churchill would say later he had been 'jostled and beaten up b

he deputy prime minister'. On the table was the critical document
ubmitted by the three Labour ministers back in June, 'The Need for
Decisions', together with a response from the late chancellor, and a
urther riposte from the Labour trio. At stake was the whole Home
ront strategy.

Attlee, first to speak, reiterated his concern that 'the formulation
f policy could not await the end of war; if decisions had not been
aken and preparatory action put in hand, the end of the war would
nd us unprepared'. Morrison backed him up, saying that 'much of
he preparatory work was now reaching a point at which decisions by
he War Cabinet were required . . . in the international field, we had
lready made a start in the discussion of post-war economic policy.
Could we not make similar progress on domestic issues?'

Churchill took what he thought was a humorous swipe at the title
f the paper. '"Need for Decisions"! Was it [the Cabinet] not always
aking decisions? A decision had been taken to have [a] Second Front.'
n the words of Rab Butler, he then proceeded to test out the Labour
ninisters 'to see if they were likely to break away'. 'There were obvious
bjections to formulating post-war policies, and still more to giving
ffect to them in legislation, if there were no assurance of the continued
o-operation of the Labour ministers after the war,' Churchill said.
he 'grimmest climax' of the conflict was approaching, he warned, and
e 'found the greatest difficulty in giving that close attention . . . to
he great social changes which were involved in the discussion of post-
var policy.'

Bevin then weighed in, suggesting there was room for compromise.
or example, he was prepared to reach agreement on questions about
griculture –'although not fully in accord with his view' – provided
 proper plan was agreed for basic services like coal, electricity and
he water supply, which 'ought to be brought under some form of
ational control'. The Education Bill was proof, he said, that it was
ot impossible to make policy on thorny issues.

The central argument shuttled back and forth, Attlee and Morrison
ressing the case for action and Churchill responding, with his natural

allies, Beaverbrook and Cherwell, largely silent. Sir John Anderson sai
progress had been made on the Beveridge Report and that he hope
shortly to be in a position to report further. At that point, Churchi
cut off Anderson, who looked set to embark on a long speech, sayin
he had to dine with the King.

On 21 October, the same group reassembled, this time joine
by Sir Archibald Sinclair and Hugh Dalton. Churchill submitted
memorandum to the meeting, and it showed that the 'going ove
he had received the previous week had forced a rethink. He wa
now prepared to concede that 'any decisions which are needed fo
the supreme objects of FOOD and EMPLOYMENT in the year
immediately after the war must be taken now, whether they involv
legislation and whether they are controversial or not'. The coalitio
should begin work on schemes for the 'transition' period, which h
proposed to define as either two years from the defeat of Germany c
four years from 1 January 1944, whichever ended sooner.

The night before, the King had come to dinner at the Annexe, wit
Attlee, Bevin, Morrison, Anderson and others in attendance. Fuelle
by a rehoboam of champagne, the talk had flowed well, alternatin
'between light badinage and intense seriousness'. It had almost certainl
helped settle the mood for the following day. Indeed, with Churchill
concessions already in place, the War Cabinet of 21 October was a
harmonious as its predecessor had been fractious. Labour ministers wer
startled, yet heartened, by Churchill's about-turn. 'Very great credit i
due to Attlee and, in a lesser degree, to Morrison for having brough
about this remarkable change in the PM's attitude,' wrote Dalton. Th
Prime Minister even warmed to the idea of post-war planning at th
meeting, laying out in 'dramatic detail' the idea of a great, thousand
page tome on the project – *The Book of the Transition* – and mooting
week of debates in the Commons, during which each minister woul
expound his own departmental plan.

Churchill's apparent determination to shape the Home Front agend
remained in evidence a week later when he invited Lord Woolton t
lunch at Downing Street. Following the two War Cabinet meeting

e had taken the decision to appoint a Minister of Reconstruction, together with a new Cabinet committee on the same subject; he offered his successful Minister of Food the job.

'He seemed to be surprised – and a little grumpy – that I didn't just jump at his offer,' Woolton recorded. 'He asked me if I had any ideas as to how it would work out under a new ministry; quite obviously he has not.' The Food Minister went away to ponder the offer. His wife Maud left him in no doubt about what she thought of the role: all the experience you have had in life has been just a preparation for this, hasn't it, so why should you hesitate?' Meanwhile Churchill's pursuit of his other option – inevitably, Beaverbrook – was brought to an abrupt end by Attlee. The Deputy Prime Minister told Dalton that he and Churchill had had 'quite a row, as we usually do, but that the result was that Beaverbrook is not to have anything to do with post-war'. A few days later, Woolton finally agreed to take on the position.

The newspaper reaction on 12 November left him in no doubt about the enormity of his task. 'WOOLTON TO PLAN NEW BRITAIN' was the Daily Mirror's front-page headline. He was 'the man on whose decisions the future of the country will depend . . . and because of the sweeping nature of his powers he will rank second only to the Prime Minister'.

'People are expecting the new heaven and the new earth . . . it terrifies me to know that I'm to be the provider of it,' Woolton wrote in his diary that night. Elsewhere, Bevin was concerned that the new minister would usurp some of his powers, and demanded – and received reassurance from Churchill that this was not the case. But Woolton's fellow welfare worker from before the First World War, Clement Attlee, was satisfied. Woolton had a good grasp of social needs and a sense of social purpose; this vital job was in the hands of someone the Deputy Prime Minister could trust.

Churchill was in buoyant mood as the third plenary session of the Teheran conference ended on the evening of 30 November. After three amicable and fruitful days with Stalin and Roosevelt, he had

successfully concluded negotiations on the grand strategy for the nex
six months of the war. They had addressed speeding up the Allie
advance to Rome, the possible wooing of Turkey, and better suppor
for Yugoslavia, but all of these were as nothing compared to the mai
agreement that *Overlord*, the American and British cross-Channe
invasion of Europe via northern France, would be launched in May
with a 'supporting operation' against the south of the country.

At the same time as Allied troops came ashore, the Red Army woul
launch a large-scale offensive to prevent any movement of Germa
forces from the east. And in the meantime – at the Russian leader
initiative – it was agreed that the military chiefs of all three power
should collaborate on joint cover and misdirection schemes: dumm
tanks, planes and airfields, and radio deception. 'Truth deserved
bodyguard of lies,' Churchill commented, quoting a phrase of Stalin'
– a Russian proverb – back at him.

It was an evening to celebrate, not least because it was the Prim
Minister's sixty-ninth birthday. But Churchill's buoyant mood evapo
rated only minutes later, when, back in his bedroom, he picked up
telegram from Clement Attlee. 'Read that,' he ordered Lord Moran, hi
doctor. 'The Government may go out over Mosley. Bevin is kicking.'

Attlee's telegram was a report of a dangerous rift in the War Cabine
with the barely disguised animosity between Bevin and Morrison no
well and truly on the surface. The home secretary's deeply controver
sial decision, announced to the War Cabinet two weeks earlier, t
release the British Fascist leader Sir Oswald Mosley from Holloway
prison on medical grounds, had provoked a storm of political and publi
protest. Mosley and his wife Diana had been interned in May 194
under Defence Regulation 18b, which allowed the home secretary t
detain anyone he believed to be 'of hostile origin or associations' an
committing acts 'prejudicial to the public safety'. A campaign for th
couple's freedom by a host of their aristocratic friends, led by Mosley
former mistress Lady Alexandra 'Baba' Metcalfe, who had sent a serie
of pleading letters to Churchill, had finally borne fruit when a confer
ence of doctors had agreed that Mosley's phlebitis was worsening, an

that there was a risk of serious complications, even danger to his life. The quandary was whether to free this leading Fascist, a sympathiser with Hitler and Mussolini, or whether to risk having a British citizen die in prison without trial,' Morrison reflected later. 'Apart from such a blot on history going back to Magna Carta, martyrdom is a very profound source of strength.'

After winning the War Cabinet's approval, on 17 November, for Mosley's release – and that of Lady Diana, on 'humanitarian grounds' – Morrison had sent a telegram to Churchill, then en route to Malta aboard the battleship HMS *Renown*. 'I highly approve your action,' came back the reply. But there had been one, serious opponent of the move: Bevin had asked for his dissent to be placed on record, saying Mosley's release 'would weaken morale and would have an unfortunate effect on negotiations and discussions in the industrial field'. Indeed, his union, the Transport and General Workers, would be at the forefront of the opposition to Morrison in the coming days.

Now, on the eve of a major parliamentary debate on the decision, it seemed Bevin was prepared to take the matter further and imperil the coalition itself. Attlee's telegram reported that the labour minister had been 'strongly critical of Morrison's action [during that day's War Cabinet meeting] and said that if there was a division he would be unable to vote with the Government and might have to resign'.

Churchill made little effort to disguise his irritation. 'We have had a grand day here, and relations between Britain, the United States and Europe have never been so cordial,' he replied. 'All war plans are agreed and concerted. Judge our astonishment to receive your telegram.' Attlee's worrying communiqué was swiftly followed by a short telegram from Lord Cherwell. 'You will have heard from Attlee about trouble in cabinet,' he wrote. 'A personal wire from you to Bevin before the division tomorrow would be helpful.'

There was still much to be done during the final days in Teheran, with tricky issues such as Poland's frontiers, Stalin's demands for compensation from Finland, and the fate of a conquered Germany yet to be resolved. Two telegrams Churchill proposed to send to Bevin and

Attlee betrayed his mounting fury at the domestic distraction thrust upon him. For Bevin he drafted the most intemperate note: 'You are the last man whom I thought would stab me in the back like this at a time when I am absent from public duty. Be assured I shall fight this matter in the House and the country with all the life and strength I possess. It is impossible for me to break up this conference in the next two critical days. You have been my loyal colleague in the sternest times, but if you bring about a series of events which lead the Labour Party to leave the Cabinet I shall still do my best to continue the war effort, and though it will be grief to me on personal grounds to part from you, my duty is plain.'

To Attlee, he was scarcely less immoderate. 'If the Labour ministers choose to leave the Government on what I can only regard as a frivolous pretext of this kind and I am entrusted by the King with the duty of carrying on the war, I shall certainly not flinch from it. I am sure that the moral sense of the British nation and their respect for humanity and fair play, even to the most unpopular figures, will vindicate itself with every step in this controversy.'

In the event, Churchill thought better of sending either telegram. Instead, in the privacy of his rooms at the legation in Teheran, he vented his frustrations upon, among others, Lord Moran. 'I said he could not govern England without Labour. It would impair unity and interfere with production. At this he shouted he could get on quite well without them. He would not get rid of them, but they could go if they wanted.'

Back in London, Brendan Bracken was given the vital task of pacifying Bevin. Bracken composed a skilful letter – a mix of flattery, exhortation and not a little blackmail – in which he told Bevin that Churchill looked upon him as the 'embodiment of loyalty and good sense. In the darkest days of the war you have always been a rock of strength to him.' But, he warned, 'If you were to publicly dissociate yourself from your colleagues in the Cabinet and fulfil your intention to resign from the Government you would add a great deal to Churchill's burdens, and the Government in the midst of some of the worst problems of the war and of reconstruction would be most seriously weakened.'

Finally, there was a salutary word on the possible consequences of his resignation. 'Most of his colleagues share the public's view that Churchill is a man of limitless physical strength and that he can cast aside the many worries which are his daily lot. I, who am more in touch with him than most persons, wish I could share this optimistic view. The facts are otherwise. He needs all the encouragement which he can get from his colleagues, and the more worries there can be kept away from him the better for his health.'

Bracken's letter did the trick. Bevin visited him in the morning and was persuaded not to move against the government. John Martin, Churchill's principal private secretary, acknowledged that Bracken had done 'most valiant work'. At the end of a gruelling all-day Commons debate, an amendment from the Labour MP Reverend George Woods (Finsbury), stating that Mosley's release would 'retard the war effort and lead to misunderstanding at home and abroad', was defeated by 327 votes to 62. Fifty-one Labour MPs voted for the amendment, a major blow to Morrison, but Bevin was not one of them. The coalition had survived.

Morrison and Churchill, despite the latter's negotiations in Cairo and Teheran, had kept in touch daily throughout the crisis, the home secretary drawing strength from the Prime Minister's unequivocal backing and shrewd advice. One curious suggestion the home secretary put to the Prime Minister did not, however, meet with his approval. 'If U.J ["Uncle Joe", i.e. Stalin] could be persuaded to say, for publication directly or indirectly, that while he does not profess to be an authority on British psychology, he is mystified by all the fuss about this unimportant individual under house arrest, and that he thought we were fighting the real big Fascists, it would be most valuable. I should be grateful if you would see what you can do with him. It would blow the agitation clean out of the water.' Churchill's reply was understandably dismissive: 'I am sure we shall not need to go to Stalin for help in defending the principles of British liberty and humanity.'

Lord Beaverbrook had, as ever, acted as Churchill's eyes and ears on the affair. He now worried that the major fallout from Mosley's release would escalate the simmering feud between the two Labour ministers. 'Everything should be done to hold the domestic situation in check until you return because the quarrel between Bevin and Morrison is continuing on other issues and sometimes appears to be serious. Certainly it is irreconcilable by anyone but yourself.'

The story told was that during a conversation between Labour MPs someone had remarked that Morrison was his own worst enemy, to which Bevin was purported to have snarled, 'Not while I'm alive, he ain't!' This may have been apocryphal, but it was essentially true. In formal situations the two men observed basic courtesies, addressing each other in committee as 'Ernest' and 'Herbert', but in War Cabinet Bevin would on occasion mutter and grumble audibly at Morrison's contributions, while in the bars and tea rooms of Westminster he would tell close colleagues 'to watch 'Erbert – and if you find the little bugger getting up to any of his tricks you tell me'.

They were like two medieval barons closely guarding their fief-doms: Bevin the trade unions, and Morrison the London Labour Party. The feud stretched back to the late 1920s when Morrison, then Minister of Transport under Ramsay MacDonald, had introduced the London Passenger Transport Bill, reorganising the city's buses, underground system and trams and bringing them under central control. For Morrison, the board running the capital's transport had to be independent and impartial, made up of executives with proven experience in 'industry, commerce or finance, or in the conduct of public affairs'. By contrast, Bevin believed in direct worker representation, and had called for a minimum number of trade unionists on the new London Transport Board.

A direct appeal to MacDonald had won Bevin some minor concessions, but it was Morrison's principle that had prevailed. In the process, the dispute had revealed the essential and enduring political difference between the two: Bevin was principally concerned for the status and welfare of the working class – 'his' people – while Morrison, the party creature, eschewed sectional interests and strove to build middle-class support for Labour wherever he could.

Political enmities are often more about character than ideology, however, and the rancour between the two was profoundly personal. Bevin was an intuitive, emotional man and would not be shaken from his prejudices once they were formed. He thought Morrison untrustworthy, 'a slick wire-puller', a political conjurer. For his part, Morrison had come to regard Bevin as a jealous bully, given to sarcasm and sneering, and always ready to use his trade union muscle to thwart his rival's ambitions.

Since joining Churchill's war ministry, they had by and large sublimated their loathing in the national interest. Skilfully managed by Attlee, they had joined forces to harry Churchill over the pace of reform. But the Mosley affair had revived all the old tensions. 'I went to the meeting of the civil defence committee with Willink . . . on the way he commented on Morrison's sullen behaviour,' Chuter Ede recorded in late December. 'I said I thought he suspected Bevin of engineering the trade union attack on him over the Mosley release.' Attlee would have more conciliatory work to do in the coming weeks.

The day after the vote on Mosley's release, Bevin – having exhausted all other methods – announced his conscription scheme for the coalfields. He told the Commons a nationwide ballot would be held of all men under the age of twenty-five, with the aim of recruiting 30,000 by 30 April 1944. Other than those who were medically unfit, the only exemptions would be for submarine mechanics, those with flying duties in the RAF or Fleet Air Arm, and a shortlist of 'highly skilled occupations'.

His cantankerous mood was hardly improved when he was questioned by MPs about why there was to be no debate on such a major decision. 'Have we not reached a most intolerable position in which ministers act in this way without consulting the House even when it is sitting? The House has become a Reichstag,' baited Aneurin Bevan. The labour minister testily told his questioners that it was his right, under the powers granted to his office, to enforce the move without further deliberation.

Twelve days later, on the morning of 14 December, twenty-two-year-old clerical assistant Betty Eileen Nunn was working, as normal, in her second-floor office in Montagu House, the Ministry of Labour's imposing headquarters on Whitehall. An Ealing grammar school girl, who had finished second in her class in the national civil service examination in 1938, Betty was one of the secretaries who served Sir Godfrey Ince, Bevin's trusted director of manpower. Like most of the junior employees in Montagu House she had great affection for her minister, referring to him as 'Uncle Ernie'. 'How are you today, my dear?' was his customary greeting if he met her in the lift, and he would usually spend a moment or two in pleasant chat.

Today Betty's work was interrupted by her supervisor, who asked if she would go down to Bevin's office on the floor below. When she entered the room, she was surprised to see a large gathering of men, which included three ministers – Bevin himself, Gwilym Lloyd George and Rab Butler – together with some senior civil servants and a few members of the press. A black homburg hat had been placed on the desk in front of her. Rab Butler gestured to her and said, 'All we want you to do, my dear, is to put in your hand and pick out a number.' Betty dipped her hand in among ten pieces of paper and drew out the number 9. Then Bevin told her to repeat the task, and this time she drew the number 0.

All young men whose National Service Registration Certificate numbers ended in those two numerals were now to become miners. This transparent, impartial method of selection would be repeated every month in Bevin's office until 23 April 1945. Only infrequently were two numbers drawn, but on this first occasion it was vital to conscript as many men as possible. The initial cohort would be sent to eleven special training centres, ready to start work in the collieries by the middle of February.

On page three of the next day's *Daily Mirror*, the paper's cartoonist 'Zec' drew Bevin as a shop assistant, tape measure around his neck, helping a young girl try on a hat in front of a mirror. Lying on the table in front of them was an apparently discarded black homburg hat with the words 'privilege and wire pulling' inscribed inside the brim. But on the girl's dress was written the word 'justice', and the label on the hat she was wearing read 'Miner's Ballot A La Bevin'. The caption to the cartoon read, 'This cap fits!' A ministry spokesman was quoted afterwards as saying that the identity of the staff member who had drawn the numbers would be kept secret 'lest she should be molested by mothers of boys who were sent to the coalmines'.

Not only was the ballot a necessary mobilisation of manpower, it became a form of social experiment. 'It doesn't seem a bad scheme – but I confess I still have my doubts about the "high and mighties" ever reaching the pit,' commented Jim Hammond, Lancashire miners' leader. 'I feel many of them will find ways of slipping through.' But the sons of lawyers, headmasters and stockbrokers would now have to take their place alongside those of engineers, gardeners and dustmen.

When Bevin eventually granted MPs a short debate about the policy on 17 December, it was greeted with near unanimous enthusiasm – as much for the social cohesion it appeared to offer as for the increased coal output it would reap. Lieutenant-Colonel Claude Lancaster, Conservative MP for Fylde and a coal industry director, enthused, 'The young miner can learn a river of life which at present flows past his narrow mountain valleys, and maybe in the learning of it he will find some of his prejudices being swept away.'

Alexander 'Sanny' Sloan, Labour MP for South Ayrshire, a miner at the age of twelve who had lost an eye in a pit accident, was equally stirred by Bevin's scheme. 'These youths may be missionaries. When they have come into mining and seen what it is like they will be able, like the Queen of Sheba, to say "The half has not been told me; the half of the misery has never yet received the light of day."'

As for the architect himself, he concluded the debate that afternoon in more prosaic style. 'We devised this scheme of selecting these lads because we thought it fair . . . I think it is coming, after all, at an opportune moment when a changed mental outlook and a change in our conception of national life is on the way.'

Chapter Twelve

'Should we tell the Russians?'

18 December 1943 to 2 June 1944

On the same day Ernest Bevin was supervising the coal ballot in his office in Whitehall, Winston Churchill dictated a telegram for the War Cabinet. In it he detailed his recommendations for the British contribution to the Allied military command structure for Operation *Overlord* and the Mediterranean. Air Marshal Arthur Tedder was to be General Eisenhower's deputy for the cross-Channel invasion, Harold Alexander or Bernard Montgomery should command the expeditionary army, and General Henry 'Jumbo' Maitland Wilson was the Prime Minister's choice to replace Eisenhower as supreme commander in the Mediterranean.

'I very much regret', the telegram concluded, 'that on account of my illness and fever – which continue – I have not been able to visit the Italian front. I still hope to do so after I have recovered.' There would be no such visit to the front; Churchill very nearly did not recover at all.

Following the summit in Teheran, and subsequent talks with Roosevelt in Cairo, Churchill had insisted on visiting Eisenhower at his villa, The White House, near Tunis. But on arrival he had been so weak he had immediately taken to bed, and in the morning he had been diagnosed with pneumonia – his second serious bout of the year. Even as he dictated that message, his temperature was still rising and the infection was spreading in his left lung. A few hours later his doctor, Lord Moran, was forced to administer digitalis for an irregular heartbeat. 'As I sat by his bedside listening to his quick breathing, I knew that we were at last right up against things.'

'Lord Moran tells me he thought the PM was going to die last night,' Harold Macmillan recorded the next day. 'He thinks him a little better as regards the pneumonia, but is worried about his heart.' On 16 December the fever began to ease and there were signs that Churchill's lungs were clearing, although his temperature was still 101°F (38.3°C). This was the fifth day of the illness, and although the War Cabinet had been kept updated – 'some of them have been getting agitated, they seem to be in a complete dither,' observed Moran – the Prime Minister's condition had yet to be revealed to the British public.

Clementine, accompanied by Jock Colville, flew out from RAF Lyneham to be at Churchill's bedside. Around midday on 16 December Attlee stood up in the Commons to deliver the news. 'The Prime Minister has been in bed for some days with a cold. A patch of pneumonia has now developed in the left lung. The general condition is as satisfactory as can be expected.' There was a gasp of concern, followed soon afterwards by loud cheers from MPs as Attlee added, 'I am sure it will be the desire of all of us that we should send our best wishes for a complete and speedy recovery.'

As the bulletins became steadily more upbeat over the following days any speculation about Churchill's fitness for office died away, at least in public. 'The circumstances certainly do not suggest any special arrangements will be necessary in connexion with the work of the war cabinet,' suggested *The Times*. However, Cecil King of the *Daily Mirror* was more ready to contemplate the worst, voicing a common line of thought in and around Westminster: 'In the event of Churchill's death, the only possible successor, in my opinion, would be Eden, though the Tories are trying to build up Anderson!'

On Christmas Day in Carthage, a recuperating Churchill hosted a conference of the five commanders-in-chief – Eisenhower, Maitland Wilson, Tedder, Alexander and Admiral Sir John Cunningham – to thrash out the strategy for *Overlord*. Then in the New Year he journeyed to one of his favourite retreats, the Villa Taylor at Marrakech, to continue his convalescence. Here he took time to consider the stalled campaign in Italy and the plans for Operation *Shingle*, the impending Allied assault on Anzio, south of Rome, whose object was to force the withdrawal of the German armies from the Gustav Line at Cassino, thus opening up the way to the capital.

On the Eastern Front, meanwhile, the momentum was now undeniably with the Red Army. 'THE GREAT RETREAT TURNS INTO ROUT' was the *Daily Express*'s description of the latest events in Ukraine, where General Nikolai Vatutin's offensive had apparently destroyed eight Panzer and fourteen infantry divisions, totalling some 250,000 men.

At the final War Cabinet of 1943, the assembled ministers took particular satisfaction from the latest evidence of the upturn in fortunes in the Arctic campaign. Details were given of the sinking on Boxing Day of the *Scharnhorst*, the German battleship that had sailed with such impunity down the English Channel in February 1942. This war had now lasted fifty-two months – exactly as long as the last one. Everywhere Hitler's army, navy and air force appeared to be either holding on or in retreat, but the biggest military challenge was yet to come.

Evidence that the second front was imminent was not hard to find, despite the censors attempting to block any informed speculation in the national newspapers. The island was crammed with foreign soldiers – mainly American and Canadian – and industry was totally geared to the war effort, with factories churning out landing craft and amphibious tanks. Builders and civil engineers, especially in and around the south coast, were particularly involved in projects for the big push; indeed, most people had a story about someone they knew who was engaged in 'secret' war work.

'I am sick of this war. Sick of everything. Sick of the waiting and the sound of bombers, of my work and my clothes and the general dullness of my complicated existence.' The weariness and frustration of Maggie Joy Blunt, a thirty-four-year-old architectural writer living alone with her cats in a cottage near Slough, mirrored the feelings of many Britons in the early months of 1944. But coupled with the general mood of lassitude and restless expectation, there was also anxiety after the return of a forgotten menace.

When Maggie Blunt spoke of the 'sound of bombers', she was referring to the renewed Luftwaffe night bombing campaign, 'The Little Blitz', which had started on 21 January and would go on until 19 April. Hitler, provoked by the RAF's saturation bombing of Berlin and other major German cities, had sent his planes back to take their revenge on London and other selected targets, including Bristol and Hull. The attacks never reached the scale of those in 1940–1, with just thirteen concerted raids spread out over the three months. But Operation *Steinbock* nonetheless sent Londoners scurrying for cover in their mothballed Anderson and Morrison shelters, and at the height of the bombing 50,000 packed into the capital's public refuges.

However, the lessons of the Blitz had been learned. This time the Heinkels, Dorniers and Junkers were up against improved anti-aircraft batteries, while the impressive de Havilland Mosquito night fighters patrolled the skies. The Luftwaffe lost 329 planes before Göring decided to preserve what was left of his bomber strength for the expected cross-Channel invasion by the Allies. Even so, by that point the raids had claimed the lives of 1,500 people – mainly Londoners – with nearly 3,000 seriously injured.

With its military campaigns stalled, or as yet unready to launch, the government was anxious to maintain morale on the Home Front. Concrete plans for reconstruction would help, and as the 'The Man Who Will Remake Britain' Lord Woolton was expected to swiftly bring forward substantial proposals on, among other matters, housing, employment and a national health service. In each case, he would be judged by the inevitable yardstick of Beveridge's detailed social insurance scheme. But first Woolton faced the problem of reconciling the differing ambitions and politics of his new reconstruction committee. It appeared to be carefully balanced: on the Labour side were Attlee, Bevin, Morrison and William Jowitt (Paymaster General), while the Conservative representatives were Butler, Lyttelton, Dominions secretary Cranborne and Henry Crookshank (Postmaster General). The Chancellor, Sir John Anderson – nominally a National Independent MP, but clearly wedded to the values and principles of the right – also took his place.

Hitherto the coalition had, by and large, suppressed its rawer political instincts in the interests of national unity. Now, with the economic future of the country to be shaped, clear party differences would surely emerge. In practice, urged on by personal political preference, pressure from their party and the clamour from the public for change, the four Labour members would prove to be the more proactive and influential.

Woolton, who had been free of party-political pressure at the Ministry of Food, now 'met the full force of the divergence' in the coalition, 'both of policy and of personalities'. 'It was a very good training ground for a sixty-year-old novice to party warfare,' he recalled. As it was, his main source of trouble came not from inside the committee, but from predictable foes outside it. Beaverbrook and Bracken regarded Woolton's project as 'socialist', a threat to the independence of doctors, managers and industrialists, and would attempt to use their influence with the Prime Minister to confound it.

Woolton's reconstruction committee now began to produce a 'White Paper chase' of suggested reform. First off the conveyor belt was a paper on health, in February, that took as its basic principle Beveridge's vision of a fully comprehensive, universal healthcare system, free at the point of delivery and available for every citizen in the land. It also introduced the concept of salaried doctors working in health centres, governed – along with public and voluntary hospitals – by new regional government authorities. What the paper did not propose, however, was a statist model. Its 'starting point' was that it was possible to 'combine public responsibility and a full service with the essential elements of personal and professional freedom for the patient and the doctor'. The latter would be allowed to continue as an independent contractor or private practitioner, and the independent, charitable 'voluntary' hospitals could carry on 'without loss of identity or autonomy', albeit encouraged to co-operate with public hospitals in their area.

It was a clear compromise, but one with which both sides of the committee appeared able to live. Attlee was concerned that state-employed doctors would favour their private patients, while Bevin would have liked greater emphasis on the development of health centres. Woolton, on the other hand, wanted to preserve the 'voluntary spirit', leaving hospitals 'as free as possible to manage their own affairs in their own ways' while accepting guidance from the new local authorities.

Woolton presented the document at a War Cabinet meeting on the evening of 9 February. He was at pains to emphasise that the scheme did not involve the abolition of private medical practice, but he did concede that any plans to establish a comprehensive service would inevitably be seen to threaten it, and he warned of strong opposition from the doctors' union. Churchill appeared content enough, although he stressed that ministers should not present the proposals as the government's final view; constructive criticism was to be welcomed. The War Cabinet also agreed to remove a reference in the introduction acknowledging Sir William Beveridge's influence on the document: this ungenerous omission was all part of an effort to emphasise the government's initiative and downplay the reformer's guiding influence.

Beaverbrook and Bracken, on this occasion, listened largely in silence. But after the meeting in the Cabinet Room was over, they stayed behind to persuade Churchill of what they considered to be the folly of Woolton's plans, in particular the attack on the 'independence' of the family doctor. As was so often the case, their arguments prevailed and Churchill was persuaded to reconvene the War Cabinet a week later to re-examine the proposals. At the same time, the Prime Minister asked Eden to confer with the Tory members of the reconstruction committee and gather details on any concerns they had. Woolton, alarmed to learn of this instruction, wrote to warn the foreign secretary, 'If the Conservatives turn down the compromise at which we have so laboriously arrived on this issue, there is little hope of getting the Socialists to arrive at a compromise on the other issues with which the committee is faced, and on which they have been publicly expressing their conviction for many years.'

At the reconstituted War Cabinet on 15 February, Bracken launched a fierce attack on both the principles and the specifics of the proposals. He feared not just the end of private practice, but the demise of voluntary hospitals, which for so long had taken the lead in teaching and research. He foresaw, too, that the new scheme would interfere with the right of doctors to set up in practice as consultants.

In the end Woolton rode the storm, and the decision taken a week earlier was reaffirmed. But Bracken and Beaverbrook's crude interference had stirred up resentment within the coalition. Lord Cherwell told Jock Colville there was 'much annoyance in Government circles because Brendan and Lord B attempt, by using their influence with the PM, to sabotage measures . . . about which they are hopelessly ignorant but which have been worked out by experts, with great pains and hard work, over a long period'.

In a two-day Commons debate on the White Paper in March, Henry Willink, health minister, and Florence Horsbrugh, his junior, had to continually reassure MPs – especially those who were doctors – that private practice was safe in their hands. In the face of a great many interruptions, Horsbrugh unflappably talked MPs through the details, assuaging their fears about doctors' independence and the future of voluntary hospitals. She finished with a flourish. 'I hope [future generations] will look back to the year 1944 when . . . at a time of increase of suffering, of wounds and maiming and crippling, we in this House launched a scheme to allay suffering, to get people made well, and in the middle of destruction, to do something constructive for the people of this country.'

One of the House's other thirteen women MPs was to make a significant intervention in a different area of reconstruction – albeit not to the government's benefit. Thelma Cazalet Kerr – Conservative member for Islington East, sister of Tory MP Victor Cazalet, and a one-time junior minister at the Board of Education – had never allowed her party loyalties to supersede a commitment to what would nowadays be termed 'feminist' politics. She had recently campaigned to press Anthony Eden to admit women to the diplomatic service, but now her principles were to stall the one piece of reforming legislation that had been progressing towards the statute book: Rab Butler's Education Bill.

Cazalet had already tried and failed (by thirty-five votes) to persuade the government to set a date for raising the school leaving age to sixteen. Now she put down an amendment that would give equal pay to women teachers. To Butler's immense annoyance, and Churchill's fury, it passed by 117 to 116; the first time in the war the coalition had been defeated in either the Commons or the Lords.

Although not the foremost advocate of women's rights, Churchill maintained he bore no ingrained hostility to the idea of equal pay. 'The amendment advocates a perfectly good principle which is not suitable for insertion in this clause. It is quite easy to have a perfectly good thing in the wrong place . . . [it] is like potato in a gooseberry pie,' he grumbled to Butler. What incensed him, as the country approached its most formidable test of the war, was what he perceived as a lack of unity in the body politic and the signal that gave to the enemy. Once apprised of the result he immediately summoned the War Cabinet to the Annexe for an emergency session at 10 p.m. the same evening. There he persuaded his ministers – with no dissenters – to reverse the vote by using the sledgehammer tactic of making it an issue of confidence.

It was a ploy that worked, even cowing the architect of the government's misfortune. In the subsequent debate on 30 March, Thelma Cazalet Kerr resignedly told the House: 'In this great democracy of ours, convention, for once, seems to have overruled commonsense. I believe in the clause as it stands, but I shall vote against it, to show my measureless confidence in the Prime Minister now, in view of the stupendous days that lie ahead.'

The government won their confidence motion by a resounding 425 votes to 23. For Rab Butler, the government's heavy-handed action 'paid a handsome dividend'. From then on, no MP was willing to press an amendment to his bill – at least, one that was unacceptable to the government – if there was any chance of it being carried. The bill progressed smoothly through the Lords that summer and became law in August. Churchill sent a congratulatory telegram to Butler, saying he had 'won a lasting place in the history of British education'.

One of the three 'assumptions' underpinning Beveridge's social insurance scheme was full employment, so early in 1944 Lord Woolton's reconstruction committee had started to turn its attention to jobs. The resulting White Paper was presented to the War Cabinet on 19 May. Churchill had not read the report, but had received a long brief from Cherwell, who had described it as a 'very bold and ably conceived plan worthy of full support'. Even so, before he committed himself the Prime Minister wanted to hear the views of Beaverbrook. 'A magnificent scheme, a first-class scheme,' was the Beaver's surprising reply. Bracken was enthused too: 'it is a document of great significance', he wrote in a memorandum that recommended maximum publicity for the plans.

So this White Paper was given a fair wind. And when it emerged few could deny that it was a landmark document: the government had finally cast aside the view that employment could not be expanded through state action. Indeed, the first words averred that 'the Government accepts as one of their primary aims and responsibilities the maintenance of a high and stable level of employment after the war'. This was taken by many as official acceptance of the doctrines of John Maynard Keynes; certainly some sections of the paper pointed towards greater government management of the economy, including a more active fiscal policy, with public works schemes and the deliberate running of deficits in times of depression. 'The Government are prepared to accept in future the responsibility for taking action at the earliest possible stage to arrest a threatened slump. This involves a new approach and a new responsibility for the State,' chapter four stated.

But this was only half the picture. The paper was a careful mix of the macro-economic thinking of the Keynesians in the Cabinet Office's Economic Section, and the orthodox micro-economic strategy of the Treasury. The first three chapters reflected the views of the latter, stressing the need to revive international trade, the importance of increased industrial efficiency and labour mobility, and the dangers of inflation.

Attlee's foreword made the compromise explicit: 'In the post-war period, the country will inevitably depend upon a mixed economy, neither wholly subject to state regulation nor wholly ruled by private enterprise; and the extent to which either one of these principles gains or loses ground will depend on the will of the post-war electorate expressed at the polls.' This position irritated many Labour backbenchers, who believed quite simply that unemployment was synonymous with capitalism. 'Shallow, empty-headed and superficial, bearing all the stigmata of its coalition origin,' was Aneurin Bevan's contemptuous verdict.

Keynes himself was underwhelmed by the White Paper. 'My own feeling is that the first sentence is more valuable than the whole of the rest,' he told fellow Cambridge economist Austin Robinson. But on the whole Woolton's proposals received a glowing response. 'GOVT PLANS JOBS FOR ALL AFTER WAR – WILL CONTROL AND AID SWITCH TO FULL PEACE PRODUCTION,' proclaimed the *Daily Mirror*. 'Irrespective of the precise nature of its contents,' wrote the *Economist*, 'this first formal resolution of democracy to shoulder anew responsibility on behalf of its members deserves a round of applause.'

At the press conference for the paper on 26 May Woolton and Bevin stood side by side, and the latter was unreserved in his enthusiasm. He reminded journalists of the Bank Act of 1844, which had set in stone a free trade system that dictated 'whenever the exchanges went wrong, you rectified them by restricting credit and producing unemployment'. Now, he said, 'instead of human beings having to fit into the international exchange system, the international exchange system must be fitted to human requirements . . . this plan leaves the 19th century behind'.

The success of the White Paper came as some relief to the Minister for Labour, who had played no small part in its development. The pit crisis still showed no signs of abating, and the first four months of 1944 had seen a wave of strikes in the coalfields, which a minimum wage award of £5 a week for underground men and £4 10s for surface workers had done little to alleviate. In March a total of 15,000 men had gone on strike in the Scottish pits, 100,000 in south Wales and 120,000 in Yorkshire. The conscription scheme for the mines was also causing trouble. There was a national strike of shipyard apprentices against their inclusion in the ballot for 'Bevin Boys', including 6,000 on Tyneside and 5,000 on Clydeside.

Then a number of court cases involving conscripts who had refused to take their places in the mines began to attract publicity (there would be 147 such refusals in 1944). One such concerned eighteen-year-old Arthur Jenner, of Bethnal Green, London, who declined to go down a Northumberland colliery. Jenner, who had joined the Home Guard at sixteen and since manned AA guns, told Old Street magistrates' court he was keen to join the forces and had been passed A1 for the army and A1 for the navy. The sympathetic presiding magistrate Mr Rowland Thomas, in adjourning the case, told him, 'It's not a matter for me, but when you have a public-spirited fellow who has been proving himself to be highly useful it does seem a thousand pities.' Bevin was indignant when told of the affair. He rebuked Thomas, although not by name, in the Commons a few days later. 'It is the duty of magistrates to enforce the law, and it is no part of their function to use the courts for expressing their personal views on the policy of that law.'

Regarding the wider problem, Bevin now decided the industrial strife had gone on too long. On 4 April, at a luncheon at the Dorchester Hotel given by the Civil Engineering Construction Conciliation Board, he launched a startling attack on the Yorkshire miners, and anyone else prepared to withdraw their labour at this time. 'What has happened this week in Yorkshire is worse than if Hitler had bombed Sheffield and cut our communications. It is the most tragic thing that in Britain you can do more harm by thoughtless action and lack of discipline than your enemy can do to you.' But a week later Bevin had negotiated a successful conclusion to the Yorkshire miners' strike, and a few days after that he achieved a national agreement on wages and conditions with the workers' leaders and the pit owners. However, he still wanted stronger powers to stamp out illegal industrial action, so on 17 April he added a new section, 1AA, to the Defence of the Realm Regulations. It was aimed at anyone inciting strikes or lockouts in an essential service, the penalty for which would be a maximum of five years' penal servitude, a fine of £500, or both, if necessary.

So soon after the vote of confidence, this seemed – and not just to the left-wing press – to be another example of an authoritarian-minded government, lashing out at straw men. On the Education Bill, rebellious MPs had been in the firing line; with 1AA, supposed bands of Trotskyist agitators were the threat. Labour MPs attacked Bevin for the 'unconstitutional' way he had imposed the new regulation, without first consulting Parliament, and argued that the miners had come out on strike because of the incompetence of his ministry, not because of any carefully orchestrated conspiracy.

But Bevin had some valuable allies that day. James ('Jimmy') Glanville, the recently elected MP for Consett, had come straight to the Commons from the pit where he had worked for forty years. Glanville reproached Aneurin Bevan for 'magnifying in high falutin' language' the implications of the new regulation, saying they existed solely in his imagination. 'This is a wartime measure and it finishes at the end of hostilities. If it is necessary that this House should collect the boys and conscript them to go and risk their lives, it is necessary to exercise severe control over the disrupters, who are preventing the workers carrying on necessary jobs.' Grateful for the backing, Bevin told MPs he hoped the new powers would never have to be used – and so it would eventually prove: there would never be a single prosecution under 1AA.

The hostile motion was defeated by 314 votes to 23, albeit just 56 out of 165 Labour MPs voted with the government (the rest either abstained or were absent). It was a political embarrassment, but memories would soon fade, as worries over industrial strife took a back seat to the war's defining military campaign, Operation *Overlord*. In the meantime, however, a yet longer-incubating matter was to occupy the minds of certain Cabinet members.

Sir John Anderson was a man ripe for caricature. For one thing, there was his face – long, forbidding, lugubrious and increasingly jowly – that seemed uncannily to have taken on the appearance of a bloodhound (a representative of which breed he would later acquire). With his customary dress of wing collar, black coat, striped trousers, immaculately folded cravat and gold watch chain, and a manner formal to the point of pomposity, he might have been mistaken for a stern butler, or perhaps an efficient undertaker. Indeed, two of the whispered sobriquets attached to him in Whitehall were 'Pompous John' and 'God's Butler'. A third, 'Jehovah', was a favourite with the War Cabinet. At one Cabinet committee meeting, as Anderson prepared to open proceedings, Clement Attlee announced in a deadpan voice, 'Well, we are all Jehovah's witnesses now!'

His portentous approach served him ill in the House of Commons. 'Is it in order for the home secretary to treat this as if we were the natives of Bengal?' an exasperated Dr Edith Summerskill had complained to the chamber in October 1939 after receiving an especially unsatisfactory answer. But whatever the demeanour Anderson presented in public – in private, colleagues attested to a more human figure, with a pawky sense of humour – no one disputed his long and considerable contribution to the British state. As secretary to the Ministry of Shipping during the previous war, he had countered the U-boat menace. As joint under-secretary to the Lord Lieutenant of Ireland in 1921, he had helped draft the treaty establishing an Irish Free State. In 1926, while at the Home Office, his meticulous preparation had enabled Winston Churchill to break the general strike. Then from 1931 to 1935 he had governed the largest Indian province, Bengal, where he had won admiration from opponents in the Congress Party for continuing to move freely among the population despite two assassination attempts.

If Anderson lacked the presentational skills of a career politician

– he was a relative novice, having only been elected MP for the Scottish Universities in 1938 – his administrative genius was undisputed. 'Anderson is the most learned of men. We can catch him out on nothing. No wonder he is a tower of strength to Winston, he settles all the quarrels in the Cabinet and knows everything,' Victor Cazalet noted in February 1942. Two years on Anderson's importance to Churchill had only grown. He was a 'friendly power of equal status rather than a satellite', was how Norman Brook, formerly his principal private secretary, would later describe Anderson's relationship with the Prime Minister by the spring of 1944.

Having shed responsibility for important economic committees to Attlee and Woolton upon becoming chancellor in July 1943, Anderson was still left – along with a brief for manpower – with two vital roles in Churchill's ministry. He was, of course, the steward of the nation's finances, but he had another, highly secretive brief, known only to the Prime Minister and a handful of colleagues. It was the latter that preoccupied him in the spring of 1944 – just as much, if not more, than his first, uncontroversial budget, introduced on 25 April.

Two days after his major financial statement – and for the second time in just over a month – Anderson had written to the Prime Minister to try and convince him that Britain's secret atom bomb project, codenamed 'Tube Alloys', should be opened up to a far wider circle of government ministers. Moreover, the Chancellor believed there should now be serious discussion about whether Britain and America might, in the interests of world security, disclose the project to the Soviet Union.

Churchill and Anderson had worked closely together on the bomb project since the late summer of 1941. The Prime Minister, whose engagement with science, though amateur, was always well-informed and imaginative, had been prescient in his analysis of the huge impact nuclear energy was likely to have on the world. In an article for the *Strand* magazine, in December 1931, entitled 'Fifty Years Hence', he had written – almost certainly influenced by Professor Lindemann:

If the hydrogen atoms in a pound of water could be prevailed upon to combine together and form helium, it would suffice to drive a 1,000-horsepower engine for a whole year. If the electrons – those tiny planets of the atomic systems – were induced to combine with the nuclei in the hydrogen, the horsepower liberated would be one hundred and twenty times greater still . . . What is lacking is the match to set the bonfire alight, or it may be the detonator to cause the dynamite to explode. The scientists are looking for this.

But for his pursuit of a career in the civil service, Anderson might have been one of those exploring scientists. A brilliant student at Edinburgh University, he had graduated with first class honours in mathematics and natural philosophy, including distinctions in physics and chemistry. Seemingly set for a career in scientific research, he had headed for the University of Leipzig, then renowned for its contributions to physics and physical chemistry. There he had chosen to study uranium, although his researches had been devoted to the chemical rather than the radioactive properties of the element. Upon his return to Edinburgh, he had written a thesis on the subject considered remarkable for its clarity and insight.

So in July 1941, after the government's Scientific Advisory Committee had produced the MAUD (Military Application of Uranium Detonation) report, with its startling suggestion that it should be possible to make an effective atomic bomb, possibly within two years, Anderson had been the obvious candidate to assume political control of this potentially potent weapon.

Anderson himself – despite the celebrated memorandum from German émigré scientists Rudolf Peierls and Otto Frisch that had made the first coherent, theoretical case for a 'super bomb', in the spring of 1940 – had been sceptical that the release of atomic energy in any useful form could be achieved soon. But he was won over by the 'sensational' prospects envisaged by the MAUD report, and lobbied strenuously to be included in any project. On the urging of the Prof, Churchill duly appointed him.

Despite his perceptive 1931 essay, Churchill had been less enthusiastic about the findings of the MAUD committee. 'Although personally I am quite content with the existing explosives, I feel we must not stand in the path of improvement,' had been his initial, muted response to Lindemann's early recommendations. Nevertheless, he sought out the view of the chiefs of staff, and when this was received, on 2 September, it was 'strongly in favour of . . . development being pressed forward in this country with the highest priority'. Although the chiefs had added that they would rather speak than write to the Prime Minister about the substance of the project, about which 'the less put on paper . . . the better'.

This strategy suited a Prime Minister who naturally inclined to the clandestine. Churchill possessed an almost boyish enthusiasm for secret information, and had been one of the earliest champions of code and cipher breaking. He relished the daily diet of raw intelligence he received from the Enigma decrypts at Bletchley Park. But at the same time he worried about the number of government officials who had access to sensitive information.

The same anxiety applied to the atom bomb project. Churchill was determined to confine the secret to as narrow a circle as possible, to the extent that he chose not to inform the War Cabinet – neither Attlee, Bevin, Morrison, Lyttelton, Cripps, Woolton, Kingsley Wood nor Greenwood were ever in the loop. Nor, it would appear, was the subject shared with the usually well-briefed Lord Beaverbrook.

The members of the government and its friends associated with the project never numbered more than a dozen. Anderson and Lindemann were the key players, while the others – with varying degrees of knowledge – were Lord Hankey (the arch-mandarin with fingers in many scientific and technical pies), Lord Halifax, Anthony Eden, the Minister of Aircraft Production John Moore-Brabazon (briefly, when the MAUD scientists had been attached to his department), Colonel John Llewellin (as the Ministry of Supply's representative in Washington), Sir Ronald Campbell (veteran British embassy diplomat in Washington), Malcolm MacDonald (former Minister of Health, now the UK high commissioner to Ottawa), and Field Marshal Jan

Smuts. Sir John Dill, who had been briefed right at the start, continued his involvement when he took up the post of chief of the British Staff Mission in the American capital; but the chiefs of staff in London, despite that initial briefing in the summer of 1941, were largely left out of the picture.

In autumn 1941, Anderson established an oversight committee of ministers and scientists, deliberately and misleadingly named the Tube Alloys Consultative Council. The Lord President (as he was then) and Wallace Akers, ICI's research director in charge of the working scientists on the council's technical committee, settled on the name 'Tube Alloys' because the phrase had the 'specious air of probability about it', and would encourage the uninitiated to believe the project was something to do with aeroplane radiators, or tanks.

To begin with, Anderson and Lindemann had resolved to make Tube Alloys an independent British venture, although they were content to share the contents of MAUD with the Americans. In any case, by the autumn of 1941 nearly all the major theoretical and practical advances had been made in Britain: the Americans, still non-combatants, had yet to display any great urgency in their fragmented and ill-directed nuclear weapons research.

Many of Britain's best scientists had been drawn into other critical war work, including the development of radar, but the presence of a number of well-qualified refugees from Germany and occupied Europe had filled the gaps. The universities of Liverpool, Birmingham, Bristol, Manchester, and King's College and Imperial College in London, had all contributed to the research effort, with the large experimental group led by Franz Simon at the Clarendon Laboratory in Oxford (working on a process known as gaseous diffusion) and the Cavendish Laboratory in Cambridge (on plutonium) having played especially crucial parts. Meanwhile, ICI and Metropolitan Vickers had embarked on preliminary industrial work, and a new factory had been established in Widnes, Lancashire, for producing pure uranium.

MAUD had impressed the Americans, and in particular the President. In October 1941 Roosevelt sent a message to Churchill, saying, 'We should soon correspond or converse concerning the subject which is under discussion by your MAUD committee . . . in order that any extended efforts may be coordinated or even jointly conducted.' His overture was ignored for almost two months, by which stage Pearl Harbor had brought America into the war and the US was fast developing its own bomb project. By the summer of 1942 Anderson realised that, despite all the intellectual talent at work in Britain, the task of building a bomb in a war-torn, still potentially vulnerable country was beyond Tube Alloys. 'It has now become clear that the production plant will have to be on such a huge scale that its erection in this country will be out of the question in the war,' he wrote to the Prime Minister on 30 July. 'The Americans have been applying themselves with enthusiasm and a lavish expenditure which we cannot rival.'

His recommendation that British design work and personnel should be moved to the United States, as part of a 'combined Anglo-American effort', had been accepted by Churchill. But over the course of the next year it proved ever more difficult to maintain an equal partnership; the US 'Manhattan Project', at Los Alamos in the New Mexican desert, had become the focus of activity, and to Anderson and Cherwell's frustration they were sidelined by politicians and scientists in Washington in an atmosphere of developing mistrust. They also faced a formidable obstacle in the project's fiercely protective senior military chief, General Leslie R. Groves. By the end of 1942 British influence on the bomb project had dwindled alarmingly.

In the early months of 1943 Churchill enlisted Harry Hopkins in an effort to break the impasse, and by the summer Roosevelt had instructed his scientific adviser Dr Vannevar Bush 'to renew a full exchange of information with the British government'. This new co-operation had led to the Quebec Agreement, signed by Churchill and Roosevelt in August, which finally formalised the Anglo-American partnership 'to bring the Tube Alloys project to fruition'. The two leaders had resolved 'never to use this agency against each other', 'not [to] use it against third parties without each other's consent', and that neither would 'communicate any information to third parties except by mutual consent'. All well and good, although they had also agreed, in the less-observed and lengthier fourth clause, that 'any post-war advantages of an industrial or commercial character shall be dealt with . . . on terms specified by the President of the United States to the Prime Minister of Great Britain. The Prime Minister expressly disclaims any interest in these industrial and commercial aspects beyond what may be considered by the United States to be fair and just and in harmony with the economic welfare of the world.' Back in London, Reginald Victor Jones, Churchill's brilliant thirty-one-year-old scientific military adviser, had concluded that herein 'we had signed away our birthright in the post-war development of nuclear energy'. But for the Prime Minister, the immediate aim of cementing the alliance between Britain and America had obscured longer-term concerns; besides, by this stage his bargaining power was on the wane.

It had been the arrival in Britain in October 1943 of perhaps the greatest nuclear physicist of the day, Professor Niels Bohr, that began to change Anderson's thinking about the bomb. Bohr, his wife and four sons and his brother had been spirited by Allied intelligence out of Copenhagen, away from the clutches of the Gestapo, and taken by boat across the Sound to Sweden. When news of his escape reached London, Cherwell sent the Danish scientist a telegram inviting him to Britain. He arrived in Scotland on 6 October in a de Havilland Mosquito, having passed out during the journey from oxygen starvation.

Thereafter, at Anderson's behest, Bohr and his son Aage, who had arrived a week after his father, joined the British Tube Alloys team at Los Alamos under the codenames 'Nicholas Baker' and 'James Baker'. Bohr was stunned by the size and ambition of the Manhattan Project, realising that the theoretical work he, as much as anyone, had laboured over had now been transformed into a potentially devastating reality. As much a philosopher as he was a scientist, he began to contemplate how the existence of such an extraordinary weapon might affect the future.

Upon Bohr's return to London, he and Anderson talked at length about their hopes and fears for the new atomic age. Bohr, the romantic idealist, had come to believe the need to prevent a nuclear war could galvanise the nations of the post-war world to overcome their differences and work together. Anderson, the pragmatic civil servant cum politician, found himself warming to the Dane's vision. In the short term, Bohr argued, the Soviets should be told the West was working on an atomic bomb; they probably knew anyway, but even if not, the longer it was hidden from them the more they would feel threatened when the secret was finally revealed. So, Anderson, now a convert, set about trying to persuade Churchill of the need to lift the blanket of secrecy over Tube Alloys.

On 21 March 1944 the Chancellor wrote a long memorandum, stating that given the vast military implications, 'it no longer seemed right' to confine knowledge to a very narrow circle. He recommended that he and Lord Cherwell should now brief all members of the War Cabinet, the three 'service' ministers (war secretary Sir James Grigg, air secretary Sir Archibald Sinclair, and First Lord A.V. Alexander), together with the chiefs of staff. He even suggested Sir Stafford Cripps (aircraft production) and Andrew Rae Duncan (supply), who 'already have some vague knowledge of the matter', should be added to the list.

He also ventured his thoughts on the shape of things to come, outlining two scenarios: 'either there will be a particularly vicious form of armaments race, in which at best the United States, or the United States and the United Kingdom working as a team, will for a time enjoy a precarious and uneasy advantage', or 'a form of international control . . . will ensure that sub-atomic energy is used for the common benefit of mankind, and is not irresponsibly employed as a weapon of military or economic warfare'. For his part, Anderson was now firmly wedded to the latter. If the Americans could be persuaded, he suggested, 'there is much to be said for communicating to the Russians in the near future . . . and for inviting them to collaborate with us'.

Churchill's notes on the memo said everything about his reaction. He ringed the words 'full', 'collaborate' and 'Chiefs of Staff' (adding 'already know'), before writing simply at the end, 'I do not agree'. But Anderson persevered. On 27 April, he tried again, this time linking his remarks to a War Cabinet paper, from minister of state Richard

Law, on a future international organisation designed to safeguard the stability of the post-war order. 'I cannot help feeling that the plans for world security which do not take into account Tube Alloys must be quite unreal,' the Chancellor wrote. 'When the work on Tube Alloys comes to fruition – as we now know it will be a comparatively short time – the future of the world will in fact depend on whether it is used for the benefit or destruction of mankind.' This time Anderson pressed Churchill to seize the initiative on greater transparency by sending Roosevelt a telegram to 'break the ice'. The President, he suggested, was hemmed in by his military chiefs who 'almost certainly want to keep Tube Alloys for the exclusive use of the US army'.

Once again Churchill was dismissive. 'I do not think any such telegram is necessary; nor do I wish to widen the circle who are informed,' was his curt reply.

Now somewhat desperate, Anderson and others, including Sir Henry Dale, Field Marshal Smuts and R.V. Jones, lobbied Cherwell to persuade the Prime Minister to speak with Bohr. Churchill, although engrossed with last-minute planning for Overlord, agreed to a meeting in Downing Street on Tuesday, 16 May. At five o'clock that afternoon R.V. Jones was returning to his office at SIS headquarters, at 54 Broadway, when he spotted the scientist approaching him. 'He seemed to be in a daze, and he walked right past me. Fearing that something was wrong I went back and stopped him, to ask how he got on,' Jones recalled. 'All he could say was, "It was terrible! He scolded us like two schoolboys!"'

The encounter had been an unmitigated disaster. Instead of being invited to speak, Bohr had been made to wait while Churchill turned on Cherwell, angrily defending himself to his scientific adviser over criticism of the Quebec agreement. That done, the Prime Minister turned to Bohr, who, now quite intimidated by his host, struggled to articulate his views on post-war nuclear proliferation, despite having prepared his statement in advance. Nor had his uncertain English and low, whispering voice done him any favours. An exasperated Churchill responded that the atomic bomb was simply a bigger one that 'made no difference to the principles of war', and had asserted that there were no problems that could not be 'amicably settled between myself and my friend President Roosevelt'.

Before departing, the disconsolate Bohr asked Churchill if he could spell out his views more clearly in a letter. 'It will be an honour for me to receive a letter from you,' the Prime Minister had replied, 'but not about politics.'

Perhaps Churchill's tetchy mood should not be judged too harshly. Weighing difficult choices about a still hypothetical nuclear future was one thing, but first there was a war to win, and its outcome would depend heavily on the success, in just a few weeks' time, of the largest seaborne invasion ever attempted.

On 19 May came news of the fall of Monte Cassino, after a gruelling 123-day siege: the road to Rome had finally been opened up. A relieved General Alan Brooke was hopeful Germany's forces would now be tied down in Italy, and Hitler's attention kept from the Channel. Six days later he was on the south coast, inspecting equipment for the artificial 'Mulberry' harbours that would be crucial to the impending landings in Normandy.

By the end of the month, a swathe of southern England fifteen miles wide resembled a huge military camp, the once picturesque fields, woods and lanes now populated by tens of thousands of Allied soldiers. Quiet country railway stations on the way to the ports of Southampton, Portsmouth and Newhaven had been transformed into mighty hubs of activity, with fourteen miles of sidings capable of holding 2,500 wagons packed with troops and supplies. Micheldever, in Hampshire, had become a vast freight yard known as the 'Woolworth Depot' because – like the eponymous high-street store – it supplied military planners with virtually everything they needed, from odd-sized nuts and bolts to entire trainloads of bombs.

All along the Southern Railway line stations resounded with thrumming and clanking as war machines were assembled, a cacophony accompanied by the banter – albeit more subdued as the hour approached – of American and British soldiers preparing their kit for battle. But on the afternoon of Friday, 2 June, Droxford, a little station on the Meon Valley branch line, twenty miles south of Micheldever, was curiously free from the bustle and clamour of the rest of the county. Indeed, it was all but deserted, except for the goods yard in Siding No. 1, south of the station near the Cutts Arch Bridge, where two saloon carriages stood in splendid isolation. Emanating from within were noises more suggestive of a Whitehall office – the clacking of typewriter keys, the continual ringing of a telephone, the barking of commands to secretaries. Later there would be the surprising sound of a man splashing in a bathtub. Droxford was located just a couple of miles from the headquarters of the Allied military commanders at nearby Southwick House, and Churchill, joined by Ernest Bevin, Field Marshal Smuts and General Ismay, had taken up residence here in order to be at heart of the action in the build-up to D-Day.

Such was the level of secrecy that the local Home Guard had not been informed of their arrival. This almost had fateful consequences when, at 1.55 a.m. the following morning, a quartermaster sergeant on guard duty at the bridge marched towards the station gates, accompanied by two privates. A Canadian major inside the compound approached and on the simultaneous cry of 'Halt! Who goes there?' both men drew their pistols. Fortunately the major broke the uneasy silence to question the Home Guard about their business. They took him to see their colonel – a very deaf, eighty-year-old old army veteran – and amicable assurances were eventually given all round.

After lunch Churchill, Smuts and Bevin departed for Southampton, where they watched the men of the 50th Durham Regiment embark onto their landing craft. Bevin found the moment deeply affecting. One of the soldiers, who happened to be a member of his union, recognised him and called out, 'You'll look after the missus and kids, won't you, Ernie?' As the labour minister walked back to the car his eyes filled with tears.

Chapter Thirteen
'Buzz bombs and flying gas mains'
6 June to 10 December 1944

I t was almost exactly four years since the evacuation of Dunkirk. For the last three of those years, the pressure on Churchill, his War Cabinet and his chiefs of staff to start a second front had been unrelenting. Finally the moment had arrived when the Allies calculated their resources were so strong, and Hitler's sufficiently weakened, that the armada could set sail across the Channel with a confident prospect of victory.

Operation *Fortitude* – the principal Allied deception plan – had been so successful that if there were any German units on extra alert along the Atlantic Wall on the morning of Tuesday, 6 June, they were in the Pas de Calais region, or Norway. In any case, the poor weather of recent days had eased the Germans' fears of an imminent attack. The Seventh Army, in charge of the defence of Normandy, had ordered all its senior commanders a hundred miles north to Rennes, in Brittany, for a map exercise, while Field Marshal Erwin Rommel, commander-in-chief of German forces in France, was back home in Herrlingen, celebrating his wife's birthday.

So the 24,000 Allied soldiers who were dropped on French soil shortly after midnight had the vital element of surprise on their side.

Behind them, a huge fleet of 7,000 ships, supported by 11,500 aircraft, negotiated the sea passage without serious interference, and the 156,000-strong force it disgorged went on to capture the Normandy beaches more easily than expected. The exception was the six-mile stretch of coast east of the Vire Estuary, codenamed 'Omaha'. Here the Germans, entrenched in heavily fortified cliff-top positions, put up prolonged resistance, continually raking the US forces in their landing craft with machine gun fire. After six hours of heavy bombardment and little progress, Lieutenant General Omar Bradley considered withdrawing the US V Corps, but by nightfall, and at the cost of over 3,500 casualties, the Americans had managed to establish a tiny, precarious bridgehead.

At 6.15 p.m. on D-Day Churchill walked into the House of Commons chamber to give MPs a brief update on the invasion's progress. The operation, he told them, was 'proceeding in a thoroughly satisfactory manner. Many dangers and difficulties which at this time last night appeared extremely formidable are behind us . . .'

While the landings had gone as smoothly as hoped, the War Cabinet had been embroiled in a stormy debate over the future administration of a liberated France. It pitted the Prime Minister against the now established axis of Eden and Attlee, and at the centre of the dispute was the haughty, indomitable figure of General Charles de Gaulle.

Churchill's relationship with the Free French leader had waxed and waned since the days of mutual admiration in June 1940, when these two intensely patriotic men had jointly embraced the Monnet–Salter plan for an 'indissoluble union' of their two nations. After four years of personal and policy differences, the Prime Minister now viewed de Gaulle with a deep suspicion that sometimes bordered on loathing. This had been fuelled by Roosevelt, who had always mistrusted de Gaulle, believing him to be only a minor figure in the resistance. But Eden and Attlee, despite the Frenchman's perpetual awkwardness, recognised his strength of character and the esteem in which he was held in occupied France. Moreover, they had identified the French Committee of National Liberation (FCNL), chaired by de

Gaulle, as the real voice of the resistance and the basis for a French future government.

In May 1943, during a trip to Washington, Churchill had written in an intemperate cable to the War Cabinet, 'I ask my colleagues to consider urgently whether we should not now eliminate De Gaulle as a political force . . . He hates England and has left a trail of Anglophobia behind him everywhere.' The Prime Minister also forwarded a personal memo from Roosevelt which described the French leader as having a 'messianic complex' with 'dictatorial tendencies', acidly suggesting, 'Perhaps you would like to make him governor of Madagascar?' But Attlee fought off the idea. His sober reply asserted that the 'removal of De Gaulle would probably have a disastrous reaction on the whole resistance movement. The resisters would consider that the Anglo-Saxons had betrayed their leader and a further swing towards Russia would be inevitable.' After detailing the adverse consequences – diplomatic and military – that would follow from breaking off relations with the FCNL, Attlee concluded, 'We are sorry not to be more hopeful, but we are convinced that the Americans are wrong in this and advocate a line . . . with possible evil consequences to Anglo-American relations.' Churchill had been forced, grudgingly, to bow to the War Cabinet's will.

A year on, with the invasion of Normandy about to begin, Attlee and Eden resolved to press de Gaulle's case once more. They were not helped, however, by a strained meeting between Churchill and the French leader in the Prime Minister's temporary headquarters at Doxford station on Sunday, 4 June. De Gaulle had been invited to the railway carriage to be briefed by the Prime Minister about D-Day, but arrived frustrated by the Allies' lack of communication with him, and seething with resentment at their reluctance to endorse his future leadership of a civil administration. Churchill, who had greeted him on the station tracks with arms outstretched, was offended by de Gaulle's sullen attitude and apparent ingratitude. Towards the end of a tense luncheon meeting the Prime Minister told him angrily, 'get this quite clear, every time we have to decide between Europe and the open sea, it is always the open sea that we shall choose. Every time I have to decide between you and Roosevelt, I shall always choose Roosevelt.'

Two days later the French leader further provoked Churchill's ire by refusing to broadcast a message to his compatriots under the terms dictated to him by the Americans. The script he had been presented with offered no recognition of his provisional government, merely saying that 'effective civil administration of France must be provided by Frenchmen'. It also instructed the French people, in the early stages of invasion, to obey the orders of the Allied command. De Gaulle feared – not without some justification – that Roosevelt intended to set up a semi-military administration until he could gauge the will of the country. As a result, the French leader forbade his liaison officers to accompany the invading forces, and he angrily opposed a plan to issue Anglo-American military currency in France – *les faux billets* (sham money), he had called it.

A week earlier, on 31 May, Attlee had written to Eden to assure him of his determination to battle Churchill and Roosevelt over the issue. 'I do not think that the President has any real understanding of the French temperament . . . nor do I think that his attitude is dictated by a zeal for democracy . . . we are the only people in this set-up who can speak as Europeans concerned with the future of Europe.' Grateful for Attlee's support, the foreign secretary chose D-Day to tackle the Prime Minister. Taking his cue from a recent telegram in which Roosevelt had insisted 'I am absolutely unwilling to police France,' he told Churchill, 'If the President renounces the paternity of France, he must allow the British to do the schooling in their own way. The present position is unfair to H.M. Government and dangerous to Anglo-American relations.' Eden and Attlee were backed by Bevin, who wrote to Churchill to explain the fear of his trade union friends in the FCNL that 'France may go completely Communist' and that unless the Free French were given the opportunity to form a government, the whole French labour movement might be driven into Stalin's hands. Whatever the flaws in de Gaulle's character, Bevin counselled, they should not be allowed to obscure the fact that the FCNL was the best option for France's future.

Late on D-Day, realising he had been backed into a corner,
Churchill exploded with rage. 'I was accused of trying to break up the
Government, of stirring up the press on this issue. He said that nothing
would induce him to give way, that De Gaulle must go,' recorded Eden.
'He said I had no right to "bully" him at this time like this . . . FDR and
he would fight the world.'

Helped by the steady progress of the troops in Normandy over the
course of the next week, slowly but surely the temperature in Downing
Street began to fall. At War Cabinet on 7 June, Eden managed to win
agreement that everything should be done to 'encourage the authority
and prestige of the FCNL as a whole, rather than De Gaulle's personal
position'; although, as a concession to the defeated Prime Minister,
the Cabinet also agreed that Churchill should advise the King not to
meet de Gaulle until the discussions over currency notes and other
matters had been satisfactorily resolved. Six days later, on the eve of
the Free French leader's first visit to his liberated homeland, Eden
hosted a dinner party for him; it was attended by five of the Cabinet,
including Attlee and Duff Cooper (by this time Churchill's liaison
minister with the Free French). During the meal, a letter was delivered
from the Prime Minister, still irritated by de Gaulle's refusal to allow
his liaison officers to go to France in the absence of agreement over the
future civil government. 'There is still time to cancel his visit,' wrote
Churchill. 'There is no harm, from our point of view, to the President's
taking the lead.'

But Eden, and Attlee, stood firm, and de Gaulle made his trip the
next day. In newly liberated Bayeux he was greeted spontaneously and
enthusiastically by cheering crowds. British newspapers carried proof
of the warmth of his reception on their front pages the next day, and
the clear success of the French leader's visit would help to mellow
Churchill over the coming weeks.

By now even Roosevelt could see the writing on the wall. In July he
would invite de Gaulle to Washington, treating him with the deference
and hospitality normally offered to a fully fledged head of state, and
granting him three tête-à-tête conversations. Yet even then the old

enmities were slow to fade; it would not be until 23 October that
Churchill and Roosevelt finally recognised the FCNL's reincarnation,
the Provisional Government of the French Republic – with de Gaulle
as its leader – as the legitimate government of France.

At first, Hitler was unperturbed by the Allied invasion. In his
increasingly deluded state of mind, he remained confident the
Wehrmacht was strong enough to repel the Allied armies. In any case,
he was fortified by the knowledge that plans were in motion to finally
put paid to the obdurate British opposition. The Führer Order of 16
May had outlined the use of new long-range weapons against England.
'The bombardment . . . will begin in the middle of June,' it had stated.
'[It] will open like a thunderclap at night.' Reviving the miseries of
the Blitz once again, *Vergeltungswaffe* (reprisal weapon) *1*, the pilotless
plane or 'flying bomb', was about to hit London.

British intelligence had received the first, tentative reports that the
Germans were developing a long-range missile programme as far back
as the autumn of 1942. Only when they listened in on a conversation
between two high-ranking German prisoners of war, on 27 March
1943, had they been finally convinced of the threat, however. One of
those officers, General Wilhelm von Thoma, a member of Rommel's
staff captured in North Africa four months earlier, had expressed
surprise that London was not already in ruins from a German rocket
attack; he had also spoken about a special site near Kummersdorf, in
Brandenburg, Germany, where the weapons were being tested.

On the recommendation of the chiefs of staff, Churchill appointed
his thirty-five-year-old son-in-law Duncan Sandys, then joint
parliamentary secretary to the Ministry of Supply, to investigate
whether the increasing intelligence on secret weapons was reliable, and
what counter-measures should be employed. Sandys was no scientist,
but his military career seemed to qualify him for the task; he had seen
action in the disastrous Norwegian campaign, he was a qualified pilot,
and he had commanded an experimental anti-aircraft rocket battery at
Aberporth in north Wales.

Sandys' biggest obstacle in Whitehall would be Lord Cherwell, piqued that this young upstart had reduced his own influence on such a vital scientific matter. In the Prof's circle of friends, what 'they' were doing with 'their' rockets did not refer to the Germans, but to Sandys and his colleagues. In fact, Cherwell had been sceptical the enemy was even pursuing a long-range rocket programme. 'I have the impression that the technical difficulties would be extreme, and I should be rather surprised if the Germans had solved them,' he told Churchill just two days after Sandys' appointment.

He had continued to hold to this position for many months, despite a convincing mass of photographic and other intelligence to the contrary. At a Defence Committee meeting on 29 June, at which his protégé R.V. Jones dramatically produced pictures of white-painted, rocket-like objects at a place called Peenemünde on the Baltic Sea, the Prof dismissed them as a great hoax, suggesting they were wooden dummies deliberately painted to show up on Allied photographs. Nearly everyone else present thought differently, however, and as a result 596 RAF bombers were sent to attack Peenemünde on the night of 17–18 August 1943. The results of the operation were mixed at best. The death toll included 730 prisoners and foreign workers, but not all the facilities were destroyed, and most of the key scientists survived. The project, it emerged later, had been delayed by just two months.

By the autumn of 1943 the focus of attention had shifted to a second type of missile, the 'pilotless plane', after Operation *Crossbow* (the codename given to the campaign against the long-range weapons programme) had begun to identify a large number of 'ski sites' – the sloping ranges needed to launch the missile – on the French coast. Once again Cherwell was dismissive: although he accepted the evidence of the threat, he advised Churchill that its scale would be 'comparatively insignificant', as the explosives carried by these weapons could weigh no more than half a ton. Herbert Morrison viewed the matter with less equanimity. In a paper prepared for the 16 November meeting of the War Cabinet, he demanded the retention of 2,700 Metropolitan Police officers and 3,500 civil defence workers, shortly due to be released from their duties, to counter the 'unprecedented strain which heavy and sustained rocket bombardment' would place on London. He also began to plot the opening of the new deep shelters he had commissioned at the time of the Blitz, and laid plans for rest centres near London to accommodate half a million refugees.

During the early months of 1944 the RAF and US Army Air Force carried out a series of successful bombing raids against the ski slopes and the pilotless plane's suspected production sites. But in mid-April Operation *Crossbow* reported that a significant number had been repaired, and that the accuracy of the weapon – which had suffered faults in the early months of the year – had been improved. On 17 April, Churchill told the War Cabinet that more effort needed to be concentrated on *Crossbow* targets, and a few days later General Eisenhower ordered US Army chief of staff General Carl Spaatz to give those attacks absolute priority 'for the time being' over all other operations.

Despite this, almost exactly a week after D-Day, the first flying bombs landed in England. In the early hours of Tuesday, 13 June one fell harmlessly in a field bordering the A2 Rochester to Dartford road in Kent, a second fell at Mizbrook's Farm near Cuckfield in Sussex, while a third crashed into a strawberry field at Crouch near Sevenoaks, Kent. Finally, at 4.30 a.m., a pilotless plane reached the real target, London, detonating on a railway bridge in Bow. Six people were killed, while twenty-eight were injured and two hundred rendered homeless.

But in Whitehall the mood was initially calm. At the chiefs of staff meeting that morning Lindemann and Sandys were in rare agreement that the defence of London should not interfere with the battle in France. And at the War Cabinet meeting at 6.30 p.m., Herbert Morrison was relieved – given previous dire predictions of ten-ton rockets – that the damage had not been worse. He reported that the weapon's effect was no greater than a parachute mine and rather less than an up-to-date 2,000lb bomb. Nonetheless, he urged that as many planes as possible should be diverted from the battlefront in Normandy to attack the ski slopes and the factories that supplied them. The War Cabinet also accepted Morrison's recommendation that the press should give out no information until the exact severity of the new menace was known.

The jet-propelled 'flying bomb' (this was Morrison's phrase) was 25ft long with a wingspan of 16ft, and weighed two tons. It travelled at up to 400 miles per hour, and was preset to a maximum range of 150 miles. The first clue it was on its way was a distant hum, growing to a distinctive tearing, rasping, chugging noise, which stopped abruptly as the engine cut out, leaving an eerie, terrifying silence of ten to fifteen seconds before it crashed to the ground, detonating the 2,000lb of high explosive in its nose. Weary, stoical Londoners found other names for the weapon: 'buzz bomb', 'doodlebug', 'zoombie' or 'robot'.

When the ban on reporting the flying bomb was lifted on 16 June, the home secretary tried publicly to shrug off the attacks. 'Dr Goebbels has painted a lurid and over-dramatised picture,' he told MPs. 'The morale of the British takes a lot of upsetting.' But some thought he had misread the mood. A few days later the *Daily Express* would capture the tension in the capital with a famous cartoon, by Giles, depicting Londoners listening with giant ears and captioned, 'It's ridiculous to say these new flying bombs have affected people in any way!'

By the end of the month, with 1,900 killed and 5,500 seriously wounded, Morrison's calm was being sorely tested. On the evening of 27 June, in the recently reopened underground Cabinet War Room, the home secretary's real anxieties were laid bare. During one of his visits to the scene of an explosion, he had been stung by 'jeering references to the impotence of the greatest military alliance in history'; he also expressed concern about the morale of the troops in France while their families were being indiscriminately bombed back home. Morrison demanded the RAF and USAF use 'maximum action' to stop the flying bombs.

Sitting across the table, General Alan Brooke was unimpressed. From his vantage point, the only priority was the battle for France, where the British were now engaged in Operation *Epsom* to capture the strategic town of Caen. '[It was] a pathetic wail from Herbert Morrison who appears to be a real white-livered specimen. He was in a flat spin . . . in fact he did not mind if we lost the war much, provided we stopped the flying bombs!' But by 3 July Churchill was in complete agreement with his home secretary, and even Brooke was acknowledging that 'the threat is assuming dimensions which will require more drastic action'. The War Cabinet, again convening underground, heard that while many Londoners had headed for the shelters, others had fled the capital in their thousands. By the end of a meeting that lasted three and three-quarter hours – one of the longest of the war so far – a comprehensive set of emergency measures had been drawn up. Civil Defence and building workers would be drafted in from outside the city to aid the victims and clear the damage; the maximum possible number of casualties should be moved to hospitals outside the capital; the evacuation of 'priority classes' would continue apace; and the homeless should be allowed to take up accommodation recently freed up by the departed US forces.

In late July, with the swarms of flying bombs still terrorising London, *Crossbow* intelligence brought news of a second, even more deadly German weapon – a missile ten to fifteen tons in weight and 46ft high. Over the next month a new Rocket Consequences Committee worked side by side with the existing Civil Defence Committee to prepare Britain for the arrival of this 'super rocket', now named the V-2. In War Cabinet earlier that month, the Prime Minister had picked up an earlier suggestion made by Morrison of using gas as a weapon of retaliation, although the idea was soon discarded. In the corridors of MI5, however, a retort far more drastic than gas was being contemplated. On 25 August, Guy Liddell, Director of Counter-Espionage, noted in his diary, 'I saw "C" [head of the Secret Intelligence Service, Sir Stewart Menzies] about the uranium bomb and put to him the suggestion that it should be used as a threat of retaliation to the Germans if they use V2. "C" said he could see no reason to think V2 was imminent, although it was possible to think it might start in the near future. He felt however that there was nothing to be lost and he would put the suggestion to the PM who might take it up on his visit to President Roosevelt, which is to take place early next month. On the other hand, he might decide to act more quickly.'

As it was, there was no need for Churchill to consider a move of such magnitude. Slowly but surely the tension in Whitehall eased as Britain's defences – much stronger than in 1940–1 – got to grips with the flying bomb, while Allied attacks slowed its production in France. Anti-aircraft guns were sited all along the coast, to tackle the V-1s long before they reached London, and two thousand barrage balloons were tethered on the southern outskirts of the capital to impede their final approach. But most importantly, the RAF's fighters were intercepting the missiles in significant numbers. Hawker Tempests, Spitfires, Mosquitos and Britain's first jet fighter, the 400mph Gloster Meteor, helped bring down 3,957 of the 7,488 flying bombs that crossed the Channel over the summer months.

By 4 September the situation had eased to such an extent that Morrison advised that the evacuation of London could be halted, and the movement of patients to hospitals outside the city should cease. On the afternoon of 7 September, at the Ministry of Information's headquarters in Malet Street, Brendan Bracken and Duncan Sandys hosted the largest press conference yet held in the war. Here Sandys, armed with the news that the recent seizure of Brussels and Antwerp had included the nearby V-1 launch sites, gave the assembled journalists an unusually detailed resume of the struggle against the flying bomb. Although he was careful to say he could give no categorical assurance that the attacks had ceased, in a dramatic flourish he told reporters, 'Except, possibly, for a few parting shots, what has come to be known as the Battle of London is over.'

Bracken telegrammed Churchill, by then aboard the *Queen Mary* en route for a conference with Roosevelt in Quebec, showering praise on the Prime Minister's son-in-law. 'His account of how the Government handled the flying bomb menace was beyond praise . . . at the end he was cheered by the Press, and as you know the Press are a hard-boiled lot.'

At the height of the Battle of London, in early July, Anthony Eden's attention had been drawn back to the plight of the Jews in the Nazis' concentration camps. On Tuesday, 4 July the Foreign Office received the first comprehensive account of the full horror of the operations at the biggest of these complexes, Auschwitz-Birkenau in southern Poland.

The information came from two Slovakian Jews, nineteen-year-old Rudolf Vrba and twenty-six-year-old Alfréd Wetzler, who had staged a remarkable breakout three months earlier, having hidden in a woodpile for three days. Without documents, compass, map or weapons they made their way southwards, carefully avoiding German 'settler' villages in Poland, before crossing the border into Slovakia and finding safe refuge. There they composed a forty-page report, giving a detailed description of everything they had witnessed at Auschwitz since their incarceration in June 1942, including the geography and management of the camps, how the thousands of prisoners lived, and how they were dying in the gas chambers. Eventually this report had been smuggled into Switzerland, and as a result of coverage in that country's press details had begun to appear in newspapers and radio broadcasts in Britain and America, first on the BBC on 15 June, and then in the *New York Times* on 20 June.

Now Eden was being pressed by representatives from the Jewish Agency on whether His Majesty's government would do anything to help stop the continuing slaughter. The focus at this moment was on the fate of Hungarian Jews, whose transportation to the death camp, which had started on 15 May, was continuing at the rate of 12,000 a day. The day after he received Vrba and Wétzler's report on Auschwitz, Eden faced questions in the House of Commons from Labour's Sidney Silverman about the killing of the Hungarian Jews. Could he confirm that 400,000 had been deported, with 100,000 already murdered? And were there 'any steps the United Nations could take to prevent . . . the total annihilation of European Jewry by Hitlerite Germany'? Without citing figures, Eden said there were strong indications from various sources of 'barbarous deportations and that in the course of them many persons have been killed'. On what to do, he offered the standard answer of the British and American governments at the time: 'the principal hope of terminating this tragic state of affairs must remain the speedy victory of the Allied nations'. But after a meeting with Jewish Agency representatives Dr Chaim Weizmann and Moshe Shertok the next day, the foreign secretary was ready to consider another option. Weizmann and Shertok had devoted the early part of the meeting to exploring whether it was still worth pursuing the Gestapo's extraordinary offer – first made in April, in a meeting between Adolf Eichmann and Joel Brand, a leading Hungarian Zionist – of 'goods for blood': the release of one million Jews in eastern Europe, in exchange for ten thousand lorries, two million bars of soap, eight hundred tons of coffee, two hundred tons of cocoa and eight hundred tons of tea.

Eden and the rest of the War Cabinet had considered this 'offer' back on 1 June and had turned it down flat, seeing it as a stunt aimed at embarrassing the Allied governments. Yet at the Foreign Office that day, Shertok suggested the 'matter was still alive, and that the Germans seemed prepared to strike a bargain'. Eden cautioned him against 'anything that looked like negotiating with the enemy'; it was too dangerous'. He was more interested in the pair's fifth and final proposal, 'that the railway line leading from Budapest to Birkenau, and the death-camps at Birkenau and other places, should be bombed'. Eden said he had already raised with Sir Archibald Sinclair the possibility of raiding the camps, and that he would now put to the air minister the additional suggestion of targeting the railway lines.

Churchill concurred with his foreign secretary about the Gestapo offer, stating bluntly, 'On no account have the slightest negotiations, direct or indirect, with the Huns.' He also supported the idea of bombing, although he rejected Eden's suggestion of wider consultation: 'Is there any reason to raise these matters at the Cabinet? You and I are in entire agreement. Get anything out of the air force you can, and invoke me if necessary.' So, on 7 July, Eden wrote to Sinclair: 'Could you let me know how the Air Ministry view the feasibility of these proposals? I very much hope it will be possible to do something. I have the authority of the Prime Minister to say that he agrees.'

Sinclair's reply, eight days later, was discouraging. On attacking the railways he wrote, 'It is out of our power. It is only by an enormous

concentration of bomber forces that we have been able to interrup
communications in Normandy; the distance of Silesia from our base
entirely rules out our doing anything of the kind.' As for the gas cham
bers, his response was equally unhelpful: 'Bombing the plant is out of the
bounds of possibility for Bomber Command, because the distance is too
great to be carried out at night. It might be carried out by the American
by daylight, but it would be a costly and hazardous operation.' Sinclair'
one positive remark was a suggestion that weapons could be dropped
into the camp, in the hope that some of the victims might fight their
way out; this had been done in a prison camp in France, and 150 men
condemned to death had managed to escape. Although he admitted
that at Auschwitz 'the chances of escape would be very small indeed'.

The air minister promised to consult the Americans about the plan
but Eden was unimpressed. 'He wasn't asked his opinion on this; he
was asked to act,' he scribbled next to Sinclair's doubts about whether
the victims would be helped. And his general comments were no les
scathing: 'A characteristically unhelpful letter. [The] department will
have to consider what is to be done about this. I think that we should
pass the buck to this ardent Zionist in due course i.e. tell Weizmann
that we have approached Sir A. Sinclair and suggest he may like to
see him.' The air minister did consult with the Americans, but his
representations fell on stony ground.

For the next six weeks the matter was passed back and forth between
the Foreign Office and the Air Ministry. The end of the deportation
of Hungary's Jews by the country's leader Miklós Horthy on 7 Jul
– though evidence of it did not filter to the West until some day
later – halted much of the impetus behind the campaign to bomb
Auschwitz, but as Isaac Linton of the Jewish Agency pointed out, in
a letter to the Foreign Office on 16 August, 'The reasons which were
advanced for the bombing of the death camps are still valid. There are
still many Jews in the hands of the Germans who can be sent to those
camps to their doom . . . [the] destruction [of the camps] would make
it difficult for them to construct new camps, and this might be the
means of saving Jewish lives.'

Despite the explicit backing of Churchill and Eden, a combination of bureaucratic infighting and inertia kept the plan bogged down. At one point the Air Ministry urgently requested the clearest and most up-to-date photographs of the camps and installations in the Birkenau area; they were not readily forthcoming. By August and September, Churchill was abroad for much of the time, first with General Alexander's troops in Italy and then in America for discussions with Roosevelt about the Pacific theatre and plans for the post-war order. At home, Eden had to chair the War Cabinet for two of those weeks, as well as cope with Stalin's refusal to aid the Polish resistance in its efforts to drive the Germans out of Warsaw. Meanwhile, the Allies had long since moved from their Normandy fastness: Paris had been set free on 25 August, and in Operation *Dragoon*, the American-led invasion of the south of France, Toulon and Marseilles had been liberated by 28 August. Many were predicting the war would be over by Christmas; once again, the overriding imperative was to hasten Germany's defeat.

Thus, on 1 September, it fell to Eden's junior minister, Richard Law, to tell the Jewish Agency that 'in view of the very great technical difficulties involved' the government had decided it had 'no option but to refrain from pursuing the proposal in present circumstances'. Twelve days later American bombers, flying from Italian bases, attacked and lightly damaged the I.G. Farben synthetic oil plant at Monowitz, just five miles away from the still active gas chambers. Jews would continue to be killed at Auschwitz until the autumn.

The armies of the United Nations are advancing on all fronts,' declared a buoyant Sir Henry Maitland Wilson, Supreme Allied Commander in the Mediterranean, on Friday, 8 September – and the news from the battlefront certainly bore him out. With the liberation of Belgium in full swing, the push to the Dutch border was now on. General Dempsey's Second British Army, having swept through Brussels, Antwerp and Ghent in previous days, was fast approaching the Albert Canal. Meanwhile, the Americans, established on five solid bridgeheads across the River Meuse, were poised to take Liège. The

Canadians, having overcome the Germans at Ypres and Passchendaele, were ready to recapture Ostend. And elsewhere, Allied troops were on the outskirts of Boulogne, the Red Army was advancing to the east Prussian border, and Bulgaria had deserted Hitler to join the Allies.

At home, blackout restrictions in homes had been scaled down to 'dim-out', with thinner curtains permitted, and street lighting was to be improved. The War Cabinet had also suspended recruitment to the Home Guard, while the last 'evacuation special' had run on 7 September, taking 600 mothers and children from Liverpool Street Station to Norfolk. Much of the newspaper coverage focused on the victory over the V-1. On the same day that Maitland Wilson hailed the Allies' onward march overseas, the front page of the Daily Worker proudly proclaimed, 'The triumph of British arms, ingenuity and steadfastness over the flying bomb makes an epic worthy to rank with the greatest feats of our nation in this war.' Just twenty-four hours later, however, all that euphoria was wiped away in an instant. At 6.34 p.m. Sandys was startled to hear a resounding thunderclap while working in his office at Shell Mex House on the Embankment. Sensing immediately that this might be the feared V-2, he rang the Home Security War Room to discover where the bomb had landed; he then called for a car to take him to the scene. R.V. Jones, in his office in Broadway, had no doubts about the cause of the noise. Turning to his assistant, he exclaimed, 'That's the first one!' The distinctive double bang they had heard was that of the supersonic rocket breaking the sound barrier and then exploding on impact.

Herbert Morrison and Ellen Wilkinson, hurrying from the Home Office, were the first ministers to reach the site of the explosion, in Chiswick, west London. In Staveley Road they found six houses destroyed and a crater 30ft deep and 8ft wide. Three people had died in the blast and seventeen others were seriously hurt, including one who died later from his injuries. Morrison's response was to impose an immediate news blackout on the rocket attacks (a second one a few seconds later, twenty miles away in Epping, had merely damaged some wooden huts).

Admiral George Thomson, the avuncular and well-liked chief censor, attended the emergency War Cabinet chaired by Attlee – Churchill was absent in Quebec – at midday on Saturday. Morrison, Bevin, Sandys, Woolton and Cripps joined them, as did the 'second eleven' of the chiefs of staff (most of their seniors were out in Canada with the Prime Minister). The rockets had come from Holland, somewhere near one of the major towns yet to be liberated by the Allies, they were told. Morrison persuaded his colleagues the news blackout should continue for at least forty-eight hours until it became clear whether this was just a one-off attack or the start of another concerted campaign similar to the flying bombs. By 18 September twenty-five rockets had reached England, fifteen of them hitting London and causing fifty-six deaths. Then came a lull of over a week as an audacious military adventure – one that would not only have halted the flow of V-2s towards London, but almost certainly hastened the end of the war – took its course in the Netherlands.

Operation *Market Garden*, the brainchild of Field Marshal Montgomery, was a two-pronged attack: *Market*, the codename for the airborne element, in which over 30,000 British and American paratroopers were dropped behind German lines to seize eight major road bridges over the River Rhine; and *Garden*, the later land link-up of General Horrocks' British armoured XXX Corps, arriving from the Belgian-Dutch border to cross those bridges. If Monty's gambit had been successful, the Allies would have outflanked the fixed German fortifications of the Siegfried Line and established a bridgehead across the Rhine, enabling them to press on towards the enemy's industrial heartland in the Ruhr Valley. In the event, the airdrop achieved complete surprise, only to meet unexpectedly strong resistance. The Allies were forced to retreat, having suffered 17,000 casualties. The failure of Operation *Market Garden* meant the Germans still occupied most of Holland and could continue to bombard both Antwerp – the major port on which the Allies depended – and Britain itself. On 25 September the V-2 campaign resumed.

In War Cabinet, there was much agonising over whether the public

should now be told about the attacks. Morrison pushed for a statemen
in Parliament, but Cripps countered that while the Germans sai
nothing it would be unwise for the government to acknowledge th
destruction and death and give Goebbels his satisfaction. On Monda
9 October Brendan Bracken informed the War Cabinet that althoug
the chiefs of staff had approached their counterparts in America t
restrain publicity, the *New York Times*' respected military edito
Hanson Baldwin had published an article giving details on the rocke
attacks. A week later, the Minister of Information came out strongl
in favour of disclosure, arguing the government was wrong to use it
powers of censorship except where security was at stake.

Baldwin's report was not picked up by the British press, howeve
so Bracken continued to be overruled by the likes of Cripps and, mor
reluctantly, Morrison. As the V-2 attacks increased in early Octobe
some Londoners came to believe – and the idea was not discourage
by Whitehall – that the mystery reverberations they were hearing, an
the fresh damage appearing on their streets, were the result of fault
gas mains. But this cover story could only last so long. After a fe
weeks, there was talk of 'ghost bombs', while the in-joke was that thes
were 'flying gas mains'.

In the end it was not the growing disbelief of the capital's populatio
that forced the government's hand, but the surprisingly belate
announcement of the V-2 attacks by Goebbels' propaganda machine
On 6 November Berlin Radio stated – quite accurately, for once – tha
the 'British Government had concealed from its people' the existenc
of this long-range weapon. Three days later, many of the Britis
newspapers reported the broadcast on their front pages: 'NAZIS GO AL
OUT ON "V2 TERROR IN LONDON" STORIES' (*Daily Mirror*), 'LONDO
UNDER FIRE, SAYS NAZIS' (*Daily Worker*) and 'V-2 HAS SMASHED EUSTO
STATION' (*Daily Express*).

Finally, on 10 November, Churchill went to the House of Common
to outline to MPs – and the country – the nature of the new threa
After informing the House that the enemy had been deploying th
weapon for the past few weeks (actually it had been in use for tw

months), he sought to calm any fears. 'There is no need to exaggerate the danger. The scale and effects of the attack have not hitherto been significant.' The following day the press, which had willingly stayed silent on the new rocket, had no regrets. 'There were excellent reasons for withholding all information while the enemy himself was so uncertain of the effect of his contrivance,' declared *The Times*.

By 20 November over two hundred V-2s had reached England, with ninety-six hitting London; 456 people had been killed – the number of deaths per incident was double that of the V-1. Five days later, a rocket hit a packed Woolworth's store in Deptford, killing 160. Yet this would prove to be the high-water mark of the offensive. In December, its intensity would diminish as the German high command concentrated on blitzing Antwerp, and over the coming months air strikes on the launch sites and the Allied advance in western Europe would render the threat far less potent.

A curious by-product of the silent V-2 was a contrary nostalgia for the noisier, slow-moving V-1. 'If I'm going to be killed, I would like to have the excitement of knowing it's going to happen,' one London woman commented sardonically. But the V-2, as George Orwell noted, successfully left its mark on a population looking forlornly for an end to terror after five years of war. 'What depresses me about these things is the way they set people off talking about the next war. Every time one goes off I hear references to "next time", and the reflection: "I suppose they'll be able to shoot them across the Atlantic by that time".'

Between August and October 1944, Churchill was abroad for seven out of thirteen weeks. A pattern had developed in which the Prime Minister concentrated almost wholly on military strategy, while Attlee presided over the Home Front and oversaw policy on post-war reconstruction.

For much of this period, despite the geographical distance between them, Churchill and the War Cabinet worked in close harmony. The likes of Eden, Anderson and Cherwell would often be at his side during foreign trips, and the normal process of consultative Cabinet government continued: the Prime Minister received approval – and took on board advice – from colleagues back in London before making vital military, political and diplomatic decisions. But Churchill's impulsive predilection for settling crucial issues one-to-one with Roosevelt or Stalin, without War Cabinet endorsement, still ruled him on occasion.

At the conference in Quebec on 15 September (codenamed 'Octagon'), Churchill and Roosevelt signed up to a startling plan, concocted by US Treasury secretary Henry Morgenthau, to dismantle the Ruhr and Saar, the industrial heartland of Germany, once the war was won so that the country's future leaders would never have the opportunity to rearm. Although Morgenthau's staff pointed out to him that fifteen million people would be put out of work, he had remained unmoved: 'Just strip it . . . I don't care what happens to the population . . . I would take every mine, every mill and factory, and wreck it.' All of which was music to the ears of Cherwell, who bore an almost unnatural loathing for the country of his birth; the Prof eagerly urged Churchill to put his name to an extraordinary paper that looked forward 'to converting Germany into a country primarily agricultural and pastoral in character'. Eden, by contrast, was appalled by Morgenthau's plan and, in the knowledge it was coming, had taken the trouble, on 11 September, to forewarn the War Cabinet, asking Sir John Anderson to prepare a paper opposing the idea on economic grounds – although the moral argument against turning Germany into an almost medieval state was as much a factor. 'It was as if one were to take the Black Country and turn it into Devonshire.'

But when the foreign secretary joined the conference in Quebec, he was horrified to discover the agreement had already been signed. Such was his dismay, he openly criticised the plan in front of the delegations – incensing Churchill – and brought forward the paper Anderson had prepared, together with another from his own officials in the Foreign Office. 'If Germany were unable to manufacture she would be unable to pay for imports. World trade would suffer and our exports along with it,' Eden recorded. Fortunately, the foreign secretary had by this point won the support of his American counterpart,

Cordell Hull, and the 'pastoralisation' plan was quietly dropped. Coming so soon after the V-1 and V-2 attacks, the incident was further evidence of the Prof's dubious judgement, and of the increasing determination of the foreign secretary – and the rest of the War Cabinet – to curb his long-standing influence over the Prime Minister.

Three days later, while closeted with Roosevelt at the President's Hyde Park home, following the conclusion of 'Octagon', Churchill bypassed his government on another major policy decision. This being the matter of the atomic bomb, however, most of the War Cabinet would learn nothing of it. And here, at least, Cherwell's was a moderating voice, as both he and Anderson still hoped Roosevelt would provide a counterbalance to Churchill's personal dislike of Niels Bohr and his reluctance to embrace the Danish physicist's idea of sharing nuclear technology with Russia. Yet the President now performed a volte-face. It is unclear whether this was due to Churchill's influence, a worry he would be painted as 'soft' during the forthcoming presidential election if he shared America's secret with an ally distrusted by most of his countrymen, or sheer frustration at Stalin's intransigence over Warsaw. Whatever the reasons, the President now disowned Bohr and his vision of nuclear co-operation.

The two leaders instead signed an aide-memoire which bluntly stated, 'The suggestion that the world should be informed regarding tube alloys, with an international agreement regarding its control and use, is not accepted. The matter should continue to be regarded as of the utmost secrecy.' The paper also noted that when the bomb was finally available 'it might perhaps, after mature consideration, be used against the Japanese'. Churchill's distrust of Bohr was evident in the final paragraph, where the two leaders agreed that 'enquiries should be made regarding the activities of Professor Bohr and steps taken to ensure that he is responsible for no leakage of information, particularly to the Russians'.

An even greater cause of anxiety for Churchill's ministers than his unblinking affection for Roosevelt were his sometimes testy meetings with 'Uncle Joe' in the Kremlin. These exchanges could be sharp, the humour raw and sometimes crude, and the confidences shared often alarmingly frank. So it was late on the evening of 9 October, the first day of the 'Tolstoy' conference between Britain and the Soviet Union, when Stalin and Churchill sat down to talk, attended only by their interpreters, and the conversation moved to south-eastern Europe and the 'spheres of influence' the two leaders wished to establish there.

The Prime Minister told Stalin he had a 'naughty document here with some ideas of certain people in London' and proceeded to lay a half sheet of paper on the table which divided the region in percentage splits between the USSR and Great Britain. Russia would control 90 per cent of Rumania, the others 10 per cent; 90 per cent of Greece would be allocated to Great Britain (in accord with the US), 10 per cent to Russia; Yugoslavia and Hungary would be divided equally between Great Britain and Russia, with 50 per cent each; and Great Britain would take 25 per cent of Bulgaria, the remaining 75 per cent going to Russia. In response, Stalin took a large blue pencil and ticked the paper before passing it back to Churchill. The Prime Minister reflected for a moment, then said, 'Might it not be thought rather cynical if it seemed we had disposed of these issues so fateful to millions of people, in such an off-hand manner? Let us burn the paper.' Stalin replied, 'No, you keep it.'

It was left to Eden to follow up this unorthodox diplomacy the following day when Stalin's foreign minister Molotov took up the percentages and proceeded to haggle over them, initially insisting on increasing Soviet influence in Yugoslavia and Hungary from 50 to 75 per cent. Eden responded with counter-proposals, before eventually calling off the whole discussion, saying he had no interest in being tied down to figures. Three days later Churchill, perhaps recognising the folly of his off-the-cuff initiative, drafted a letter to Stalin in which he admitted the percentages could never form the basis of any public agreement between the Allies, and indeed 'would be considered crude, and even callous if they were exposed to the scrutiny of the Foreign Office and diplomats all over the world'. Yet even now he suggested 'they might, however, be a good guide for the conduct of our affairs'.

When Averell Harriman, Roosevelt's special envoy to Russia, was shown this letter he warned Churchill candidly that the President and Cordell Hull would wash their hands of it. Poland, in particular, was too serious a problem to be dealt with in such summary fashion. So the message was never sent. Then, a few hours later, the Prime Minister deemed it politic to send by telegram to the War Cabinet an explanation of his 'naughty document'. He told Attlee and his colleagues that 'the system of percentage . . . is not intended to be more than a guide . . . nor does it attempt to set up a rigid system of spheres of interest.'

Regardless, Churchill's manoeuvring had been not only premature, but probably also futile. The hard decisions about eastern Europe would be taken at the Yalta conference in January, and even then the unspoken reality, as Stalin tightened his stranglehold on much of the Balkans, was that possession would prove to be nine-tenths of the law.

Churchill had been greatly distracted by the military campaigns in Europe throughout much of 1944, and had left his Cabinet wide scope on the Home Front. But by the autumn of that year, with the moves towards social reform back home gathering pace, he and Lord Woolton became concerned that the shape of post-war Britain was being too significantly moulded by the powerful Labour triumvirate of Attlee, Bevin and Morrison. As Woolton told Rab Butler, the 'Reconstruction Committee should see to it that the Conservative element pulled its weight rather more than it had done'. And when Attlee requested that Labour's Lord Listowel be allowed to attend meetings, Churchill drafted a reply (which he never sent) declaring his reluctance to appoint the peer because 'a solid mass of four [William Jowitt, the new Minister of National Insurance, was the fourth] Socialist politicians . . . all working together, very much dominates this committee'.

Nonetheless, Woolton and his colleagues had been collaborating to great effect, as shown by the near universal public acclaim for the White Paper on social insurance published on 25 September. This was not altogether surprising given it had stayed faithful to the spirit of Beveridge's plan, embodying almost all of its proposals and even paying a belated tribute to the Liberal reformer's 'comprehensive and imaginative report'. Britain now had a government blueprint for a scheme of social insurance in which the whole working population would participate, paying in flat-rate contributions in return for the entitlement to claim flat-rate benefits. Only in three areas did the White Paper diverge from Beveridge. The idea of an unlimited duration of unemployment benefit was rejected in favour of a thirty-week cut-off; for some this evoked the memory of the dreaded means test. Second, the amount of benefit paid, at 24s a week for a single person, was not a subsistence rate; it was designed to act as an incentive for claimants to seek work. And finally, Beveridge's plans for industrial retraining for the unemployed and working-class life assurance were deemed too costly and quietly shelved.

Once again, the paper represented a compromise between Labour and Conservative instincts. But despite the inevitable cheese-paring, the government's Home Intelligence reports recorded widespread approval from the public. The mere establishment of a Ministry of National Insurance appeared to instil confidence that 'the Government means business'. Concern remained about the possible encouragement of thriftlessness: some resented providing incomes for the 'work-shy'; others worried the scheme would be difficult to finance in a crippled post-war world economic environment. But the overall message from the people was, 'If we can pay for the war, we can pay for the peace.'

The other piece of work to come out of the Reconstruction Committee that autumn proved far more contentious – indeed, at one moment it looked as if it might bring down the coalition. After the destruction wrought on the nation's towns and cities in 1940–1, it was clear that in peacetime town and country planning would be needed on a scale hitherto unknown. Politicians of the left, previously uninterested in a subject thought either dull or arcane, now seized on it as another potential tool for social engineering; moreover, in the area of land reform, there was an opportunity for radical redistribution of wealth.

Sir John Reith, in charge of works and planning from 1940 to 1942, had been the first of Churchill's ministers to tackle the country's physical reconstruction. The 'building arbitrator of Britain' (to quote Beaverbrook) had encouraged local government officials from Coventry and Plymouth to 'think big' when imagining the future of their blitzed cities and not to worry about the limitations imposed by the existing pattern of land ownership or planning laws. Reith had also set up the Uthwatt Committee to look at the issues of 'compensation and betterment', and by April 1941 this had returned with some findings anathema to many Conservatives – namely that a central planning authority should be established (with a national plan), and that planning should be viewed not simply as an issue of land use but as a means of 'control of economic development through taxation and regulation'.

Reith's 'socialistic' ideas had begun to concern the property-owning members of the Tory party, and his dismissal from office in February 1942 had been as much to do with his views on national planning as with his boorish and inflexible relations with his colleagues. Now the subject was back on the agenda, however: the Town and Country Planning Bill was designed to enable local authorities to compulsorily acquire bomb-damaged areas for redevelopment on payment of compensation to their owners. But for many Conservatives, who had watched the build-up of radical proposals in health, employment and social insurance with mounting alarm, this was a bill too far. Lord Selborne, Minister of Economic Welfare, claimed it cut 'fundamentally at the rights of property and disregards equity between the State and the individual'.

Much time was spent wrangling over the compensation clauses of the bill; on 2 October the War Cabinet discussed the subject for nearly three hours. 'It revealed . . . the profound cleavage between the two wings of the coalition,' recorded Leo Amery. 'Winston handled the debate with considerable skill and impartiality, but the nearer we get to reconstruction the more difficult it will be to keep the team together.' On 10 October Labour's chief whip William Whiteley disclosed to education minister James Chuter Ede that Tory backbenchers had been to see Churchill and 'threatened trouble'. A fortnight later, the prospect of mass backbench revolt was still on the cards, with Beaverbrook gossiping to Hugh Dalton that 'Anderson had made a complete mess of' explaining the government's latest compensation plans at the 1922 Committee.

Eventually William 'Shakes' Morrison, the minister in charge, quelled much of the rebellion with a substantial concession, fixing compensation at levels that reflected the increase in land prices since 1939. When the final vote was taken, only fifty-six Tory backbenchers went into the opposition lobby, and, on 17 November, the bill followed the Education Act onto the statute book. But along the way it had widened the fault lines in the coalition, and there was little prospect of them now narrowing. Having strained its co-operation to the limit in hours of fierce argument over the various White Papers, the government was fast running out of compromises. Legislation had formally prolonged the life of the parliament until November 1945, but the odds were shortening on the war being over in six months, and normal political hostilities were breaking out again.

Chapter Fourteen
'A light shining on every helmet'
13 December 1944 to 28 May 1945

By December 1944, the Allies were bogged down on the Western Front. All six of their armies had launched a general offensive in mid-November, but although the French 1st and US 7th Army had reached the River Rhine in Alsace, there was precious little progress elsewhere. On 11 December, Ernest Bevin told the War Cabinet that in trade union circles, the impression was 'that the position was slipping and was not being properly gripped'. He himself worried that 'a continuance of the present position might have serious effects on the coalition government'. Yet there were more immediate problems for Churchill and his ministers that day. They had been plunged into a serious political and military crisis over Greece, which was threatening to undermine the whole of the war effort.

After the last German troops had fled the Greek mainland two months earlier, the War Cabinet had authorised a force of 5,000 paratroopers, under the command of Lieutenant General Sir Richard Scobie, to help keep the peace while a new representative, democratic government was established. At first a population starved and brutalised for four years by its German oppressors greeted Scobie's men rapturously as liberators. But by the beginning of December, the mood had changed.

The powerful left-wing alliance EAM (National Liberation Front) the main resistance movement during the occupation, contained a significant communist element and had walked away from a carefully constructed coalition government led by Georgios Papandreou, the social democratic leader who headed the Greek government-in exile. Negotiations over the disarming of the various rebel groups – o which EAM's military wing, ELAS, was by far the most powerful – had broken down. With the political vacuum yet to be filled, Athens had become a dangerous city thronging with thousands of well-armed ELAS guerrillas, spurred on by leaders who were determined to exploit their strength and block any attempt by the provisional government to return to the old days of monarchical rule.

The crisis erupted on Sunday, 3 December, when Greek gendarmes fired on an EAM-inspired demonstration of over 100,000 in Constitution Square in the centre of Athens, killing twenty-eight – some of them children – and injuring 148. For *The Times'* correspondent, this was when 'the seeds of civil war were well and truly sown'. Although no British soldier had played any part in the shooting, the newspaper reported that armoured cars had been present beforehand, and had been reinforced later by tanks and patrols of the Parachute Regiment Since then the population had turned on General Scobie and his men accusing them of association with this 'Fascist action' and of interfering in Greek internal affairs.

When Stalin and Churchill 'carved up' Europe during their late-night meeting at the Kremlin, in October, the former had conceded that Greece was to be in Britain's 'sphere of influence'. So far there was no reason to doubt his word, no hint of interference from Moscow, but Churchill feared that if he failed to act quickly a communist-led EAM could drag the country into the ambit of the Soviet Union. Greece was Britain's major strategic lifeline to the oilfields of the Middle East and to India; the Prime Minister was prepared to countenance the toughest action to restore order.

Having received reports of growing violence in the streets and the seizure by ELAS of many police stations in Athens, Churchill, entirely on his own initiative, issued unambiguous orders to Scobie: 'Do not hesitate to fire at any armed male in Athens who assails the British authority or Greek authority . . . act as if you were in a conquered city where a local rebellion is in progress.' Thus a full-blown armed confrontation began. On 7 December, the British public woke up to bewildering newspaper headlines: 'RAF STRAFE GREEK PARADE' on the front page of the *Daily Mirror*, 'SPITFIRES BLITZ ATHENS TROOPS' in the *Daily Express*. Many had been unable to understand why Britain was interfering so forcefully in the affairs of a liberated country; why were British troops firing on allies when there was a war still to be won against Germany? To all intents and purposes, the action looked like support for a right-wing government against a popular uprising.

In America, the new secretary of state Edward Stettinius Jr was provoked to issue a rebuke. Ostensibly criticising Britain's attempt to stop Count Sforza, deemed untrustworthy by Churchill, becoming foreign minister of Italy – 'We expect the Italians to work out their problems of government along democratic lines without influence from outside' – his comments were widely interpreted as a display of the administration's anger at events in Greece. Members of Congress had begun to ask why Lend-Lease supplies should be used to kill Greeks who had resisted fascism.

The disquiet was such that the government was unable to resist a full-scale Commons debate on the matter. Held on 8 December, it was a rollicking, partisan affair, with no quarter asked or given by Churchill or his critics. Seymour Cocks, the Labour MP who introduced the censure motion, likened the deaths in Constitution Square to the killing of peaceful protestors during the Peterloo Massacre in Manchester in 1815, and wondered if Churchill was claiming the right to appoint the leaders of allied states just 'as Hitler appoints gauleiters in the different countries that come under his sway'. But the Prime Minister appeared unabashed. 'Democracy is no harlot to be picked up in the street by a man with a tommy gun . . . when countries are liberated it does not follow that those who have received our weapons should use them in order to engross themselves by violence and bloodshed all those powers and traditions and continuity which many countries have slowly developed.'

In the end the motion was defeated, by 279 to 30, but only twenty-three Labour MPs supported the government; the rest abstained. Worse, the Prime Minister's plan to re-establish Greece's traditions by restoring to the throne King George II – a monarch widely disliked in his own country for his blessing of the pre-war neo-fascist Metaxas regime – was winning few supporters among his ministers. Most were becoming exasperated by Churchill's predictable and interminable expositions at War Cabinet meetings, and his inability – or reluctance – to persuade the Greek king to step aside and allow a regent, Archbishop Damaskinos of Athens, to take over as an interim leader.

By Wednesday, 13 December, disaster beckoned. In Greece, General Scobie's men were trapped in a small pocket in the centre of Athens, hard pressed to protect British embassy staff and keep ELAS at bay; while in Britain, the government's actions were attracting fierce opposition from the left. Churchill had urged his colleagues to 'put our case to the world', and the first to answer the call was Ernest Bevin. The Minister of Labour decided to face the government's critics head-on at the Labour conference, where the party's fury over what it considered the acquiescence of its leaders in an 'imperialist' venture was boiling over.

When Bevin lumbered onto the platform in Central Hall, Westminster, on the morning of 13 December, cheers were still resounding for John Benstead, general secretary of the National Union of Railwaymen, who had just declared that nothing could be more repugnant to British workers than the 'utilization of our splendid British boys to shoot down the Greek guerrillas'. Undaunted, the labour minister waited for the applause to die down, and then made a passionate and unequivocal defence of the War Cabinet's decision to intervene in Greece.

First, he gave the delegates a stiff lesson in the responsibilities of government. 'If we win the next election you will find that you cannot govern this world by hard emotionalism. It will call for hard thinking and great decisions, tremendous willpower will have to be applied, and the Labour movement will have to learn to ride the storms of life as these great issues arise from time to time.'

Banging the table in front of him, he proclaimed, 'I say boldly that I will hide behind no one. I am a party to all the decisions taken. I cannot say that any one of them was wrong. This step taken in Greece is not the decision of Winston Churchill. It is the decision of the Cabinet.'

Bevin's strong medicine worked. Supported by the block vote of his Transport and General Workers' Union, a resolution uncritical of the government duly passed by 2,455,000 votes to 137,000. Friend and foe alike hailed Bevin's speech as a turning point in the struggle for hearts and minds over the Greek question. Churchill was delighted. 'Ernest Bevin's speech to the Labour Conference won universal acclaim,' he pointed out to Roosevelt.

On 14 December, the British 4th Infantry Division arrived in Greece from Italy – to be followed later by the 46th Division – and over the course of the next few days the military situation was partially stabilised. Finding a political solution proved more difficult, however. In London Churchill and Eden spent fruitless hours talking to the obdurate King George II, who remained unwilling even to countenance the idea of a regent, or indeed any other settlement that did not involve his immediate restoration. And Churchill appeared similarly stubborn. At War Cabinet, two days later, frustrations boiled over when the Prime Minister once again refused to accept Archbishop Damaskinos as a suitable candidate for regent, protesting, 'I won't install a dictator – a dictator of the left.' An exasperated Attlee responded, 'We often heard you say that, but you haven't produced a scintilla of evidence to support your thesis.'

Churchill and Eden now decided to forgo their Christmas holiday and fly to the Greek capital in an effort to find a way through the impasse. It was a mission fraught with danger: EAM only abandoned a plan to blow up the British military headquarters at the Hotel Grande Bretagne when they learned, just hours before his arrival, that the Prime Minister would be in the building.

The negotiations themselves – held on Boxing Day in a sparse room at the Ministry of Foreign Affairs – took place in an atmosphere of intense theatricality, with tanks on guard outside and Spitfires and Beaufighters patrolling ceaselessly overhead. 'When we entered the room all was in murky shadow except for a long table down the middle,' Eden recorded. 'There a few hurricane lamps broke the darkness and played upon the glittering epaulets of the chief of the Soviet Mission . . .'

When the three EAM/ELAS representatives arrived, dressed in khaki battledress, they were forced to hand in their weapons outside the door. Churchill then assured them, 'We want nothing from Greece, not an inch of her territory. We must, of course, ask acceptance of General Scobie's terms. But we hope this conference may restore Greece to her place among the Allies.' The leader of the trio, Dimitrios Partsalidis, the general secretary of EAM, replied smoothly and courteously, thanking the 'Prime Minister of our great ally, England', and assuring him that the clashes between the two sets of troops 'will not shake the traditional relations of the Greek people with the British people'. Churchill then passed down both sides of the long table, shaking hands with all members of the Greek government, before finishing with the EAM/ELAS group, 'whose bows could not have been lower, handshakes warmer nor protestations more friendly had they been ambassadors of a party under the deepest obligation to Great Britain'. He and Eden and the other foreign representatives then left the room to allow the warring Greek parties to get down to business.

The intervention broke the deadlock. Archbishop Damaskinos, whose humour and quiet determination at a meeting prior to the talks had eventually melted Churchill's hostility, reported the next day that there had been unanimous agreement to establish a regency. Back in London, with the help of a persuasive letter from Roosevelt, Churchill and Eden also prised a declaration of consent from a reluctant George II, albeit only after keeping him locked away with them at the Downing Street Annexe until 4 a.m. on 30 December. 'W was very firm and steady,' Eden recalled.

On 5 January EAM/ELAS was forced to flee Athens under pressure from the British forces; six days later it signed a ceasefire. The following month the Treaty of Varkiza was drawn up, instituting a definitive political settlement to the fifty-day armed resistance. A plebiscite on the country's governmental system was promised, to be held within twelve months and followed by free parliamentary elections. When Churchill and Eden returned to Athens two days later, on 14 February, to put their stamp of approval on the agreement, an enthusiastic crowd of 40,000 cheered them as they were driven through the city in an open-topped car. Churchill had achieved his objectives. The communist threat of EAM/ELAS had been defeated, and Britain's vital 'sphere of influence' in the Balkans had been preserved. But it had been a close-run thing, and another cause of division within the coalition.

In Italy, the transfer of those British divisions to Greece had further depleted the Allied ground forces – already reduced since D-Day – and their American commander, General Mark Clark, had been forced to consolidate and wait for better weather before attempting the push north, through the country's treacherous mountainous regions, towards the German 'Gothic Line'. At the same time, a far more serious setback had come in a surprise German counter-offensive in the Ardennes region of Belgium, France and Luxembourg, where on 16 December twenty-eight divisions punched a big hole through the Allied front, splitting the American and British armies in two. Ultimately, the Wehrmacht advance had foundered on a lack of supplies and strong resistance from General George S. Patton's Third Army, and by 3 January Patton and Field Marshal Montgomery – by then in temporary command of the American First and Ninth Armies in the north of the 'Battle of the Bulge' – had begun to push the Germans back; but it had been a costly campaign, with American casualties eventually numbering 100,000.

Back in Britain, the early weeks of 1945 had seen tensions continue to rise within the government. One of the major factors was the hold Beaverbrook and Bracken continued to exert over Churchill. Attlee, for one, had finally lost patience; on 19 January, he wrote a letter to the Prime Minister setting out a devastating critique of his handling of the Cabinet and his favouritism towards his two 'cronies'. The Deputy Prime Minister's frustration had soared following a series of War Cabinet meetings badly managed by an occasionally ill, often tired and invariably distracted Churchill. On 2 January, for instance, ministers spent a good part of what Brooke called a 'ghastly' three-hour Cabinet listening to the Prime Minister fulminate against the BBC and Reuters over their news coverage of the Greek crisis, before he finally turned to Attlee's paper on a V-2 warning system for London Underground stations. A week later Leo Amery noted that items regarding Italian claims against Germany and constitutional policy in Malaya had taken an hour and a quarter to discuss when 'they need not have taken five minutes . . . Winston had not looked at the papers and had no idea what they were about, but talked away at large and would not hear when things were explained to him.'

In his letter Attlee confronted Churchill over this time wasting. Busy ministers, he wrote, spent much time preparing succinct memoranda for their colleagues to read for War Cabinet meetings. 'What happens then? Frequently a long delay before they can be considered. When they do come before the Cabinet it is very exceptional for you to have read them. More and more often you have not read even the note prepared for your guidance. Often half an hour and more is wasted in explaining what could have been grasped by two or three minutes reading of the document.'

Yet 'worse than this', Attlee moved on to explain, was the destructive influence of Beaverbrook and Bracken. 'Conclusions agreed upon by a committee on which have sat five or six members of the Cabinet and other experienced ministers are then submitted with great deference to the Lord Privy Seal [Beaverbrook] and the Minister of Information [Bracken], two ministers without cabinet responsibility, neither of whom has given any serious attention to the subject. When they state their views it is obvious that they know nothing about it . . . Time and again important matters are delayed or passed in accordance with the decision of the Lord Privy Seal.' This was, Attlee suggested, 'a serious constitutional issue'. He concluded, 'I do not think you can complain of any lack of loyalty on my part, but I think that your cabinet colleagues have the right to ask that in matters to which you cannot give your personal attention you should put confidence in them.'

Churchill was stunned by the letter; his anger at it was nothing short of apoplectic. After phoning Beaverbrook to share his fury, he began drafting a derisive reply. But upon consulting the members of his inner circle, he was surprised to discover the Deputy Prime Minister had their support. Jock Colville recorded, 'Greatly as I love and admire the PM, I am afraid there is much in what Attlee says, and I rather admire his courage in saying it.' Bracken himself told Churchill, 'Attlee's quite right,' while Clementine, always honest with her husband, replied, 'I admire Mr Attlee for having the courage to say what everyone is thinking.' Most surprising of all was Beaverbrook's acknowledgement that it was a 'very good letter'. After this, Churchill put aside his withering response and instead sent a short, courteous reply:

My Dear Lord President,
    I have to thank you for your Private and Personal letter of January 19. You may be sure I shall always endeavour to profit by your counsels.

Yours sincerely,
Winston Churchill

Yet the following day's War Cabinet, on Monday, 22 January, provided little evidence that the leopard had changed its spots. Brooke wrote, 'At 5.30 War Cabinet, drawn out by the usual endless statements by Winston. My God! How I loathe these Cabinet meetings. The waste of time is appalling.' Nor was there any sign of contrition from either Beaverbrook or Bracken, despite their acceptance of the force of Attlee's argument. Two days later they sent a joint, mocking letter to Churchill about the Labour leader – who had also been complaining about non-attendance at the Lord President's Committee – in which they quoted from Samuel Taylor Coleridge's *Rime of the Ancient Mariner*:

> Our attention has been called to the lament of Mr Attlee in his paper L.P. (45) 17 that ministers do not attend his committee. We now offer to fill two of the vacant places. We are moved to this offer by the sad plight of the Lord President.
>
> 'Alone, alone, all, all alone,
> Alone on the wide wide sea',
>
> Yours ever,
> B.
> B.B.
>
> P.S Our offer depends of course on the approval of the Lord President.

Meanwhile, Lord Woolton's Reconstruction Committee had virtually run its course. The King's Speech at the end of 1944 had promised only two new items of policy: one was Bevin's inspiration, establishing wages councils to set minimum pay levels and encourage collective bargaining, while the other was Hugh Dalton's Distribution of Industry Bill, which would give the government greater powers to locate new manufacturing in areas of heavy industry blighted during the depression.

But Parliament's principal legislative preoccupation in early 1945 was the Family Allowances Bill. This was an outcome of the Social Insurance White Paper and took up a key principle of Beveridge's plan, which had proposed an allowance of 8s a week for all children after the firstborn, graduating with age. In the end the Cabinet had decided on a lower sum of 5s a week – intended to supplement a family's income, rather than provide for the needs of the child in full – but even this represented a milestone in the history of social reform, as well as a personal triumph for the backbench MP Eleanor Rathbone, who had been campaigning for the measure for twenty years. Before it reached the statute book, however, the government faced another Commons rebellion, as Rathbone mounted a final battle to have the payment made to the mother, rather than the father.

On 6 March, just two days before the bill's second reading, Eden, as Leader of the House, and Sir William Jowitt, national insurance minister, met a group of MPs including Rathbone, Beveridge (now elected as a Liberal) and Labour's Edith Summerskill to hear the rebels' case. By now 180 MPs from all parties had signed a motion in favour of the mother being the recipient, and Rathbone's delegation suggested to Eden that the matter should be left to a free vote. At War Cabinet a little later that afternoon – still being held underground, as the sporadic V-2 attacks continued – there was an hour-long discussion on the subject. Morrison made it clear he favoured the mother. 'She controls the household budget . . . and it is in accord with modern ideas,' he said. Churchill responded, 'Wages will be paid to the mother next! But this is not a matter for Government to force.'

Eventually they agreed to allow a free vote, and the debate on 8 March revealed almost unanimous support for Rathbone's cause. Although some MPs were reluctant to back the move under the banner of 'women's rights', most agreed with the Conservative Lady Astor's observation that 'When family allowances were first mooted people on this side of the house said it would break up the home, and the Labour Party and the trade unions would not have them at all. We have come a great way since then, and all because of one revolutionary woman.'

The Family Allowances Act would be the last major reform to emerge from Churchill's war ministry. The other White Papers were now bogged down by party disputes and resistance from vested interests. The White Paper on health, for example, had run into the brick wall of the leaders of the British Medical Association, who continued to resist the proposal that GPs should become salaried state employees. And Herbert Morrison's attempt to push for nationalisation of the electricity industry was stymied by the Tory members of the Reconstruction Committee.

Without a common legislative project, the coalition began to succumb to old-fashioned partisanship. And of the many individual Labour–Tory alliances that had made it so effective in earlier times, the first to collapse was the Churchill/Bevin axis. The trigger was the Prime Minister's refusal to consider changes to the Trade Disputes and Trade Unions Act of 1927, drawn up after the general strike of 1926 by Stanley Baldwin's government – when Churchill had been chancellor – and which had declared any sympathetic ('secondary') strike action illegal, had outlawed mass picketing, and had forced trade union members to make a positive decision to pay a political levy to a political party ('contracting-in' rather than 'contracting-out').

Over the previous four years the act had been the target of repeated lobbying by Walter Citrine, general secretary of the Trades Union Congress. Bevin meanwhile, who had long regarded it as 'petty vindictiveness inspired by class and party spite', saw its repeal as the minimum reward for the hard work done by trade unionists in factories up and down the country to supply the war effort. Yet on 9 March, knowing the Conservative Party would reject the change, Churchill wrote to the TUC council to say any amendment was out of the question prior to a general election.

This alone was enough to provoke Bevin's ire, but worse was to follow six days later, in Churchill's speech to the Conservative Party conference. Standing on the same stage in Central Hall, Westminster, where the labour minister had so loyally rallied to his side four months earlier, the Prime Minister warned, 'Our Socialist friends have officially committed themselves, much to the disgust of some of their leaders, to a programme for nationalizing all means of production, distribution and exchange . . . these sweeping proposals . . . imply not only the destruction of the life of the whole of our existing system of society and life and labour, but the creation and enforcement of another system or systems borrowed from foreign lands and alien minds.'

Churchill then turned to wartime controls, which covered not only rationing and prices but also wages and production and had already been a target of Beaverbrook's *Daily Express* for many weeks. 'Control for control's sake is senseless. Controls under the pretext of war or its aftermath which are, in fact designed to favour the accomplishment of totalitarian systems however innocently designed or whatever guise they take . . . are a fraud which should be mercilessly exposed to the British public. At the head of our mainmast we fly the flag of free enterprise.'

As Minister of Labour and National Service, charged with directing Britain's workforce and industries to sustain the war effort, Bevin had implemented many of those 'controls'; the link with totalitarianism infuriated him. 'He's all right as a national leader, but when he turns into the leader of the Tory Party you can't trust him an inch,' Bevin complained to Dalton. He retaliated in a series of cutting speeches in the north of England on the weekend of 7 and 8 April. In Leeds he reminded his audience that the Tory Party 'which had a majority for nearly 20 years . . . completely failed to prepare for defence or adequately to warn the country where it was heading. It ran a foreign policy which nearly brought us and the whole of civilisation to the dust.' And on the specific question of controls, he said the Conservatives were creating a bogey. 'Come out into the open. Is it your intention to take off the control of food and let prices rise? Do you mean you are going to take off the price control of clothing, furniture and other things?' If that was the case, Bevin claimed, the resulting inflation would cut the value of the public's savings in half. In Blaydon-on-Tyne in Durham, on the Sunday, he went so far as to invent his own totalitarian threat. Hitler had received his money and power from big business, Bevin claimed; now 'big business here might join up with the big business of the Nazis', leaving Labour as the sole force to fight oppression.

This provided the pretext for Brendan Bracken to enter the fray. 'I can hardly avoid saying something about his blitz on the Conservative Party,' he told Holborn Tories on Monday, 9 April. 'Britain will never accept the sort of totalitarian state desired by the Socialists . . . as a nation of enterprises our future is boundless. As a nation of form fillers and restrictionists we have the bleakest of futures.'

Not only had the government's unanimity broken down, its splits were now being paraded openly. Yet the Prime Minister appeared outwardly relaxed about this newfound spirit of disunity. The day after Bracken's broadside against Bevin, during questions in the House about the future of the Ministry of Information, Labour's Manny Shinwell suggested mischievously that following such a partisan speech the former's salary should now be borne by Tory Central Office. At which Churchill shot the arch riposte, 'The minister of information was speaking in his capacity as a member of His Majesty's Government – in which, at present, great freedom appears to be allowed . . .' provoking laughter in the chamber.

The gloves were off, and the press now hummed with talk of an immediate break-up of the coalition and an early general election. 'Just a Big Happy Family' was the caption to a Low cartoon in the *Evening Standard* on 12 April. In it, Bevin and Bracken, their arms in slings, glared at each other across the Cabinet table; the gnome-like Beaverbrook peered up from under the table next to Bracken, holding a book entitled 'Unarmed Combat'; and Churchill, presiding with cigar in mouth, told his ministers, 'Remember gentlemen, no questions asked about our private lives outside . . .but all is peace and loyalty within.' It was a far cry from 'All Behind You, Winston'.

The 'Big Three' conference at Yalta, in February, had seen the post-war territorial settlement dictated by the brute fact of the Soviet Union's overwhelming military presence in eastern Europe. Of all the concessions to Stalin, perhaps the most ignominious was that Poland's new frontier to the east would follow the Curzon Line – a return, effectively, to the carve-up of the Molotov–Ribbentrop pact. By way of compensation the Poles had received a 'substantial accession of territory' from Germany in the north and west, but within weeks it had become clear that their future would be bleaker even than this.

On 6 March Eden reported to the War Cabinet that Stanislaw Mikolajczyk, leader of the Polish government-in-exile, looked certain to be excluded from a new provisional administration at the behest of Molotov, the Soviet foreign minister. Meanwhile the Foreign Office had received disturbing reports of mass arrests of intellectuals in the Cracow area, the transportation of thousands to labour camps at Voroshilovgrad, and the detention of 6,000 former Home Army resistance officers in a camp near Lublin run by Russian officials.

Churchill and Eden, unwilling to concede they had been betrayed by Stalin at Yalta, wondered whether there might be another explanation. Churchill even speculated to the War Cabinet, 'The change of atmosphere since Yalta suggests that Stalin is not in supreme control.' But his overriding reaction was gloom: 'What alternative [is there] – unless you are prepared to fight against Russia . . . Russia is fastening [her] own types of government in all other countries, including now Vienna, Czechoslovakia, Poland and Yugoslavia.' Writing in his diary on 23 March, Eden conceded, 'Altogether our foreign policy seems a sad wreck and we may have to cast about fresh.'

Five days later the War Cabinet debated a pledge made by Churchill in the Commons, on 27 February, that citizenship of the Empire should be offered to those Polish troops who had fought 'so valiantly' under British command in France and Italy, but who had no desire to return to a homeland increasingly under Soviet diktat. Herbert Morrison expressed doubts about the commitment: 'Many of those who have passed through the army are pretty poor people . . . many also are Fascists. Lots of other foreigners want to stay here – many have "fought" in Pioneer units to escape internment. They will press for what you give to the Poles.' The home secretary returned to an argument with which his colleagues were all too familiar. 'Any large increase in the foreign population increases the risk of disorder – anti-Semitism is just below the surface.'

Churchill's response was brusque. 'I'm concerned only with Poles – and Poles who have really fought. We have a sacred duty to them. They are not without their troubles, and they have been led on by pledges and promises of ours.' He was backed by Sir Archibald Sinclair, who reminded his colleagues of the 'indispensable reinforcement' provided by Polish pilots in the Battle of Britain. 'They had a very good reputation in Scotland, in spite of being Roman Catholics . . . the claims of the Teutonic Jews are not to be compared with them.'

The pledge would be honoured, but it was at best a gesture, and a small one at that. Five and a half years before, Germany's invasion of Poland had been the act that had finally stirred Britain from her slumber. Now the same people were falling under the yoke of a new dictatorship, but this time the oppressor was Britain's ally. So long as the war against Germany was yet to be won, the plight of the Poles would have to be overlooked.

The previous month, on Friday, 16 February, the strategy behind the RAF's bombing campaign in Germany had, quite by accident, finally spilled out into the open. In a briefing at SHAEF (Supreme Headquarters Allied Expeditionary Force) in Paris, Air Commodore Colin Grierson had taken questions from reporters about the recent raids on Dresden, during which huge numbers were killed (estimates of 70–100,000 were being made, although the death toll would later be calculated at around 30,000) after hundreds of tons of incendiary bombs unleashed a firestorm on the city.

When asked whether the main aim of attacking Dresden had been to cause confusion among fleeing refugees, or to hit trucks carrying military supplies to the Russian front, Grierson replied that the primary objective was to prevent the Germans transporting military equipment to the battlefront, but added, in a later aside, that the raid had helped destroy 'what is left of German morale'. In his report on the press conference, Associated Press correspondent Howard Cowan then wrote, 'Allied air bosses have made the long-awaited decision to adopt deliberate terror bombing of the great German population centres as a ruthless expedient to hasten Hitler's doom.' The following day newspapers all over America ran the startling headline 'TERROR BOMBING GETS ALLIED APPROVAL AS STEP TO SPEED VICTORY'.

In London, Cecil King, executive editor of the *Daily Mirror*, was appalled by the report. 'This is entirely horrifying. Not only does it make nonsense of all our protestations about our war aims and about our bombing policy; it gives official proof for everything that Goebbels ever said on the subject. It is wicked as well as being typically un-British.' Nonetheless, although the censor Admiral Thomson had approved Cowan's story, King and others in Fleet Street successfully lobbied for its suppression.

It was not until Tuesday, 6 March, when Richard Stokes, one of a lonely trio of parliamentary campaigners against the bombing campaign (the Bishop of Chichester, George Bell, and Stokes' fellow Labour MP Arthur Salter were the others), stood up in the Commons chamber to reveal the Associated Press report, that MPs and the public learned of the policy for the first time. Stokes chose as the occasion for his intervention the annual Air Estimates debate, in which Sir Archibald Sinclair had earlier praised the work of Bomber Command. 'Allied air bombing is on such a colossal scale that Dr Goebbels has had to admit "it can now hardly be borne",' the air minister told MPs. In response Stokes, after reading out the banned AP story, asked, 'Is terror bombing – perhaps the minister will answer me – now part of our policy? And why is it that the British people are the only people who may not know what is done in their name?'

'I leave out the moral issue,' he said resignedly. 'I have given up in despair trying to persuade people on that issue. On the strategic issue, what are you going to find with all the cities blasted to blazes and diseases rampant? May you not well find that you will simply be overtaken by your own weapons, and that the disease, filth and poverty, which will arise, will be almost impossible either to arrest or to overcome . . .'

Of course the 'news' in the AP dispatch was over three years old. The RAF's switch from 'precision' targeting to 'area' bombing had followed the publication of the Butt Report in September 1941, which revealed that only one in three aircraft had got within five miles of its target. A directive to Bomber Command on 15 February 1942 stated that in the campaign to strike at the industrial heartlands of the Ruhr and Rhineland, 'the primary object of your operations should now be focussed on the morale of the enemy civil population and, in particular, that of industrial workers'. The only time in the subsequent three years when the War Cabinet had seriously dissented from the strategy had occurred during the build-up to D-Day, when Eisenhower insisted on blitzing multiple French communication and industrial centres at the cost of thousands of civilian lives. And even then Britain's objections – led by Churchill – had been swiftly overruled.

If Sir Archibald Sinclair, in charge of the political direction of policy, had any moral qualms about the bombing of population centres, he kept them well hidden. In May 1942 Geoffrey Shakespeare, National Liberal MP and a former junior minister for Dominion Affairs, wrote to the air minister in support of the campaign: 'I am all for the bombing of working class areas in German cities. I am Cromwellian – I believe in "slaying in the name of the Lord" because I do not believe you will ever bring home to the civil population of Germany the horrors of war until they have tasted it in this way.' Sinclair replied that he was 'delighted to find that you and I are in complete agreement about . . . bombing policy generally'.

There is, however, evidence that Churchill harboured some doubts about the campaign. On the night of 27 June 1943, just days after the RAF had dropped 15,000 tons of bombs in twenty nights as part of the 'Battle of the Ruhr', Australian Richard Casey, the War Cabinet's minister resident in the Middle East, was among those with the Prime Minister at Chequers when he was shown a graphic film of the bombings. 'WSC suddenly sat bolt upright and said to me "Are we beasts? Are we taking this too far?" . . . I said we hadn't started it, and that it was them or us.'

The same scruples may have inspired an extraordinary memorandum Churchill drafted to the Chief of the Air Staff, Sir Charles Portal, and his colleagues on the Chiefs of Staff Committee, on 28 March 1945. 'It seems to me that the moment has come when the question of bombing of German cities simply for the sake of increasing terror, though under other pretexts, should be reviewed,' the Prime Minister wrote. 'Otherwise we shall come into control of an utterly ruined land . . . The destruction of Dresden remains a serious query against the conduct of Allied bombing.'

What prompted this volte-face is unclear. But a volte-face it certainly was, for it had been a curt instruction from Churchill, back on 26 January, that set in train the bombing of Dresden. Having asked Sinclair, the night before, what plans he had for 'basting the Germans in their retreat from Breslau' – a remark that revealed his eagerness to curry favour with Stalin ahead of the forthcoming Yalta conference – the Prime Minister had urged his air minister to consider whether 'Berlin, and no doubt other large cities in East Germany, should not now be considered especially attractive targets'. After a conversation with Sinclair the following day, the air chiefs immediately set about planning strikes on Dresden, Chemnitz and Leipzig.

In fact, by the time Churchill drafted his later memorandum, the area bombing campaign was already in its final throes; there were few strategic targets left to strike. What had changed, perhaps, was that news of the scale of the carnage at Dresden was now reaching the West, and the authorities were being furnished with disturbing reconnaissance photographs of the devastated city. Or maybe Churchill had succumbed to one of his periodic bouts of introspection, prompted by the realisation that the military campaign was finally, irrevocably, winding down. 'AT LAST – COLLAPSE,' was the headline in Beaverbrook's *Daily Express* on the day the Prime Minister wrote to the air chiefs. It was now apparent that all organised resistance along the 700-mile Western Front had ceased; all that remained was for the Allied forces to capture the ruins of Berlin and link up with the Soviets.

Whatever the reason, Air Chief Marshal Sir Charles Portal would have no truck with Churchill's self-critical minute. Four days later the Prime Minister was persuaded to withdraw it, and substitute it with something altogether milder for the record. In the new version, there was no mention of Dresden, no reference to 'increasing terror', and no hint of a 'serious query' against the bombing strategy. With the punch taken out, the opening merely stated, 'It seems to me that the moment has come when the question of the so-called "area bombing" of German cities should be reviewed from the point of view of our own interests.'

The strategic air offensive formally ended on Monday, 16 April. From then on, Portal directed, the RAF's remaining tasks would be to give 'direct support to the land battle and . . . continue their offensive against the sea power of the enemy which they have already done so much to destroy.'

On the afternoon of Thursday, 12 April, while sitting for a portrait at his favourite retreat in Warm Springs, Georgia, President Roosevelt collapsed and died of a cerebral haemorrhage. The sixty-three-year-old had appeared tired and sick at Yalta two months earlier, but his death nonetheless came as a shock in Downing Street. The following morning Churchill told the War Cabinet he felt 'profound sorrow and a deep sense of personal loss'; he initially planned to attend the funeral, but later asked Eden to go in his place.

Roosevelt's successor, Harry Truman, a farmer's boy and former county judge from Independence, Missouri, was little known on the international stage, and there was concern about how this modest, unassuming sixty-one-year-old would engineer an end to the Pacific war and manage the tricky transition to peace in Europe alongside the wily Stalin. 'I felt like the moon, the stars, and all the planets had fallen on me,' an apprehensive new president told reporters soon after taking the oath of office.

The day before Truman was sworn in, the US Third Army's 80th Infantry Division reached the gates of the Buchenwald concentration camp, in Weimar, Germany, and thus became the first Allied soldiers to confront evidence of the singularly depraved nature of Hitler's regime. Buchenwald had been in operation for seven years, during which around 240,000 prisoners had been incarcerated there – many Jews, but also Poles, Slavs, the mentally and physically disabled, Roma, homosexuals, and various religious and political prisoners. Large numbers had been worked to death in local arms factories. Many had died after being experimented upon. Others had been arbitrarily murdered, taken into the woods nearby and shot or hung from trees.

On 18 April General Eisenhower met Churchill in London, and persuaded him to quickly dispatch parliamentarians and journalists to the camps, before they were cleaned up and it was 'too late to see the full horrors'. Three days later a British delegation of ten MPs and two peers arrived at Buchenwald to view the piles of dead bodies and talk to the remaining, starved inmates. The sole woman in the party was Mavis Tate, Conservative MP for Frome, a striking, unconventional advocate of women's rights. She had been asked to record her impressions of Buchenwald for a British Pathé News film. Thousands in cinemas up and down Britain would later hear her voice, poised but seemingly on the edge of anger, deliver a narrative about the camp over images more awful than anything they had seen in all the previous five years of war.

'Some people believe that the reports of what happened there are exaggerated,' she began. 'No words could exaggerate. We saw – and we know.' Then, to pictures of scores of naked and half-naked corpses piled up on top of each other next to a giant woodpile, she told the audience, 'Much as they shock you, do believe me when I tell you that the reality was indescribably worse than these pictures. You can't photograph suffering – only its results. In pictures you have no smell of disease or death. You see just a fragment of the full pattern of horror.' Tate returned from Buchenwald convinced that the restoration of democratic government would not, by itself, be sufficient to solve the German problem. 'There is indubitably a deep streak of evil and sadism in the German race, such as one ought not to expect to find in a people who for generations have paid lip service to Western culture and civilisation.'

In War Cabinet in April there had been fierce debate about what punishments the Nazi hierarchy should suffer for having ordered this slaughter. The Americans wanted some kind of quasi-judicial process; they suggested that 'arch criminals' like Hitler, Göring and Goebbels should first be served with a 'document of arraignment', alleging they were responsible for a plan to establish Nazi domination over the world, before being brought before an inter-Allied tribunal. Stafford Cripps, the lawyer, disliked the idea: 'It mixes political and judicial decisions with disadvantage to both. It will give him [Hitler] the chance to harangue . . . it would be better to make a political decision in favour of punishing them by forced labour.' Morrison and Churchill saw no point in a trial of any kind. 'All major allies are committed to the execution of Hitler,' said the home secretary. 'This mock trial is objectionable . . . better to declare that we shall put them to death.' Field Marshal Smuts, however, advised against summary executions, saying it would 'set a dangerous precedent'.

Then, on the night of 1 May, came the news, via Hamburg radio, that Hitler was dead, having 'fallen at his command post in the Reich Chancellery fighting with his last breath against Bolshevism'. Churchill, who had been discussing future election strategy over dinner with Beaverbrook, Minister of Production Oliver Lyttelton and the Tory chief whip James Stuart, remarked, 'Well, I must say I think he was perfectly right to die like that.' A sceptical Beaverbrook retorted that he 'obviously did not', a judgement borne out some days later, when it was revealed that the Führer and his mistress Eva Braun had committed suicide in his bunker. Elsewhere, Alan Brooke 'remained completely unmoved . . . I think I have become so war weary with the continual strain of war that my brain is numbed, and incapable of feeling intensely.'

The War Cabinet's earlier preference for summary execution now gave way to America and Russia's insistence that the major war criminals should face full state trials. But two days after the announcement of Hitler's death, Churchill still wondered whether they should 'negotiate with Himmler, and bump him off later'. 'Quite entitled to do so,' agreed Morrison. The horrific scenes from Buchenwald were fresh in ministers' minds, and when the war secretary Sir James Grigg suggested the atrocities there and at the other concentration camps – all of which were under Himmler's command – did not qualify as 'war crimes', the Prime Minister responded sharply: 'Don't quibble; he could be summarily shot, in respect of some of those in the camp.'

The war was now hurtling towards its conclusion. On 2 May the Red Army completed the capture of Berlin, and in Italy nearly a million German soldiers laid down their arms. The following day the British 7th Armoured Division entered Hamburg, the last remaining defence for the Germans in the north. Meanwhile, as Japan's defences crumbled in Burma, Major General Henry Chambers' Indian 26th Division marched into Rangoon. Then, at 6.30 p.m. on 4 May, in a carpeted tent on a wind- and rain-swept Timeloberg Hill at Wendisch Evern, in Lower Saxony, Field Marshal Montgomery accepted the unconditional surrender of German forces in north-west Germany, Holland and Denmark. Soon afterwards Churchill summoned his chiefs of staff to the Cabinet Room at 10 Downing Street, where, with tears in his eyes, he thanked them for everything they had done over the last five years, before shaking them each by the hand.

It would be another three days before General Alfred Jodl arrived, at 2.40 a.m., at General Dwight Eisenhower's temporary headquarters in a small schoolhouse in Rheims, France, to sign the final unconditional surrender. Churchill was informed at 7 a.m., and then spent a frustrating day on the telephone in tortuous negotiations with President Truman and Stalin – in particular, about how to synchronise the announcement that the war was over. Meanwhile word about the German surrender had got out, and crowds began to gather outside Buckingham Palace, shouting 'We want the King.' In response, despite the absence of any official confirmation that hostilities had ceased, the Home Office issued a circular instructing the nation on how they could celebrate: 'Bonfires will be allowed, but the government trusts that only material with no salvage value will be used.' Bell ringers were put on alert for a nationwide celebratory peal.

At War Cabinet that evening, Churchill recounted his discussions with an obdurate Stalin – whom he remained unwilling to upset, even at this late stage – and told his colleagues that the victory and end of the war would be formally announced at 3 p.m. the next day. But given the outpouring of joy, all present agreed that it was impossible not to say something before then. The Ministry of Information therefore put out a short statement a little while later, saying simply: 'In accordance with arrangements between the three great powers, tomorrow, Tuesday, will be treated as Victory in Europe Day and will be regarded as a holiday.'

Perhaps appropriately, there was no meeting of the War Cabinet on the morning of VE Day. As the lunchtime speaker at a wallpaper industry exhibition at the Suffolk Street Galleries, Ernest Bevin was in reflective mood. After admiring the exhibits, he told fellow diners he had no doubt that the harmony of colour on the walls contributed to happier minds and happier homes. He 'looked forward to the time when the housewife would display her new wallpaper to her friends as she now expectantly displayed her new jumper'. After lunch, Bevin, like his fellow ministers, made his way to the Houses of Parliament to await the arrival of the Prime Minister, who was due to speak following his victory broadcast from the Cabinet Room in Downing Street at 3 p.m.

In the Lords, at 3.15, it fell to Lord Woolton to read out Churchill's statement. This disclosed that hostilities would officially end at one minute after midnight, but that in the interests of saving lives the ceasefire had been sounded along all fronts the previous day. In the Commons, as the clock ticked by with no sign of the Prime Minister, it was left to Sir John Anderson, acting Leader of the House in Eden's absence, to fill in. The Chancellor, hardly a natural extemporiser, attempted to spin out a series of good-humoured answers to spurious questions, prompted on occasions by Morrison and A.V. Alexander who sat alongside him. In danger of drying up, he had just responded to a further supplementary question with a terse 'No, Sir, I do not know,' when Churchill finally walked into the chamber at 3.23 p.m.

The MPs rose as one to greet him, waving their order papers, their cheers combining with those from the side galleries and Strangers' Gallery to produce a truly thunderous welcome. The Prime Minister then read his broadcast statement once more, before giving 'hearty thanks to men of all parties . . . for the way in which the liveliness of parliamentary institutions had been maintained under the fire of the enemy'. Once he had sat down, in lines of three, peers and MPs left the chamber and then walked slowly through an avenue of onlookers across the road to St Margaret's Church for a service of remembrance.

Afterwards Churchill and his War Cabinet – minus Attlee and Eden, who were in America – went to Buckingham Palace for tea with the King and Queen, accompanied by Sir Archibald Sinclair, the chiefs of staff and Sir Edward Bridges, the Cabinet secretary. Later, they returned to Whitehall, where a vast crowd had massed, filling the road from the end of Downing Street to Parliament Square. Here Churchill and his colleagues took to the balcony of the Ministry of Health, which had been brightly decked out with Union flags. The Prime Minister was flanked on his right by Oliver Lyttelton, smiling urbanely, and on his left by Ernest Bevin. The other three architects of victory on the Home Front, Anderson, Woolton and Morrison, made up the rest of the group.

'God bless you all,' Churchill told the crowds through the loud and sustained cheering, his voice carried resonantly by the surrounding loudspeakers. 'This is your victory! In our long history, we have never seen a greater day than this. Everyone, man or woman, has done their best.' He asked Bevin to come forward to share the applause, but the Labour man declined, saying, 'No, Winston, this is your day.' The Minister for Labour beat time as the crowd sang 'For He's a Jolly Good Fellow', and led them in giving three cheers for the Prime Minister, to which they responded loudly and fervently.

The celebrations would continue all through the night and well into the following morning. Thereafter, some of the men on that balcony would return their attention to the task of saving the coalition – or, for others, hastening its collapse.

It had long been agreed that once the war was over, normal party politics would resume as soon as practicable. The coalition members had been drawn from a Parliament that was now ten years old, and Churchill had told MPs, 'I cannot think of anything more odious than for a Prime Minister . . . to try to grapple with the perplexing and tremendous problems of war and peace, and of the transition from war to peace, without being refreshed by contact with the people.' So an election would take place at the end of hostilities – but which hostilities? When he moved to extend Parliament by a further year back in October 1944, Churchill had anticipated – correctly as it turned out – that the German war would end 'in March, April or May' of 1945, but he had foreseen that the Japanese could go on fighting for another eighteen months, into the middle of 1946. So he had made it quite clear that 'we must look to the termination of the war against Nazism as a pointer which will fix the date of the General Election'.

Now he had changed his mind. With relations between the western Allies and the Soviet Union ever more strained, he was reluctant to disband a team that had weathered so many storms together. Moreover, he had no great relish for a return to partisan politics: he was happy as a national leader.

Attlee, Bevin and Dalton agreed with Churchill on postponing the election until the defeat of Japan, accepting the need to present a united front on international affairs. But neither the Prime Minister nor his Labour colleagues had a free hand: there were other forces at play. On the Conservative side, Beaverbrook and Bracken were furiously lobbying Churchill to exploit his popularity and go for a June election; Eden, too, was keen for a quick ballot. Whereas for Labour, Herbert Morrison, who was increasingly setting the pace on policy, had set about rallying support for an October election, thus allowing time for the majority of servicemen to return home and vote, and for an up-to-date, accurate electoral register to be compiled.

Others were in less haste. Rab Butler wanted the coalition to continue, 'preferably until the social reforms upon which we were in general agreement had been passed; this seemed best in the national interest'. From a purely party perspective, he recognised that the Tory machine was in a 'parlous' state, hit much harder than Labour by the absence of its agents and organisers on war service.

'The coalition is getting more and more threadbare,' observed *The Economist*, reflecting on recent failures to agree legislation on social insurance, land values and coal. The reality was that the War Cabinet was now so divided over domestic policy, and the pressures from MPs and the rank and file of both major parties for a parting of the ways so strong, that a general election looked likely sooner rather than later. October seemed a long way away.

When Churchill and Attlee first sat down to seriously discuss the disbandment of the coalition in early April, prior to the Labour leader's departure for America with Eden on the 17th, the Prime Minister had assured his deputy that there was no question of breaking up the government or of dissolving Parliament in his absence. But a few days later the electioneering had started in earnest, and Labour – in particular Morrison – had been quickest out of the blocks. On 21 April the home secretary (who was also his party's campaign manager) launched what was to all intents and purposes Labour's election manifesto, *Let Us Face the Future*. An unabashed 'instalment of socialism', it set out a massive programme of public ownership – of the fuel and power industries, iron and steel, inland transport, and also the Bank of England. And in addition to a commitment to implement Butler's Education Act, it planned to raise the school leaving age to sixteen as soon as possible.

The Tories had responded in a series of weekend speeches. Party chairman Ralph Assheton told an audience in Newcastle upon Tyne that only a system of free enterprise could ensure full employment. In an early display of the uninhibited scaremongering that lay ahead, he predicted that Labour's nationalisation plans would not only fail but would also 'create such fear in all other industries that there would be a general paralysis of trade . . . We have been fighting totalitarianism in Germany, and do not wish to adopt as our creed German-made doctrines of Karl Marx.' Morrison had countered with a major speech in Bristol on 29 April in which he argued that central banking policy should be in the hands of the state so as to ensure full employment and avoid inflation. Thereafter political hostilities had been largely suspended again; first while Sir John Anderson presented an uncontroversial budget – although he promised tax cuts by the end of the financial year – and then by the general rejoicing over the end of the war in Europe.

Meanwhile, Eden and Attlee had been in San Francisco, negotiating for Britain at a momentous gathering of fifty countries to discuss the creation of the United Nations. The British delegation also included Ellen Wilkinson and Florence Horsbrugh, both now Privy Councillors. Wilkinson's stock – she was due to chair the Labour Party conference at the end of May – was particularly high. An *Observer* profile confidently stated, 'Nobody with any knowledge of politics would lay any money against her becoming the second woman cabinet minister in our history . . . and an extremely efficient one she will make.'

On 11 May Churchill met with Bevin and Morrison and warned them that although he personally wished to postpone the general election until after the defeat of Japan, he was coming under pressure from his own party to go to the polls in June. The Labour pair had earlier consulted the party's National Executive Committee, and gave the Prime Minister its view that the national interest would be best served by an election in October. They also shared their personal positions, however, Morrison making it clear that he was keen for an immediate election, Bevin admitting he still saw the value in preserving the coalition until the war in the Pacific was over.

Five days later Attlee returned from America. Just hours after stepping off his plane, he headed for Downing Street and a late-night meeting with Churchill. During an amicable discussion that lasted into the early hours, they had a meeting of minds. Attlee too wished to prolong the government until after Japan's defeat, but both men now recognised that neither of them was in tune with the majority feeling in their respective parties, so Churchill set about drafting a compromise letter that might just bridge the gap. Attlee would then present it to his colleagues at the Labour conference in Blackpool.

But when the first draft arrived, Ernest Bevin realised it would have little chance of winning acceptance. At his insistence, a new sentence was inserted that gave a pledge that the coalition would continue to press on with social reform. 'In the meanwhile', it read, 'we would together do our utmost to implement the proposals for social security and full employment contained in the White Papers which we have laid before Parliament.' In the document the Prime Minister had included the rather odd idea that another extension of the parliament – and thus the coalition – might be put to the people, via a referendum.

Labour's National Executive Committee assembled in Blackpool's Town Hall after tea on Sunday, 20 May to consider Churchill's offer. Attlee remained detached, coolly presenting both sides of the argument, while Bevin and Hugh Dalton did their best to advocate an extension of the coalition. But Morrison's powerful advocacy for a return to party independence in October received the backing of, among others, Ellen Wilkinson, Aneurin Bevan, Harold Laski and Emmanuel Shinwell. Just three members of the committee wanted to prolong the government until the absolute end. Churchill's gambit had failed.

This meeting had been the mirror image of one held almost exactly five years previously. Then, Labour's National Executive Committee, sitting in a basement conference room at a seaside hotel, had taken a decision that consigned Chamberlain's Conservative-led national government to history. Now, although the world and the country had changed irrevocably, here was the same body, with the majority of the same members, back in a seaside hotel, passing a very similar vote to deal a fatal blow to Churchill's administration.

When the conference delegates supported the NEC decision the following morning – just two out of 1,100 voted for Churchill's proposals – Attlee sat down in the Clifton Hotel to write a letter he surely knew would bring his five-year partnership with the Prime Minister to a sudden end. This was no private letter of regret that all the work they had done together was over, however; it was a blunt, detailed, public rebuttal of Churchill's offer that reflected the will of his party. It included strong criticism of the idea of a referendum. 'I could not consent to the introduction into our national life of a device so alien to all our traditions . . . which has only too often been the instrument of Nazidom and Fascism. Hitler's practices in the field of referenda and plebiscites can hardly have endeared these expedients to the British heart.' There was also an accusation that Churchill's rejection of an autumn election had been made purely on 'considerations of political expediency'. 'It appears to me', Attlee wrote, 'that you are departing from the position of a national leader by yielding to the pressure of the Conservative Party, which is anxious to exploit your great services to the nation in its own interest.' And there was a final barb: 'I would earnestly ask you to reconsider your decision to hold an election in circumstances which are bound to cause bitter resentment among the men of the fighting services.'

It was Whit Monday, and Churchill was dining at Chequers, with a party that included his son Randolph and Harold Macmillan. From his hotel room in Blackpool, Attlee telephoned the Prime Minister to read the letter to him, leaving Churchill surprised and disappointed that the Labour leader had failed to carry his party with him. 'Winston was hurt at the unnecessarily waspish and even offensive tone of Attlee's reply,' recorded Macmillan. The die was cast.

Churchill drafted a reply to Attlee the following day. At Beaverbrook's insistence, he omitted a warm tribute to the Labour leader and his colleagues for their war work. Indeed, he composed a riposte as harsh as the rejection he had received. 'I regret the aspersions with which you have darkened this correspondence,' he wrote. 'It is odd that you should accompany so many unjust allegations with an earnest request that we should go on bickering together until the autumn. Such a process would not be a decent way of carrying on a British government.' His anger was echoed by supportive growl from the Beaverbrook press. 'Who brands the greatest Englishman of his time as a rogue and a scoundrel?' asked the editorial in the *Daily Express* on Wednesday, 23 May.

At noon that day the Prime Minister went to Buckingham Palace for an audience with the King, to tender his resignation. At 4 p.m. he returned, to be formally asked to form a new, caretaker administration. Parliament would be dissolved on 15 June, the election would take place on 5 July, and the result would be declared on 26 July after all the ballot papers from servicemen abroad had been gathered in.

Churchill had led his 'Great Coalition' for a total of five years and thirteen days. When the leader writers penned their obituary notices in Thursday's papers, there was near universal acclaim. 'This has been a great administration,' said *The Times*. 'Its members have worked together in harmonious cooperation and mutual loyalty to a degree never surpassed, and seldom approached, in the history of the many coalition governments that have held office in England.' The *Yorkshire Post* was equally, if not more, effusive in its praise. 'No-one can question the brilliant success of this Government of all the talents . . . its close comradeship and steady teamwork will be cited by future historians as an inspiring example of what a free people can accomplish in defence of their common life and liberties.'

At the Labour Party conference the same day, delegates stood and cheered wildly as Ellen Wilkinson passed a resolution expressing the party's heartfelt gratitude to, and admiration of, 'all British forces, men and women, who are serving the nation on and over the seas, in India, and at home'. It also pledged the party to 'render to the Services every support in the war against Japan'. There was then a moment of silence in memory of those who had never come back.

Monday, 28 May had been a grey, cheerless day in London, and at 4.30 p.m., as the members of the disbanded coalition made their way to 10 Downing Street for a final farewell, the rain started to fall.

Most of the retiring ministers were chauffeured up to the familiar black door in their big, polished, official cars, with the word 'Priority' emblazoned in red lettering on the front windows. The exceptions were Herbert Morrison and Ellen Wilkinson, who bounded jauntily along the street in a small, private vehicle, and then walked in together, the home secretary smiling jovially at the gathering of photographers.

Inside, with painters and decorators at work, there was a feel of renewal, and as the guests entered the Cabinet Room, they were greeted by the cheerful sight of four magnificent clusters of double peonies spaced across the wide oval table, which was otherwise laden with cups of tea and a buffet. Winston Churchill was 'At Home', hosting a party to thank his colleagues for their unstinting efforts in the fight for their country's survival.

Nearly all of Labour's former ministers had joined him – Bevin, Attlee, Morrison, Dalton, Jowitt – and a fair smattering of Tories and Liberals, too. Lord Beaverbrook and Brendan Bracken were, however, conspicuous by their absence. Sadly, the renewal of political hostilities and the strident tone of the parties' rhetoric in recent days meant the atmosphere was more strained than it might have been. 'Clem Attlee adopted a very correct and chilly attitude. He did not allow his humour off the chain,' observed Oliver Lyttelton. 'Ernie Bevin looked shaken and anxious, Morrison expectant.'

Once tea had been served, Churchill moved to the head of the table, first assuring his guests that although this was a tea and not a cocktail party – 'nothing so flippant' – other drinks that 'were capable of local adjustment' would be made available. Then, visibly moved, with tears starting to stream down his cheeks – as they so often did on such occasions – he began to pay his tributes.

He warmly thanked his Labour and Liberal colleagues for the last five years, asserting that they had been 'surely been the most glorious in our history'. If the Cabinet had not stood together as a united band of friends, Britain 'might have been wiped out'. Posterity would hail their achievements, and a 'light would shine on every helmet' of each man and woman in the room. If another mortal danger threatened, he knew the response would be exactly the same, because that was the mettle and character of this country's leaders.

For his former deputy he had a special promise. In the coming weeks, when he negotiated with Stalin and Truman, he wanted his 'good friend, Clem Attlee' by his side. 'How can you speak for your country when an election is pending? I shall say, the alternative prime minister is with me. We are agreed. On these issues whoever is returned at the election will be supported by the other.'

Attlee and Archibald Sinclair gave brief replies, the former saying simply that 'we had given a practical example of democracy at work', and everyone had 'subordinated their own policies to the necessities of the state'. Then the outgoing Minister of Economic Warfare, Lord Selborne, called for a group photograph and everyone walked out into the garden of Number 10. With no sign of a break in the rain, the Prime Minister joked, 'We'd better finish this as my political opponents will say this is a conspiracy on my part to give them all rheumatism.' Thereafter the party gradually dispersed. Conservative ministers returned to their Whitehall offices to get to grips with their new briefs; their Labour colleagues, once again in their all too familiar role of opposition, could resume the drafting of election speeches.

'Salute the Great Coalition 1940–45' was the motto Churchill had inscribed on the medal he gave to every member of his war ministry. Britain had turned to coalition governments before, but never one so broadly based, never one that had lasted so long, never one that had worked in such harmony, and never one that affected the lives of its citizens so greatly. In her hour of need, this 'Ministry of All the Talents' had served Britain well.

POSTSCRIPT

Churchill began the 1945 general election campaign in seemingly relaxed vein. On the weekend before his farewell party for the 'Great Coalition', he had embarked on a tour of his new constituency of Woodford, Essex, in an open-topped car, accompanied by his wife Clementine. At one stage he had called in at a children's tea party, where he had donned a paper hat and kissed several of the toddlers for the benefit of the accompanying press pack. Later he had dealt firmly with a group of hecklers who had shouted, 'What about the food shortage?' by retorting, 'I have not come here to promise you beer and skittles.'

The lobby correspondents of left-wing newspapers had quickly dubbed his temporary, two-month administration 'the caretaker government', but he had turned that ridicule to his advantage. 'They call us the "caretakers",' he told a crowd outside the working men's club in Woodford High Road, addressing them from his car in the persistent drizzle. 'We endorse the title because it means that we shall take every good care of everything that affects the welfare of Britain and of all classes in Britain.' This good-humoured, consensual approach had been well received. But ten days later, on Monday, 4 June, Churchill made an abrupt and damaging misstep.

In his first election broadcast on the BBC, live from his study at Chequers, he claimed that 'socialism is inseparably interwoven with totalitarianism' and portrayed the state as a malign individual, a dictator, 'the arch-employer, the arch-planner, the arch-administrator and ruler, the arch-caucus boss'. This by itself might have been forgiven as no more than characteristically robust campaigning, but one particularly intemperate passage was to ensure the speech's notoriety. 'No Socialist Government conducting the entire life and industry of the country could afford to allow free, sharp, or violently worded expressions of public discontent. They would have to fall back on some form of *Gestapo*, no doubt very humanely directed in the first instance. And this would nip opinion in the bud; it would stop criticism as it reared its head, and it would gather all the power to the supreme party and the party leaders, rising like stately pinnacles above their vast bureaucracies of civil servants, no longer servants and no longer civil.'

Churchill was far from alone in hurling insults inspired by the vanquished Nazi regime. Bevin's speech in Leeds in April had suggested British big business might ally with 'Nazi big business', while Attlee had linked the Prime Minister's idea of a referendum on prolonging the life of the parliament to Hitler's 'practices' in the field of plebiscites. But the use of 'Gestapo', in the context of this already lurid broadcast, gave the Labour leadership potent ammunition, and they used it cannily: not to criticise Churchill himself – still the acclaimed war leader – but to suggest he had been unduly influenced by those familiar, malign influences behind the throne.

Bevin was the first to attack. 'It was Churchill at Beaverbrook's worst,' he told the Press Association that night. For Morrison, 'This broadcast will, I fear, go down in history as Churchill's Crazy Broadcast . . . the best excuse I can find is that Mr Bracken, and not the prime minister, must have written it.' In fact Beaverbrook and Bracken were blameless: neither had contributed to the speech. But it was Attlee who was most withering. 'I realised at once what was his object,' he explained in his own BBC address the following evening. 'He wanted the electors to understand how great was the difference between Winston Churchill the great leader in war of a united nation, and Mr. Churchill, the party leader of the Conservatives. He feared lest those who had accepted his leadership in war might be tempted out of gratitude to follow him further. I thank him for having disillusioned them so thoroughly. The voice we heard last night was that of Mr. Churchill, but the mind was that of Lord Beaverbrook.'

To his Conservative Cabinet colleagues, Churchill's speech was an evident disaster. 'A fantastical onslaught on Socialism which, while cheering a good many of our supporters, will put off a lot of those who might otherwise have voted on the main international issue,' reflected Leo Amery. Anyhow, its authorship was not the central issue. What bewildered the public was the unreal ring to Churchill's words. For five long years they had been assured that all these socialists had worked in great harmony with the Prime Minister in the national interest; now they were expected to believe they were malevolent outsiders, plotting to bring about a totalitarian state.

In the end, the 'Gestapo' speech was merely a symptom of the Conservatives' malaise, rather than a material cause of their defeat. During wartime, 'fair shares for all' and a genuine equality of sacrifice had been the overriding mood; the country had been 'socialised', to use Churchill's phrase, and had not objected. Thus the election on 5 July proved to be a stunning triumph for Labour, the scale of which surprised even the most optimistic of the party's leaders. The electoral system amplified a popular vote of 48.8 per cent into a tally of 39? House of Commons seats. Although the Conservatives captured ten million votes (compared to Labour's twelve million), they could only muster 213. The resulting rout saw Leo Amery, Brendan Bracken, Sir James Grigg, Harold Macmillan, Richard Law, Ernest Brown, Florence Horsbrugh and Duncan Sandys, the Prime Minister's son-in-law, all defeated. And to compound Churchill's misery, his son Randolph failed to win either of the two seats available in Preston.

It was an equally disastrous election for Sir Archibald Sinclair's Liberal Party, which had hoped to profit from the presence and influence of their recently elected MP, Sir William Beveridge. The great reformer's vision undoubtedly played a major part in the outcome of the election, but his was not the party to benefit; the Liberals won a paltry twelve seats. Beveridge himself was defeated in Berwick-upon-Tweed, Sinclair came a shocking third in Caithness and Sutherland, and Violet Bonham Carter also placed last, in Wells.

'Seldom has an electorate gone to the polls with more deliberate purpose. Seldom has an electorate been more clearly aware of what it was voting against and what it was voting for – against the past, and for the future,' was the view of the American magazine *Time*. The Tories were held responsible for Munich and appeasement, for the sharp class divisions that were now only just beginning to erode, and for the harsh economic policies of the 1930s. Moreover, the party's lacklustre election manifesto had been seen to fall short in addressing the people's needs and aspirations for the post-war period.

Labour had offered a far more coherent and ambitious prospectus, but before the new government could embark upon it, Attlee and Bevin (now foreign secretary) had to replace Churchill and Eden at Potsdam for the final Big Three conference of the war. There, with Truman and Stalin, they concluded negotiations on a final agreement on the governance of occupied Germany, with zones for Britain, America, the Soviet Union and France, and an Allied Control Council to co-ordinate overall administration. Less trumpeted, however, was the final abandonment of Poland. In recognising the Soviet puppet government, rather than the London-based Polish government-in-exile, Britain and America implicitly conceded de facto Russian occupation of central and eastern Europe.

There was also the Potsdam Declaration, signed by America, Britain and China, demanding the unconditional surrender of all Japanese forces – the refusal of which would necessitate Japan's 'prompt and utter destruction'. Without explicitly referring to the atom bomb, Truman casually mentioned to Stalin that America now possessed a 'new weapon of unusual destructive force'; the Soviet dictator merely replied that 'he hoped we would make good use of it against Japan'.

His apparent indifference reflected the fact that his spies had already provided him with details of the recent successful test explosion in the New Mexico desert.

When the first atomic bomb landed on Hiroshima on 6 August – the immediate blast and resulting firestorm killing close to 80,000 – the enormity of the event took some hours to absorb. 'It has been interesting to watch the growing understanding of Londoners of what the atomic bomb means,' wrote the Foreign Office diplomat Pierson Dixon, who had been by Bevin's side at Potsdam, 'The prepared announcements on Monday were received with polite interest. It was evidently thought that this was merely an expanded high explosive. [But] the Japanese reports of the destruction of Hiroshima have swept England in a wave of horror.'

Those events at last brought the work of Sir John Anderson and Tube Alloys (although it was not referred to by name) to public attention. Attlee left Churchill to issue a long, detailed and characteristically colourful account of the Anglo-American bomb project, while Anderson himself gave a rare interview to the Evening Standard. 'It is the biggest thing ever to be developed,' he told the newspaper. 'It might be a valuable treasure awaiting full development in the interests of mankind. On the other hand it might be the release of a maniacal bomb of death and destruction. God grant this may not be so.'

Anderson remained Attlee's chief adviser on nuclear policy for another year. The new Prime Minister showed no more enthusiasm than his predecessor for airing the subject in Cabinet, preferring to confine discussion to a small, secret sub-committee. Ernest Bevin, worried at Soviet belligerence and concerned about Britain's loss of prestige in the world, drove forward the argument for a homegrown atomic bomb: 'we've got to have this thing over here whatever it costs . . . we've got to have the bloody Union Jack on top of it'. Thus on 8 January 1947, a Cabinet committee led by Attlee and Bevin would eventually commit Britain to becoming a nuclear power.

The Japanese surrender left the United States free to re-evaluate major areas of her foreign policy. One of these was the Lend-Lease agreement, which was terminated with brutal haste on 21 August, partly due to a suspicion (which proved accurate) that if left in place it would be used to fund Labour's 'socialist' industrial and welfare reforms. John Maynard Keynes, now advising the new Labour government, spoke of the severing of this lifeline as a 'financial Dunkirk'. Unless new American financial aid was forthcoming, he warned the Cabinet, a greater degree of austerity would be necessary than we have experienced at any time during the war'.

Disaster was averted in December, however, when Keynes negotiated a $3.75 billion loan and secured a final $650 million of Lend-Lease assistance. In return Britain had to commit to the establishment of an international free trade organisation, pledge not to discriminate against US imports, and accept that there could be no devaluation of sterling without the approval of the new American-dominated International Monetary Fund. Britain agreed to pay off the 1945 loan in fifty annual instalments, starting in 1950. It would take until 29 December 2006 – when a final payment of $84 million was made – for another Labour government, under Tony Blair, to fully settle that debt.

In the debate on the King's Speech on 29 November 1944, at the zenith of coalition co-operation on social reform, Churchill had cast his mind forward to the aftermath of the coming election. 'There is one thing that is quite certain,' he told MPs, 'all the leading men in both the principal parties – and in the Liberal Party as well – are pledged and committed to this great mass of social legislation, and I cannot conceive that whatever may be the complexion of the new House, they will personally fail to make good their promises and commitments to the people.'

So it fell to Attlee, Morrison, Bevin, Bevan, Cripps and others to build on the work of Lord Woolton's Reconstruction Committee. As it was, their 'New Jerusalem' would come to eclipse it. The 1945 Parliament produced an astonishing 347 acts. Beveridge's report was finally cast in stone, with the National Insurance and National Assistance Acts, and another of his three prerequisites for effective social insurance, a National Health Service, was inaugurated in 1948. The new government also raised the school leaving age to fifteen, and implemented much of Rab Butler's Education Act, introducing free secondary education for all.

Where Attlee and his ministers clearly struck out on their own was with the nationalisation of key areas of British industry, including the coal mines, the railways, gas and electricity, together with the Bank of England. Externally, Labour also pursued a path a Churchill administration would surely not have followed, by granting independence to India, Pakistan, Ceylon and Burma, and pulling out of the latter. Attlee's government also helped to set up an important new security pact, the North Atlantic Treaty Organisation (NATO).

There had, of course, been pockets of resistance to the collectivist ethos of the war years – in constituency Conservative associations, employers' organisations, insurance companies and the upper echelons of the British Medical Association. Moreover, political thinkers on the right had been energised by the publication of Friedrich von Hayek's *The Road to Serfdom* (1944), which had challenged the emerging orthodoxy by putting notions of economic liberalism and individual freedom to the fore, warning that the socialist welfare state contained within it the seeds of totalitarianism. But despite Churchill's 'Gestapo' speech, it was clear that a new political consensus had grown out of the deliberations of Lord Woolton's committee.

Indeed, at the reforming height of its work, in the autumn of 1944, Ellen Wilkinson had even wondered whether the left's thunder had been stolen. 'What were we going to fight about?' she had asked an NEC meeting. 'Certain legislation had been placed on the statute book by the coalition government, for which the Labour minister and the Labour Party were entitled to a large measure of credit. There was other important legislation, such as Full Employment, Social Security, Health Service etc which it was hoped would become law before the Government broke up. What, therefore, would remain to be incorporated in our programme specifically for the General Election?'

Since the publication of the Beveridge Report both main parties had embraced the idea of full employment, a welfare state, a mixed economy and the involvement of 'both sides of industry' in political and economic decision-making. The Tories would not have carried out Labour's programme of state ownership but neither would they seek immediately to reverse it. Although Rab Butler's 1947 'Industrial Charter' talked of rolling back some of the frontiers of the state, it also put forward the notion of a 'Workers' Charter'. And by 1954 *The Economist* had coined the term 'Butskellism' to express the notion that there was precious little to distinguish between the two parties on economic policy (Butler became Chancellor of the Exchequer in Churchill's second administration, 1951–5, and Hugh Gaitskell was his Labour shadow). Only in 1979 when Margaret Thatcher came to power, fired by Hayek's ideas, had the wartime consensus between Beveridge and Woolton finally run its course.

That it lasted so long was, in part, due to the domination of British politics by the personnel of the 'Great Coalition' during the 1940s, 50s and 60s. Churchill's first administration spawned five prime ministers: after Attlee (1945–51), he himself returned to Downing Street in 1951–5, followed by Eden (1955–7), Macmillan (1957–63), and finally – from the wartime civil service – the young economist and statistician who had helped alleviate Bevin's problems with the miners, J.H. (Harold) Wilson (1964–70 and 1974–6). Lord Woolton, who finally joined the Conservative Party after the election defeat of 1945, went on to become a successful party chairman, using all the communication skills he had employed so adroitly at the Ministry of Food; he later served in the Cabinet again, for four years from 1951 to 1955. And Anderson too was offered a place in Churchill's 1951 government, as some kind of 'overlord' to the main economic ministries, but he resisted; although he did accept a place in the House of Lords as Viscount Waverley when his university seat in the Commons was abolished.

The only two women to have served in the coalition both achieved Cabinet rank, and in the same post, as education secretary. Neither realised her true potential. Ellen Wilkinson's tenure lasted just eighteen months, cut tragically short by her death in February 1947. Florence Horsburgh had to wait until September 1953 before Churchill finally gave her a seat at the top table, but with the government's spending priorities on housing, not education, she had a troublesome time.

Whenever leading politicians die of a non-infective condition, it is almost taken for granted that their untimely deaths have been brought about by the strains of their 'unnatural lives'. Churchill's wartime ministers, many working up to sixteen hours a day for five years, with the nation's very existence at stake for the first of those, inevitably suffered more than most. If Anthony Eden had been a more forceful presence during the 1945 general election campaign, rather than convalescing after a duodenal ulcer, the mistakes of the 'Gestapo' speech, and much else, might have been avoided. In 1953, he would suffer a botched operation to remove gallstones, and his premiership was continually dogged by ill health, necessitating three major operations.

During the war Wilkinson suffered crippling bouts of bronchial asthma, accelerated by nervous tension. She was on a cocktail of drugs and an overdose of one of them – barbiturates – contributed to her death from 'heart failure as a result of emphysema, acute bronchitis and bronchial pneumonia'. She was just fifty-five. Ernest Bevin did not die in office, like Wilkinson, but just a month after Attlee had persuaded him to step down as foreign secretary, in March 1951, because of heart problems. In some ways it was a miracle he lived until seventy – he smoked, ate and drank to excess, and his doctor once quipped that the only sound organs in his body were his feet.

Sir Stafford Cripps, by contrast, appeared to lead a puritanically healthy lifestyle, built around his vegetarianism. Yet he had long suffered from colitis, brought on by stress, and during his time as Chancellor of the Exchequer under Attlee he would be forced into frequent absences. After leaving office in October 1950, he was eventually diagnosed with bone marrow cancer. He died in 1952, aged sixty-two.

Perhaps the saddest casualty of all was Sir Archibald Sinclair, who was ennobled as Lord Thurso in 1952. Diagnosed with dangerously high blood pressure at the start of the war, he had survived it on a strict fat-free diet. But he suffered two serious strokes, in 1952 and 1959, the latter leaving him in a coma for six months. Thereafter he was permanently bed-bound until his death in 1970. His old adversary Beaverbrook proved again his capacity for private generosity and thoughtfulness when, on Sinclair's seventy-second birthday, he wrote to Lady Thurso, 'My Dear Marigold. This is a message to Archie which I ask you to read to him. He did so much over five years and worried so greatly on account of the boys who lost their lives that it is no wonder that he is now a war casualty.'

Churchill, whose extraordinary working regime and fondness for rich living might have been expected to take their toll far sooner, outlasted the majority of his colleagues. Two years after his return to Downing Street in 1951, aged seventy-seven, he suffered a life-threatening stroke that was carefully kept secret by his inner circle in alliance with the major newspaper proprietors. Even so, he soldiered on as Prime Minister for two more years. His death at the age of ninety, on 24 January 1965, prompted national mourning the like of which had never previously been seen for a prime minister.

Looking back over his time in the War Cabinet, Anthony Eden could recall 'sharp debate' and 'occasional outbursts of anger or indignation'. But his abiding memory was one of 'no continuing tension or intrigue, on the contrary respect, friendship and even affection among those who bore the chief burden. I doubt if it would have been tolerable otherwise.' Sir Archibald Sinclair wrote to Churchill on 24 May 1945, 'We have done something together in the past five years . . . For my part, I can imagine no greater honour than to have served in your war administration, which now passes not ingloriously into history.'

History must surely credit that administration not only for winning the war, but also with beginning the vital work of framing the future political and social structure of Britain.

REFERENCES

AB – Maud Committee
  (atom bomb project)
CAB 65 – Cabinet minutes
CAB 66 – Cabinet memoranda
CAB 120/127 – Tube Alloys
  (atom bomb) papers
CAB 195 – Cabinet transcripts
CO – Cabinet Office
FO – Foreign Office

FRUS – Foreign Relations of the
  United States
HO – Home Office
INF – Ministry of Information
IWM – Imperial War Museum
NA – National Archives
PREM – Prime Minister's Office
WO – War Office

Prologue

p5 He seemed tired – Channon, *Diaries* p244
p5 We had an – *Hansard*, 7 May 1940
p6 The minister of – ibid.
p6 You have sat – ibid.
p6 This was – ibid., 8 May 1940
p7 Jackals – Reith, *Diaries* p7
p7 It was a – Williams, *Politics Grave and Gay* p112
p8 I thought – Dalton, *Memoirs*, pp306–7
p8 I believe – *The Times*, 9 May 1940
p8 The PM – Halifax, *Diaries* p114
p8 Winston, with suitable – ibid. p115
p9 bit evasive – ibid. p116
p9 Mr Prime Minister – Williams,

A Prime Minister Remembers p33
p10 although not at – NA CAB 65/7
p10 I propose to – US Ambassador J. Kennedy to State Dept, Tel No 1158
p10 It was the – Channon, *Diaries* p249
p10 Recent events – *Hull Daily Mail*, 10 May 1940
p11 Neville is inclined – Templewood papers XII
p11 It's as hard – Dalton, *Second World War Diary* p9
p11 Not at all – quoted in Prior, *When Britain Saved the West* p43
p11 The Labour Party – Dalton, *Memoirs* p310

p11 it would look – Dalton, *Memoirs* p311

p12 indignant – Eden, *The Reckoning* p97

p12 Personally, I think – ibid.

p12 calm and charming – Channon, *Diaries* p249

p12 little effects – ibid. p240

p14 the strongest – Dalton, *Memoirs* p312

p15 It helped some – ibid. p311

p15 The National Executive – NEC minutes, 10 May 1940

p15 If you don't – Dalton, *Memoirs* p311

p16 He [Hitler] – *The Times*, 11 May 1940

p17 The good clean – Colville, *Fringes of Power 1939–41* p14

p17 What a moment – Bonham Carter, *Champion Redoubtable* p212

1 A Ministry of all the Talents

p18 Is there a – *Hansard*, 21 May 1936

p18 When Winston – quoted in Gilbert, *Prophet of Truth* p741

p19 I am interested – Gilbert, *The Challenge of War* p31

p20 He has been – Beaverbrook to J.L. Garvin, Beaverbrook papers BBK/C/140, Jan 1932

p21 the strategic – Attlee, *As It Happened* p41

p22 Sir, we have – quoted in Hore, *Nelson's Band of Brothers* p153

p23 I was very – Williams, *A Prime Minister Remembers* p35

p23 was absolutely – ibid. p35

p24 It is probably – Churchill, *Their Finest Hour* p8

p24 too old – Dalton, *Second World War Diary* p12

p24 too slow – ibid.

p24 pleasant talk – Churchill, *The Gathering Storm* p256

p25 You helped to – Williams, *A Prime Minister Remembers* p36

p25 You have sprung – ibid. p36

p25 a glorified – ibid, p34

p26 this is a – Hunter, *Winston and Archie* p223

p26 it didn't sound – Dalton, *Memoirs* p311

p27 He looked ill – Eden, *The Reckoning* p98

p28 He said, I – *Manchester Guardian*, 23 May 1944

p28 Nevertheless, he – ibid.

p28 How filthy this – Reith, *Diaries* p251

p29 little patience with – *Daily Mirror*, 13 May 1940

p32 My dear Malcolm – MacDonald, *Titans & Others* p94

p32 I want you – ibid.

p32 Did he also – ibid.

p32 Let him who – Giuseppe Guerzoni, *Garibaldi*, Barbèra Firenze 1882, p245

p32 on account of – *Hansard*, 13 May 1940

p33 Our leader, the – ibid.

p33 You may be – Gilbert, *Finest Hour* p331

p34 monstrous and imbecile – James, *Churchill, Complete Speeches* p1028, 4 May 1908

p34 Our whole nation – *Dundee Courier*, 7 June 1915

p34 It is not – Evans, *Bevin*, p102, speech in Swansea, Apr 1929

p34 It is imperative – Churchill papers 20/11/59–60

p36 the battle that – NA CAB 65/13, 13 May 1940

p37 Do Greenwood, Attlee – Cadogan, *Diaries* p283

p37 there is no – Halifax, *Diaries* p123

p37 Attlee, Greenwood – Ironside, *Diary* p306

p38 [Bracken] sat up – Nicolson, *Diaries* p85, 13 May 1940

p38 Humble Suggestions – Churchill papers 20/11

p42 From Lord Lloyd – Macmillan, *Blast of War* p78

2 'No longer two nations but one'

p44 This red line – Horne, *To Lose A Battle* p372

p44 I expected the – Eden, *The Reckoning* p103

p44 impossible and – NA CAB 65/13, 18 May 1940

p45 After this – *Daily Express*, 20 May 1940

p45 The Minister of – *Hansard*, 22 May 1940

p45 Horny-handed – *Time*, 3 June 1940

p46 came near to – *The Times*, 23 May 1940

p46 British strategy – NA CAB 66/7, 25 May 1940

p47 We had to – NA CAB 65/13, 9 a.m. 26 May 1940

p47 doubted whether – NA CAB 65/13, 2 p.m. 26 May 1940

p47 Herr Hitler – ibid.

p48 Being in a – NA CAB 65/13, 4.30 p.m. 27 May 1940

p48 the suggested – ibid.

p48 If it got – ibid.

p48 increasingly opposed – ibid.

p48 I thought Winston – Halifax, *Diaries* p142

p48 I can't work – Cadogan, *Diaries* p291

p48 Nonsense – ibid.

p48 full of apologies – Halifax, *Diaries* p142

p49 stunned, bewildered – Addison and Crang, *Listening to Britain* p45

p49 public confidence – NA CAB 65/7, 11.30 a.m. 28 May 1940

p49 extremely grave – *Hansard*, 28 May 1940

p49 The sky out – MacDonald, *Titans & Others* p96

p50 it might be – NA CAB 65/13, 4 p.m. 28 May 1940

p50 did not feel – ibid.

p50 nothing in his – ibid.

p50 the chances of – ibid.

p50 magnificent performance – Dalton, *Second World War Diary* p26

p51 We shall go – ibid. p28

p51 We had a – Amery, *Empire at Bay* p619

p52 the most unforgettable – MacDonald, *Titans & Others* p98

p52 the only man – Dalton, *Second World War Diary* p26

p52 Yes, that was – ibid.

p52 dramatic, unreal, insincere – Reith, *Diaries* p255

p52 in reaching – NA CAB 65/13, 7 p.m. 28 May 1940

p52 evidently reinforced – Spears, *Assignment to Catastrophe* p251

p53 I had perhaps – IWM H.S.L. Dundas interview, Cat 10159

p53 You couldn't – IWM Ron Tomlinson interview, Cat 9728

p54 We shall fight – Butler, *Art of the Possible* pp85–6

p54 our thankfulness – *Hansard*, 4 June 1940

p55 Tours airfield – Ismay, *Memoirs* p145

p55 Whether or not – Spears, *Assignment to Catastrophe* p519

p55 else he could – ibid. p520

p56 I replied that – Alanbrooke, *War Diaries* p81

p56 dramatic gesture – Amery, *Empire at Bay* p622

p57 too gloomy – NA CAB 65/13, 15 June 1940

p57 I thought it – Amery, *Empire at Bay* p624

p57 It is an – de Gaulle, *Memoirs* Vol. 1 p243

p58 The two Governments – NA CAB 65/7 Annex 1, 16 June 1940

p58 warm support – NA CAB 65/7, 3 p.m. 16 June

p59 with an air – Churchill, *Their Finest Hour* p184

p59 Does he agree – Spears, *Assignment to Catastrophe* p589 p59 He was transfigured – ibid.

p59 Who knows – Colville, *Fringes of Power 1939–41* p187

p60 Some were astonished – Spears, *Assignment to Catastrophe* p595

p61 The ships might – NA CAB 65/13, 22 June 1940

p61 We could not – NA CAB 65/7, 22 June 1940

p62 the first shot – Smith, *England's Last War Against France* p74

p63 I leave the – *Hansard*, 4 July 1940

p63 This is heartbreaking – Colville, *Fringes of Power 1939–41* p216

p63 It will wake – Amery, *Empire at Bay* p630

3 The Beaverbrook Effect

p65 rammed into – quoted in Bungay, *The Most Dangerous Enemy* p150

p66 Very few – Holland, *The Battle of Britain* p545

p67 the complete – King, *With Malice Toward None* p49

p67 They delighted – Bonham Carter, *Churchill As I Knew Him* p444

p68 He [Churchill] is – Churchill Archives, Thurso papers

p70 dislocating the pattern – Low, *Autobiography* p174

p71 I asked him – Crozier, *Off The Record* p172

p72 Archie was – Balfour, *Wings Over Westminster* p121

p72 Grenville lived – Taylor, *Beaverbrook* p242

p72 diverting comedy – Menzies, *Dark and Hurrying Days*, 7 Mar 1941

p73 It was the – Churchill Archives, Boyle papers 1E

p74 What have you – Boyle, *Poor Dear Brendan* p256

p75 Lord Beaverbrook has – Hunter, *Winston and Archie* p226

p75 I would like – Beaverbrook papers, BKK C/311, 4 Jan 1940

p75 By all means – ibid., 7 Jan 1940

p75 the Air Ministry – Colville, *Fringes of Power 1939–41* p193, 18 June 1940

p76 Churchill treated – IWM, Ronald Melville interview, Cat 13078

p76 Churchill had – Morrison, *Autobiography* p214

p76 the abuse – Brabazon, *The Brabazon Story* p206

p76 [H]e receives – Dalton, *Second World War Diary* p102, 15 Nov 1940

p76 Archie Sinclair – Halifax, *Diaries* p121

p76 Max makes – Chamberlain, *Diary Letters* p540

p77 There is one – Hunter, *Winston and Archie* p277

p77 I am definitely – Churchill papers 20/13

p77 Better a – quoted in Len Deighton, *Fighter* p164

p77 I earnestly trust – Hunter, *Winston and Archie* p255

p77 I am not – Taylor, *Beaverbrook* p443

p77 I require you – ibid.

p78 I am distressed – Beaverbrook papers BBK/D/5, 4 Sep 1940

p79 I heard the – Colville, *Fringes of Power 1939–41* p261

p79 W[inston] is convinced – ibid.

p80 You lay in – Cowles, *Looking For Trouble* p404

p81 consumed with – Colville, *Fringes of Power 1939–41* p263

p81 I felt sick – Ismay, *Memoirs* p181

p82 The Lord President – Colville, *Fringes of Power 1939–41* p263

p82 Don't speak – Ismay, *Memoirs* p182

p82 Like the Mississippi – *Hansard*, 20 Aug 1940

p82 power . . . dogged fighting – ibid.

p83 The House would – ibid.

p83 As far as – IWM, Ronald Melville interview, Cat 13078

p84 The Air Ministry – NA CAB 66/11, 20 Aug 1940

p84 Max . . . always – Halifax, *Diaries* p250

p84 There have been – NA CAB 66/11 'RAF Training', 20 Aug 1940

p84 We must take – NA CAB 65/14, 30 Aug 1940

p84 Our reserves – ibid.

p85 We had no – ibid.

p85 Archie came back – IWM, Ronald Melville interview, Cat 13078

p86 Everyone getting – Koa Wing, *Our Longest Days* p44

p86 The Berliners – Shirer, *Berlin Diary*, 26 Aug 1940

p87 First of all – Alanbrooke, *War Diaries* p105

4 'A troglodyte existence'

p88 Derrick Clewley – author interview, 10 July 2014

p91 crowds of – Maisky, *Memoirs* p108

p92 Good old Winnie – Ismay, *Memoirs* p185

p94 Apart from – *Hansard*, 21 Dec 1938

p94 'YOU HAVE RECEIVED' – *Daily Worker*, 22 Apr 1939

p95 This proposal – Wallace, *Diary*

p95 There was – *Daily Telegraph* ,13 Sep 2009

p96 showing reluctance – NA CAB 65/9, 13 Sep 1940

p96 Even though victory – North, *The Many Not The Few* p217

p97 This day our – Taylor, *Beaverbrook* p448

p97 Hitler will invade – Lee, *Journal* p60

p98 I went to – Eden, *The Reckoning* p139

p98 If it's good – www.communist-party.org.uk

p99 episodes of this – NA CAB 65/9, 16 Sep 1940

p100 Is that the – Bennett, *John Anderson* p253

p100 cartoon – *Daily Worker*, 21 Sep 1940

p100 dusty, dirty – NA HO 205/40, 26 Sep 1940

p101 we must take – ibid.

p101 You will not – *Sunday Graphic*, 20 Oct 1940

p102 not attain – Self, *Neville Chamberlain* p443

p102 unshaken nerve – Churchill papers 2/393

p104 anything like – BBC broadcast, 3 Nov 1940

p105 promised his – *Daily Worker*, 4 Nov 1940

p105 I do so like – Nicolson, *Diaries* p128

p105 After I had – *Tribune*, 28 May 1940

p106 woman triumphs – *Daily Express*, 4 Nov 1936

p106 impressive mixture –Horsbrugh papers HSBR 2/11

p106 This has been – *Daily Express*, 11 Oct 1940

p107 No distasteful – ibid.

p108 There seems – Wallace, *Diary*, 11 Oct 1940

p108 undefended state – NA PREM 3/108, 7 Nov 1940

p109 I was horrified – Wheeler-Bennett, *King George VI* p478

p109 local people – NA CAB 65/10, 18 Nov 1940

p110 mothering the city – *Daily Mirror*, 18 Nov 1940

p110 one of the – Horsbrugh papers HSBR 2/11

p112 That's the one – Baker papers LDBA 1/63, Churchill Archives

p112 the worst of – *Evening News* (London), 17 Dec 1940

5 'A New Magna Carta'

p113 The crazy villain – NA PREM 3/496/1, Jan 1941

p113 The PM promised – Colville, *Fringes of Power 1939–41* p408, 25 Jan 1941

p114 the invasion – NA WO 193/141, 31 Oct 1940

p114 I always disliked – Meacham, *Franklin and Winston* p5

p114 ruthless war – *Evening Standard*, 10 Dec 1937

p115 Passionately though – Roosevelt, 'Fireside Chat', 3 Sep 1939

p115 How glad – Meacham, *Franklin and Winston* p45

p115 I trust you – Churchill papers 20/14

p116 A step of – NA PREM 3/468, 17 May 1940

p117 I cannot – NA PREM 3/462/2/3

p117 We are already – NA CAB 66/10, 18 July 1940

p118 All this is – *Bases for Destroyers*, J. Balfour papers, NA FO 800/433

p118 Only a war – quoted in Costello, *Ten Days That Saved The West* p381

p118 Those bloody – *Bases for Destroyers*, J. Balfour papers, NA FO 800/433

p119 an openly – quoted in Kershaw, *Fateful Choices* p219

p119 fully aware of – NA CAB 65/14, 22 Aug 1940

p119 we ought to – ibid.

p120 American sympathy – Woolton, *Diaries*, 14 Oct 1940

p120 We are deeply – Beaverbrook papers, BBK D/45, 15 Dec 1940

p120 Well, boys – Bennett, *King George VI* p521

p121 I do not – NA FO 371/24249

p121 Germany does not – *The Times*, 31 Jan 1935

p122 He was not – Lee, *Journal* p174

p122 useless to help – NA CAB 65/10, 2 Dec 1940

p123 The moment – Churchill papers 23/4

p123 I'm terribly sorry – quoted in Cull, *Selling War* p123

p124 it is a blow – Nicolson, *Diaries* p130

p124 instinctive sense – *Hansard*, 17 Dec 1940

p124 another victim – Halifax, *Diaries* p361

p124 I had at – Colville, *Fringes of Power 1939–41* p371, 13 Dec 1940

p124 knowledge of munitions – Colville, *Fringes of Power 1939–41* p367, 12 Dec 1940

p125 It is an – Halifax, *Diaries* p367

p125 I got the – Lee, *Journal* p225

p125 The US would – Halifax, *Diaries* p369 20 Dec 1940

p125 an opportunity – ibid. p371

p125 We still hold – *New Republic*, 30 Dec 1940

p125 I have worked – Dalton, *Second World War Diary* p130, 22 Dec 1940

p126 get rid of – FDR Library website (text of 'firehose' press conference)

p126 We must be – Roosevelt, 'Fireside Chat', 29 Dec 1940

p127 I am much – NA PREM 4/17/1, 89–91

p127 We are deeply – NA PREM 4/17/1, 77–8

p128 It was raining – Eden, *The Reckoning* p185

p129 a man of – John Buchan, quoted in Stevenson, *A Man Called Intrepid* p140

p129 Never have – *Hansard*, 11 July 1940

p130 It is an – Halifax, *Diaries* p389, 3 Feb 1941

p131 try to get – Sherwood, *White House Papers* p237

p131 His sonorous – Chandos, *Memoirs* pp165–6

p131 Well, Prime Minister – ibid., p165

p131 had made him – Colville, *Fringes of Power 1939–41*, 12 Jan 1941

p132 The people here – Sherwood, *White House Papers* p244

p132 The most important – ibid., p257

p132 we should – NA CAB 65/17, 20 Feb 1941

p133 A financial problem – Halifax, *Diaries* p402

p133 stripping us – quoted in Steil, *The Battle of Bretton Woods* p110

p134 The Government – Hansard, 12 Mar 1941

p134 Many thousands – NA FO 371/26169

p135 turned over – Library of Congress Archives, Roosevelt, 4 Nov 1939

p135 I have always – NA FO 371/26169

p135 would give – ibid.

p135 it ought not – ibid.

p136 I prefer this – ibid.

6 'Uncle Fred's Recipe for Survival'

p138 [I thought] it – Woolton, *Diaries*, 18 Mar 1941

p138 It was clear – Woolton, *Memoirs* p176

p139 Is it worse – Woolton, *Diaries*, 12 July 1940

p139 My mail – ibid., 13 July 1940

p139 Almost all – Churchill papers 20/2

p139 I always felt – Woolton, *Memoirs* p184

p140 Lunched with Woolton – Reith, *Diaries*, 30 July 1940

p140 one of the – Woolton, *Diaries*, 25 Oct 1940

p140 Churchill is not – ibid., 7 Nov 1940

p140 The Prime Minister – ibid., 28 Nov 1940

p140 saw a new – ibid., 24 Dec 1940

p141 receptive and helpful – ibid.

p141 tinge of jealousy – see Boothby, *Recollections of a Rebel* p64

p142 woman of some – Woolton, *Memoirs* p1

p142 Few things affected – ibid. p2

p143 very dangerous house – ibid. p30

p143 I am a – ibid.

p143 Here was an – ibid.

p144 high-powered rocket – ibid. p132

p145 It was the most – ibid. p259

p145 I made it – ibid. p171

p145 Seldom have I – *Life*, 7 Feb 1944

p146 Lord Woolton was – Boothby, *Recollections of a Rebel* p165

p146 A man of – Chandos, *Memoirs* p300

p146 I made the – Woolton, *Memoirs* p188

p147 That short morning – ibid. p189

p147 I always kept – ibid. p251

p148 The only way – ibid. p248

p151 Distressing! – Colville, *Fringes of Power 1939–41* p426

p152 Arrivals Much – NA CAB 66/14, 29 Jan 1941

p152 the average round – ibid.

p153 The fire will – Crozier, *Off The Record* p211

p153 to enable us – Churchill papers 23/9

p154 Every effort – ibid. 20/49

p154 perhaps too – Ismay, *Memoirs* p163

p154 The issue was – Brabazon, *The Brabazon Story* p206

p154 had not a – Colville, *Fringes of Power 1939–41* p443

p154 He at once – Roskill, *Hankey Man of Secrets* p501

p155 He burst out – ibid.

p155 The Prime Minister – Hansard, 7 May 1941

p155 It was not – ibid.

p155 Never have I – Channon, *Diaries* p303

p155 Winston . . . made – Headlam, *Parliament and Politics* p251

p155 He went to – Colville, *Fringes of Power 1939–41* p456

p156 At last he – Eden, *The Parliament Book* p12

p156 Something bad – Mortimer, *The Longest Night* Ch 16

p157 Satrap of the – Chandos, *Memoirs* p223

p158 bold and bloody – Crozier, *Off The Record* p218, 21 May 1941

p158 I do not know – Taylor, *Beaverbrook* p471

p158 Truth to tell – Woolton, *Diaries*, 5 June 1941

p158 as it does – Churchill papers 20/24

p158 is going to – Orwell, *Diary*, 20 Mar 1941

p160 Hearty congratulations – quoted in Williams, *Battle of the Atlantic* p140

p160 To celebrate – Woolton, *Memoirs* p229

p160 flagrantly violated – *Ottawa Citizen*, 21 June 1941

p160 There wasn't much – Woolton, *Diaries*, 13 June 1941

p161 Cricket gives me – Woolton, *Diaries*, 21 June 1941

7 'Riding the dung cart'

p162 The Prime Minister's – Eden, *The Reckoning* p270

p162 We savoured – ibid.

p162 from every source – NA PREM 3/230/1

p163 Winant . . . suspects – Colville, *Fringes of Power 1939–41* p481, 22 June 1941

p163 I was happy – Foot, *Debts of Honour* p99

p164 Russia will assuredly – Colville, *Fringes of Power 1939–41* p480

p164 I see Russian – *Yorkshire Post*, 23 June 1941

p165 It seems grand – Koa Wing, *Our Longest Days* p90

p165 cleverest speeches – ibid.

p165 After hearing – Maisky, *Memoirs* p159

p165 We are next – *Daily Express*, 23 June 1941

p165 politically Russia – NA CAB 65/22, 23 June 1941

p165 should continue – NA CAB 65/18, 23 June 1941

p166 poor, overlain – *Daily Express*, 14 July 1941

p166 one of the – *Daily Mirror*, 14 July 1941

p168 His best yet – Addison and Crang, *Listening to Britain* p50

p169 had instituted – *Daily Herald*, 26 July 1940

p169 You are bloody – *Daily Mirror*, 19 July 1940

p170 This is spreading – NA INF 1/251, undated

p170 passed into – *Hansard*, 23 July 1940

p170 A monster had – Duff Cooper, *Old Men Forget* p285

p170 the enemy within – Reith, *Diaries* p270, 6 Nov 1940

p170 they ought to – ibid.

p171 tell them exactly – *Daily Mirror*, 27 Jan 1941

p171 I am very – Churchill papers 20/36

p171 I feel that – Nicolson to Monckton, NA INF 1/912, 13 May 1941

p172 In future – NA CAB 66/17, 21 June 1941

p172 The cabinet has – ibid., 24 June 1941

p172 The publication – ibid., 26 June 1941

p172 The Ministry of – ibid., 28 June 1941

p173 I have come – BBC broadcast, 15 July 1941

p173 He was a – Williams, *Nothing So Strange* p165

p174 Here is a – Kennedy, *The Business of War* p80

p174 They quarrelled – Boyle, *Poor Dear Brendan* p250

p174 He had the – Selborne papers, Bodleian Library, 23 July 1941

p174 I hope that – *Hansard*, 28 July 1939

p175 I am a – *Daily Mirror*, 24 July 1941

p175 drill sergeant – Lord Birkenhead, quoted in Lysaght, *Brendan Bracken* p218 p175 he seems to – Nicolson, *Diaries* p183, 29 July 1941

p176 The result was – Tree, *When The Moon Was High* p173

p176 I should be – NA INF 1/869, 17 May 1940

p176 in wartime – *Hansard*, 23 Oct 1941

p177 What is the – *Hansard*, 11 Sep 1940

p178 There must be – NA CAB 66/23, 10 Apr 1942

p178 You know perfectly – NA INF 1/859, 2 June 1942

p179 Make sure you – Churchill papers 20/36

p179 Beaverbrook has – Sherwood, *Roosevelt and Hopkins* p391

p180 both racketeers – Liddell Hart papers, King's College, LH/11/1942/14

p180 We had got – Sherwood, *Roosevelt and Hopkins* p388

p180 Stalin must be – BBC, 9 p.m. 29 Oct 1941

p181 Bevin was the – Macmillan, *Blast of War* p128

p181 Bevin said the – Reith, *Diaries* p270, 14 Nov 1940

p182 What a wonderful – IWM, Trevor Evans interview, Cat 2764

p182 very *unsafe* – Leasor, *War at The Top* p110

p182 Lord Beaverbrook – quoted in Taylor, *Beaverbrook* p499

p182 I would serve – Beaverbrook papers, BBK/C/85-87

p183 I do not – Churchill papers 20/12

p183 I have done – Beaverbrook papers, BBK/C/85-87

p183 Dear Ernie – ibid. BBK/C/38

p183 Dear Max – ibid.

p184 sorry that I – ibid.

p185 working on the – *Hansard*, 2 Dec 1941

p185 I would rather – ibid., 4 Dec 1941

p185 The best speech – Headlam, *Parliament and Politics* p282, 4 Dec 1941

p185 A stirring call – *Daily Mirror*, 3 Dec 1941

p185 After twenty-seven – *Yorkshire Post*, 3 Dec 1941

p186 Today all of – Churchill papers 20/46, 8 Dec 1941

p186 In the past – *Hansard*, 8 Dec 1941

p186 The next few – Amery, *Empire at Bay* p753, 7 Dec 1941

p186 I could not – Eden, *The Reckoning* p286

8 'The Ascendancy of Stafford Cripps'

p188 It is almost – *Western Daily Press*, 9 Feb 1942

p189 Your individual effort – *Daily Mirror*, 9 Feb 1942

p189 Last night he – *Gloucester Citizen*, 9 Feb 1942

p190 had always been – Eden, *The Reckoning* p539

p190 A lunatic – Colville, *Fringes of Power 1939–41* p368, 12 Dec 1940

p191 Stafford saw – Thomson, *Vote of Censure* p79

p191 they should vanish – Ismay, *Memoirs* p242

p192 very much older – NA CO 967/77, 18 Dec 1941

p193 both Mr Attlee – Harvie-Watt, *Most of My Life* p69

p194 coronary insufficiency – Moran, *Churchill At War* p18

p194 Events have – *Daily Mirror*, 18 Dec 1941

p194 We hear of – Woolton, *Diaries*, 11 Jan 1942

p194 There is no – Headlam, *Diary* p289, 22 Jan 1942

p195 He said there – Harvie-Watt, *Most of My Life* p73

p195 wrapped up – *Hansard*, 29 Jan 1942

p195 It is not – *Hansard*, 27 Jan 1942

p196 I say that – ibid.

p196 We have passed – *Yorkshire Post*, 5 Feb 1942

p196 For an imaginative – *Spectator*, 5 Feb 1942

p196 There must – Churchill Papers 20/70

p196 so long as – ibid.

p197 Owing to losses – ibid. 20/73

p197 heavy and – BBC Written Archives Centre, 15 Feb 1942

p197 It was a – Woolton, *Diaries*, 15 Feb 1942

p197 Unfortunately he – Nicolson, *Diaries* p211

p197 because he didn't – Harvie-Watt, *Most of My Life* p78

p197 Bracken now knows – Harvey, *War Diaries* p94, 12 Feb 1942

p198 We are in – Templewood papers, Feb 1942

p198 If I were – Woolton, *Diaries*, 13 Feb 1942

p198 Mr Bevin has – *Daily Mirror*, 11 Feb 1942

p198 leave Lord B – Baroness Spencer-Churchill papers, 12 Feb 1942

p198 I have reached – Churchill, *The Hinge of Fate* p67

p199 He could have – Crozier, *Off the Record* p298, 20 Feb 1942

p199 for the first – *Time*, 23 Feb 1942

p200 Hide them – National Gallery Archives, Kenneth Clark letters

p200 Because London's face – *The Times*, 3 Jan 1942

p201 seditious Middle Temple – Gilbert, *Prophet of Truth* p390

p201 Invite Herr Hitler – *Harijan*, 6 Jul 1942

p201 for an act – NA CAB 66/21, 2 Feb 1942

p202 temporary dominion – FRUS p615, 10 Mar 1942

p202 post-dated cheque – Taylor, *English History 1914–45*, p545

p203 The truth is – Harvey, *War Diaries* p116

p203 We have done – Churchill Papers 20/73

p204 mystery man – *Daily Express*, 12 June 1942

p204 I don't know – Maisky, *Memoirs* p267

p205 skilful handling – NA CAB 65/30, 26 May 1942

p205 full understanding – *Hansard*, 11 June 1942

p205 as keen and – *Western Daily Press*, 22 June 1942

p205 Cripps was annoyed – Morrison, *Autobiography*, p215

p206 the War Cabinet – *Hansard*, 20 May 1942

p206 There must be – *Daily Express*, 4 May 1942

p206 uncompromisingly – Nicolson, *Diaries* p225, 3 May 1942

p206 I cannot help – Orwell, *Diary*, 7 June 1942

p207 a very large – NA PREM 3/11/4, 20 May 1942

p207 The British are – Goebbels, *Diaries* p186, 26 Apr 1942

p207 there was little – NA CAB 65/26, 1 June 1942

p208 [The] German responds – ibid.

p208 likely news for – ibid.

p208 The news from – Woolton, *Diaries*, 15 June 1942

9 'Ringing the bells of victory'

p209 Tobruk has – Churchill, *The Hinge of Fate* p343

p209 What can we – Ismay, *Memoirs* p255

p210 defeatist attitude – NA CAB 65/30, 21 June 1942

p210 When General – ibid.

p210 Of course there – Eden, *The Reckoning* p332

p211 Undoubtedly the – Headlam, *Diary* p321, 23 June 1942

p211 This wicked – *Yorkshire Post*, 29 June 1942

p212 It is being – Harvie-Watt papers, 25 June 1942

p212 too many committees – *Hansard*, 1 July 1942

p213 one object – ibid.

p214 The country is – ibid.

p214 bitter animosity – ibid., 2 July 1942

p215 Winston wound up – Eden, *The Reckoning* p332

p215 the House was – Woolton, *Diaries*, 2 July 1942

p215 Your presence – Amery, *Approach March* pp308–9

p215 a sparrow and – Beaverbrook papers BBK/C/307-308

p216 He is the – Churchill, *The Hinge of Fate* p337

p216 I had to – Attlee Collection, Bodleian Library, 9 Aug 1942

p217 PM now away – Alanbrooke, *War Diaries* p211, 15 Dec 1941

p217 Attlee . . . does – Amery, *Empire at Bay* p828, 17 Aug 1942

p217 No one – quoted in Crowcroft, *Attlee's War* p137

p217 would prefer – *Hansard*, 28 July 1942

p217 He gives me – Dalton, *Second World War Diary* p477, 19 Aug 1942

p218 I am a good – quoted in Harris, *Attlee* pp585–8

p219 to withdraw our – Churchill Papers 20/67

p219 scourge the Third – *Daily Mirror*, 29 July 1942

p219 immense advantages – NA PREM 3/76A/1, 29 July 1942

p220 Winston was – Tedder, *With Prejudice* p320

p221 I fear – Eden, *The Reckoning* p339

p221 I issued orders – Montgomery, *Memoirs* p100

p222 our intention – NA CAB 127/23, 12 Aug 1942

p222 This is the – NA PREM 3/76A/9, 13 Aug 1942

p222 meet the hand – ibid.

p223 I do not – quoted in Sherwood, *Roosevelt and Hopkins* p620

p223 It is my – NA PREM 3/76A/9, 14 Aug 1942

p223 the greatest – ibid., 16 Aug 1942

p223 something could be – NA CAB 127/23, 12 Aug 1942

p224 lessons learned – NA CAB 65/31, 6 p.m. 20 Aug 1942

p224 reflected the – ibid.

p224 I don't think – Halifax, *Diaries* p677

p224 The air support – NA CAB 65/31, 20 Aug 1942

p225 My general – Churchill Papers 20/87

p225 As executed – quoted in North, *Inappropriate Conduct*

p225 He takes a – Dalton, *Second World War Diary* p478

p225 The casualties – Alanbrooke, *War Diaries* p317

p225 Stalingrad is in – Grossman, *A Writer At War* p125

p226 I would leave – NA CAB 195/1, 10 Aug 1942

p227 Stafford Cripps' shares – *Champion Redoubtable* p241

p227 This has enraged – Nicolson, *Diaries* p241

p227 Why encourage – NA CAB 195/1, 9 Sep 1942

p227 I do not – NA CAB 127/85

p227 surprised and – Churchill Papers 20/54

p228 The first hour – Eden, *The Reckoning* p342

p228 If 'Torch' failed – ibid. p343

p228 You have not – Churchill Papers 20/56

p228 If 'Torch' fails – Harvey, *War Diaries* p165

p229 one of the – NA CAB 65/30, 9 Nov 1942

p229 It is the – ibid.

p229 thus breaking – Hansard, 11 Nov 1942

p229 He switched – Morrison, *Autobiography* p216

p230 very skilfully – Dalton, *Second World War Diary* p522

p230 withdrawal from – *The Times*, 23 Nov 1942

p230 working up – NA CAB 195/1, 16 Nov 1942

p230 It was a – ibid.

p230 US reaction – NA CAB 195/1, 18 Nov 1942

p230 When opinion – ibid.

10 'Slaying the five giants'

p232 Freedom from want – *Social Insurance and Allied Services*, HMSO 1942, p461

p233 The European House – *The Times*, 1 July 1940

p234 kicked upstairs – Harris, *William Beveridge* p376

p235 The state in – *Social Insurance and Allied Services*, pp6–7

p235 All social insurance – *Daily Mirror*, 2 Dec 1942

p235 If not – NA PREM 3/168/7B, 8–15 Dec 1942

p235 People in – ibid.

p236 The younger – Harvie-Watt papers, 3 Dec 1942

p236 brilliance and – quoted in Harris, *William Beveridge* p139

p236 If you are – ibid.

p237 an awful windbag – Harvie-Watt, *Most of My Life* p117

p237 May he bring – ibid. p127

p237 A dangerous – NA CAB 65/33, 12 Jan 1943

p238 Can you spare – NA PREM 4/89/2, 30 Jan 1943

p238 Man cannot live – *Daily Mirror*, 16 Feb 1943

p238 bringing the magic – NA CAB 66/34, 15 Feb 1943

p239 I doubt whether – Attlee papers 2/2, undated

p239 If the PM's line – NA CAB 195/2, 15 Feb 1943

p239 Our first promise – ibid.

p240 If we accept – ibid.

p240 is indeed a – Hansard, 16 Feb 1943

p241 [The] general – NA CAB 195/2, 17 Feb 1943

p241 fought like a – Dalton, *Second World War Diary* p554

p241 [I] didn't come – NA CAB 195/2, 17 Feb 1943

p241 peril to financial – ibid.

p241 If we said – ibid.

p242 My plan was – ibid.

p242 classed as a – ibid., 18 Feb 1943

p242 The Beveridge Plan – Hansard, 18 Feb 1943

p243 not to make – *The Times*, 22 Mar 1943

p244 bringing the magic – ibid.

p244 It was a – Woolton, *Diaries*, 21 Mar 1943

p244 proclamation of – *The Times*, 22 Mar 1943

p244 We refused to – NA CAB 66/38, 26 June 1943

p245 Not a step – Stalin's Order No. 227, 28 July 1942

p246 He is trying – quoted in Karsten Friedrich, *The Cruel Slaughter* p171

p247 could not recall – Eden, *The Reckoning* p358

p247 reliable reports – Hansard, 17 Dec 1942

p247 eloquent and just – ibid.

p247 Is it possible – ibid.

p247 We stood for – Channon, Diaries p347

p248 whole districts being – Churchill papers 9/152

p248 The Pole – NA FO 371/26515, 19 Nov 1941

p248 called to solve – Berenbaum, The Holocaust in History p42

p249 I can assure – The Times, 10 July 1942

p250 most bestial – Hansard, 8 Sep 1942

p250 ferocity . . . with – ibid., 7 Oct 1942

p250 At first it – introduction to ITV's The World At War, 'Genocide', 1973

p251 did not underestimate – Lambeth Palace Library, Temple papers 54/135

p251 There are many – NA CAB 66/29, 23 Sep 1942

p252 I have seen – Hansard, 19 June 1936

p252 I ask honourable – ibid., 23 May 1939

p253 the only real – ibid., 19 Jan 1943

p253 Of the six – Gollancz, Let My People Go p1, emphasis original

p254 Fourth Horseman – Yorkshire Post, 15 Mar 1943

p255 public opinion – quoted in Wasserstein, Britain and the Jews p187

p255 There has been – NA CAB 195/2, 22 Feb 1943

p255 If we do – FRUS, 27 Mar 1943

p256 To 5,000,000 – New York Times, 4 May 1943

p256 [It was] encouraging – NA CAB 195/2, 10 May 1943

p256 that when you – ibid.

p257 rate of extermination – Hansard, 19 May 1943

p257 breathed the very – ibid.

p257 All I can – ibid.

p258 I know some – ibid.

p258 painful and – The Times, 20 May 1943

p258 We have had – Manchester Guardian, 20 May 1943

11 'A grand job to be done for the nation'

p260 growing size – Hansard, 3 June 1943

p261 The Navy – NA CAB 66/11, 3 Sep 1940

p261 the defeat of – quoted in Terraine, The Right of the Line p441

p262 I cannot mention – Daily Express, 21 July 1943

p263 a fair, honest – ibid.

p263 My boy did – ibid.

p263 I was afraid – Hansard 28 May 1941

p263 This Government – Daily Express, 24 June 1941

p265 a sort of – Orwell, Road to Wigan Pier p18

p266 anti-war people – Birmingham Daily Post, 2 Oct 1943

p266 I am convinced – NA CAB 66/41, 7 Oct 1943

p267 The principle – Hansard, 13 Oct 1943

p267 It is clear – ibid.

p267 There's a grand – Gloucestershire Echo, 12 Nov 1943

p267 We were deeply – Longmate, How We Lived Then p202

p269 the Labour wing – Amery, Empire at Bay p942, 21 Sep 1943

p270 I think you – Howard, Rab p109

p270 I hope our – The Times, 22 Mar 1943

p270 frightful row – Dalton, Second World War Diary p657, 21 Oct 1943

p271 the formulation – NA CAB 65/40, 14 Oct 1943

p271 'Need for Decisions' – ibid.

p271 to see if – Chuter Ede, Labour and the Wartime Coalition p147

p271 There were obvious – NA CAB 65/40, 14 Oct 1943

p271 although not fully – ibid.

p272 any decisions – NA CAB 66/42, 19 Oct 1943

p272 between light – Lascelles, *King's Counsellor* p172

p272 Very great – Dalton, *Second World War Diary* p655

p273 He seemed to – Woolton, *Diaries*, 1 Nov 1943

p273 all the experience – ibid.

p273 quite a row – Dalton, *Second World War Diary*, 3 Nov 1943

p273 People are – Woolton, *Diaries*, 12 Nov 1943

p274 Truth deserved – Gilbert, *Road to Victory* p586

p274 Read that – Moran, *Churchill At War* p175

p275 The quandary – Donoughue and Jones, *Herbert Morrison* p222

p275 I highly approve – NA PREM 4/39/5

p275 would weaken – NA CAB 65/40, 17 Nov 1943

p275 strongly critical – NA PREM 4/39/5

p275 We have had – ibid.

p275 You will have – ibid.

p276 You are the – ibid.

p276 If the Labour – ibid.

p276 I said he – Moran, *Churchill at War* p176

p276 embodiment of – NA PREM 4/39/5

p277 most valiant – ibid.

p277 retard the war – *Hansard*, 1 Dec 1943

p277 If U.J – NA PREM 4/39/5

p277 I am sure – ibid.

p278 Everything should – NA PREM 4/39/5

p278 industry, commerce – London Passenger Transport Act 1933

p279 I went to – Chuter Ede, *Labour and the Wartime Coalition* p160, 31 Dec 1943

p279 Have we not – *Hansard*, 2 Dec 1943

p280 Uncle Ernie – information from Liz Todd

p280 All we want – ibid.

p281 This cap fits! – *Daily Mirror*, 15 Dec 1943

p281 lest she should – Evans, *Bevin* p197

p281 It doesn't seem – *Daily Worker*, 4 Dec 1943

p281 The young miner – *Hansard*, 17 Dec 1943

p281 These youths – ibid.

p281 We devised this – ibid.

12 'Should we tell the Russians?'

p282 I very much – NA CAB 65/40, 14 Dec 1943

p283 As I sat – Moran, *Churchill At War* p185

p283 Lord Moran – Macmillan, *War Diaries* p327

p283 some of them – Moran, *Churchill At War* p186

p283 The Prime Minister – *Hansard*, 16 Dec 1943

p283 The circumstances – *The Times*, 19 Dec 1943

p283 In the event – Cecil King, *With Malice Toward None* p237

p284 the great retreat – *Daily Express*, 31 Dec 1943

p284 I am sick – Koa Wing, *Our Longest Days* p198

p286 met the full – Woolton, *Memoirs* p298

p287 If the Conservatives – Woolton papers, 10 Feb 1944

p288 much annoyance – Colville, *Fringes of Power 1941–55* p97, 5 Mar 1944

p288 I hope – *Hansard*, 17 Mar 1944

p289 The amendment – Chuter Ede, *Labour and the Wartime Coalition* p179

p289 In this great – *Hansard*, 30 Mar 1944

p289 paid a handsome – Butler, *Art of the Possible* p122

p290 won a lasting – ibid.

p290 very bold – Dalton, *Second World War Diary* p747

p290 A magnificent – ibid.

p290 it is a document – NA CAB 66/50, 16 May 1944

p290 the Government – NA CAB 65/42

p291 In the post-war – ibid.

p291 Shallow, empty-headed – Foot, *Aneurin Bevan* p413

p291 My own feeling – Moggridge, *Keynes* p709

p291 Govt plans – *Daily Mirror*, 27 May 1944

p291 Irrespective of – quoted in *Social Security Bulletin* p22, Sep 1944

p291 whenever the – *Yorkshire Post*, 27 May 1944

p292 It's not a matter – *Dundee Evening Telegraph*, 18 May 1944

p292 It is the – *Hansard*, 25 May 1944

p292 What has – *Daily Express*, 5 Apr 1944

p293 magnifying in – *Hansard*, 28 Apr 1944

p294 Well, we are – *Onward* magazine, Apr 1954

p294 Is it in order – *Hansard*, 31 Oct 1939

p295 Anderson is the – James, *Victor Cazalet* p273

p295 friendly power – Sir John Anderson papers

p296 super bomb – NA AB 1/210, Mar 1940

p297 Although personally – quoted in Gowing, *Britain and Atomic Energy* p106

p297 strongly in – NA HO 205/240, 2 Sep 1940

p298 specious air – Gowing, *Britain and Atomic Energy* p109

p299 We should soon – NA CAB 127/201

p299 It has now – NA HO 205/240

p299 to renew a – Hewlett and Anderson, *The New World 1939–46* p274

p299 to bring the – NA CAB 127/201

p300 we had signed – Jones, *Most Secret War* p474

p301 it no longer – NA PREM 3/139/2

p302 I cannot help – ibid.

p302 I do not think – ibid.

p302 He seemed to – Jones, *Most Secret War* p477

p302 made no difference – ibid.

p303 It will be – quoted in Rhodes, *The Making of the Atomic Bomb* p530

p304 Halt! Who goes – *Heritage Railway* no. 201, Apr–May 2015

p304 You'll look after – Bullock, *Life and Times of Ernest Bevin* p318

13 'Buzz bombs and flying gas mains'

p306 proceeding in a – *Hansard*, 6 June 1944

p307 I ask my – quoted in the *Guardian*, 5 Jan 2000

p307 messianic complex – ibid.

p307 removal of – NA CAB 65/42

p307 get this – Lacouture, *De Gaulle* p521

p308 effective civil – *Sarasota Herald-Tribune*, 6 June 1944

p308 I do not think – NA FO 954/9, 31 May 1944

p308 I am absolutely – ibid., 6 June 1944

p308 If the President – ibid.

p308 France may go – ibid.

p309 I was accused – Eden, *The Reckoning* p455

p309 encourage the – NA CAB 65/42, 7 June 1944

p309 There is still – NA FO 954/9, 13 June 1944

p310 The bombardment – Trevor-Roper, *Hitler's War Directives* p239

p311 I have the – Lindemann papers G410/1

p311 comparatively insignificant – ibid. G420/23

p312 unprecedented strain – NA CAB 66/58, 16 Nov 1943

p313 Dr Goebbels – *Hansard*, 23 June 1944

p313 It's ridiculous – *Daily Express*, 1 July 1944

p313 jeering references – NA CAB 66/51, 27 June 1944

p313 [It was] a pathetic – Alanbrooke, *War Diaries* p563

p314 the threat is – ibid. p565

p314 I saw 'C' – Liddell, *Diaries* p223

p315 Except, possibly – *Daily Mirror*, 8 Sep 1944

p315 His account – NA PREM 3/111A, 7 Sep 1944

p316 any steps – *Hansard*, 5 July 1944

p317 matter was still – quoted in Gilbert, *Auschwitz* pp268–9

p317 that the railway – ibid.

p317 On no account – NA PREM 4/51/10, 7 July 1944

p317 Could you let – NA FO 371/42809/142, 7 July 1944

p317 It is out – ibid., 15 July 1944

p318 He wasn't – ibid., 16 July 1944

p318 The reasons – NA FO 371/42814, 16 Aug 1944

p319 in view of – quoted in Wasserstein, *Britain and the Jews* p317

p319 The armies – *Daily Express*, 8 Sep 1944

p320 That's the first – Jones, *Most Secret War* p459

p322 There is no – *Hansard*, 10 Nov 1944

p323 There were – *The Times*, 11 Nov 1944

p323 If I'm going – private information

p323 What depresses me – *Tribune*, 1 Dec 1944

p324 Just strip it – Blum, *Morgenthau Diaries* p327

p324 to converting Germany – ibid. pp371–2

p324 It was as – Eden, *The Reckoning* p476

p325 The suggestion – NA CAB 127/201

p326 naughty document – NA CAB 120/158

p326 Might it not – Churchill, *Triumph and Tragedy* p198

p326 would be considered – ibid. pp201–5

p327 the system of – Gilbert, *Road to Victory* p1004

p327 Reconstruction Committee – Butler papers G16, 8 Sep 1944

p327 a solid mass – NA PREM 4/88/1, 20 Nov 1944

p328 the Government – NA INF 1/292, Oct 1944

p329 building arbitrator – Reith, *Diaries* p267, 6 Oct 1940

p329 fundamentally – quoted in Jefferys, *The Churchill Coalition* p178

p329 It revealed – Amery, *Empire at Bay* p1016

p330 threatened trouble – Chuter Ede, *Labour and the Wartime Coalition* p191

p330 Anderson had – Dalton, *Second World War Diary* p797, 23 Oct 1944

14 'A light shining on every helmet'

p331 that the position – NA CAB 65/48, 11 Dec 1944

p332 the seeds of – *The Times*, 4 Dec 1944

p333 Do not hesitate – Churchill papers 20/176, 5 Dec 1944

p333 We expect the – FRUS Vol 3 p1162, 5 Dec 1944

p333 as Hitler – *Hansard*, 8 Dec 1944

p333 Democracy is no – ibid.

p334 put our case – NA CAB 65/48, 13 Dec 1944

p334 utilization of – *Daily Express*, 13 Dec 1944

p334 If we win – ibid.

p335 Ernest Bevin's – NA FO 954/11, 14 Dec 1944

p335 I won't install – Cadogan, *Diaries* p689, 21 Dec 1944

p335 We often heard – ibid.

p336 When we entered – Eden, *The Reckoning* p501

p336 We want – Moran, *Churchill at War* p258

p336 Prime Minister – Greek NLF 'White Book', http://www.redstarpublishers.org

p336 whose bows – Colville, *Fringes of Power 1941–55* p181

p336 W was very – Eden, *The Reckoning* p502

p338 ghastly – Alanbrooke, *War Diaries* p641

p338 they need not – Amery, *Empire at Bay* p1023

p338 What happens – Attlee papers Atle 2/2

p339 Greatly as I – Colville, *Fringes of Power 1941–55* p192, 20 Jan 1945

p339 Attlee's quite right – ibid.

p339 I admire Mr – quoted in Wrigley, *Winston Churchill* p34

p339 very good – Colville, *Fringes of Power 1941–55* p193, 21 Jan 1945

p339 My Dear – Gilbert, *Road to Victory* p1156

p339 At 5.30 – Alanbrooke, *War Diaries* p648

p340 Our attention – Taylor, *Beaverbrook* p558

p341 She controls – NA CAB 195/3, 6 Mar 1945

p341 When family – Hansard, 8 Mar 1945

p342 petty vindictiveness – Bullock, *Life and Times of Ernest Bevin* p378

p342 Our Socialist – *Daily Express*, 16 Mar 1945

p343 He's all right – Dalton, *Second World War Diary* p852, 19 Apr 1945

p343 which had – *Yorkshire Post*, 9 Apr 1945

p343 big business – ibid.

p343 I can hardly – *Daily Express*, 10 Apr 1945

p344 The minister of – Hansard, 10 Apr 1945

p345 The change of – NA CAB 195/3, 10 Mar 1945

p345 Altogether our – Eden, *The Reckoning* p525

p345 Many of those – NA CAB 195/3, 28 Mar 1945

p345 I'm concerned – ibid.

p345 indispensable reinforcement – ibid.

p346 Allied air – Associated Press, 18 Feb 1945

p346 This is entirely – King, *With Malice Toward None* p290

p347 Allied air bombing – Hansard, 6 Mar 1945

p347 Is terror bombing – ibid.

p347 the primary – Webster and Frankland, *Strategic Air Offensive* p323

p348 I am all – De Groot, *Sinclair* p190

p348 delighted to find – ibid.

p348 WSC suddenly – Gilbert, *Road To Victory* p437

p348 It seems to – Webster and Frankland, *Strategic Air Offensive* p112

p349 basting the – Air Historical Branch file, Freeman minute, 26 Jan 1945

p349 It seems to – Webster and Frankland, *Strategic Air Offensive* p112

p350 direct support – Portal to Harris, Air Historical Branch file, 16 Apr 1945

p350 profound sorrow – NA CAB 65/50, 13 Apr 1945

p350 I felt like – Truman Library website, 'Senate to the White House'

p351 too late to see – NA PREM 4/100/11, 19 Apr 1945

p351 Some people – British Pathé News, May 1945

p351 There is – *The Spectator*, 3 May 1945

p351 document of – NA CAB 66/64, 9 Apr 1945

p351 It mixes – NA CAB 195/3, 12 Apr 1945

p352 All major – ibid.

p352 fallen at his – *Daily Express* 2 May 1945

p352 Well, I must – Colville, *Fringes of Power 1941–55* p242 p352 remained completely – Alanbrooke, *War Diaries* p686

p352 negotiate with – NA CAB 195/3, 3 May 1945

p352 Don't quibble – ibid.

p354 looked forward – *Yorkshire Post*, 9 May 1945

p354 No, Sir – Wheeler-Bennett, *John Anderson* p314

p354 hearty thanks – *Hansard*, 8 May 1945

p355 This is your – *Yorkshire Post*, 9 May 1945

p355 I cannot think – *Hansard*, 31 Oct 1944

p356 we must look – ibid.

p356 preferably until – Butler, *Art of the Possible* p126

p356 The coalition – *The Economist*, 24 Mar 1945

p357 instalment of – *Daily Mirror*, 21 Apr 1945

p357 create such fear – *Daily Express*, 23 Apr 1945

p358 Nobody with – *Observer*, 20 May 1945

p358 In the meanwhile – Harris, *Attlee* p250

p359 I could not – Williams, *A Prime Minister Remembers* p64

p360 Winston was – Macmillan, *War Diaries* p762

p360 I regret the – *Daily Express*, 23 May 1945

p361 This has been – *The Times*, 24 May 1945

p361 No-one can – *Yorkshire Post*, 24 May 1945

p361 all British – ibid., 25 May 1945

p362 Clem Attlee – Chandos, *Memoirs* p323

p362 nothing so – Chuter Ede, *Labour and the Wartime Coalition* p221

p362 were capable of – ibid.

p362 surely been – Dalton, *Second World War Diary* p865

p362 How can you – Chuter Ede, *Labour and the Wartime Coalition* p221

p362 we had given – ibid.

p363 We'd better – Dalton, *Second World War Diary* p865

Postscript

p364 What about the – *Adelaide Advertiser*, 28 May 1945

p364 They call us – ibid.

p365 socialism is – *Daily Express*, 5 June 1945

p365 It was – *Evening Standard*, 5 June 1945

p365 This broadcast – *Daily Herald*, 5 June 1945

p365 I realised – *Daily Mirror*, 6 June 1945

p366 A fantastical – Amery, *Empire at Bay* p1046, 4 June 1945

p367 Seldom has an – *Time*, 6 Aug 1945

p367 new weapon – Harry S. Truman, *Years of Decisions* p242

p368 It has been – Dixon, *Double Diploma* p178

p368 It is the biggest – *Evening Standard*, 7 Aug 1945

p368 we've got to – quoted in Hennessy, *Cabinets and the Bomb* p48

p369 financial Dunkirk – NA CAB 128-1, 23 Aug 1945

p369 There is one – *Hansard*, 29 Nov 1944

p370 What were – quoted in Addison, *Road to 1945* p284

p372 heart failure – *Lancashire Evening Post*, 28 Feb 1947

p373 My Dear – Beaverbrook papers BBK/C/ 311

p373 sharp debate – Eden, *The Reckoning* p552

p373 We have done – Hunter, *Winston and Archie* p419

BIBLIOGRAPHY

Private Papers

Bodleian Library, University of Oxford
Sir John Anderson papers
Ava Anderson papers
Lord Woolton papers

Cambridge University Library
Lord Templewood papers

Churchill Archive Centre, Churchill College, Cambridge
Clement Attlee papers
Sir Winston Churchill papers (CHAR & CHUR)
Andrew Boyle papers
Lawrence Burgis papers
Sir Alfred Duff Cooper papers
Sir Maurice Hankey papers
Sir George Harvie-Watt papers
Florence Horsbrugh papers
Sir Archibald Sinclair papers

House of Lords Record Office
Lord Beaverbrook, Beaverbrook papers

Nuffield College Library, University of Oxford
Sir Frederick Lindemann papers

Trinity College, Cambridge
Lord Butler papers

Diaries

Alanbrooke, Field Marshal Lord (ed. Alex Danchev and Daniel Todman), *War Diaries 1939–45*, Phoenix 2001

Amery, Leo (ed. John Barnes and David Nicholson), *The Empire at Bay 1929–45*, Hutchinson 1988

Cadogan, Sir Alexander (ed. David Dilks), *Diaries 1938–45*, Faber Finds 1971

Channon, Sir Henry (ed. Robert Rhodes James), *Chips – The Diaries of Sir Henry Channon*, Phoenix Giant 1999

Colville, John, *The Fringes of Power – Downing Street Diaries*, Volume 1, 1939–41, Hodder and Stoughton 1985

Colville, John, *The Fringes of Power – Downing Street Diaries*, Volume 2, 1941–April 1955, Hodder and Stoughton 1985

Dalton, Hugh (ed. Ben Pimlott), *Second World War Diary 1940–45*, Jonathan Cape 1986

Ede, James Chuter, *Labour and the Wartime Coalition 1941–45*, Historians' Press 1987

Goebbels, Joseph, *The Goebbels Diaries 1942–43*, Fireside Press 1948

Halifax, Lord, *Diaries*, University of York (online)

Harvey, Oliver (ed. John Harvey), *War Diaries*, Collins 1978

Headlam, Sir Cuthbert (ed. Stuart Ball), *Parliament and Politics in the Age of Churchill and Attlee*, Cambridge University Press 1999

Ironside, William Edmund, *Time Unguarded: Diaries 1937–40*, Greenwood Press 1962

King, Cecil, *With Malice Toward None*, Sidgwick & Jackson 1970

Lascelles, Sir Alan (ed. Duff Hart-Davis), *King's Counsellor – Abdication and War*, Phoenix 2007

Macmillan, Harold, *War Diaries – The Mediterranean 1943–45*, Macmillan 1984

Moran, Lord Charles, *Churchill At War 1940–45*, Constable & Robinson 2002

Nicolson, Harold, *Diaries and Letters 1939–45*, William Collins 1967

Orwell, George (ed. Peter Davison), *The Orwell Diaries*, Penguin Classics 2010

Reith, Sir John (ed. Charles Stuart), *The Reith Diaries*, Collins 1975

Wallace, Captain David Euan, *Diary*, Bodleian Library

Woolton, Lord, *Diaries*, Bodleian Library

Autobiographies & Memoirs

Attlee, C.R., *As It Happened*, Heinemann 1954

Balfour, Harold, *Wings Over Westminster*, Hutchinson 1973

Boothby, Lord, *Recollections of a Rebel*, Hutchinson 1978

Brabazon, Lord, *The Brabazon Story*, Heinemann 1956

Butler, Lord, *The Art of the Possible*, Hamish Hamilton 1971

Chamberlain, Neville (ed. Robert Self), *The Neville Chamberlain Diary Letters* Vol. 4, 1934–40, Ashgate 2005

Chandos, Lord, *Memoirs*, Bodley Head 1962

Churchill, Winston, *My Early Life*, Thornton Butterworth 1930

— *The Gathering Storm*, History of the Second World War Vol. 1, Penguin Classics 2005

— *Their Finest Hour*, History of the Second World War Vol. 2, Penguin Classics 2005

— *The Grand Alliance*, History of the Second World War Vol. 3, Mariner Books 1985

— *The Hinge of Fate*, History of the Second World War Vol. 4, Penguin Classics 2005

— *Closing the Ring*, History of the Second World War Vol. 5, Penguin Classics 2005

— *Triumph and Tragedy*, History of the Second World War Vol. 6, Penguin Classics 2005

Dalton, Hugh, *Memoirs 1931–45*, Frederick Muller 1957

De Gaulle, Charles (trans. Griffin, Jonathan), *War Memoirs Volume I: The Call to Honour 1940–42*, Viking Press 1955

Doenitz, Grand Admiral Karl, *Memoirs*, Da Capo Press 1997

Duff Cooper, Alfred, *Old Men Forget*, Faber and Faber 2011

Eden, Anthony, *The Reckoning: Memoirs*, Cassell 1965

Harvie-Watt, G.S., *Most of My Life*, Springwood Books 1980

Ismay, General Lord, *Memoirs*, Viking Press 1960

Kennedy, Sir John, *The Business of War*, Hutchinson 1957

Low, David, *Autobiography*, Michael Joseph 1956

MacDonald, Malcolm, *Titans & Others*, Collins 1972

Macmillan, Harold, *The Blast of War 1939–45*, Macmillan 1967

Montgomery, Field Marshal Bernard, *Memoirs*, Collins 1958

Morrison, Herbert, *An Autobiography*, Odhams Press 1960

Shakespeare, Sir Geoffrey, *Let Candles Be Brought In*, Macdonald 1949

Woolton, Earl of, *Memoirs*, Cassell 1959

Secondary Sources

Addison, Paul, *Churchill on the Home Front 1900–55*, Faber Finds 2013
  – *The Road to 1945*, Pimlico 1994
  – and Crang, Jeremy (eds), *Listening to Britain*, Vintage 2011
Amery, Julian, *Approach March*, Hutchinson 1973
Anderson, R.G., and Hewlett, O.E., *The New World 1939–46*, Pennsylvania State University Press 1962
Barker, Elizabeth, *Churchill and Eden At War*, St Martin's Press 1978
Beckett, Francis, *Clem Attlee*, Richard Cohen Books 1997
Beevor, Antony, *D-Day: The Battle for Normandy*, Penguin Books 2009
Beevor, Antony, *The Second World War*, Phoenix 2012
Berenbaum, Michael, *Holocaust in History*, Indiana University Press 1998
Beveridge, Janet, *Beveridge and His Plan*, Hodder & Stoughton 1954
Birkenhead, Earl of, *The Prof in Two Worlds*, Collins 1961
Blum, John Morton, *From the Morgenthau Diaries 1941–45*, Houghton Mifflin 1970
Bonham Carter, Violet, *Champion Redoubtable*, Weidenfeld & Nicolson 1999
Bonham Carter, Violet, *Winston Churchill As I Knew Him*, The Reprint Society 1965
Boyle, Andrew, *Poor Dear Brendan: The Quest for Brendan Bracken*, Hutchinson 1974
Breitman, Richard, *Official Secrets*, Allen Lane 1998
Broad, Richard, and Fleming, Suzie (eds), *Nella Last's War*, Profile Books 2006
Brookes, Pamela, *Women at Westminster*, Peter Davies 1967
Bullock, Alan, *The Lives and Times of Ernest Bevin: Ministry of Labour 1940–45*, Heinemann 1967
Bungay, Stephen, *The Most Dangerous Enemy: A History of the Battle of Britain*, Aurum Press 2010
Burridge, T.D., *British Labour and Hitler's War*, Andre Deutsch 1976
Calder, Angus, *The People's War*, Pimlico 1992
Campbell, Christy, *Target London: Under Attack from the V-Weapons during WWII*, Abacus 2012
Castle, Barbara, *Fighting All The Way*, Macmillan 1993
Charmley, John, *Churchill: The End of Glory*, Hodder & Stoughton 1993
  – *Duff Cooper: The Authorised Biography*, Weidenfeld & Nicolson 1986
Chisholm, Anne and Davie, Michael, *Lord Beaverbrook: A Life*, Alfred Knopf 1993
Churchill, Winston, *Savrola*, Longmans Green 1900

Clarke, Peter, *The Cripps Version – The Life of Sir Stafford Cripps*, Allen Lane 2002

Collins, Canon L. John, *Faith Under Fire*, Leslie Frewin 1966

Colville, John, *The Churchillians*, Weidenfeld & Nicolson 1981

Costello, John, *Ten Days That Saved The World*, Bantam Press 1991

Cowles, Virginia, *Looking for Trouble*, Hamish Hamilton 1941

Crowcroft, Robert, *Attlee's War*, I.B. Tauris 2011

Crozier, W.P, *Off The Record: Political Interviews 1933–43*, Hutchinson 1973

Cull, Nicholas John, *Selling War: The British Propaganda Campaign Against American Neutrality in World War II*, Oxford University Press 1995

De Groot, Gerard, *The Life of Sir Archibald Sinclair*, Hurst & Co 1993

Dixon, Piers, *Double Diploma: The Life of Sir Pierson Dixon*, Hutchinson 1968

Donoughue, Bernard and Jones, C.W., *Herbert Morrison: Portrait of a Politician*, Phoenix Press 2001

Eden, Guy, *The Parliament Book*, Staples Press 1953

Edgerton, David, *Britain's War Machine*, Penguin Books 2011

Evans, Trevor, *Bevin*, Allen & Unwin 1946

Farrer, David, *G – For God Almighty: A Personal Memoir of Lord Beaverbrook*, Weidenfeld & Nicolson, 1969

– *The Sky's The Limit*, Hutchinson, 1943

Foot, Michael, *Aneurin Bevan Vol 1*, Tribune Publications 1962 ·

– *Debts of Honour*, David-Poynter 1980

Fort, Adrian, *Prof – The Life of Frederick Lindemann*, Pimlico 2004

Friedrick, Karsten, *The Cruel Slaughter of Adolf Hitler*, self-pub 2012

Gilbert, Martin, *Finest Hour*, Heinemann 1983

– *Road to Victory*, Heinemann 1986

– *Never Despair*, Heinemann 1988

– *The Challenge of War*, Minerva 1990

– *Prophet of Truth*, Minerva 1990

– *Auschwitz and the Allies*, Pimlico 2001

Gowing, Margaret, *Britain and Atomic Energy 1939–45*, Macmillan 1964

Grossman, Vasily, *A Writer At War*, Pimlico 2006

Harris, Jose, *William Beveridge: A Biography*, Oxford University Press 1977

Harris, Kenneth, *Attlee*, Weidenfeld & Nicolson 1984

Hastings, Max, *Finest Years: Churchill as Warlord 1940–45*, Harper Press 2009

– *All Hell Let Loose: The World at War 1939–45*, Harper Press 2011

Hennessy, Peter, *Cabinets and the Bomb*, Oxford University Press 2007

Hickman, Tom, *Called Up, Sent Down: The Bevin Boys' War*, The History Press 2010

Holland, James, *The Battle of Britain*, Corgi 2011

Hore, Peter, *Nelson's Band of Brothers*, Seaforth Publishing 2015

Hough, Richard and Richards, Denis, *Battle of Britain*, Pen & Sword 2007

Howard, Anthony, *Rab: The Life of R.A. Butler*, Jonathan Cape 1987

Hunter, Ian (ed.), *Winston and Archie*, Politico's 2005

Irving, David, *Churchill's War*, Avon Books 1991

Jablonsky, David, *Churchill: The Great Game*, Routledge 1991

James, Robert Rhodes (ed.), *Winston Churchill, His Complete Speeches 1897–1963*, Chelsea Home 1974
    – *Victor Cazalet*, Hamish Hamilton 1976

Jefferys, Kevin, *The Churchill Coalition and Wartime Politics*, Manchester University Press 1995

Jenkins, Roy, *The Chancellors*, Macmillan 1998
    – *Churchill*, Macmillan 2001

Johnson, Boris, *The Churchill Factor*, Hodder & Stoughton 2014

Jones, R.V., *Most Secret War*, Penguin Books 1978

Kennedy, Sir John, *The Business of War*, Hutchinson 1957

Kershaw, Ian, *Fateful Choices*, Penguin Books 2007

Keyes, Roger, *Outrageous Fortune*, Secker & Warburg 1984

Kimball, Warren F., *The Most Unsordid Act: Lend-Lease 1939–41*, Johns Hopkins Press 1969

Koa Wing, Sandra (ed.), *Our Longest Days: A People's History of the Second World War*, Profile Books 2008

Krauss, Rene, *The Men Around Churchill*, J.B. Lippincott 1941

Lacouture, Jean, *De Gaulle The Rebel 1890–1944*, W.W. Norton 1993

Lee, J.M., *The Churchill Coalition*, Archon Books 1980

Lee, General Raymond E., *The London Observer 1940–41*, Hutchinson 1972

Longmate, Norman, *How We Lived Then*, Pimlico 2002

Lukacs, John, *Five Days in London: May 1940*, Yale University Press 1999

Lysaght, Charles, *Brendan Bracken*, Allen Lane 1979

Maisky, Ivan, *Memoirs of a Soviet Ambassador*, Hutchinson 1967

McKinstry, Leo, *Operation Sealion*, John Murray 2014

McLaine, Ian, *Ministry of Morale*, Allen & Unwin 1979

Meacham, Jon, *Franklin and Winston*, Random House 2003

Menzies, Robert, *Dark and Hurrying Days, 1941 Diary*, National Library of Australia 1993

Moggridge, Donald, *Maynard Keynes*, Routledge 1992

Mortimer, Gavin, *The Longest Night: Voices from the Blitz*, Orion 2005

North, Don, *Inappropriate Conduct*, iUniverse 2013

North, Richard, *The Many Not the Few*, Continuum 2012

Pedersen, Susan, *Eleanor Rathbone and the Politics of Conscience*, Yale University Press 2004

Pimlott, Ben, *Harold Wilson*, HarperCollins 1992

Prior, Robin, *When Britain Saved The World*, Yale University Press 2015

Reynolds, David, *In Command of History: Churchill Fighting and Writing the Second World War*, Penguin Books 2005

Rhodes, Richard, *The Making of the Atomic Bomb*, Simon & Schuster 2012

Rhodes James, Robert, *Victor Cazalet – A Portrait*, Hamish Hamilton 1976

Roberts, Andrew, *The Holy Fox – The Life of Lord Halifax*, Weidenfeld & Nicolson 1991

Roskill, Stephen, *Hankey Man of Secrets*, Vol III, 1931–63, Collins 1974

Self, Robert, *Neville Chamberlain: A Biography*, Ashgate 2006

Sherwood, Robert, *Roosevelt and Hopkins*, Harper 1948
  – *The White House Papers of Harry Hopkins*, Eyre & Spottiswode 1948

Shirer, William L., *Berlin Diary 1934–41*, Black Dog & Leventhal 2005

Smart, Nick, *The National Government 1931–40*, Macmillan 1999

Smith, Colin, *England's Last War Against France*, Phoenix 2010

Spears, General Sir Edward, *Assignment to Catastrophe*, The Reprint Society 1961

Steil, Benn, *The Battle of Bretton Woods*, Princeton University Press 2013

Stevenson, William, *A Man called Intrepid*, Lyons Press 2009

Stowe, Peter, *Manny Shinwell: An Authorised Biography*, Pluto Press 1993

Strauss, Patricia, *Bevin & Co*, Books for Libraries Press 1941

Sweet, Matthew, *The West End Front*, Faber & Faber 2011

Taylor, A.J.P., *English History 1914–45*, Oxford University Press 1965
  – *Beaverbrook*, Hamish Hamilton 1972

Tedder, Lord, *With Prejudice War Memoirs*, Cassell 1966

Terraine, John, *The Right of the Line*, Hodder & Stoughton 1985

Thompson, Laurence, *1940*, Collins 1966

Thompson, R.W., *Churchill and Morton*, Hodder & Stoughton 1976

Thomson, George Malcolm, *Vote of Censure*, Secker & Warburg 1968

Tree, Ronald, *When The Moon Was High*, Macmillan 1975

Trevor-Roper, Hugh, *Hitler's War Directives 1939–45*, Birlinn 2004

Vernon, Betty D., *Ellen Wilkinson*, Croom Helm 1982

Wasserstein, Bernard, *Britain and the Jews of Europe 1939–45*, Oxford University Press 1979

Webster, Sir Charles, and Frankland, Noble, *Strategic Air Offensive Against Germany 1939–45*, Naval & Military Press 2006

West, Nigel (ed.), *The Guy Liddell Diaries*, Vol. 2, 1942–45, Routledge 2009

Wheeler-Bennett, John Wheeler, *King George VI: His Life and Reign*, Macmillan 1958

– *John Anderson Viscount Waverley*, St Martin's Press 1962

Williams, Andrew, *The Battle of the Atlantic*, BBC Worldwide 2002

Williams, Francis, *Ernest Bevin*, Hutchinson 1952

– *A Prime Minister Remembers*, William Heinemann 1961

– *Nothing So Strange: An Autobiography*, Cassell 1970

Williams, Sir Herbert, *Politics Grave and Gay*, Hutchinson 1949

Wrigley, Chris, *Winston Churchill: A Biographical Companion*, ABC-CLIO 2002

Young, Kenneth, *Churchill and Beaverbrook*, Eyre & Spottiswoode

Websites

www.battleofbritain1940.net (Battle of Britain Historical Society)

www.bbc.co.uk/history/ww2peopleswar

British Newspaper Archive

EUReferendum.com ('Shelter War')

(Official UK history of WW2)

UKpressonline

INDEX